ANALECTA BIBLICA
INVESTIGATIONES SCIENTIFICAE IN RES BIBLICAS
82

FROM EYE-WITNESSES TO MINISTERS OF THE WORD

ROMAE
E PONTIFICIO INSTITUTO BIBLICO
1978

RICHARD J. DILLON
St. Joseph's Seminary, Dunwoodie
Yonkers, New York

FROM EYE-WITNESSES TO MINISTERS OF THE WORD

Tradition and Composition in Luke 24

ROME
BIBLICAL INSTITUTE PRESS
1978

PRINTED IN ITALY

TYPIS PONTIFICIAE UNIVERSITATIS GREGORIANAE — ROMAE

Dedication

To my Father, Edward F. Dillon († 1970).

PROLOGUE

Our discussion is unusually easy to introduce. Its subject is crucial, its previous treatments, astonishingly few. A paradox, this, which could be both a joy and a dispair to the doctoral student. — The celebrated Easter narrative of Lk 24 is the crossroads of the two-volume opus of St. Luke, as the reader can tell when he finds it being repeated, in condensed and slightly varied form, at the beginning of the second volume. The function of such an " axis " composition must be to demonstrate the concerns that are common to the two books, and to show how such concerns are to be pursued from the first book, which this story terminates, to the second, which it inaugurates. Indeed, Easter is the point of connection between the ministry of Jesus and the mission of his followers ; and these are the two topics, respectively, of the gospel of Luke — where his is one voice among four in the New Testament — and the Acts of the Apostles, where his testimony practically stands alone.

The unique situation of one gospel among several, extended into a book altogether unique in the canon, has made the gospel into what one of its foremost students has called " the practice-field of redaction-criticism " (H. Conzelmann, *TRu* 37 [1972] 264). Is it possible that, in such well-quarried terrain, anything could be left to say about the composition that holds that key position at the nuclear center ? But precisely here the dearth of concerted study defies explanation. The essay everyone quotes is a slender, apparently hasty work on " The Structure and Significance of Luke 24," by P. Schubert (1954), now over twenty years old and scarcely yet equipped with the mature perspectives of *Redaktionsgeschichte*. Otherwise, there are but a handful of brief essays (including the rather insightful one of M. Brändle, 1960) and some commentary of the popular (E. Lohse) and non-scientific (H. Gollwitzer) vein, — and that is all ! One is then relegated to the equally sparse studies of individual pericopes in Lk 24, of which the only one that is at all beneficiary of recent and comprehensive treatment is the Emmaus story, to which the welcome monograph of J. Wanke (1974) helped our access enormously. Of specific studies of Luke's tomb sequence there are none, to our knowledge ; and on the third pericope, fewer than the fingers of one hand.

After this meagre bibliography on the material proper of Lk 24, one is cast out upon a vast and amorphous literature. The commentary situation on the third gospel is notoriously bad, with H. SCHÜRMANN already creating an encyclopedia where he has been stopped for eight years (Lk 9,51), and other scientific commentary decades old (E. KLOSTERMANN, J. M. CREED, *et al.*). A welcome relief from this drought has been the Regensburg commentary of J. ERNST (1977), appearing just as this endeavour was in the typing stage (cf. chap. II, n. 6). — Redaction-historical works on Lk too often make desultory, passing reference to the Easter story in support of certain tenets, usually determined *aliunde* (so H. CONZELMANN, H. FLENDER, M. RESE, F. SCHÜTZ, U. WILCKENS). The exceptions to this rule are few : H.-W. BARTSCH (some good observations in pursuit of an inscrutable overview of the Lucan purpose), C. H. TALBERT (greater space allotted in pursuit of an unacceptable view of Luke's purpose), and recently, R. GLÖCKNER (a welcome rebellion against mainstream *Lukasanalyse*, with some precious pages devoted to Easter). It is symptomatic, I think, that where one has protest against the *opinio communis* on Lk — whether in what we consider the right or the wrong direction — there one finds greater attention paid to the Easter story ! The exception to this that one hastens to add is G. LOHFINK (*Himmelfahrt*) : an excellent book, extremely helpful to us, and very much mainstream.

Striking out on the densely packed shelves of resurrection monographs, one is either weary or confused, for the most part. Some of these are repetitive, some embarked on massive reconstruction projects for which the reader soon loses the blueprints. One thing is the rule here : Lk 24 will not be heard out on its own terms ! It is usually refractory of reconstructions of either Easter *Historie* or Easter *Überlieferung*, and these have the upper hand in the resurrection books. Nevertheless, we have quarried what we could from this vast literature, and not a little of the guidance our project received came from this quarter, directly or indirectly. Beside the hoary, older works, U. WILCKENS, C. F. EVANS, and R. H. FULLER were helpful guides in this category, with the late-comer, J. E. ALSUP, furnishing much good information amidst a single-minded reconstruction project which made it all but impossible for him to hear the individual voices, like Luke's, among his witnesses.

This being the research situation, painted with a thick brush, it was clearly not desirable to present a *Forschungsbericht* on Lk 24 as a whole. Our predecessors are simply too few and too scattered. We shall set forth the *status quaestionis* on each of the three Easter pericopes, as we perceive it. Our wish here is to raise several questions directed at the widespread opinion on Luke which has been forged by M. DIBELIUS and H. CONZELMANN, convinced as we have become that several of their major tenets cannot withstand the test of a carefully examined Lucan Easter story. Let us list these matters briefly: (1) A most influential judgment dates back to M. DIBELIUS (*Formgeschichte*, 14): Luke's purpose, supposedly defined by his prologue, was to give *not the content* of Christian preaching, but a " warranty " or *historical foundation* for that content. H. CONZELMANN took this up, maintaining that the gospel of Lk furnishes a " Zweites zum Kerygma ... (das) nicht selbst Kerygma (ist), sondern gibt dessen geschichtliche Voraussetzungen " (*MdZ*, 3). These judgments purport to render the objective announced at Lk 1,4 (ἵνα ἐπιγνῷς ... ἀσφάλειαν). (2) From here, dramatic consequences of a systematic nature are urged concerning Luke's project. The basic one is that he has made salvation a matter of an *historical process*, depriving the kerygma of its vital address to the " *now* " of the hearer, and requiring communion with the sacred past through legitimate tradition (G. KLEIN) and " early-Catholic " institution (E. KÄSEMANN, S. SCHULZ). (3) The mediators of Luke's " legitimate tradition " are, of course, the apostles in this view, and their unique, eyewitness experience of the origins guarantees transmission of saving effects to those who receive their tradition through its restricted channels. (4) Concomitant with this concentration on the sacred past and its guarantors is the view that Luke emphasizes *deeds and facts over the interpretative word* (cf. our debate with CONZELMANN on this, pp. 127ff. and n. 172 on p. 127). Faith is supported by historical reasoning, and the room for God's *sola gratia* summons to the individual is drastically restricted by measures of human verification and testimony. (5) Finally, since the deed of God in Christ has become sacred past, and a preordained historical process at that, there is now the commonplace denial that the death of Jesus has soteriological value of its own in Luke's schema (cf. chap. I, n. 84). This stands in fascinating contrast to the threefold explanation of the meaning of the death in the Easter story, as we shall see, but many are convinced the cross can be no more than an historic misdeed of man which God has reversed, — as KÄSEMANN crassly put it, " a malfunction of world-history " which " God repaired at Easter " (quoted p. 289 below).

Much of this criticism ignores the *dialectical moment* in Lucan thought, which comes into its own in the Easter narrative (as we read it) and was brought out with particular emphasis in the monograph of H. FLENDER (recently endorsed in this by R. GLÖCKNER). We shall be intent on probing what has appeared to us as a *denial of the primacy of empirical fact and human experience* in Luke's Easter narrative, and this precisely through a *dialectic of human perception and divine disclosure* dedicated to bringing out just what Luke is not supposed to stand for: Easter revelation as the *pure gift* of God, conveyed only through the personal presence and conclusive *word of the risen Christ.* In the course of this, we shall be inclined to find other answers to the issues posed above than the views we stated there (cf. the fuller discussion of them in chap. IV/pt. ii, esp. in notes 110ff.).

In order to carry out this dialogue with contemporary Lucan criticism, we shall have to approach our subject-matter systematically and methodically, hearing it out patiently on its own terms and applying to it sound norms of both *tradition-* and *redaction*-criticism. What seems most difficult, and what has not as yet succeeded, is the delineation of the source-material the evangelist utilized in his two appearance stories. Yet some such determination, as well as a decision concerning his dependency in the tomb story, will be indispensable to our accurate probing of his mind in telling the Easter story. Our method will be mainly to probe his *selection, coordination, and enlargement of source-material*, both in the material we are studying and in other, related passages. This is, to our mind, the primary procedure for any student of Luke's mind to follow. The method of linguistic and stylistic measurement must be employed in subsidiary status, to confirm or suggest the presence of editorial (or traditional) matter; but as J. Wanke discovered in his minute language-analysis of the Emmaus story, this is an evangelist who has too thoroughly mastered his source-material for any strict dissociation to be made between tradition and composition in terms of vocabulary alone (cf. pp. 79f. below). Not the immanent features of a pericope by themselves, but the measurement of it in terms of the trends established throughout the two volumes of Luke's project: this alone seems the adequate means of access to his mind.

In the unsettled matters of the text of Lk 24, we shall be generally opting for the non-" Western," longer readings, as we shall set forth in each instance, most fully *ad* 24,12 (pp. 59ff. below; also pp. 182ff.).

———————

May I thank, with more feeling than this page can convey, all of those who have made the pursuit and termination of this labor possible. First, I wish to thank Fathers Martini and Vanhoye, who have guided and encouraged me during a period that has lasted longer than anyone expected. They patiently dealt with material submitted irregularly and in haste, and I am grateful for their unfailing kindness and complete availability in spite of their many commitments. I am grateful, too, to my Archbishop, Terence Cardinal Cooke, and to the archdiocesan Department of Education in New York, for unconditional support and financial assistance through my entire course of studies. Special thanks are then due to my Scripture colleague at St. Joseph's Seminary, the Rev. John P. Meier, who preceded me in completing his doctoral work at the Institute, and in doing it quickly and well, goaded me to complete the labors I was too inclined to postpone. My colleague at Fordham University, Dr. Madeleine Boucher, was generously helpful in the preparation of bibliography and manuscript, and I thank her with special emphasis.

Finally, I offer homage to the man who started me on the path of Scripture study years ago, the Rev. Msgr. Myles M. Bourke, now pastor of Corpus Christi parish in New York City, but for many years one who ignited the interest of fledgling seminarians towards probing the inexhaustible riches of τὰ γεγραμμένα.

May 16, 1977 R. J. Dillon

TABLE OF CONTENTS

CHAPTER I

THE DISCOVERY OF THE EMPTY TOMB (Lk 23,55 - 24,12)

(1) *Methods and Presuppositions*:

Amongst the exegetes who have contributed to the mainstream of its modern interpretation, there is nearly universal agreement that Mk 16,1-8 is the literary point of departure for the synoptic tradition of the " empty tomb ".[1] This means, of course, that Mark's version of the story is the one which the other Synoptics develop and adapt (Mt 28,1-8; Lk 24,1-12; cp. Jn 20,1-2.11-13). Further questions concerning the course of this development, possible alternate versions to Mark's which influenced his successors, and the connection of the grave stories to a pre-canonical passion narrative, are all unfinished business and do not give us firm presuppositions for our inquiry. We must take a position on these matters, and yet we cannot settle them. It seems best, therefore, to adopt a working hypothesis on each, in the expectation that close analysis of Luke's text will bear out or modify our judgments in due course. The objective, after all, is to distinguish as clearly as possible our evangelist's raw materials from his editorial initiatives in the one section of Lk 24 where both can be measured by synoptic comparison. Because this is the only Lucan Easter story with formal synoptic parallels, it is the passage from which to expect the soundest clues to a compositional plan for the Easter chapter as a whole.

Whether or not a consecutive account of Jesus' final hours came into writing before Mark and became a common exemplar of the canonical accounts,[2] it is fairly clear that many episodes of the story

[1] Among others: R. BULTMANN, *GsT*, 311; J. FINEGAN, *Überlieferung*, 87; E. HIRSCH, *Auferstehungsgeschichten*, 27; H. von CAMPENHAUSEN, *Ablauf*, 21; W. NAUCK, *ZNW* 47 (1956) 251; G. KOCH, *Auferstehung*, 33; E. M. DHANIS, *Greg* 39 (1958) 370; U. WILCKENS, in *Festschr. F. Smend*, 39, und in *Zur Bedeutung*, 59; G. KEGEL, *Auferstehung*, 21; J. DELORME, in *La résurrection*, 111f.; W. MARXSEN, in *Zur Bedeutung*, 19, and *Auferstehung*, 47; J. KREMER, in *Resurrexit*, 146, 153-154; J. D. CROSSAN, in W. H. Kelber, ed., *The Passion in Mk*, 135ff.

[2] The so-called *Urpassion* — a continuous, organically connected, written account that preceded Mk's — is still very much in dispute, as we learn from

preexisted the writing as independent pericopes, much like the rest of the synoptic tradition, undergoing development of their own at both spoken and written stages.[3] The traditions surrounding Jesus' grave seem to belong to this category. The accounts of the burial and the

---

the recent surveys of G. SCHNEIDER (*BZ* 16 [1972] 222-244) and J. R. DONAHUE (in W. H. Kelber, ed., *The Passion in Mk*, 8-16). The early judgments of the form-critics on this issue were more assumptions than conclusions of adequate literary analysis, e.g. K. L. SCHMIDT, *Rahmen*, 303ff.; M. DIBELIUS, *Formgeschichte*, 21f., 178ff.; R. BULTMANN, *GsT*, 297f., 301f. Even from the earliest days of form-criticism the objection has been heard that, contrary to appearances, "the passion story as well consists of individual pericopes" (G. BERTRAM, *Leidensgeschichte*, 8, 101), and the *opinio communis* is still contradicted on occasion, as recently by E. LINNEMANN (*Studien sur Passionsgeschichte*, 54), who sought to show that the primitive passion tradition was made up, "from beginning to end," of "independent pieces of tradition" whose amalgamation was Mk's work and no one's before him. So also W. H. KELBER, in *The Passion in Mk*, 56 n. 35, 157. — Such departures from the standard consensus show that the usual arguments for the pre-Marcan continuum, of which the unwonted Johannine coincidence with the synoptic sequence (at least from the arrest onward) is undoubtedly the most effective (G. SCHNEIDER, *art. cit.*, 229ff.), do not make the case by themselves and stand in need of thorough-going literary analysis to delineate the alleged ancient account (*ibid.*, 227, 242ff.). — More recently, tentative steps towards filling the gap with adequate, full-scale literary analysis have been taken by L. SCHENKE, *Der gekreuzigte Christus. Versuch einer literarkritischen und traditionsgeschichtlichen Bestimmung der vormarkinischen Passionsgeschichte* (SBS 69; Stuttgart: Katholisches Bibelwerk, 1974), and W. SCHENK, *Der Passionsbericht nach Markus. Untersuchungen zur Überlieferungsgeschichte der Passionstraditionen* (Gütersloh: Gerd Mohn, 1974), lately also D. DORMEYER, *Die Passion Jesu als Verhaltensmodell. Literarische und theologische Analyse der Traditions- und Redaktionsgeschichte der Markuspassion* (NTAbh 11; Münster: Verlag Aschendorff, 1974). All three of these monographs defend and delineate the pre-Marcan narrative by means of literary analyses which will not command universal assent but may advance the *Urpassion* hypothesis, nevertheless, by securing certain evidences for it and encouraging further analysis of this indispensable kind.

[3] Thus did R. BULTMANN (*GsT*, 297ff.) modify the assumptions of SCHMIDT and DIBELIUS, hence taking a position closer to BERTRAM's on the matter. The passion story's components seem often to be episodes which oral tradition developed separately, before and apart from the literary versions, by continuing to recount them as single anecdotes (so BERTRAM, *Leidensgeschichte*, 4). Obvious examples are the stories whose independent existence is documented in other NT books than the gospels: the eucharistic institution account (I Cor 11,23-26) and the death of Judas (Acts 1,18-20). By analogy with these instances, one readily projects an independent function and history for the anointing at Bethany, the denial of Peter, and certain scenes peculiar to one gospel or the other (e.g. Lk's Herod episode and "women of Jerusalem" scene). There is especially good reason for thinking that the introduction to the synoptic passion sequence, including the Bethany anointing, the last supper preparation and component scenes, and the Gethsemane episode, consists of these separate pieces that were not joined in the tradition before Mk's writing (so G. SCHNEIDER, *BZ* 16 [1972] 242, 243, citing with approval L. SCHENKE, *Studien zur markinischen Passionsgeschichte. Tradition und Redaktion in Mk.* 14,1-42 [Forschungen zur Bibel 4; Würzburg: Echter-Verlag, 1971] 12-66, 119-140).

women's visit stand in immediate sequence at Mk 15,42 – 16,8 and in subsequent gospel versions,[4] but the Marcan sequence belies a definite incongruence of the two episodes. The burial account portrays Joseph's service as normal and complete, raising no expectation of the additional ministration of the women.[5] Moreover, the women appear abruptly at the tail-end of Mk's account (15,47) and do not participate at all in its action. Their mention at the burial is an afterthought and suggests secondary tailoring of that story for its connection to the account of Easter morning.[6] Because of the notorious difficulties caused by Mk's separate listings of the women's names, first at the crucifixion scene (15,40) and then in both grave stories (15,47; 16,1), it would appear that the women's association with the burial, and consequently also the problematic sequence of the two grave episodes, might well antedate Mk's composition.[7] Whether this fusion was intended to furnish an Easter climax to a pre-Marcan passion sequence[8] or was the fruit

---

[4] The insertion of Mt 27,62-66 between the two stories is a secondary development related to the episode, equally peculiar to Mt, of the chief priests' bribe (Mt 28,11-15). The apologetic concerns behind these pericopes, and likewise the addition of the guards to the "empty tomb" story (Mt 28,4), clearly came at an advanced phase of the tomb tradition close to Mt and his community. They effectively remove these passages from consideration with the earliest materials of the tomb tradition (cf. H. GRASS, *Ostergeschehen*, 23ff.; H. von CAMPENHAUSEN, *Ablauf*, 28ff.; W. NAUCK, *ZNW* 47 [1956] 254; U. WILCKENS, in *Festschr. Smend*, 32; I. BROER, *Grab*, 60-78 [extensive analysis showing the passages to be Matthean constructs expanding Mk]; R. H. FULLER, *Formation*, 72-73; Ph. SEIDENSTICKER, *Auferstehung*, 87).

[5] This and the obvious problem of the intervening days make the women's subsequent service historically difficult, as many exegetes have pointed out. Cf. R. BULTMANN, *GsT*, 308; H. GRASS, *Ostergeschehen*, 20; J. FINEGAN, *Überlieferung*, 79; I. BROER, *Grab*, 135f.; R.H. FULLER, *Formation*, 51f.; L. SCHENKE, *Auferstehungsverkündigung*, 31ff.; J. BLINZLER, in *Resurrexit*, 63.

[6] J. FINEGAN, *Überlieferung*, 79; I. BROER, *Grab*, 92, 103, 113-116. — Or else the women are original to the tomb tradition in both instances (*pace* L. SCHENKE, *Auferstehungsverkündigung*, 18f., 27f.; J. BLINZLER, in *Resurrexit*, 65), and then one has to find a convincing reason for their mere supernumerary status in the burial story. J. BLINZLER reasons solely on the basis of the differing names in the Marcan lists, and L. SCHENKE argues from his dubious hypothesis of the tradition's origin in Christian services at the tomb site, for whose location the women's witness was supposedly being invoked.

[7] So H. GRASS, *Ostergeschehen*, 181; I. BROER, *Grab*, 135-137; cf. also Ph. SEIDENSTICKER, *Auferstehung*, 62ff. — Because he understands Mk 15,47 to be part of the original burial story, and the story itself to have been the conclusion of the *Urpassion*, L. SCHENKE contends it was Mk who first brought the formerly unrelated burial and empty tomb pericopes into conjunction (*Auferstehungsverkündigung*, 29).

[8] É. DHANIS, *Greg* 39 (1958) 392, 395ff.; U. WILCKENS, in *Zur Bedeutung*, 59, and *Auferstehung*, 55-64; R. H. FULLER, *Formation*, 53; M. HENGEL, in *Festschr. O. Michel*, 246, 253. This position, often argued with little more than arguments *ex convenientia* which assume that narrative and kerygmatic traditions

of some early observance at the Saviour's tomb [9] is an issue we need not explore. Our concern is the question of the Marcan versus alternate sources in Luke's account of the tomb happenings. If we should decide that his departures from Mk in this sequence are consistent and momentous enough to justify the hypothesis of an alternate source,[10] we shall leave to further research the matter of that source's origin and contours.

Many scholars confidently insist, however, that Mk was Luke's controlling source material in the composition of his tomb stories.[11] By this we understand that, whatever modifications of this material might have reached him from oral tradition or an alternate written source,

---

were continuous in the early Church, now receives some analytical support from W. SCHENK, *Passionsbericht* (cited in n. 2 above) 259-271.

[9] W. NAUCK, *ZNW* 47 (1956) 260-263; L. SCHENKE, *Auferstehungsverkündigung*, 86ff.; J. DELORME, in *La résurrection*, 123-132. — A modified liturgical *Sitz-im-Leben*, without dubious assertions about the tomb-site of Jesus, is proposed by X. LÉON-DUFOUR, *Résurrection*, 158f.

[10] Some exegetes maintain that Lk relied *principally* on an alternate, non-Marcan source for his composition of the grave sequence. Thus W. GRUNDMANN, *Lk.*, 436, 439, thinks of a special Lucan source to which the evangelist united " some elements " from Mk. Vincent TAYLOR (*Third Gospel*, 60-66, and *Passion Narrative*, 99ff., 103ff.) proceeds with a mechanical source-criticism, understandably of pre-*redaktionsgeschichtlich* vintage, to his conclusion of a con current, non-Marcan source supposedly dominant in the stories of the burial and women's discovery (but for the old matrix of the former and small elements in the latter). — Other scholars, sensitized by recent trends in redaction-analysis, prefer to keep Mk in the foreground of Lk's source-material but, nevertheless, to invoke special sources generously in analyzing Lk's version of these stories. Thus G. SCHNEIDER, *Verleugnung*, 155; U. WILCKENS, in *Festschr. Smend*, 35f. (but cf. 36); R.H. FULLER, *Formation*, 95ff.; E. L. BODE, *Easter Morning*, 70; J. KREMER, in *Resurrexit*, 154. — J. SCHMITT, *RvScRel* 25 (1951) 123, 127, followed by X. LÉON-DUFOUR, *Résurrection*, 208, propounded the idiosyncratic view that Lk used Mk and Mt *ex aequo*, but one can report no acceptance or development of this suggestion.

[11] Even B. H. STREETER, who formulated an influential argument for a concurrent Lucan *Hauptquelle* in the third gospel's passion and Easter stories (*Four Gospels*, 207f.), nevertheless held that in Lk 23,33-24,10a the evangelist " reversed his usual procedure " and make Mk his main source (*ibid.*, 217). — J. FINEGAN (*Überlieferung*, 86-88), H. GRASS (*Ostergeschehen*, 35), and R. BULTMANN (*GsT Ergänzungsheft*[4], 103) argue one-sidedly for Lk's exclusive dependence on Mk in 24,1-11, but of course this argument rests on the older consensus that v. 12 was a secondary interpolation in Lk's text, — a view which better knowledge of both Lk himself and of the ms. tradition is making more and more questionable. As a result, we shall keep an open mind towards eventual auxiliary source material, particularly at the conclusion of the empty tomb pericope, while maintaining Mk's predominant influence on Lk's narrative through 24,11 (sharing, more or less, the position of J. WELLHAUSEN, *Lc.*, 137; J. M. CREED, *Lk*, 289f.; E. KLOSTERMANN, *Lk.*, 229; W. MICHAELIS, *Erscheinungen*, 49f.; A. DESCAMPS, *Bib* 40 (1959) 737f.; E. LOHSE, *Auferstehung*, 14; B. RIGAUX, *Dieu l'a ressuscité*, 209; J. WANKE, *Emmauserzählung*, 73; R. MAHONEY, *Two Disciples*, 169.

he was composing here *in conscious and deliberate dialogue with his canonical predecessor*; and even such additional changes of the material as might have originated in other sources — for example, the added apostolic presence at the tomb (Lk 24,[12].24) — were made as part of that same dialogue with Mk. Let us attend, first, to preliminary observations which favor Luke's direct use of Mk in the account of the "empty tomb."

(a) It has been observed often that Mt and Lk go their separate ways in the Easter story after recording the events at the tomb (Mt 28,9ff.; Lk 24,13ff.), which means that they jointly used Mk up to 16,8.[12] The later versions of the empty-tomb story, besides taking the obvious step of "improving" Mk's abrupt and disconcerting outcome,[13] appear to follow two general trends:[14] verification of the women's story by prominent disciples (Lk 24,[12].24); Jn 20,3-10) and the addition of an appearance of the risen Lord at or near the tomb-site (Mt 28, 9-10; Jn 20,11-18).[15] Of course, these two trends involve a complicated

---

[12] This is, of course, the most persuasive argument in favor of accepting Mk 16,8 as that gospel's original and intended conclusion (rightly W. Nauck, *ZNW* 47 [1956] 252 n. 46; H. Grass, *Ostergeschehen*, 17 [who nevertheless cannot come to terms with such an original intention]; W. G. Kümmel, *Introd. N. T.*[17], 100f.; W. Michaelis, *Erscheinungen*, 7-9; W. Marxsen, *Einleitung*[3], 125; B. Rigaux, *Dieu l'a ressuscité*, 187). On the compelling evidence for Marcan originality in the shift to a carrying out of the angelic command, cf. also E. Hirsch, *Auferstehungsgeschichten*, 27; H. von Campenhausen, *Ablauf*, 39; M. Hengel, in *Festschr. O. Michel*, 254. W. Michaelis (*op. cit.*, 9) and H. von Campenhausen (*op. cit.*, 25) were already able to take note of the more recent preference of exegetes for the view that Mk 16,8 was the intended termination of the gospel, "... a climax which is consistent with and satisfactory in view of everything which led up to it" (P. Schubert, in *Ntl. Studien f. Bultmann*, 167). As is often verified in such recent opinion trends, it is a better understanding of Mk's own way of thinking, particularly his all-embracing "messianic secret" theory, which has won exegetes over to accepting his intention to close his book so abrasively (cf. W. Marxsen, *Der Evangelist Markus*, 59, 142; J. Delorme, in *La résurrection*, 109f., 134; U. Wilckens, in *Zur Bedeutung*, 59, and *Auferstehung*, 52-53; R.H. Fuller, *Formation*, 64).

[13] Cf. E. Hirsch, H. von Campenhausen, M. Hengel, cited in prev. note. Mk's abrupt conclusion would motivate enterprising ms. copyists to fill in missing appearance accounts (hence Mk 16,9-20 *l.v.*), and Mt and Lk both show the change from the women's puzzling and disobedient concealment of their experience to an obedient announcement to the disciples (Mt 28,8; Lk 24,9). These joint revisions are not immediately to be credited to a non-Marcan source. Surely the mere coincidence of ἀπαγγεῖλαι/ἀπήγγειλαν between Mt and Lk does not establish a common source, *pace* J. Schmitt, *RvScRel* 25 (1951) 126; rightly R. H. Fuller, *Formation*, 100.

[14] U. Wilckens, in *Festschr. Smend*, 40, *Zur Bedeutung*, 59, and *Auferstehung*, 66ff.

[15] Although the empty tomb and appearance stories were originally separate narrative traditions, with little demonstrable interconnection (even Mk 16,7 is secondary to its present context) (cf. H. Grass, *Ostergeschehen*, 86-88), the deve-

tradition process which goes well beyond the activity of these few authors. Our point is, the basic Marcan version of the story was such as to motivate Mt and Lk either to employ alternate information from other auspices or to revise details of his themselves. The diverging paths of enlargement upon Mk separate Lk from Mt, then converge in the highly developed Easter story of Jn.

(b) The citation of Jesus' own promise by the angel at the tomb (Mk 16,7) occasions different adjustments by Mt and Lk for different reasons. Mk's ἐκεῖ αὐτὸν ὄψεσθε, καθὼς εἶπεν ὑμῖν [16] is clearly meant to evoke the promise attached to Jesus' prophecy of the disciples' defection (Mk 14,28 / Mt 26,32; wanting in Lk),[17] but Mt found no mention of "seeing" there, hence shifted καθὼς εἶπεν to a partnership with ἠγέρθη which more accurately echoes the promise (28,6). — Lk, on the other hand, had reported neither the disciples' flight nor the prophecies related to it (Mk 14,26-28), but he retained the tomb story's retrospect upon dominical prophecies by making a full citation of the earlier passion predictions become the focus of the angels' message (24,7). Considering that echoes of those predictions furnish his Easter story's *Leitmotiv* (cf. Lk 24,26.46), and given Lk's unilinear geographical schema, his concentration of the central events at Jerusalem, and the artful twist which made the Galilee of Marcan promise become the Galilee of memory and retrospect (24,7f.), it is difficult to account the novelty of Lk's angelic pronouncement to anything other than this

loping Easter story tended to draw them together and intermingle them, so that the tomb story "drew the appearances irresistably to itself" in the traditions' course (H. GRASS, *op. cit.*, 121; cf. also U. WILCKENS, in *Festschr. Smend*, 31).

[16] It is highly selective vision which allows J. SCHMITT (*RvScRel* 25 [1951] 125) to conclude that, because Mt has attached καθὼς εἶπεν to the resurrection announcement (28,6) and Lk proceeded to quote Jesus' passion prophecy in full (24,7), Lk is consequently dependent upon Mt (!). This is typical of the kind of conclusion that can be drawn when literary analysis is carried on by mechanical comparison, without awareness of the *motivating impulses* which account for specific differences amongst the synoptic texts.

[17] Prevailing opinion seems to classify both Mk 16,7 and 14,28 as redactional contributions to pre-existing, traditional contexts (cf. L. SCHENKE, *Auferstehungsverkündigung*, 43-53; W. MARXSEN, *Evangelist Markus*, 48, 51; U. WILCKENS, *Auferstehung*, 51; G. KEGEL, *Auferstehung*, 70; but already R. BULTMANN, *GsT*, 287, 309, among many others). It is rare that either of these promises is considered original to its present context (as *pace* H. von CAMPENHAUSEN, *Ablauf*, 37 n. 147, re. 16,7, and *pace* M. DIBELIUS, *Formgeschichte*, 182, 184, 190f., re. 14,28; cf. E. LOHMEYER, *Galiläa*, 29, 34). It is true that the promise itself is probably traditional, and not the invention of Mk (cf. B. RIGAUX, *Dieu l'a ressuscité*, 218f. n. 38), but its present position in both the supper passage and the tomb story is clearly the result of interpolation by the redactor into preexistent, coherent sequences (rightly C. F. EVANS, *Resurrection*, 78-79; E. L. BODE, *Easter Morning*, 35-37).

evangelist's deliberate editing of Mk. In fact, this is a point of nearly universal consensus amongst the authors we have studied.[18]

(c) The fact that Mk's tomb stories both lay before Lk is apparent from the noticeably reduced role of the "stone," which has been eliminated from Lk's account of Joseph's provisions (cp. Mk 15,46c) and the women's trek to the tomb (cp. Mk 16,3) but is suddenly encountered at Lk 24,2: εὗρον δὲ τὸν λίθον κτλ. We know of "the stone" indeed, but from Mk, not Lk! In just such ways does our evangelist betray his debt to his principal source-text.[19]

In the course of these preliminary observations, we have noticed that Lk's burial story, too, seems to have been adapted by him mainly from the Marcan source.[20] Indeed, the sequence of the two tomb episodes might well have been refashioned by our evangelist in critical reaction to Mk's narrative.[21] Let us admit, however, that our observations thus far suffice neither individually nor in sum to solve the

---

[18] Among others: H.-J. Holtzmann, *Synoptiker*³, 421; J. Finegan, *Überlieferung*, 87; E. Hirsch, *Auferstehungsgeschichten*, 14; W. Michaelis, *Erscheinungen*, 48ff.; H. Grass, *Ostergeschehen*, 33; H. Conzelmann, "Zur Lukasanalyse," in Braumann-*LkEv*, 59, and *MdZ*, 85f., 188; P. Schubert, in *Ntl. Studien f. Bultmann*, 168; M. Brändle, *Orientg* 24 (1960) 86, 89; U. Wilckens, in *Festschr. Smend*, 34 n. 13, and *Missionsreden*, 116; E. Lohse, *Auferstehung*, 18f.; H.-W. Bartsch, *Wachet*, 20-21; J. Riedl, *BibLit* 40 (1967) 102; G. Kegel, *Auferstehung*, 87; C. F. Evans, *Resurrection*, 103; R. H. Fuller, *Formation*, 97-98; B. Rigaux, *Dieu l'a ressuscité*, 207; and all the commentaries.

[19] The "stone" motif is carried out integrally in the three Marcan references (cf. H. Grass, *Ostergeschehen*, 20; E. Meyer, *Ursprung und Anfänge* I, 20; H. von Campenhausen, *Ablauf*, 25; L. Schenke, *Auferstehungsverkündigung*, 37ff.; C. F. Evans, *Resurrection*, 77; R. H. Fuller, *Formation*, 51), but that integrity has been broken by Lk for the purpose, as we shall suggest, of bringing the women's ministrations into closer conjunction with Joseph's. — If the use of μνῆμα (Lk 23,53; 24,1) alongside the more usual μνημεῖον (Lk 23,55; 24,2.9.12. 22.24) were already verified in the Marcan tomb sequence, as some authors assume (e.g. U. Wilckens, in *Festschr. Smend*, 34; L. Schenke, *Auferstehungsverkündigung*, 40-41; I. Broer, *Grab*, 169; J. Wanke, *Emmauserzählung*, 71; B. Rigaux, *Dieu l'a ressuscité*, 188), this would be a further persuasive argument for Lk's reliance on Mk in the tomb sequence. The same duality of *vocabula* is verified, in any case, at Mk 5,2ff. (*par.* Lk 8,27), but the mss. are not agreed on μνῆμα in Mk 15,46b or Mk 16,2, so we do better not to rely on this argument.

[20] This is admitted by even so strong an advocate of a proto-Lucan *Sonderquelle* as V. Taylor (cf. *Third Gospel*, 59f., and *Passion Narrative*, 100, re. Lk 23,50-54). Cf. also J. Finegan, *Überlieferung*, 35; I. H. Marshall, *TyndB* 24 (1973) 65; J. Blinzler, in *Resurrexit*, 70f., and the convincing demonstration of Mk's originality in the burial pericope, and the use of him by Mt and Lk, given by I. Broer, *Grab*, 44-59.

[21] R. Bultmann, *GsT*, 296f.; U. Wilckens, *Festschr. Smend*, 33f.; Ph. Seidensticker, *Auferstehung*, 63 n. 6. The improved connection between the two pericopes was also noticed by J. Schmitt (*RvScRel* 25 [1951] 131,134) but was wrongly accounted by him to Lk's use of a non-Marcan, "Jerusalem source."

literary problem of the first Easter pericope. We have yet to show *why* Lk observed the Marcan sequence so closely, or what he meant to say about these episodes *beyond what Mk had said.* To secure our judgment of the genesis of Lk's text and, more importantly, to draw *interpretative results* out of it, we must follow the text in detail, noting the distinctive turns of Lucan language and thought over against the source-text, and searching for an emerging picture of the Easter events which will coherently explain the various editorial initiatives we discern. For our purposes, the emergence of such a *coherent interpretative pattern* of modifying Mk in the tomb stories will both confirm Lk's purposeful dialogue with his predecessor and give us a tentative compositional design to be verified in the remaining Easter pericopes. A circle of mutually reinforcing hypotheses, drawn to connect recurrent themes of the Lucan *opera,* on the one hand, and divergences from Mk in the tomb sequence, on the other hand: this is the course we intend to follow in pursuit of the test-pattern for the rest of Lk 24.

(2) *The Women at the Tomb* (Lk 23,[49]55 – 24,1):

Lk draws more out of the women's part in the *triduum sacrum* than Mk had.[22] A series of participles typical of his narrative style[23] impresses on us the totality of their exposure to the Lord's journey and its ending: συνακολουθοῦσαι (23,49), κατακολουθήσασαι ... συνεληλυθυῖαι (23,55), φέρουσαι ... εἰσελθοῦσαι (24,1.3), ὑποστρέψασαι (24,9; 23,56). The confusion of Mk's listings of the women's names is avoided, and one list is proposed at the end of the sequence (24,10). Lk accentuates what is the more important matter for him: these are the women who "*have come up from Galilee*" with Jesus, hence they are members of

[22] In Mk the women had provided continuity of witness during the *triduum sacrum,* but had borne this task alone since all the disciples had fled the scene of the passion at Mk 14,50 (cf. H. GRASS, *Ostergeschehen,* 181; L. SCHENKE, *Auferstehungsverkündigung,* 22f., 26f.; Ph. SEIDENSTICKER, *Auferstehung,* 62f.). However one explains the variation of the three Marcan lists (cf. possibilities in I. BROER, *Grab,* 104-105), the fact that there are three, and their location at cross, burial, and empty tomb episodes, all derive from the developing concern for continuity of witness. "Man versteht, dass sie unter diesem Gesichtspunkt mit Nachdruck genannt und hervorgehoben werden" (H. von CAMPENHAUSEN, *Ablauf,* 23). — We do not mean, of course, that the motif of the women's witness was created out of apologetic need, given the flight of the disciples before Jesus' death (so R. BULTMANN, *GsT,* 296). J. FINEGAN (*Überlieferung,* 77) and H. GRASS (*Ostergeschehen,* 182) are quite correct in opposing BULTMANN's hypercriticism on this issue. Cf. also J. BLINZLER, in *Resurrexit,* 66f.

[23] J. H. MOULTON, *A Grammar of N. T. Greek,* vol. III: Syntax, by Nigel TURNER (Edinburgh: T. & T. Clark, 1963) 158. Cf. also A. PLUMMER, *Lk,* lxii.

that stable gallery of " witnesses " who provide a crucial continuity-factor in the whole story of Lk-Acts.[24]

Of course, neither as credential of discipleship nor as experience of the women-witnesses does the *anabasis*-motif originate with Lk. He has drawn it quite directly from Mk (10,32 ; 15,41), but he has accentuated it as a criterion of discernment for the nascent missionary church. It was from the ranks of συναναβάντες ἀπὸ τῆς Γαλιλαίας that the missionary μάρτυρες πρὸς τὸν λαόν were recruited by the risen Christ (Acts 13,31), just as that same circle (συνελθόντες ... ἐν παντὶ χρόνῳ) furnished the candidates for the vacant position of Judas amongst the special Twelve (Acts 1,21ff.). The women's part in the momentous dominical journey, expressed with the nuance of its permanent effect through the perfect participle συνεληλυθυῖαι (23,55), qualified them for membership in the same *nucleus of the primitive church* (Acts 1,14). That nuclear circle belongs to the framework and continuum of Lk's Easter narrative, together with the sustained " third day " timing and stable Jerusalem locale (Lk 24,9.13.33 ; *vide infra*)[25], all of which will demonstrate the direct birth of the Christian mission from the *vita Jesu* (Lk 24,44-49). Our evangelist carefully safeguards the integrity of the formative witness-circle at every step of his story, even back at the crucifixion scene (23,49), where he put πάντες οἱ γνωστοὶ αὐτῷ next to the Galilean women, whom Mk had standing alone ἀπὸ μακρόθεν (Mk 15,40f.). This Lucan initiative was possible, we recall, because the Marcan prophecy and report of the disciples' flight from the passion scene (Mk 14,27.50 *par*. Mt) had been passed over in Lk (note the contrasting πάντες in Mk 14,50 and Lk 23,49 !).

A significant Lucan variation on Mk's theme of the Galilean women appears in the fact that Lk was not introducing them for the first time on Calvary. He had already placed them alongside the Twelve back in the Galilean phase of Jesus' ministry (Lk 8,1-3), in a passage

[24] On the *anabasis* from Galilee as basic criterion of Lucan witness, cf. G. KLEIN, *Zwölf Apostel*, 207f., and in *Zeit und Geschichte*. *Festschr*. *Bultmann*, 201-205 ; H. FLENDER, *Heil*, 110 ; W. C. ROBINSON, *Weg*, 39 ; E. NELLESSEN, *Zeugnis*, 206ff. As we shall see later on (in chap. IV), G. KLEIN's insistance on narrowing the group of ἀναβάντες to the Twelve, making theirs an " official " witness for the legitimation of the Lucan historiography, is not supported in the text of Lk-Acts and needs the correction it has now gotten from E. NELLESSEN, and others.

[25] On this conscious Lucan " framing " of the Easter story, aimed at drawing the episodes together into an integral picture held together by common time, place, and witnesses, cf. L. BRUN, *Auferstehung*, 85ff. ; H. GRASS, *Ostergeschehen*, 114 ; E. MEYER, *Ursprung und Anfänge* I, 33f. ; J. KREMER, *Osterbotschaft*, 80 ; A. GEORGE, in I. de la Potterie, éd., *De Jésus aux évangiles*, 117-119 ; A. DESCAMPS, *Bib* 40 (1959) 738 ; C. F. EVANS, *Resurrection*, 95ff. ; J. WANKE, *BZ* 18 (1974) 187.

which proves to be a skillful blending of his own special tradition with the Marcan sequence.[26] The women come on stage there just as Lk is returning to the Marcan material after his " lesser insertion " of Q and *Sondergut* passages, Lk 6,20 – 7,50. They are introduced with names which, but for " Mary called Magdalene," occur only at this point in the gospel tradition,[27] just as only this passage informs us of the healed sick and demoniacs among the women, including Mary herself. On the other hand, Mk 15,41 is clearly echoed at Lk 8,3b [28] (ἕτεραι/ἄλλαι πολλαί ... διηκόνουν) and is probably responsible for the location of Lk's first report of the women-followers back in the story of the Galilean ministry.

There is a further aspect of the positioning of Lk 8,2-3 which may clarify Lk's intentions in reechoing those verses at 23,49 and 24,10. The list of indebted women following the Master in Galilee directly

[26] H. CONZELMANN, *MdZ*, 41: " Das Motiv von den galiläischen Frauen hängt natürlich mit Mc 15,40 zusammen. Dass die Namen variieren, weist zwar auf Seitenüberlieferung, aber nicht notwendig auf eine neue ' Quelle ' im spezifischen Sinn." I. BROER agrees that the appearance of the women in Lk's Galilean narrative is a conclusion drawn from Mk 15,40f. (*Grab*, 101); similarly E. MEYER, *Ursprung und Anfänge* I, 185 n. 1; J. FINEGAN, *Überlieferung*, 34; and in a detailed demonstration, J. DELOBEL, " L'onction par la pécheresse. La composition littéraire de Lc., VII, 36-50," *ETL* 42 (1966, 415-475) 445-449. — The names, of course, derive from Lk's *Sondergut*, but Lk 8,3 shows the influence of Mk 15,41 (rightly G. LOHFINK, *Sammlung Israels*, 67). This combination of dependencies is probably correctly stated by CONZELMANN and LOHFINK, but others prefer to think of Lk 8,2f. and Mk 15,40f. as " zwei ältere Traditionsstücke verschiedener Herkunft " (M. HENGEL, in *Festschr. O. Michel*, 247; cf. also H. SCHÜRMANN, *Lk.* I, 448).

[27] Beside Mary Magdalene and the certain Susanna, never elsewhere mentioned, Lk 8,3 mentions " Joanna, the wife of Chuza, Herod's steward," and this lady appears as a witness of the empty tomb, expressly named at 24,10. This specific information might have something to do with Lk's special interest in the house of Herod (Lk 1,5 [Herod the Great]; 3,1 [Herod Antipas, and his brother Philip]; also 3,19f.; 8,3; 9,7-9; 13,31; 23,7; Acts 13,1; Acts 12 [Herod Agrippa]; cf. M. HENGEL, in *Festschr. O. Michel*, 246) as well as in Herod's adversary stance towards the ministry of Jesus (cf. Lk 13,31ff.; 23,7-12). For her husband's service to the hated puppet ruler of the Romans, Joanna would hardly have been more highly regarded than the tax-collectors and sinners in Jesus' following by the leadership and mainstream adherents of Palestinian Judaism. She is therefore not to be considered an exceptional woman of high station among the others, as if she were more likely to alter the official criticism of Jesus' company.

[28] J. DELOBEL, *ETL* 42 (1966) 448: " L'ensemble de ces trois versets (Lk 8,1-3) est, bien sûr, à mettre en rapport avec Lc., XXIII, 49 ... et Mc., XV, 41 .... Ce dernier verset semble avoir inspiré les deux passages chez Lc. Notons que Luc préfère ἕτεραι à ἄλλαι et αἵτινες à αἵ. Nous estimons pouvoir conclure que Lc., VIII, 1-3 est une composition rédactionelle de Luc, qui transpose logiquement le motif de Mc., XV, 41 dans la période galiléenne." Cf. also G. LOHFINK, *loc. cit.* in n. 26.

adjoins the celebrated story of the *sinful woman who anointed the neglected Houseguest and received forgiveness for her loving gesture* (Lk 7, 36-50). It is never explicitly reported that this forgiven sinner joined the ranks of Jesus' feminine followers, but in our opinion that very suggestion is contained in the sequence of her story with 8,2f. and in certain editorial touches in the story itself.[29]

The " sinful woman " pericope is non-Marcan, like the " lesser insertion " in which it is found, but it includes a few details evoking comparison with the anointing story used by Mk and the other evangelists as a prelude to the passion of Jesus (Mk 14,3-9 / Mt 26,6-13 / Jn 12,1-8). Although Lk has omitted the Marcan story *in situ*, he seems to have incorporated some of its language into his own story, perhaps after the tradition before him had fused the anointment motif to an original foot-cleansing with tears and hair.[30] The center of the two anointing stories is not the same, of course. Lk's focuses on the vindication of the repentant sinner over the self-righteous *homo religiosus*, whereas Mk's makes the woman's gesture a preparation for Jesus' burial (Mk 14,8 & par.). Lk seems to have sacrificed the *anointing for burial* by omitting the Marcan story *in situ* (cf. Lk 22, 2/3).[31] But has he suppressed that point after all ? Could the slight

[29] E. KLOSTERMANN (*Lk.*, 95) takes note of the view that Lk 8,2f. was intended as a companion picture to Lk 7,36-50, and H. SCHÜRMANN (*Lk.* I, 447) positively favors it, noting that both the healed women and the forgiven sinner are presented as recipients of the free gift of the Saviour's mercy. It is, moreover, a compositional technique which Lk learned well from Mk to juxtapose individual episodes and generalized summaries denoting the same or related activities (cf. H. J. CADBURY, *The Making*, 58 ; M. DIBELIUS, *Aufsätze zur Apg.*, 15f.).

[30] Cf. W. GRUNDMANN, *Lk.*, 170 ; G. BOUWMAN, " La pécheresse hospitalière (Lc., VII, 36-50)," *ETL* 45 (1969, 172-179) 174 ; J. DELOBEL, *art. cit.* (in n. 26) 467ff. ; E. HAENCHEN, *Weg Jesu*, 470-472. U. WILCKENS prefers to think of direct Lucan retouching of the story with the anointment motif as well as the Marcan vocabulary (" Vergebung für die Sünderin [Lk 7,36-50]," in P. Hoffmann, hrsg., *Orientierung an Jesus. Zur Theologie der Synoptiker, für J. Schmid* [Freiburg/Basel : Herder, 1973, 394-424] 398f., 417, 421), whereas others posit literary dependence of Jn on Lk for the detail of the foot-anointing (so Hans DREXLER, " Die grosse Sünderin Lukas 7,36-50," *ZNW* 59 [1968, 159-173] 162). Since Jn 12,3 contains the curious detail of the *anointing* of the feet (just as in Lk 7, 38), as well as the washing of them, it is preferable to think of an assimilation process in the oral tradition between two basic stories : one of a woman's anointing Jesus' *head* with ointment, another of a sinful woman's bathing his *feet* with her tears. — J. DELOBEL (*ETL* 42 [1966] 468) specifies the verbal similarities between Mk 14,3 and Lk 7,37 : ἐν τῇ οἰκίᾳ (Σίμωνος), κατακειμένου/κατάκειται, ἦλθεν/καὶ ἰδοὺ γυνή, ἀλάβαστρον μύρου.

[31] H. DREXLER, *art. cit.* (prev. note) 161f. It is hardly just the usual Lucan tendency to avoid doublets that accounts for the omission of Mk 14,3-9 (H. SCHÜRMANN, *Traditionsgesch. Untersuchungen*, 279-289 ; 286), given that some fifteen instances of genuine doublets can be counted in his gospel (*ibid.*, 272-278), to say nothing of the well-known repetitions in Acts. It is wiser to accord this skillful author the presumption that his editorial decisions are never mech-

assimilation to Mk 14,3ff. in the account of the sinful woman have had the purpose of subtle anticipation of the women's presence at Jesus' tomb?

The possibility that Lk indeed intended an implicit relation between the forgiven sinner of 7,36ff. and the corps of feminine attendants to Jesus' *anabasis*, is enhanced by a detail of Lk 23,56. Here the women observers, returning from Jesus' tomb, are said to prepare " spices *and ointments* " in order to play their part in his burial. Only apparently is this a casual addition of μύρα to the ἀρώματα of Mk 16,1! " Precious ointment," μύρον, is just what the sinful woman had used to anoint the Master's feet (Lk 7,37.38.46), the one item most evidently borrowed by Lk from the Marcan story of the woman's burial preparation (Lk 7,37 / Mk 14,3: ἀλάβαστρον μύρου). Now both the literary juxtaposition of Lk 7,36ff. and 8,2f. and the precious ointment's reappearance in the tomb sequence, both literary initiatives of this skillful manager of his traditions, form a combined argument for including the forgiven sinner among the Galilean wayfarers who became witnesses of the *triduum paschale*. Though it is admittedly a subtle detail of literary arrangement, it is fully consonant with Lk's sustained portrayal of Jesus' following (cf. Lk 15,1), and it will have added significance in view of the conjunction of forgiveness-preaching and witness mandates in 24,47f. (*q.v.*).

This fuller Lucan background of the women at the tomb, resting mainly on the foundation of Mk, explains, in turn, the more *active role* Lk assigns them in Jesus' burial, in contrast to their secondary, passive presence in Mk 15,47.[32] In Lk they take note not just of *where* the burial was done (Mk) but of " *how his body was laid* " (ὡς ἐτέθη ... Lk 23,55).[33] They return immediately and prepare " spices and ointments "

---

anical but always made for a reason dictated by his overall design. In that case, we should better speak of a conscious anticipation at Lk 7,36-50 of the passion-oriented anointing of Mk 14,3ff. (rightly J. DELOBEL, *ETL* 42 [1966] 468 n. 205).

[32] H. GRASS, *Ostergeschehen*, 32; R. H. FULLER, *Formation*, 95f. The women's seeming " close cooperation with Joseph of Arimathea " (FULLER) is prepared for by the mention of " *all his acquaintances* " together with the women at 23,49 (*diff.* Mk 15,40). The words οἱ γνωστοὶ ... ἀπὸ μακρόθεν are an allusion to Ps 38,12 and Ps 88,9.19; but taken together with v. 51 (*diff.* Mk 15,43), they permit the implication that Joseph was among the followers of Jesus who stood observing the crucifixion scene (cf. H. GRASS, *Ostergeschehen*, 174).

[33] H. GRASS, *Ostergeschehen*, 32; J. BLINZLER, in *Resurrexit*, 64, 70f. n. 48. Aside from passages he has received from his sources (Lk 11,34.36; 12,4.22f.; 17,37 from Q; 22,19; 23,52 from Mk), Lk seems to prefer the application of σῶμα to the dead body in his own writing (Lk 23,55; 24,3 [*diff.* Mk 16,5]; 24, 23; Acts 9,40). In any case, he does not adopt the alternate πτῶμα (Mk 15,45;

to complete what is now shown to be *an incomplete burial*! No stone was rolled across the tomb's entrance by Joseph (Mk 15,46), as if to preclude or obstruct the further ministrations of the women (Mk 16,3). Lk's transfer of their preparations to the burial episode, *before* the intervening sabbath (cp. Mk 16,1), is therefore part of a deliberate involvement of the women in the action of burial, hence a skillful *fusion of the two, awkwardly related Marcan pericopes into one*! It is not just " smoothing out the narrative sequence "[34] or making room " to locate all the appearance traditions on Easter day "[35] that Lk is about; he is paring two pericopes down to a *single episode*, with the women becoming central figures throughout. The new, single episode, fashioned within the restraints of the Marcan *Vorlage*, may then be expected to form the threshold, by way of coherence or contrast, for the main Easter narratives that follow it.

Our evangelist's contouring of the grave stories as one is also manifest in the series of *time notices* which he inherits from Mk but rearranges.[36] The first of these, significantly enough, has been transferred from the beginning of the burial pericope, where it referred to Joseph's initiative, to a position following Joseph's activity, where it now pertains to *the women's ministrations* (Lk 23,54). The new wording of the notice is a typically economical Lucan recasting of Mk 15, 42.[37] Now we understand how the women, hastening to prepare ma-

also Mt twice) in reproducing the present passage. Cf. J. WANKE, *Emmauserzählung*, 71.

[34] U. WILCKENS, in *Festschr. Smend*, 34.

[35] J. WANKE, *Emmauserzählung*, 74. Still less is it just accentuating the pious, loving deliberation of the women (J. FINEGAN, *Überlieferung*, 35). — Because R. H. FULLER discerns only " an attempt to wrestle with the difficulties of the Marcan version " (*Formation*, 96) in these changes, rather than a conscious editorial pursuit of Lk's own objectives, he is content to speak of changes already introduced in the pre-Lucan tradition (*ibid.*, 95).

[36] J. SCHMITT (*RvScRel* 25 [1951] 131) points these out correctly, but he insists they come from a gratuitous "Jerusalem source." Rightly, *e contra*, J. WANKE, *Emmauserzählung*, 73f., and *BZ* 18 (1974) 186.

[37] From ἤδη ὀψίας γενομένης, ἐπεὶ ἦν παρασκευή, ὅ ἐστιν προσάββατον ... (Mk), we now read: ἡμέρα ἦν παρασκευῆς, καὶ σάββατον ἐπέφωσκεν (Lk). — ἐπιφώσκειν, " shine forth," " dawn," " break in," has rare attestation, but it seems always to refer to real dawn where it is found, e.g. in the papyri or LXX variant readings (at Job 41,10; cp. ἐπιφαύσκειν at Job 25,5; 31,26; διαφαύσκειν at Gen 44,3; Jgs 16,2; 19,26; I Kgs 14,36; II Kgs 2,32; Jth 14,2, occasionally supplanted by διαφώσκειν in the mss.). There is no reason, therefore, to hold that ἐπιφωσκούσῃ in Mt 28,1 is an original tradition, reflecting rabbinical adaptation of the verb to the onset of the Jewish day at sunset, whereas Mk mistook the reference and interpreted it with ἀνατείλαντος τοῦ ἡλίου (Mk 16,2; *pace* E. L. BODE, *Easter Morning*, 12f., following M. BLACK, *An Aramaic Approach to the Gospels and Acts* [3rd ed.; Oxford, 1967] 136-138). The instances just cited, together with the two uses of the verb in *Evang. Petri* (9,34.35; cf. K. ALAND,

terials for the embalming, are overtaken by the sabbath (Lk 23,56b) and have to suspend their participation in the burial during it. The women's sabbath rest is clearly a conclusion drawn from Mk 16,1 and requires no other source-basis.[38] Its particular value to Lk, however, is that it sets the stage, chronologically, for the subsequent phases of the paschal happenings: " the first day of the week " (24,1 = Mk), when the action can continue, and the distinctively Lucan kerygmatizing thereof: " *the third day* " (24,7.21b.46). In short, here is the carefully constructed *time-framework* in which the Lucan Easter story will be told.[39] The imposition of an exact chronological schema on his narrative is one of Lk's devices for bringing out the theological significance of the events recounted.[40]

Their sabbath rest brings the women back to the tomb " on the first day of the week " (24,1), in accordance with the original introduction of the empty-tomb story. Not that Lk is the rationalist concerned with the implausibility of such a belated embalming,[41] but at least now we have it that their intention did not originate on the " third day " but was forcibly suspended by the sabbath. Lk replaces Mk's λίαν πρωί with an accentuated notice of the early hour: ὄρθρου βαθέως (*prima luce*), and typically omits Mk's duplicative ἀνατείλαντος τοῦ ἡλίου, as Mt also does (28,1).[42] The noun ὄρθρος (here and Acts

Syn. 4. Evang., §§ 351, 352) which, like Mt, seem indeed to refer to early "dawn" (9,34: πρωίας δὲ κτλ., and 9,35 in context), show that Mt is more likely interpreting and condensing Mk at 28,1 in accordance with the more common sense of this verb (so F. NEIRYNCK, " Les femmes au tombeau: étude de la rédaction matthéenne [Matt. XXVIII. 1-10]," *NTS* 15 [1968-69, 168-190] 190 n. 4). NEIRYNCK's study demonstrates that Mt 28,1-10 is based on no tradition independent of Mk 16,1-8 (cf. esp. *art. cit.*, 170-176), and particularly Mt 28,1, with its harmonization of Marcan names (*ibid.*, 187 n. 6), is a secondary composition unlikely to hold any glimmers of primitive tradition. — If Mt and *Evang. Petri* attest ἐπιφώσκειν in its usual sense of real dawn, Lk's usage at 23,54 is then an independent accomodation of the verb to the onset of the sabbath at sunset. No common source is to be defended on the basis of this unusual word.

[38] J. FINEGAN, *Überlieferung*, 35; J. BLINZLER, in *Resurrexit*, 71. On the supposed conflict between the Lucan sabbath rest and the actual prescriptions of rabbinical law permitting such ministrations as the women wished to perform (*pace* FINEGAN), cf. BLINZLER, *loc. cit.*, n. 50.

[39] Cf. note 25 above, and especially C. F. EVANS, *Resurrection*, 95f.; A. GEORGE, in *De Jésus aux évangiles*, 118.

[40] Emphasized by H. CONZELMANN, " Zur Lukasanalyse," in Braumann-*LkEv*, 62, and *MdZ*, 27.

[41] The changes of Mk's account made in Lk are not mainly attempts to deal with the " difficulties " of Mk's version (*pace* R. H. FULLER, *Formation*, 95f.). Lk is not engaged in legitimating a naive story for sophisticated readers, for his intentions with the empty tomb are by no means apologetic.

[42] It is common that Mt and Lk jointly eliminate such duplicative expressions in Mk, which are typical of the less cultivated style of the earliest evangelist (cf. examples in J. B. HAWKINS, *Horae syn.*, 110-112). A closely parallel

5,21 only), together with the verb (Lk 21,38 only) and adjective (Lk 24,22 only) of the same root, constitute an exclusively Lucan word-group in the NT. Consequently, our author's revision of Mk 16,1-2 will not require the hypothesis of a concurrent, non-Marcan source to explain it. Lk 24,1 is a tersely effective clasp between the previously disjointed burial and empty-tomb pericopes, with the combination of its main clause and participial supplement displaying the newly fashioned unity of the two.

So much for Lk's paragraph concerning the women who came to the tomb. We have seen that its intent was to make the women function actively in Jesus' burial just as they had formerly in the empty tomb story alone. By taking this initiative Lk fulfilled the hint of (Marcan) burial anticipation he had instilled in the story of the sinful woman, with its adjoining summary depicting Jesus' Galilean following (Lk 7,36-8,3). He has also condensed the burial and the women's discovery into a single, progressive sequence at Jesus' tomb,[43] so that the newly fused pericopes can function together as a *prelude to the great awakening of Easter faith.* How the tomb sequence thus functions will emerge as our treatment continues. — For the moment, neither in 23,55 – 24,1 nor in the preceding burial report have we found any reason to maintain Lk was working on any source other than Mk. Apart from a fragment or two of the oral tradition which had repeated the story many times after, or apart from, Mk's work,[44] Lk has been forming his composition thus far on the basis of Mk, but in conscious, critical dialogue with him.

---

instance is Mk 1,32 (ὀψίας δὲ γενομένης, ὅτε ἔδυσεν ὁ ἥλιος), where Mt eliminates the second temporal clause, Lk eliminates the first.

[43] Cf. X. Léon-Dufour, *Résurrection*, 200. The " empty tomb " had its own independent function in Mk since it contained only a short prophecy of the appearances to follow (16,7) and the latter were not to be narrated thereafter. Now that two apparitions of the risen One follow on the same " day " in Lk's narrative, and are recounted as the tomb story's aftermath, the latter appears only as a preliminary and inconclusive episode in the Easter sequence (rightly G. Koch, *Auferstehung*, 32).

[44] Oral tradition's influence can be sensed, for example, in the descriptions of Joseph's sepulchre : " hewn out of rock " (Mk 15,46), " new " (Mt 27,60), " where(in) no one had yet been laid/buried " (Lk/Jn) (I. H. Marshall, *TyndB* 24 [1973] 64). The tradition's edifying impulses carried this motif along without benefit of literary borrowings, for the most part. Similar edifying changes in the image of the suffering and crucified Jesus were carried out in oral developments of the passion-narrative tradition (cf. I. Broer, *Grab*, 54ff., citing Mk 11,2 / Lk 19,30 as an expression parallel to the sepulchre descriptions).

(3) *The Women's Discovery* (Lk 24,2-3):

The most noticeable departure from Mk in this passage is the absence of the women's concern about the great stone which would block their way (Mk 16,3). The same element is missing from Mt's account, but then so is the women's embalming project itself, whose implausibilities Mt apparently sensed.[45] Lk's omission of the question about the stone is understandable because he also omitted mention of the stone in the first place, to maintain, as we proposed, the unity of burial service by Joseph and the women. Since, however, the stone is finally mentioned as part of the women's discovery in 24,2, Lk might just as well have included Mk's deliberative question since it might have diminished the jolting impression that his single mention of " the stone " presently makes. Clearly, his omission of the question is not sufficiently motivated by the mere omission of the stone from the burial scene.

To find the real reason for this gap, we have to inquire what the women's question, and indeed the whole " stone " motif, contributes to the Marcan narrative. On this there happens to be substantial agreement.[46] The women's concern for the great stone is not well-timed for psychological verisimilitude but is perfectly timed for dramatic effect, for it builds the narrative's momentum towards their shocking discovery. An impressive contrast results between the women's project and the reality proclaimed in the angel's kerygma.[47] The preparations and uncertainties of the embalming mission are a *foil* for what the heavenly messenger discloses: the Easter tidings of earliest Christendom. Even if Mk proceeds to veil this tomb revelation with his familiar messianic secret, for good reasons of his own,[48] the force of the original narrative's

---

[45] U. Wilckens, in *Festschr. Smend*, 32. — Besides, having put the tomb under guard (Mt 27,62-66), Mt could hardly retain the women's anointing project (F. Neirynck, *art. cit.* [in n. 37 above] 175).

[46] See note 19 above, and also X. Léon-Dufour, *Résurrection*, 154ff.; B. Rigaux, *Dieu l'a ressuscité*, 191f. — The feeling is widespread amongst the authors cited that the stone-motif is the Marcan redactor's enrichment of the tomb stories (cf. also S. Schulz, *Stunde*, 140; J. Kremer, in *Resurrexit*, 152; extensively L. Schenke, *Auferstehungsverkündigung*, 38ff.). The most plausible explanation is that the stone references in Mk 16,3-4 have been infused into the story by Mk in order to connect it with the tradition of the burial, with which it was not originally associated (cf. Mk 15,46 *fin.*), which is basically the view these authors adopt.

[47] U. Wilckens, *Auferstehung*, 47: " Diese Verkündigung ist der eigentliche Kern der Geschichte." Cf. also C. F. Evans, *Resurrection*, 76-78; H. Grass, *Ostergeschehen*, 20f.; G. Koch, *Auferstehung*, 29f.; L. Schenke, *Auferstehungsverkündigung*, 54, 70f., 72ff.

[48] Certain suggested " reasons " are surely to be rejected. The " secrecy " motif is hardly serving the self-critical purpose of explaining why the empty

dialectical movements is still plain as day. — When, therefore, Lk diminishes the tension-building component of the women's project, mentions "the stone" only in haste towards the real "finding" (vv. 2f.), and transfers the women's perplexity (ἀπορεῖσθαι) from Mk's stone-query to the discovery inside the tomb (v. 4),[49] we realize that the original story's momentous contrast has less importance in his composition. Not only is the "foil" of the women's project much less emphatic, but what breaks forth from the *angeli interpretes* in vv. 5ff. is something less than the joyous Easter message of Mk's account. It has, in fact, more the nature of a reproach, a scolding reminder,[50] than a breaking of joyous news. The implication is that a proper under-

tomb story was unknown at earlier stages of the tradition (*pace* M. Dibelius, *Formgeschichte*, 190; R. Bultmann, *GsT*, 308; H. Grass, *Ostergeschehen*, 22; G. Kegel, *Auferstehung*, 71; H.-W. Bartsch, *Wachet*, 20; S. Schulz, *Stunde*, 141). Such an explanation smacks of the discredited explanation W. Wrede gave of the whole messianic secret motif (*Messiasgeheimnis*, 209-229; cf. the critical survey of W. C. Robinson, Jr., "The Quest for Wrede's Secret Messiah," *Interpr* 27 [1973] 10-30), which fell under the sway of the very historicism Wrede thought he was combatting. — Even more untenable is the notion that Mk 16,8b suggests a formation of the primitive community at Jerusalem rather than Galilee, contrary to what the evangelist propounds as the prophecy and frustrated wish of the Lord himself (! — so L. Schenke, *Auferstehungsverkündigung*, 49-52 n. 71; B. Steinseifer, *ZNW* 62 [1971] 255f.). Are we really to imagine that a NT author could entertain such a thought? — The correct solution of the problem, in our opinion, follows the direction that most now seem to prefer: that the women's silence preserved the primacy of the apostolic witness; that the appearances of the risen Lord to Peter and the others, not the women's word or the phenomenon of the empty tomb, were the first source of the Easter faith (so H. von Campenhausen, *Ablauf*, 37, 39; G. Koch, *Auferstehung*, 30; U. Wilckens, *Auferstehung*, 53; R. H. Fuller, *Formation*, 64; J. Riedl, *BiLit* 40 [1967] 99; apparently also X. Léon-Dufour, *Résurrection*, 181). Still other explanations are found: a paradoxical human reaction to a divine event (C. F. Evans, *Resurrection*, 79; E. L. Bode, *Easter Morning*, 42ff.); merely temporary silence, but afterward the women did report the event (surely a harmonistic approach, taken by B. Rigaux, *Dieu l'a ressuscité*, 196f., suggested by A. Descamps, *Bib* 40 [1959] 728). Most of these authors acknowledge the affinity between Mk's report of the women's reaction and similar notices regarding the disciples' reaction to Jesus' words and deeds earlier in the gospel. Mk 16,8b is clearly part of the Marcan *Geheimnismotiv* and a product of the readactor's hand (so also J. Kremer, in *Resurrexit*, 151).

[49] All these touches are wrongly considered by R. H. Fuller (*Formation*, 96) to be a sign that Lk is preferring an alternate source of the story to his Marcan source. Fuller has not adequately probed Lk's reasons for altering Mk of his own accord. On the other hand, B. Rigaux takes note of the substantial changes in Lk *vis-à-vis* Mk but correctly accounts these to "une 'lucanisation' accentuée de la tradition" rather than an integral non-Marcan source (*Dieu l'a ressuscité*, 205).

[50] G. Kegel, *Auferstehung*, 87; F. Schnider - W. Stenger, *BZ* 16 (1972) 102. Kerygma is included (v. 6a), as in v. 26, but is framed by the reproach, as in vv. 25f.

standing of past experiences would have precluded surprise and perplexity at the empty tomb. In this respect, the angels' reproach of the women parallels the risen Lord's words to the Emmaus disciples (Lk 24,25f.), at which point the reality of Easter has yet to take hold of those who have observed all the material facts of Easter!

It looks, therefore, — at least from our present vantage point — as if the counterpoint drama which Mk had built into the narrative of the women's experience at the empty tomb has been shifted in Lk's editing. Now the contrast is not between the women's project and the angelic Easter tidings but between *the whole experience at the tomb and the subsequent birth of the Easter faith*! The tomb experience seems to conclude an observation of all the material *facta paschalia*, but after it faith is yet to be born. The final word from the witnesses' standpoint is Lk 24,24: αὐτὸν δὲ οὐκ εἶδον. — Not that Mk's affirmation was any different. The beginning of the Easter faith seems to be put off beyond the empty tomb by him also, through the editorial conclusion at 16,8b.[51] Indeed, it is not this point that Lk is altering but the *structure of its statement*. The abrupt ending of Mk's episode is something of an anticlimax to its rhetorical counterpoint between anointing project and Easter kerygma, whereas Lk shifts the counterpoint to a position where it can truly dramatize the transition from *Ostererfahrung* to *Osterglaube*. — But we are ahead of ourselves. We mean only to observe Lk's removal of Mk's accentuated stone-motif, to note the effect of this on our story's overall structure, and to anticipate the direction in which all this is leading us.

Lk 24,2f. emphasizes the women's *discovery* as a *non-finding*: εὗρον δὲ ... οὐχ εὗρον, a double employment of εὑρίσκειν where the expression ἀναβλέψασαι θεωροῦσιν had stood in Mk (16,4). To show that the direct dialogue with Mk's text is still being held, we observe, first, that the verb εὑρίσκειν is favored by our author throughout Lk-Acts (80 occurrences) as both an improvement upon the language of source-texts[52] and an evocative (biblical) idiom for being, perceiving, choosing, and judging (Lk 1,30; 9,36 [diff. Mk]; 17,18; Acts 5,39; 7,46; 8,40; 27,28; cp. 13,22 [Ps 89,21]). Moreover, the verb's two-fold occurrence here signals the fact that it is not the displaced stone only that the women

[51] So also W. NAUCK, *ZNW* 47 (1956) 251 n. 45: "Steht dahinter vielleicht der Gedanke, dass nur die Selbstoffenbarung des Auferstandenen die Furcht, den Unverstand und die Unfähigkeit angemessener Rede von Gottes wunderbarem Handeln überwinden kann?" See again note 48 above. — G. KEGEL (*Auferstehung*, 21) and S. SCHULZ (*Stunde*, 142) also recognize this as the point of Mk's tomb story, but they still hold the older form-critics' explanation of Mk 16,8b (cf. note 48).

[52] Cf. Lk 5,19; 6,7; 8,35; 9,12.36; 19,48; 24,2.3, all *diff.* Mk. Further, Lk 1,30; 2,12.45f.; 4,17; 15,6.8f.24.32; 17,18; 18,8; 23,2.4.14.22; 24,23f.33, all S-Lk.

" found " (Mk) but the *fact of the empty tomb* as well (οὐχ εὗρον τὸ σῶμα κτλ., v. 3).[53] For the first time in the story's tradition, the women actually *verify the fact* of the absence of Jesus' body from the tomb. Mk's εἰσελθοῦσαι appears in its place, but it is the οὐχ εὗρον that it modifies, not the angelic encounter, which comes only after the fact has been verified. The integrity of the women's experience is guaranteed by the earlier Lucan mention of their scrutiny of the burial (23,55: ὡς ἐτέθη τὸ σῶμα αὐτοῦ), hence the two revisions of Mk clearly go hand in hand.

It is a mistake to jump to the obvious conclusion from this innovation of our author. At first glance the concern seems to be an apologetic improvement of the story, establishing the " empty tomb " beyond the eventual doubts one could entertain on reading the earlier versions.[54] Lk is indeed intent on demonstrating the *totality of observation* on the women's part, as the improved nexus between the tomb pericopes and the emphatic ταῦτα πάντα of 24,9 bring out. But one will account this to apologetic interests only if he ignores the *dialectic* in Lk's Easter narrative, suggested by us shortly ago in our discussion of the revised Marcan counterpoint. If the whole tomb experience is now to become a contrasting episode to the risen Lord's own instilling of the Easter faith (24,25ff.), then the painstaking establishment of all the *bruta facta* of the experience will serve only as the foil *ex parte hominis* to the risen One's activity! That is precisely the role we shall assign to this first Easter experience in Lk's thinking.[55] And we find support for this immediately in what he presents as the consequence of the discovery: ἐν τῷ ἀπορεῖσθαι αὐτάς (v. 4). The *fact* of the empty tomb begets *perplexity* and requires the *interpreting word* of the angels.[56]

[53] H. GRASS, *Ostergeschehen*, 32. — On the phrase τοῦ κυρίου Ἰησοῦ, considered " almost certainly a later addition " by C. F. EVANS (*Resurrection*, 102), note the attestation now in P-75 and the remarks of K. ALAND, *Studien zur Überlieferung des NTs*, 165f.

[54] I should not even think a first hesitating step is taken towards later apologetic exploitation of the story in Lk's version (*contra* W. NAUCK, *ZNW* 47 [1956] 252f., who admits how slight any such movement is in Lk). Rightly H. VON CAMPENHAUSEN, *Ablauf*, 35: " Lukas ist der einzige Evangelist, der sich in seiner Darstellung von solchen Rücksichten (*sc.* apologetic - R. D.) frei oder so gut wie frei gehalten hat ...." Cf. also J. DELORME, in *La résurrection*, 135; X. LÉON-DUFOUR, *Résurrection*, 162; J. KREMER, *Osterbotschaft*, 55, and in *Resurrexit*, 139.

[55] G. KEGEL, *Auferstehung*, 88: " Worauf es letztlich ankommt, drückt V. 24 negativ aus(:) αὐτὸν δὲ οὐκ εἶδον." Cf. also W. MICHAELIS, *Erscheinungen*, 125; W. MARXSEN, *Auferstehung*, 53. That Lk's point is precisely to separate the empty tomb from the birth of the Easter faith is held by M. BRÄNDLE, *Orientg* 24 (1960) 86; J. RIEDL, *BiLit* 40 (1967) 89-91; J. KREMER, *Osterbotschaft*, 60; H.-W. BARTSCH, *Wachet*, 21, 22; R. GLÖCKNER, *Verkündigung*, 204f., 207f.

[56] W. NAUCK, *ZNW* 47 (1956) 253; Ph. SEIDENSTICKER, *Auferstehung*, 95. —

Here we encounter the first of three combinations of *unintelligible facts* versus *elucidating word* which will constitute the controlling pattern of this chapter's design (vv. 2-3 *vs.* 5-7; 19-24 *vs.* 25-27; 36-43 *vs.* 44-49).

(4) *The Heavenly Message* (Lk 24,4-7)

The problem of non-Marcan source-material in our passage becomes acute at v. 4, with its semitic syntax and its doubling of the angelic embassy. Even careful interpreters yield almost at once to the syntax argument,[57] even though the same construction, (καὶ) ἐγένετο ἐν τῷ ... with infinitive, followed by main clause with καί,[58] is found in such unimpeachably Lucan sentences as the introductions to the great "journey" narrative (9,51) and the vocation of Peter (5,1f.). It recurs in the

---

As against G. KEGEL (*Auferstehung*, 87), we would insist that the ἀπορεῖσθαι of the women is not "gelöst" by the angels' message. Lk's account does not indicate understanding on the women's part (or anyone else's) as the consequence of the angelic appearance. What the angels reiterate, as we shall maintain, is the *mystery of the messiah's destiny*, to which the fact of the empty tomb belongs as final enigma. — Re. the phrase ἀπορεῖσθαι περὶ τούτου cp. Acts 25,20 (the verb is rare — 3 times assured — in the rest of the NT).

[57] U. WILCKENS, in *Festschr. Smend*, 36 n. 18. More to be expected is the argument of T. SCHRAMM (*Markus-Stoff*, 94-95), for whom Lk's semitisms are ready arguments for a semitizing, non-Marcan source. — For a recent, very thorough discussion of the matter of semitizing language in Lk-Acts, cf. F. NEIRYNCK, in *L'évang. de Luc. Mém. Cerfaux*, 179-193.

[58] In the present instance, the flavor of biblical Hebrew in the sentence is further intensified by the καὶ ἰδού of the apodosis (as in Lk 5,12). The phrase καὶ ἰδοὺ ἄνδρες δύο sounds an intentional echo, we think, of Lk 9,30 and Acts 1,10, and it seems to be an instance of Lk's appropriation of OT language for its evocative effect, in this case evocative of OT apparitions (cf. Peter FIEDLER, *Die Formel "und siehe" im Neuen Testament* [StANT 20; München: Kösel-Verlag, 1969] 37). — A. PLUMMER's useful listing of the variety of constructions used with the basic ἐγένετο ἐν τῷ ... (= וַיְהִי circumstantial clause) in Lk-Acts begins with the statement: "More than any other Evangelist Lk makes use of the Hebr. formula, ἐγένετο δὲ or καὶ ἐγένετο" (*Lk*, 45). The accompanying constructions range from very hebraistic types (καί plus finite verb in the apodosis) to classical Greek usage (accompanying infinitive); and whereas the former are common in the gospel and very rare in Acts, the classical syntax is frequent in Acts and most rare in the gospel. It appears, in other words, that the ἐγένετο construction serves as a flavor-ingredient of this author's language to help him recreate the atmosphere of the events he is narrating. The gospel's circumstances make the evoking of semitic, biblical backgrounds appropriate, whereas the world-mission in Acts unfolds against mainly the background of the hellenistic world-culture. Says PLUMMER: All the facts of this usage are "quite what we might have expected," given the different scenarios of Lk's narratives. — On the importance of imitative style in Lk's milieu, amongst Greek-speaking audiences sensitive to variations of style and impressionable by archaizing and mimetic idiom, cf. H. J. CADBURY, *Making*, 122-123; E. PLÜMACHER, *Lukas als hell. Schriftsteller*, 50-79.

Easter chapter at v. 15, announcing the encounter of the journeying disciples with the unknown Stranger (cp. also v. 30). Whereas every such passage must be analyzed on its own terms, it is quite impossible to maintain that a semitizing source is indicated every time Lk uses this construction in modifying Mk.[59] The imitation of familiar hebraisms from his own bible, the Greek Old Testament, is known to be a feature of Lk's narrative style when he is operating independently, as in editorial summaries (9,51) and pericope introductions (5,1f.).[60] Where clear trends of editing Mk can be diagnosed in a passage, therefore, as we believe to be the case in the pericope at hand, the presence of a hebraism cannot immediately and solely cancel other arguments favoring direct use of Mk. In such cases we should think "rather of Lk's imitation of a style that struck him as hieratic than of any influence of semitizing sources." [61] In the present instance, as in Lk 1,8ff.; 3,21; Acts 9,3; 22,6 (all more or less modified uses of the ἐγένετο construction), Lk seeks to evoke the atmosphere of the earthly appearance of heavenly beings, a particularly sacred occasion which the Old Testament always cloaked in numinous glow and solemn language. In fact, is it not the same situation which the biblical idiom adorns in 24,15?

Still another feature of v. 4 which suggests the influence of an alternate source-narrative is the appearance of *two angels* (ἄνδρες δύο ... ἐν ἐσθῆτι ἀστραπτούσῃ), a detail which Lk has in common with Jn 20, 12 and at variance with the one figure of Mk 16,5 and Mt 28,2f. In fact, one cannot exclude the influence of a different version of the tomb story in this detail, for this is the kind of touch which came readily out of an active oral tradition, whether due to the narrators' predilec-

---

[59] This is true especially since, as T. SCHRAMM failed to notice, ἐγένετο ... (καὶ) + *verbum finitum* belongs among the favored Lucan formulas of *introduction* (ca. 25 times in the gospel). And if we include the usage with infinitive complement, we find 26 occurrences of the construction at the beginning of pericopes, where editorial activity is usually heaviest. Cf. F. NEIRYNCK, in *L'év. de Luc. Mém. Cerfaux*, 184; J. B. HAWKINS, *Horae syn.*, 37. — The presence of LXX imitation in the ἐγένετο + καί and finite verb combination is made the more probable by the fact that the apodosis nearly always begins with καὶ αὐτός rather than the finite verb (e.g. Lk 24,15). This word-order is almost never found in Hebrew, hence "retrotranslation" cannot be direct (so K. BEYER, *Semitische Syntax im Neuen Testament* I/1 [StUNT 1; Göttingen: Vandenhoeck und Ruprecht, ²1968, 29-62] 55f., 62).

[60] On LXX imitation as a consistent and planned feature of Lucan writing, cf. J. M. CREED, *Lk*, lxxviii *ff.*, H. J. CADBURY, *Making*, 218ff.; E. HAENCHEN, *Apg.*, 66f.; H. CONZELMANN, *Apg.²*, 4; W. G. KÜMMEL, *Introd. N. T.¹⁷*, 138; U. WILCKENS, *Missionsreden*, 11; F. NEIRYNCK, *L'év. de Luc. Mém. Cerfaux*, 190; (on specifically the Acts sermons:) E. PLÜMACHER, *Lukas als hell. Schriftsteller*, 38-50.

[61] J. WANKE, *Emmauserzählung*, 29. Cf. also E. PLÜMACHER, *op. cit.*, 68f.

tion for twofold enumeration [62] or under the influence of legal requirements for legitimate witness.[63] Yet we shall miss an important *redactional* interest that Lk has in the two figures if we let such explanations satisfy us. Let us observe the language more closely:

First of all, the use of ἀνήρ as cryptic synonym for ἄγγελος (cf. 24, 23) is a *proprium* of Lk in the NT. Cf. again in Acts 1,10 and, in a combination like the present one, Acts 10,30 *vs.* 10,22. — The verb ἐφίστημι is almost exclusive to Lk-Acts (18 times), but for two occurrences in the epistles; and nearly always Lk's usage is the intransitive second aorist, as here, which can acquire the nuance of a *sudden* appearance in context. The same usage occurs in classical Greek depicting appearances, dreams, visions, etc. (cf. A. Plummer, *Lk*, 55), and in Lk this applies at Acts 12,7; 23,11 in addition to Lk 2,9; 24,4. Finally, the words depicting the visitors' clothing — ἐσθής ("fine apparel" in Lk 23,11; Acts 12,21; angelic garments in Acts 1,10) and ἀστράπτω ptc. (only here and Lk 17,24, "lightning," in all the NT) — are also indicative of Lk's hand. Consequently, wherever the two *angeli interpretes* originated, the language which describes their appearance to the women is Lk's language. This observation prepares us to find a special interest of his in the visitation of the two mysterious "men".

The visitation of heavenly figures, cryptically designated as ἄνδρες δύο, occurs on three occasions in Lk-Acts, and the three may intentionally echo one another: [64] the transfiguration scene (Lk 9,30), the empty tomb (Lk 24,4), and the ascension (Acts 1,10). Rare participles describe heavenly apparel at both the transfiguration (9,29: ἐξαστράπτων = N.T. *hapax leg.*) and the tomb (ἀστραπτούσῃ), revising Mk's language in both

[62] J. Finegan, *Überlieferung*, 86, citing L. Brun, *Auferstehung*, 24; R. Bultmann, *GsT*, 345 (doubling of supernumeraries); H. Grass, *Ostergeschehen*, 32f.

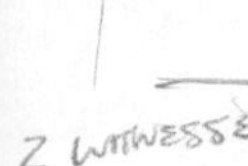

[63] Ph. Seidensticker, *Auferstehung*, 93f., makes much of this alleged motif. Lk is supposed to be stressing the trustworthiness of the Easter message in accordance with the Jewish legal requirement of two witnesses to guarantee a testimony (cf. Dt 17,6; 19,15; Mt 18,16, etc.). The same principle was extended to legitimate embassies (Mk 6,7; Lk 10,1; Acts 13,2; 8,15, etc.). This view also proves attractive to X. Léon-Dufour, *Résurrection*, 209, but I should think that, at least at Lk's own level, it runs counter to the intention of the narrative of the narrative as a whole, which, as we shall stress repeatedly, does not make the empty tomb the site of faith's emergence or the basis of a convinced Easter witness. If Lk was in search for evidence supporting a "Rechtssicherheit" of the Easter message, in accordance with the aim stated at Lk 1,4, his presentation of the women's experience at the tomb is not such as might suggest conviction on the basis of the material event. Nevertheless, cf. also B. Rigaux, *Dieu l'a ress.*, 206f.

[64] Cf. A. R. C. Leaney, *Lk*, 71; E. L. Bode, *Easter Morning*, 60f. (who then also favors the "legitimate witness" approach); J. Wanke, *Emmauserzählung*, 74.

cases. When the ἄνδρες δύο return for the third time at the ascension, it is the noun ἐσθής which makes the additional verbal echo there (Acts 1,10). Common to all three passages is the hebraizing καὶ ἰδού, typically adorning the numinous event with biblical phraseology.

It is most unlikely that the resemblance of these passages is accidental. The transfiguration story, after all, was uniquely expanded by Lk with a conversation between the heavenly figures which anticipated the events the women have just witnessed in full: ἔλεγον τὴν ἔξοδον αὐτοῦ, ἣν ἤμελλεν πληροῦν ἐν Ἰερουσαλήμ (Lk 9,31).[65] That celestial dialogue remained hidden from Peter and his companions, however, whose eyes were "heavy with sleep" during it (Lk 9,32; cp. Mk 14, 40; Lk 22,45f.[66]). It was thus the *hidden destiny of the Messiah* — the necessity of his passion and resurrection (Lk 9,20-22)[67] — that Moses and Elia discussed with him during his heavenly transport. Correspondingly, it will be a restatement of the Lord's own prophecy of his passion that the heavenly visitors make to the women here at v. 7, repeating words which this evangelist had repeatedly and emphatically bonded

---

[65] On the transfiguration's Lucan function as announcement of the passion, cf. H. CONZELMANN, *MdZ*, 50, 183; H.-W. BARTSCH, *Wachet*, 87ff.; F. SCHÜTZ, *Christus*, 67. — Note the direct anticipation of Lk 9,51 (ἀνάλημψις) in the ἔξοδος ... ἐν Ἰερουσαλήμ of the heavenly figures' colloquium (9,31). There is a complementary relation between this ἔξοδος and the εἴσοδος of Jesus' ministry (Acts 13,24; cp. Acts 1,21) as well as his εἰσελθεῖν εἰς τὴν δόξαν αὐτοῦ (Lk 24, 26), but this does not mean that the reference of ἔξοδος has to be punctually and exclusively to Jesus' impending death. It is better taken as a term deliberately chosen by Lk because it is unspecific enough to embrace the whole conclusion of Jesus' "way," including his resurrection and ascension (so A. GEORGE, *RB* 80 [1973] 215; also G. SCHNEIDER, *Verleugnung*, 199 [but cf. 178 n. 62]; R. GLÖCKNER, *Verkündigung*, 73; and with ample argumentation, P. von der OSTEN-SACKEN, *EvT* 33 [1973] 482ff.). In this respect, the term's meaning is unduly restricted, it seems, by G. LOHFINK, *Himmelfahrt*, 213 (but cf. 256); G. FRIEDRICH, in *Orientierung an Jesus*, 73.

[66] On the relation of the disciples' sleep to the concealment motif, cf. H.-W. BARTSCH, *Wachet*, 88, 94f.; R. GLÖCKNER, *Verkündigung*, 157. The disciples' failure to hear the heavenly prophecy is connected with the inappropriateness and confusion of Peter's response to the vision (Lk 9,33: μὴ εἰδὼς ὃ λέγει / cp. Mk 9,6). The Marcan messianic secret included both motifs, the sleep of the disciples on the eve of Jesus' death (Mk 14,37-41; cf. W. WREDE, *Messiasgeheimnis*, 103) and their not knowing what to say to Jesus (cf. G. MINETTE de TILLESSE, *Secret messianique*, 275).

[67] In favor of this fuller sense of ἔξοδος, including possibly even the ascension, cf. n. 65 above. Lk's focusing of the messianic concealment on the messianic passion is observable already where the confession of Peter adjoined the first passion prediction in the Marcan source-text (Mk 8,29ff. / Lk 9,20ff.). Separate sentences contained the secrecy injunction and passion prediction in Mk (8,30.31), whereas they have been made into one sentence in Lk 9,21f. through the connecting participle εἰπών (cf. W. WREDE, *Messiasgeheimnis*, 175f.; U. WILCKENS, *Missionsreden*, 162; H. SCHÜRMANN, *Lk*. I, 533).

to the *mystery of Jesus' person,* concealed from the hearers' perception as if by divine design (cf. the passive forms: παρακεκαλυμμένον [ἵνα μὴ αἴσθωνται] in Lk 9,45; κεκρυμμένον in 18,34).[68] W. WREDE correctly pointed out, as others have after him,[69] that in Lk the *Messiasgeheimnis* of Mk has become a *Leidensgeheimnis,* with the Marcan incomprehension motif specifically bound to Jesus' predictions of his own passion (and resurrection)[70] and the latter developed even beyond their ample Marcan range to express the central divine plan of salvation revealed in the Old Testament scriptures.[71] Uniquely Lucan is the three-fold association of the passion prophecies with the Easter narratives, following a planned allotment of one restatement of the prophecies to each of the three narratives (cf. 24,7.26.46; also v. 20).[72] By thus forming the structural mainstays of Lk's Easter story, the restated passion formulas seem to suggest that *Easter revelation is essentially the unlocking of the mystery of the messiah's passion,* which his followers were prevented from understanding until this point.

It is therefore very much in Lk's interest to evoke the " hidden

[68] On the implication of divine agency in these passive forms, cf. A. GEORGE, *RB* 80 [1973] 206f., and the commentaries of A. PLUMMER (256), W. GRUNDMANN (196), and H. SCHÜRMANN (I, 573). With PLUMMER and SCHÜRMANN we should think that ἵνα μὴ αἴσθωνται αὐτό in 9,45 should be allowed its full telic force, not reduced to a consecutive clause (*pace* GRUNDMANN). We shall have an occasion later to discuss the relation of these texts to similar passives of divine agency in the Emmaus story, Lk 24,16.31.35.

[69] W. WREDE, *Messiasgeheimnis,* 166ff.; H. CONZELMANN, *MdZ,* 49, 56-57, 184f.; W. GRUNDMANN, *Lk.,* 189; H. FLENDER, *Heil,* 33, 43; F. SCHÜTZ, *Christus,* 65; J. WANKE, *Emmauserzählung,* 88; R. GLÖCKNER, *Verkündigung,* 156f.

[70] The connection is clearest in the second and third predictions, to which explicit notices are attached of the disciples' incomprehension of τὸ ῥῆμα τοῦτο (Lk 9,45; 18,34, *diff.* Mk 9,32; 10,32), but it is also found in the one-sentence combination of concealment-command and prediction in 9,21f. (cf. n. 67 above). On the connection of Lk's *Leidensgeheimnis* and the passion formulas, besides the authors cited in n. 69, cf. A. GEORGE (*loc. cit.* in n. 68) and F. NEIRYNCK, in *L'év. de Luc. Mém. Cerfaux,* 174f.

[71] Cf. U. WILCKENS, *Missionsreden,* 112ff.; P. SCHUBERT, in *Ntl. Studien f. Bultmann,* 180ff.; J. WANKE, *BZ* 18 (1974) 191. The imposition of the secrecy injunction, followed by the first passion prophecy, directly adjoins Peter's confession of Jesus at Lk 9,20 as τὸν χριστὸν τοῦ θεοῦ, a Lucan formula which bespeaks his being the chosen instrument of God's grand design of *salvation-history* (cf. also Lk 23,35; Acts 3,18 [cp. 4,27]; related expressions in Lk 2,26; 2,11; U. WILCKENS, *Missionsreden,* 159-163; H. SCHÜRMANN, *Lk.* I, 530f.). The same christology comes to expression when the passion prophecy is begun in 9,22, as in Mk 8,31, with the word δεῖ, *terminus technicus* for the inexorable course of sacred history as charted by the divine will. Lk is the evangelist who has given the δεῖ-pattern of both Jesus' destiny and his followers' mission the broadest development in both the gospel and Acts (cf. E. FASCHER, " Theologische Beobachtungen zu δεῖ," in *Ntl. Studien f. Bultmann* [BZNW 21, 228-254] 245ff.).

[72] U. WILCKENS, *Missionsreden,* 116; J. WANKE, *Emmauserzählung,* 90f.

revelation" of the transfiguration episode by reintroducing the "*two men*" at the tomb and creating the verbal echoes we pointed out. He remains within the constraints of his source material by later identifying the visitors as "angels" rather than the OT figures of the first visitation, but it is the content of their discourse, not their personal identity, which he means to place in close connection. Both at the transfiguration and at the tomb, the heavenly figures articulate the *mystery of the passion*, which only the risen Lord will unveil.

First, it seems inescapable that the heavenly figures' colloquium with the transfigured Jesus (Lk 9,30-33a) is Lk's redactional contribution to that pericope (rightly H. SCHÜRMANN, *Lk.* I, 559; F. NEIRYNCK, in *L'évang. de Luc. Mém. Cerfaux*, 173). The figures of Moses and Elia embody the Jewish scriptures in their totality and their promissory attestation of Christ.[73] The passion predictions in Mk had already made an implicit connection between the necessity (δεῖ) of Jesus' death and the fulfillment of the Scriptures, which document the divine will (cf. Mk 9,12; 14,21; H.-E. TÖDT, *Menschensohn*, 174-178); but it is Lk who brings out that connection most clearly and makes it a *Leitmotiv* of his composition (cp. Lk 22,22 with Mk 14,21; Lk 18,31 with Mk 10,32f.; note the three-fold elaboration of the δεῖ in Lk 24, 6f.26-27, culminating at 24,44ff. with δεῖ πληρωθῆναι ....[74]) One now better appreciates the Lucan logic which connects the conversation on the mount of transfiguration to the first passion prediction (Lk 9,22): the prediction had made the messiah's destiny, veiled in mystery (vv. 21f.), a matter of divinely decreed "necessity" (δεῖ), and now the hidden discourse of the heavenly figures gives a confirmation "from the world beyond" (SCHÜRMANN) that Jesus' impending ἔξοδος is truly a δεῖ παθεῖν by divine decree.[75] To enhance this understanding of the whole scene as a heavenly endorsement of the foregoing

[73] H. CONZELMANN, *MdZ*, 155f. In Lk's understanding the OT is not divisible by content, as e.g. "the Law" as command *vs.* "the Prophets" as promise; it is *prophetic* in its entirety, meaning that it embodies the "promise" of Christ throughout (rightly H. CONZELMANN, *op. cit.*, 148; J. ERNST, in *Schriftauslegung*, 179). — This understanding is reflected at Lk 4,17f., where Jesus' *lectio divina* in the synagogue is limited to the prophet's text (cf. H. SCHÜRMANN, *Lk.* I, 229), as well as Lk 24,27.44; Acts 24,14.

[74] U. WILCKENS, *Missionsreden*, 158f.; G. SCHNEIDER, *Verleugnung*, 180f. The full sense of this association is expressed at Acts 3,18 and 13,27ff. Elsewhere, a use of OT proof-texts occurs in connection with the "necessity" motif (e.g. Acts 2,23ff.; 4,25ff.).

[75] S. SCHULZ, *ZNW* 54 (1963) 107f.: "Die in dem Vorsehungsratschluss gegründete Planmässigkeit der Passion Jesu geht vor allem aus dem lukanischen Interpretament zur traditionellen Verklärungsgeschichte ... hervor: Mose und Elia erscheinen Jesus deshalb auf dem Verklärungsberg, um ihn seinen Ausgang mitzuteilen, der er erfüllen musste (ἤμελλεν) in Jerusalem! Dieser Satz des Lukas ist zentral in seinem Evangelium. Zum ersten Mal nämlich wird nicht nur ausdrücklich von der Passion Jesu gesprochen, sondern der Grund der Passion Jesu angegeben."

passion instruction (Lk 9,22-27), Lk has given it an introduction of his own at 9,28, couched in his familiar and hieratic ἐγένετο ... καὶ construction (= 24,4 !), which locates the transfiguration eight days μετὰ τοὺς λόγους τούτους, hence giving it an explicit connection with the passion instruction which effectively defines its function (cf. H. SCHÜRMANN, *Lk.* I, 555).

Now it seems fully justified to maintain that, whatever source-impulse he might have had to double the angelic embassy to the tomb, Lk had ample reason in his own plan of composition to evoke 9,30f. and its context at this point. When the angelic figures, so cryptically introduced, give their message in vv. 6-7 to explain the women's perplexing experience, they are renewing the heavenly testimony given at the transfiguration and once again endorsing the words of Jesus' own prophecies. Moreover, the veil of the *Leidensgeheimnis* remains drawn over their testimony at the tomb, it would seem. Since they only repeat words the Master had spoken to uncomprehending ears (9,45; 18,34), the women's "remembering" at 24,8 cannot be taken as comprehension without an explicit statement to that effect. So far from hinting any breach in the mystery at the empty tomb, the evangelist carefully keeps all the witnesses in the dark throughout the account: first, with the women's ἀπορεῖσθαι ... περὶ τούτου (v. 4), then with the cryptic designation of the heavenly interpreters, the subsequent dismissal of the women's report as λῆρος (v. 11), and the last word spoken about the tomb in v. 12 (assuming its authenticity, for the moment): ... ἀπῆλθεν πρὸς ἑαυτὸν θαυμάζων τὸ γεγονός. When the tomb sequence ends with the cover of the passion *mysterium* still intact, we understand that Lk has made his version of the *Messiasgeheimnis* into an instrument of the literary counterpoint that is abuilding in the Easter narrative: the tension between *Easter phenomena and Easter faith* that we have already begun to observe.

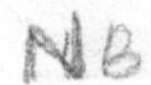

Verse 5 records the women's fear and homage before the heavenly visitors. Indeed, the tempo of their reactions has been quickened in Lk *vis-à-vis* Mk. Whereas the latter had them "astonished" at the sight of the angel and seized by fear at his message in Mk (16,5.8), Lk has them "perplexed" by the fact of the empty tomb and terrified by the sight of the angels. In part this description is unmistakably Lucan, and in part it is redolent of other scenes of heavenly apparitions:[76]

[76] The word ἔμφοβος in the NT, invariably used with γίνεσθαι, is almost confined to Lk (but for Apoc 11,13): Lk 24,5.37; Acts 10,4; 24,25 (cf. A. PLUMMER, *Lk*, 548). — The phrase κλινουσῶν τὰ πρόσωπα εἰς τὴν γῆν is peculiar to this text but presents standard descriptive features of the biblical apparition: the dazzling light, the thundering voice, and the earthlings' fright and prostration

Of the standard descriptive features of the heavenly apparition, which include the dazzling light, the thundering voice, and the prostration of the terrified earthling (G. LOHFINK), all three are present in the three Acts accounts of Paul's conversion. There is the light, the awesome voice, and prostration ἐπὶ τὴν γῆν (Acts 9,4; 26,14) or εἰς τὸ ἔδαφος (Acts 22,7). The heavenly light so bedazzles the earthling (Acts 26,13f.) that he can only shield his face by pressing it to the ground, a posture which, in Saul's case, effectively displays the sudden powerlessness of the mighty one! — The analogy between the women's experience and Saul's is merely a formal one, of course, except that in both cases, too, the message from heaven *does not win inmediate understanding but awaits clarification* at a further stage.[77] In such cases the dazzling apparition does not cancel the divine plan's concealment but actually enhances it.

In the comparison of Lucan apparitions that we are making, delayed understanding of the vision is a common element. Saul became part of the divine plan in the event on the road to Damascus, but his eyes were not opened to perceive this until he heard the interpreting word of Ananias, the young church's representative (Acts 9,6.17-18; 22,10-16). Just so, the women's experience at the tomb will await the further interpretative word of the risen Lord, without which it remains productive only of confusion and doubt (Lk 24,11-12.22-24).

The angelic words that follow are a drastic revision of Mk's account which, as many agree,[78] represents deliberate editorial work on our evangelist's part. Pursuing our hypothesis that Lk is presenting his statement on the empty tomb in conscious dialogue with the Marcan text, we look first to the famous question: τί ζητεῖτε τὸν ζῶντα μετὰ τῶν νεκρῶν; Aside from the word ζητεῖτε, the first part of the announcement in Mk has nothing in common with Lk (cf. Mk 16,6). In Mk's case the angel acknowledges the women's quest of "Jesus of Nazareth,

(cf. on this G. LOHFINK, *Paulus vor Damaskus. Arbeitsweisen der neueren Bibelwissenschaft, dargestellt an den Texten Apg.* 9,1-19; 22,3-21; 26,9-18 [SBS 4; Stuttgart: Katholisches Bibelwerk, 1965] 69ff.). Example: of the three apparition features, the light and voice are present, along with the witnesses' fear, in the three synoptic accounts of the transfiguration (Mk 9,2-8 par.), but Mt adds the element of prostration (Mt 17,6), according to formula.

[77] With face to the ground, Saul saw nothing but the dazzling light, according to the clear implication of Acts 9,3ff.; and that means, of course, that the fall to the earth is directly connected to Saul's blindness (9,8) and his need for the healing and direction of Ananias (cf. Chr. BURCHARD, *Zeuge*, 92).

[78] Even those who readily assert the admixture of a second source in our pericope are inclined to view the angels' words as direct Lucan revisions of Mk; thus e.g. W. GRUNDMANN, *Lk.*, 441; R. H. FULLER, *Formation*, 97. B. RIGAUX observes quite correctly: "Nulle part dans Lc 24,1-11, on ne se rende mieux compte du travail littéraire de Lc que dans *la déclaration angélique*" (*Dieu l'a ressuscité*, 207; ital. his). See note 18 above.

the one who was crucified," while in Lk their quest is rebuked as a futile search of " the *living one* among the dead." This reproachful question has been prepared for by precisely Lk's revised version of the women's experience at the tomb : εὗρον δὲ ... οὐχ εὗρον ... ἀπορεῖσϑαι (vv. 2-4a), whereas Mk did not include a search for the body explicitly. The angels' rebuke is a further indication that the women at the tomb are *without understanding,* even after the verification of the missing body ; and this reinforces the reprise of the *Leidensgeheimnis* which we have detected in our passage.[79]

A confirmation of our literary analysis comes from a comparison of Lk's question with its Marcan exemplar. The question cancels the positive acknowledgement of the women's search for the Crucified which had furnished the basis for Mk's association of the Easter kerygma with the fact of the empty tomb. The announcement, ἠγέρϑη, οὐκ ἔστιν ὧδε, could thus be reinforced positively by the exclamation, ἴδε ὁ τόπος ὅπου ἔϑηκαν αὐτόν (Mk 16,6). There is to be no such positive correlation between the fact of the tomb and the reality of Easter in Lk, on the other hand. With the omission of " behold the place ..." the evidential function of the tomb is ignored,[80] and the censuring question rather stigmatizes the tomb as part of *the realm of the dead* (μετὰ τῶν νεκρῶν), where no one would seek Jesus who had understood his teaching ! Suddenly, with only the negative factor of the body's *non*-discovery established thus far, that mystery is already hinted which will prove so important to Lk as the distant horizon of the Jesus-event : χριστὸς ὁ παϑητός has become πρῶτος ἐξ ἀναστάσεως νεκρῶν, according to " what the prophets and Moses said would come to pass " (Acts 26,22-23).[81]

The distinctively Lucan phrasing of the angels' question is hardly in doubt. It compares directly with the editorial resumé of the post-Easter period that we read at the beginning of Acts : οἷς καὶ παρέστησεν ἑαυτὸν ζῶντα μετὰ τὸ παϑεῖν αὐτόν ... (Acts 1,3). The disciples' account of the women's experience, given to the Stranger on the road to Emmaus, faithfully reflects the present passage : οἵ λέ-

---

[79] In agreement with J. WANKE, *Emmauserzählung*, 74.

[80] P. SCHUBERT, in *Ntl. Studien f. Bultmann*, 176f. ; W. NAUCK, *ZNW* 47 (1956) 262 ; U. WILCKENS, in *Festschr. Smend*, 34.

[81] The Christian message can be summed up under the heading, " Jesus and the resurrection," in Acts 17,18. And the divisive issue between Christianity and Judaism, as Lk sees it, is no longer the law but the resurrection ; consequently the Sadducees are the main adversaries rather than the traditionalist Pharisees (cf. Acts 4,1-2 ; 5,17 ; 23,6-9 ; 24,15.21 ; E. HAENCHEN, *ZNW* 54 [1963] 157f. [= *Die Bibel und wir*, 341] ; U. WILCKENS, *Missionsreden*, 61). Cf. H. CONZELMANN, *MdZ*, 191-192, on Lk's view of the redemptive significance of the resurrection. On the resurrection as *articulus stantis vel cadentis* of the Christian message in Acts, also E. KRÄNKL, *Jesus*, 146f.

> γουσιν αὐτὸν ζῆν (Lk 24,23). In the account of Paul's disputes with the Jews given by Festus to King Agrippa, we read that the issue was περί τινος Ἰησοῦ τεθνηκότος, ὃν ἔφασκεν ὁ Παῦλος ζῆν (Acts 25,19).

Recalling, moreover, the title given to the risen One in Peter's temple kerygma — τὸν δὲ ἀρχηγὸν τῆς ζωῆς ἀπεκτείνατε, ὃν ὁ θεὸς ἤγειρεν ἐκ νεκρῶν (Acts 3,15)[82] — we can begin to grasp Lk's reformulation of the angels' address of the searching women in terms of his overall soteriology of Easter, developed hereafter through the book of Acts.

The same comprehensive view of Lk's soteriology will also help us to understand why the angels' query necessarily replaced the positive statement of the women's quest by the Marcan angel: Ἰησοῦν ζητεῖτε Ναζαρηνὸν τὸν ἐσταυρωμένον (Mk 16,6). A prominent feature of that utterance is the perfect passive participle, ἐσταυρωμένον, which proves to be rather exceptional in the synoptic tradition. For the most part, the exponents of that tradition, particularly the narrators of the passion, did not make the manner of Jesus' death an object of special theological reflection. Aside from the symbolic use of the cross in the instruction on discipleship (Mk 8,34 par.), the statement of Mk 16,6 is a rare exception to that general rule.[83] The perfect tense, denoting past situation with perduring effect, suggests that Jesus remains "the Crucified" for the Easter church and continues to affect her as such. Such is surely Paul's thought when he employs the same participle, at any rate (I Cor 1,23; 2,2; Gal 3,1). Perhaps Mk's angelic address is to be taken as rejoining the instruction on the disciple's cross-bearing (8,34), thus comforting the church called to share the destiny of ὁ ἐσταυρωμένος with the evidence of his ultimate victory at the tomb. — Lk's elimination of this expressive participle is probably not accidental and poses the difficult question of the theological significance he assigns to Jesus' death.[84] We shall address this crucial issue of *Lukasanalyse*

---

[82] Cf. U. WILCKENS, *Missionsreden*, 175-177. The statement containing the title (Acts 3,15) is identified as the center of gravity of the Lucan redaction of the speech by K. KLIESCH, *Heilsgeschichtliche Credo*, 149.

[83] H.-W. KUHN, "Jesus als Gekreuzigter in der frühchristlichen Verkündigung bis zur Mitte des 2. Jahrhunderts," *ZTK* 72 (1975, 1-46) 21, 23. — On the importance of the participle in Mk's passage, cf. also G. KOCH, *Auferstehung*, 29; B. RIGAUX, *Dieu l'a ressuscité*, 194.

[84] The absence of a soteriological significance of Jesus' death in Lucan theology, at least in terms of the atonement and forgiveness of sins, is widely held by contemporary scholars; for example: J. M. CREED, *Lk*, lxxii; Ph. VIELHAUER, *Aufsätze*, 22; H. J. CADBURY, *The Making*, 280, and in *Beginnings* V, 366; H. CONZELMANN, *MdZ*, 187f.; C. K. BARRETT, *Lk the Historian*, 23, 59f.; U. WILCKENS, *Missionsreden*, 126, 185, ^{2}216f., ^{3}196ff.; S. SCHULZ, *Stunde*, 236, 289; E. HAENCHEN, *Apg.*, 82; E. KÄSEMANN, *Exegetische Versuche*, I, 199, and *Der Ruf der Freiheit* (Tübingen: J. C. B. Mohr, ^{4}1968) 167-168; G. VOSS, *Christologie*,

later on (chap. IV/ii), but for now we observe that Mk's perfect participle has become the *aorist* infinitive σταυρωθῆναι in the passion-prophecy formula repeated by the angels (Lk 24,7). This corresponds to the exclusive use of the aorist in the Acts kerygmata of Jesus' death, the σταυροῦν statements in particular.[85] Like the passion prophecies, the Acts kerygma confines the Lord's death to the status of a " station " along the way to the triumphal ἀναστῆναι/ἐγερθῆναι, which embodies the divine vindication of the outraged, murdered messiah.[86] Indeed, all of the kerygmatic language in Lk-Acts reinforces this view of the death as an intermediate, now finished phase of the journey of Jesus into glory.

Most compelling in this perspective is Lk 24,26, the " kerygma " of the risen One himself, where a past-tense ἔδει with παθεῖν expresses a phase of sacred history's course prior to the messiah's εἰσελθεῖν εἰς τὴν δόξαν αὐτοῦ, the latter phase succeeding the first by the same necessity of divine decree (cp. Acts 17,3 ; G. LOHFINK, *Himmelfahrt*, 236). — So it is that his messianic exaltation succeeded Israel's sinful onslaught against Jesus of Nazareth in Acts 2,36 (... ὃν ὑμεῖς ἐσταυρώσατε, *aor.*). — The Jews were unconscious instruments of the divine will in putting Jesus to death (Acts 3,17-18 ; 4,27f. ; 13,27.29), but their action was overcome in God's " raising up " their victim, thus carrying his " definite plan " (Acts 2,23) to its triumphal climax. Both stages of the " plan " are " fulfilling " it, but it is interesting that πληροῦν can be used to express this *in the perfect tense with reference to the " raising up " only* (Acts 13,33 : ἐκπεπλήρωκεν ... ἀνα-

---

130 ; M. RESE, *Altt. Motive*, 98ff., 158 ; A. GEORGE, *RB* 80 (1973) 198 ; E. KRÄNKL, *Jesus*, 118-124, 209 ; I. H. MARSHALL, *Luke*, 174-175 ; E. FRANKLIN, *Christ the Lord*, 65ff. — Of these scholars, KÄSEMANN takes the extreme and immoderate position, while VOSS and GEORGE devote themselves to an alternate perspective which might preserve some positive soteriological moment for the death in Lucan thinking (so also H. FLENDER, *Heil*, 140ff., and now R. GLÖCKNER, *Verkündigung*, § B-III). F. SCHÜTZ also, after admitting the absence of any atonement doctrine in Lk's theology, or at least the retreat of that idea (*Christus*, 93 ; similarly W. G. KÜMMEL, " Luc en accusation ...," in *L'év. de Luc. Mém. Cerfaux*, 103 [= in Braumann-*LkEv*, 428f.]), nevertheless insists that the question of a soteriological value is still open. Neither his own suggestions on the passion as formative of the gospel-community's self-understanding (*Christus*, 105-112), nor the similar ones of G. VOSS on the passion as model and prototype (*Christologie*, 118-130), nor even the several perspectives developed by GLÖCKNER (*loc. cit.*), can be said to have brought the discussion to a satisfactory pass ; but at least they have taken an important new direction in Lucan studies which must continue to be developed. We hope to contribute to the discussion in chap. IV/ii.

[85] Acts 2,23.36 ; 3,13-15.18 ; 4,10 ; 5,30 ; 10,39 ; 13,27-29. The σταυροῦν statements are Acts 2,36 and 4,10 (cp. Lk 24,7.20).

[86] Cf. U. WILCKENS, *Missionsreden*, 126, 129, 135 ; J. DUPONT, in *L'év. de Luc. Mém. Cerfaux*, 337-339 ; H.-W. KUHN, *art. cit.* (in n. 83) 20.

στήσας Ἰησοῦν)[87], whereas it is used only in the *aorist* when it refers to the past moment of the messiah's death (cf. Acts 13,27.29: κρίναντες ἐπλήρωσαν ... ἐτέλεσαν πάντα τὰ περὶ αὐτοῦ γεγραμμένα / also Acts 3,18: ὁ δὲ θεος ... παθεῖν τὸν χριστὸν ἐπλήρωσεν οὕτως). Perduring effect " for us " can be predicated of the Easter " fulfillment " in Acts 13,33, since it not only succeeds and completes the steps of Jesus' course initiated by his εἴσοδος (13,24) but subdues and reverses the crucifixion, with which the men of Jerusalem thought to put an end to that course.

Our grammatical survey of Lucan kerygmatic and " fulfillment " statements thus shows that perfect-tense forms can be applied to resurrection statements as well as aorist forms can, but only the latter can be applied to statements of Jesus' death. This furnishes some illuminating commentary on both the structure of the apostolic kerygma in Acts[88] and the recasting of the angelic address of the women at Jesus' tomb.

At *Lk* 24,6, in the statement οὐκ ἔστιν ὧδε, ἀλλὰ ἠγέρθη, we encounter the first important case of words omitted from this chapter's text in the Western manuscript tradition. As we shall do in the several prominent " Western non-interpolations " of Lk 24, we side here with K. ALAND[89] in treating the longer text as the original one and the shorter, Western text, as the product of the westerners' instinct to harmonize within the chapter, between the tomb story and its resumé in the Emmaus dialogue (24,22-24). Nor does v. 6a undermine Marcan priority in that Mt and Lk jointly transpose οὐκ ἔστιν ὧδε.[90] Their common impulse to correct Mk is understandable since that phrase

[87] The Easter reference of Acts 13,33 is required by the context; so rightly E. HAENCHEN, *Apg.*, 353 n. 3; H. CONZELMANN, *Apg.*², 85; U. WILCKENS, *Missionsreden*, 51 n. 3; E. KRÄNKL, *Jesus*, 137f.; K. KLIESCH, *Heilsgeschichtliche Credo*, 131f., 166; J. DUPONT, *Études sur les Actes*, 296.

[88] The decisive Lucan authorship of the kerygma in this respect is asserted by U. WILCKENS (*Missionsreden*, 137) and J. DUPONT, in *L'év. de Luc. Mém. Cerfaux*, 339. — Something of the nuance of finality of the Scripture-fulfillment in the death of Jesus, over against the perduring effect of the resurrection-fulfillment, is found in the alternation of ἐπλήρωσαν and ἐτέλεσαν in Acts 13, 27.29.

[89] *Studien zur Überlieferung des NTs ...*, 167f. — Amongst recent defenders of the Western reading are R. H. FULLER (*Formation*, 97) and Ph. SEIDENSTICKER (*Auferstehung*, 94 n. 62). In taking the same position, P. SCHUBERT surprising misrepresents the ms. evidence (*Ntl. Studien f. Bultmann*, 168 n. 10). D and it omit the disputed words, they do not add them in a typical " ' Western,' harmonizing interpretation " (!). SCHUBERT argues, as many do, that the resumé of the tomb story in Lk 24,23 argues against the longer version of v. 6. But precisely the opposite might better be the case: given the " Western " harmonizing proclivities, the conflict between vv. 12 and 23 might have occasioned the excision of v. 12.

[90] So J. SCHMITT, *RvScRel* 25 (1951) 124.

following after ἠγέρθη (Mk) would strike anyone as banal, whereas οὐκ ἔστιν ὧδε in prior position furnishes the smoother progress of thought *a minori ad maius*, from the obvious to the unsuspected. Mk's sentence proceeds from the marvelous to the obvious, hence speaks the kind of flawed rhetoric that Mt and Lk would both be moved to correct, each with his own new wording.

What function does the disputed sentence have in this context? It does seem integral to the angelic speech,[91] providing the transition between rebuke and recollection. Moreover, now that its partnership with "*behold the place* ..." (Mk) has been broken, it stands alone as a capsule statement of Lk's assessment of the whole tomb experience, viz. the latter's contrapuntal effect *vis-à-vis* the revelation of Easter. The adversative ἀλλά no longer stands between ἠγέρθη and ὄψεσθε, as in Mk 16,6f., but stands now between ὧδε and ἠγέρθη · — which means it stands right at the breach between what the observer could perceive and what the believer can affirm.[92] That is the breach that will be crossed only under the self-disclosing word of the risen Lord, as we shall see. As yet, ἠγέρθη (Lk 9,21f.) and ἀνέστη (Lk 18,33f.; 24,7) remain the language of the messianic *mysterium*, whose web is thickened, not broken through, by the fact of the empty tomb.

V. 6b brings the most distinctive feature of Lk's angelic message. Instead of pointing *forward* to a presence of the risen One in Galilee (Mk 16,7; Mt 28,7), the angels point *back* to the instruction of Jesus in Galilee, when all that has happened was foretold: μνήσθητε ὡς ἐλάλησεν ὑμῖν ἔτι ὢν ἐν τῇ Γαλιλαίᾳ .... Exegetes are impressively united in explaining this as a purposeful and skillful Lucan remolding of Mk.[93] It is wholly consonant with both the chapter's and the gospel's plan since, in fact, the Easter appearances are to be confined to locations in and around Jerusalem; and this not just in fact, but in principle (Lk 24,49; Acts 1,4). The promise of Mk 16,7 could therefore not be recorded, nor could the earlier promise to which it responded (Mk 14, 28). To pave the way for this stabilization of the Jerusalem locale, the Marcan προάγειν to Galilee is avoided altogether, as is any departure of the disciples from the scene of Jesus' arrest or prophecy thereof (Mk 14,27-28.49b-50). At Lk 23,49, the whole corps of followers is presum-

---

[91] J. Schmitt is right on this, *art. cit.*, 125.

[92] Precisely that breach seems to involve the essence of the Easter faith as a faith that can transcend appearances. The *meta-historical* nature of the Easter event derives from its quality of *eschatological* event, defying observation and certification in this-worldly terms (R. H. Fuller, *Formation*, 22f.; cf. also U. Wilckens, in *Die Bedeutung*, 56-59, and with reference specifically to Lk's view of the Easter event, R. Glöckner, *Verkündigung*, 57ff., 204-210; already, too, H. Flender, *Heil*, 143).

[93] Cf. the list in n. 18 above.

ably still on hand. The path which led from Galilee to Jerusalem (Lk 9,51; 23,5.49.55; Acts 10,37.39; 13,31) was obviously an irreversible one, according to the uniquely expressive geography of this evangelist.[94] Why that is so becomes a matter of definite importance to our inquiry.

Where Lk's enterprise is understood exclusively in terms of a definition of legitimate tradition, based upon a methodically delimited sacred past, the formula "*Galilee to Jerusalem*" is explained as a geographical fixation of the normative *vita Jesu*, corresponding to the chronological definition of that period in texts like Acts 1,22 ("from the baptism of John till the day he was taken up ...").[95] We are not yet prepared to join the issue of whether this view of Lk's work is correct (cf. chap. IV/ii), but we note that its founding and leading exponent, H. CONZELMANN, was not content with this merely historiographical position of Galilee as "beginning" of the Lucan *argumentum*.[96] According to CONZELMANN's suggestions, if not his clearly expounded solution of the problem, Galilee's meaning to Lk should be sought in the *christological implications of the "journey" motif*, which proves such a prominent organizational principle in the third gospel's composition.[97] In point of fact, something of a summary characterization of the "Galilean phase" of Jesus' ministry is given where Lk begins the narrative of the public life, Lk 4,14f.: καὶ ὑπέστρεψεν ... εἰς τὴν Γαλιλαίαν κτλ. Here actually "begins" the activity ἐν τῇ δυνάμει τοῦ πνεύματος for which the baptism, with its Spirit-bestowal, had endowed the man from

[94] Cf. E. LOHSE, "Lukas als Theologe ...," in Braumann-*LkEv*, 70; H. CONZELMANN, "Zur Lukasanalyse," in *ibid.*, 47.

[95] So G. KLEIN, in *Zeit und Geschichte*, 201 (= Braumann-*LkEv*, 181f.); W. C. ROBINSON, *JBL* 79 (1960) 27ff.; U. WILCKENS, *Missionsreden*, 106-107; M. VÖLKEL, *ZNW* 64 (1973) 229ff. Evidence of the desire for a legitimating criterion is taken to be Lk's concern to circumscribe the *vita Jesu* (with prepositions ἀπό and ἕως) in both chronological and spatial terms. The *terminus a quo* is given in chronological terms as "the baptism of John" (Acts 1,22; 10, 37), the *terminus ad quem* as the day of Jesus' ἀνάλημψις (Acts 1,22; cp. Lk 9,51; Acts 1,2). Geographically, the circumscription is "from Galilee to Jerusalem" (Lk 23,5; cp. Acts 13,31; 10,37.39).

[96] CONZELMANN speaks of a "sachlich-charakterisierende" sense to be attributed to Lk's Galilee, and specifies that this has to do with Galilee as a "christologische Entwicklungsstufe" of the gospel's "journey" (cf. *MdZ*, 24, 40), but he never clearly expounds what he means; nor is his reference to E. LOHMEYER, *Galiläa und Jerusalem*, 41ff., at all enlightening on the stage of christological perception which Galilee might represent. Actually, the elements for the solution of this matter that we shall adopt are all present in CONZELMANN's analysis but, typically of his manner of exposition, they are at loose ends and must be drawn together by his reader.

[97] CONZELMANN: "Als christologische Stufe ist die Reise Element eines völlig originalen Entwurfes des Lebens Jesu, der den Weg von der ἀρχή in Galiläa über das Leidensbewusstsein bis zur Erhöhung gliedert" ("Zur Lukasanalyse," in Braumann-*LkEv*, 54; cf. also *ibid.*, 62, and *MdZ*, 24, 40, 66).

Nazareth (cf. 4,21 : ἤρξατο δὲ λέγειν). In its character of editorial summary, Lk 4,14f. might be taken as the description of an *epoch*, a phase of the public life with fixed *termini* and the all-pervading feature of *pneumatic teaching in the territory of the Jews.*[98] As a distinct stage of Jesus' ministry, this period seems to end at Lk 9,51, where the " journey " begins which has Jerusalem as its divinely appointed destination (Lk 13,33).[99] Could it be that " *Galilee to Jerusalem,*" as geographical summation of Jesus' activity on earth, expresses a *journey in christological understanding* as well as a pragmatic arrangement of the traditions ? In other words, since Galilee is *terminus a quo* of the gospel's " journey," might it also be symbolic of a stage of understanding and associating with the earthly Jesus, so that the journey " from Galilee to Jerusalem " would depict an irreversible progress in discipleship ?[100]

---

[98] K. L. SCHMIDT, *Rahmen*, 37f. : " Mehr als die Sammelberichte des Mk und Mt tragen so die lukanischen Verse den Charakter einer Überschrift über das Folgende." So also H. CONZELMANN, *MdZ*, 24 (quoting SCHMIDT with approval, and adding re. 4,14-15 : " eine Überschrift über den gesamten ersten Zeitraum des Wirkens Jesu "). — It is quite true, as M. VÖLKEL has brought out, that Galilee does not at any time circumscribe the *audience* of Jesus in Lk's narrative, even though it does remain the principal *theatre* of his ministry. The Galilean audience is quickly and decisively surpassed at the conclusion of Lk 4, where the teacher-healer resists the bid to keep him in Capernaum, " a city of Galilee " (4,31), and is found thereafter preaching " in the synagogues of Judaea " (4,44). VÖLKEL correctly insists on " Judaea " as the *lectio difficilior* in 4,44, to be taken as authentic (cf. *ZNW* 64 [1973] 227), not least of all because of the pairing of Galilee and Judaea elsewhere in reference to the terrain of Jesus' ministry (cf. Acts 10,37.39 ; Lk 23,5). In Lk 5,17, Jesus' audience is said to come from all over Galilee, *Judaea and Jerusalem*, and it is depicted in even more expansive geographical terms in 6,17. Clearly, it is *Palestinian Jewry as a whole* which Lk assembles before Jesus in this first phase of his ministry, exemplarily so at 6,17 as prelude to the great sermon (6,20-49) (cf. G. LOHFINK, *Sammlung Israels*, 39f.). The same combination of Galilean " beginning " with total activity " in the country of the Jews and in Jerusalem " is observed in the retrospective resumés of Acts 10,37.39. The Galilean ministry of Jesus is therefore already a time when the word is out to *all Israel*, right in her principal forum of instruction and amongst all her people.

[99] " Galilee " disappears after Lk 8,26, to reappear at 17,11. The latter text seems to indicate Galilee as continuing scene of certain aspects of Jesus' ministry (cf. Lk 13,31-33 ; H. CONZELMANN, *MdZ*, 63). In any case, the exposition of Lk 9, pursuant to the question posed by " the tetrarch " (9,7) (" of Galilee ", 3,1), reminds us that the activity, personages, and *argumentum* of 9, 1-50 still belong to the ministry's " Galilean " phase, though the prophetic instructions of the Master prepare for the inception of the " journey," at 9,51.

[100] Rightly P. von der OSTEN-SACKEN, *EvT* 43 (1973) 491 : " So nimmt der Reisebericht in jenem christologischen Klärungsprozess die zentrale Stelle ein." Similarly, with emphasis on the Davidic eschatology associated with Jerusalem, E. LOHMEYER, *Galiläa und Jerusalem*, 46. — I cannot agree, in any case, with M. VÖLKEL's denial that the Lucan data are substantial enough to establish a " wie immer geartete(n) Galiläer-Ideologie " (*ZNW* 64 [1973] 226f. n. 24).

If Galilee can be given such a christological symbolism, it must have something to do with that prevailing " pneumatic " feature of Jesus' mission there, during which Galilee was filled with reports of his teaching ἐν ἐξουσίᾳ καὶ δυνάμει (Lk 4,36f. *diff.* Mk; cf. 4,14.31). If we take that feature as focal point of the Galilean " beginning," it sheds some light upon the point where Lk begins the πορεύεσθαι εἰς Ἰερουσαλήμ of the Master and his followers. This happens after Jesus' passion has been forecast three times (9,22[31].44) without ever being understood by his followers (9,33.45). When we are informed most emphatically of their incomprehension of the Master's destiny, at 9,45, this is pursuant to a prophecy which put the impending passion of the Son of Man in the starkest contrast to the *wonder of the miracles* (vv. 43-44), as if the latter perception stood in the way of the first. This is a clue to the sense of the " journey," for if Galilee is anything consistently for our redactor, it is *the land of miracles* and, correspondingly, of the lust for miracles among Jesus' public (Lk 9,43f.). This last point requires some specific data in its support.

The Nazarenes, at the beginning of the Galilean phase, are foreseen by Jesus to demand to have ὅσα ἠκούσαμεν γενόμενα εἰς τὴν Καφαρναούμ done in their midst also (Lk 4,23; cp. 8,20 [101]), and the people of Capernaum, a " city of Galilee " (4,31), are shown to seek to keep him with them after the day of wonders they had witnessed (4,42). Herod, " tetrarch of Galilee " (3,1), was moved by the δύναμις and ἐξουσία exerted by Jesus through his emissaries (9,1-6) to pose the christological question, τίς ἐστιν οὗτος περὶ οὗ ἀκούω τοιαῦτα (9,9), and the section 9,10-45 appears to be assembled from a drastically curtailed Marcan *Vorlage* as an answer to Herod's query.[102] In the end the tetrarch, confronted with Jesus on trial because the accused was a " Galilean " (23,6f.), is shown to be still in quest of miracles (23,8) and contemptuous of Jesus when his craving is not gratified. As Galilee's ruler, Herod is perhaps prototypical in his lust for the miraculous and his rejection of the miracle-worker. An apparently innocent but, nevertheless, a puzzling geographical detail which introduces the pericope of the " ten lepers " (17,11; cf. H. CONZELMANN, *MdZ*, 60ff.), may also contribute to this portraiture of

[101] On the interrelation of Lk 4,23 and 8,20 within Lk's theory of election, and the final definition of the kinsfolk's desire to " see " Jesus in terms of miracle-enthusiasm at Lk 23,8, cf. H. CONZELMANN, *MdZ*, 29.

[102] H. CONZELMANN, " Zur Lukasanalyse," in Braumann-*LkEv*, 53: " Lk schafft einen grossen Sachkomplex: Manifestation durch Wunder — Bekenntnis — Leidensidee — Verklärung. Wie wichtig der Zusammenhang ist, zeigt z.B. Lk 9,23: immer noch ist das Volk aus der Speisungsszene da. Mk 8,32f. fällt. Die Szenerie wird auf die typisch lukanische Doppelheit stilisiert: Esoterik — Wendung zur Offentlichkeit (stark betont in 8,23 [*sic* for 9,23] gegen Mk!)." Cf. also E. E. ELLIS, " The Composition of Luke 9," in *Current Issues* ... (ed. G. F. Hawthorne), 121-122.

the Galileans. The episode is located on the border between "Samaria and Galilee," and the only one of those who sought the miraculous cure to return and offer thanks (εὐχαριστῶν) is reported to be a "Samaritan" (17,16). Is Jesus' command to the thankful Samaritan, πορεύου, a bid to join the "journey" to Jerusalem, in view of the man's saving πίστις and the use of the thematic πορεύεσθαι in the pericope's introduction ?[103] And are we not to conclude that *nine Galileans* (v. 17) had sought Jesus' healing but had not been brought to πίστις by it ? In any case, the mention of the Galilean border does seem to be connected to the revival of both the ministry of miracles and the faithless lust for them !

To support our understanding of the gospel's "journey" in terms of this christological trajectory, we observe that something of a *caesura* in Lk's account of the public life is reached at the scene of the Master's approach to the Mount of Olives, when the exultant disciples are *looking back* upon the great wonders they have witnessed (Lk 19,37 *diff.* Mk 11,9) while he himself is pressing forward to meet his destiny at Jerusalem (cf. 19,28).[104] Here, as the goal of the "journey" is about to be reached, the veil of the "passion mystery" has not yet been lifted (cf. 18,34). Indeed, when the facts overtake the followers who thus prefer to look back on the dominical thaumaturgy, they become distraught and manage only to reiterate hopes for redemption based on the impression of those wondrous deeds (Lk 24,21 ; cp. Acts 1,6). The backwardlooking "men of Galilee" will also be reproached by the angels at the scene of the Lord's ascension (Acts 1,11), as if to show that their messianic vision of miracles and the early Kingdom is yet to be fully penetrated by the imperatives of suffering and mission, the twin objectives of the journeying Master's instruction during the ἡμέραι τῆς ἀναλήμψεως αὐτοῦ (Lk 9,51f.).[105]

---

[103] We shall discuss this pericope briefly later in our study (chap. IV/i-2a), but we take note for now of the agreement among recent exegetes on the origin of the framework statement (17,11) at the hand of the redactor (cf. H.-D. Betz, "The Cleansing of the Ten Lepers (Luke 17 : 11-19)," *JBL* 90 [1971, 314-328] 314f. ; R. Pesch, *Jesu ureigene Taten*? 116ff.). My analysis shows that I should not be persuaded by Pesch's ascription of διὰ μέσον Γαλιλαίας to the pre-Lucan tradition of this miracle story (cf. *op. cit.*, 118f.). The mention of the two regions in the introduction, with conclusions to be drawn as to the citizenship of the nine miracle-seekers who did not return to the Master, belongs very much to the redactor's plan for the pericope, in my opinion.

[104] H. Conzelmann, *MdZ*, 70f., 185. H. Flender, too, taking note of the actual cessation of miracles after 18,35-43 (moved into direct sequence with the third passion prediction through the elimination of Mk 10,35-45), maintains that the cessation becomes a dividing line between distinct periods of Jesus' ministry through Lk's insertion of 19,37 (cf. *Heil*, 34, 113).

[105] We quite agree with C. H. Talbert on the literary relation of Lk 9,51 and Acts 1,11 (ἀνάλημψις αὐτοῦ / ὁ ἀναλημφθείς) (cf. *Jesus and Man's Hope* I,

Cumulatively, this evidence points to a christological symbolism of Galilee beyond its function of geographical *terminus a quo* of Lk's Jesus-story. The " beginning in Galilee " appears to represent a point of *christological perception to be surpassed* by the follower of Jesus' " journey " who accompanies him to his ἀνάλημψις. When the angelic interpreters at the tomb point back beyond the journey's inception to Jesus' words ἔτι ὢν ἐν τῇ Γαλιλαίᾳ, one should remember, first of all, that the listeners at the tomb are *beneficiaries of Jesus' miraculous healings* (τεθεραπευμέναι, Lk 8,2), hence " women from Galilee " in this fuller Lucan sense (23,49). To them the angels recall the words of the passion prophecies (24,7), and this combination evokes the great christological exposition of Lk 9 — miracle, confession, passion prophecy, and transfiguration (9,10-45) — which gave answer to the query of Galilee's prototypical miracle-enthusiast: τίς δέ ἐστιν οὗτος περὶ οὗ ἀκούω τοιαῦτα; (9,9). Heavy editing of Mk achieved a coherent *argumentum* through the several episodes which form a threshold of the " journey-narrative," Lk 9,51ff.: the prophet acclaimed for his *wondrous deeds* is God's messiah *destined to passion and death.*[106] When that christological preparation for the " journey " ended, the disciples to whom the second passion prediction was addressed were shown to be in similar condition to Herod's and the crowds' (9, 45): miracle-enthusiasts (9,43) to whom the prospect of a suffering messiah remained incomprehensible! Even at the end of the " journey," when the miracles ceased (Lk 18,35-43 is the last, and is back to back with the third passion prophecy[107]),

173, 176f.), and we shall discuss the overall christological conception which inspired it in chap. IV/ii-2 (cf. note 129 there).

[106] F. SCHÜTZ, *Christus*, 66-67, makes much of the combined motifs of wonder-working and passion in Lk 9, maintaining, in fact, that the connection between thaumaturgy and destination to suffer is a specifically Lucan contribution to NT messianism (*ibid.*, 75). We shall have an occasion to study this conjunction of motifs more closely in our analysis of the Emmaus dialogue (24,19ff.). — On the connection of messiahship and passion in the framework of the messianic *krypsis*, cf. the magistral observation of H. CONZELMANN: " Das Missverständnis kann sich erst erheben, wenn die besondere Art der Messianität — als leidende — an den Tag tritt. *Das* bleibt den Jüngern verborgen — bis zur Auferstehung. Bei Mc geht es darum, *dass* er der Messias ist, bei Lukas, *wie* er es ist " (*MdZ*, 57 — italics his).

[107] By his omission of Mk 10,35-45, Lk brings this last miracle story (= Mk 10,46-52) into direct linkage with the third passion prediction and its misunderstanding (Lk 18,31-34/Mk 10,32-34). The sequence is similar to Lk 9,37-45 (a tailored version of Mk 9,14-32), except that the order is reversed. The combination *miracle* → *passion* of Lk 9 becomes *passion* → *miracle* in Lk 18, since the Master is now leading on to his destiny at Jerusalem while the disciples still look back upon the wonder of his miracles, and the tension of these two perspectives is fully brought out at Lk 19,37. — In keeping with the cessation of miracles before the entry to Jerusalem, the fig-tree episode (Mk 11,12-14/20-26) is eliminated by Lk (cf. H. CONZELMANN, *MdZ*, 69f.).

the uncomprehending disciples were looking back on them (19,37), just as Herod would still be seeking signs at the hour of Jesus' trial (23,8). — It appears, after all, that the men of Galilee were at one with their ruler (3,1 ; 23,6f.) in eagerness for wonders and incomprehension of the messiah ! *Miracle-enthusiasm is the christology of Galilee*, and the disciple's journey from it to the christological climax at Jerusalem is irreversible. Lk's geography is thus at the service of his christological portraiture, here as elsewhere. This explains conclusively, in our opinion, why the Galilee of the future in Mk 16,7 had to become the Galilee of retrospect in the angelic message at the tomb.

Verse 7 now records the passion prophecy which had been the heart of the christological exposition in Lk 9. It is surprising that the women were not mentioned amongst the uncomprehending hearers of that earlier teaching.[108] Moreover, there is some new wording in the formula the angels use : ἁμαρτωλῶν is new *vis-à-vis* 9,44, and σταυρωθῆναι is a concrete specification of παραδοθῆναι which does not occur in the Lucan predictions or their Marcan exemplars. However, there is no need to look elsewhere than to our author's own procedures to explain these peculiarities. The women are not so much in focus as the evangelist's own audience is in the ὑμῖν (v. 6b) of the angels' reminder.[109] Too, " studied variations of phrase and exchange of synonyms " is a frequent feature of Lucan composition, especially where repetition of themes and cross-referencing occur which mean to impress this history's continuity upon the reader.[110] We shall therefore not be deterred by the novelties of v. 7 from considering it a key statement of the evangelist himself, carefully inserted by him in his editorial dialogue

---

[108] It were better not to make too much of this discrepancy, however, since Lk's portrayal of Jesus' ever-widening circle of disciples seems to imagine that, once won over to the Master, they become part of a fixed gallery which never left the scene of the ministry (cf. R. BULTMANN, *GsT*, 368-370, 390f.). Moreover, note the deliberately accentuated shift between the audience of Lk 9,22 (= v.18) and that of 9,23ff. The change is based on Mk, but the πάντες of 9,23 has the effect of raising the following instruction to the level of a universal summons, applying ultimately to the universal church and its mission (so H. SCHÜRMANN, *Lk.* I, 540). The disciples are also specified at 9,44, over against the broader group of πάντες at 9,43. Lk faithfully reflects Mk in restricting the passion prophecies to the disciples of Jesus, but the alternation of disciples and a larger public reflects Lk's inclination to show, in this pictorial fashion, the accountability of the disciples to the world beyond their ranks (cf. Lk 6,17ff. ; Acts 2, 5ff.), but also the gradual process by which " the true Israel " is gathered into Jesus' following (cf. G. LOHFINK, *Sammlung Israels*, 76ff.).

[109] U. WILCKENS, in *Festschr. Smend*, 34 n. 13.

[110] On " repetition and variation " as hallmarks of Lucan style, cf. H. J. CADBURY, " Four Features of Lucan Style," in *StLA*, (87-102) 88-97. A " forward and backward look " characterizes Lk's literary style and his theology of history, according to P. SCHUBERT, *Ntl. Studien f. Bultmann*, 185.

with the Marcan source. Of course, this view must be borne out by a closer look at the language of the passion formula at hand.

The importance of the prediction formula to the construction of this Easter chapter would be clear at first reading. It recurs, with characteristic variation, as the core of the risen Lord's instruction of the Emmaus disciples (24,26) and those gathered at Jerusalem (24,46). It seems also to inspire the reportage of events by the uncomprehending Cleopas at 24,20. Moreover, the purpose of this unprecedented repetition is clarified when the risen Lord recalls (24,44), just as the angels had at the tomb (24,6), that " these are my words which I spoke to you while I was still with you ...." It is to establish the connection between the instruction of the earthly Jesus and the kerygma of the risen Lord that the formula recurs in all three Easter episodes.[111] The predictions are the words in which his passion and resurrection had been prophesied by the earthly Jesus; as such, they are prime hermeneutical devices for Lk's demonstration of continuity between the earthly Jesus and the risen Lord, hence between the *vita Jesu* and the mission of the Church.

It will be worthwhile to observe how the angels' use of the prediction formula prepares for the risen Lord's and differs from his. The key difference involves the title *Son of Man*, which is still the formula's subject as the angels speak it, just as it invariably was in the prophecies of the earthly Jesus (Lk 9,22.44; 18,31; also 22,22; 17,25).[112] When the risen One takes up the formula for his instruction, however, the subject is no longer " the Son of Man " but " *the Christ* " (24,26.46)! The transition occurs here in reverse which came earlier between " the Christ of God " in Peter's confession and " the Son of Man " of the Master's prophecy directly adjoining each other (9,20.22). It is clear that the use of the Son of Man in these formulas *coincides with the*

[111] U. WILCKENS, *Missionsreden*, 98. — This point is missed by J. DUPONT in *L'év. de Luc. Mém. Cerfaux*, who does not explore at all the connection between the gospel prophecies (and their Marcan parentage) and the kerygmatic schema of the Acts sermons; and for this reason, he does not explore, either, the way the schema is intended to serve Lk's demonstration of continuity between the *vita Jesu* and the mission of the Church.

[112] The contrast between men's onslaught against the Son of Man and the latter's triumphal ἀναστῆναι is the constitutive element of all the Marcan formulas, hence they have the title bespeaking transcendent authority as their subject (rightly U. WILCKENS, *Missionsreden*, 114, in dependence on the analysis of H.-E. TÖDT, *Menschensohn*, esp. 172, 185, 199ff., 252). The circles in which these formulas were developed were probably close to Mk's own, considering it is he alone who has infused them into the synoptic tradition. Since Mk's community is hardly close to the oldest Palestinian communities in time or place, as even TÖDT himself admits (*op. cit.*, 134), it would be better not to insist on great antiquity for this distinctive strand of kerygmatic formularies (so G. STRECKER, *ZTK* 64 [1967] 27, noting TÖDT's inconsistency on this point).

duration of the passion's concealment. The cryptic name of the apocalyptic deliverer and magistrate replaced ὁ χριστός at the very same juncture of Mk's narrative (8,29.31), and there, too, it signaled the beginning (ἤρξατο διδάσκειν ...) of the instruction on the necessity of the messiah's passion, cloaked immediately by the *mysterium* (Mk 8,30 / Lk 9,21f.) and constituting the nerve and focus thereof.[113] Lk's innovation is to shift *back* to the χριστός -title in using the passion formula as the heart of Easter's revelation. This could take place only in the speech of the risen One himself, and by this device Lk can demonstrate the *end of the messianic concealment.* Such a *terminus ad quem* of the concealment could only be foreshadowed in the economy of Mk (9,9: ὅταν ὁ υἱὸς τοῦ ἀνθρώπου ἐκ νεκρῶν ἀναστῇ [114]) but comes to be expressly narrated in Lk's composition. One can see how he has taken the raw materials of Mk's narrative and reconstructed them in a development which is crowned by his Easter story! Illustrative of this project is the concluding remark of Lk's transfiguration story, which revises the secrecy injunction of Mk 9,9 and makes the concealment of Jesus' destiny a state of affairs prevailing ἐν ἐκείναις ταῖς ἡμέραις (Lk 9,36), hence explicitly a matter of *the time before Easter.*[115] The necessity

---

[113] That this was already the case in Mk is shown by G. MINETTE de TILLESSE, *Secret messianique*, 370; also H. CONZELMANN, in *Zur Bedeutung des Todes Jesu*, 41f.; E. SCHWEIZER, "Zur Frage des Messiasgeheimnisses bei Markus," *ZNW* 56 (1965, 1-8) 2. — For Lk, W. DIETRICH judges correctly: "Das Petrusbekenntnis bildet bei Lukas die christologische Zäsur im Leben Jesu" (*Petrusbild*, 103); but because he gives scant attention to the all-important passion-mystery, he passes over the function of the Son-of-Man title in the confession/instruction passage (*ibid.*, 101). DIETRICH insists Lk meant to make Peter's confession a fully correct understanding of Christ on the apostle's part (*ibid.*, 102), only then he asserts that Lk accentuated the inappropriateness of Peter's offer during the vision on the mount (*ibid.*, 113f.). The element that is missing from this author's exegesis is an adequate understanding of Lk's *Leidensgeheimnis*.

[114] The case for making this verse the key to the Marcan secrecy motif was the crucial argument of W. WREDE's *Messiasgeheimnis*, 66-67.

[115] W. WREDE, *Messiasgeheimnis*, 167f., 175, 176. "Noch ist die Zeit nicht da, wo Jesus als der Christus Gottes dastehen kann; erst muss er noch leiden, sterben und auferstehen" (*ibid.*, 176; cf. also H. SCHÜRMANN, *Lk.* I, 563). In revising Mk 9,9 at the end of the transfiguration story, Lk is reinforcing the passion-mystery motif which was already present in the sequence of heavenly conversation and disciples' sleep (cf. text above, p. 23). His statement reads: καὶ αὐτοὶ ἐσίγησαν καὶ οὐδενὶ ἀπήγγειλαν ἐν ἐκείναις ταῖς ἡμέραις οὐδὲν ὧν ἑώρακαν (Lk 9,36). It is not Jesus who imposes the silence, as in Mk, it is rather the *time* during which the status of Jesus cannot yet be known or understood (9,45; 18,34). In interpreting the period of *krypsis* thus as a phase of *Heilsgeschichte*, Lk removes from it the component of dispute between Master and disciples over his embrace of passion as messianic destiny. Mk 8,33 is dropped, as is the disciples' flight (Mk 14,50) and most of the unfavorable portrait of their following that Mk had drawn. The *Leidensgeheimnis* in Lk does not consist in an

of the messiah's passion could simply not be known before he himself could make it the matter of *Easter revelation.* And by Easter revelation, as Lk 24 shows us, the evangelist understands the meaning of all the Scriptures, imparted solely by the risen Lord after the events of his passage.[116]

The sense which the title " Son of Man " obtains when it is the subject of passion statements was already indicated by the context Mk constructed for the first passion prediction (Mk 8,27-9,1).[117] The combination of Mk 8,38 and 9,1, coming after the passion prophecy and associated instruction on the following of the Crucified (8,31-37), brought the eschatological " coming " of the Son of Man into direct connection with his historic existence and radical summons to follow a rejected messiah.[118] Separate strands of Son-of-Man tradition are thus intermingled in Mk with the effect of identifying the judge of the world with the sufferer who exerted a paradoxical authority in his call to discipleship.[119] — Once again, an implicit association thus made editorially by

opposition or disharmony on the matter between Jesus and his followers; it is simply a matter of their historical position " in those days," when the divine plan kept the knowledge of Jesus' destiny from them (hence the passive forms, — text, p. 24). Lk's elimination of passages like Mk 8,16-21, and his modification of the disciples' crass persistence in sleep as the hour of the passion drew on (Lk 22,45: ἀπὸ τῆς λύπης), exemplify his concern to lessen the distance between Master and disciples, even while accentuating the design of God which kept the messianic destiny of passion and resurrection a mystery unbroken until Easter day.

[116] W. WREDE, *Messiasgeheimnis*, 171. Cp. W. DIETRICH, *Petrusbild*, 116; R. Glöckner, *Verkündigung*, 58.

[117] Cf. E. HAENCHEN, " Die Komposition von Mk vii(i) 27 – ix 1 und Par.," *NT* 6 (1963) 91-109, esp. 88ff.; N. PERRIN, *What is Redaction Criticism* ? (" Guides to Biblical Scholarship "; Philadelphia: Fortress Press, 1969) 40-57; N. PERRIN, *A Modern Pilgrimage in New Testament Christology* (Philadelphia: Fortress Press, 1974) 109; M. HORSTMANN, *Studien zur markinischen Christologie. Mk 8,27 – 9,13 als Zugang zum Christusbild des zweiten Evangeliums* (NtAbh 6; Münster: Verlag Aschendorff, 1969) 26-31.

[118] As E. HAENCHEN points out (*NT* 6 [1963] 95), the traditions of the " Son of Man " in Mk 8,31 and 8,38 do not belong to the same stratum of tradition about Jesus. The " coming " Son of Man is attested in all strata of the synoptic tradition, the suffering and rising Son of Man only in the material emanating from Mk. — On the mingling of the two strands in this Marcan context, cf. also M. HORSTMANN, *op. cit.* (prev. note) 49, 54-56.

[119] The identification is again clear in the question and answer of the trial scene (Mk 14,61-62), on which H. CONZELMANN writes (in *Zur Bedeutung des Todes Jesu*, 47): " Markus gestaltet die Antwort Jesu so, dass im Widerspiel von Frage und Antwort die sachliche Identität der drei christologischen Titel Messias, Gottessohn und Menschensohn klar wird, also die Einheit von Werk und Weg Jesu, von Taten, Passion und künftiger Parusie. Der Leidende stellt sich als der Kommende vor, das heisst in die Perspektive der nachösterlichen Gemeinde übertragen: Der Erwartete ist der, der ' gelitten ' hat. Als solchen ' sieht ' sie ihn." — The paradoxical authority of the Son of Man amidst his

Mk came to be explicitated in Lk. Our evangelist has put one of his several repetitions of the passion-prediction formula in a direct conjunction with traditional (Q) sayings on the future "day" of the Son of Man (Lk 17,24 / Mt 24,27).[120] After the saying which compares the advent of the Son of Man "on his day" (Mt: his "parousia") to the sudden glare of lightning across the whole sky, Lk adds:

> πρῶτον δὲ δεῖ αὐτὸν πολλὰ παθεῖν καὶ ἀποδοκιμασθῆναι ἀπὸ τῆς γενεᾶς ταύτης (Lk 17,25; cp. 9,22 / Mk 8,31).

Here, with the express identification of the "coming" and the suffering Son of Man, the passion is assigned its place in the eschatological drama which is now unfolding by inexorable divine plan. His suffering and his "coming" are shown to be necessary, connected steps on the one journey of the Son of Man;[121] and so the tension between the two strains of tradition is resolved in a coherent historical process (as in Lk 24,26), — a solution wholly characteristic of our evangelist!

The context of the sudden passion prophecy in Lk 17,25 is illuminating in another respect. The oracles stressing the suddenness of the Perfecter's coming (... like lightning, as amongst the unsuspecting contemporaries of Noe and Lot, etc.) bring out the *hiddenness* of the divine plan of which the Son of Man is executor.[122] It catches careless

---

passion at men's hands is shown to be the point of the Marcan passion formulas by H.-E. Tödt, *loc. cit.* in n. 112.

[120] Recognizing Lk's own redactional operation in this are H.-E. Tödt, *Menschensohn*, 102f.; W. Grundmann, *Lk.*, 342; H. Conzelmann, *MdZ*, 115 n. 1; G. Strecker, *ZTK* 64 (1967) 19-20; R. Geiger, *Endzeitreden*, 83; J. Zmijewski, *Eschatologiereden*, 419, 525f.; F. Schütz, *Christus*, 67. — The influence of older "Son of Man" traditions on the formulation of Lk 17,25 can be noticed in the conflict with ἡ γενεὰ αὐτή (cf. Lk 11,30-Q/cp. Mt 12,39ff.), which is that total eschatological contest in which "prophets and apostles" alike are involved (Lk 11,49-51 *diff.* Mt) and the membership of the Christian church is to be ferreted out (Acts 2,40). A solidarity of the Son of Man and his followers in the suffering brought on by this conflict may therefore be hinted in the insertion of 17,25 (so R. Schnackenburg, "Der eschatologische Abschnitt Lk 17,20-37," in A. Descamps & A. de Halleux, éds., *Mélanges bibliques en hommage au R. P. Béda Rigaux* [Gembloux: Éditions J. Duculot, 1970, 213-234] 222f., 230; also R. Geiger, *Endzeitreden*, 83, 84f.). In any case, Schnackenburg views the redactional origin of 17,25 as "so gut wie sicher" (*art. cit.*, 222); cf. also G. Schneider, in *Jesus und der Menschensohn*, 275-276.

[121] H.-E. Tödt, *Menschensohn*, 103; R. Geiger, *Endzeitreden*, 77, 84; G. Schneider, in *Jesus und der Menschensohn*, 276.

[122] R. Schnackenburg, *art. cit.* (in n. 120) 218. As J. Zmijewski rightly explains (*Eschatologiereden*, 414f.), the point is made *via negativa* in the traditional (pre-Lucan) couplet 17,23f.: there should be no search for the Son of Man "there ... or here," because when that heavenly figure finally comes out of *hiding*, he will be visible everywhere (like lightning)! "Weil der Menschensohn erst an 'seinem Tage' wie ein Blitz erscheinen wird, ist es unmöglich, ihn schon

men unawares since it follows a hidden timetable (Lk 17,22) and gives rise to false claims and apprehensions (17,23). Lk furnished a most appropriate introduction to this Q sequence in Jesus' exchange with the pharisees over " when the Kingdom of God was coming " (17,20f.), found in this gospel only.[123] Jesus' answer is : οὐκ ... μετὰ παρατηρήσεως, οὐδὲ ἐροῦσιν · ἰδοὺ ὧδε ἤ · ἐκεῖ. The design of God for the eschatological consummation is thus being carried out in a *hidden* fashion, without " observation," right in the midst of those seeking evidence of it (ἐντὸς ὑμῶν); and the " Son of Man " is the one whose determined course is carrying it out. The mystery of the suffering and rejected Son of Man (17,25) is therefore part of the great *mysterium* of God's plan for the end of things.[124] Lk 17,20-30 thus furnishes a background and rationale for the messianic *Leidensgeheimnis*, which still covers the fact of the empty tomb. It also shows that the Son-of-Man title in Lk expresses the suffering Christ's instrumentality in the *hidden* divine master-plan for the eschaton, which will also be served by his followers' persecuted " testimony " according to Lk 21,12ff. (cf. chap. IV/ii-3 below). " Hid-

---

jetzt zu *sehen* " (ZMIJEWSKI, *op. cit.*, 427). By joining this Q couplet to the introduction to his series (17,20-21), Lk accentuated the implication of the *hiddenness* of the Son of Man *in the present* which was already contained in vv. 23f.

[123] As against R. SCHNACKENBURG, who is convinced that Lk 17,20b-21 was already united with the following catena of sayings at the level of Lk's source, presumably Q (cf. *art. cit.* [in note 120] 214ff.), I should prefer the view of most others that, whatever the traditional basis of 17,20b-21 (S-Lk), the combination of it with vv. 23f. is Lk's doing, and v. 22 is the redactional clasp between the two (so H. CONZELMANN, *MdZ*, 114f.; R. GEIGER, *Endzeitreden*, 47ff., 85-86; J. ZMIJEWSKI, *Eschatologiereden*, 390, 519f.). All things considered, I find ZMIJEWSKI's literary criticism of the passage most satisfying: vv. 20b/21b *Sondergut*, vv. 23f./26ff. *Q*, vv. 20a/21a/22/25 redaction. Admittedly, SCHNACKENBURG's view that Lk's version of Q had already associated some form of vv. 20f. with the sayings on the " day " of the Son of Man cannot be excluded with full certainty.

[124] The *hiddenness* of the Son of Man before his " apocalypse " (Lk 17,30) is a motif of Jewish Apocalyptic (e.g. I Enoch 48,6ff.) which had its impact on the tradition of Jesus' sayings (cf. G. MINETTE de TILLESSE, *Secret messianique*, 382-383). H.-E. TÖDT warns, however, that the Jewish apocalypses cannot account for the motif of messianic concealment in the Jesus-tradition because the notion of pre-existence is essential to their portrait of the Son of Man but absent from the synoptic tradition of Jesus' sayings (*Menschensohn*, 202, 271ff.). The connection between the Son of Man and the concealment motif is therefore secondary in the gospel tradition and due, in large measure, to the redactional activity of Mk. If this is correct, then we might say that Lk understood the connection between the Son of Man and God's hidden designs which Mk had already established and developed it within the framework of his own theory of the divine guidance of sacred history.

denness" is, we think, a special nuance of Lk's usage of the title, "Son of Man."[125]

We should consequently be convinced by the title's occurrence in the angel's message at the tomb that the passion-mystery still prevails there. That Lk means to make precisely that suggestion *via* the title is suggested by its unusual proleptic position[126] in v. 7: λέγων τὸν υἱὸν τοῦ ἀνθρώπου ὅτι κτλ. Speaking of *the Son of Man,* Jesus said he must ..., etc. The title is hardly "just a literary cross-reference to the three passion prophecies"[127] when it is accorded such an emphasis in the reformulation. A deliberate contrast is being established between the angels' words and the subsequent instructions of the risen Lord, and the *krypsis* still prevailing at the tomb is the point of contrast.

The remaining words of the passion-prophecy's restatement by the angels can now be considered in brief, for we shall return to these crucial formulas in each of the succeeding sections of our study. First, the word δεῖ, septuagintal innovation in the biblical tradition[128] bespeaking a divine superimposition of absolute necessity on the order of things,[129] presents an idea for which Lk's special predilection is very

---

[125] We should not agree with U. WILCKENS, therefore, that the title "Son of Man" had lost its meaning for Lk and was retained by him only for its certain "archaizing" flavor (*Missionsreden*, 118). Similarly negative on a Son-of-Man christology in Lk, H. CONZELMANN, *MdZ*, 159 n. 2. *E contra*, and rightly in our opinion, H.-E. TÖDT, *Menschensohn*, 101; G. SCHNEIDER, in *Jesus und der Menschensohn*, 281. It is especially noteworthy that Lk "die traditionellen Gruppen von Menschensohnworten miteinander *verbindet* und sie in seine christologische Gesamtkonzeption vom Weg Christi *integriert*" (G. SCHNEIDER, *art. cit.*, 282). The concept of hiddenness developed in the sayings concerning the suffering and rising Son of Man involves the *paradox* that the One whom he invested with ultimate authority, God consigned to the control and apparent conquest of men (H.-E. TÖDT, *op. cit.*, 202, 272). Precisely these dialectically related steps comprise the *way* that was determined for the Son of Man, according to the sayings tailored or composed by Lk (22,22.48b.69; 24,7) and the Lucan combination of 17,24-25. This is why the concealment motif is also important to Lk in connection with the title.

[126] BLASS-DEBRUNNER, § 476.

[127] U. WILCKENS, *Missionsreden*, 118 n. 1.

[128] The words δεῖ and δέον reflect thought-patterns at home in a Greek and hellenistic environment, where they were originally associated with the deity who determined the course of the world (cf. E. FASCHER, "Theologische Beobachtungen zu δεῖ," in *Ntl. Studien f. Bultmann*, 228ff.). It is hardly surprising that there is no OT idea or vocabulum to which this word corresponds. It gained its entrance to the biblical tradition, nevertheless, through the LXX, with the first generalized usage, in terms of δεῖ γενέσθαι and in eschatological perspective, found in Dan 2,28-29 LXX, the seer's interpretation of Nebuchadnezzar's dream, considered as retrospective interpretation of history rather than an intrusion of the notions of fate or destiny *ab extra* (so E. FASCHER, *art. cit.*, 229).

[129] A. PLUMMER, *Lk*, 247: δεῖ is the expression of logical necessity rather than moral obligation (ὀφείλει) or suitability (πρέπει).

well known.[130] With reference specifically to Jesus' passion prophecies, Lk has accentuated the δεῖ motif by employing the word every time he reapplies the Marcan prediction formula to new settings:[131] Lk 17, 25; 22,37; 24,7.26.44(→46); Acts 17,3; cp. Lk 13,33. In these new and original contexts, the particular understanding comes to light which Lk has added to the older concept. In Lk 24,26 the divinely disposed "necessity" is predicated of the messiah's "way," which steadily followed the steps which God predetermined. The same point is made of Jesus' earth-bound steps at Lk 13,33. Moreover, Lk firmly and explicitly equates "*it is necessary*" with "*it is written,*"[132] whereas this association was implicit in Mk's formulas. The statements combining δεῖ with scripture-fulfillment in the messiah's destiny (Lk 22,37: τελεσθῆναι · 24,44: πληρωθῆναι) are exclusively Lk's own; and, correspondingly, he can use κατὰ τὸ ὡρισμένον as a self-understood substitute for Mk's καθὼς γέγραπται in reference to the πορεύεσθαι of the Son of Man (Lk 22,22/*diff.* Mk 14,21; cp. Acts 2,23; 4,28). The "determined plan and foreknowledge of God" (Acts 2,23) made Jesus' passion part of a "universal history of divine providence" which runs its course according to plan, despite and even by means of every form of human resist-

[130] Of 102 NT occurrences, Lk-Acts accounts for 44: 19 in the gospel (2 from Mk, 1 from Q, 16 S-Lk) and 25 in Acts. Among the gospel occurrences peculiar to Lk, those which express the "necessity" of Jesus' course predominate, as in 2,49 (ἐν τοῖς τοῦ πατρός μου ... εἶναι); 4,43 (preaching throughout the Jewish land); 13,33 (πορεύεσθαι to Jerusalem and death); 24,26 (εἰσελθεῖν εἰς τὴν δόξαν αὐτοῦ after the messianic παθεῖν), as well as five other uses bearing directly on the messianic passion (9,22[Mk]; 17,25; 22,37; 24,7.44, all S-Lk). Except noted, all these statements of the "necessity" of Jesus' course, from its beginning through the passion to glory, occur uniquely in Lk and constitute a special theologoumenon of his (cf. E. Fascher, in *Ntl. Studien f. Bultmann*, 245ff.; H. CONZELMANN, *MdZ*, 141-144; U. WILCKENS, *Missionsreden*, 140f., 158f.; S. SCHULZ, *ZNW* 54 [1963] 104-116; H. FLENDER, *Heil*, 129-131; I. H. MARSHALL, *Luke*, 105-115; R. GLÖCKNER, *Verkündigung*, 155f.).

[131] As an expression of the divinely determined necessity of the messiah's παθεῖν etc., δεῖ occurred only once in Mk, viz. with the first passion prediction (Mk 8,31/*par.* Lk 9,22). This was the only occasion, apart from the καθὼς γέγραπται of Mk 14,21, that Lk's predecessor spoke of the "necessity" of Jesus' passion. The fact that the motif remains thus undeveloped in Mk argues for its place in the oldest tradition of his passion formulas (so H.-E. TÖDT, *Menschensohn*, 174-178; U. WILCKENS, *Missionsreden*, 140; G. STRECKER, *ZTK* 64 [1967] 26), where it probably expressed the apocalyptic necessity of the conflict between the "Son of Man" and "men," without yet being referred specifically to the fulfillment of scripture (so M. HORSTMANN, *Studien zur mk. Christologie* [cited in n. 117 above) 24; *e contra*, H.-E. TÖDT, *Menschensohn*, 177, 251).

[132] Cf. the authors cited in n. 130 above, especially H. CONZELMANN, *MdZ*, 147f.; U. WILCKENS, *Missionsreden*, 158f.; I. H. MARSHALL, *Luke*, 111. — One should probably not insist on the heavy admixture of Greek *Providentia* and *Anagkè* doctrines in Lk's thought which S. SCHULZ propounded (*ZNW* 54 [1963] 111); rightly H. FLENDER, *Heil*, 130 n. 257; MARSHALL and GLÖCKNER (n. 130).

ance."[133] The operation of τὸ ὡρισμένον and ἡ ὡρισμένη βουλὴ καὶ πρόγνωσις τοῦ θεοῦ through unknowing human instruments (Lk 22,22f.; Acts 3,17-18; 4,27-28; 13,27) echoes our explanation of the apocalyptic logia into which Lk 17,25 has been inserted. Divine and human designs work together in counterpoint,[134] and so the rule *of God* is brought about, — gradually, mysteriously, unobservably. This accounts for the close relationship of δεῖ with the passion-mystery and its disclosure in Lk. The riddle of the δεῖ is dissolved by the Easter instruction of the risen Lord, and that it is probably why we find the word only once in Acts associated with the passion kerygma (17,3 — and there closely attended by the "opening" of the scriptures, as in Lk 24,26f. and 24,44ff.). Like the title "Son of Man," the unelucidated δεῖ, prior to the "opening" of the Scriptures, remains a symptom of the concealed destiny of the messiah, which the angels' words at the tomb cannot yet bring out of the realm of mystery.

The expression, παραδοθῆναι εἰς χεῖρας ἀνθρώπων (ἁμαρτωλῶν), employs the full flavor and word-play of semitic idiom to bring out the clash between present and future ages around the person of the Son of Man.[135] The word ἁμαρτωλῶν intensifies the suggestion of that conflict since it designates the counter-movement to God's sovereignty which, paradoxically, gains sway over the very one appointed to pronounce

---

[133] S. SCHULZ, *ZNW* 54 (1963) 108.

[134] H. FLENDER, *Heil*, 130; S. SCHULZ, *art. cit.*, 109ff. — One should therefore beware reductions of the contrast-moment in Lk's versions of the passion formulas, as *pace* U. WILCKENS, *Missionsreden*, 159, echoed by J. WANKE, *Emmauserzählung*, 91. At least there should not be talk of this in those versions of the formula which are recorded by Lk *before* the Easter solution of the mystery of his person by the risen Christ (therefore, up to 24,7).

[135] The primitive nucleus of the Marcan passion formulas is found in this expression by H.-E. TÖDT, *Menschensohn*, 148ff., and, following him, F. HAHN, *Hoheitstitel*, 52; U. WILCKENS, *Missionsreden*, 114. On the other hand, G. STRECKER finds the *Vorform* in Mk 8,31 and considers Mk 9,31 a redactional epitomizing of the longer formula (*ZTK* 64 [1967] 29). R. PESCH has recently argued for a relationship of the Marcan formulas to the oldest passion narrative, with Mk 9,31 possibly going back to the speech of Jesus, — a debatable exercize of *Traditionsgeschichte* which does not seem to take the enterprise of the second evangelist sufficiently into account (cf. "Die Passion des Menschensohnes ...," in R. PESCH & R. SCHNACKENBURG, hrsg., *Jesus und der Menschensohn, für A. Vögtle* [Freiburg/Basel: Herder, 1975] 166-195). — The word-play "Son of Man"/ "men" could also be used to good effect by an author writing in Greek (instance Mt 9,6/8), so the mere occurrence of that combination does not prove a statement's origin in the semitic speech of Palestine (rightly G. STRECKER, *ZTK* 64 [1967] 30). It seems more likely that the Marcan formulas are traceable to bilingual northern Palestine (*ibid.*, 32ff.) than to Aramaic-speaking Palestinian Christians (H.-E. TÖDT, *Menschensohn*, 186) or the speech of Jesus himself (*pace* R. PESCH, *art. cit.*, 192ff. — how explain the formulas' restricted entrée to the synoptic tradition?).

its doom.[136] The word appeared in Mk 14,41, the Gethsemane announcement which Lk did not reproduce *in situ* and which presented an editorial variation on the second passion prophecy, Mk 9,31. Considering that the words of the angels' pronouncement bear the closest resemblence to that second prophecy (παραδίδοσθαι εἰς χεῖρας ἀνθρώπων, Lk 9,44 / Mk 9,31), we can readily conceive the process of editorial conflation (Mk 9,31 + 14,41) by which our skillful manager of his sources composed the pronouncement. Small wonder that he chose for this purpose a version of the formula which expresses the apparent triumph of the ἁμαρτωλοί, for that *seeming* state of affairs is taken to be the real one by followers as yet unable to comprehend the ἀναστῆναι of the Son of Man. This is precisely the misapprehension voiced by the Emmaus disciples to the Stranger in 24,20f. as the reason for their perplexity and sadness.

σταυρωθῆναι is a secondary addition to the vocabulary of the Marcan passion formulas, as yet unused even in the prior Lucan predictions to which cross-reference is being made here.[137] It appears at this point first of all, as we have suggested (pp. 29f.), because Lk is remolding the angelic pronouncement of Mk 16,6a and making the crucifixion a finished stage of the Saviour's passage rather than a perduring vision for the believer. As part of a resumé of finished events which fulfilled the Master's own forecasts, the fact of his crucifixion can serve to complete the *listing of observable facts* in which the divine purpose *still lies hidden* from the perception of the followers. Again, that is the word's function when it recurs in the recital of empirical paschal events by Cleopas (24,20), where the totality of empirical observation by the travelers acts as a foil to the actual inception of their Easter faith *in verbo Domini*. Here at the tomb, the generalized language of the passion predictions begins to be enhanced by the specific details which the paschal witnesses have observed but not understood. This is the way our evangelist builds the climactic momentum of his narrative, gradually and dialectically, towards the moment when Easter revelation breaks the grip of the mystery of the suffering messiah.

τῇ τρίτῃ ἡμέρᾳ has been carefully retained by Lk in all versions of the passion prophecy which include resurrection statements: 9,22; 18,33; 24,46, and here. It is significant, too, that Lk is the only evangelist to associate this formula with the Easter narratives. It

[136] H.-E. Tödt, *Menschensohn*, 173.

[137] Cf. the different context of Mt 26,2, and H.-E. Tödt, *Menschensohn*, 139, 141. This is a detail which Lk will emphasize in the Acts kerygmata, both by incorporating the word itself into them (Acts 2,36; 4,10; cp. Lk 24,20) and by using other vocabulary to focus on the manner of Jesus' death. So Acts 2,23: διὰ χειρὸς ἀνόμων προσπήξαντες ἀνείλατε· Acts 5,30; 10,39: κρεμάσαντες ἐπὶ ξύλου (Dt 21,22); cp. Acts 13,29.

becomes part of his precise chronological framework of the Easter happenings, as we have observed (cf. 23,54.56b ; 24,1.7.13.21b.33.46), making all of them " third-day " events. Indeed, since they have been concentrated in the one day's time, we might say " the third day " is their *redemptive-historical dating*, drawn from prophecy (Os 6,2) and, perhaps, eschatology. " It is this theology (of history) which determines (Lk's) chronological interest. The latter does not determine his theology." [138]

Finally, the intransitive ἀναστῆναι is the expression of Jesus' *rising up* from death which reflects the consistent usage in the Marcan prediction formulas (Mk 8,31 ; 9,31 ; 10,34 ; cp. also Mk 9,9) [139]. In these formulas, the intransitive forms (ἀνιστάναι, 2nd aor. and fut. mid.) had the effect of asserting the paradoxical triumph of the Son of Man, who retains and reaffirms his exalted sovereignty at the very moment the evil generation appears to vanquish him.[140] Lk preserves this frame-

---

[138] P. SCHUBERT, in *Ntl. Studien f. Bultmann*, 185. — The convenient summary of views on the origin of " the third day " offered by R. H. FULLER (*Formation*, 23ff.) arrives at the conclusion which one would be inclined to make his own: not the text of Os 6,2 by itself (*pace* H. GRASS, *Ostergeschehen*, 127-138, 304-305), but the late-Jewish *eschatology* which understood the " third day " as *the day of salvation*, based on numerous OT situations which were commented upon in the *targumim* and *midrashim* : Gen 22,4 ; 42,17 ; Jon 2,1 ; Esth 5,3, as well as Os 6,2 (documented fully [from STR.-BILL. I, 747] by K. LEHMANN, *Auferweckt*, 262ff.). This is the full background which makes FULLER's own solution plausible, viz. that late-Jewish eschatology viewed "the third day" after the world's end as the day of the general resurrection, hence may be the inspiration of the belief in Jesus' resurrection from the dead on the third day. Osee's passage by itself poses the difficulty that it never appears among the OT testimonies used in the early Christian preaching or apologetic, at least not early enough to explain NT usage. The general apocalyptic tenet, on the other hand, goes further in the direction of a solution to the problem. Cf. also F. MUSSNER, *Auferstehung*, 41ff.

[139] Aside from the Marcan formulas, only in I Thess 4,14. So harsh and unusual did the usage sound to Mt that he consistently restored the apposite forms of ἐγείρειν (Mt 16,21 ; 17,23 ; 20,19 ; 17,9). Lk, however, allows the intransitive form to stand in all his accomodations of the Marcan formula save the first (9,22 : ἐγερθῆναι, *diff.* Mk 8,31). In the kerygma of Acts, the two verbs will be combined (cf. note 143 below), but the intransitive form of ἀνιστάναι will reappear only at Acts 10,41 & 17,3.

[140] Thus, in agreement with H.-E. TÖDT (*loc. cit.*, n. 112 above), F. HAHN, *Hoheitstitel*, 49 ; G. KEGEL, *Auferstehung*, 30. The association of ἀνιστάναι with the passion formulas antedates Mk, considering the latter's own preference for ἐγείρειν (6,14.16 ; 14,28 ; 16,6 ; cf. G. STRECKER, *ZTK* 64 [1967] 25 n. 21). The stereotyped nature of the resurrection statement in the formulas need not mean subsequent addition to fixed formularies (*pace* HAHN, *op. cit.*, 52) ; after all, the rest of the formulas had to do with empirical events, hence could be amplified with different descriptive details, whereas the resurrection statement dealt with the *eschatological* reality, the heart of the paradox enunciated by these formularies, which was quite beyond description or descriptive variation.

work of the eschatological combat, " Son of Man " *vs.* " men," in the kerygmatic statements he comes to model after the predictions.[141] In the Acts kerygma addressed to the Jews, however, it is the dialectic of men's onslaughts against the messiah versus *God's* mighty deliverance of him which turns the argument, and this in order to motivate the call to repentance which is the climax of the sermon structure.[142] God is kept in the center of this kerygma as its single agent, working all phases of sacred history and completing it through Jesus as his instrument. Consequently, God is the subject of the two resurrection verbs used in the sermons,[143] and whereas this is familiar usage in the case of ἐγείρειν, it is a novel situation with ἀνιστάναι, whose transitive (1st aor.) form, with God as subject, is a usage peculiar to Acts. It seems clear that this results from a refashioning of the Marcan prediction formulas, retaining the verb becaused it echoed the words of Jesus himself, yet adjusting the form to express the distinctively Lucan theology of history in the mission preaching of the apostles.[144] — In this respect, as in all others, one can see that Lk's accomodations of the passion-prophecy formula in his Easter story serve him as an all-important transition from the words of Jesus himself to the proclamation of the apostolic missionaries after Easter.[145]

After our lengthy analysis of the angels' message, which forms the core of Lk's tomb story as it did of Mk's, let us draw some conclusions and take stock of our position : (a) We found no reason to depart from our working hypothesis that Lk composed this pericope in sustained dialogue with Mk, his principal source. (b) The motif we found to dominate this passage, and to be revived by cross-reference to earlier texts throughout it, was the mystery of the messianic passion, conjured

---

[141] U. Wilckens, *Missionsreden*, 115ff., ²190, ³196. It is the schema of the Marcan predictions, not that of I Cor 15,3-5 (*pace* J. Dupont, *L'év. de Luc. Mém. Cerfaux*, 354), that is operative in the Lucan kerygmata (cf. Wilckens, *op. cit.*, 80).

[142] U. Wilckens, *Missionsreden*, 97f., 119, and earlier, M. Dibelius, *Formgeschichte*, 15f., and *Aufsätze*, 97f., 142. — In his various surveys of the call to repentance that is the climax of the sermons, J. Dupont correctly analyzes this point but does not keep in view the close connection of this concluding summons to the preceding moments of the sermon-schema (cf. *L'év. de Luc. Mém. Cerfaux*, 344-345 ; more amply : *Études*, 433-440, 460-465).

[143] Of ἐγείρειν in Acts 3,15 ; 4,10 ; 5,30 ; 10,40 ; 13,30.37 ; of the transitive (1st-aor.) ἀνιστάναι in Acts 2,24.32 ; 13,33.34 ; 17,31. Cf. H. Braun, " Zur Terminologie der Acta von der Auferstehung Jesu," in *Gesammelte Studien zum N. T. und seiner Umwelt* (Tübingen : J. C. B. Mohr, 1962) 173-177 ; E. Kränkl, *Jesus*, 130.

[144] U. Wilckens, *Missionsreden*, 137-140.

[145] On the function of the Acts discourses in the demonstration of continuity between the time of Jesus and the mission of the Church, cf. U. Wilckens, *Missionsreden*, 92-96.

up first by the women's perplexity and the " two men " who reminded us of the transfigured Christ's companions, then by the words the visitors spoke, redolent as they were of the passion prophecies that Lk had wrapped in an unbroken cover of mystery and incomprehension. (c) The angels' rehearsal of the passion prophecy gave utterance once again to Lk's view of the inexorable but hidden course charted by the divine will, whose goal, the " Kingdom of God " (Lk 17,20), comes to be without observable signs, right in the midst of its opponents and those calculating its portents. God's adversaries became his unconscious instruments in staging their onslaught against the " Son of Man," whose cryptic person enacts the final divine purpose. This dialectic between observable phenomena and unobservable purpose pervades all the events of Jesus' course, including those of the *triduum sacrum*. For Lk, the tomb has become the final factor in the mystery of the suffering messiah (cf. 24,22-24); it does not yet disclose God's hidden purpose, but only reiterates an enigmatic promise that can only be kept by the living person of the one who made it ! (d) The angels' reprise of the passion prophecy was the first of three in the Easter story, each forming the central instructional content of the episode to which it belongs (cf. 24,26.46). If we found the first of these to be a highly expressive composition of the evangelist himself, refashioning his predecessor's texts to express his own overarching themes and design, then we shall be prepared to reach the same conclusion in the case of the other two repetitions. As our comparison of the kerygmata of the Acts speeches with these passages showed, the passion formulas' rehearsals in the Easter story are meant to establish the connecting link between the instruction of the earthly Jesus and the kerygma of the apostolic church.[146]

[146] This preoccupation goes hand in hand with a second concern which we note throughout Lk 24, and which is already present in the recollection of the earthly Jesus' words at the tomb, viz. establishing that the Jesus of earthly memory and the risen Christ are one and the same (cf. E. LOHSE, *Auferstehung*, 20; R. GLÖCKNER, *Verkündigung*, 206ff.). To connect the Master's teaching and the Church's proclamation is to see the historical Jesus and the heavenly Kyrios as one. This underlines the importance of recognizing his living presence in his *word* (GLÖCKNER, *op. cit.*, 208), — a tenet that is no less Lk's than other NT authors', though it has been obscured in much recent Lucan redaction-analysis. (We shall take up this point in chap. IV/ii.) — In this connection, J. DUPONT's essay in *L'év. de Luc. Mém. Cerfaux* (329-374) illustrates recurring patterns with full textual citation, but fails to probe sufficiently the theories of this author which inspired these ample harmonies between the gospel and the Acts.

(5) *The Observers' Reaction* (Lk 24,8-12)

In view of the understanding of this pericope that we have been able to formulate thus far, it will be impossible to see in its concluding verses anything like the birth of the Easter faith.[147] V. 8 records: καὶ ἐμνήσθησαν τῶν ῥημάτων αὐτοῦ. There is not even the "fear and great joy" of Mt 28,8, and even this might not be affirming true belief, as we shall find out at Lk 24,41. — Let us consider what it is that the women "remembered"; it is the ῥήματα of the Master. The same word occurs as a designation of the second and third passion prophecies in Lk (9,45[2*x*], based on Mk 9,32[1*x*]; 18,34 *diff.* Mk); and each time it specifies the "word" of prophecy as absolutely *hidden and incomprehensible* to the disciples! Emphatic wording declares Lk's intended meaning: οἱ δὲ ἠγνόουν τὸ ῥῆμα τοῦτο ... περὶ τοῦ ῥήματος τούτου ... ἦν τὸ ῥῆμα τοῦτο κεκρυμμένον ἀπ' αὐτῶν .... Demonstratively and specifically, it is the prophecy of the *passion* that is shown to be hidden, inaccessible truth when the Master uttered it. (There is even no resurrection statement in the first of these instances.) If those "words" were not comprehended by the disciples when they were uttered, the "remembrance" of them now cannot be taken to imply faith or understanding unless the shift is explicitly noted.[148] Since there is not a διανοίγειν τὸν νοῦν nor συνιέναι noted as the effect of the angels' words, as there will be later with respect to the words of the risen Lord (24,45; cp. 24,31.32), we can establish only that the *riddle of the suffering and rising Son of Man* is recalled to the women at the tomb; indeed, that the experience of the empty tomb is being *inserted into the framework of that mystery*, whose veil is still drawn at this point.

---

[147] *Pace* H. GRASS, *Ostergeschehen*, 33; J. SCHMITT, *RvScRel* 25 (1951) 123 ("une foi plénière en la Résurrection"!); E. L. BODE, *Easter Morning*, 67 ("seems implied"); C. F. EVANS, *Resurrection*, 104 ("presumably"). — BODE and EVANS give good example of how *not* to proceed! The end of mystery of the messiah's destiny is hardly a point to be passed over by Lk with implication and presumption, after having so emphatically noted the concealment (9,45; 18,34) and prior to the dramatic eye- and mind-*openings* at 24,31.45.

[148] Thus the angels' words have not dispelled the perplexity, *pace* E. L. BODE, *Easter Morning*, 70. And it is sheer phantasy that we hear from J. SCHMITT: "Marie de Magdala et ses compagnes crurent dès la déclaration des anges; mieux: elles éprouvèrent quelque remords de n'avoir point cru dès la découverte du sépulcre vide (v. 8). De plus, elles se rendirent aussitôt ches les 'Douze' (*sic*) et les autres 'disciples' pour les informer des faits *et leur confesser leur croyance*" (ital. mine). Where is all this in the text? What "faith," "rather tardy and as if imposed by the facts" does Lk record? Is his concept of faith such that he could have recorded such a "faith"? (Cf. SCHMITT, *RvScRel* 25 [1951] 125, 126, 128.) Similar to SCHMITT, but without scientific pretensions: H. GOLLWITZER, *Jesu Tod und Auferstehung* ...[5], 94.

Only later in our chapter, when we hear of the " opening " of eyes (v. 31) and minds (v. 45), will we be entitled to speak of a lifting of that veil.

Not that v. 8 records no step at all towards faith's — and the church's — inception. Remembrance and retrospect will be very much part of the dialogue with the risen Christ which makes believers out of uncomprehending followers. The Lord's instructions will be reformulations of the very prophecy that the angels repeated, but then it will have become Easter revelation through its incorporation into an integral vision of sacred history taught — in fact, embodied — by the risen Lord. The believing community begotten of the Easter revelation will have its life determined by a fundamental, *retrospective relationship with the life of Jesus,*[149] such as will be illustrated by the Easter story in several ways: its " recognition " motif (vv. 31, 39), its recital of the words spoken by the Lord ἔτι ὢν σὺν ὑμῖν (v. 44), and its artful evoking of past situations through echoing the language of earlier narratives (e.g. Lk 9 throughout, the meal scene in vv. 29f. in particular). " Remembrance " will be an important ingredient of the Easter revelation's integrated view of sacred history, in the interests of which " backward " and " forward " cross-references are built into Lk's narrative as a matter of course.[150] — These are the terms in which the place of v. 8 in the Easter story can be properly understood.

V. 9 further records the women's reaction to their experience : they " announced all these things " to " the Eleven and all the rest." Two features of the reaction, the remembering and the announcing, constitute a full departure from the conclusion of Mk's story, and one can explain this as a sudden recourse to non-Marcan source material[151] or a deliberate redactional change in the interests of a new conception this evangelist is sponsoring.[152] That Lk already knew a version of the story which included the expected disclosure of their experience by the women, we have no means of refuting. But that v. 9 represents this

[149] U. WILCKENS, *Missionsreden*, 94 : "... der Verlauf der Kirchengeschichte in ihrer grundsätzlichen Rückbezogenheit auf die Zeit Jesu theologisch erklärt und begründet wird." Cf. also H. CONZELMANN, *MdZ*, 174.

[150] Cf. note 110 above.

[151] U. WILCKENS, in *Festschr. Smend*, 36, 40. WILCKENS believes that vv. 9.11 constitute a smooth sequence belonging to a pre-Lucan, non-Marcan souce, while v. 10 has been inserted by Lk and has disturbed the sequence. The narrative sequence associating the women at the tomb with a verification of their experience by the disciples (Lk/Jn) was already a datum of the tradition before either Lk or Jn wrote. On this assertion we might well agree, but we balk at finding that pre-Lucan tradition so clearly traceable in 24,9ff. To our mind, Lk is still holding his dialogue with Mk during most of the empty-tomb narrative.

[152] J. FINEGAN, *Überlieferung*, 86f. ; R. H. FULLER, *Formation*, 100 ; J. E. ALSUP, *Appearance Stories*, 114.

other tradition, we should want to question. The language is thoroughly typical of this evangelist and, moreover, what is said here is still part of his conscious critique of the Marcan source, in our opinion.

A first, very noticeable sign of Lk's hand is the word ὑποστρέψασαι, a favored vocabulum and device of this evangelist.[153] The gospel has the word 21 times, as against no occurrence in the other three gospels; and the Acts shows it 11 times, with only three, then, in all the rest of the NT.[154] Especially at the conclusion of episodes does Lk have a predilection for recording the *return* of main characters: Lk 1,23.56; 2,20.39; 4,14; 5,25; 7,10; 23,48.56; 24,9.33.52. The list includes, as one can see, a " return" of agent-personnel at the conclusion of each of the three Easter episodes, and each time the Jerusalem community of the Lord's followers is involved in the " return," either as destination (vv. 9.33) or as itself returning *in sedem* (v. 52). In Jerusalem and its community of disciples we have, as we pointed out before (p. 9), essential elements of the *framework* of Lk's Easter narrative, — meaning the editorial connective tissue by which the evangelist gave three disparate traditions sequence, thematic coherence, and salvation-historical relevance. The " return " motif serves to restore this framework to focus after the action of each pericope has been completed. The framework's importance in Lk 24 can be appreciated considering the fact that a three-fold ὑποστρέφειν marks the conclusion of as many episodes here. Consequently, the word in v. 9 is part of the editorial device favored by *this* author, and nowhere so consistently as in *this* chapter. In no way does it show the presence of a non-Marcan source.

Hand in hand with the " return " in Lk's redactional operation goes the expression, " *the Eleven and all the others*," as we suggested (cf. v. 33: τοὺς ἕνδεκα καὶ τοὺς σὺν αὐτοῖς). This is the " gallery " whose lingering presence during the *triduum sacrum* unifies the account of the paschal happenings. The reader is given the impression that the circle of "Eleven," as if a *collegium* residing and teaching *in cathedra*, was gathered at Jerusalem the whole day long, surrounded by a wider group of disciples (representative of the Church ?). "This circle

[153] G. LOHFINK, *Himmelfahrt*, 174; J. WANKE, *Emmauserzählung*, 47f. Note the return of persons and groups in the following Lucan passages, with special attention to the structurally functional passages of the Easter story: Lk 1,23.56; 2,15.20.39.43.45.51; 4,1.14; 5,25; 7,10; 8,37.39.40; 9,10; 10,17; 17,15.18; 19,12; 23,48.56; 24,9.12.33.52; Acts 1,12; 4,23; 5,23; 8,25.28; 12,25; 13,13; 14,21; 17,15; 20,3; 21,6; 22,17; 23,32.

[154] Especially diagnostic of the redactor's interest is the pattern of texts like Lk 4,14 (= summary, *diff.* Mk 1,14); 5,25 (*diff.* Mk 2,12); 8,37.40 (*diff.* Mk 5, 18.21); 24,9 (*diff.* Mk 16,8); also Lk 4,1 and 7,10, both framing Q pieces. — The motif of *return to Jerusalem* is a very special Lucan pattern, found at Lk 2,45; 24,33.52; Acts 1,12; 8,25 (12,25); 13,13; 22,17.

constitutes the center of the Easter happening. Only for a brief time do some disciples set out away from this center (Lk 24,12 *l.v.*; 24,13. 22.24), and yet it seems always taken for granted that they soon return to it." [155] — "The Eleven" is an expression which takes for granted the pre-Easter choice of "the Twelve" (Lk 6,13 / Mk 3,14) and the defection of Judas from the plenary group (cf. Acts 1,15-26). Even if the traditions of I Cor 15,5.7 were wholly reconcilable with Lk's Easter "Eleven" [156] and the apparently taxative application of the name "apostles" in Lk 6,13, the enumeration which takes account of Judas' departure is made repeatedly by Lk (24,9.33; Acts 1,26; 2,14) and elsewhere only by Mt (28,16; cf. Mk 16,14). Our evangelist was especially concerned to record the restoration of the plenary group of "twelve" (Lk 22,30) at the beginning of his second volume, where they will become collegial "witnesses of his resurrection" (Acts 1,21-26).[157] As we shall have added reason to observe when we analyze 24,33f., Lk saw in "the Eleven" surrounded by "all the others" on Easter day the beginning and the model of every subsequent ecclesial gathering, poised to function fully as "church" when the outermost circle of humanity rejoins them on Pentecost (Acts 2,5ff., as in Lk 6,17) and the worldwide mission is inaugurated.

Those concentric circles — the Twelve, then "the other disciples" gathered about them, and then a cosmopolitan public hearing the word from within the circle — are a schematic Lucan arrangement depicting the process by which, under the power of Word and Spirit, the *true Israel* is to be assembled by Jesus' "witnesses" (24,47f.).[158] The concentric arrangement was already drawn up, through skillful editing of

---

[155] J. Wanke, *Emmauserzählung*, 48; cf. *BZ* 18 (1974) 186f. In the same vein, H. Grass, *Ostergeschehen*, 33: "Die Jünger sind vielmehr, wie die lukanischen Ostergeschichten zeigen, als ein geschlossener, wenn auch ratloser und hoffnungsloser Kreis in Jerusalem geblieben."

[156] The only path of such reconciliation, of course, is to suggest that Paul's reference is inexact, using still the hallowed number despite the defection, while the evangelists' "Eleven" (Mt 28,16; Lk 24,9.33; Acts 1,26) is a pedantic adjustment taking account of the defection. Cf. G. Klein, *Apostel*, 34ff., and W. Schmithals, *Das kirchliche Apostelamt. Eine historische Untersuchung* (FRLANT 81; Göttingen: Vandenhoeck und Ruprecht, 1961) 58ff.

[157] Cf. most recently J. Jervell, *Luke*, 79-82; E. Nellessen, "Tradition und Schrift in der Perikope von der Erwählung des Mattias," *BZ* 19 (1975, 205-218) 205ff.; E. Nellessen, *Zeugnis*, 169ff.; Chr. Burchard, *Zeuge*, 134ff. — The boundary between older and more recent approaches to this passage was set by E. Haenchen, "Tradition und Komposition in der Apg.," *ZTK* 52 (1955, 205-225) 206-208 (= *Gott und Mensch*, 207-209), but the older approach reappeared in K. H. Rengstorf, "Die Zuwahl des Matthias," *ST* 15 (1961) 35-67, and more recently in S. G. Wilson, *Gentiles*, 111ff.

[158] Brought out rather effectively by G. Lohfink, *Sammlung Israels*, esp. 74-77.

Mk, at Lk 6,13-17, making Jesus' first recorded instruction a foretaste of the world-mission.[159] The same circles have gradually to be restored through the events of Easter, the interim replenishment of " the Twelve " (Acts 1,21ff.), and the Pentecost (Acts 2,5ff.41). The nuclear Twelve bespeak Jesus' claim upon Israel, of course (Lk 22,30), and this means that the formation of his church will be the gathering of a faithful Israel of the last days (Acts 2,17-21.39), heir to the expectations and promises of the entire biblical tradition.[160] — This is the sweeping pattern of which Lk 24,9 is a part. In no sense is it indicative of pre-Lucan source-material. It is the fruit of this author's innovative commentary on Mk, and very much part of the linkage he creates between his two volumes.

We are interested, finally, in the expression ταῦτα πάντα characterizing the content of the women's announcement on their return. The emphasis is on the *totality* of the women's reportage, and the phrase is echoed in reference to the wayfarers' discussion at 24,14, περὶ πάντων ... τούτων, and in their resumé of recent events in 24,21, σὺν πᾶσιν τούτοις. We have already observed our evangelist's interest in the integrity of the women's witness (p. 19): first at Lk 23,55, when they saw not just " where " (Mk) but " how " Jesus' body was buried; then at 24,3, when they were made to observe the *fact* of the body's absence for the first time in the story's tradition. We insisted that this redac-

[159] H. Conzelmann, *MdZ*, 38 (brief literary analysis; more ample interpretation:) H. Schürmann, *Traditionsgeschichtliche Untersuchungen*, 291-293, and *Lk.* I, 311f.; G. Lohfink, *Sammlung Israels*, 63ff. I agree with Lohfink, against Schürmann (I, 319), that Lk 6,12-20 results from a repositioning of Marcan materials, not the use of Q or some other *fons*.

[160] The gathering of the " true Israel " was begun by Jesus and mandated to his apostles by his commission (so G. Lohfink, *Sammlung Israels*, 83). This means that the Church does not lay claim to Israel's status as an outsider, she has rather developed organically and gradually from the womb of Israel, as the result of a sundering of repentant and obstinate Israelites that began during Jesus' lifetime and was carried on *vis-à-vis* the preaching of the apostles (*ibid.*, 74; — cf. the last such sundering at Rome in Acts 28,24 !). The process of the ingathering can be observed in Lk 23: the people and their leaders are together in condemning Jesus at 23,4f.13, but the two groups become disunited under the cross, the folk looking on, the leaders mocking (23,35); then finally, at 23,48, the multitude is shown beating its breast and returning home. This seems to foreshadow the repentance that is called for, after the accusation of their sin in rejecting Jesus, by the apostolic preachers to Jewish audiences (cf. Acts 2,37ff.; and esp. Acts 3,13-19). " In der Zeit der ersten apostolischen Predigt sammelte sich aus dem jüdischen Volk das wahre Israel ! Und jenes Israel, das dann noch in der Ablehnung Jesu beharrte, verlor sein Anrecht, das wahre Gottesvolk zu sein ..." (G. Lohfink, *op. cit.*, 55 [all in italics]; cf. also 43, and H. Conzelmann, *MdZ*, 135ff.). — A. George misses the point of the crowd's change of attitude in Lk 23 when he tries to maintain their disposition was uniquely favorable. He must then account the accusation in the Acts speeches to the early kerygma rather than the intent of the author (cf. *RB* 75 [1968] 503f.).

tional trend did not have the straightforward apologetic purpose one might expect, but had the *dialectical force* of building a total experience *bereft of understanding and belief*, so that faith's inception should prove to be the independent gift of the risen Lord. This dialectical pathos will become especially strong when the tomb experience is rehearsed anew by the travelers to Emmaus. Their account of " *all* these things " simply underscores the futility of a self-reliant human perception *vis-à-vis* the paschal happenings, which stood as *bruta facta* in the travelers' view, bereft of all their redemptive logic and significance.[161]

The case for a tomb-story *Vorlage* other than Mk, which has been inconsequential thus far, gains a certain allure at *v.* 10. We are learning the women's names here for the first time, since our author passed over the earlier points of Mk's conflicting lists with no mention of names (Mk 15,40.47 ; 16,1). The names we encounter now are in agreement with no previous listing, neither Mk's nor Lk's own of 8,2f. What we have is a selection from the variant lists : " the Magdalene, Mary, then Joanna, and Mary (mother [162]) of James " ; and a certain method in the combining makes the redactional character of the passage reasonably clear.[163] The first name in each of Lk's sources, Mk 16,1 and Lk 8,2f. (S-Lk), is the same, while the remaining two in each differ. Consequently, the name that is common heads the present list, and then follows the second name in each of the sources : Joanna, from Herod's court (Lk 8,3), and " Mary of James " (Mk). The third name from each of the source-lists is dropped, suggesting that the ternary number was required throughout the different stages of the tradition.[164] The names omitted are subsumed, of course, in αἱ λοιπαὶ σὺν αὐταῖς, somewhat similar to Mt's recourse to " the other Mary " to reconcile Mk's lists (Mt 27,61 ; 28,1). Beyond any concern for legally

[161] Brilliantly commented by H.-D. Betz, *ZTK* 66 (1969) 10, 11. " Obwohl sie die Tatsachen kennen, wissen sie nichts damit anzufangen."

[162] I. Broer, *Grab*, 97-99 : the *genitivus originis* could mean " mother of," but need not. One would more readily think of " wife " or, in the case of an unmarried woman, " daughter." Broer thinks this is a good indication that Mk 15,40, the only text which specifies " mother " for " Mary of James " (Mk 16,1) and " Mary of Joses " (Mk 15,47), is a redactional fusion of the two other texts, making the eventually different " Marys " into one the only way that was possible, viz. as " mother " of the two men.

[163] So rightly M. Hengel, in *Festschr. O. Michel*, 248 ; W. Grundmann, *Lk.*, 441 ; A. Dauer, " Das Wort des Gekreuzigten an seine Mutter und den ' Jünger, den er liebte '. Eine traditionsgeschichtliche und theologische Untersuchung zu Joh. 19,25-27," *BZ* 11 (1967, 222-239) 228 ; R. Mahoney, *Two Disciples*, 120, 166.

[164] M. Hengel (*Festschr. O. Michel*, 248) cites other important ternary groups, including the inner circle of Jesus' companions (e.g. Mk 5,37 ; 9,2 ; 14,33 ; but cf. 13,3), who were admitted, like the women, to special revelatory events.

prescribed witness-number that the older tomb tradition might have had, Lk's interest in the names seems rather that of sustaining the motif he had instilled in his narrative back in its Galilean phase. The two leading names on his present list, after all, are from the list of those the Master had exorcized in Galilee, so their mention now reinforces the Galilean "remembrance" evoked by the angels (v. 6). These women's participation in the Jesus-story is truly complete, for they have both experienced his healing-ministry in Galilee and have been amongst the συναναβάντες from there. Their names demonstrate that full participation through the schema of Lk's narrative.[165] In short, the list of women's names in v. 10 still finds Lk composing according to his overall narrative plan and to sustain his own themes. If an alternate version of the empty-tomb story associated these non-Marcan names with that episode, the present verse will not bear the weight of proof for the existence of such a version.

This judgment can be sustained despite an apparent syntactical irregularity in v. 10, which some take to betray a redactional seam.[166] The phrase ἦσαν δὲ ..., coming before the names, would appear to associate them with the announcement of v. 9 (ἀπήγγειλαν), whereupon a second announcement (ἔλεγον) is ascribed to αἱ λοιπαὶ σὺν αὐταῖς in v. 10b. The scribes who undertook revisions of convenience, such as dropping the initial phrase or inserting αἵ before ἔλεγον, cannot be followed, of course.[167] The original text included ἦσαν δέ, and the problem of an apparent duplication of announcements must be faced. If the hypothesis of a redactional suture be adhered to,[168] we own we find this a most unusual situation for this evangelist, who otherwise masters his sources so thoroughly as never to leave their loose ends hanging! We suggest a closer look at the function of v. 10.

What is to be noticed about the second announcement (ἔλεγον) is that it sets a new sequence in motion, especially if the disputed v. 12

---

[165] The unusual way in which the Magdalen's name is recorded here is no sign of independent source material underlying the text. The form is ἡ Μαγδαληνὴ Μαρία, but Lk's earlier S-Lk reference in 8,2 read: Μαρία ἡ καλουμένη Μαγδαληνή, and its special stress on Mary's surname accounts for the latter's prior position in our text, which clearly means to echo it. — Joanna too, of course, arouses memories of Galilee for the reader who recalls her connection with Herod's court (8,3).

[166] E.g. J. WANKE, *Emmauserzählung*, 75.

[167] *Contra* E. KLOSTERMANN, *Lk.*, 233, and J. M. CREED, *Lk*, 294, who follow WELLHAUSEN in omitting the first phrase. P-75 now adds further support to the consensus of textual critics in favor of ἦσαν δέ.

[168] *Pace* J. WANKE, *loc. cit.* in n. 166; cf. also P. SCHUBERT, in *Ntl. Studien f. Bultmann*, 174. Both scholars, like WILCKENS (in n. 151), seem to rely on criteria of source-analysis which recent Lucan criticism has steadily undermined and which at least WANKE and WILCKENS would usually abjure!

is accepted as original to Lk's text. After we hear of the women's announcement to the Jerusalem assembly (v. 9), we are reminded of the pedigree and credibility of the observers (v. 10). But typically of this chapter's *argumentum*, such amplification of the speakers' *credibility* is only building up *via contraria* to the *incredulity* of the apostolic leadership, whom neither the stature nor the number of the observers impressed. The names emphasized that long-standing companions of the Lord's " way " had seen the realization of his Galilean prophecies; and the voices of " the others who were with them " took up their report, addressing it specifically to " the apostles," who are thus identified with " the Eleven " by familiar Lucan presumption.[169] *Typical amplification of the strain between Easter phenomena and disciples' perception*: facts are recited *totally*, by observers who had participated in Jesus' ministry *fully*, before those related to Jesus' earthly life and mission program *most intimately*. And still, *only disbelief results*! — In v. 12, it is one of the inner circle, the principal one, who runs to the tomb to verify the women's story; and so *ultimate authority, and paradoxically, ultimate incomprehension ex parte hominis, are accorded the fact of the empty tomb*! Thus will v. 12 cap the dialectical story of the tomb perfectly, — if we can make its authenticity solidly probable.

Recapitulating the thought-sequence of this section: (a) " Remembrance " and report to the Jerusalem assembly (v. 9); (b) assurance that it was long-standing followers who testified (v. 10a); (c) confirmation of their report by " the others with them," and assurance that the report reached the very innermost circle, " the apostles," Jesus' " chosen " ones (v. 10b; cp. 6,13); (d) *and still the report was branded " non-sense "* (λῆρος) and disbelieved (v. 11), except that (δέ) (e) Peter, the leading " apostle," ran to the tomb to verify the women's report for himself, and came away " wondering " at what had occurred (θαυμάζων τὸ γεγονός — v. 12).

V. 12 can thus be integrated into our pericope's texture, and not only within the sequence of thought, as we sought to show, but also in the grammatical structure of vv. 10f. After the new sequence is begun with δέ in v. 10, there follows a paratactical series which is unusual in Lk: καὶ αἱ λοιπαὶ ... καὶ ἐφάνησαν ... καὶ ἠπίστουν ...[170] The effect

[169] Cf. Lk 22,14/Mk 14,17 (!); Lk 17,5; Lk 6,13 & Acts 1,2. It is probably correct, however, that Lk does not make either a delimiting definition of " apostle " or the taxative application of the word to " the Twelve " a matter of his special concern or personal statement (with E. NELLESSEN and S. G. WILSON [n. 157 above] *contra* G. KLEIN, *Apostel*, 202ff.; similarly against KLEIN, W. SCHMITHALS, *Apostelamt* [cited in n. 156 above] 236 n. 80, 237 n. 89).

[170] Cf. J. C. HAWKINS, *Horae syn.*, 121, on Lk's preference for the alternate καί and δέ instead of Mk's monotonous parataxis. On the other hand, A.

of the series is to accumulate strength in the moment of apostolic incredulity, which is prelude to the apostolic verification, introduced by δέ. Without v. 12, we should expect that v. 11 would have been introduced by δέ, which would give it a final adversative thrust against the women's report and enable it to conclude the pericope on that note. Instead, with v. 12, the final word of the pericope is not disbelief but wonder, and a perplexity comparable to the women's (v. 4). This grammatical argument only creates a positive disposition towards accepting v. 12 as Lk's own. A much fuller discussion of the problem is required, however.

The Problem of V. 12 : The textual criticism of this verse has been discussed often enough to excuse us from a complete review of the matter.[171] The *status quaestionis* can be resumed in propositions affecting three aspects of the question : (a) the state of manuscript evidence has been irreversibly altered by the discovery of 𝔓-75, which contains the Western omissions in Lk 24 and has lately won for them the assent of prestigious textual critics ;[172] (b) the internal arguments against v. 12 are more or less what they always were : a coincidence with Jn 20,3-10 *etiam ad verba* which suggests interpolation ; some non-Lucan language ; clash with 24,24 (a two-edged argument, witness 24,51 !) ; abrupt non-reliance on Mk ;[173] (c) exegetical opinion seems as divided as ever,

---

PLUMMER (*Lk*, li) stresses Lk's freedom in composing and his occasional recourse to a series of δέ phrases where the effect of such might be desired.

[171] The latest discussions : in favor of authenticity, J. MUDDIMAN and F. NEIRYNCK, *ETL* 48 (1972) 542-553 ; J. WANKE, *Emmauserzählung*, 76-82 ; against authenticity, R. MAHONEY, *Two Disciples*, 41-69.

[172] Cf. B. M. METZGER, *Textual Commentary*, 183f., 186f., 189-193, with report on p. 193 of the discussions of the U. B. S. international committee of textual scholars which led to a majority's acceptance of the non-Western readings in Lk 24 (with a minority in vigorous opposition). The implications of P-75 constituted the decisive factor, as the noted essay of committee-member K. ALAND makes clear (*Studien zur Überlieferung* ..., 162-171, esp. 168 re. 24,12). The state of external evidence on the matter is quite accurately summarized by R. MAHONEY, an opponent of authenticity : " we are left ... with a very fine text of established antiquity showing certain longer readings, over against an admittedly capricious text of perhaps equal antiquity [?] showing uncharacteristically shorter readings. The question is whether or not that canon of criticism which prefers the shorter reading can prevail against the Alexandrian text as seen in the new light of P-75. To answer we must turn to what is known as the internal evidence " (*Two Disciples*, 53). — The internal evidence is what the Western text's partisans have long relied on since the weight of authority has always been against it. Cf. C. F. EVANS, *Resurrection*, 97 ; G. HARTMANN, *ZNW* 55 (1964) 204 n. 18.

[173] These arguments are amplified but, in our opinion, not improved by R. MAHONEY, *Two Disciples*, 53ff. Our verse is one of several in the chapter which are close enough to Jn 20 in wording to suggest interpolation from there ; but the two others, vv. 36 and 40 (*pace* C. F. EVANS, *Resurrection*, 58), occur in a passage which represents a parallel *tradition* to that of Jn 20,19ff. (so most

except that a slight shift in favor of the verse is noticeable of late.[174] — Our response to this three-fold *status quaestionis* is this: (a) ac-

scholars judge — cf. chap. III/1a, note 13), and that promises an alternate explanation to ms. interchange both there and in the present text. Those, like MAHONEY, however, who urge that the coincidences between Lk 24,12 and Jn 20,3-10 go beyond what common tradition can account for (*loc. cit.*), rely on the following arguments: -i- verbal coincidences: (προ-)έδραμεν, not overly compelling; παρακύψας (Jn 20,5.11, never elsewhere in Lk-Acts); βλέπει in the historical present, quite usual for Jn, most unusual for Lk (but cf. precisely the exception, Lk 16,23: ὁρᾷ, an other-worldly *sight*!); τὰ ὀθόνια (4*x* in the Jn context, here only in Lk, nowhere else in the NT); κείμενα is uncertain in the ms. tradition of Lk 24,12, and is almost certainly imported from Jn (therefore wisely ignored by MAHONEY, *op. cit.*, 55); finally, the curious correspondence of ἀπῆλθεν πρὸς ἑαυτὸν κτλ. to Jn's ἀπῆλθον ... πρὸς αὐτούς (preferring Lk's wonted employment of the reflexive pronoun with preposition, with J. WANKE, *Emmauserzählung*, 79f., and noting that Lk has a significantly different alignment of the phrase than Jn 20, permitting Jerome's *secum mirans* since θαυμάζων follows; cp. Lk 22,23). -ii- Unlucan style-traits: the uncorrected *praesens historicum* is unusual for Lk, but not unique. Only one of 92 instances has been allowed to stand in Marcan material (Lk 8,49/Mk 5,35), and eight of nine other uses in Lk-Acts are in verbs of saying, a vernacular habit. Lk 16,23 approaches our case, and we indicated above that we regard it as a significant parallel to the present one. (On the matter in general, cf. J. C. HAWKINS, *Horae syn.*, 22.) — θαυμάζειν is normally used with a preposition rather than a direct object in Lk (2,33; 4,22; 9,43; 20,26), and yet cf. Lk 7,9 and Acts 7,31, where traditions in use may account for the unwonted direct object. Moreover, the presence of the direct object might possibly indicate that πρὸς ἑαυτόν was intended to accompany θαυμάζων after all (*pace* Vulg.) and a duality of prepositional phrase was avoided. -iii- Comparison with Lk 24,24 is urged against v. 12 at some risk, as R. MAHONEY himself admits (*Two Disciples*, 58). On the same token, and *not* with less probability, *pace* MAHONEY, "the same consideration could have caused an early literary-minded editor to have (*sic*) omitted the verse." Contrasts with both v. 24 and Jn 20 make scribal elimination of v. 12 a strong possibility (rightly J. SCHNIEWIND, *Parallelperikopen*², 88f.; K. H. RENGSTORF, *Lk.*¹³, 280; R. SCHNACKENBURG, "Der Jünger, den Jesus liebte," *EKK Vorarb.* 2 [97-117] 103; J. E. ALSUP, *Appearance Stories*, 103f.). Of course, any interpretation of the passage which defends the authenticity of v. 12 must also come to terms with its divergences from v. 24 and Jn 20, and we plan to do that in the course of our discussion. -iv- The Source-Question receives an enticingly simpler answer when v. 12 is removed from the text (e.g. H. GRASS, *Ostergeschehen*, 34f.), but v. 24 shows that Lk was acquainted with the separate tradition of the disciples' visit in any case. Whereas we think we have shown that the empty-tomb story is best understood as a critical dialogue between Lk and Mk up through v. 11, v. 12 is a different story and is, whether interpolated or not, a reflection of the same tradition found in Lk 24,24 and Jn 20,3-10 (cf. U. WILCKENS, *Festschr. Smend*, 40, and *Auferstehung*, 66f.; R. H. FULLER, *Formation*, 103). — By way of brief *animadversio*: I do not think F. NEIRYNCK made a successful case for the derivation of Lk 24,12 from the Marcan text, with βλέπει echoing the similar historical present, θεωροῦσιν, in Mk 16,4 (cf. *ETL* 48 [1972] 548-553), although I found many of his observations quite provocative and helpful.

[174] The decision against v. 12 was easier for older interpreters, such as J. M.

knowledging the altered weight of the manuscript evidence, we are also convinced that (b) the case against v. 12 on internal grounds stresses factors which also show another side of the coin in the verse's favor.[175] (c) We are therefore inclined to accept some fairly persuasive arguments offered recently [176] in favor of the preservation in v. 12 (as well

---

CREED, *Lk*, 294; A. PLUMMER, *Lk*, 550; E. MEYER, *Ursprung und Anfänge* I, 27 n. 1; E. KLOSTERMANN, *Lk.*, 233 (" so ... fast alle Kritiker, doch vgl. LOISY, 578 "); E. HIRSCH, *Auferstehungsgeschichten*, 12; J. FINEGAN, *Überlieferung*, 87; H. GRASS, *loc. cit.* above; H. von CAMPENHAUSEN, *Ablauf*, 35 n. 139; P. SCHUBERT, in *Ntl. Studien f. Bultmann*, 172 n. 18; E. LOHSE, *Auferstehung*, 21. The problems discussed in n. 173 still cause hesitation among exegetes, with some suspending judgment (e.g. W. DIETRICH, *Petrusbild*, 162; W. MARXSEN, *Auferstehung*, 53f.), others complicating the matter with fragile source-evaluation which makes Lk 24,12 an intrusion from a pre-Johannine source, but an intrusion nevertheless (so R. E. BROWN, *The Gospel according to John XIII-XXI* [Anchor Bible 29A; New York: Doubleday, 1970] 969, 1000). Even such recent scholars as still uphold the Western " non-interpolation " in this instance must take note of a rising trend of critical opinion in its favor (so Ph. SEIDENSTICKER, *Auferstehung*, 93 n. 58). Even if it is not quite true that recent studies have created a *status quaestionis* fully favorable to the authenticity of v. 12 (*pace* J. E. ALSUP, *Appearance Stories*, 103), it might be said that " the recent trend seems clearly toward acceptance as genuine " (so R. MAHONEY, *Two Disciples*, 43), — and this not only in Germany, as MAHONEY seems to wish to limit it, considering A.R.C. LEANEY, J. SCHMITT, P. BENOIT, X. LÉON-DUFOUR, J. MUDDIMAN, F. NEIRYNCK, E. L. BODE, and J. E. ALSUP, to be mentioned in the subsequent note 176!

[175] To wit: -i- Vocabulary common to Lk 24,12.24 and Jn 20,3-10 is such as favors the common tradition view rather than scribal insertion. After all, the *specifica* of Jn's narrative — the race of *two* disciples, the details of the tomb, and the one disciple's *belief* at the tomb — are not verified in Lk, either verse! At very least, an interpolator would have provided for the two disciples at v. 12 and the emergent faith in both verses (cf., respectively, R. LEANEY, *NTS* 2 [1955-56] 114; R. SCHNACKENBURG, *art. cit.* [in n. 173] 103). -ii- Of supposedly non-Lucan style-traits it should be said that fully Lucan expressions stand right beside them, a situation which also argues for common tradition rather than interpolation. The pleonastic ἀναστάς is often introduced by Lk into a gospel pericope (Lk 4,29.38; 11,7f.; 15,18.20; 17,19) and is used frequently and distinctively by him in Acts. The word θαυμάζειν, usually followed by a preposition, is nevertheless found taking a direct object only at Lk 7,9 (cp. Mt 8,10) and Acts 7,31 in all the NT. τὸ γεγονός is very much a Lucan expression, found in all the NT only in Lk-Acts: Lk 8,34.56 [*diff.* Mk]; 2,15; Acts 4,21; 5,7; 13,12. Concerning ἀναστάς, it admittedly precedes a proper noun as a rule, but the change in ordinary usage can surely be understood from the thought-structure in vv. 10b-12 and the necessary adversative (δέ) emphasis on Peter, making his trip of discovery amongst the general disbelief of the apostles. -iii- The relation of v. 12 to v. 24 proves to be according to a pattern of Lucan use of sources, the technique of " cross-reference," as we explain on p. 65 below.

[176] The case was made as far back as J. SCHNIEWIND, *Parallelperikopen*², 89. Cf. also R. LEANEY, *NTS* 2 (1955-56) 111, and *Lk*, 28f.; W. GRUNDMANN, *Lk.*, 439f.; U. WILCKENS, in *Festschr. Smend*, 35 n. 16; H.-W. BARTSCH, *Wachet*, 16,

as v. 24) of " a tradition separate and distinct from, younger than and supplementary to the older form of the tomb story " (J. E. ALSUP), in which a visit to the tomb by disciples of Jesus and confirmation of the great discovery were recorded. This " disciple-oriented tradition," variously adapted by the two evangelists (Lk: concentration on Peter alone in v. 12; Jn: identification of two figures) was added to the older form of the story as an insertion in Jn, an appendage in Lk, but both times " reflecting a distinctly separate and supplementary development of the tradition as a whole, a development arising out of the further process of reflection .... " [177]

If a common tradition explains the convergence of Lk and Jn on the presence of disciples at the tomb, it must be admitted that the disciples' number remains a problem, at least in Lk. V. 24 (τινες τῶν σὺν ἡμῖν) is in accord with the two disciples of Jn 20, but v. 12 has it rather emphatically that only Peter made the trip. Is v. 12 an older version of the tradition, with v. 24 and Jn 20 representing further developments, or does Lk deliberately limit the visit to Peter in v. 12, knowing well (and providing in the Emmaus retrospect) that more than one were recorded by the tradition? [178] This latter alternative is the one we shall defend, and we shall advance some considerations to show its coherence with Lucan redactional policies. A comparison with Lk 5,1-11 helps us make that case, together with an observation of typical editorial procedure on Lk's part.

As is well known, *Lk* 5,1-11 contains a story of Peter's vocation which has remarkable literary rapports with the Easter episode in Jn 21,1-

---

23, and *Auferstehungszeugnis*, 11 n. 24; P. BENOIT, in *Festschr. Jeremias*, 142-144, and with M.-É. BOISMARD, *Synopse* II, 445-446 (both positing use by Lk of pre-Jn source-writing); E. L. BODE, *Easter Morning*, 68-70; X. LÉON-DUFOUR, *Résurrection*, 163f., 224-225; F. NEIRYNCK, *ETL* 48 (1972) 548ff.; (J. MUDDIMAN, in the companion piece to NEIRYNCK's in *ibid.*, 542ff., defends the authenticity of v. 12 but does not probe its traditional roots); J. WANKE, *Emmauserzählung*, 78; J. E. ALSUP, *Appearance Stories*, 105, 114. — The case for literary interdependency at the level of the finished products of Lk/Jn is not broadly accepted. J. SCHMITT defends the authenticity of Lk 24,12 and believes it is the basis of Jn's text (despite the many Johannine elements that remain thus unexplained; cf. *RvScRel* 25 [1951] 219-228). The dependency was asserted in the opposite direction by A. LOISY, but this was in the framework of his curious theory on the last sections of Lk (cf. *Luc*, 578). As C. H. DODD rightly judged, it is scarcely probable that either evangelist (Lk or Jn) used the other's text for the report of the disciples' trek to the tomb (cf. *Historical Tradition in the Fourth Gospel* [Cambridge: Cambridge Univ. Press, 1963] 141f.).

[177] J. E. ALSUP, *Appearance Stories*, 105. In defense of the common tradition hypothesis, also R. SCHNACKENBURG, *EKK Vorarb.* 2, 103f.

[178] J. KREMER seems to hold the first of these views (*Osterbotschaft*, 57), while J. WANKE correctly insists upon the second (*Emmauserzählung*, 80).

14. A long history of modern criticism [179] has not brought the issue of this relationship to rest, but our purposes are served, for the moment, by a careful look at the *miraculous haul of fish* which the two passages have in common. This episode represents the only real point of intersection between Lk and Jn, for Lk is lacking any accompanying meal shared by the wonder-worker and the fishermen (and also the Easter recognition-motif associated therewith), and Jn lacks the framework of the Lord's instruction (Lk 5,1-4a) and the call to discipleship joined to the miracle (Lk 5,10-11); and precisely the unjohannine elements give the miracle story its focus and purpose in the Lucan version.[180] Lk's pericope thus has two distinct sources: an old story of the miraculous draught of fish [181] and the Marcan vocation scene (1,16-20), with schematic seashore scenario also from Mk (4,1-2; 2,13; 3,7.9).[182] The hypothesis that Lk's pericope is a transposed Easter story, frequently posited but seldom given substantial analytical support, has lost ground in recent discussion,[183] and deservedly so, we think.

---

[179] Recounted in R. Pesch, *Fischfang*, 13-52, and in "La rédaction lucanienne du logion des pécheurs d'homme (Lc., V,10c)," in F. Neirynck, éd., *L'év. de Luc. Mém. Cerfaux*, (225-244) 226-235.

[180] Rightly R. Pesch, *Fischfang*, 63-64.

[181] In Lk 5,4b-9 and Jn 21,2(*part.*)-4a.6.11, according to R. Pesch, *Fischfang*, 86. Greater scope is given the miracle story by B. Steinseifer, who restricts the appearance episode to 21,9b.13 (*ZNW* 62 [1971] 261-262, 264), and greater scope is given to the appearance story by J. E. Alsup, who implausibly includes the night spent without a catch (Jn 21,3c) in it (cf. *Appearance Stories*, 201-203). While these authors disagree on the delineation of the strands, they agree, as we do, on the principle of tradition-historical dissociation of miracle story and appearance story.

[182] The Marcan "scenario" passages are then omitted in their proper sequence by Lk, confirming his conscious incorporation of them into the one *mise-en-scène* of Lk 5,1-4a (cf. R. Pesch, *Fischfang*, 53ff., 64ff.). The case for Marcan dependency in the scenario is so strong that even ready advocates of alternate Lucan sources recognize the priority of Mk in it (e.g. T. Schramm, *Markus-Stoff*, 28f.). W. Dietrich is therefore in the minority when he asserts the integrity of the introduction and the vocation scene already in pre-Lucan tradition (*Petrusbild*, 25-38). In our opinion, Dietrich offers no data that are not better explained by Lk's conflation of the "great catch" tradition (Jn) with Mk's scenario and vocation apophthegm.

[183] Cf. R. Pesch, *Fischfang*, 86-110. Also M.-É. Boismard, "Le chapitre XXI de saint Jean. Essai de critique littéraire," *RB* 54 (1947, 473-501) 495; C. K. Barrett, *The Gospel according to Saint John* (London: SPCK, 1955) 483; W. Grundmann, *Lk.*, 127 n. 1; R. Fortna, *The Gospel of Signs. A Reconstruction of the Narrative Source Underlying the Fourth Gospel* (SNTS 11; Cambridge: Cambridge Univ. Press, 1970) 87-98; B. Steinseifer, *ZNW* 62 (1971) 260; R. H. Fuller, *Formation*, 151f.; H. Schürmann, *Lk.* I, 273f.; R. Schnackenburg, *Johannesevangelium* III, 410-413; W. Dietrich, *Petrusbild*, 54ff.; apparently also B. Rigaux, *Dieu l'a ressuscité*, 241f., 252 n. 55. — The hypothesis of a transposed Easter story in Lk 5, hence the tradition-historical priority of Jn 21, scarcely survives careful literary criticism of both passages. The proponents, mostly older-vintage form-critics (cf. the listing in Schürmann, *loc. cit.* in n. 273),

An interesting datum in both the Marcan and Lk/Jn sources of Lk 5,1-11 is that Peter was participating in a scene *with others*, and any special prominence of his role is missing in Mk, present but still understated in Jn. Mk's vocation pericope has the focal pronouncement, parallel to Lk 5,10c, addressed plurally to Andrew as well as Peter (Mk 1,17); and there are successive calls to Peter with Andrew, then James and John, Zebedee's sons. The same Zebedees are on the scene of the Johannine fishing miracle (21,2), along with other disciples elsewhere brought forward in the fourth gospel; and consequently, the fishing story, with its dominical command and miraculous draught (21,6), is told with *plural* verbs referring to the several disciples involved. — Now, of course, the peculiarity of the Lucan version can be seen more clearly. The story concentrates on Peter, even to setting the scene with him and the Master apparently alone in the boat (vv. 3-4). But then a puzzling alternation of *singular and plural* verbs (vv. 4-6) abruptly reminds us that other disciples are present, hence that *Lk is mindful of the plurality of disciples in the tradition even while he deliberately concentrates on Peter* ![184] The same is even more striking at vv. 10-11:[185] the Zebedees suddenly appear at v. 10, after an episode in which they have not been mentioned, only then to have Jesus address his vocational command to *Peter only* (καὶ εἶπεν πρὸς τὸν Σίμωνα· [Mk's Andrew having vanished altogether]... ἀνθρώπους ἔσῃ [!] ζωγρῶν). Yet finally they *all* — *plural* — leave everything and follow Jesus, as in Mk 1,18.20.

The pattern is clear: reminiscence of sources in which a plurality of disciples were involved, but concentration on Peter. The latter's name-change, incidentally, is observed by Lk consistently after the call of

never accorded the passages that kind of literary analysis, more often than not assuming the relationship rather than demonstrating it. Typical is the argument of Th. LORENZEN, *ZNW* 64 (1973) 215-216, which presents a kind of specious reasoning which is not of the nature of literary criticism at all.

[184] Given the similar alternations of singular and plural in vv. 4b-6 and 10-11, I do not agree with R. PESCH (*Fischfang*, 76f.) that the hand of Lk was not at work in 4b-6. The plurality of disciples is the tradition's "given," and it is Lk who creates the impression of Peter's acting alone, — based, perhaps, on his having already obtained a position of leading exponent in the traditional story; so W. DIETRICH, *Petrusbild*, 53).

[185] And here admitted by R. PESCH (*Fischfang*, 69-76, and *art. cit.* [in n. 179] 237ff.). — On the basis of the change from μέταχοι to κοινωνοί in vv. 7/10, W. DIETRICH builds a very fragile hypothesis which would make the mention of the Zebedees at v. 10 independent of Mk and part of the original, pre-Lucan vocation story (*Petrusbild*, 74f.). The unmotivated vocabulary change reflects, *pace* DIETRICH, the preeminence of a leadership triumvirate at the pre-evangelical stage of the tradition. But since D. admits the philological inconclusiveness of his own argument (71), we do not feel compelled by it to revise our critical assessment of Lk's source-material in 5,1-11.

the Twelve at 6,14, though it is already anticipated in the adoration scene of 5,8. While still known as Simon, he is the only one of the eventual disciples to be introduced in Lk's narrative prior to his vocation (4,38; 5,3). He is also specially highlighted in Marcan passages redacted by Lk.[186] — All this emphasizing of Peter in the gospel obviously builds towards his special role in the inaugural period of the Church, narrated in Acts. The momentous transition between these periods is marked by the Easter narrative, where the traditional announcement of the first Easter appearance, at Lk 24,34, and probably also this concluding experience at the empty tomb, continue Lk's policy of making Peter stand out amidst momentous events of which he will become the leading "witness."

In Lk's adaptation of the distinct tradition of the disciples at the tomb, Peter is thus made to stand out at v. 12, but the Emmaus disciple's resumé acquaints Lk's reader with the plurality (τινές) of disciples provided for by the tradition (24,24). Here we encounter the Lucan technique of *cross-reference*, by which allusion is made to other versions or traditions of an event while Lk concentrates on his own rendering.[187] It is as if concession were being made to the perceptive reader who knows the other information Lk is not recording! The instance of this involving Peter's solo role in Lk 5,1-11 seems to us a perfect counterpart of what we understand to be Lk's procedure in the Easter story. Of the two reports of the grave visit in Lk 24, v. 12 bears the special stamp of the evangelist's interest in Peter, while v. 24 is a casual reference to the tradition many already knew: that *more than one* of the disciples' company went to verify the women's tale.

Inquiring into Lk's purpose in thus concluding the tomb story with his "Petrine" version of the disciples' jaunt, we might suggest the obvious relation of this to the report of the first Easter appearance in 24,34. There, in the Jerusalem assembly's announcement to the returning travelers, the word ὄντως with ἠγέρθη ὁ κύριος κτλ. reflects the disbelief and puzzlement with which the disciples, and principally Peter, had reacted to the fact of the empty tomb.[188] Thus the Easter faith, born amidst human befuddlement and in the blind alley of human perceptions by the gift of the risen Lord, occurred first in the appearance to Peter. The temporal priority of that experience, brought

[186] Lk 8,45 *diff.* Mk 5,31; Lk 9,32 *diff.* Mk 9,4; Lk 22,8 *diff.* Mk 14,13; Lk 22,55.58.60.61/cp. Mk 14,66-72 (and the whole revision of the trial sequence *vis-à-vis* Mk to put the denial integrally first). Cf. also Lk 12,41/Mt 24,44 (Q); *Lk* 22,31 (S); 24,34 (S); Acts 1,15-12,17 *passim.* Cf. W. DIETRICH, *Petrusbild*, 16-18, 323ff.

[187] P. SCHUBERT, in *Ntl. Studien f. Bultmann*, 173.

[188] W. DIETRICH, *Petrusbild*, 160; J. WANKE, *BZ* 18 (1974) 187; F. NEIRYNCK, *ETL* 48 (1972) 550.

out in the very abruptness of v. 34, bespeaks the real, founding priority of Peter's witness.[189] And corresponding to that primacy of Easter witness, in the dialectic which controls Lk's narrative, is an *ultimate observation and ultimate incomprehension at the empty tomb* ![190] If v. 12 is original, after all, Peter's wonderment, θαυμάζων τὸ γεγονός, is the "last word" of the tomb story, — the last human observer of the fact, uncomprehending of the fact (on θαυμάζων, see below). Standing up front at the breach between human experience and the transcendent reality of Easter (v. 12), Peter will be the first summoned to cross it by command of "the living One" (v. 34). There is visible symmetry between his roles at the end of both the tomb story and the Emmaus story. They are very much part of the *dialectic of human experience and Easter revelation* which has furnished our chapter's design and pathos.

The redactional theme of the tomb sequence is thus brought to a climax in v. 12. When we read that Peter left the tomb πρὸς ἑαυτὸν[191] θαυμάζων τὸ γεγονός, we are tempted to give the verb the sense of puzzlement (as in Lk 1,21), making it correspond to the women's ἀπορεῖσθαι in v. 4. Observe the parallel development which results :[192]

Women : ἦλθον (v. 1) — εὗρον (vv. 2f.) — ὑποστρέψασαι (v. 9)
Peter : ἔδραμεν – – βλέπει – – – – ἀπῆλθεν (v. 12 ; cf. similar triad in vv. 22f.)

Women : ἀπορεῖσθαι (v. 4)
Peter : θαυμάζων (v. 12)

The rhythms of the two experiences, the women's and the disciple's (disciples'), are recorded in a fashion which reflects a skillful editorial hand ; and they are echoed just as skillfully in vv. 22-24, with its climax in ἀπῆλθον — εὗρον — οὐκ εἶδον. It is not clear, however, that we have captured the full nuance of θαυμάζων by making it a mere synonym for perplexity. In fact, there seems to be a more specific meaning of the verb, closely related to Lk's development of the mystery of Jesus' person.

The verb's prevailing sense in this author's usage is "*marvel*," as in the appropriate human reaction to otherworldly events (Lk 2,18.33 ;

[189] With the temporal priority of Peter's Easter experience "ist deutlich eine sachliche Priorität angezeigt" in 24,34, writes J. WANKE, *Emmauserzählung*, 52. Cf. also P. SCHUBERT, in *Ntl. Studien* ..., 168f.

[190] On the climax-effect of v. 12 in this respect, cf. J. ROLOFF, *Apostolat*, 189 n. 64, and F. NEIRYNCK, *loc. cit.* in n. 188.

[191] Following J. WANKE in this reading, based on habitual Lucan usage, as we observed above, n. 173 (under -i-).

[192] F. NEIRYNCK, *ETL* 48 (1972) 552, astutely observed this pattern in the passages of Lk 24 dealing with the tomb (vv. 1-12.22-24).

Acts 2,7; 3,12; 4,13; 7,31) and to the extraordinary teaching (Lk 4, 22; 20,26) and *miraculous activity* of Jesus (Lk 8,25; 9,43; 11,14) in particular. In fact, Lk places this verb, which was infrequent in Mk, alongside the verbs φοβεῖσθαι, ἐκπλήσσεσθαι, and ἐξίστασθαι, with which Mk had characterized human reaction to Jesus' powerful and mysterious ministrations. Given Mk's well-known *Leitmotiv*, these words were so many expressions of the *messianic secret*.[193] In Lucan partnership with the three verbs mentioned, θαυμάζειν also enters into the *argumentum*: powerful deeds *vs.* hiddenness and mystery in the ministry of the messiah.[194] An especially important passage establishing that connection is Lk 9,43, where ἐκπλήσσεσθαι and θαυμάζειν occur together. The verse is a redactional coupling between the exorcism story and the second passion prophecy (*diff.* Mk), and it shows that the people's "amazement" at God's power shown in the exorcism became a *diversion from understanding the destiny of the messiah.* Jesus' prediction of his passion, spoken to the disciples πάντων δὲ θαυμαζόντων ἐπὶ πᾶσιν οἷς ἐποίει, met total incomprehension. As we discussed previously (pp. 37f.), the "miracle-enthusiasm" of Galilee was the phase of christological recognition prior to, and somewhat obstructive of, the "journey" of the suffering Christ. The *Leidensgeheimnis* had much to do with the dialectical relationship of the two christological phases.

Against this background, we can understand the partnership of Peter's θαυμάζων (24,12) with the rapturous astonishment (ἐξέστησαν ἡμᾶς) reported by the Emmaus traveler (24,22; cp. Mk 16,8). These are terms which describe men under the spell of the messianic *mysterium*, stunned by the numinous effects of divine action yet unable to grasp its meaning. The terminology confirms our exegesis of vv. 6ff.: that the experience and angelic interpretation at the tomb still lay within the economy of the Lucan *Leidensgeheimnis*, from which only the word of the risen Lord, alive and fully present to his followers, would finally rescue them.

---

[193] Cf. G. MINETTE de TILLESSE, *Secret messianique*, 265.

[194] θαυμάζειν occurs with φοβεῖσθαι at Lk 8,25, where Mk 4,41 only had the latter, describing the disciples' reaction to the stilling of the storm. With their fear and wonder went the question, "*who is this?*" — The verb ἐξίστασθαι, and the noun ἔκστασις, were favorite Marcan vocabula for the rapture of those witnessing numinous events: cf. Mk 2,12 (vb.)/Lk 5,26 (n.); Mk 5,42 (vb.+n.)/Lk 8,56 (vb.); Mk 16,8 (n.)/Lk 24,22 (vb.). Both the verb and the noun are taken up abundantly in Acts with the same reference: the verb 8 times, the noun 4 times. θαυμάζειν occurs alongside ἐξίστασθαι at Acts 2,7, depicting public reaction to the Pentecost miracle. — Finally, θαυμάζειν at Lk 4,22 replaces ἐκπλήσσεσθαι in Mk 6,2 (the Nazarenes' reaction to Jesus' dazzling speech and deeds), whereas Lk preserves ἐκπλήσσεσθαι in the Capernaum sequence (Lk 4,32/Mk 1, 22). The two verbs occur together in Lk 9,43, the most important one so far as our argument is concerned.

(6) *Results for Our Further Investigation*:

By understanding Lk's empty-tomb story as mainly a conscious, critical dialogue with Mk, his principal source, we found that the effect of his editing was to fuse separate tomb stories, hitherto awkwardly interrelated, into a single, organic sequence which serves as a counterpoint prelude to the personal disclosures of the risen Christ. By then judging v. 12, like v. 6a, an authentic part of Lk's original text, we recognized that he also adopted a second, younger and supplementary tradition of the apostles' presence at the tomb, which he shared with Jn and adapts differently at vv. 12 and 24. The admission of this separate tradition serves the self-same dialectic as had been brought out in the Marcan story, and does so by augmenting *ad extremum* the tomb story's paradoxical combination of authoritative observers and uncomprehended phenomena. In Lk's story of Easter, Peter completes at the tomb the *testimonium paupertatis* of Jesus' entire retinue, whose paschal *experience* will become paschal *faith* only in the personal presence of the Easter Christ and under his instruction.

Redaction-analysis of the tomb story also showed how our evangelist worked out of the Marcan " raw material " what it was that blocked the observers' understanding of the empty grave. Heavy editing of the women's encounter with the angels produced " flash-backs " to the great christological treatise of Lk 9, where the specifically Lucan *Leidensmysterium* had been expounded for the first time. By changing the angelic tidings from the promise of a Galilean future to the remembrance of a Galilean past, Lk introduced the first of three Easter reprises of the dominical passion and resurrection prophecies, which the gospel had recorded under an accentuated cover of messianic concealment (Lk 9,45; 18,34). The three rehearsals of these prophecies form centerpieces of the Easter episodes, and they give us to understand that Easter revelation in our chapter will consist in a lifting of the veil which shrouded this teaching of the earthly Master concerning his own mission and destiny.

Two major acquisitions, therefore, with which to move on to the study of the remaining Easter pericopes: a greatly intensified contrast between the Easter faith of Christians and the *brutum factum* of the empty tomb (to be reinforced at 24,22-24); and closely connected to this, a vital connection between the messianic *mysterium*, inherited from Mk, and the basic content of the Easter revelation.

Chapter II

THE EMMAUS NARRATIVE (Lk 24,13-35)

(1) *Introduction: State of the Question and Method*

Like the chapter of which it is a sparkling centerpiece, this " most extensive," " loveliest and most impressive " [1] of the Easter narratives has suffered inexplicable neglect in contemporary gospel scholarship.[2] Whether this is because of its complexity and the uncertainty of its traditional substratum, or because of its resistance to the broad patterns pursued by form- and redaction-criticism,[3] the fact is that until within two years of this writing we were without a comprehensive modern study of the Emmaus story. Now this unfortunate dearth has been remedied by the work of J. Wanke, whose listing of predecessors embraces over seventy-five years but only one monograph (1906) and some forty-three articles. Of the latter, twenty-one are less than five [4] pages long, another nine, less than ten pages; and most deal with the

---

[1] H. Grass, *Ostergeschehen*, 35. Cf. also J. M. Creed, *Lk*, 290; C. R. Bowen, *Biblical World* 35 (1910) 235; U. Wilckens, *Auferstehung*, 78; R.H. Fuller, *Formation*, 104.

[2] J. Wanke, *Emmauserzählung*, 1; A. Ehrhardt, in *Mullus*, 93: " ... in der modernen Exegese eine deutliche Vernachlässigung ...."

[3] Our story's refractory characteristics include its obscure personages, the unusual mode of the appearance it recounts, and the absence from it of motifs which elsewhere accompany the Easter tradition's development, principally the risen One's mission mandate and the (apologetic) demonstration of his physical reality. As C.H. Dodd notes (*More N. T. Studies*, 108), it is clear that we have here " no mere expansion of the general pattern, but a carefully composed statement ...," contributing little to systematic views of either the Easter tradition or the Easter happenings. On this latter issue, the story's resistance to historicizing harmonizations (noted by A. Ehrhardt, in *Mullus*, 93, and *NTS* 10 [1963-64] 194) is the dispair of those who wield form-criticism in the interests of historical reconstruction. Instance H. Grass: " Was ergibt sich aus der Emmauserzählung an geschichtlichem Ertrag für das Ostergeschehen? Herzlich wenig " (*Ostergeschehen*, 40). Some, like H. von Campenhausen (*Ablauf*, 46), are beguiled by the story's depiction of the disciples' state of mind following Good Friday; but they quickly admit that history is reconstructed in that respect only *ex convenientia*, not on solid criteria of historicity applied to the narrative (cf. also G. Bornkamm, *Jesus von Nazareth* [Stuttgart: W. Kohlhammer, 1956] 158; R. H. Fuller, *Formation*, 105, 110).

[4] *Emmauserzählung*, IX-X.

obscure circumstances and personalities of the story. Of concerted endeavours to interpret the pericope as a whole, employing an integrated critical methodology of the post-war era, there are a meagre handful of articles on the list.[5]

Significant studies of this passage can also be sought, of course, within larger works: the few scientific Lucan commentaries,[6] but more

---

[5] In my estimation, only the studies of J. DUPONT, A. EHRHARDT, H.-D. BETZ, and F. SCHNIDER / W. STENGER, qualified for this category before the efforts of J. WANKE, and after him one can mention only the short piece of D. A. LOSADA (*RBibArg* 35 [Buenos Aires, 1973] 3-13) as deserving of serious attention. — J. DESREUMAUX ("Les disciples d'Emmaüs," *BiViChr* n. 56 [mars/avril 1964] 45-56) is homiletic and wholly innocent of critical trends, while J. MAGNE (L'episode des disciples d'Emmaüs et le récit du paradis terrestre," *CahCerclERenan* 8 [1971] 29-32) is idiosyncratic and unrepresentative. Several other pieces which I have left unmentioned I would place in one of these categories or the other. To the genus of scriptural reflection-without-criticism (or true exegesis) also belongs the essay of H. SWANSTON, "The Road to Emmaus," *CleR* 50 (1965) 506-523, whose value for spiritual reading or homiletic purposes I am not thereby denying. — I have not been able to obtain E. LIPINSKI, "Les disciples d'Emmaüs," *Rev. ecclésiastique de Liège* 53 (1967) 220-226, which I presume to belong to the order of *haute vulgarisation,* considering the author-forum combination there. — Three pieces under J. DUPONT's name on WANKE's list (*Misc. Ubach, LumVie* n. 31 [1957] 77-92, and in J. Delorme, ed., *The Eucharist and the New Testament* [London, 1964] 105-121) are really reducible to one, since the second and third are condensations, in French and English respectively, of the very estimable essay that appeared originally in 1953 in the Ubach Festschrift.

[6] A generally dismal state of affairs in this category has just been altered — at the point of this study's final typing, in fact! — by the advent of the Regensburg Lk-Commentary of Josef ERNST (Regensburg: F. Pustet, 1977), which I have been able only to collate with my work here and there. It is clear that this is a long-awaited antidote to the dearth of scientific commentary on the third gospel, remedied previously only to Lk 9,51 by H. SCHÜRMANN. The commentary on Lk 24 is well-informed, judicious, and (like W. GRUNDMANN) rather inclined to maximize the contribution of Lucan *Sonderquellen* at the expense of an adequate sounding of this author's thought. This commentary combines critical detail with theological depth, however, in a manner which has not often been realized in the Lucan commentaries of our century. We might say that, with SCHÜRMANN's, the ERNST commentary will be the first to realize in commentary dimension the enormous strides of the redaction-historical criticism of the last two decades. — Of the antecedent commentaries on Lk 24, I have judged their contribution to my work as follows: A. PLUMMER and E. KLOSTERMANN are principally valued for their philological precision, as befits their genus; W. GRUNDMANN was occasionally useful for his expository line, not for his critical detail (and the same can be said of the more popular efforts of K. H. RENGSTORF, J. SCHMID, and E. LOHSE, *Auferstehung*, 23-33). Among these, there is little success at explaining the evangelist's overall intention for the Emmaus narrative, with E. LOHSE making at least a brief attempt at doing so. — The English-language commentaries of E. E. ELLIS and A. R. C. LEANEY are fragmentary and symptomatic of the draught prevailing in this area. They are gaited to a broad readership and only intermittently helpful to the scholar.

especially, general monographs on the NT Easter traditions. Treatments of this last kind, however, are mostly pursuing partial aspects of the pericope in the interest of broader arguments, either composite histories of the Easter events[7] or tradition-histories of the Easter witness.[8]

— One concludes by mentioning A. LOISY (*Luc*, 572-584): idiosyncratic, disorganized, but occasionally rising to insightful comment.

[7] J. FINEGAN, *Überlieferung*, 90-91; H. GRASS, *Ostergeschehen*, 32-40; R. H. FULLER, *Formation*, 103-113. — A deluding example of superficial literary criticism dedicated to Easter *Historie* is I. H. MARSHALL, *TyndB* 24 (1973) esp. 78-91.

[8] No hypothesis that would make a tradition-historical milestone of the Emmaus account has won widespread adherence. The suggestion of R. BULTMANN that the account is " in its content the oldest of the synoptic resurrection stories " (*GsT*, 314), remains undeveloped because it was posited without substantiating evidence (as it is likewise by J. E. ALSUP, *Appearance Stories*, 194; cp. M. DIBELIUS, *Formgeschichte*, 191). The same can be said of the notion that, considering its style, this might be a " Galilean-type " Easter epiphany, secondarily located in Jerusalem's environs (so G. KITTEL, as cited by H. GRASS, *Ostergeschehen*, 121 n. 1; also G. KOCH, *Auferstehung*, 50). Nor is X. LÉON-DUFOUR noticeably more successful in arguing that the story belongs to a " Jerusalem type " of Easter story: first, because this scholar's typologies are peculiarly reductionistic to start with, and second, because even he has to acknowledge that Emmaus " brise la structure précédente " (*Résurrection*, 128). A similarly unconvincing schematism of " Jerusalem " *vs.* " Galilean " appearance traditions urged by Ph. SEIDENSTICKER (*Auferstehung*, 64ff., 96ff.) fails to envelop our passage successfully. Still less does the sweeping tradition-historical panorama of F. HAHN (*Hoheitstitel*, 387-390). — One readily agrees with the useful distinction between " experiences of identity " (Lk 24,13ff.; Jn 20,11ff.) and " demonstrations of identity " (Lk 24,36ff.; Jn 20,19ff.) in the developing Easter-narrative traditions (U. WILCKENS, *Auferstehung*, 80-85), but it is anything but clear that the second category is a direct outgrowth of the first (*pace* WILCKENS), unless one can accept the obviously late and compounded narrative of Jn 21 as a middle stage in this process. — The same uncertainty applies to other proposed growth-patterns in the Easter tradition, such as the popular hypothesis that the christophany portrayals developed from " heavenly apparitions " to highly objectified pictures of a restored " earthly " presence (so E. HIRSCH, *Auferstehungsgeschichten*, 17-18; H. GRASS, *Ostergeschehen*, 45, 48ff., 88; U. WILCKENS, *Auferstehung*, 96ff.; R. H. FULLER, *Formation*, 5, 115; C. F. EVANS, *Resurrection*, 65-66, 105): one cannot gainsay the phenomenon itself, but evidence is lacking for any theory which tries to delineate distinct and independent narrative traditions (say, " Galilean " *vs.* " Jerusalem," *pace* HIRSCH) based on the phenomenon. The supposed development of a view of the Easter christophanies as confined to a temporary *Zwischenzustand* between earthly existence and heavenly glory (GRASS) finds no particular illustration in the Emmaus story, however much one might contend that view affected Lk's composite Easter presentation. Other patterns of the developing tradition as well — the doubt and verification motifs, the disciples' commission — are wanting in our story, with the result that, generally speaking, it functions poorly for the exegete looking to trace the history of the resurrection narratives. Before this story can furnish data for such a quest, it has to undergo a painstaking critique to unravel tradition and composition, such as J. E. ALSUP undertook (*Appearance Stories*, 190ff.) before he juxtaposed Emmaus with Jn 20,11ff. and Jn 21 in pursuit of common elements ascribable

Since the Emmaus story is more refractory than functional in such reconstructions, it has had few ample treatments in this category either. And the focus of interest is equally restricted in most monographs devoted to Lucan *Redaktionsgeschichte*, of which one can cite scarcely a one which accords more than passing references to the story, and usually to its more celebrated statements, vv. 26 and 34.[9] Finally, a few studies of the eucharist in the NT have devoted significant pages to the Emmaus repast,[10] but the meal scene and its terminology naturally occupy their restricted horizon of interest.

Given such a state of research, one has to reach far and wide for insights on this challenging pericope, attempting to coordinate the various approaches in a comprehensive interpretation of the whole. J. WANKE has culled for us the major currents of criticism in his fine *Forschungsbericht*,[11] and one sees that he has ferreted them out of a broad and disparate literature. We can review and partly reorganize the stages of investigation sketched by WANKE in order to situate our own study in respect to its predecessors.

(a) Studies of an earlier vintage concentrated on issues connected with the *historical setting* and nature of the Emmaus experience.[12] But

---

to an appearance-story *Gattung* (*ibid.*, 211ff.). Whether ALSUP's effort can be judged successful or not, we believe the method he has followed is the one that must be employed before the Emmaus narrative can be serviceable to the tradition-historian.

[9] H. CONZELMANN's very brief treatments of Lk 24 (cf. *MdZ* index) are the rule in redaction-analyses, not the exception. The same situation is found in the works of H. FLENDER, W. C. ROBINSON, M. RESE, G. VOSS, I. H. MARSHALL, — in fact, almost anyone we wish to name. It is very rare that the Easter narrative is accorded even so much as a chapter or section of its own, as occurs only in H.-W. BARTSCH, *Wachet* (23-25 on Emmaus), and R. GLÖCKNER, *Verkündigung*, 202-227 (nothing in specific detail on Emmaus), and these treatments are much too limited thus far to represent major contributions to the discussion of this pericope.

[10] The only treatments offering specific coverage of the Emmaus narrative in this category are W. SCHENK, in *Theol. Versuche* II, 77-81; M. KEHL, *GeistLeb* 43 (1970) 101ff.; J. WANKE, *Eucharistieverständnis*, 31-44. One might also mention J. ROLOFF, *Kerygma*, 254-258, although this treatment of the Emmaus meal denies it had properly eucharistic reference for either the evangelist or his tradition (a view that is now rather exceptional). — Other studies on the eucharistic language and allusions of the gospel tradition, which might bear indirectly on Lk 24,29ff. but do not dwell on it specifically: J. JEREMIAS, *Abendmahlsworte*³, 166ff., and (on Lk) H. PATSCH, *ZNW* 62 (1971) 210-231.

[11] *Emmauserzählung*, 1-19.

[12] A favorite topic was the locale, of course, since no verifiable site agrees with both the name and the distance given by Lk 24,13 (cf. the bibliography in J. WANKE, *op. cit.*, 37f.). — Nor is it difficult to understand the fascination held by the two obscure travelers, Cleopas and companion, for generations of Christian interpreters. What is somewhat harder to understand is that twentieth-century expositors should employ the tools of criticism refined in their times to

of course, the era of form-criticism has enormously complicated the task of historical reconstruction from the NT texts. It has held before the exegete in a new form that principle that should never have been forgotten: that the intention of the sacred author, not the exact contours of what he recounts, is the first order of exegetical inquiry! Speculative reconstructions of events behind the text should never gain the upper hand in an investigation which must come to terms, first and foremost, with the narrator's point of view, his circumstance, and his intention. That crucial, prior question has become the burden of all mainstream exegesis in our century. " Contentons-nous donc de ce que l'évangéliste a cru bon de nous apprendre "![13]

(b) The quest for *religio-historical analogies* to the Emmaus story has yielded but modest fruits as yet for interpretation. The appearance of the risen Lord as an unknown wanderer, whom his followers encounter and entertain unawares, suggests a host of more or less appropriate parallels in other religious traditions.[14] But one must not

---

carry forward unscientific speculation on the bewitching figures' identity. N. Huffman's attempt to identify the unnamed companion as Peter is a case in point: a critical hypothesis is advanced suggesting differentiated levels of the tradition, the uneasy appendage of v. 34, etc., all in the service of an idea which was often hazarded but has no real foundation in the text: that this was originally a Peter-story, but Lk secondarily adjusted its locale to fit his own Easter geography (cf. *JBL* 64 [1945] 219ff., and the similar hypotheses of J. H. Crehan, *CBQ* 15 [1953] 418-426; R. Annand, " ' He was seen of Cephas '. A Suggestion about the First Resurrection Appearance to Peter," *ScotJT* 11 [1958] 180-187; P. Winter, *ST* 8 [1954, 138-172] 139 n. 1; A. Ehrhardt, *NTS* 10 [1963-64] 182f.). — Further discussions, already vigorous in patristic times, concerned the nature of the meal shared by the Emmaus travelers. Augustine's contention that it was truly the sacramental Eucharist (*Epistula* 149,32 [*CSEL* XLIV 38, 7]; so also Jerome, *Epistula* 108,8 [*CSEL* LV, 314]) seems also to hold sway in our own day, except, of course, that moderns are careful to pose the question in terms of the narrator's point of view before they wonder about the event itself. The broad agreement of contemporary exegetes in this matter is noted by M. Kehl, *GeistLeb* 43 (1970) 101, and X. Léon-Dufour, *Résurrection*, 214. The argument of J. Dupont would be accepted by most: " Avant de se demander ce qui s'est passé à Emmaüs, il faut commencer par la question: à quoi Luc pense-t-il, que veut-il dire ?... Pour nous, Luc est un chrétien et il écrit pour des chrétiens. Quand il donne tant d'importance à un repas ..., comment pourrait-il ne pas vouloir suggérer qu'il s'agit de l'eucharistie ? " (*Misc. Ubach*, 363). Some prefer to think of a common meal on which Lk himself conferred the touches suggestive of the Eucharist (so A. Loisy, *Luc*, 581; R. Orlett, *CBQ* 21 [1959] 219), but separation of tradition and composition at this point is an uncertain endeavour. — As noted in n. 10, J. Roloff (*Kerygma*, 257) resists a strong consensus in denying the eucharistic complexion of the Emmaus meal.

[13] *Misc. Ubach*, 351.

[14] Pointing out that the story is " age-old in its format," H. Gunkel maintained that, at least in this respect, " it could stand as easily in the book of Genesis ": the divine being is encountered in plain human dress, reveals his secret identity in certain of its aspects, then, as soon as he is recognized, dis-

invoke them prematurely, on the basis of mere resemblance, as instruments of interpretation. Beyond our story's familiar format, which was certainly known and diversely utilized by the ancients, any more specific elucidation of the text from the history of religions must be consequent upon, not prior to, a study of Lk's *argumentum* on its own terms. Eventual hellenistic antecedents of the story, especially such as already belonged to acculturations of the Jewish scriptures,[15] can be considered plausible *apriori*, but where they are to affect the interpretation process positively, they must be refined and demonstrated in detail.

(c) *Form Criticism* brought recognition of the all-important nexus between the story's literary form and its meaning to those who told it. It does not seem that the nexus is correctly depicted, however, by the

---

appears (cf. *Zum religionsgeschichtlichen Verständnis des Neuen Testaments* [FRLANT 1; Göttingen: Vandenhoeck und Ruprecht, 1903] 71, and the approving endorsements of A. LOISY, *Luc*, 584, and R. BULTMANN, *GsT*, 310, among many others). OT analogies would include the Genesis stories of Hagar (16,7ff.) and Abraham's guests (18,1ff.), and perhaps the Manoah episode in Jgs 13,11-20. — But more appropriate than the hidden presence of a divine being might be the analogy of the θεῖος ἄνθρωπος unexpectedly returned from death, of which pattern there are numerous instances in hellenistic literature brought forward by A. EHRHARDT (*NTS* 10 [1963-64] 194ff., and in *Mullus*, 94ff.): the Greek Romulus legend, transmitted in the *Antiquitates Romanae* (II 63,3f.) of Dionysius of Halicarnassus, and the interesting apparition of Apollonius of Tyana to two disciples after his martyrdom (in Philostratus, *Vita Apollonii* VIII, 11f., thought by EHRHARDT to be modeled after Lk). Cf. also H.-D. BETZ, *ZTK* 66 (1969) 9 n. 8, who adduces Herodotus IV, 13-15 (Aristeas of Proconnesus); IV, 94f. (Zalmoxis); Lucian of Samosata, *De morte peregrini* 28 (Peregrinus Proteus). — In this connection, we are attracted by the suggestion of G. FRIEDRICH: " Lukas benutzt bewusst Motive aus der *Entrückungsanschauung*, um seinen Lesern die Auferstehung Jesu verständlich zu machen " (in *Orientierung an Jesus*, 56; italics ours). For the Emmaus episode, FRIEDRICH cites (*ibid.*, 56-59) the motifs of the journey encounter, non-finding and non-seeing of the *assumptus*, εἰσελθεῖν εἰς τὴν δόξαν αὐτοῦ (v. 26 = NT *hapax* !), and ἄφαντος γενέσθαι (v. 31), as topical to the literary form of heavenly assumptions, well known in hellenistic culture at large, and hellenistic Judaism in particular (on which cf. also G. LOHFINK, *Himmelfahrt*, 34-50). — Since individual features of our story are redolent of still other narrative forms (e.g. the blindness-eye-opening sequence of the Elisha narrative, 2 Kgs[LXX 4 Kgs] 6,18-20, on which cf. J. DUPONT, in *Misc. Ubach*, 365; J. WANKE, *Emmauserzählung*, 36f.), our composite picture is of a rich fusion of ancient motifs, not a single-minded emulation of any one of them.

[15] Lk's indebtedness to *Jewish* traditions of the hellenistic Diaspora is getting increased attention in recent study. The fact that he had overlooked this factor in earlier editions, to the detriment of his tradition-historical analysis, is now admitted by U. WILCKENS, in *Missionsreden*³, 187-224, esp. 207ff., 217ff. The same factor is brought out emphatically in the very recent essay of G. SELLIN, " Lukas als Gleichniserzähler," *ZNW* 66 (1975) 47f., 55-59. " Die Konsequenz dieser Deutung (i. e. the universal covenant-relationship set forth in the Samaritan parable — R.D.) ist die Vermutung, dass das lukanische Christentum bedeutend stärker vom (hellenistischen) Judentum geprägt ist, als dies allgemein angenommen wird " (*ibid.*, 57).

widely accepted characterization of "legend,"[16] which contains an element of truth[17] but invites measurement of the passage by the usual legendary goals of aetiology and edification,[18] whereas this story is a magistral lesson in the central tenets of Christian belief and nothing less. Further refinements of a form-critical classification came from M. ALBERTZ[19] and L. BRUN,[20] who recognized a category of christophany distinct from those with apostolic commissions as focal points, ascribing Jn 20,11-18 to this separate class together with our passage (and *Ev. Heb.* — ALAND, *Syn.* 4 *Evang.*, § [361]) and calling them *scenes of personal recognition.* This rubric, and variants of it, have become fixed in the literature, with C. H. DODD[21] introducing the comparison of the

[16] In addition to GUNKEL and BULTMANN (n. 14 above): M. DIBELIUS, *Formgeschichte*, 191; H. GRASS, *Ostergeschehen*, 35, 40; E. LOHSE, *Auferstehung*, 32; H.-W. BARTSCH, *Wachet*, 23; H.-D. BETZ, *ZTK* 66 (1969) 8; J. KREMER, *Osterbotschaft*, 70 n. 41, and numerous others.

[17] The truth in the designation is that the narrator's objective does not lie in the event which is *prima facie* recounted but in the Christian experience which is captured and typified in the recounting (cf. H.-D. BETZ, *ZTK* 66 (1969) 13; J. KREMER, *Osterbotschaft*, 71f.). To the extent that one identifies as the narrative's purpose a model-portrayal of the Christian liturgical experience, with Scripture exposition and eucharistic meal as its two component parts (so W. SCHENK, in *Theologische Versuche* II, 81; J. WANKE, *Eucharistieverständnis*, 44, and [with reservations] *Emmauserzählung*, 120ff.), one gives fuller legitimacy to the "legend" designation in its proper form-critical sense.

[18] M. DIBELIUS offered the magistral treatment of the "legend" as *Gattung* in *Formgeschichte*, 101ff., and carefully avoided confusing judgments of its literary earmarks with those of its historical veracity in specific instances (cf. *ibid.*, 106, 110, 119). The question of historicity must be decided in each instance, based on the individual features and content of a given passage. The "legend" classification itself remains a literary description, not (as in conventional usage) an evaluation of historicity (cf. J. KREMER, *Osterbotschaft*, 24 n. 11; 70 n. 41; I. H. MARSHALL, *TyndBull* 24 [1973] 84). — Despite this precaution, however, it is still not clear that this classification does right by the kerygmatic focus of the Emmaus account (rightly J. WANKE, *Emmauserzählung*, 9). As centerpiece of the Easter chapter and thus a principal ingredient in the connective tissue of the two Lucan volumes, the Emmaus pericope is above all "theological doctrine and preaching" in narrative form (so H.-D. BETZ, *ZTK* 66 [1969] 13), so we shall not probe its true literary character until we adequately acknowledge Lk and his predecessors as *preachers and church-builders* in it. Aetiology and edification do not adequately embrace the story's objectives.

[19] *ZNW* 21 (1922) 260: "Diese drei Erzählungen stellen in den Mittelpunkt das Wiedererkennen an dem vertrauten Namen in der aramäischen Muttersprache (Maria), oder am Brotbrechen (Emmaunten) oder — materialistischer — am Brotessen (Jakobus [*Ev. Heb.* — R.D.]) und betreffen sämtlich Menschen, die nicht zum Kreise der Zwölf, sondern zur nächsten Verwandtschaft Jesu gehören..." (*sic* !).

[20] *Auferstehung*, 48.

[21] "The Appearances of the Risen Christ," in *More N. T. Studies*, 107-108. This motif is now commonly cited as the central one of the original Emmaus story; thus: P. SCHUBERT, in *Ntl. Studien f. Bultmann*, 172; W. GRUNDMANN,

ἀναγνώρισις device known to Greek dramaturgy: delayed recognition, remembrance process, then recognition at a point coinciding with the completion of the *argumentum* of the author. L. BRUN, too, saw how auxiliary motifs served the dynamic of remembrance and recognition between the Stranger and the travelers, accounting for a dual point of focus in the narrative: Scripture reflection on Jesus' passion and death, and reenactment of meals shared by the earthly Master and his followers.[22] In a most important step in the progress of our study, BRUN opined that, of the two stages of that "recognition" process, the Scripture reflection, conducted by the still unknown Jesus, was "peculiarly Lk's own,"[23] while the meal, where the *Wiedererkennen Jesu* finally occurs, belonged to a traditional — possibly historical — fundament of the story. Subsequent studies have tended to endorse this analysis since, on the one hand, the "argument from prophecy" (Lk 24,25-27) is one that is sustained throughout Lk's history,[24] and the combination of "recognition" and Easter meal (Lk 24,28-31), on the other hand, appears to be comparable to Jn 21,12-13 and may even represent a tradition-historical bonding of the two texts.[25]

Although studies since BRUN's have not succeeded in making a secure delineation of tradition and composition in the Emmaus narrative, his lasting influence can be seen in the widespread agreement forged by P. SCHUBERT[26] that the narrative framework, with its meal-scene

---

Lk., 442; U. WILCKENS, *Auferstehung*, 78; F. SCHNIDER / W. STENGER, *BZ* 16 (1972) 112; J. WANKE, *Emmauserzählung*, 5; D. A. LOSADA, *RBibArg* 35 (1973) 5-7; J. E. ALSUP, *Appearance Stories*, 196ff. — Strictly speaking, the "recognition" category includes the "identity-experiences" reported in our text, Jn 21,4ff., and Jn 20,14ff., but it is also extended to include the "identity-demonstrations" like Lk 24,36ff. and Jn 20,19ff. (according to the distinction made by U. WILCKENS, *Auferstehung*, 84-85). The emphatic probative steps of the second group are missing in the first; and on the other hand, the feature of delayed recognition is no longer present in Jn 20,19ff. (except in one disciple's case).

[22] L. BRUN, *Auferstehung*, 56.

[23] *Ibid.*, 48.

[24] P. SCHUBERT, in *Ntl. Studien f. Bultmann*, 174, 176; J. DUPONT, in *Misc. Ubach*, 358f.; J. ERNST, in *Schriftauslegung*, 177ff.

[25] So U. WILCKENS, *Auferstehung*, 81f., 85; M. KEHL, *GeistLeb* 43 (1970) 106; H. KASTING, *Mission*, 50f.; X. LÉON-DUFOUR, *Résurrection*, 133ff.; Th. LORENZEN, *ZNW* 64 (1973) 219; J. WANKE, *Emmauserzählung*, 102ff., and *BZ* 18 (1974) 183-184; R. SCHNACKENBURG, *Johannesevangelium* III, 412. Less specific: R. PESCH, *Fischfang*, 132, 133; J. E. ALSUP, *App. Stories*, 204ff.

[26] In *Ntl. Studien f. Bultmann*, 174; but cf. already N. HUFFMAN, *JBL* 64 (1945) 219-220; J. SCHMITT, *RvScRel* 25 (1951) 237. — Variations of the SCHUBERT hypothesis are proposed by J. ROLOFF, *Kerygma*, 256; W. MARXSEN, *Auferstehung*, 163f.; U. WILCKENS, *Auferstehung*, 78-80; F. SCHNIDER / W. STENGER, *BZ* 16 (1972) 100-102; X. LÉON-DUFOUR, *Résurrection*, 210; R. H. FULLER, *Formation*, 106; D. A. LOSADA, *RBibArg* 35 (1973) 4; J. E. ALSUP, *Appearance Stories*, 194. — B. RIGAUX, while disowning the delineation SCHUBERT sponsored,

denouement, constitutes an Emmaus *tradition*, and the extensive dialogue of the travelers, the pericope's centerpiece, is an enlargement of the older story originating in the *composition* of the evangelist. The problems attending this convenient hypothesis are not to be swept under the rug, however,[27] nor is one to regard it as anything more than a beginning of further analysis to refine it and make it serviceable to the interpretation of Lk's mind and background.

The necessary form-critical quest for a *Sitz-im-Leben* of the hypothetical Emmaus tradition has been far less conclusive. Beyond the merely local interest to tell the story in the locale where the apparition occurred,[28] it has been suggested that the tradition might have served the legitimation of certain kinds of missionary endeavour in the primitive church.[29] Suggestions along these lines have usually not been

---

nevertheless acknowledges the meal-recognition as the primordial nucleus of the tradition (cf. *Dieu l'a ressuscité*, 230-232). SCHUBERT ascribed vv. 13, 15b, 16, 28-31 to the Emmaus tradition, and the rest to Lk's composition.

[27] C. H. DODD warned against the attempt to ferret out a primitive matrix from the existing story, calling this "an unprofitable task" (in *More N. T. Studies*, 118). Most agree, of course, that the pericope is not of a single piece; exceptional are the contentions that Lk took the story over more or less as it stands, possibly excepting 33-35 in whole or in part (so H. GRASS, *Ostergeschehen*, 36; A. R. C. LEANEY, *Lk*, 29; A. EHRHARDT, *NTS* 10 [1963-64] 183-185; tentatively also F. HAHN, *Hoheitstitel*, 388 n. 1). The strength of Lk's hand in reformulating and expanding his material is acknowledged by most interpreters (so J. FINEGAN, *Überlieferung*, 90; R. LEANEY, *NTS* 2 [1955-56] 110; J. SCHMITT, *RvScRel* 25 [1951] 237; J. DUPONT, in *Misc. Ubach*, 350, 361; J. WANKE, *Emmauserzählung*, 109, 112, 123, and *BZ* 18 [1974] 181), and yet few would accept the old suggestion of C. R. BOWEN that it is wholly the creation of Lk, without a traditional background (*Biblical World* 35 [1910] 236, 243). — The difficulty of any exact delineation of tradition and composition, like SCHUBERT's, is that it cannot be supported by clear alignments of vocabulary and style. J. WANKE's careful analysis left no doubt of this: "Es gibt keinen Vers, ja keine zusammenhängende Wendung, die nicht luk Spracheigentümlichkeiten oder luk Vorzugsvokabeln enthält" (*Emmauserzählung*, 109). If any refinement of previous tradition-analyses can still be hoped for in the case of the Emmaus story, it will therefore have to be through careful and comprehensive motif-analysis, pursuing both patterns of Lucan editing throughout the two volumes and possible underlying fabric which can be identified as the foundation Lk worked on. This will be our method of approach to this complex study.

[28] So G. SCHILLE, *Anfänge der Kirche*, 168; U. WILCKENS, *Auferstehung*, 79: "Man nahm dort für sich in Anspruch, jene Erscheinung Jesu beim Mahl sei der Ursprung der eigenen Gemeinde gewesen."

[29] So already C. R. BOWEN, *Biblical World* 35 (1910) 234-245; J. A. GRASSI, *CBQ* 26 (1964) 463-467. According to GRASSI, "Luke may be teaching us that the mysterious stranger in the Emmaus account is Christ himself, manifesting himself through the traveling apostle, the stranger who meets new people in new places" (465). As a matter of fact, we think this suggestion has merit and intend to follow it up, though we must also admit that GRASSI's hypothesis is unaided by the kind of redaction-analysis we think is indispensable to its re-

accompanied by careful evaluation of Lk's interests *vis-à-vis* the tradition he used, and that is precisely what has to be done before they can contribute substantially to the interpretation process. Hard as it unquestionably is to sift the strands of tradition and composition so expertly interwoven in a passage like this, any accurate form-critical analysis still relies on the distinction of the two strata and, in fact, cannot gain a sure footing without it.

(d) *Redaktionsgeschichte*, the form-critic's inquiry extended to the circumstances of the gospel's composition, was thus the forward step which the study of the Emmaus pericope desperately needed. It called for a thorough evaluation of the passage as *a Lucan statement*, and it furnished comparative data for such an approach in the works which first tilled this comparatively new terrain of modern criticism. Even though the unavailability of parallel texts of the gospel tradition poses an acute problem in this instance, as in other Lucan *Sondergut*, we do have the benefit of the unique situation of our author's companion volume to his gospel, which often shows how he managed certain themes over the whole of the two volumes to demonstrate the all-important historical continuity which is their basic and sustained argument.[30] J. DUPONT and P. SCHUBERT seized that special Lucan advantage in pilot essays of the new course of gospel research, each showing our story's significant pooling of major themes developed over the two volumes.[31]

---

finement and support. As a form-critical objective, the "life-situation" of a pericope requires the clearest possible definition of the structure and focus of the original narrative. The difficulty of this step leaves GRASSI's idea before us as an interesting but still speculative path to follow. — Some critics have been stressing precisely that connection between the risen Lord's appearances and the *credentials* of persons and groups in the earliest churches, so GRASSI's issue deserves to be debated. Cf. (on said connection): U. WILCKENS, in *Dogma und Denkstrukturen*, 75ff., and *Auferstehung*, 26; R. H. FULLER, *Formation*, 29f., 48, 49. Although I do not agree with these scholars' artificial separation of the ὤφθη-formulas from the properly kerygmatic formulas of the early mission, I do think there is merit in their suggestion that part of the "message" was formulated precisely to accredit the "messengers." It might well be that certain of the appearance stories had this function, so we shall be watching for signs of mission-orientation in the matter of the present study.

[30] M. DIBELIUS, in many ways the prime mover of Lucan *Redaktionsgeschichte*, brought out repeatedly the comprehensive design according to which, throughout his two volumes, Lk can assign a *Richtungssinn* to every event he records (cf. esp. "Der erste christliche Historiker," in *Aufsätze zur Apg.*, 108-119, esp. 110, 118). This "directional thrust" of each event or circumstance is its contribution to the divinely constituted continuum of sacred history. Lk is conscious of the compelling logic of that continuum at every step of his two-volume narrative (cf. also M. VÖLKEL, *NTS* 20 [1973-74] 289-299; W. C. ROBINSON, *Weg*, 34, 40ff.).

[31] P. SCHUBERT, in *Ntl. Studien f. Bultmann*, 174, 176, 183; J. DUPONT, in

Despite these promising efforts, no substantial efforts of redaction-analysis followed them for a full twenty-years, until the monograph of J. WANKE, student of H. SCHÜRMANN, broke the unfortunate silence. His teacher's influence shows in what WANKE proposes as his contribution to a lagging discussion: a language- and style-analysis of the whole narrative, such as no previous study had carried out. This scrutiny, alongside motif-comparison within the Lucan books, was expected to put the analysis of Lk's own intentions for the celebrated appearance story on firmer ground (cf. *Emmauserzählung*, 19ff.). But WANKE, too, found the solid cover of Lk's own writing to block any exact delimitation of a source-narrative.[32] His own position rejoins, tentatively and cautiously, the trend set by BRUN, SCHUBERT, *et al.*, in making the meal-scene the story's traditional nucleus, secondarily enriched by the *Weggespräch* as Lk's own interpretation of the scene (*ibid.*, 119, 122ff.). But throughout, there is a prudent refusal to draw clear lines between the older story and its editorial adaptation; and there are some nuances over the *opinio communis*, so the line is not drawn woodenly between narrative and dialogue.[33] — An important

Misc. Ubach, 352-361. Cf. also the words of J. SCHMITT: " A dire vrai, il s'en sert (sc. de l'épisode — R. D.) comme d'une occasion pour fournir au lecteur un exposé type de son message pascal " (*RvScRel* 25 [1951] 237). — SCHUBERT and DUPONT, though their essays antedate the more momentous turns of Lucan redaction-analysis, were able to point out the obviously planned resonances between the " kerygmatic " formulae which punctuate the Emmaus narrative (vv. 19-21.23.25-27.34) and both the passion predictions of Jesus (esp. SCHUBERT) and the apostolic preaching in Acts (esp. DUPONT). In addition, DUPONT showed the hand of the evangelist in the composition of the meal scene (vv. 28ff.) on the basis of its repetition of eucharistic formulae used elsewhere in Lk's history (esp. Acts 2,42; Lk 9,12-17; 22,19; Acts 20,7.11). Concludes DUPONT: his formulaic language suggests Lk was rewriting his traditions from the vantage point of the ecclesiastical life of his own time, demonstrating in the Emmaus christophany the manner of the church's encounter with her unseen Lord through word and sacrament (cf. *Misc. Ubach*, 364 and n. 43; also R. ORLETT, *CBQ* 21 [1959] 218; H.-D. BETZ, *ZTK* 66 [1969] 12f., 16f., 20; J. WANKE, *Eucharistieverständnis*, 41, 43, and *BZ* 18 [1974] 184f., 192). Cp. n. 17 above.

[32] WANKE's argument has been mentioned already in n. 27 above. According to his researches in *Emmauserzählung*, " there is no verse " of the Emmaus story, " nor even an integral turn of phrase, that does not contain properties of Lucan usage or words of Lk's preference " (109). " The synopsis (of his language-analysis, pp. 110-112) does not permit the judgment that certain parts of the narrative partake in greater or lesser degree of Lk's linguistic refurbishments " (112). " This negative evidence must warn us against all tradition-historical hypotheses which pretend to assure the circumference and format of the pre-Lucan account on the basis of language-indications .... Anyone who brackets anything out of Lk 24,13-35 destroys an integral whole " (114). Invalid, therefore, is any " *Distillationsverfahren* " by which the older narrative is made to crystallize, as if by critical magic, from amidst this thoroughly and concertedly Lucan text (*BZ* 18 [1974] 181).

[33] WANKE believes that the encounter with Jesus as itinerant stranger cer-

second step in WANKE's procedure is the analysis of the pericope's rapport with the rest of the Easter chapter, and this is where we believe we can complement his work from the scope we have set for the present study. WANKE wrote: " The Emmaus narrative, given its specific and unique character, cannot be interpreted with attention only to the immanent features of the pericope itself; rather, it must be illumined from the perspective of its position in the Easter chapter taken as a whole (which is, in turn, the concluding chapter of the gospel!) " (*Emmauserzählung*, 35). His study therefore combines word-study with motif-analysis in a comprehensive, redaction-analytical pursuit of Lk's mind. This is the path we think is right and wish to follow; and after the labors of J. DUPONT, P. SCHUBERT, J. WANKE, *et al.*, we can still observe that it is as yet but lightly trodden.

It is incumbent upon us, however, to locate the *specificum* of our own labors, and that must lie, of course, in a new assessment of the pericope in its relation to the Easter story at large, for our thesis is dedicated to the whole complex of which Emmaus is only one portion, albeit a central and most important one. We therefore reiterate the objective set at the beginning of the treatment of the tomb sequence (pp. 1, 8 above): sounding Lk's Easter perspectives in a passage where his critical dialogue with a source-text was measurable, we would then purpose to seek verification of those perspectives in the *Sonderstücke* that follow. In other words, it was the *voice we heard in dialogue with Mk over the mystery of the tomb that we shall now listen for* in the walk to Emmaus, using the redactional motifs and stratagems observed in

tainly belonged to the original story, as did his reception " from outside " into meal companionship (whether from a journey shared with him or at his bid for rest as a weary traveler); and the situation was rendered the more mysterious and dramatically taut by the normal, everyday humanity of the *Viator* (*ibid.*, 34f.). Lk himself filled out the story's brief non-recognition phase with the travelers' colloquium, replete as it is with vocabulary and doctrines of his. He also wove this new material harmoniously together with the older account by means of the motif of the " eye-restraining " (v. 16) *vs.* " eye-opening " (v. 31), which both sustains the dramatic momentum through the expansive colloquium and permits the fusion of Scripture-understanding and meal-recognition in the unified climax of the " opening " (vv. 31, 32; cf. WANKE, *Emmauserzählung*, 31f., 35f.). In this last argument, WANKE emerges in (we think) successful debate with U. WILCKENS, who saw a clue to the demarcation of tradition and redaction in the two " openings " (dual reference of the verb διανοίγειν): " The *opening* of their eyes to the messianic prophecy of Scripture (v. 32) prepared for the *eye-opening* to recognize (Jesus) himself (v. 31). From this different reference of the same key-word '*opening*' one realizes that the colloquium during the journey was put into the story by Luke " (*Auferstehung*, 80 [italics mine]; cf. the scripture " opening " again at Lk 24,44-46). WANKE's view is that the διανοίγειν motif is wholly redactional, hence its dual application to scriptural exposition and breaking of the bread is not the result of a redactional imposition upon the older story. Our investigation will bear out this view.

the first pericope as pointers to the plan of composition — and thus also the substratum of tradition — in the travelers' saga. WANKE pursued this method only for Lk 24,22-24, where the tomb story's echoes are explicit (*op. cit.*, 73-76), but we wish to extend it to as much of the second pericope as it might (even unexpectedly) elucidate. Then, incorporating some indispensable tests of Lucan vocabulary and style, and observing how the story both receives and emits thematic resonances heard throughout the two volumes, we might hope to be exerting a comprehensive criticism of this most challenging of the Easter narratives.

(e) In the contemporary exegetical climate, one must consider *structural analysis* part of a comprehensive criticism, and surely a story with such a high degree of editorial originality and such a strong concentration of Lucan themes must be prime material for that methodology. In fact, it has received tentative efforts along these lines from scholars who have by no means renounced historical criticism, notably X. LEON-DUFOUR [34] and the companion scholars, F. SCHNIDER and W. STENGER.[35] Because of our own personal training and dispositions, we can use this approach only sparingly, for we are neither practiced in it nor aware that it has contributed significantly to the understanding

[34] LÉON-DUFOUR finds a fairly perspicuous concentric pattern framing the story's dual components, the dialogue and the meal (cf. *Résurrection*, 212ff.), as follows: (a) outer circle, vv. 13/33: ἐν αὐτῇ τῇ ἡμέρᾳ ἦσαν πορευόμενοι ... ἀπὸ 'Ιερουσαλήμ / αὐτῇ τῇ ὥρᾳ ὑπέστρεψαν εἰς 'Ιερουσαλήμ ...· (b) next circle, vv. 14/32: ὡμίλουν πρὸς ἀλλήλους / εἶπαν πρὸς ἀλλήλους· (c) next circle, vv. 15/31b: ἐγγίσας συνεπορεύετο αὐτοῖς / ἄφαντος ἐγένετο ἀπ' αὐτῶν. (d) Inner circle, vv. 16/31a: οἱ δὲ ὀφθαλμοὶ αὐτῶν ἐκρατοῦντο τοῦ μὴ ἐπιγνῶναι αὐτόν. / αὐτῶν δὲ διηνοίχθησαν οἱ ὀφθαλμοὶ καὶ ἐπέγνωσαν αὐτόν· (e) *center*, vv. 17-30: *colloquium and breaking of the bread*. So far, of course, no one could deny the definite pattern of the writing. It corresponds to the dramatic movement of the story and attests the stylistic skill and economy of our author. When LÉON-DUFOUR seeks, however, to extend the concentric pattern to smaller units of the pericope — say, the colloquium — too much manipulation and transposition is required to verify the design. In just the few pages this exegete devotes to our passage, therefore, we witness both the validity and the limits of the structural analysis he sponsors. — Cf. also the essays of Sr. JEANNE D'ARC (bibliog.).

[35] In their "Beobachtungen zur Struktur der Emmausperikope," SCHNIDER and STENGER renounce any "monism of method" and propose to combine structural analysis with the perspectives of contemporary *Traditionsgeschichte*. Their trouble is, however, that they commit themselves prematurely to the rigid separation of narrative (= tradition) from colloquium (= redaction), following P. SCHUBERT, and set about analyzing the narrative as if it were a block of pre-Lucan material. Valuable observations are advanced to reinforce the Lucan character of the colloquium and to define the dynamics of the narrative. Hence, though we shall take note of the authors' helpful observations in both these matters, we are unable to follow their basic approach or to agree that it will function in smooth partnership with historico-critical study (to which our endeavour is steadfastly devoted).

of the texts under discussion. And we remain opposed to any " immanent analysis " that prescinds from the genus and formation of texts of the gospel tradition, for these were, after all, the end-products of a rich and varied early Christian transmission, not the creations *ex nihilo* of single hands obeying individual minds!

Informed now by both our conclusions from chapter I and our survey of the exegetical *status quaestionis*, our treatment of the Emmaus story can begin with observation of what we have repeatedly found to be the most prominent rationale of the Easter chapter's composition: its *framework of time, place, and persons*, which effects our author's peculiar condensation of the Easter events in his narration. Since the framework unites three rather diverse episodes and is uniformly imposed on all of them, we shall be diagnosing redactional activity where we find it; and we shall move from the passages which display it to the interior of the pericope, hoping to move concurrently *from composition back towards the tradition* in steps suggested by substantial consensus, comparison of Lucan editorial trends, and some efforts at tradition-historical detection. — Our path will lead us from the framework passages (vv. 13f. 33-35. 21b-24) to the travelers' colloquium (vv. 17-27), and finally to the narrator's exposition (vv. 15f.) and meal scene (vv. 28-32). The studies surveyed above (pp. 74ff.) have suggested to us that this might well be a path from the editorial to the traditional level of our celebrated Easter narrative.

(2) *The Lucan Framework* (Vv. 13f. 33-35. 21b-24)

To the " framework " (*Rahmen*) of a pericope belongs, according to form-critical canons,[36] whatever confers upon a pre-existent, self-sufficient traditional story a " location " in the secondary sequence of the written gospel. In our chapter, material belongs to the *Rahmen* of the three episodes which not only documents Lk's Easter continuum of time, place, and persons, but also creates the explicit sequence of one pericope and another, — say, between the Emmaus episode and the tomb story, whose connection almost certainly does not antedate Lk's redaction.[37] The strained attachment of these first two Easter episodes is already apparent in the introduction to the Emmaus narrative.

---

[36] K. L. SCHMIDT, *Rahmen*, V *f.*, 317; R. BULTMANN, *GsT*, 3-4, 362; J. ROHDE, *Redaktionsgesch. Methode*, 10, 13, 17, 21.

[37] The obvious lack of an inherent sequence between Lk's first two Easter episodes is recognized by most critics, following the lead of A. LOISY, *Luc*, 573; R. LEANEY, *NTS* 2 [1955-56] 111; J. FINEGAN, *Überlieferung*, 90; H. GRASS, *Ostergeschehen*, 36; J. DUPONT, in *Misc. Ubach*, 361 n. 40, and others; most recently, J. E. ALSUP, *Appearance Stories*, 115-116. — The suggestion that the tomb and Emmaus stories had been fused in the tradition before Lk (H.-D.

Vv. 13*f.*: καὶ ἰδού belongs among the LXX semitisms whose planned profusion in the gospel, and corresponding retreat in Acts, partake of the evangelist's linguistic techniques for recreating the mood and aura of events narrated.[38] We spoke of this already in the exegesis of 24,4 (pp. 20f.). Having found the Lucan tomb sequence to be a newly unified episode, we now note that καὶ ἰδού also began the burial account (Lk 23,50/*diff.* Mk 15,42f.); and in a fashion similar to the present passage, the expression introduced Joseph of Arimathea as putatively stepping forth from the γνωστοί of Lk 23,49, just as now the δύο are explicitly brought forth from the followers mentioned in vv. 9ff. The tomb sequence and the Emmaus appearance story thus have parallel beginnings, with καὶ ἰδού in each case bringing forward the main figure(s) from the stable coetus of paschal witnesses: πάντες οἱ γνωστοί of 23,49, πάντες οἱ λοιποί of 24,9.[39]

Persons: The phrase ἐξ αὐτῶν with δύο maintains the continuity of persons in the Easter experiences. As yet it is unclear what circle the "two" have come from, and not until v. 18 will we learn that it is not the inner circle of "the apostles" — as the more proximate antecedent of αὐτῶν would require (v. 11) — but the broader group of πάντες οἱ λοιποί, v. 9. This abrupt alternation of "the Eleven" and the wider circle is a distinct compositional trend here at the axis of the two Lucan volumes; it is not maladroit suturing of source-texts.[40]

BETZ, *ZTK* 66 [1969] 9; R. H. FULLER, *Formation*, 105, 113) has no substantial evidence in its favor. We hope to demonstrate that the main connective tissue between the two stories, vv. 22-24, is the work of the evangelist and no one before him.

[38] On the narrative καὶ ἰδού in Lk and Acts, cf. P. FIEDLER, *Die Formel "und siehe"*... [cited in chap. I, n. 58] 35-38, 65-67. Lk's dependence on Septuagintal style is apparent in the fact that καὶ ἰδού, most often accompanied by ἀνήρ (ἄνθρωπος) or γυνή, introduces to his reader persons previously unmentioned who are nevertheless important for the progress of his narrative. The idiom occurs 16 times in gospel narratives, only 4 times in Acts narratives (plus Acts 10,30 and 11,11, narratives attributed to speakers, and Acts 10,17 *l.v.*), and it disappears after Acts 16,1 altogether. — A novelty in Lk 23,50 and 24,13 (also 10,25), over against the LXX and NT (Mt) usage, is that this idiom is used to introduce new pericopes that are without inherent sequence with what precedes them in the text (so P. FIEDLER, *op. cit.*, 37).

[39] καὶ ἰδού also introduces main actors of episodes in Lk 2,25; 5,12.18; 7,37; 8,41; 10,25; 13,11; 14,2; 19,2. And they are similarly made to stand apart from a larger group of *adstantes* in 5,18 and 8,41.

[40] Cf. A. LOISY, *Luc*, 570; J. WANKE, *BZ* 18 (1974) 186. In view of πρὸς τοὺς ἀποστόλους in v. 10, there is not an "immediate connection" between the αὐτοί of vv. 11 and 13, *pace* W. GRUNDMANN, *Lk.*, 444. — On the alteration of the (eleven) apostles and the larger group of disciples in the Easter complex, cf. G. LOHFINK, *Sammlung Israels*, 66. The pattern is sustained by Lk's editing: "Sosehr die Zwölf aus dem Jüngerkreis herausgehoben werden, so sehr gehören sie ihm andererseits doch auch wieder an" (*ibid.*, 64). — "Aus den genannten

The distinction of the " two " from " the Eleven " becomes definitive at v. 33. The important thing about the travelers is that they belong to the corps of paschal observers. That is what ἐξ αὐτῶν means to express, and it prepares the reader for the return of the two to the full assembly at the conclusion of the story (v. 33). The observers' circle is portrayed, as we have noted, in constant " plenary session " at Jerusalem during Easter day. The phrase ἐξ αὐτῶν is therefore plainly part of Lk's editorial structure, even if it does not smooth over these pericopes' disconnectedness with complete success. — The travelers' two-fold number, on the other hand, is not so easily diagnosed. Unlike the one traveler's name given at v. 18, which is likely a datum of the original tradition (along with the Emmaus locality), the two-fold number might have resulted from a special interest of the redactor's. This is suggested, first, by the fact that the second personage is never named, and second, by an echo of Lk's *Sonderstück* in 10,1ff. which could prove part of an editorial pattern he intended. The sending out of the " Seventy(-two) *others* " ἀνὰ δύο occurred in a passage which pointedly segregated them from " the Twelve " in similar fashion (cf. parallelism of 9,1ff. and 10,1ff., and the specification ἑτέρους in 10,1).[41] We are not yet in a position to justify this suggestion, however. Let us leave it as a mere whimsical impression and hope it might gain some support in the course of our treatment.

Time: ἐν αὐτῇ τῇ ἡμέρᾳ[42] extends to the new pericope the careful time-framework of Easter " day," whose artful construction we have already observed in the tomb sequence (Lk 23,54.56; 24,1.7). It connects the episode at hand with the women's discovery at the tomb since its present reference can only be back to 24,1. It is also paralleled by the similar αὐτῇ τῇ ὥρᾳ at the end of the pericope (v. 33), which

---

Texten folgt, dass für Lukas die Zwölf trotz aller Heraushebung integrierender Bestandteil des grösseren Jüngerkreises um Jesus sind " (*ibid.*, 67). The best example of editing along these lines is Lk 6,13-20, where the choice of " the Twelve " as " apostles " brings them emphatically to the fore, from amidst the ranks of the greater number of disciples; and yet they then melt back into the larger group when the great sermon is introduced (v. 20).

[41] Cf. chap. IV below, n. 131. The identification of the Emmaus disciples as members of the " Seventy(-two) " goes back to the Fathers of the Church, according to E. KLOSTERMANN, *Lk.*, 234.

[42] The expression is characteristically Lucan. The intensive adjective/pronoun itself, αὐτὸς ὁ, occurs mainly in Lk (11 times) among the Synoptics (only twice in Mt and Mk, once in Mk postscript). Moreover, in 9 of 11 uses in Lk's gospel, the use is with time-terminology: ἡμέρα, ὥρα, καιρός (also 2*x* in Acts) (cf. J. B. HAWKINS, *Horae syn.*, 14; H. SCHÜRMANN, " Protolukanische Spracheigentümlichkeiten ? " in *Traditionsgeschichtliche Untersuchungen*, 221; A. DENAUX, " L'hypocrisie des pharisiens et le dessein de Dieu. Analyse de Lc., XIII, 31-33," in F. Neirynck, ed., *L'év. de Luc. Mém. Cerfaux*, [245-285] 258f.; J. WANKE, *Emmauserzählung*, 24f.).

sets the final events of the chapter in rapid motion. These two "framework" notices point within the pericope to the traveler's still puzzled reference to "the *third* day" (v. 19b), the day of Jesus' prophecy (v. 7). The Easter event thus runs its course in full keeping with the will of God, reflected in Jesus' prophecies and still hidden in the scriptures. The time-notices document the fulfillment of both to the letter! [43]

As we have pointed out before, the *time*-framework functions for Lk as an *idea*-framework since the events woven together into the *chronological* integrity of the "third day" also fit together into the *theological* integrity of Lk's Easter panorama. We shall see that the *time*-connective in v. 33 is very much an expression of the *thought*-connection between the Emmaus experience and the Easter confession of the assembled disciples. No less is the present notice expressive of the logical sequence between the experience of the empty tomb and what now follows.[44] As yet, our explanation of that logical sequence is not complete, but the assertion of it *via* the chronological continuity endorses our method of interpreting the two pericopes as closely conjoined expressions of our author's mind.

An additional point of reference for this initial time-reference is the preface of the Emmaus meal scene, v. 29: κέκλικεν ἤδη ἡ ἡμέρα (cp. Lk 9,12). The theological function of that chronology, introducing the travelers' Easter repast as the Lord's Supper, is as clear as day and will come under discussion in its turn. For now, we reiterate our evangelist's intense interest in this chapter's many time-notices, hence the great probability of their origin at his hand.

Place: Jerusalem's function for Lk as the geographical focus of the saving events also derives from Jesus' prophecies (Lk 13,33; 18,31),

---

[43] The use of ἡμέρα to depict the stages of sacred history's fulfillment is familiar Lucan usage, redolent again of LXX usage. To take only instances of the noun in the singular, we can cite Lk 1,80; 6,23 *diff.* Mt; 17,22.24.30.31 *diff.* Mt; 19,42; 21,34; Acts 1,2.22; 2,1.41; (8,1). For precisely the motif of "*the third day*" as expression of fulfillment, cf. Lk 13,32: ... σήμερον καὶ αὔριον, καὶ τῇ τρίτῃ τελειοῦμαι. Here, as in 13,33, the three days are certainly not mere material chronology, any more than τελειοῦμαι expresses merely the termination of Jesus' miracles in Herod's territory. Whatever be the precise point of τελειοῦμαι in this text (cf. the survey of exegetes' perplexity in K. LEHMANN, *Auferweckt*, 235ff.), the "days" clearly express the stages in which God, and he alone, will bring the mysterious consummation about (cf. H. CONZELMANN, *MdZ*, 57, 60, 184; also, with different sense and persuasive OT antecedents, A. DENAUX, in *L'év. de Luc. Mém. Cerfaux*, 271-274, 278ff., esp. 280).

[44] The practice of signaling *content*-connections through *time*-connections (cf. H. CONZELMANN, "Zur Lukasanalyse," in Braumann-*LkEv*, 62), which we are positing in the cases of Lk 24,13 and 24,33, is not altogether new with Lk. Note the introduction to the Q-logion containing the Revealer's cry of jubilation, Lk 10,21 / Mt 11,25, where the notice of the "same hour/time" (Lk/Mt) is likely a connective original to the source and expressive of an idea-connection (cf. P. HOFFMANN, *Logienquelle*, 105, 286f., 305; D. LÜHRMANN, *Redaktion*, 64).

along with the chronology of the third day. Time and place together demonstrate that fulfillment is at hand. — What of the city's position in the present verse, however, where it is only the reference-point for the location of Emmaus ? The latter, of course, is hardly expressive of any special Lucan interest but is rather a basic traditional component of the appearance story.[45] But the fact that the town is located with reference to Jerusalem does place the present passage in comparison with the one other instance of such referential geography in Lk-Acts, Acts 1,12, which also involves Jerusalem. The Acts text, which terminates the narrative of the risen Lord's appearances just as our passage inaugurates it, places the appearance- (and ascension-) site " a sabbath's journey distant " from Jerusalem (σαββάτου ἔχον ὁδόν). But that phrase accompanies, and is clearly meant to expand upon, the preceding ἐγγὺς Ἰερουσαλήμ, which negates any real shift of locale in the final Easter encounter. That is, in fact, the point of the " sabbath's journey." The Mount of Olives was *a mere sabbath's journey*, no real distance at all ![46] By comparison, perhaps even by the strength of a literary parallelism it forms with Acts 1,12, we take our passage to mean much the same thing : " Emmaus lay *at most* 60 *stades distant* " (11.5 km.),[47] hence still very much in Jerusalem's vicinity. The only purpose of such information is thus to maintain the locale of the paschal happenings at sacred history's focal point and the geographical symbol of its fulfillment-phase. So it is with the story of the travelers, who otherwise might be thought to take the story beyond that divinely determined area.[48]

---

[45] Rightly U. WILCKENS, *Auferstehung*, 79 ; B. STEINSEIFER, *ZNW* 62 (1971) 265 ; J. WANKE, *Emmauserzahlung*, 123, and *BZ* 18 (1974) 182.

[46] G. LOHFINK, *Himmelfahrt*, 207. Cf. also H. J. CADBURY, *The Making*, 248 : " Perhaps it is noteworthy that the only measures of geographical distance in either volume occur in indicating the relative nearness to Jerusalem of the two places outside of that city where Jesus was seen, Emmaus, sixty stadia away, and the Mount of Olives, only a sabbath day's journey." — The rabbinical law of the sabbath journey was based on Ex 16,29 (" ... let no man go out of his place on the seventh day "), interpreted with recourse to Num 35,5 (the 2000-cubit radius prescribed for the cities of the Levites). A sabbath day's journey was thus 2000 cubits, or 6 stadia outside a town (= slightly more than half a mile ; cf. K. LAKE & H. J. CADBURY, *Beginnings* IV, 10).

[47] G. LOHFINK, *Himmelfahrt*, 208, 264 ; J. WANKE, *Emmauserzählung*, 33.

[48] J. WANKE, *Emmauserzählung*, 41 : " Lukas braucht für die Erzählung — so wie er sie berichten will — ein Emmaus in nur geringer Entfernung von Jerusalem. Dann ist verständlich, dass beide Wanderer noch am Abend zurückkehren können." Cf. also R. H. FULLER, *Formation*, 120. — We note that the Emmaus story retains Lk's focus on the events " at Jerusalem " (v. 18) and leads to the conclusion that involves the travelers' return to the city (v. 33). It is therefore no departure from Lk's theological interest in Jerusalem's centrality (*pace* E. LOHMEYER, *Galiläa*, 24) but precisely a confirmation of it (rightly P. ZINGG, *Wachsen*, 140 n. 5).

On the question of the *Emmaus locale itself*[49] we have nothing new to say and doubt that, barring sudden archeological revelations in Jerusalem's suburbs, there will be much new to say in the near future. We are convinced, as many are, that the site referred to is the town of Maccabean times (I Macc 3,40; 4,3; 9,50), later *Nicopolis*, today's *'Amwas*, which is the only place sanctioned by the tradition of the ancient church.[50] Other claims, like the variant readings of the distance, all derive from the fact that the Maccabean town is appreciably farther from Jerusalem than Lk's "60 stades," more like the 160 stades substituted for it by diligent scribes of the Palestinian ms. tradition.[51] Like most practitioners of Lucan redaction-criticism, we prefer to think that the problem was created by our evangelist's scant acquaintance with the area's topography and his even scanter interest

---

[49] The excursus of J. WANKE (*Emmauserzählung*, 37-42) contains as complete a bibliography and exposition of the issue as one could desire. To his bibliography I should add only Jack FINEGAN, *The Archeology of the New Testament. The Life of Jesus and the Beginning of the Early Church* (Princeton: Princeton Univ. Press, 1969) 177-180, and the reprinted edition of Gustaf DALMAN's *Orte und Wege Jesu*[3] (Gütersloh, 1924) augmented from the author's own notes by Alfred Jepsen (Darmstadt: Wissenschaftliche Buchgesellschaft, 1967; cf. pp. 241-246, 429). — The literature in the listing of WANKE is all at least fifteen years old, much of it considerably older. One has the impression of a stalemated question.

[50] Since the original Hebrew text of I Macc is not extant, it is already a hellenized form of the name that we find in Palestinian sources (אמאוס, עמואס); but if the derivation from חָמַם, "be warm," is correct, the presence of warm springs on the site would be indicated (G. DALMAN, *Orte und Wege*, 242), and only the Maccabean site, with its two fountains of tepid water (*ibid.*, 243), would pass that test. Too, it is undoubtedly the Maccabean town to which Josephus refers in *Bell.* II 5,1, 71 ('Αμμαοῦς) and *Ant.* XVII 10,7 282 ('Εμμαοῦς), whereas the occurrence of the same appelation in *Bell.* VII 6,6 217, in reference to a settlement of army veterans established under Vespasian (*Colonia*, Arab. *Qaloniyeh*) only 30 stadia from Jerusalem, probably results from a scribal error in the transmission of the historian's text (so G. DALMAN, *op. cit.*, 244). There is thus little save the interpreter's convenience to recommend the site of the Roman barracks as the Emmaus of the Easter walk, even though it continues to be favored by some exegetes (cf. K. KLOSTERMANN, *Lk.*, 234; R. H. FULLER, *Formation*, 107). — A medieval competitor of *'Amwas* for veneration as Lk's site was *El-Qubeibeh*, located the appropriate distance northwest of the city on the road to Jaffa (60 stadia = 11 km./7 mi.) and boasting a large, 19th-century Franciscan church built on the ruins of another which the crusaders had built (cf. J. FINEGAN, *Archeology*, 177). The trouble here is that nothing can be established at the site beyond the crusaders' veneration, and this is more likely the result of harmonizing with the gospel datum than an authentic discovery of the medieval pilgrims (so G. DALMANN, *op. cit.*, 241f.; E. LOHSE, *Auferstehung*, 25; J. WANKE, *Emmauserzählung*, 40).

[51] Although "the most elementary rules of textual criticism" force the choice of "60 stadia" over 160 as the original reading (J. DUPONT, in *Misc. Ubach*, 369), and even though it is understandable that the higher figure should have emerged in the Palestinian textual tradition, G. DALMAN's later notes

in such detail for its own sake.[52] So long as one understands the distance statement in light of Acts 1,12, with the integrity of the unifying Jerusalem locale as our author's main concern, the actual locality involved in the story becomes a point of peripheral interest. *Jerusalem*[53] is the Easter narrative's focal point, hence ἀπὸ Ἰερουσαλήμ with distance-datum is a preparation for this narrative's conclusion in the return εἰς Ἰερουσαλήμ of the travelers (v. 33). Emmaus, on the other hand, was furnished by the tradition of the mysterious wayfarer and was hardly dispensable for the evangelist in view of the *travel*-setting that is so important to his own use of the tradition.

---

indicate he was of a mind to endorse F.-M. ABEL's choice of the Palestinian reading (cf. *Orte und Wege*, 429; F.-M. ABEL, *RB* 34 [1925] 347-367). This option is perhaps as understandable in the geographer as in the ancient scribe acquainted with the Palestinian landscape. It is not a sound option for the textual critic, however, who must prefer the *lectio difficilior* here if anywhere!

[52] H. CONZELMANN, *MdZ*, 86; J. DUPONT, in *Misc. Ubach*, 369f.; E. LOHSE, *Auferstehung*, 25; G. LOHFINK, *Himmelfahrt*, 207f.; W. ELTESTER, in *Jesus in Nazareth*, 85; J. ERNST, *Lk.*, 659. — The inexactitude of Lk's geography was brought out years ago by C. C. McCOWN ("Gospel Geography: Fiction, Fact, and Truth," *JBL* 60 [1941, 1-25] 14ff.), who showed that the inconsistencies and errors of detail in the central "journey" section could be explained only by recognizing Lk's geography as a "literary device." At most, Lk could be called a "desk geographer," who leaves one in doubt whether he ever visited Palestine (*art. cit.*, 18)! — Clearly, rather than seek some dubious Emmaus site at the requisite distance from Jerusalem, one should pursue the problem at the level where it is posed: the level of *Lk's composition* and its distinctive concerns (rightly J. DUPONT, in *Misc. Ubach*, 368; J. WANKE, *Emmauserzählung*, 41).

[53] The hebraic form of the city's name, Ἰερουσαλήμ (= יְרוּשָׁלַיִם), is, of the two forms current in the Gk of NT times, the one used almost exclusively by Jewish authors. It had the dignity and sacral ring of the old biblical language, hence it is preferred by authors (like Heb and Rev) who write of Jerusalem in its theological or eschatological significance. Mk and Jn always use the hellenizing Ἱεροσόλυμα, the name associated with profane usage and preferred both by Greek authors and Jewish authors addressing Greek audiences (cf. the recent survey of J. JEREMIAS, "ΙΕΡΟΥΣΑΛΗΜ-ἹΕΡΟΥΣΟΛΥΜΑ," *ZNW* 65 [1974] 273-276). In the use of the "sacral" form, Lk distinguishes himself markedly from the other evangelists (elsewhere, only Mt 23,37 Q). He rewrites all Mk's references to the city with this form, and uses the profane form only 4 times of 31 in the gospel. In Acts 1-7 he keeps to the sacral form, whereas in Acts 8ff. he employs both forms (Acts statistics: 36*x* sacral, 23 profane). Although the pattern of this usage is not always clear, it would seem that our author's concern for the sacred meaning of the city and his generalized use of evocative language patterns furnish the best explanation for the choices. In general, the sacral form, evocative of the OT "sacred prose," is used while Lk's story is in its Palestinian phase and wherever Jerusalem's role in prophecy and sacred history is being highlighted. The Greek spelling begins to predominate, on the other hand, when the mission's course into the Greek-speaking world is being recounted, as also when non-specific, chronicle-type references are made to the city. — Similar patterns are observable in other proper-name variations in Lk-

The *travel* momentum of the Emmaus account is instilled in it from the outset with ἦσαν πορευόμενοι, an instance of Lk's frequent recourse to periphrasis with the present participle.[54] " The reason for periphrasis is the emphasis on duration," such that it " readily denotes the ' frame of reference '" for an event or narrative (Bl-Deb § 353-1). That is clearly what it does in our text, where the journey-setting is to be the consistent framework of the event that is central to the pericope, the appearance of the risen One. In fact, Lk elsewhere uses such periphrasis — or, as we saw in 24,4, the equally " semitizing " ἐγένετο ἐν τῷ ... construction (cf. v. 15) — to depict the attendant circumstance of heavenly visions and appearances (cf. Lk 2,8f.; Acts 1, 10). In all these instances, " the declaration of the background circumstance is by no means accidental. It stands rather in close relation to the appearance that follows in each case .... For the correct interpretation of any of these texts, one has to consider carefully the complementary effect of ' background ' and ' action '." [55] In our text, this means that the *appearance* of the risen Lord is to be understood in close relation to the background of the *wayfaring*, and with the latter, of course, the wayfarers' dialogue (v. 15).

With the verb πορεύεσθαι, of course, we have a vocabulum of Lk's preference (Lk *ca.* 50*x* / Acts 39*x* *vs.* *ca.* 33*x* in the rest of the NT) and the echo of perhaps the most important editorial schema of the gospel,

---

Acts (cf. H. J. CADBURY, *The Making*, 225-227), so that even scholars who readily posit source-material mirrored in Lk's writing hesitate to make spelling variations like this one a basis for arguing to the existence of such sources (e.g. P. WINTER, " ' Nazareth ' and ' Jerusalem ' in Luke chs. I and II," *NTS* 3 [1956-57, 136-142] 141). Such variations as narrative *vs.* direct or indirect discourse, persons portrayed as speaking Aramaic or Greek, and the like, also play their part in Lk's choice of spellings (cf. J. WANKE, *Emmauserzählung*, 27).

[54] Bl-Deb n. 353: Hellenistic Greek saw this development only to a limited degree, whereas it increases considerably in NT Greek with the support of the frequent such semitic paraphrases, especially in the imperfect tense. Of NT authors, Lk uses this type of expression most frequently, with typical concentration in the gospel and the first half of Acts. This unequal distribution is indeed " suspect," but not for the reason T. SCHRAMM thinks (*Markus-Stoff*, 101), viz. as a sign of non-Marcan source-material in the gospel (*ibid.*, 85). Semitic flavoring in Lk's narrative is intentionally evocative of the theatre and portent of the events being narrated. We are not surprised, therefore, that it is found in the editorial connective tissue between pericopes and at junctions of sources (H. J. CADBURY, *The Making*, 224 n. 18), hence paraphrases abound in passages like Lk 4,31.44; 5,16.17; 9,45; 18,34, etc., where even SCHRAMM is hard-put to maintain the presence of independent source-material (cf. *op. cit.*, 101 n. 6). The periphrastic conjugation is a particularly graphic way of stressing the continuation of action or circumstance, and while it was not altogether offensive to the Greek ear (A. PLUMMER, *Lk*, li), it flourishes in Lk where the evangelist's evocative style calls for a semitic seasoning of the narrative.

[55] G. LOHFINK, *Himmelfahrt*, 194.

the "journey" motif.[56] It is not clear immediately that the "journey" of the disciples with the hidden Master (v. 15: συνεπορεύετο αὐτοῖς) to Emmaus has anything to do with the "itinerary" of the earlier chapters, but surely the ideas orchestrated earlier by the "journey to Jerusalem" are to be rehearsed again in the *Weggespräch* with the risen One: the mystery of his destined passion is to be expounded anew, as at Lk 13,33 and 18,31ff., apparently because it had not been grasped during that original exposition. Whether this renewed exposition required a travel setting of the appearance story, and if so, why it did, we are not yet in a position to say. Our decision awaits the exegesis of the content of this new "journey," namely, the colloquium with the risen Lord.

V. 14 associates the travelers' dialogue with their journey and does so with some distinctively Lucan vocabulary. The unemphatic καὶ αὐτός/καὶ αὐτοί, continuing discourse concerning the third person, is an imitative semitism peculiar to Lk's style.[57] ὁμιλεῖν occurs only in this passage and Acts 20,11; 24,26 in the NT, and the substantivized participle τὸ συμβεβηκός / τὰ συμβεβηκότα (="the event[s]") occurs only at Acts 3,10 and here.[58] In a sentence thus replete already with

[56] H. Conzelmann, *MdZ*, 61; also W. C. Robinson, *Weg*, 40: "Entsprechend dem lukanischen Verständnis der Heilsgeschichte, das in Wegterminologie zur Sprache gebracht wird, zeigt sich in dem ... (Reise-)bericht eine geordnete Bewegung auf einem 'Weg' oder einem 'Lauf'." In pericope introductions, where the verb quite clearly comes from the pen of the evangelist: Lk 7,11; 9,51.57; 10,38; 17,11; 19,28; (cp. 1,39; 2,41).

[57] The expression καὶ αὐτός is good Greek only if it introduces a new subject that is in some kind of contrast with the previous subject, or if some other kind of emphasis on the subject is required (cf. W. Michaelis, "Das unbetonte καὶ αὐτός bei Lukas," *ST* 4 [1950, 86-93] 86). And while it is not always easy to determine the presence of special emphasis, the expression is extraordinarily frequent in Lk (39 examples), compared to no usage in Mt and only three introducing sentences in Mk. "As more or less clear instances of unemphatic usage only Lk 4,15; 15,14; 16,24; 17,13; 19,2 (*bis*); 24,14 qualify"; elsewhere, especially where Jesus is the pronoun's antecedent, some intended emphasis has to be reckoned with (so Michaelis, *art. cit.*, 88, 90). — The LXX renders a little more than half the corresponding expressions of MT with καὶ αὐτός, and sometimes it supplies the phrase for clarity's sake where MT does not prompt it. Lk's usage is thus most likely a "Septuagintalism," not a pointer to any hebraizing source (Michaelis, *art. cit.*, 92-93; *contra* E. Schweizer, "Eine hebraisierende Sonderquelle des Lukas?" *TZBas* 6 [1950, 161-185] 163; cf. also T. Schramm, *Markus-Stoff*, 98).

[58] Participles with the article in place of substantives (Lk 2,27; 4,16; 8,34; 22,22; 24,14, etc.) are a Lucan predilection (cf. A. Plummer, *Lk*, lxii; J. Wanke, *Emmauserzählung*, 28). In particular, τὰ συμβεβηκότα = "events" is a classical expression, found also in I Macc 4,26; Ep. Arist.; Jos. *Bell.* 4,43; Jos. *Ant.* 13, 194 (cf. Bauer, *Wb.*, 1539). — For the expression πρὸς ἀλλήλους with verbs of speaking: Lk 2,15; 4,36; 6,11; 8,25; 20,14; *24,14.17.32*; Acts 4,15; 26,31; 28,4.25.

this evangelist's vocabulary and style, we note that περὶ πάντων συμβεβηκότων τούτων still belongs very much to the connective tissue between the new pericope and what preceded it in the *gospel text*. Together with the data of persons, time, and place in v. 13, therefore, it is to be included in the " framework " of the Emmaus account, fitting the latter into the larger literary context of Lk 24. We recognize in this phrase also a redactional motif brought to light in our study of the tomb story: the *totality of the facts observed* by the befuddled followers on the third day (pp. 55f.). The travelers are thus found to be discussing the *bruta facta paschalia* (v. 18: τὰ γενόμενα), which still lie under the veil of the great *mysterium*. They will likewise recite them in their *totality* for their fellow traveler in vv. 20-24, prior to the latter's self-revelation and as something of a foil for it. In other words, the topic of the *Weggespräch* is already known to us as the dialectical factor in the evangelist's portrayal of the Easter awakening. In its reprise here at the second pericope's introduction, therefore, we recognize his design and compositional dexterity. We are inclined, in fact, to view v. 14 with v. 13 as integrally *from Lk's hand*, as he deftly fashions a " framework " for the Emmaus story and thus fastens it to his total Easter construct.[59] Besides the name of the travelers' destination, we do not think we have yet encountered any substantial component of the Emmaus tradition that was already told before Lk's writing. We expect to have this judgment borne out in the remainder of our study.

Vv. 33-35

Moving to the story's conclusion, we encounter verses that are considered a redactional enlargement of it by a clear majority of our fellow interpreters.[60] In support of this we find assembled already in v. 33 the familiar " framework " factors, now in the order: time – place – persons. As we shall see, this repetition of the chapter's framework factors does double duty here: it both concludes the second pericope,

---

[59] The same conclusion is reached by J. WANKE, *Emmauserzählung*, 33: " Lukas hat also mit Sicherheit am Anfang der Erzählung selbst formuliert."

[60] A. R. C. LEANEY, *Lk*, 30; P. SCHUBERT, in *Ntl. Studien f. Bultmann*, 174; A. EHRHARDT, *NTS* 10 (1963-64) 182f.; H.-D. BETZ, *ZTK* 66 (1969) 13; J. ROLOFF, *Kerygma*, 256; F. SCHNIDER / W. STENGER, *BZ* 16 (1972) 102; J. WANKE, *Emmauserzählung*, 48, and *BZ* 18 (1974) 182, 186ff.; G. LOHFINK, *Himmelfahrt*, 264; F. SCHNIDER, *Prophet*, 127; C. H. TALBERT, *Literary Patterns*, 60; D. A. LOSADA, *RBibArg* 35 (1973) 4; J. E. ALSUP, *Appearance Stories*, 194. — F. HAHN also acknowledges the secondary character of vv. 33-35 with respect to the preceding narrative, but he supposes, without analysis, that this expansion was made at a stage of the tradition's growth prior to Lk's writing (*Hoheitstitel*, 388 n. 2).

bringing the action back where it started, so to speak, and it introduces the third episode, furnishing both the stage and the actors for the chapter's finale. Vv. 33f. is thus a connective passage, not merely a conclusion. It is the more certainly a redactional product for this double service, and it fastens together stories which nearly everyone recognizes as indepedent entities, unconnected before this evangelist's composition.[61]

Time: καὶ ἀναστάντες αὐτῇ τῇ ὥρᾳ maintains the chapter's compressed time-framework and, in fact, dramatically increases the compression. Moving from " that same day " at the beginning (v. 13) to " that same hour " at the end, we feel the tempo of the narrative quickening noticeably. The present expression is, in G. LOHFINK's word, " vorwärtsdrängend," [62] especially when read together with the words that introduce the third episode: ταῦτα δὲ αὐτῶν λαλούντων (v.36). A pressure is thus created, an urgent momentum, which impels the ensuing narrative towards the end and climax of the chapter, the ascension. That momentum will unify vv. 36-53 as a single concluding episode of the " third day " and the whole gospel.

Place: ὑπέστρεψαν εἰς Ἰερουσαλήμ. We have already discussed Lk's predilection for ὑποστρέφειν and the motif of " return " at the conclusion of episodes (cf. pp. 53-54 above). What is to be noted here is that this is the first time we are given the explicit information that the two disciples' journey had been *from Jerusalem*. V. 13 did not state the fact, and it was only implicit in the resumé of recent happenings in the city given to the Stranger by Cleopas (vv. 18ff.). Are we to understand special intent and meaning in the fact that, whereas

---

[61] So rightly J. WELLHAUSEN, *Lc.*, 141; A. LOISY, *Luc*, 584; L. BRUN, *Auferstehung*, 44; P. SCHUBERT, in *Ntl. Studien f. Bultmann*, 173; H. GRASS, *Ostergeschehen*, 39; E. LOHSE, *Auferstehung*, 34f.; G. LOHFINK, *Himmelfahrt*, 147; H.-W. BARTSCH, *Wachet*, 26; C. F. EVANS, *Resurrection*, 107f., and almost everyone we could name. It is hard to follow U. WILCKENS, therefore, in his assertion that departure from, and return to, Jerusalem already belonged to the oldest Emmaus tradition (cf. *Dogma und Denkstrukturen*, 77, and *Auferstehung*, 79). Were it not for v. 33, we should have no clear statement that the Easter travelers had set out *from Jerusalem* at all (rightly F. SCHNIDER / W. STENGER, *BZ* 16 [1972] 98). Others who hold that the second and third episodes of Lk 24 had come together at vv. 33 & 35 before Lk's writing, with only v. 34 forced into the junction by him (so R. H. FULLER, *Formation*, 105, 111f., following WILCKENS), are ignoring the plainly Lucan character and wording of the whole connective tissue joining the episodes. Ph. SEIDENSTICKER speaks similarly of pre-Lucan association of the pericopes, with the older connection even including v. 34 (!); but he can do this only because he ignores the matter of Lk's composition altogether (cf. *Auferstehung*, 96-97). — Once one subscribes to the *opinio communis*, it becomes extremely difficult to demonstrate analytically any other agent of the two pericopes' combination than Lk himself.

[62] *Himmelfahrt*, 113. — On the αὐτὸς ὁ usage as a Lucan trait, particularly with time-reference, cf. note 42 above.

the departure *from* Jerusalem was only implicit in the story, the return *to* Jerusalem is now made explicit? Does this "return" imply that the disciples' journey was a theological event,[63] as we suspected when we met the word συμπορεύεσθαι in the introduction?

Our answer to these questions is tentatively affirmative. The evangelist's *mise-en-scène* established, we recall, a close, complementary relation between the risen Lord's appearance and its journey-situation. The story also makes it clear that their *journey* coincided with the duration of the disciples' *blindness* (v. 16), since the eye-opening came only when the συμπορεύεσθαι had terminated in the eucharistic κατακλιθῆναι (vv. 30-31). Now, accompanying the eye-opening with punctual exactitude (αὐτῇ τῇ ὥρα), comes an explicit return to Jerusalem at the story's end. We suspect now that, in a fashion not unknown to our author, the simultaneity of time bespeaks a real conceptual connection of *recognition* and *return*.[64] The travelers left Jerusalem in confusion and disappointment; they now return there aglow with the revelation of the risen Lord. There is thus the closest relationship between the "journey" motif, with its contrasting moments of *concealment* and *revelation*, and the return to Jerusalem, presented almost as a homecoming. With ample reason one can argue that if the evangelist is found responsible for one of these, he is *pari passu* found responsible for the other.[65] But what overall design of his is served by the combination?

Of special moment in Lk-Acts is unquestionably the dialectic "*to* Jerusalem / *from* Jerusalem," which our story obtains retroactively from

[63] Rightly so, F. SCHNIDER / W. STENGER, *BZ* 16 (1972) 99f.: In their colloquium with Jesus, the disciples' journey is shown to be an expression of their shattered hopes and deficient faith. "Darum kann sich die Rückkehr nach Jerusalem ... zum Ausdruck ihrer wiedererweckten Hoffnung und ihres wiedergefundenen Glaubens werden." — Similarly G. LOHFINK, *Himmelfahrt*, 264; J. WANKE, *Emmauserzählung*, 47: "Der Ausgangspunkt Jerusalem qualifiziert den Weg der Jünger als ein theologisches Ereignis."

[64] See again n. 44 above, and observe especially Lk 7,21 (ἐν ἐκείνῃ τῇ ὥρᾳ), a time-notice from Lk's hand (cp. Mt) which makes the Johannine disciples' inquiry simultaneous with Jesus' miraculous healings "in order very emphatically to render these disciples eye-witnesses of Jesus' healing miracles" (A. VÖGTLE, *Das Evangelium und die Evangelien. Beiträge zur Evangelienforschung* [Düsseldorf: Patmos, 1971] 220). On the redactional origin and function of Lk 7,21, cf. also K. L. SCHMIDT, *Rahmen*, 117; R. BULTMANN, *GsT*, 22; W. GRUNDMANN, *Lk.*, 162; H. CONZELMANN, *MdZ*, 178f.; P. HOFFMANN, *Logienquelle*, 192, 193.

[65] F. SCHNIDER / W. STENGER, *BZ* 16 (1972) 100, 102. — U. WILCKENS correctly perceives that the moments of departure and return belong together at the same stage of the story's formation, but he is wrong in making that the stage of the pre-Lucan tradition (cf. *Dogma und Denkstrukturen*, 77 n. 55). As we hope our treatment will show, it is Lk's hand which has instilled in the Emmaus tradition its *theological relationship to Jerusalem*, of which the motifs of the "journey" and "return" are dramatically expressive components.

its conclusion. After all, these are the geographical trajectories which characterize, respectively, the *life of Jesus* and the *mission of the Church* in Lk's schema; and Jerusalem serves as a fixed symbol of the continuity between them.[66] The risen Lord himself, in this very chapter, will program the universal mission "from Jerusalem" (v. 47: ἀρξάμενοι ἀπὸ Ἰερουσαλήμ) with words that stand in hardly accidental contrast to the resumé of Jesus own mission to the Jews: ἀρξάμενος ἀπὸ τῆς Γαλιλαίας ἕως ὧδε (Lk 23,5; cp. Acts 10,37; 1,22). Jerusalem is, by sacred necessity, where Jesus completed the prophets' experiences by undergoing death (Lk 13,33), by rising from the dead, and by bestowing the Spirit for a *universal prophetic mission* (Acts 2,14ff.). The unity of place for all these phases of his saving deed is made a matter of principle in 24,49.[67] Because all the prophets were put to death not only *in* Jerusalem but *by* Jerusalem, according to the tradition Lk has very strongly endorsed (cf. 13,33ff.; 18,31ff.; Acts 13,27ff., etc.; cp. Acts 7,52 in context),[68] the missionaries of the Church will have to continue to tread the path *to Jerusalem* to the extent that their ministry remains qualified and legitimated by a basic relation to Jesus' own (cf. e.g. Acts 21,13 !).[69] The Church will thus live a strained existence which combines the *outward* paths of the world-mission with the *return* to Jerusalem to embrace the prophetic destiny of the Master.[70] — Our question is: does the Emmaus experience, with its two-fold trajectory and its central instructional content (vv. 25f.), already offer a portrait-in-miniature of the dual path of the Church's mission ? That depends, of coure, on what additional *ecclesial* references we are able to verify in this pericope, and whether perhaps the successive roles of the risen One in the story — as fellow-traveler, houseguest, and host at table — bear some allusion to familiar situations of the early Christian mission. We shall pursue these matters as our texts bid us.

Persons: καὶ εὗρον ἠθροισμένους τοὺς ἕνδεκα καὶ τοὺς σὺν αὐτοῖς, λέγοντας ὅτι ...· The corps of disciples is back at center stage in its

[66] H. CONZELMANN, *MdZ*, 124; U. WILCKENS, *Missionsreden*, 150f.; P. ZINGG, *Wachsen*, 143-144; but most especially, G. LOHFINK, *Himmelfahrt*, 263.

[67] H. CONZELMANN, *MdZ*, 199: "... nicht nur faktisch, sondern notwendig an Jerusalem gebunden."

[68] H. CONZELMANN, *MdZ*, 125, 186.

[69] On this qualification and legitimation: H. CONZELMANN, *MdZ*, 173ff. (and on the deliberate parallelism of Lk 23,5 and 24,47: 197 n. 1); U. WILCKENS, *Missionsreden*, 94ff. Cf. also S. SCHULZ, *Stunde*, 255ff.; W. C. ROBINSON, *Weg*, 28f.; G. SCHNEIDER, *Verleugnung*, 208f.

[70] Cf. P. ZINGG, *Wachsen*, 141 n. 2, and chap. III below, pp. 210ff. (*ad* 24, 47) for a fuller explanation. — In a sense, these contrasting momentums correspond to the dialectic within Lk's writing between the once-for-all uniqueness of the *historia Jesu* and its paradigmatic value for the present (cf. H. CONZELMANN, *MdZ*, 173; W. C. ROBINSON, *Weg*, 29; H. FLENDER, *Heil*, 131ff., esp. 144; J. WANKE, *Emmauserzählung*, 122, and *BZ* 18 [1974] 191).

role of *ecclesia in partu*, which we discussed above in reference to 24,9 (pp. 54-55). Regarding the manner of the nuclear group's reintroduction here, however, it is an exegetical commonplace that the nexus between vv. 33 and 34 is maladroit; that is, the story's conclusion is abruptly an announcement *by* the assembly *to* the homecomers rather than, as expected, their relating of what had just occurred. Attempts to repair this dissonant twist in the narrative were made in the ancient manuscript tradition, where the Codex Beza and Origen already witness the variant reading, λέγοντες.[71] Modern interpreters, acknowledging the weight of the witnesses and the *lectio difficilior* canon favoring λεγοντας, still feel its interruption of "the flow of the narrative," taking "the wind out of the sails of the Emmaus disciples" with a "surprising reference to the primary appearance to Peter, which nowhere else in Luke is either narrated or even mentioned."[72] V. 34 is therefore declared by many[73] an inserted statement by the evangelist, interrupting the smooth and natural sequence of vv. 33 and 35 and preserving the primacy of Peter's Easter witness according to the *regula fidei* of the primitive kerygma (I Cor 15,5). If this view is found convincing, we shall have to admit that vv. 33 and 35 are not part of our evan-

[71] A. LOISY (*Luc*, 582-583) is among the few modern interpreters inclined to propose this old *échappatoire* (cf. also E. KLOSTERMANN, *Lk.*, 238f.; J. H. CREHAN, *CBQ* 15 [1953] 422). Difficulties are not obviated by this reading either, as LOISY admits, since the story gives no basis for knowledge of an appearance to Peter on the wayfarers' part, should they be the speakers in v. 34. One has either to imagine Peter as the unnamed companion of Cleopas (CREHAN) or arbitrarily eliminate Σίμωνι as a secondary gloss in v. 34 (LOISY, KLOSTERMANN).

[72] R. H. FULLER, *Formation*, 112. Cf. also W. DIETRICH, *Petrusbild*, 161. The Marcan epilogue is silent on the first appearance to Peter when it relates the appearance of the two wayfarers and has them reporting their experience to incredulous disciples (Mk 16,12-13). We shall have occasion later to discuss the Emmaus reference in this passage, and we shall find no reason to depart from the majority opinion that it contains no independent tradition of the Emmaus appearance. For now, we observe only that the Deutero-Marcan passage should not be invoked in support of reading λέγοντες at v. 34, any more than it should be urged to support a prior version of the Emmaus story without v. 34. Pseudo-Mk's report that their confreres disbelieved the two disciples' account is not supported by Lk's text but is "at best an impression derived from vv. 36f." (J. M. CREED, *Lk*, 298). Moreover, the Easter summary of the Marcan postscript is organized around the motif of the disciples' *unbelief* (Mk 16,11.13.14 *vs.* 16,20), and this, rather than any variant tradition, accounts for the independent twist of Mk 16,13 (rightly H. GRASS, *Ostergeschehen*, 39, *contra* J. KREMER, *Osterbotschaft*, 67 n. 39). Cf. pp. 147f. below.

[73] U. WILCKENS, *Missionsreden*, 79, and in *Dogma und Denkstrukturen*, 76f.; J. KREMER, *Osterbotschaft*, 71; G. KEGEL, *Auferstehung*, 88; W. MARXSEN, *Auferstehung*, 55 (by Lk or predecessor); C. F. EVANS, *Resurrection*, 107; R. H. FULLER, *Formation*, 112.

gelist's own writing but belong to an older Emmaus account that came into his hands.

Yet commonplace that it might be, the criticism of v. 34 as " awkward " and " disruptive " needs to be reviewed. For one thing, there has not been enough attention paid to the connection between the participles ἠθροισμένους and λέγοντας.[74] Granted their relation is not one of logical sequence, so that a καί might be in place before λέγοντας,[75] our text's principal assertion will be diluted if we fail to recognize the *deliberate and theologically expressive juxtaposition* of the two words. The first, ἠθροισμένους, is the perfect passive participle of ἀθροίζω, which is not found elsewhere in the NT save in its compound, συναθροίζω, which our author employs at Acts 12,12 and 19,25. Both the tense and the prominent position of the participle suggest that it expresses an important feature of the returning travelers' discovery. And, in point of fact, this is the very first mention of an actual *gathering together* of " the Eleven " and their fellows; the two groups were mentioned in 24,9ff., but their " togetherness " remained unspecific there and was only allusively hinted in the τινες τῶν σὺν ἡμῖν of 24,24. Obviously the forming of the Easter congregation is being brought out in the same cumulative literary pattern as fashions other motifs of our chapter.[76] " The Eleven and their company," *definitively* " gathered " (= perf. ptc.[77]) for their announcement of the Lord's resurrection, presents a real climax of previous references to the gallery of *triduum* observers.

---

[74] H.-W. BARTSCH, *Wachet*, 23, suggests the connection but is content to view v. 34 as independent of its present context, having preexisted the story, hence presumably a subsequent insertion into it.

[75] Rightly J. WANKE, *Emmauserzählung*, 44, rejecting CREHAN's contention (*loc. cit.* in n. 71) that the absence of καί at v. 34 favors the reading λέγοντες.

[76] On the literary and theological " climax " movements in Lk 24, cf. P. SCHUBERT, in *Ntl. Studien f. Bultmann*, 176-177: from perplexity and disbelief to witness appointment and joy; from remembrance of Jesus' words to universal kerygma. — G. LOHFINK adds (*Himmelfahrt*, 113-114): the heavenly appearance, from angels to the Stranger known but for an instant, to the Lord of Easter in full personal disclosure; circle of observers, from the women to unknown disciples to Peter to the Twelve *and* the other disciples together. — Through these steadily augmented, progressive themes of the Easter story, " Lk 24 legt ausführlich dar, wie die Zeugen zum Glauben an den Auferstandenen kommen " (R. GLÖCKNER, *Verkündigung*, 57), — and, we would add, how they become active, mission-appointed believers, not just assenters to the Easter fact.

[77] It would be incorrect to suggest that the apparently " attributive position " of ἠθροισμένους, preceding τοὺς ἕνδεκα κτλ. (cf. J. WANKE, *Emmauserzählung*, 44), gives the participle an attributive *function* in v. 33. The sense of the verse is surely not: " they found the Eleven and their company who were assembled ...," but rather: " they found *that the* Eleven and their company were assembled ..." (NEB), giving the participle a *supplementary* (Bl-Deb n. 416) or " predicative " function (cf. N. TURNER, in J. H. MOULTON, *Grammar of N. T.*

Confirming the participle's pregnant sense is the frequent association of this verb with "gatherings" of the *religious and cultic community* of Israel in the literature of hellenistic Judaism. This is especially true of the compound συναθροίζω (usage reflected at Acts 12,12)[78] but it is also verified often in the use of ἀθροίζω.[79] Considering both this traditional (LXX) flavoring of the verb and the tense of the participle, we are entitled to suggest the Emmaus disciples "found," on their return to Jerusalem, the risen Lord's definitive reconstitution of his assembly of followers. And this suggests, in turn, the close conceptual relationship between the two participles, "*gathered*" and "*saying*": the content of the disciples' confession (λέγοντας) is the event which was the basis of their regrouping (ἠθροισμένους) as the "church-to-be."

> "24,33f. relates that ... the primitive community of disciples was assembled on the strength of this appearance of the resurrected One before Peter. The appearance to Peter thus reassembled the disciples in the congregation of whose previous dispersal the Emmaus pericope

---

Greek III, 160ff.). A predicative function of the participle with verbs of perception and cognition (on Lk's use of εὑρίσκειν as such, cf. chap. I, n. 52) is a classical usage well preserved in the NT; and where the participle refers to the object of cognition, it occasionally precedes the object (e.g. in Acts 7,12; 24,10; II Cor 12,2) rather than follows it (as in Lk 24,2). Lk himself offers, so far as we know, the only three NT instances, apart from the present one, in which εὑρίσκειν is followed immediately by the supplementary participle and the object thereafter: Lk 8,35 (*diff.* Mk 5,15); Lk 22,45 (*diff.* Mk 14,37 / Mt 26,40); Acts 10,27. In both gospel instances, the synoptic parallels display the more conventional word-order (object first), indicating that the front-running participle is a turn of phrase favored by Lk for the sake of emphasis. — The nuance of the *perfect passive* participle, i.e. completed action with perduring effect, gives a pregnant sense to "*were assembled*" and precludes the attributive function, which would make this equivalent to a retrospective relative clause. No "assembling" of the disciples has been mentioned before this, after all; nor has it been said explicitly that "the others" — the broad circle of οἱ γνωστοὶ αὐτῷ (Lk 23,49) — were "with" the Eleven, though 24,24 is an allusive step in that direction. Not that any scattering of the band of followers was reported either, except that the Emmaus wanderers might be taken as a hint of that. We are simply bound to take every word of our skillful author with its proper weight and in its proper order. And following this principle, we are not over-interpreting if we understand the perfect passive ἠθροισμένους to express a *definitive gathering* of the disciples of Jesus. The wayfarers returned thus to a newly and permanently "gathered" Jerusalem community. If he did not intend this special nuance, Lk might better have written ἀθροισθέντας and placed it after τοὺς ἕνδεκα κτλ.

[78] LXX: Ex 35,1; Jos 22,12; I Kgs 7,7; 8,4; 25,1; 28,4; II Kgs 2,30; 3, 21; III Kgs 12,24; 18,19. — Also IV Kgs 10,18 (Aq.); Jos. *Bell.* 2, 289; *Ant.* 3, 84. Cp. I Clem 6,1.

[79] LXX: Gen 49,2; I Kgs 7,5; I Chr 16,35; Ez 36,24. — Also I Macc 3, 44 (ἡ συναγωγή· cp. 3,13: ἄθροισμα καὶ ἐκκλησίαν); 13,2; 14,30; Jos. *Ant.* III, 300: Μωυσῆς εἰς ἐκκλησίαν ἀθροίζει τὸ πλῆθος.

itself bears witness. Hence in this formulary of community tradition which has been inserted into the Emmaus pericope, the appearance to Peter is ... designated as the basis of the new gathering of the corps of disciples .... Jesus, the Kyrios, has summoned the congregation together. As risen Lord, he is the foundation of its existence. It is from this perspective that we are to understand the legend of the Emmaus disciples " (H.-W. BARTSCH, *Wachet*, 23).[80]

The fact that " the Eleven and their company " are the speakers of the formative confession, and that they speak it *first* before the travelers' report, is all true to the Lucan concept of the apostolic circle as primary μάρτυρες τῆς ἀναστάσεως αὐτοῦ (Acts 1,22).[81] This view of the church's origins accounts for the unexpected conclusion Lk composed for the Emmaus narrative. The Eleven *et al.* speak first of the founding Easter experience of Peter, and only then (v. 35) do the two pilgrims announce their experience. The Petrine apparition and the testimony of the apostolic circle thus obtain logical priority in the building of the church. Not that the travelers' encounter is thereby devalued; Lk has recounted it first, after all! On the contrary, the happening " on the road " is authenticated and confirmed by being incorporated into the united Easter witness of the apostolic assembly.[82] This is why v. 34 must precede v. 35 and must be written as it is. — Nothing in this sequence compels us to look beyond the pen of Lk for the source of this pericope's conclusion. Why it is that an apostolic encounter was not *narrated* first, instead of this wayfaring experience of unknown disciples, is an important question which awaits an answer from our further analysis of the pericope and the chapter; but

[80] Cf. also W. DIETRICH, *Petrusbild*, 162f., 175; W. MARXSEN, *Auferstehung*, 56: " Mann weiss also nur von der Erscheinung vor Simon und gründet darin seinen Glauben: Jesus lebt." — On the comparably fundamental, *ecclesial* moment of the Petrine appearance in the confessional formula of I Cor 15,3-5, cf. H. CONZELMANN, " Zur Analyse der Bekenntnisformel I. Kor. 15,3-5," *EvT* 25 (1965, 1-11) 8f.

[81] We believe, however, that this is based on salvation-historical priority (" the Twelve " - destination Israel), not the unique authority of " the Twelve " to vouch for the facts of the Jesus-period, although this idea is favored by Chr. BURCHARD, *Zeuge*, 134f.; G. KLEIN, *Apostel*, 204ff.; U. WILCKENS, *Missionsreden*, 146ff.; S. SCHULZ, *Stunde*, 261; J. ROLOFF, *Apostolat*, 196-198 (more nuanced); N. BROX, *Zeuge*, 50ff.; G. SCHNEIDER, *Verleugnung*, 203ff.; J. WANKE, *Emmauserzählung*, 53. — More on this problematic in chap. IV/ii.

[82] J. WANKE, *BZ* 18 (1974) 187: " Das Erlebnis der Emmauswanderer soll mit dem Credo der Kirche in Verbindung gebracht werden und von diesem her seine Legitimation erhalten." Cf. also WANKE, *Emmauserzählung*, 115; also U. WILCKENS, *Missionsreden*, 147, on the founding function of the witnesses in the schema of salvation-history. — Acknowledging this clear and well-known Lucan framework, we need not follow Ph. SEIDENSTICKER's suggestion that v. 34 devalues the Emmaus disciples' experience (*Auferstehung*, 97).

it is a distinct question which does not affect our diagnosis of the verses at hand.

V. 34 poses well-known questions of provenance which we shall not delve into. Whether it is itself a kerygmatic utterance of the early Church [83] or was composed by Lk from the language of the credal formulas,[84] what matters to us is its function in the evangelist's framework of the Easter story. It seems safe to say, in any case, that the prefatory ὄντως comes from Lk's hand [85] and is meant to make a cross-reference within the larger story of this "third day." Indeed, it is clearly a response to the incredulity of the disciples at the news of the empty tomb (24,11) and, of course, is the more effective and pointed reminder of that in the event that 24,12 proves authentic. The report of Peter's jaunt to the tomb, which brought out the complete and ultimate quandary of human observation of the fact, echoes in the present verse and was its intended prelude. The truth that the tomb did not divulge is now out, for the resurrected One himself, the Kyrios,[86] has "appeared"[87] to Simon,[88] the last of the tomb's observers.

---

[83] H. Grass, *Ostergeschehen*, 107, 186f; J. Dupont. in *Misc. Ubach*, 352ff.; C. H. Dodd, in *More N. T. Studies*, 126; U. Wilckens, *Missionsreden*, 79f.; H.-W. Bartsch, *Wachet*, 23; Ph. Seidensticker, *Auferstehung*, 96, 98; W. Dietrich, *Petrusbild*, 159f. ("... da man bei freier Ausgestaltung eine Angleichung an den Kontext erwarten sollte" [!]).

[84] J. Wanke, *Emmauserzählung*, 50.

[85] On the editorial function of ὄντως: J. Dupont, in *Misc. Ubach*, 353; J. Wanke, *Emmauserzählung*, 44, 45f.

[86] The presence of this title, in place of the expected χριστός, may be an argument against considering v. 34 an integral formulary of pre-Lk kerygmatic usage. The *Christos* title is consistently found in death/resurrection statements amongst NT kerygmata, while *Kyrios* belongs mainly to parousia statements (— this according to W. Kramer's widely accepted analysis of the tradition-history of NT confessional formulae: *Christos - Kyrios-Gottessohn* [AbhTheolA/NTs 44; Zürich/Stuttgart: Zwingli Verlag, 1963] ## 3, 15). Besides, as J. Wanke points out (*Emmauserzählung*, 49f.), there is no similar bipartitle formula (resurrection & appearance) found elsewhere in the NT, hence Lk's statement is hardly fixed usage (*contra* U. Wilckens, in *Dogma und Denkstrukturen*, 73).

[87] ὤφθη is *terminus technicus* of the kerygmatic formulas and not of the Easter narrative tradition, where it does not appear. As standard LXX terminology for appearances of *heavenly personages*, rather than persons reappearing in the circumstances of earthly life (cf. U. Wilckens, in *Dogma und Denkstrukturen*, 82ff., and *Auferstehung*, 38f., 89ff., R. H. Fuller, *Formation*, 30-32), this word's absence from the narrative tradition may suggest a later, "materializing" conception of the risen Lord's appearances in that tradition (so H. Grass, *Ostergeschehen*, 197). If this be the case (cf. the caution of G. Koch, *Auferstehung*, 59, 68ff.), one must conclude that the church-founding appearance to Peter never underwent such a development but remained on the conceptual (and traditio-historical) level of the earlier statements. — Concerning these statements, however, I do not think that U. Wilckens and R. H. Fuller have made a successful case for separating them from the kerygma and establishing a separate

The wayward disciple, who both denied the Master on trial (Lk 22,34. 54ff.) and could only wonder at the sight of the empty tomb, has presumably " turned " and can now " strengthen " his brothers (Lk 22,32 S).[89] Thus is the dialectic of human experience *versus* Easter revelation, which controls the composition of Lk 24, dramatically focused in the person of Peter, who appears so abruptly at corresponding terminal points of the adjoining Easter episodes (vv. 12.34). His was the last word of human incomprehension, the first word of divinely bestowed belief in the risen One!

But there is more to say about ὄντως. It might also be taken to signal an unexpected state of affairs, brought about by God against all human calculation and capability. In this respect, the two occurrences of the word in Lk are noticeably similar: the truth that Jesus " lives," formerly considered ὡσεὶ λῆρος (24,11), is like the truth which the centurion on Calvary " gave glory to God " by acknowledging: ὄντως ὁ ἄνθρωπος οὗτος δίκαιος ἦν (Lk 23,47).[90] The content of the two " confessions " is, in fact, more closely related than appears at first sight. Considering that the words of the Crucified which precede the centurion's are taken from the prayer of the confident sufferer of Ps 31 who ultimately celebrates his *victory* as " *righteous one*," [91] it is probable

category of " legitimation-formulas " as their form-critical explanation (cf. WILCKENS, in *Dogma und Denkstrukturen*, 74ff., 81, 93f.; FULLER, *Formation*, 29f., 48, 49; note 29 above).

[88] The occurrence of Σίμων here (also Lk 22,31), in contrast to Lk's systematic use of Πετρός after the account of Peter's call (Lk 5,1-11), should not be prematurely invoked to support the classification of v. 34 as a pre-Lk confessional statement (as e.g. by W. DIETRICH, *Petrusbild*, 159). An author as skillful as Lk in the use of evocative language may be aiming at precisely a resonance of the vocation epiphany, where Peter's given name is used throughout and the astonished fisherman is transformed into Jesus' leading apostle. Moreover, since the original name also recurred at the supper (22,31), where Jesus explained the fisherman's role in the mystery of the passion and promised his recovery from Satan's snare to lead his fellows once again, the thread connecting these three stages of his experience as disciple — vocation, temptation, conversion and paschal witness — may just be evoked in the echo of the name between 5,3ff.; 22,31; 24,34.

[89] Cf. W. DIETRICH, *Petrusbild*, 173ff. The explanation of the promise in Lk 22,32 in terms of Easter and afterward seems to me much more plausible than that of S. BROWN, *Apostasy and Perseverance*, 72ff., where a peculiar brand of *eisegesis* obtains a triumph of apostolic faith over Satan *during the passion*, which is Satan's onslaught. This interpretation, for which I find no positive support in the texts, must gloss over the problem of disbelief and perplexity at the empty tomb (*ibid.*, 74ff.), alleging that only the women were disbelieved, not the truth; that the Emmaus travelers' *testimonium paupertatis* did not affect the apostles; that v. 12 cannot be integral to Lk's text, etc. The evangelist's mind is not to be learned between his lines in this fashion!

[90] W. DIETRICH, *Petrusbild*, 160.

[91] Lk's version of the cry of the Crucified (23,46/cp. Mk 15,34) suppresses

that the centurion's δίκαιος is, in fact, the *messianic victor* about to be vindicated by God in spite of the human onslaught against him (Acts 3,14f.).[92] If this exegesis (in terms of the wording and context of Ps

---

the Marcan cry of dereliction and seems to articulate, instead, the final "shout" of Mk 15,37 with an accomodation of Ps 31(LXX 30),6: Πάτερ, εἰς χεῖράς σου παρατίθεμαι τὸ πνεῦμά μου (alterations of LXX wording being the result of accomodation to the context; cf. R. BULTMANN, *GsT*, 304; M. RESE, *Altt. Motive*, 200ff.; T. HOLTZ, *Altt. Zitate*, 58f.). Together with Pss 22 and 69, Ps 31 is among the Psalter's laments of the *suffering righteous man* that have the strongest echoes in the canonical passion narratives, and especially in the accounts of the crucifixion (cf. M. DIBELIUS, *Formgeschichte*, 187; E. LOHSE, *Geschichte des Leidens und Sterbens*, 15f.; Lothar RUPPERT, *Jesus als der leidende Gerechte? Der Weg Jesu im Lichte eines alt- und zwischentestamentlichen Motivs* [SBS 59; Stuttgart: Katholisches Bibelwerk, 1972] 50f.; Ellen FLESSEMAN-VAN LEER, "Die Interpretation der Passionsgeschichte vom Alten Testament aus," in H. Conzelmann, *et al.*, *Zur Bedeutung des Todes Jesu*, [79-96] 91f.). — What is special about Ps 31 is that it is the only one among the three which explicitly names "*the righteous one*" as its praying subject (v. 19 [ψ 30,19:] ἄλαλα γενηθήτω τὰ χείλη τὰ δόλια τὰ λαλοῦντα κατὰ τοῦ δικαίου ἀνομίαν...). Moreover, of the standard "thanksgivings" that conclude each of the three psalms and celebrate their sufferers' deliverance (Pss 22,23-32; 31,20-25; 69,31-35), making each composition an appropriate picture of the passion *and resurrection* of Jesus, Ps 31 has perhaps the most exuberant announcement of *salvation already granted* "*the righteous one*" in answer to his confident pleas (cf. esp. vv. 22-23 after vv. 17-19). As L. RUPPERT observes (*op. cit.*, 51), the use of such a composition to illustrate fulfillment of the divine will in the passion of Jesus "... kann ... schwerlich mit Zufall und ohne Rücksicht auf die endgültige Errettung und Verherrlichung des leidende Jesus an Ostern geschehen sein." (For a similar argument re. Ps 22,23ff., cf. H. GESE, "Psalm 22 und das Neue Testament," *ZTK* 65 [1968, 1-22] 11ff. [cf. 16 on Lk's substitution of Ps 31].) — It cannot be accidental, then, that Lk's centurion responds to the cry of the Crucified with a recognition of the sufferer as δίκαιος! The victory celebrated by "the righteous" in the psalm is already in view at the Lucan scene of the crucifixion. The unlikely victor is thus identified with the assistance of the adverb ὄντως. The intent to present the first martyr's death in closest conformity to the passion of his Lord has often been noted as the compositional plan of Acts 6,11ff./7,54ff. (cf. E. LOHSE, "Lukas als Theologe ...," in Braumann-*LkEv*, 86; H. FLENDER, *Heil*, 53; W. GRUNDMANN *Lk.*, 388; J. BIHLER, *Stephanusgeschichte*, 18f.; M. HENGEL, *ZTK* 72 [1975] 190, with the reservations of Chr. BURCHARD, *Zeuge*, 29f.). The protomartyr boldly accuses his accusers of having betrayed and murdered "the righteous one" (Acts 7,52), then faces his own death with the prayer of the Crucified on his lips: Κύριε Ἰησοῦ, δέξαι τὸ πνεῦμά μου (Acts 7,59), yet another accomodation of the prayer of Ps 31. Passion and victory as "righteous ones" thus unite Master and martyr!

[92] Lk has accentuated the *innocence* of Jesus by elaborating a three-fold declaration of it by Pilate (cf. Lk 23,4.14f.22[τρίτον]), and also with the words of the repentant thief that are peculiar to his account (23,41). This is all part of a controlling *passio iusti* theme which runs through the Lucan narrative (cf. M. DIBELIUS, *Formgeschichte*, 202-204; E. LOHSE and H. FLENDER, *loc. cit.* in n. 91 above; G. VOSS, *Christologie*, 110f., 118ff.; L. RUPPERT, *Jesus als der leidende Gerechte?* [cited in n. 91] 57f.; — attributed to the alleged pre-Lucan

31) can be sustained, then a bond of anticipation is seen to unite the two ὄντως proclamations: the reality hidden *sub contrario* and confidently declared in both cases is the triumph of God's "righteous One," crucified by sinful men but about to be raised up by God (Lk 24,7). The prophecies are in the process of being fulfilled as the centurion speaks; they are already fulfilled as the Jerusalem assembly speaks. Each confession affirms the triumph of God's cause which the scriptures forecast: the "righteous One," apparently vanquished by the enemies who plotted his death (Ps 31,14),[93] is "*really*" himself their conqueror since he placed his life in God's hands. Indeed, Lk's revision of the centurion's confession was done in the interests of more than a plausible narration.[94] It involved a typical, two-level presentation of the event:[95]

passion source, along with 23,47, by G. SCHNEIDER, *Verleugnung*, 181 and n. 76). This theme prepares for an important structural component of the Acts kerygma: the guilt of the Jewish populace (leaders and people together; cp. Lk 23, 13ff. with Acts 3,17; 13,27) who, μηδεμίαν αἰτίαν θανάτου εὑρόντες (Acts 13,28), nevertheless gave their "holy and righteous" messiah over to death κατὰ πρόσωπον Πιλάτου, κρίναντος ἐκείνου ἀπολύειν (Acts 3,13f.). Because of the theme of Jesus' innocence, developed in steady counterpoint to the denunciations of the people and their leaders in Lk's passion story, some remain satisfied with a non-messianic sense of "innocent" in the cry of the centurion (so RSV, NEB, NAB, and U. WILCKENS, *Missionsreden*, 169f.). If that is the only meaning of δίκαιος there, however, it is difficult to see why Lk should have introduced it so solemnly as a δοξάζειν τὸν θεόν on the soldier's part (rightly F. SCHÜTZ, *Christus*, 102 n. 483). Acts 7,52 and 22,14 show that Lk is acquainted with ὁ δίκαιος in its titular, messianic usage (admitted by WILCKENS, *op. cit.*, 168f., who nevertheless refuses to extend that sense to Acts 3,14; *e contra*, and rightly, J. DUPONT, *Études sur les Actes*, 147). The fact that the cry of the Crucified in the words of Ps 31 and the recognition of the centurion have been brought into direct juxtaposition, with intervening Marcan material (Mk 15,34-39) either eliminated or transposed by Lk, indicates to us that the profounder sense of *messianic* δίκαιος was intended by him as at least what the sensitive believer was to overhear in the passage. — For background of the titular ὁ δίκαιος· Wis 2,18; PssSol 17,35; rabbinical interpretation of Jer 23,5f.; 33,15; Zech 9,9 (cf. G. SCHRENK, *TWNT* II, 188f.).

[93] The second narrative phase of Ps 31 brings out the menace of *death* under which the sufferer stands (vv. 10-14) The highpoint of that description comes with the לָקַחַת נַפְשִׁי of v. 14 (LXX Ψ 30,14: τοῦ λαβεῖν τὴν ψυχήν μου ἐβουλεύσαντο). Cf. H.-J. KRAUS, *Psalmen* I (Bibl. Komm. A.T. XV/1; Neukirchen: Neukirchener Verlag, ²1961) 247-252.

[94] Such is the only concern that E. LOHSE could suggest as motivating the change (*Geschichte des Leidens und Sterbens*, 98f.).

[95] H. FLENDER (*Heil*, 43ff., 133ff.) makes much of the Lucan *double entendre* involving the human, historical aspect of the *vita Jesu*, observable to all witnesses, and the divine event in him that is visible only to the eye of faith. F. notes the "Spannung von berichtender und auf Glauben zielender Aussage" (133) which one ignores at the expense of adequate interpretation of this author's mind. Ignoring the tension, one obtains an historiography dedicated only to the empirically plausible and demonstrable aspects of the life of Jesus, and it is

that of the pagan observer's reaction at face value, which does have greater verisimilitude than Mk's christological confession; but then, secondly, the level of the astute reader's perception, attuned by the adjoining psalm-verse to the imminent triumph of the messianic " righteous One " in the seemingly dire events at hand. — Now one sees that the parallel confession of the Easter community, for whom the risen Lord's appearances finally bring human perception and revealed truth into harmony, is the announcement that the unexpected victory has been disclosed to Simon. It is he, in fact, who will unite the two confessions in his missionary preaching (Acts 3,14-15): ὑμεῖς δὲ τὸν ἅγιον καὶ δίκαιον ἠρνήσασθε ... ὃν ὁ θεὸς ἤγειρεν ἐκ νεκρῶν· — to which Peter is uniquely qualified to add — οὗ ἡμεῖς μάρτυρές ἐσμεν.

It was thus in the disciples united in proclaiming an Easter truth that transcends empirical observation (ὄντως) that the Christian church was conceived.[96] In fact, however, Lk has yet to recount the apparition in which the risen Lord became known to the whole group of followers. This is why, with apparent inconsistency, he will portray that same group in the next pericope (vv. 36ff.) as quite undisposed to recognize the risen One on his coming into their midst. The self-same dialectic of material fact *vs.* revealed truth will then set in in the third pericope, dividing its exhaustive but fruitless demonstration of the Master's physical reality (vv. 36-43) from the words of instruction and commission (vv. 44ff.) which finally bring belief and witness. In this dialectical structure, as we shall see, the Emmaus and Jerusalem pericopes are fully parallel. And we discovered this basic dynamism of Lk's Easter story already in his adaptation of the empty-tomb tradition.

V. 35, in which the returning disciples can finally relate their experience, furnishes a succinct, two-pronged conclusion to the whole pericope. Indeed, τὰ ἐν τῇ ὁδῷ and ὡς ἐγνώσθη αὐτοῖς ἐν τῇ κλάσει τοῦ ἄρτου recapitulate the entire passage in its two components, the travelers' dialogue and the meal scene. The sentence thus reflects the fully developed story as the evangelist wrote it, rather than any prior, preliterary version.[97] Its form and language, too, support attribution of

---

just such understanding of the Lucan project that is under review in current Lucan studies. — Cf. Acts 22,14 for the association of the titular ὁ δίκαιος with the risen Christ.

[96] This combination of features in Lk's Easter story — the transcendent " inevidence " of the Easter truth and the church-founding orientation of the appearances — is brought out in the essay of M. Brändle, *Orientierung* 24 (1960) 87, 89.

[97] J. Wanke, *Emmauserzählung*, 46, 53f.; also D. A. Losada, *RBibArg* 35 (1973) 8f.; John E. Alsup, *Appearance Stories*, 197. The combination of a concluding " account " of an event with the " return " from it (e.g. Acts 4,23; 9,27; 10,8; 12,17) seems to be a distinctive feature of Lk's narrative style, as Wanke points out. He reminds us, too, that " accounts " of missionaries return-

it to the evangelist. — Regarding form, first of all: the concluding account of an event by its main protagonists, often accompanying their return *in sedem* (Acts 4,23; 9,27; 14,27; cp. also 10,8; 12,17), qualifies as a " stable element of Lucan narrative style " and possibly derives from a commonplace of mission-journey accounts.[98] So far as vocabulary is concerned, the situation is the familiar one of Lk's specialties throughout,[99] of which we devote our attention to two, ἐγνώσθη and ἡ κλάσις τοῦ ἄρτου.

First of all, *re-cognition* (ἐπι-γινώσκειν) is clearly a key concept of the Emmaus story, coming in pivotal points, the beginning (v. 16), the climax (v. 31), and the conclusion (v. 35) of the pericope. Our concluding verse is stating in this respect what the narrative already made clear: that although the travelers' hearts were " burning " during the Stranger's Scripture exposition " on the road " (v. 32), it was properly ἐν τῇ κλάσει τοῦ ἄρτου that the recognition of the risen One occurred (v. 31). The two moments of the encounter belong very closely together, as v. 35 makes clear; hence one may speak of a " hermeneutical function " of the Easter meal in Lk's understanding.[100] This does not mean, however, that it is the reenactment of the familiar ritual that revives the disciples' memories, as if by " something in His manner of taking and breaking the bread, and of uttering the benediction ...." [101] Rather, the emphatic *passive* verb-forms of the narrative — ἐκρατοῦντο in v. 16, διηνοίχθησαν in v. 31, and ἐγνώσθη at hand — express the exclusively *divine action* which brought about the sequence of blindness

---

ed from their journeys are also a feature of this author's books (cf. following note).

[98] Lk 9,10; 10,17; Acts 14,27; cp. the stereotyped statements in Acts 15,3.12; 21,19. The significance of this possible mission-*topos* is enhanced by the parallelism between the Emmaus story and the Philip-sequence of Acts 8,26-40, which we shall consider presently (pp. 111f.).

[99] ἐξηγεῖσθαι = " recount " is Lucan (Acts 10,8; 15,12.14; 21,19; elsewhere in the NT, with different meaning, only Jn 1,18). — τὰ ἐν τῇ ὁδῷ displays both the favored " journey " motif (of which we spoke in explaining 24,13, pp. 89f.) and the kind of substantivizing idiom Lk favors (cf. also 24,19: τὰ περὶ Ἰησοῦ · 24,27; τὰ περὶ ἑαυτοῦ · also Lk 22,37 S; Acts 18,25; 23,11.15; 28,31). — γινώσκειν occurs in Lk most frequently of the Synoptics (28*x* vs. 20 Mt, 12 Mk), and its passive usage occurs also in Lk 8,17 *diff.* Mk; 12,2(Q); Acts 9,24. Note, too, the threefold (ἐπι-) γινώσκειν in the present pericope (vv. 16.31.35). — ἡ κλάσις τοῦ ἄρτου, characterizing the eucharistic meal (and as a *terminus technicus*) is exclusively Lucan (Acts 2,42; cf. the verbal expression κλάσαι τὸν ἄρτον in Acts 2,46; 20,7.11; 27,35).

[100] J. WANKE, *Eucharistieverständnis*, 41. Cf. also F. MUSSNER, *Auferstehung*, 141.

[101] A. PLUMMER, *Lk*, 557 (although P. recognizes the force of the passives as implying " divine interposition "); also D. P. FULLER, *Easter Faith*, 231. It is equally irrelevant how the disciples' " wearied physical and mental faculties " were " restored " (A. R. C. LEANEY, *Lk*, 293).

and recognition.[102] In the travelers' encounter with the risen Christ, culminating in his " breaking of the bread " with them, the divinely appointed moment for the lifting of the veil of mystery over his person and destiny had come to pass.[103] The messianic *krypsis* was a matter of time precisely ordained and delimited by the divine will (cf. pp. 40f.), which arranged all of sacred history with the Easter Christ as its focal point (cf. 24,27). " Only personal encounter with the resurrected One could produce faith " in his person,[104] hence the moment of recognition in the Easter story was punctually determined by the Will which had charted Jesus' course (24,26). It is simply not a question of the rhythms and motives of human knowledge ! — But granting this, why was the *fractio panis* the moment ? Why was it precisely that which brought the decisive disclosure (ἐγνώσθη) ? Better still : what is the relationship between the " eye-opening " of the *fractio* and the " scripture-opening " of the journey (τὰ ἐν τῇ ὁδῷ) in the scrupulous economy of Lk's narrative ?

A closer analysis of his *fractio*-motif may give us an answer to our question. The expression, both in its nominal (Acts 2,42 and here) and verbal forms (Acts 2,46 ; 20,7.11 ; cp. Lk 9,16[Mk]; 22,19[Mk]; 24,30 [S]), serves our historian as a " connecting link " between the meals of Jesus with his disciples and the eucharistic repasts of the early Christian churches.[105] But this linkage of terminology only directs our attention to more important aspects of continuity in the meals. In both ministries, the Lord's and the church's, the " breaking of the bread " is associated with the *instruction concerning his person and mission* of which he, the earthly Master, had established the prototype. In the episode of the feeding of the mutitude, for example, whose echoes are so strong in the Emmaus meal-scene (Lk 9,10b-17/24,29-30),

[102] Rightly C. R. Bowen, *Biblical World* 35 (1910) 239, 241 ; A. Loisy, *Luc*, 581 ; H. Grass, *Ostergeschehen*, 37f. ; E. Lohse, *Auferstehung*, 30 ; E. Earl Ellis, *Lk*, 277 ; A. Ehrhardt, *NTS* 10 (1963-64) 184 ; J. Reidl, *BibLit* 40 (1967) 90 ; C. F. Evans, *Resurrection*, 106 ; J. Schmid, *Lk.*, 356, 359, and J. Ernst, *Lk.*, 659, 663f. (both less specifically, but equivalently). The same point seems to be made also by B. Rigaux, *Dieu l'a ressuscité*, 230, but with unperspicuous attempts at clarification. More to the point : J. E. Alsup, *Appearance Stories*, 196f.

[103] We shall take up later the relationship between the passive forms of this account and the comparable ones which accompany the passion prophecies at Lk 9,45 and 18,34 (cp. 19,42), on which cf. chap. I, p. 24 and note 68. Cf. the discussion *ad* v. 16, under no. 4 below.

[104] X. Léon-Dufour, *Résurrection*, 215.

[105] J. Wanke, *Eucharistieverständnis*, 40 ; also 43 : " Die Ostererscheinung beim Mahl wird durch die Interpretation mit Hilfe des Terminus ' Brotbrechen ' zu einem Urbild des Gemeindemahles. Was dort zu Emmaus geschah, wiederholt sich nach Auskunft des Evangelisten im eucharistischen Tun der Gemeinde." Cf. also D. A. Losada, *RBibArg* 35 (1973) 10ff. ; J. Ernst, *Lk.*, 664, 665f.

Lk redefines the dominical διδάσκειν prefacing Mk's miracle (6,34) as a λαλεῖν περὶ τῆς βασιλείας τοῦ θεοῦ (Lk 9,11), the very same instructional program that was to mark the appearances (and meals!) of the risen Christ according to Acts 1,3f.[106] Moreover, we recall with what drastic curtailment of Mk's sequence the feeding of the multitude was made to adjoin directly the beginning of Jesus' instruction on *the mystery of his passion* (Lk 9,18ff.; cf. chap. I, n. 102). This redactional "splicing" of Mk created a sequence of *meal-scene and passion-forecast* which made all the beneficiaries of the miraculous *fractio* become the audience straightway instructed on following the suffering messiah (Lk 9,23: ἔλεγεν δὲ πρὸς πάντας)![107] — The very same sequence recurs in Lk's account of the Lord's Supper. There, too, the Marcan sequence is broken after the institution narrative for the insertion of a lengthy *instruction concerning the Master's destiny* (22,22.37) *and his disciples' participation therein* (22,24-38).[108] — Taken as ensembles, therefore, the

---

[106] Due to the rarity of συναλιζόμενος in Acts 1,4, one cannot be fully certain of the sequence of λέγων τὰ περὶ τῆς βασιλείας κτλ. and eucharistic repast in Acts 1,3f., although Lk 24,43 and Acts 10,41, and the resumptive pattern followed in Acts 1,2ff., make it more probable that the disputed word does mean "eating together with" (root ἅλς; cf. E. HAENCHEN, *Apg.*, 110 n. 1; H. CONZELMANN, *Apg.*², 25 [inclination]; J. ROLOFF, *Kerygma*, 254ff.; R. PESCH, in *EKK Vorarb.* III, 24; M. WILCOX, *Semitisms of Acts*, 106-109, esp. 108).

[107] H. CONZELMANN, "Zur Lukasanalyse," in Braumann-*LkEv*, 53: "... immer noch ist das Volk aus der Speisungsszene da."

[108] It seems clear that, whatever the origin of the special traditions he transcribes in 22,14-38, Lk is himself the designer of the ensemble, which he has shaped into something of a "eucharistic parenesis" (A. VÖÖBUS, *ZNW* 61 [1970] 108; cf. also M. DIBELIUS, *Formgeschichte*, 201f.; R. BULTMANN, *GsT*, 302; E. ELTESTER, in *Jesus in Nazareth*, 132-134), as against the unviable prior-document hypotheses of H. SCHÜRMANN, *Jesu Abschiedsrede*, 140; G. SCHNEIDER, *Verleugnung*, 142, 149. — The passion-mystery is the *necessity* of the messiah's passion, as we have seen, and Lk interprets that necessity in terms of the fulfillment of the scriptures in Jesus' "way" (cf. p. 45 above). It is this combination that we discern between 22,22 (κατὰ τὸ ὡρισμένον) and 22,37 (τοῦτο τὸ γεγραμμένον δεῖ τελεσθῆναι...). The citation of Is 53,12 at Lk 22,37 has influenced Lk's passion narrative, as can be seen from the insertion of 23,32 (*diff.* Mk/Mt), the addition of κακοῦργοι (cf. 23,32: ἕτεροι δύο σὺν αὐτῷ) in 23,33, and the uniquely Lucan scene in 23,39-43. Considering these factors, M. RESE considers the addition of the fulfillment-citation in 22,37 to be the evangelist's initiative and theologoumenon (cf. *Altt. Motive*, 160, 164), although the prophecy could as well have been cited by the tradition beforehand. It suffices to notice how, with his solemn introduction to the Isaian citation there, Lk has created something of a literary inclusion with the beginning of the supper dialogue (v. 22: κατὰ τὸ ὡρισμένον); and it was very probably his initiative which transferred the mysterious reference to Judas's treachery from its Marcan position prior to the institution account (Mk 14,21) to the position *directly* following it. We have, in other words, a well-rounded sequence following the institution account that *Lk himself* has assembled and designed as a discourse of the Master on the mystery of his destiny and its implications. The association of this instruc-

sequences of Lk 9,10-27 and 22,14-38 are symmetrical combinations of dominical *feeding and self-revelation.* In Lk's mind, *the Master breaking bread with his followers is the Master sharing his mission and destiny with them*! This is why the order is reversed, but the combination of self-disclosing instruction and "breaking of the bread" is the same in the Emmaus story. It corresponds perfectly, and in chiastic design, to the pattern of self-revelation already set in those earlier episodes of feeding and instruction. It expounds, as they had, the combination of *messianic destiny and Master-disciple solidarity* which, for Lk, forms the heart of the christological revelation formerly veiled in cryptic *gesture-and-word* of the earthly Jesus, but fully accessible in the Easter Christ's lucid *word-and-gesture.*

> When the "*breaking of the bread*" is encountered as a community meal in Acts, there is likewise a fixed association of missionary instruction with it.[109] On one occasion, this instruction reflects the confidence of the missionary in the face of the mortal danger he constantly faces. For the intrepid Paul "breaking bread" on the stormy seas (Acts 27,33-36), the circumstance of life endangered on the path of the mission is surely not a neutral detail in the narrative.[110] "Breaking bread" on the threatening seas, Paul is clearly

tion with the "breaking of the bread" is the result of his construction here, as also in the cases of Lk 9 and Lk 24.

[109] The first "summary" passage in Acts, offering a condensed portraiture of the apostolic community rendered *church* by the Pentecost Spirit-outpouring, combines the διδαχὴ τῶν ἀποστόλων and the common life with ἡ κλάσις τοῦ ἄρτου and "the prayers" (Acts 2,42). With this close association of *didache* and *fractio,* Lk may be attesting the formation already in his own day of a Christian divine service consisting of both proclamation of the word and eucharistic repast (cf. R. ORLETT, *CBQ* 21 [1959] 218; J. JEREMIAS, *Abendmahlsworte*³, 112), or he may not (E. HAENCHEN, *Apg.*, 153; H. CONZELMANN, *Apg.*², 37); the point is that, in keeping instruction and *fractio* together, Lk means to show how the apostolic church continued to observe the practice of the Lord himself. If "breaking bread" was the framework of the Master's sharing his own mission and destiny with his followers, then the church remained true to this commission by continuing to instruct the meal-participants concerning the Lord's saving mission. — Is it not the intention of Lk to imply the association of such instruction with the meal by imposing the liturgical framework upon the anecdote of Paul at Troas, Acts 20,7-12 (cf. M. DIBELIUS, *Aufsätze zur Apg.*, 22-23; H. CONZELMANN, *Apg.*², 125; W. SCHENK, in *Theol. Versuche* II, 76f.; J. WANKE, *Eucharistieverständnis*, 21f.)? The miracle worked by the missionary ἐν τῇ μιᾷ τῶν σαββάτων (!), in which the young man become νεκρός (v. 9) is restored to life (v. 12: ζῶντα), demonstrates in so many words the close connection between the mystery of the Lord's passage and the "breaking of the bread" (vv. 10f.). The missionary is steward and dispenser of the power of that mystery.

[110] Aptly A. VÖÖBUS, *ZNW* 61 (1970) 104: "In Trübsal und Lebensgefahr auf den Wellen des Mittelmeeres — ganz allein solch ein Hintergrund muss den Leser schon dazu angeregt haben, sich tiefere Gedanken zu machen — nimmt Paulus das Brot, bricht und isst es .... Seine (des Lk) eigentliche Absicht kommt

Lk's exemplar of the charismatic, itinerant missionary, pursuing his task in the face of the lethal dangers he shares with the Master before him, and finding strength in the latter's promise: θρὶξ ἐκ τῆς κεφαλῆς ὑμῶν οὐ μὴ ἀπόληται (Acts 27,34/cp. Lk 21,18 / [Lk 12,7 Q]).

Now we better understand how the two stages of the Emmaus story — τὰ ἐν τῇ ὁδῷ and ἡ κλάσις τοῦ ἄρτου — form an integral christological revelation according to established Lucan pattern. Instruction on the destiny and following of the messiah falls together consistently with breaking of the bread to illustrate how the Master bequeathed his own mission integrally to his followers. One might say the Emmaus story displays the moment and mode of his bequest. The design and composition of the whole pericope can be seen to be substantially Lucan, following a pattern clearly discernible elsewhere in this author's combinations and framings of traditional material. — To the extent that the association of passion destiny and *fractio panis* belongs to a Lucan blueprint of the itinerant Christian mission, of which Acts features Paul as heroic prototype, we might have a clue to the *ambient* whence some of Lk's traditions derive and/or to which his writing is addressed. But lest we run on ahead of our analysis, let us return to discussing the framework passages of our appearance story.

Cleopas's Account of the "Third Day" (Lk 24,21b-24)

The familiar details of time, place, and persons stand out in the resumé of recent events given to the Stranger by Cleopas: the "third day" in v. 21b, Jerusalem in v. 18, the stable *coetus personarum* in vv. 22, 24. This observation, plus the fact that Cleopas is made to rehearse *Lk's own rendition* of the Jesus-tradition, particularly of the *triduum sacrum*, ought to alert us to the likelihood that the evangelist himself composed the traveler's *relatio* in its entirety.[111] Nevertheless

in den knappen Bemerkungen klar genug zum Vorschein: εὔθυμοι δὲ γενόμενοι. Ohne Zweifel sollen diese Worte auf die Gabe des Herrenmahles hindeuten." — Considering the reservations of E. HAENCHEN (*Apg.*, 632 n. 2), H. CONZELMANN (*Apg.*², 155), and H. PATSCH, *ZNW* 62 (1971) 217, 225f., we should think only in terms of a eucharistic figure, not a meal of the same sacramental kind as at Troas. Yet, "eucharist or no eucharist" may be a false alternative, as J. WANKE contends (*Eucharistieverständnis*, 28f.). Without concerning himself about the practical probabilities of the situation, Lk meant to teach what v. 34b expresses, viz.: "den Sinn der Mahlzeit damals und der Eucharistie für jede Zeit ...: τοῦτο γὰρ πρὸς τῆς ὑμετέρας σωτηρίας ὑπάρχει."

111 Correctly A. LOISY, *Luc*, 577; also E. MEYER, *Ursprung und Anfänge* I, 26 n. 1. — On Lk's version of the Jesus-tradition in vv. 18ff.: J. DUPONT, in *Misc. Ubach*, 355-357, and *L'év. de Luc. Mém. Cerfaux*, 337; P. SCHUBERT, in *Ntl. Studien f. Bultmann*, 177. Cf. also I. H. MARSHALL on the integrity of this passage, otherwise wholly in the historicizing vein and scarcely helpful for critical analysis (*TyndB* 24 [1973] 89f.).

some exegetes, concentrating on the supposedly better sequence of v. 21(a) and v. 25 and the apparently digressive character of vv. (21b) 22-24, prefer to distinguish a prior and final version of the passage on this basis. They thus ascribe vv. (21b)22-24 to Lk or some other interpolator, and suggest that one or the other expanded the original account in the conviction that " the two disciples would certainly have related everything that had occurred up to that moment." [112] But this view lacks a sound foundation in literary criticism, for the whole account of Cleopas is of a piece and v. 25 builds as readily on v. 24, the observers' conundrum at the empty tomb, as on the frustrated messianic hopes of v. 21a.[113] — Let us approach this passage, first, by reassuring ourselves that it comes from the hand of the designer of the Easter story as a whole, and then by posing the question whether it is an attachment to a preexistent context or integrally part of a larger compositional unit.

First, on the *issue of Lucan authorship*: the literary device of resuming and varying previously narrated events in direct discourse is a familiar feature of this author's historiography.[114] No independent source-material need be invoked, therefore, to explain the unprecedented details of what is, on the whole, a perfect précis of *Lk's* empty-tomb episode, vv. 22-24. The phrase ἐξέστησαν ἡμᾶς (v. 22) echoes Mk 16,8 and belongs to the vocabulary of messianic concealment, as we brought out above, *ad* 24,12 (p. 67).[115] The phrase ὀπτασίαν ἀγγέλων ἑωρακέναι (v. 23) represents the same variation on ἄνδρες δύο in 24,4 as occurs between ὑπὸ ἀγγέλου ἁγίου in Acts 10,22 and ἰδοὺ ἀνὴρ ἔστη in Acts 10,30. Moreover, as we also proposed *ad* 24,12, τινές in v. 24, in con-

---

[112] H.-D. BETZ, *ZTK* 66 (1969) 10. Cf. also J. WELLHAUSEN, *Lc.*, 140 (Glossator); H. GRASS, *Ostergeschehen*, 36 (Lk or Glossator); P. WINTER, *ST* 8 (1954) 167f. A pre-Lk expansion is supposed by R. H. FULLER (*Formation*, 105, 113) and BETZ (*art. cit.*, 9). Supporting Lk's own insertion of the digression into an antecedently formed context: M. DIBELIUS, *Formgeschichte*, 191; N. HUFFMAN, *JBL* 64 (1945) 219; E. LOHSE, *Auferstehung*, 27f.; H.-W. BARTSCH, *Wachet*, 23; G. KEGEL, *Auferstehung*, 88; J. KREMER, *Osterbotschaft*, 62, 67.

[113] Rightly J. M. CREED, *Lk.*, 296, and J. WANKE, *Emmauserzählung*, 82f.

[114] The verbal summaries of earlier narrative are especially noticeable in Acts, of course, where the second and third accounts of Paul's conversion (22, 3-21; 26,4-20), the resumés of the Cornelius episode by Peter (11,5-17; 15,7-9), and the letter of Claudius Lysias (23,26-30) are perhaps the most familiar examples. — We have already had occasion to cite " repetition and variation " as an important technique of this author (chap. I, n. 110), dedicated to demonstrating the divinely guided continuity of his story. We are encountering a significant instance of this in the Emmaus traveler's retrospect.

[115] With ἐξέστησαν cp. ἐξιστάνων in Acts 8,9, referring to the sensation caused by the preternatural arts of Simon Magus at Samaria. These are the only two instances of a transitive use of the verb(s) in the NT (cf. A. PLUMMER, *Lk*, 554).

trast to Peter alone at v. 12, results from typical, cross-referential procedure on the evangelist's part, showing a tradition here which he had altered for his own purposes in the earlier statement (cf. p. 65 above). — So far as the rest of vv. 22-24 is concerned, its derivation from *Lk's editing* of the empty-tomb story is made clear as day by its concise, resonating language.[116]

So much for vv. 21b-24. So obviously do these verses reinforce the Emmaus story's Easter-day framework (hence its incorporation into Lk 24), and so unmistakably do they resume and condense the Lucan *specifica* of vv. 1-12, that we can be secure in ascribing them to the hand of our evangelist. — But are these verses different in this respect from what surrounds them? Cannot the same compositional origin be argued for the travelers' dialogue as a whole, both the *relatio* by Cleopas (in which the "digression" plays an integral part) and the response by the Stranger? Once again, it is our exegesis of the tomb story which suggests the further look at Lk's designs for the whole dialogue.

We pointed out above (p. 18) that the concluding words of Cleopas, αὐτὸν δὲ οὐκ εἶδον (v. 24), effectively capture Lk's point in editing the tomb sequence since they express the ultimate perplexity of the observers which was that episode's only outcome. We took special note of the contrast Lk developed between the observers' verification of *all* the *bruta facta paschalia* and their ever-deepening incomprehension of what they meant (pp. 55f.). To dramatize this complete *échec* of human cognition, and consequently the wholly gratuitous gift of the Easter faith, Lk has employed the motif of empirical totality to link the empty-tomb and Emmaus narratives, carrying the idea along pointedly from the women's report (v. 9) to the wayfarers' discussion (v. 14) and, finally, to the account given to the Stranger (v. 21b). Within the Emmaus dialogue itself, there is a studied continuity between πάντων τῶν συμβεβηκότων τούτων of the initial discussion (v. 14), οἱ λόγοι οὗτοι of the Stranger's query (v. 17), τὰ γενόμενα... ἐν ταῖς ἡμέραις ταύταις (v. 18), τὰ περὶ Ἰησοῦ τοῦ Ναζαρηνοῦ (v. 19), and σὺν πᾶσιν τούτοις (v.

---

[116] So rightly J. WANKE, *Emmauserzählung*, 73ff.; F. SCHNIDER / W. STENGER, *BZ* 16 (1972) 101f.: ὀρθριναί (v. 22) corresponds to ὄρθρου βαθέως of 24,1 (*diff.* Mk); μὴ εὑροῦσαι τὸ σῶμα αὐτοῦ and οἳ λέγουσιν αὐτὸν ζῆν of v. 23 both correspond to unique traits of the Lucan tomb story (24,3.5), due, as we saw, to purposeful revising of Mk. Lk alone among the evangelists recorded the *non-finding* of the *body* and placed this before the angelic encounter (so v. 23), thus accentuating the dichotomy between empirical observation, producing only ἀπορεῖσθαι (24,4), and the faith that was still unborn at the tomb. We saw, too, how the angels' chiding question concerning the women's quest of ὁ ζῶν in the realm of the dead (24,23: οἳ λέγ. αὐτὸν ζῆν) was Lk's purposeful suppression of a positive correlation between the Easter truth and the fact of the empty tomb.

21b) of the disciple's response. All this is calculated dramatization of the human observers' *aporia* (v. 24); the *totality of facts* is developed in ironic counterpoint to their *total incomprehension* by those who experience and recount them. Rescue from this *aporia* will come only *sola gratia* with the resurrected Lord's instruction, and that is the climax towards which Lk's composition builds.

Our survey urges that the dialogue en route to Emmaus came integrally from the same hand as refashioned the Marcan tomb story. The same dialectic is instilled in both, and the " totality " of Cleopas's account is essential to that dialectic.[117] Not only is the " digression " of vv. 21b-24 integrally part of its context, but both are the product of the larger compositional plan which this evangelist followed in creating his own Easter story. — We hope now to reinforce this assessment with analysis of the whole dialogue, vv. 17-27.

(3) *The Travelers' Dialogue* (24,17-27)

A vivid exchange leads up to the disciple's recital of recent events and deluded hopes. One of our evangelist's special skills is recognizable in the way the scene is now enlivened and elucidated by the *dialogue*.[118] In particular, the *leading questions* of a protagonist, often the main one, are used to advance the author's perspectives, and this both where he appears to be composing freely[119] and where he is adhering closely to source-material.[120] So here, too, the Stranger's questions build pathos and anticipation towards the point where he himself, the questioner, will become the teacher uttering the final answer (v. 25: καὶ αὐτὸς εἶπεν πρὸς αὐτούς·).[121] This dialogue-sequence, with its engaging pedag-

[117] A. LOISY, *Luc*, 577. Cf. also H.-D. BETZ, *ZTK* 66 (1969) 10: " Kleopas und sein Freund wissen im Grund nicht, was dort geschehen ist, obwohl sie Augenzeugen der sogenannten 'reinen Tatsachen' gewesen sind, während dieser Reisende im Verlauf der Erzählung ihnen offenbaren wird, was 'in Wahrheit' geschehen ist." — In ascribing the whole of the dialogue to the evangelist, we join forces with (and hopefully enhance the view of): P. SCHUBERT, in *Ntl. Studien f. Bultmann*, 174f.; U. WILCKENS, *Auferstehung*, 79ff.; F. SCHNIDER / W. STENGER, *BZ* 16 (1972) 100-102; F. SCHNIDER, *Prophet*, 124ff.; J. WANKE, *Emmauserzählung*, 118ff.; J. E. ALSUP, *Appearance Stories*, 192ff.

[118] H. FLENDER, *Heil*, 79ff.; E. HAENCHEN, " Tradition und Komposition in der Apg.," *ZTK* 52 (1955, 205-225 / now in *Gott und Mensch*, 206-226:) 212/213: " Er lehrt nicht wie ein Dogmatiker, sondern eher wie ein Dramatiker." Cf. also J. WANKE, *Emmauserzählung*, 56f.

[119] Acts 1,6; 2,37; (cp. Lk 3,10-13); 4,7; 8,30-31.34; 16,30; 17,18.19; 19, 2.3, etc. Perhaps also Lk 1,34. — W. GRUNDMANN (*Lk.*, 100) notices how often question/answer combinations occur in the *Sondergut*.

[120] Lk 3,10-13; 13,23 (red. introd. to v. 24); 17,37 (red. link between vv. 35 and 37b), etc.

[121] H.-D. BETZ (*ZTK* 66 [1969] 11, 12) comments on the exchange of roles: questioner/teacher, guest/host. The latter was noticed by C. R. BOWEN, *Biblical World* 35 (1910) 238.

ogy, reminds us of the very similar encounter between Philip, the itinerant preacher from the " hellenist " ranks, and the Ethiopian eunuch en route to Jerusalem (Acts 8,26-39). The parallel design of the two passages has been pointed out frequently,[122] and some suggest that their analogy is meant to press a point of continuity between the Easter *wayfarers'* experience and the exposure of the nascent Gentile churches to the comings and goings of wayfaring missionaries.[123] Philip, like the risen Lord, comes on the scene as a stranger. His questions lead to a travelers' dialogue, and the dialogue builds to his *christological exposition of the scriptures,* with focus on the mystery of the *messiah's passion* (Acts 8,32ff.; cp. Is 53,7-8 LXX). A sacramental action, baptism, and the strange expositor's disappearance conclude the scene, just as the sacramental repast and the Lord's disappearance close the Emmaus episode. — It would be hard to deny that the composing hand in both these passages is the same. Indeed, " Luke, who composed both accounts and put his personal stamp on them, shows us here a manner of narrating that is proper to him. It was not in his sources that he found the schema of these narratives; he constructed them himself." [124] This judgment does not settle all tradition-historical questions raised by the parallelism of the two passages; but for the moment we shall be satisfied with what it contributes to the analysis of the composition at hand.

First, we observe that the journey and its dialogue are swiftly brought to the point of the messianic *Leidensgeheimnis* in the Philip episode (vv. 30-34), and it seems to us that there is no delay in getting to that point on the road to Emmaus, either. The Stranger's leading question reflects the thematic connection of *journey* and *discussion of the facta paschalia* (v. 17: ἀντιβάλλετε ... περιπατοῦντες), and the same connection had been established in the evangelist's introduction (vv. 13f.: ἦσαν πορευόμενοι ... καὶ αὐτοὶ ὡμίλουν). Clearly the connection is

[122] A. Loisy, *Luc*, 574; J. Dupont, in *Misc. Ubach*, 361f., 372; J. Grassi, *CBQ* 26 (1964) 464f.; J. Kremer, *Osterbotschaft*, 68ff.; X. Léon-Dufour, *Résurrection*, 213f.; M. Kehl, *GeistLeb* 43 (1970) 103f.; J. Wanke, *Emmauserzählung*, 122, and *BZ* 18 (1974) 192; I. H. Marshall, *TyndB* 24 (1973) 79 (and n. 92), 85; D. A. Losada, *RBibArg* 35 (1973) 11f.

[123] So C. R. Bowen, J. Grassi, J. Wanke, and D. A. Losada, listed in the previous note. Writes Wanke: " Was in der Aethiopiergeschichte exemplarisch als missionarisches Bemühen der Kirche herausgestellt wird, hat nach Auskunft des Evangelisten seine Grundlegung im Tun (Lk 24,25ff.) und Auftrag (24,44ff.) des Auferstandenen." Wanke leaves a more exact determination of the *Sitz-im-Leben* of the tradition in the status of unanswered question (*op. cit.*, 125), and most others who mention the mission situation do so only by way of speculative suggestion. We wonder if some definite clues might be sought, at least.

[124] J. Dupont, in *Misc. Ubach*, 362. Even I. H. Marshall has to acknowledge the literary interdependency of the two passages, though he insists this does not prejudice the historicity of either (*TyndB* 24 [1973] 88).

a concept of Lk himself. — Next, introducing the response of Cleopas, we hear that the travelers stood still, σκυθρωποί (" with gloomy looks "); and rather than imagining the actual psychological state of the followers after Good Friday which might be authentically captured here,[125] let us ask again, insistently: what does our author understand by it? Does he not intend to portray the travelers *still under the pall of the passion-mystery*? At least once before, the sentiment of " sorrow " (λύπη) was associated with the concealment of Jesus' destiny, still incomprehensible to the dozing disciples (Lk 22,45) on the threshold of the terrible events themselves.[126] Besides, if we make σκυθρωποί a partner of two other descriptive expressions which come after the disciple's *relatio*, viz. ἀνόητοι, and βραδεῖς τῇ καρδίᾳ (v. 25), we can see that the whole *relatio* has been placed in a framework of expressions belonging to the theme of the *Leidensgeheimnis*. All three descriptions belong to the motif of the disciples' bewilderment and incomprehension under the pall of the great *mysterium*. The journey-discussion format is thus reminiscent of the great " journey " of the gospel, which was also framed by the exposition and atmosphere of the mystery.[127] Whether this reminiscence is intended or not requires further probing, of course.

The first rejoinder of Cleopas (v. 18) betrays its articulation by Lk immediately. Not only the Jerusalem locale of the sacred events but their unrestricted *publicity* among the Jews[128] is of special interest to him and gets repeated emphasis in his writing. The witness of " *all the people* " is thus invoked by Cleopas as it is on numerous occasions

[125] Emphasized by VON CAMPENHAUSEN, BORNKAMM, and FULLER (*loc. cit.* in n. 3 above). The fascination held for some by Lk's portrayal of the disciples' state of mind becomes obstructive of sound interpretation when the exegete will not see beyond a supposed pre-Easter, " disappointed " understanding of Jesus in 24,19ff. — The interesting variant reading of v. 17 in A²D it*var* sy*rsc* has ἐστε in place of ἐστάθησαν, hence carries the Stranger's question forward to σκυθρωποί rather than stopping it at περιπατοῦντες. This reading is favored in nearly the entire Latin textual tradition, but it has been given up by most moderns, who find ἐστάθησαν the most likely source of the variants (including ἔστησαν in L; cf. A. PLUMMER, *Lk*, 552).

[126] Cf. again Lk's anticipation of the Gethsemane sleeping scene at Lk 9,32 (in light of our remarks on p. 23 and n. 66 [chap. I] above).

[127] Lk 9-18, framed by 9,18-45 and 18,31-34. By the separation of the third passion prediction from the sequence of the first two (hence also from the rhythm of Mk's placement), Lk was able to make the mystery of the passion the framework of the " journey " section (H. CONZELMANN, *MdZ*, 57 n. 2). On the essential relation between passion-mystery and " journey " narrative, cf. *MdZ*, 184, 185 n. 1; H.-W. BARTSCH, *Wachet*, 94f., and pp. 34ff. above.

[128] On the characteristic Lucan emphasis on the publicity of Jesus' deeds, cf. H. SCHÜRMANN, *Lk.* I, 260, 322; F. SCHNIDER, *Prophet*, 124f.; M. VÖLKEL, *ZNW* 64 (1973) 226ff. CONZELMANN speaks of the dialectic of publicity and secrecy as a " typisch lukanische Doppelheit," brought out strongly at Lk 9,21f.23, *contra* Mk (cf. Braumann-*LkEv*, 53).

elsewhere (v. 19 : ἐναντίον τοῦ θεοῦ καὶ παντὸς τοῦ λαοῦ · cp. Lk 2,52 ; — other occasions [*diff.* Mk :] Lk 8,47 ; 9,13 ; 20,45 ; [*diff.* Mt :] Lk 3, 21 ; [S-Lk :] 1,10 ; 2,10.31 ; 4,14f.[red.] ; 7,29[red.] ; 18,43. Cp. Acts 4,10 ; 2,47 ; 3,9.11 ; 5,34). Indeed, the impact of Jesus' ministry on " all the people " was the consequence of its extension to *all* the precincts of Palestinian Jewry (cf. Lk 23,5[= Acts 10,37; cp. Lk 4,14f. 43f. ; 5,17 ; 6,17] ; 19,48 ; 21,38).[129] In no sense were τὰ γενόμενα[130] hidden from anyone's sight (cf. Acts 2,22 ; 26,26 : οὐ γάρ ἐστιν ἐν γονίᾳ πεπραγμένον τοῦτο) ; yet, paradoxically, their meaning evaded all, even the disciples ! The " totality " motif merely sharpens the dichotomy between man's vision and God's revelation, and so the unrestricted *openness* of the messiah's ministry stands in a highly expressive Lucan contrast to the undiluted *mystery* of his person and destiny. The events, universally witnessed and nowhere really understood, represent *God's* kingdom ἐντὸς ὑμῶν, *God's* action ἐν μέσῳ ὑμῶν (Lk 17,21 ; Acts 2,22). They can be understood as divine, saving events only through the gift of the Easter Christ, whom *God* ἔδωκεν ... ἐμφανῆ γενέσθαι (Acts 10,40). — In other words, the Lucan publicity motif, like the detailed observations of the paschal onlookers, functions within an overall dialectical argument advanced by this author. Its purpose is not the straightforward evidential argument of the apologetic historian.[131]

" *The Things Concerning Jesus of Nazareth* " (24,19ff.)

The retrospect of Cleopas begins with a depiction of Jesus as divinely endowed *prophet* : ἀνὴρ προφήτης δυνατὸς ἐν ἔργῳ καὶ λόγῳ. This characterization, together with the assertion of full publicity amongst the people, contains pointed echoes of Lk's introductory summary of Jesus' ministry ἐν τῇ δυνάμει τοῦ πνεύματος (Lk 4,14 ; cp. Acts 10,38).[132] The

---

[129] Similarly the ministry of the Baptist : Lk 3,15.18.21 ; Acts 13,24.

[130] Also a turn of phrase typical of our author ; cp. Lk 2,15 : τὸ ῥῆμα τοῦτο τὸ γεγονός · Acts 10,37 : τὸ γενόμενον ῥῆμα · Lk 13,17 ; and esp. Lk 8,34 *diff.* Mk ; 8,56 ; 23,47 *diff.* Mk/*par.* Mt.

[131] Cf. H. Flender, *Heil,* 64, 149, on the importance of Lk's dialectic of observable fact and sacred truth.

[132] On the close and systematic connection made by Lk between πνεῦμα ἅγιον and δύναμις (= miracle-power), cf. G. W. H. Lampe, in *Studies in the Gospels,* 171-172, 194ff. ; H. Conzelmann, *MdZ,* 170f. ; U. Wilckens, *Missionsreden,* 108. By using the Spirit as motivating factor in the successive changes which inaugurate Jesus' public ministry (Lk 4,1 ; 4,14f.) — thus carrying the Spirit-endowment forward editorially from the scene of the baptism (Lk 3,22 ; cf. K. L. Schmidt, *Rahmen,* 37) — Lk shows his prime interest in drawing a *pneumatic portrait* of the Master ministering to Israel (cf. H. Schürmann, *Lk.* I, 222 ; F. Hahn, *Hoheitstitel,* 318f.). The broad generalization in the summary of Lk 4,14-15 gives it the character of a title-sentence for the ministry-phase that it inaugurates, — and this much more clearly than in the counterparts of Mk 1,

δύναμις of his deeds and words was the fruit of his " Spirit " endowment (Lk 3,22 ; 4,1), and this was programmatic of Lk's account of the public ministry. Its first display was in the charismatic dominical *teaching* (Lk 4,14f.22.32.36), but then it was seen as the " power " to exorcize (Lk 4,36) and to heal (Lk 5,17 ; 6,19 ; cp. 8,46[Mk]). As Lk tells the story, it was first of all as pneumatic teacher and healer that the messiah was presented to Israel (Lk 4,17ff. ; 6,17-19 ; Acts 10,37-38), " accredited " by God before " the men of Israel " by " *acts of power* and wonders and signs that God performed through him " in their midst.[133] The same pattern of presentation and accreditation applied to the messiah's followers in the worldwide mission (Lk 9,1: ἔδωκεν αὐτοῖς δύναμιν [*diff.* Mk 6,7] ; Lk 24,49 S : ἕως οὗ ἐνδύσησθε ἐξ ὕψους δύναμιν), hence the motif of the Spirit's *dynamis* can also permeate the story of the nascent church (Acts 1,8 ; 3,12 ; 4,7.33 [= the Twelve] ; 6,8 [Stephen] ; 8,13 [Philip] ; 19,11-12 [Paul]). Moreover, corresponding to the articulation of the messianic ministry in powerful " deed and word " (Lk 24,19 ; Acts 1,1) is the combination of wondrous things " seen and heard " as credentials of the Lord's witnesses (Lk 7,22 ; 10,24 ; Acts 4,20 ; cp. Acts 22,15 ; 2,33). — All of which illustrates our evangelist's special interest in the charismatic, *thaumaturgical* feature of both the ministry of Jesus and the mission of the church.[134] This interest is often discussed in terms of an intensified Lucan portraiture of Master and disciples after the image of the hellenistic wonder-men, the θεῖοι ἄνδρες,[135] a model appropriated by both Jewish and Christian

14-15 and Mt 4,23ff. (cf. K. L. Schmidt, *op. cit.*, 37f. ; H. Conzelmann, *MdZ*, 23ff. ; G. Voss, *Christologie*, 134f.).

[133] The Acts kerygma which depicts the public ministry of Jesus (esp. 2,22 ; 10,37ff.) adheres closely to the pattern of presentation in the third gospel, hence is to be judged the author's own (rightly U. Wilckens, *Missionsreden*, 109, 121ff. ; E. Kränkl, *Jesus*, 98-101).

[134] The presentation of Paul's ministry in Acts is representative of this interest and, as such, presents certain contrasts to the Apostle's own definition of the *essential nature* of his apostolic ministry, e.g. in II Cor 10-13, where he opts for the *cruciform* apostolate as against the charismatic (cf. G. Bornkamm, *Paulus*[2] [Stuttgart/Berlin : Kohlhammer, 1969] 91ff. ; also 81ff. ; H.-W. Kuhn, *ZTK* 67 [1970] 304). It is not that the Paul of Acts does not embrace the Master's cross ; he precisely does as soon as he sets his course to Jerusalem, according to the Lucan schema (Acts 19,21). The question is, has Lk, in making Paul's successes in the mission mainly a matter of successful thaumaturgy against pagan rivals (Acts 19,20 ! ; cf. the particularly massive portrayal in Acts 19,11f.), not shown himself a more attentive student of the growing Pauline legend of early Christendom than of the Paul we know from the epistles (cf. C. K. Barrett, " Pauline Controversies in the Post-Pauline Period," *NTS* 20 [1973-74, 229-245] 240 ; H.-M. Schenke, " Das Weiterwirken des Paulus und die Pflege seines Erbes durch die Paulus-Schule," *NTS* 21 [1974-75, 505-518] 511f.) ?

[135] H. Köster, in Robinson-Köster, *Trajectories*, 191, 218f. ; H.-D. Betz, " Jesus as Divine Man," in F. T. Trotter, ed., *Jesus and the Historian, written*

propagandists[136] and a probable developmental impulse in the gospel tradition.[137] While it would not appear that Lk, any more than his fellow evangelists, gives complete endorsement to such a christological model,[138] his emphasis on miracles and Pneuma-power as a major continuum between the missions of Jesus and his followers cannot be disputed.[139] Just how this factor is seasoned by this evangelist and

---

in Honor of Ernest C. Colwell (Philadelphia: Westminster, 1968, 114-133) 126; H.-W. KUHN, *ZTK* 67 (1970) 303f.; S. SCHULZ, *Stunde*, 281, 286.

[136] The most thorough and frequently cited exposition of this model in the religious propaganda of the period is D. GEORGI, *Die Gegner des Paulus*, 145ff., 210ff. (specifically on Lk 24,19, cf. 217). Cf. also H. WINDISCH, *Paulus und Christus. Ein biblisch-religionsgeschichtlicher Vergleich* (*UntNT* 24; Leipzig: J. C. Hinrichs, 1934) 101ff., 115ff.; H.-W. KUHN, *ZTK* 67 (1970) 304ff.; P. J. ACHTEMEIER, *Interpr* 26 (1972) 187ff.; S. SCHULZ, *Stunde*, 68f. Cf. also M. DIBELIUS, *Formgeschichte*, 93f.

[137] R. BULTMANN, *GsT*, 256; H. BRAUN, "Der Sinn der neutestamentlichen Christologie," in *Gesammelte Studien zum N. T. und seiner Umwelt* (Tübingen: J. C. B. Mohr, 1962, 243-282) 255ff.; D. GEORGI, *Die Gegner des Paulus*, 213ff., 289; F. HAHN, *Hoheitstitel*, 295-308; S. SCHULZ, *Stunde*, 67ff.; H. KÖSTER, in *Trajectories*, 187ff.; P. J. ACHTEMEIER, *Interpr* 26 (1972) 174-197; H.-W. KUHN, *Ältere Sammlungen im Markusevangelium* (StUmweNT 8; Göttingen: Vandenhoeck und Ruprecht, 1971) 192ff. — I do not mean to ignore the legitimate objections raised against the use of the Greek rubric, θεῖος ἀνήρ, as if it embodied a uniform conception. The miracle-men to whom scholars usually attach the expression emerge in *written* sources only of the late second century (E. SCHWEIZER, *Jesus*, 127 n. 10). Moreover, witnesses of the biblical tradition generally avoid the term and concept θεῖος, as L. BIELER was careful to point out (ΘΕΙΟΣ ΑΝΗΡ II, 24-25); and the designation itself tends, in recent discussion, to suppress a broad diversity of traits in the sources with a synthetic conglomerate idea that could apply partially to anyone, wholly to no one (so D. L. TIEDE, *Charismatic Figure*, 246, 254f.). Cf. also the caution expressed by H. CONZELMANN, *TRu* 37 (1972) 244; H. C. KEE, *JBL* 92 (1973) 402-422; U. LUZ, "Das Jesusbild der vormarkinischen Tradition," in G. Strecker, hrsg., *Jesus Christus in Historie und Theologie. Ntl. Festschrift für H. Conzelmann* (Tübingen: J. C. B. Mohr, 1975, 347-374) 362-365.

[138] Just as Mk seems to follow Paul in placing the charismatic and thaumaturgical portraits of Christ under the shadow of the Crucified (S. SCHULZ, *Stunde*, 75ff.; H. KÖSTER, in *Trajectories*, 189; K. KERTELGE, *Die Wunder Jesu im Markusevangelium. Eine redaktionsgeschichtliche Untersuchung* [StANT 23; München: Kösel-Verlag, 1970] 38), apparently applying the messianic-secret motif to this end (so H. CONZELMANN, in *Zur Bedeutung des Todes Jesu*, 41f.; L. E. KECK, "The Introduction to Mark's Gospel," *NTS* 12 [1965-66, 353-370] 368), so it would seem that Lk intends to teach the christological unity of the two portraits (*contra* H.-D. BETZ, *art. cit.* [in n. 135 above] 129). Both images have their place in Jesus' course, though perhaps Lk does insist more than the other evangelists do on the "accrediting" force of the miracles (e. g. Acts 2,22) (cf. P. J. ACHTEMEIER, *JBL* 94 [1975] 552ff.).

[139] H. CONZELMANN, *MdZ*, 171f.; S. SCHULZ, *Stunde*, 288; H.-W. KUHN, *ZTK* 67 (1970) 305; G. W. H. LAMPE, "Miracles in the Acts of the Apostles," in C. F. D. Moule, ed., *Miracles: Cambridge Studies in their Philosophy and History* (London: A. R. Mowbray, 1965) 165-178.

integrated into his christology, we shall attempt to discover in analyzing the passage at hand, — though we already have a suggestion for the path of synthesis from our study of the passion mystery in the empty-tomb story (*ad* 24,6b, pp. 33-38).

Prophet: An important frame of reference for the traveler's charismatic portrait of his Master is the title "prophet," which will offer us crucial clues to Lk's integrated christology and its tradition-historical background. Because the title occurs only in maxims quoted by Jesus (Lk 4,24; 13,33) and witness-reactions (Lk 7,16; [7,39;] 9, 8.19; 24,19) in the gospel and is something less than a mainstay of the kerygma in Acts (3,22f. [= Dt 18,15f.]; 7,37 [= Dt 18,15]), some interpreters insist that Lk employs it only as a deficient christological model, to be counteracted or corrected by the fuller *argumentum* in which it occurs.[140] Others accept it as a positive component of Lk's christology,[141] noting both the title's relative prominence in his gospel (7*x* compared to Mt 2*x*, Mk 1*x*, Jn 4*x*, and 5*x* of 7 in S-Lk) and the considerable importance to him of the tradition of the prophets' destiny in Israel as a key to understanding Jesus' own (cf. Lk 13,33; 4,24ff.; Acts 7,52, etc.). We are in agreement with this positive evaluation of the title in Lucan usage, and to support it we point out, first of all, the echo created between the words of Cleopas and the Jewish public's reaction to the raising of the widow's son at Nain:

> The words of Cleopas join ἀνὴρ προφήτης δυνατὸς κτλ. to the expectation of ὁ μέλλων λυτροῦσθαι τὸν Ἰσραήλ (24,19.21), and the crowd reaction at Nain was similarly bipartite: προφήτης μέγας ἠγέρθη ἐν ἡμῖν, and ἐπεσκέψατο ὁ θεὸς τὸν λαὸν αὐτοῦ (Lk 7,16). If the second member of this acclamation correctly assesses the situation (cp. Lk 19,44; 1,68), so also must the first; and in fact, the combination of the two places Jesus' mighty prophecy in a unique, eschatological framework.[142] On the other hand, situating the Nain story (from his

---

[140] U. WILCKENS, *Missionsreden*³, 201 n. 5; H. SCHÜRMANN, *Lk.* I, 402f., 507f.; M. RESE, *Altt. Motive*, 206; J. WANKE, *BZ* 18 (1974) 189, and *Emmauserzählung*, 60ff.

[141] F. GILS, *Jésus Prophète*, 45; A. HASTINGS, *Prophet and Witness*, 50-75; G. VOSS, *Christologie*, 155-170; A. DENAUX, in F. Neirynck, éd., *L'év. de Luc. Mém. Cerfaux*, 282; F. SCHNIDER, *Prophet*, 237f.; W. RADL, *Paulus und Jesus*, 281ff.; R. GLÖCKNER, *Verkündigung*, 164ff.; J. NAVONE, *Themes*, 132-140; E. FRANKLIN, *Christ the Lord*, 67ff.

[142] Note especially the adjective μέγας with προφήτης, and the eschatological implications of the divine "visitation" (F. HAHN, *Hoheitstitel*, 392; G. FRIEDRICH, *TWNT* VI, 847f.; cp. also M. RESE, *Altt. Motive*, 168). The absence, however, of both the definite article with προφήτης and any allusion to Dt 18,15 or Moses makes it inadmissible to posit the figure of the *Mosaic* prophet at this point (rightly F. SCHNIDER, *Prophet*, 110; H. SCHÜRMANN, *Lk.* I, 402 n. 104; *contra* K. H. RENGSTORF, *Lk.*, 97; F. HAHN, *loc. cit.*).

Sondergut) in conjunction with the great christological testimony to the Baptist's envoys (Lk 7,18ff. / Mt 11,2ff. -Q), Lk has given the crowd's reaction at Nain a much fuller context; and he has also furnished a fuller documentation of the answer to John's query concerning *the messiah*, ὁ ἐρχόμενος, whose mighty deeds are now *shown* to include: νεκροὶ ἐγείρονται (Lk 7,22 Q).[143] Now, too, the wonder-worker of the special source-narrative, who repeated Elia's mediation of divine power in a beleaguered widow's behalf,[144] is shown to be the one who fulfills the *messianic* expectation, the *Kyrios* himself (Lk 7,13[19*l.v.*]). " In a certain sense, then, Lk has ' christologized ' the source here, hence ' corrected ' it also, but without eliminating the assertion that, in Jesus, God raised up a great prophet for his people. For Lk also, Jesus remains the great prophet of God " (F. SCHNIDER, *Prophet*, 115). — No one maintains that the pre-Lucan choral conclusion[145] *adequately* expressed Lk's understanding of Christ. But neither is the designation " prophet " to be considered false or misleading just because it is *preliminary* (rightly F. SCHÜTZ, *Christus*, 35 n. 114). Lk is not arguing dialectically when he applies the title to Christ; he is building positively towards a fuller portrait of him.[146]

By attaching the Nain story to Jesus' statement to the Baptist, as the latter's prelude, Lk thus indicates one trajectory of his christological argument, which is: the *prophet*, acclaimed for mighty works, is the *messiah*, ὁ ἐρχόμενος (7,16.19f.). But that is not all. The Q sequence inaugurated by the Baptist's question (Lk 7,18-35/cp. Mt 11,

[143] H. SCHÜRMANN, *Lk.* I, 404; J. ERNST, *Lk.*, 242; F. SCHNIDER, *Prophet*, 112f.; H. CONZELMANN, *MdZ*, 197 n. 1. The same concern to " document " Jesus' claim of 7,22 can be seen in the special mention of sight restored to " many blind folk " in the redactional v. 21 (cf. n. 64 above), for whereas this category of healings comes first in the response (v. 22 Q), none has yet been narrated in Lk (cf. E. KLOSTERMANN, *Lk.*, 90). On the basis of such preparations for v. 22, Lk could change the words " see and hear " there to the *aorist* ἃ εἴδετε καὶ ἠκούσατε (cp. Mt 11,4), " denn er weist historisierend auf die Taten zurück, welche die Boten — nach Vers 21 — selbst sahen und von denen sie hörten " (P. HOFFMANN, *Logienquelle*, 193).

[144] On the influence of I (LXX III) Kgs 17,8-24 on the Nain story, including verbal echoes at Lk 7,11 (I Kgs 17,9-10) and 7,15 (17,23), cf. F. GILS, *Jésus prophète*, 26f.; H.-W. BARTSCH, *Wachet*, 80f.; J.-D. DUBOIS, *RHPhilRel* 53 (1973) 168. — We leave the question of a direct literary modelling open; F. SCHNIDER (*Prophet*, 109) is in favor, H. SCHÜRMANN (*Lk.* I, 405) is opposed. The verbal resonances do not seem to be accidental, in any case.

[145] Such " choral conclusions " as Lk 7,16 represent one way of recording a miracle's impact on the witnesses; as such, they belong to the miracle-story form, hence Lk 7,16 was wholly or partially in the traditional pericope as Lk received it (cf. M. DIBELIUS, *Formgeschichte*, 71f.; R. BULTMANN, *GsT*, 230; H. SCHÜRMANN, *Lk.* I, 402f.; F. SCHNIDER, *Prophet*, 108).

[146] *Contra* SCHÜRMANN and WANKE. At least the latter concedes that the evangelist does not throw the prophet-model out of court altogether (*Emmauserzählung*, 61; cp. SCHÜRMANN, *Lk.* I, 530).

2-12.16-19) embraces two crucial aspects of the ministry of Jesus which Lk associates with his *prophetic* role: it begins with a demonstation of the *mighty works* of ὁ ἐρχόμενος (7,22) and ends on the note of the people's *rejection* of the two envoys of Wisdom (7,31ff.).[147] Here are the two contrasting phases of Jesus' " way " which we brought out once before in explaining the gospel's program of christological exposition (cf. p. 37 above): the ministry of *wondrous deeds*, which we associated with Galilee and Galilean aspirations, and the *destination to violent rejection*, which we understood to be the rationale of the Lucan " journey " to Jerusalem. Now we take note of the fact that both of these christological phases, so dramatically confronted at Lk 9,43f. and 19, 37ff., belong to the *prophet's role* attributed to Jesus by Lk. Each phase has its programmatic episode: the Nazareth scene in the first phase (Lk 4,16-30),[148] the Lord's statement in response to Herod's threat (Lk 13,31-33)[149] as thematic principle of the " travel " sec-

[147] Cf. D. LÜHRMANN, *Redaktion*, 31, speaking of the Q-passage without the addition of Lk 7,29-30; on the latter, cf. P. HOFFMANN, *Logienquelle*, 194ff.

[148] H. SCHÜRMANN's dubious source-analysis of the Nazareth pericope, which seeks to derive the narrative and its summary introduction (4,14f.) from Q (cf. *Mélanges Rigaux*, 200ff.), allows him to ascribe the strong prophet-model of the passage to the source (*ibid.*, 190), hence remove it from Lk's own proper interest (cf. also *Lk.* I, 229 n. 59, 243; also J. WANKE, *Emmauserzählung*, 61). It is puzzling, too, that F. SCHNIDER denies that the model is specifically prophetic in Lk 4,24-27, only to conclude: " Das Verständnis von Jesu Geschick als Prophetenschicksal nimmt darin eine untergeordnete Rolle ein, darf aber nicht übersehen werden " (*Prophet*, 166, 167). — Rightly C. Voss, *Christologie*, 158: " Die mit ἐπ' ἀληθείας eingeleiteten folgenden Verse (4,25ff. - R. D.) zeigen, dass προφήτης kein für das tertium comparationis nebensächlicher Bestandteil dieses Sprichwortes (i.e. 4,24 – R. D.) ist, dass vielmehr der Ton gerade darauf liegt, dass Jesus als *Prophet* ... zu ihnen gekommen ist " (emph. his). Cf. also F. HAHN, *Hoheitstitel*, 395f.; P. STUHLMACHER, *Evangelium* I, 226ff.; M. RESE, *Altt. Motive*, 143-154. — However one deals with the question of prior source-material in the Nazareth pericope, he must acknowledge at least that Lk knew Mk 6,1-6a and the Marcan sequence and chose to revise both for this inaugural episode of the public life (cf. H. CONZELMANN, *MdZ*, 26). Even if one is not willing to opt simply for a Lucan reconstruction of Mk here (as favored by W. ELTESTER, in *Jesus in Nazareth*, 135-136, and R. C. TANNEHILL, *ibid.*, 52), one should admit minimally that Lk is responsible for the position of the Nazareth episode and the choice of a version of the story which best served his own requirements for a full-scale, programatic overture to the public life. (We shall express our preference for S-Lk derivation in chap. IV/i lc.)

[149] The connection of the two themes here is most probably Lk's work, considering the difficult conjunction of vv. 32 and 33 and the latter's focus on the Lucan " journey " (πορεύεσθαι). It is likely that the original apophthegm contained only the warning to Jesus and his response that his mission would be guided to its completion (τελειοῦμαι) undeterred by Herod's threat (v. 32). V. 33 would then be an insertion by the evangelist, furnishing a transition to the Q piece, 13,34f., and a thematic explanation of the " journey " presently in course. This hypothesis of O. STECK (*Israel*, 43ff.) is also favored by K. LEH-

tion.[150] Both key passages coordinate the two phases, mighty works and violent rejection, as two necessary steps in Jesus' mission. Indeed, the Herod response makes them both matters of the ultimate, divinely ordained necessity : δεῖ ! Moreover, at what we might call the dividing line between the two phases, the confession of Peter (Lk 9,18ff.),[151] the popular enthusiasm for Jesus as " Elia ... (or) one of the *prophets* of old " has been recorded twice in the immediate context, on either side of the feeding miracle right before the confession (9,8.19).[152] Lk's severe editing of Mk here has intensified both the circumstance of Jesus' (and his disciples') thaumaturgy [153] and the public acclaim of him as

MANN, *Auferweckt*, 234f. ; F. SCHNIDER, *Prophet*, 168ff. ; M. MIYOSHI, *Anfang*, 23f. ; P. von der OSTEN-SACKEN, *EvT* 33 (1973) 487 n. 41. In any case, the redactional origin of v. 33 is widely accepted, whether one considers its content to be a traditional prophet's maxim (U. WILCKENS, *Missionsreden*³, 201 ; cp. F. SCHNIDER, *Prophet*, 172 : open question) or a construction of Lk himself (O. H. STECK, *op. cit.*, 46f., following A. LOISY, *ad loc.*).

[150] The redaction-critics have sensitized us to the function of 13,33 as key to the whole program and theology of the Lucan " travel " section ; so H. CONZELMANN, *MdZ*, 57 (" in diesem Worte steckt das sachliche Darstellungsprinzip des Abschnitts ...") ; A. HASTINGS, *Prophet and Witness*, 109 ; W. OTT, *Gebet und Heil*, 34 ; G. LOHFINK, *Himmelfahrt*, 213. It is no longer satisfactory to view 13,31-33 as an old tradition simply taken over by the evangelist (*pace* R. MEYER, *Prophet*, 121 ; J. SCHNEIDER, in *Synoptische Studien*, 215). Yet it would seem excessive to make the three verses wholly a construct of the evangelist, as A. DENAUX has done (in F. Neirynck, éd., *L'év. de Luc. Mém. Cerfaux*, 252ff.). In our opinion, the analysis of STECK (prev. note) represents the viable, form-critically defensible middle-ground which is best taken on this passage.

[151] W. DIETRICH, *Petrusbild*, 103 ; P. von der OSTEN-SACKEN, *EvT* 33 (1973) 478.

[152] The two Marcan recordings of public opinion about Jesus, one connected with Herod's quandary (Mk 6,14-16) and the other with Peter's confession (Mk 8,27f.), have been drawn much closer together in Lk 9,7-9.18f., with massive elimination of Marcan material in between (Mk 6,17-29.45-56 ; 7,1-8,26). H. SCHÜRMANN observes : " Wenn Kunst im Weglassen besteht, dann hat Luk diesen Können hier meisterhaft unter Beweis gestellt " (*Lk.* I, 526). Only the feeding of the five thousand (Lk 9,10b-17 / Mk 6,32-44) separates the two public-opinion passages after Lk's curtailments, so that the " messianic question," articulated almost identically in both instances, both frames the feeding miracle and prefaces the sequence of messianic confession and passion instruction. — On this editorial operation, cf. H. CONZELMANN and E. E. ELLIS, cited in chap. I, n. 102.

[153] No less important to Lk's new construct in chap. 9 is the older Marcan sequence of the disciples' mission and Herod's question (Mk 6,6b-16), which Lk has retained in 9,1-9 but with a characteristic redoubling of emphasis on the *thaumaturgical* aspect of both pieces. Note the additions to Mk : δύναμιν καὶ / καὶ νόσους θεραπεύειν (9,1) ; καὶ ἰᾶσθαι (9,2) ; θεραπεύοντες πανταχοῦ (9,6) ; τὰ γινόμενα πάντα (9,7) ; τίς δέ ἐστιν ... ἀκούω τοιαῦτα ; καὶ ἐζήτει ἰδεῖν αὐτόν (9,9 — cf. chap. I, n. 101). Notice also the elimination of Mk's καὶ ὅσα ἐδίδαξαν (Mk 6,30) and consequent focus exclusively on ὅσα ἐποίησαν in Lk 9,10. Lk thus instills the motive for the question of Jesus' identity (Mk 6,14) more specifically into the sequence of events surrounding it, so that both t mes the ques-

prophet[154] in direct preparation for Peter's confession and the subsequent passion instruction. When these follow next in Lk's story (9,20ff.), the familiar lines of christological argument are completed which were already set down in Lk 4 and Lk 7: the *mighty prophet* is God's *messiah*, the *miracle man* is now destined for *violent rejection* (πολλὰ παθεῖν καὶ ἀποδοκιμασθῆναι). These are the intersecting paths our author repeatedly follows in setting forth the mystery of Christ.

Prophet (*like Moses*) *Mighty and Rejected*! The christological schema we have been exploring resulted in all cases from *redactional* selection and combination of source-materials. The same interest accounts fully for the words of Cleopas in 24,19ff., just as the evangelist's "passion-mystery" accounts for the fact that he utters them without under-

---

tion is raised we know exactly what public opinion is reacting to, viz. *the abundance of mighty works* both performed and deputed "every-where" by this mystery-man!

[154] The three-fold division of public opinion reported in both Lk 9,7f. and 9,19 is reducible to one opinion: that a great *prophet* has come back from the other world (H. SCHÜRMANN, *Lk.* I, 507), either being "raised up" or, in Elia's case, "appearing," according to their mode of departure from this world formerly. As against SCHÜRMANN, who concentrates on the fallacy of all three views, it is important to recognize that, for Lk, there is *quid verum, quid falsum* in the three opinions, whose syntactical parallelism in 9,7f. (*diff.* Mk) shows that they are being considered *per modum unius*. There are several reasons for thinking that the prophet-assertion reductively asserted in all three is no longer being taken as a mere foil for the Petrine confession, as in Mk, but forms a positive threshold for the messianic statement, with the three variants building up to the apostle's utterance in something of a climax-pattern (so H. FLENDER, *Heil*, 50; J. ERNST, *Lk.*, 295). First, the opinions are attributed to the well-disposed ὄχλοι (cf. G. LOHFINK, *Sammlung Israels*, 40ff.) rather than the adversary ἄνθρωποι of Mk 8,27.33. Moreover, although Lk's new version of the third opinion (προφήτης τις τῶν ἀρχαίων ἀνέστη) contains the mistaken notion that Jesus is τις τῶν ἀρχαίων, the rest of the opinion — προφήτης ἀνέστη — will be equivalently stated in the temple speech of Peter, Acts 3,22.26, in assertion of the fulfillment of Dt 18,15 (also Acts 7,37): προφήτην ὑμῖν ἀναστήσει κύριος ὁ θεὸς κτλ. (cf. ἀναστήσας, Acts 3,26). It is premature to be speaking yet of Mosaic-prophet christology in Lk 9, as M. RESE tentatively does (*Altt. Motive*, 206; rightly J. ERNST, *Lk.*, 288). But certain aspects of what the crowds say are surely right: that a prophet has arisen, that he is recognizable as such because his great deeds remind one of οἱ ἀρχαῖοι. The missing dimensions are basically those that will also be missing from Peter's confession: the harsh destiny that awaits this prophet, just like the ἀρχαῖοι, and the fuller sense of ἀνέστη that will be said of him after he has suffered that fate (Acts 3,22). As we shall see, it is only after Easter that Lucan christology can assimilate the motif of the *Mosaic prophet*, fulfillment of all Moses wrote and "like him" in both wonders and rejection (Acts 7,35ff.), whom God truly "raised up" in fulfillment of Moses' promise. — We conclude: the popular opinions about Christ in Lk are not simply false and diversionary; they build up climactically to Peter's confession, forming with it the progression *prophet-messiah* which we already observed in Lk 7, 16ff. The third of the three opinions, summing up and generalizing the other two, brings out the one note about Christ which prepares the crowds for genuine understanding of him.

standing. In the first place, it is now fully understood that his characterization of Jesus as wonder-working prophet — ἀνὴρ προφήτης κτλ. — is not the survival of some primitive and flawed christological viewpoint,[155] it is specifically and recognizably Lucan, depicting the first phase of Jesus' mission and the first step in understanding him. The traveler's words are echoed almost exactly in Stephen's eulogy of Moses: ἦν δὲ δυνατὸς ἐν λόγοις καὶ ἔργοις αὐτοῦ (Acts 7,22), and the martyr's argument is that the combination in Moses' mission of mighty works and rejection by the Israelites (7,35-36) is what made his promise of the future prophet *like himself* authentic (7, 37: οὗτός ἐστιν ὁ Μωϋσῆς ...).[156] Correspondingly, when Cleopas next, in familiar sequence, gives a material description of the prophet's dire fate, in words redolent

---

[155] *Pace* F. HAHN, *Hoheitstitel*, 388; R.H. FULLER, *Formation*, 110; I.H. MARSHALL, *Luke*, 125f.; J. ERNST, *Lk.*, 657, 660. That Lk 24,19 is "archaic christology" is frequently heard, but none the more accurate for the frequency of the assertion!

[156] The most distinctive feature of the Mosaic messianism that comes into its own in Acts is the depiction of Moses and Jesus as *leaders rejected by the Israelites* (cf. F. SCHNIDER, *Prophet*, 98-99; J. DUPONT, *Études*, 250; F. SCHÜTZ, *Christus*, 34f.). Note the parallel statements of this motif in Acts 3,14f. (Jesus) and Acts 7,35 (Moses). In connection with the motif in Acts 7, and as preamble to the christological application of Dt 18,15 in 7,37, there is the companion picture of Moses as *wonder-worker*. This parallelism between the two speeches elucidates the core of Peter's kerygma at the temple gate, where the miracle performed by the power of Jesus' "name" furnishes that member of the partnership thaumaturgy/rejection. This is the mystery whose full dimensions could only appear when Easter had illumined all the scriptures: the wonder-working *prophet* in Moses' image is the *messiah* rejected by God's people, as Moses had been; thus did God bring to fulfillment the unanimous prophetic testimony, παθεῖν τὸν χριστὸν αὐτοῦ (Acts 3,17). The speech in Acts 3 brings the Mosaic-prophet and servant designations together (ἀνιστάναι related to both: 3,22.26; cp. 3,13), and Moses emerges as the messiah's prototype as well as his principal prophetic witness (cf. G. VOSS, *Christologie*, 183f.; F. SCHÜTZ, *Christus*, 83). In explaining the miracle preceding the speech, Peter addresses the misunderstanding that the apostles have worked it ἰδίᾳ δυνάμει ἢ ἀσεβείᾳ (3,12), whereas it is rather God's "servant," Jesus, whom he has "glorified," in whose name — hence by whose mediation of divine δύναμις — the wondrous deed was done (vv. 13.16; cp. 4,30). Whereas the "servant" statement of 3,13 is usually explained as an allusion to Is 52,13 (e.g. by J. DUPONT, *Études*, 260; U. WILCKENS, *Missionsreden*, 38; K. KLIESCH, *Credo*, 128f.), the statement of v. 26, which echoes and resumes it, is plainly linked by ἀναστήσας to the citation of Dt 18,15 in v. 22 (cf. U. WILCKENS, *op. cit.*, 43; F. HAHN, *Hoheitstitel*, 385f.; H. CONZELMANN, *Apg.*², 41; M. RESE, *Altt. Motive*, 70; J. ERNST, in *Schriftauslegung*, 181f.). Moses, as messianic prototype and principal scriptural prophet, is truly the focus of the argument from prophecy in the temple sermon. Consequently, the strong resonance between 3,14f. and 7,35 is comparable to the resonance between Lk 24,19 and Acts 7,22. Mosaic-prophet christology is important to Lk, but he must wait until Easter and afterward to instill it fully into his narrative.

of the Lord's own passion prophecies (Lk 24,20),[157] he is articulating the second christological phase, successor to the first in Lk's schema (v. 19), but as yet uncomprehended by him. This second phase set in in the wake of Peter's confession and gave to the gospel's central section the literary form of a "journey" from Galilee to Jerusalem.[158] It constitutes the essence of Jesus' messiahship, in Lk's thinking;[159] it is the critical step in faith's understanding of him, and it can come — so our chapter teaches — only in the form of the risen Lord's *gift*, imparted with his personal presence and clarifying word of instruction.

Why precisely *miracles and* passion in Lk's schema? Why his repeated emphasis on this partnership?[160] — First of all, it furnishes a *salvation-historical schema* through which the continuity of Jesus' mission with his predecessors' (the prophets') and his successors' (the Christian missionaries') can remain constantly before Lk's reader. It is thus made into a *literary schema*, a principle for the arrangement, enlargement, and fusion of sources, hence a pattern of *editorial comment upon the sources.* (Lk 9,43-45, where the miracle story is directly connected to the second passion prophecy, and the latter is pared to focus on the passion-destiny alone, is an excellent case in point.[161]) By means of this literary schema Lk constantly instills the *law of the prophets' destiny* which governs the missions of Jesus (Lk) and his witnesses (Acts), just as it had governed the prophets' ministries of old, led by Moses and including the Baptist.[162]

---

[157] U. WILCKENS, *Missionsreden*, 116. — Instances: παρέδωκαν ... ἐσταύρωσαν (cf. 24,7); εἰς κρίμα θανάτου· cp. Mk 10,33 *diff*. Lk 18,31! and Lk 23,40; οἱ ἀρχιερεῖς καὶ οἱ ἄρχοντες· Lk 23,13 (9,22).

[158] F. SCHÜTZ's attempt to remove the passion from the motive of the journey in Lk 13,33 (*Christus*, 70) is unsuccessful and careless of the differences between the christological phases of Lk's narrative. The prospect of Jesus' rejection does accompany him in earlier stages of the gospel (*ibid*., 81), but the narrative from Lk 9,51 onward is a formal preparation of the *reader* for the story's denouement and its existential implications.

[159] Reread H. CONZELMANN, *MdZ*, 57, quoted in chap. I, n. 106.

[160] Pointed out, but without considerable exegetical consequence, by H. FLENDER, *Heil*, 35 n. 113, and F. SCHÜTZ, *Christus*, 67; more expansively by U. BUSSE, *Wunder*, 372ff. It is true that Mk set the pattern of juxtaposing the traditions of wonder-worker and sufferer in his version of the gospel; but it is Lk who makes this juxtaposition systematic and explicit, and he finds salvation-historical basis for this pattern in the perennial experiences of the prophets.

[161] In this case, an implicit dialectic in Mk's sequence is given explicit commentary (9,43b), so that the tension between wondrous deeds and imminent passion can be understood as a factor in concealing the latter from the disciples (9,45). The incomprehension motif is not thereby psychologized; rather, the divinely disposed succession of "days" (Lk 9,36) is better illustrated as a succession of stages of christological revelation (— and assimilation!).

[162] Apart from Mk 6,14, miracles are not associated with John the Baptist

It is fairly clear how the schema works in the *composition of Acts*. The sequence of *cc. 3-4*, for example, begins with the apostles' miracle and continues with the account of their rejection and trial. The kerygmatic discourse in between (3,13-26) sets forth the prophetic models of Jesus and Moses, and the community prayer following the apostles' release again coordinates the motifs of rejection (4,25-29) and miracles (4,30). — *Acts 5* is even more clearly arranged according to the schema: miracles (vv. 1-16), rejection (vv. 17-42, including kerygmatic discourse). — The experience of *Stephen* extends the prophetic law, and its literary schema as well, to the mission of the "Hellenists." Stephen's "great wonders and signs" (6,8) immediately precede his trial (6,9ff.) and ultimate martyrdom after the pattern of Jesus' own (6,11-14; 7,54-60); and the great discourse in between fully expounds the salvation-historical pattern which unites Moses, Jesus, and the protomartyr in the bitter experience of Israel's rejection (cf. 7,51-52). — *Philip's ministry* of miracles in Samaria follows the great persecution (8,1ff.), and then Philip the *thaumaturge* becomes Philip, the expositor of scripture, setting forth the *mystery of the passion* for the Ethiopian traveler (8,26ff.). — Finally, *Paul's ministry*, though we cannot probe it in great detail here, also displays the pattern several times (cf. esp. cc. 14, 16, 19). There seems to be deliberate tailoring of the sequence in *Acts 19,21 - 21,17* after the model of the gospel's "journey" to Jerusalem, as the strong echo of Lk 9,51 in 19,21 clearly indicates (cf. W. RADL, *Paulus und Jesus*, 103-126). This announcement of Paul's πορεύεσθαι εἰς Ἱεροσόλυμα amounts to a "passion-prediction" of the great missionary, in view of its parallels in Acts 20,22 and 21,13. But what is especially interesting to us is the fact that the "prediction" follows directly upon what appears to be the climax of Paul's *thaumaturgy*, viz. his triumph over the magical arts at Ephesus. The editorial conjunction shows that Paul's ministry is being divided here as Jesus' was: οὕτως κατὰ κράτος τοῦ κυρίου ὁ λόγος ηὔξανεν καὶ ἴσχυεν. Ὡς δὲ ἐπληρώθη ταῦτα κτλ. (Acts 19,20f.).[163]

in the sources known to us. Whether miracles of John were once narrated by his followers and suppressed in the NT tradition (cf. Jn 10,41; R. BULTMANN, *GsT*, 22; R. MEYER, *Prophet*, 40, 115, 142 n. 171) need not be decided by us. Lk does include traditions of the Baptist's wondrous birth, as well as the promise depicting his coming before the Lord ἐν πνεύματι καὶ δυνάμει Ἠλίου (Lk 1,17). These items probably stem from traditions nurtured in Baptist circles, whether or not they formed an integral "Johanneslegende" (so M. DIBELIUS, *Formgeschichte*, 120f.; Ph. VIELHAUER, "Das Benedictus des Zacharias," in VIELHAUER, *Aufsätze zum N. T.* [München: Kaiser-Verlag, 1965, 28-46] 29-34).

[163] Paul's "journey to Jerusalem" is clearly under the divine disposition that controlled the destiny of Jesus' witnesses. "Wie Christus starb, so enden auch seine Zeugen" (E. LOHSE, "Lukas als Theologe ...," in Braumann-*LkEv*, 86; also W. RADL, *Paulus und Jesus*, 126; A. HASTINGS, *Prophet and Witness*, 136; H. FLENDER, *Heil*, 119). For this reason, Acts makes no mention of the "collection" or other practical motives of the historic Paul's journey (cp. Rom

A second interest Lk has in the christological combination of wonder-worker and sufferer appears in the Pentecost sermon of Peter and is closer to the theological heart of the matter. In words reminiscent of the account of Cleopas, Peter identifies the object of his audience's murderous rejection: ἄνδρα ἀποδεδειγμένον ἀπὸ τοῦ θεοῦ εἰς ὑμᾶς δυνάμεσι καὶ τέρασι καὶ σημείοις ... (Acts 2,22). The construction of the passage shows that its main assertion is the accusation of the Jerusalem audience: προσπήξαντες ἀνείλατε, whereas the preceding reference to the accrediting wonders, like the subsequent resurrection statement, is only a subordinate clause to that main assertion.[164] The contrast thus established between the action of God in Jesus (ἐποίησεν δι' αὐτοῦ ὁ θεὸς ... ὅν ὁ θεὸς ἀνέστησεν) and men's sinful action against him pervades and controls the whole sermon's content, as the summary verse 36 brings out.[165] If men's rather than God's action is the center of the kerygmatic statement, this can only be for the purpose of motivating the call to repentance, which is the sermon's goal (vv. 38f.); and the call to repentance, in turn, serves the historiographical purpose of illustrating the birth of a repentant, forgiven people (vv. 40-41) from the womb of a collectively accused, partially remorseful nation of Israel (Acts 2,22.36; cf. Lk 23,48; Acts 3,17ff.).[166] The motivation of the call to repentance, and therefore of an essential impulse to the birth of the Christian church, is thus the collision of divine and human actions in the person of the messiah. The miracles, like the conclusive divine act, ἀνέστησεν, demonstrate and dramatize that collision! That is doubtless why, even when miracles of Jesus are not among the explicit kerygmata of the discourses to Jewish hearers (as in Acts 2,22;

15,25; H. Conzelmann, *Apg.*², 121; Flender, *op. cit.*, 119 n. 196). Acts 23,11 shows the unity of the divine δεῖ governing the journeys to Jerusalem and Rome: "Im Rahmen dessen, dass sich das Evangelium durch Leiden ausbreitet, kommt auch das Evangelium nach Rom, indem Paulus als Gefangener in die Reichshauptstadt gebracht wird" (F. Schütz, *Christus*, 112).

[164] Correctly stressed by U. Wilckens, *Missionsreden*, 34.

[165] The reference of ἐποίησεν ὁ θεός to the whole kerygmatic statement of the sermon, rather than exclusively to vv. 32-35, is rightly maintained by U. Wilckens, *Missionsreden*, 36, 173, ³238; W. Dietrich, *Petrusbild*, 205; H. Conzelmann, *MdZ*, 162 n. 3; M. Rese, *Altt. Motive*, 65f. with n. 96; K. Kliesch, *Credo*, 147. This is apparently also the conclusion of G. Voss (*Christologie*, 143f.), although by concentrating on the parallel between 2,36 and 5,31 (*ibid.*, 135) and ignoring the more immediate relation to 2,22, Voss reaches no conclusive position on the meaning or function of the verse. — *E contra*, defending the more common view that 2,36 refers only to its immediate context, hence to a messianic installation of Jesus first on his resurrection and exaltation, are J. C. O'Neill, *Theol. of Acts*, 124; apparently E. Haenchen, *Apg.*, 150; J. Dupont, *Études*, 147ff.; J. Kremer, *Pfingstbericht*, 175, 208; E. Kränkl, *Jesus*, 159ff.

[166] Cf. chap. I, n. 160, for our explanation of the development in Lk's passion narrative and its relation to the pattern of the apostolic sermons.

10,38), miracles done in his name by his spokesmen furnish a contextual threshold for the discourses (Acts 3,12 ; 4,9-10 ; 5,19ff.32.39 ; 6,8 ; 13,6-12).

A clue to the traditional inspiration of the belief in miracles as divine accreditation is furnished by Lk's adaptation of the Joel prophecy as *ductus* from Pentecost wonder to Pentecost sermon (Acts 2, 16-21 / Joel 3,1-5 LXX).[167] By repeating καὶ προφητεύσουσιν in his transcription of the prophet's words, directly prior to the promise : καὶ δώσω τέρατα ... καὶ σημεία κτλ. (vv. 18f.),[168] our author seems to associate the apostles' miracle with those of Jesus (v. 22) as *accrediting signs of the eschatological prophecy*.[169] This observation, besides confirming the relationship of Peter's statement to that of Cleopas, shows how important Lk's (Mosaic) prophet-christology is to his understanding of the necessity of the Lord's passion (and the suffering of his witnesses as well). Prophecy, as a principal form of communion between God and man, is inevitably also a volatile ground of contention between the two realms. Precisely the one whom God *accredits*, man *repudiates* ; thus it is that divine forgiveness and human conversion become the prerequisites of God's rule, and thus is the bitter course charted for all who stand in the prophets' tradition, — principally, of course, the *summus propheta* and his emissaries.

---

[167] Rightly asserting this compositional function of the Joel citation as the " hinge " by which the Pentecost happening can be interpreted by the Pentecost kerygma : U. Wilckens, *Missionsreden*, 34 ; M. Rese, *Altt. Motive*, 38 ; K. Kliesch, *Credo*, 127.

[168] The repetition of καὶ προφητεύσουσιν is deliberate (rightly U. Wilckens, *Missionsreden*, 32 ; W. Dietrich, *Petrusbild*, 201f. ; C.H. Talbert, in *Jesus and Man's Hope* I, 175f.) and not simply an inadvertent repetition of v. 17b/c somewhere in the textual tradition (*pace* E. Haenchen, *Apg.*, 142 n. 4 ; T. Holtz, *Altt. Zitate*, 11f.), for the intrusion of ἐπὶ πᾶσαν σάρκα in like manner was avoided.

[169] On σημεῖα καὶ τέρατα as accreditation of the prophet like Moses, cf. LXX Ex 7,3 ; especially *Dt 34,11-12* in relation to 18,15ff. ; also 13,2f. — It is hard to know why σημεῖα ... κάτω would be added to the prophet's text in v. 19b if not for the purpose of connecting the wonder just witnessed (v. 2 : ἐκ τοῦ οὐρανοῦ ... ὅλον τὸν οἶκον, etc.) with the δυνάμεις καὶ τέρατα καὶ σημεῖα (v. 22) by which Jesus was " certified " (so O. Bauernfeind, *Apg.*, 46 ; U. Wilckens, *Missionsreden*, 33 ; M. Rese, *Altt. Motive*, 49f., 52ff. ; K. Kliesch, *Credo*, 144). The word τέρας with σημεῖον for the miracles : Acts 2,43 ; 4,30 ; 5,12 ; 7,36 (=Ex 7,3) ; and with δύναμις added : Acts 6,8 as well as 2,22. Obviously this LXX language serves Lk by sustaining the motif of prophetic accreditation from Moses, as prototype, to Jesus and the early witnesses, including Stephen (cf. T. Holtz, *Altt. Zitate*, 13 n. 3). — On the other hand, in none of these instances nor in the Pentecost sermon is this vocabulary associated with anything of the messianic woes or the judgment, such as might be implied in Joel's language of vv. 19c-20. If Lk was applying the prophet's words in that direction, we should certainly expect to find evidence of his intention in Peter's exegesis of the prophet's text (*contra* J. Kremer, *Pfingstbericht*, 173 ; E. Kränkl, *Jesus*, 192).

A corollary of this forms a significant issue of Lucan studies: the soteriological paradox of the *approbatus interemptus* forbids the view that, for Lk, the mighty deeds of Jesus have acquired an independent evangelical moment, apart from the interpretative, hortative *word* of the preaching. H. CONZELMANN[170] has sponsored this view and, with inconclusively selective data, has unfairly subjected Lk to the pressure of modern systematic debate on the issue.[171] Our own analysis of Lk 24, on the other hand, makes us wary of attributing to the evangelist any conviction of the transparency of historical facts and deeds. Until the risen One speaks in vv. 25ff. of the Emmaus pericope, there is no understanding of the wonder of the empty tomb, only perplexity and amazement (vv. 4.11.12.22). Indeed, the mystery of the passion consistently prevented wonder over the miraculous from becoming christological comprehension. The two stand in apparent conflict in Cleopas's words (vv. 19-20), just as they stood when Jesus prophesied his passion and death (Lk 9,43-45). It is precisely here, at the breach of human understanding between wonder and passion — the breach made by v. 20 in the account of Cleopas — that the clarifying, summoning *word* of the risen Lord must be spoken.[172] Without it, the veil of the passion-mystery remains drawn, and faith, genuine christological understanding, remains impossible.

---

[170] *MdZ*, 177-180; and in apparent agreement, U. WILCKENS, *ZNW* 49 (1958) 233, and *Missionsreden*, 108. Even more emphatic: S. SCHULZ, *Stunde*, 281; E. KÄSEMANN, "Das Problem des historischen Jesus," in *Exegetische Versuche* I, 199.

[171] In that he allegedly stresses Jesus' deeds as objective historical verification of the divine action in him, Lk is judged to depart from the vital center of NT thought and deprive the Christian gospel of its *skandalon*. The systematic prejudgments involved in such an assessment have been rightly diagnosed by H. FLENDER, *Heil*, 11ff.; W. G. KÜMMEL, "Luc en accusation ...," in F. Neirynck, éd., *L'év. de Luc. Mém. Cerfaux*, 100, 105 (= Braumann-*LkEv*, 425, 431f.); cf. also U. WILCKENS, in *StLA*, 71ff., and R. GLÖCKNER, *Verkündigung*, 30ff. and *passim*.

[172] H. CONZELMANN takes note of the "breach" we are emphasizing but does not do it justice: "The sign is granted — it cannot be demanded. It works as attestation, in fact as proof — yet it is misunderstood" (*MdZ*, 180). An author who taught us so well concerning the significance of Lk's *Leidensgeheimnis*, and the connection of the "journey" pattern therewith, might be expected to draw more measured conclusions concerning the supposed primacy of Jesus' mighty works in Lk's conception. For one thing, traditional expressions like "*see and* hear," "*do and* teach," "*work and* word," etc., should not be pressed to express an author's priorities. CONZELMANN admits this (179), yet he cannot resist the temptation to press (178 n. 2)! — Moreover, for as many Lucan passages as might suggest a primacy of fact over deed, especially for the requisite experience of the witnesses (Lk 10,24 Q; Acts 4,20; 2,33; 22,15), there are also crucial decisions of Lk's editorializing which tend to instill the primacy of Jesus' *word*. For example, the combination of inaugural summary and first act of public ministry at Nazareth (Lk 4,14-30) demonstrates a messianic *coming in the*

Lk 24,20, as renewed expression of the humanly insurmountable messianic *paradoxon*, contains echoes of the passion prophecies (n. 157 above) which are now ironic, of course, on the lips of a disciple who had heard the prophecies from the Lord's own mouth. The evangelist's authorship of v. 20 is indicated by both its resemblance to v. 7 (παρέδωκαν ... ἐσταύρωσαν) and its implied distancing of the people from their leaders, the latter now in progress since Lk 23,35.48 and the basis, as we have argued, of the apostolic preachers' first appeals (cf. p. 125 and n. 166 above). In our view, it is this verse alone which reflects the travelers' deficient understanding of their Master. And it does so not because its details are incorrect (cf. Lk 23,13-25; Acts 3,13-14.17; 13, 27-28), but because it articulates what is still, by divine ordination, the great mystery of the messiah and, by consequence, the unhealed breach in the disciples' understanding. The statements on either side of v. 20, expressing the prophet christology and the messianic hope for Israel, are both sound tenets of our author's teaching. They simply cannot be put together, however, without the linkage of v. 20. This linkage, as we have said, only the risen Lord can instill.

The soundness of v. 19 is clear, we hope, from what we have proposed. What of *v.* 21? Does not ἡμεῖς δὲ ἠλπίζομεν κτλ. introduce an expectation that was not to be fulfilled and should not have been entertained? Indeed, is this not the "particularistic hope for redemp-

word (H. SCHÜRMANN, *Lk.* I, 221), for both the summary (v. 15) and the Nazareth episode stress Jesus' impressive διδάσκειν and omit, but for the presumption of v. 23, the expected mention of miracles as evidence of the δύναμις τοῦ πνεύματος (v. 14). Jesus' teaching is similarly emphasized throughout Lk 4 (cf. vv. 15.18f.21.24ff.31f.43.44), while the miracles subsequently reported are treated as themselves "word-events" (vv. 33ff.38.41), functioning as certification that his was a "*word* spoken with authority" (4,32). — CONZELMANN urges that the first summons of disciples was made *via* an expressive epiphany-miracle (5,1-11), ignoring the teaching and hearing of the word of God which Lk used as an introduction and framework of the miracle (5,1.3). In fact, when the "apostles" are singled out as chosen witnesses from amongst the "disciples" (6,13) and a cosmopolitan crowd gathers "to *hear* him and be healed" (6,18), it is *first* his *teaching* that is given in detail (6,20-49), and only then are miracle stories related (7,1-17), — a sequence which repeats that of Lk 4. In other words, a schematic presentation of the ministry of Jesus with *preaching and instruction before miracles*, the latter illustrating and confirming the former, proves to be the Lucan pattern at variance with the one proposed by CONZELMANN (cf. the critique of M. RESE, *Altt. Motive*, 152 n. 39; also W. DIETRICH, *Petrusbild*, 280). — Jesus is said to have "*spoken* to them of the Kingdom of God," then "healed those in need of healing" (Lk 9,11; cp. 4,43f.); and in similar "summary" passages, "hearing" the dominical word precedes "being healed" as the craving of the masses who pursued him (Lk 5,15; 6,18; cp. Acts 4,29f.). Corresponding to this priority is the "hearing" that must precede the "doing" of the word of God (Lk 8,21; 11,28). — Cf. P. J. ACHTEMEIER, *JBL* 94 (1975) 550-551, 559f., for a much sounder assessment of the ex aequo relationship of miracles and teaching in Lk.

tion" confined to "Israel," whereas Lk will shatter such a restriction with announcements of salvation for "all peoples" (Lk 24,47; cp. Acts 1,8; 13,38f.46-47; 28,20.28)?[173] — In fact, it does not seem that this is Lk's mind at all, for the word "Israel" does not function in his pages as a one-dimensional name of the people that rejected its messiah. Quite the contrary, the name Ἰσραήλ, like the designation λαός, forms a salvation-historical continuum which includes the adherents of Jesus and from which the Jews who reject him are excluded.[174] This is why the celebration of Israel's "redemption" and "consolation" in the infancy narrative (Lk 1,68; 2,25.32) can still be a matter of Paul's kerygma at Acts 13,23 and his service in chains at Acts 28,20. Not that the name is ever explicitly given to Gentile groups;[175] but then, neither is λαός so applied, except in the significant statements of Acts 15,14 and 18,10.[176] Both words belong to the vocabulary of the LXX and bespeak the ideals and aspirations begotten by God's historic choice of a people as his own possession. In Lk's understanding, those ideals were not cancelled by Christ but brought to realization by him; they belong, therefore, to all who adhere to him, as do the biblical names which express them. The extension of the gospel to the Gentiles thus results from God's disposition to take ἐξ ἐθνῶν λαὸν τῷ ὀνόματι αὐτοῦ (Acts 15,14), just as the disciples' query to the risen One concerning the *time* of *Israel's* restoration brought the familiar answer rejecting only the *time* question, while commissioning their witness ἕως ἐσχάτου τῆς γῆς (Acts 1,6-8).[177] — In other words, though

[173] J. Wanke, *Emmauserzählung*, 67f. Cp. J. Bihler, *Stephanusgeschichte*, 103f., 61f.

[174] H. Conzelmann, *MdZ*, 135ff., 152ff.; W. Eltester, in *Jesus in Nazareth*, 125ff.; G. Lohfink, *Sammlung Israels*, 55, 58, 62. — Those striving for nuances in the matter — e.g. a distinction between the empirical and the eschatological Israel, or some developmental idea — are H. Flender, *Heil*, 107, 120ff., and A. George, *RB* 75 (1968) 522f. — The uncertainty whether the concept of a "true Israel" is appropriate (cf. Lohfink, *op. cit.*, 55, 60, 74, *contra* Conzelmann and Eltester) shows the need for care in rendering Lk's mind. As Lohfink shows, the new community of the "saved" is one that was born out of the Israel of old, not an extraneous group laying claim to Israel's status. The criterion of "Israel" after Jesus' death is repentance and belief, not physical descendancy.

[175] As J. Jervell objects against Conzelmann, in *Lk and the People of God*, 49, 72 n. 22. Jervell's view is that Israel for Lk refers not to the church composed of Jews and Gentiles but to the repentant portion of the empirical Israel, whereas the church extends beyond Israel's borders and no longer lays claim to the name (*ibid.*, 43). The disagreement shows one has to pursue a more nuanced understanding of the biblical terms of the question than has been developed hitherto.

[176] On which cf. J. Dupont, *Études*, 361-365; H. Flender, *Heil*, 120; A. George, *RB* 75 (1968) 523f.; G. Lohfink, *Sammlung Israels*, 58ff.

[177] G. Lohfink, *Sammlung Israels*, 79. The *time*-emphasis of the question

the biblical *vocabulary* is kept mainly in the "Jewish" phases of the story, in typical Lucan economy, the broader scope of the divine election expressed by the names is the consistent anticipation and goal of Lk's writing.

The sundering process within Jewish ranks that is recorded in Lk's narrative has the formation of a *true, redeemed Israel* as the object of the *argumentum*.[178] Each time the split is mentioned or implied, it is to remind the reader that the sacred process of the redeemed people's formation is in progress: at the Cross (Lk 23,35.48), on the "third day" (Lk 24,20), and under the powerful surge of the Easter witness (Acts 3,17ff.; 4,21). Large-scale Jewish resistance to Paul effects a consolidation of the ranks (Acts 14,5), but the split is still yielding believers to the new people when Acts comes to an end, at Rome (Acts 28,24). The prototypical impenitence of the ἄρχοντες consigns them to unbelieving Judaism, which will have no part in the *Israel* of the restoration. This is suggested when Peter, at Acts 3,17, mentions the *unknowing* agency of *both* leaders and people in the παθεῖν of God's messiah, but seems to extend the opportunity of repentance and conversion only to the people. The purpose of this suggestion comes to light when we hear, at Acts 4,4f., that a large number of Peter's hearers became believers while the ἄρχοντες gathered to challenge his preaching (cf. also 4,16-17). — These analyses of guilt and conversion are not polemical, of course, but *historiographical*. They are meant to explain how the Christian church came into being, not as a separate body laying claim to the *propria* of Israel, but as *redeemed Israel herself*, born from the ranks of the old, reaching out to embrace the Gentiles.[179]

(H. CONZELMANN, *MdZ*, 112) is clearly determined by the answer, hence it is not a "worldly, nationalistic" messianism that is repudiated (*pace* A. WIKENHAUSER, *Apg.*, 27) but the anticipation of a proximate parousia (F. MUSSNER, "Die Idee der Apokatastasis in der Apg.," in H. Gross & F. Mussner, hrsg., *Lex tua veritas. Festschrift für H. Junker* [Trier: Paulinis-Verlag, 1961, 293-306] 297; but cf. H. SCHLIER, *Besinnung auf das N. T.*, 234f.). — The phrase ἐπ' ἐσχάτου τῆς γῆς anticipates Acts 13,47, with its citation of Is 49,6, hence it makes the risen Lord's command the fulfillment of the divine plan of election already revealed in OT prophecy (J. DUPONT, *Études*, 403f.).

[178] H. CONZELMANN, *MdZ*, 136, 173; G. LOHFINK, *Sammlung Israels*, 41-43, 50ff., 62.

[179] The use of ἄρχοντες (pl.) for the Jewish leaders is peculiar to Lk among the Synoptics (J. WANKE, *Emmauserzählung*, 58). Perhaps their prototypical role accounts for his choice of this categorical term, with its transcendental dimensions. LOHFINK writes: "In der Zeit der ersten apostolischen Predigt sammelte sich aus dem jüdischen Volk das wahre Israel! Und jenes Israel, das dann noch in der Ablehnung Jesu beharrte, verlor sein Anrecht, das wahre Gottesvolk zu sein — es wurde zum Judentum" (*Sammlung Israels*, 55). Lk thus makes the redeemed people a matter of genuine continuity, and unbelieving Judaism a matter of defection!

Against this background, one perceives the authentically Lucan nexus in the words of Cleopas between 24,20 and 21. The fact that the speaker makes " our chief priests and rulers " the agents of the great prophet's death already reflects their separation from the redeemed " Israel," to whose formation the apostolic summons will be dedicated (cf. Acts 3,17-21). Cleopas reinforces the separation: ἡμεῖς δὲ ἠλπίζομεν ..., and it becomes clear that the lost hope was a valid one; moreover, it is about to be fulfilled unexpectedly since he will be among the first of the redeemed people!

Finally, the expression λυτροῦσθαι τὸν Ἰσραήλ (cp. Lk 1,68; 2,38) rejoins the Mosaic typology of v. 19, as a glance at Acts 7,35 will establish. For one thing, one cannot fail to notice the structural similarity between Stephen's statement about the rejected Moses and the kerygmatic declarations of God's vindication of the messiah who was put to death (Acts 2,36; 5,30f.).[180] Moreover, the same statement stands in a sequence (7,35-37) containing crucial elements we have noted in our present passage:[181] prophet-title, wondrous works, public repudiation. Whether or not Lk also infused these elements into the martyr's speech,[182] the remarkable parallelism of the passages elucidates

---

[180] λυτροῦν and related nouns belong to the LXX vocabulary of redemption, esp. (in the case of the verb) that of the Psalter and the Deutero-Isaiah (cf. J. WANKE, *Emmauserzählung*, 153 n. 447). — Structural similarities between the mission sermons and the speech of Stephen are concentrated, so far as the latter is concerned, in v. 35, with its paradox of the *approbatus negatus* (τοῦτον ... ὃν ἠρνήσαντο ... τοῦτον ὁ θεὸς ... ἀπέσταλκεν κτλ.). The verb ἀρνεῖσθαι also occurs in the kerygma of Acts 3,13f., a passage with strong literary relationships with the martyr's speech (cf. n. 156 above). As CONZELMANN remarks, in Acts 7,35 " die Moses typologie schafft sich hier stilistischen Ausdruck " (*Apg.*², 54; cf. also J. BIHLER, *Stephanusgeschichte*, 60ff., 104.

[181] On the relationship of the Emmaus dialogue to Stephen's speech, cf. M. H. SCHARLEMANN, *Stephen*, 86ff.

[182] H. CONZELMANN, *Apg.*², 57, thinks that points of abrupt transition from positive Scripture exposition to polemic are probable signs of redactional expansion of the *Vorlage*; and he includes vv. 35 and 37 among these. Cf. also J. ERNST, in *Schriftauslegung*, 180f. — Somewhat simpler is the view of M. DIBELIUS, for whom a neutral presentation of sacred history concludes at v. 34, with signs of tendentious application (= Lk) beginning at v. 35 (*Aufsätze*, 144). Undoubtedly an oversimplification. — E. HAENCHEN (*Apg.*, 240), M. RESE (*Altt. Motive*, 78-80), and T. HOLTZ (*Altt. Zitate*, 95-98), are all inclined to view 7,35-(36)37 as Lucan redactional enlargement of an older text. — After DIBELIUS' case, we should also judge oversimplified the view that Lk composed the whole of the martyr's speech (so J. BIHLER, *Stephanusgeschichte*, 86; J. KILGALLEN, *The Stephen Speech*, 121, 163; apparently also S. G. WILSON, *Gentiles*, 149; *e contra* rightly M. HENGEL, *ZTK* 72 [1975] 186). It may also be oversimplified to regard the whole as adopted from the source, without infusion of Lucan interests (*pace* U. WILCKENS, *Missionsreden*³, 208ff., basing himself on O. H. STECK, *Israel*, 265-269; cf. also O. BAUERNFEIND, *Apg.*, 110ff.; F. HAHN, *Hoheitstitel*, 383-385).

the one at hand. Jesus and Moses, precisely as *mighty prophets rejected*, are the two historic " deliverers " of God's people. The combination of Moses' titles, ἄρχοντα καὶ λυτρωτήν, associates the " deliverance " with the exodus journey, which Moses led by performing his prophetic " wonders and signs " (Acts 7,36). Given the all-important " journey " framework of the third gospel's christology, and specifically the expression thereof in Lk 9,31.51, we are convinced that a *positive Mosaic-prophet typology* is intended by the evangelist in the words of Cleopas. These are not mistaken or inadequate phrases but the very basis of the scriptural " necessity " which the risen One is about to expound in v. 26. Nor will it be by accident, of course, that his exposition will be made ἀρξάμενος ἀπὸ Μωϋσέως (v. 27), for Moses, as *prototype of the rejected prophet*, is the key to the passion mystery that is about to be broken.

So much for the afflicted traveler's words. We can be certain that they are words from our *evangelist*, and no one else. Every aspect of our investigation supports that conclusion : the patterns already observed in the tomb story, the combinations and modifications of sources elsewhere in Lk and Acts, and the compositional traits and vocabulary that are so distinctively Lucan. The traveler's christological resumé was strictly according to the arrangement and perspective of the third gospel. The facts recited were all correct, the hope expressed was authentic. The only thing missing was the *meaningful connection of the three elements*: wondrous deeds, rejection, redemption ! The traveler obviously wanted to move from the first to the third, according to hopes held out for the eschatological prophet.[183] The great prophet's *violent rejection* he could not grasp, and so the remainder of his recital is of empirical events without sense or connection (vv. 21b-24). Such is the *cul-de-sac* of human perceptions to which that mysterious fellow-traveler must now address himself.

The " Opening " of the Scriptures (24,25-27)

Several previous phases of our study prepare us for the momentous turn which the Easter story now takes. The dialogue's shift is accentuated with the emphatic : καὶ αὐτὸς εἶπεν πρὸς αὐτούς, as the Stranger seizes the platform from the confused disciple. His reproach — ὦ ἀνόητοι καὶ βραδεῖς τῇ καρδίᾳ — rejoins the descriptive σκυθρωποί of v. 17, and together they enclose what is spoken in between within the framework of the messianic passion-mystery (cf. p. 113 above). We are also reminded of the parallelism, pointed out *in loco*, between the

[183] Concerning which, cf. chap. IV, n. 54. — We fully endorse P. von der OSTEN-SACKEN when he rejects the view that v. 21 is only a foil for v. 26 (*EvT* 43 [1973] 489).

angels' reproach of the women (24,5b-7) and the present passage: in both cases it is implied, by reference to the prophecies of Jesus himself, that the lack of understanding should not be. And yet, paradoxically, the passive voice formulations attached to the passion prophecies (παρακεκαλυμμένον 9,45; κεκρυμμένον 18,34) were echoed in the ἐκρατοῦντο of our present context (24,16) to suggest that the concealment of the matter that is about to be disclosed was really a matter of divine plan. To reinforce this, Lk 9,45 read: (τὸ ῥῆμα τοῦτο) ἦν παρακεκαλυμμένον ἀπ' αὐτῶν ἵνα μὴ αἴσθωνται αὐτό· and the conjunction there of evocative passive form and ἵνα-clause makes it arbitrary to deny that a *purposeful schedule of concealment and disclosure, divinely appointed*, coordinates the two stages of the Emmaus narrative.[184] The veil of mystery is now to be lifted, according to divine determination, in the only way it could be lifted: by the personal presence and instruction of the risen Lord, who "opens" the scriptures by showing their realization in himself (v. 27: διηρμήνευσεν αὐτοῖς ἐν πάσαις ταῖς γραφαῖς τὰ περὶ ἑαυτοῦ). The "things concerning Jesus of Nazareth" that the travelers could not grasp (v. 19) are now the focal point of the Easter exposition of all Scripture. No more than the events themselves could the Scripture by itself beget faith in the messiah's triumph; *only he can bestow that as his personal gift*.[185] — The mystery was a matter of that certain *duration*, which Lk brings out through noticeable resonances between this passage and the transfiguration scene, especially the εἰσελθεῖν/ἔξοδος correspondence we observe between v. 26 and Lk 9,31 (cf. p. 30 above). In recasting Mk's secrecy injunction at the descent from the mount (Mk 9,9), Lk produced the statement that the witnesses told the vision to no one ἐν ἐκείναις ταῖς ἡμέραις (Lk 9,36; cf. pp. 40f. above), which made the messianic *krypsis* a delimited *season* coursing towards an anticipated end. Now, as the One stands before the disciples in whom all the scriptures reach their goal and fulfill-

[184] On the divine intervention implied in the passive forms accompanying the passion prophecies, cf. A. GEORGE, *RB* 80 (1973) 206f., and the commentaries of A. LOISY, K. H. RENGSTORF, W. GRUNDMANN, J. SCHMID, and J. ERNST (near unanimity among the commentators, so far as we can see) *ad* Lk 9,45; 18,34. Most recently and emphatically, J. ERNST (*Lk.*, 310): "Das finale 'damit' macht sogar deutlich, dass dies so sein muss, Gott hat es so gewollt, er hat das Geheimnis des Leiden-Müssens vor ihren Augen verhullt, damit sie nicht begreifen, also mit voller Absicht." J. ERNST (*ibid.*, 508) joins E. KLOSTERMANN (*Lk.*, 183) in suggesting the relationship between the divinely willed concealment and the disclosure on the road to Emmaus. In this economy, the disciples are kept in the dark by the evangelist up to the great *peirasmos* of the passion, "um ihnen dann vom Auferstandenen denn Sinn erschliessen zu lassen (24,32)."

[185] H. GOLLWITZER, *Jesu Tod und Auferstehung*, 99: "Er will offenbar selbst den Augenblick bestimmen, wo man ihn erkennen kann, er hat das ganz in der Hand; wer ihn erkennt, empfängt in dem Erkennen Christi Geschenk." Also M. BRÄNDLE, *Orientierung* 24 (1960) 87.

ment, the season of *krypsis* — and the longing of generations — is over! It is not that the Master did not instruct his followers during the great "journey" concerning the very same matter; it is simply that he could not demonstrate the τελεσθῆναι[186] of all the scriptures except *in his own person, risen and victorious.*[187] Only Christ *risen* is fully sacred history's *telos.*

We begin to perceive that closer connection between the Emmaus journey and the gospel's "journey" which we held an uncertain possibility at the beginning of this study (p. 90). The travelers here are indeed caused to recapitulate the gospel's "journey," for they are now, at last, in the presence of the scriptures' and the "journey's" *end* (vv. 26f.). Only in the risen One's presence and under his instruction can both be understood. With this *telos* of the prophetic testimonies comes the *telos* of the period of concealment. Indeed, only because they have been in the risen One's presence can the travelers be called in any sense ἀνόητοι κτλ., the kind of reproach Lk avoided altogether in connection with the concealment prior to Easter (*diff.* Mk!). — So it is, with emphasis on the scriptural attestation of the messianic δεῖ and the appointed time of its concealment, that Lk is able to include in his book what Mk's had only anticipated (9,9) but left untold: the *end* of the mystery surrounding the messiah, his entry into glory.

The *appeal to the Scriptures and their characterization* in our passage bear the unmistakable trademark of this evangelist. First, the conviction is expressed that they bear witness to Christ in their *totality*[188] (v. 25: ἐπὶ πᾶσιν οἷς ἐλάλησαν· v. 27: ἀπὸ πάντων τῶν προφητῶν ... ἐν πάσαις ταῖς γραφαῖς). Here is a counterpart in the argument from prophecy to the emphasis we found earlier in the chapter on the *totality*

[186] The use of τελέω for Scripture fulfillment is exclusive to our author: Lk 18,31 (at the end of the "journey" section!); 22,37 (accompanied by: καὶ γὰρ τὸ περὶ ἐμοῦ τέλος ἔχει, as the supper instruction ends and the passion sequence begins). We would suggest that the essential connection of the "journey" framework with the passion as messianic destiny is responsible for this innovation. τελεῖσθαι and τέλος properly refer to a *course* or *way* that is completed, after all, and "Lukas scheint sich die Kontinuität der Heilsgeschichte als Lauf (δρόμος) oder als Weg (ὁδός) vergegenwärtigt zu haben ..." (W. C. ROBINSON, *Weg*, 39).

[187] H.-W. BARTSCH, *Wachet*, 25: "Das Alte Testament wird nur vom Auferstandenen her recht verstanden. Das will die Gemeinde mit dieser Legende bezeugen." Cf. also H. CONZELMANN, *MdZ*, 151f.; J. ERNST, in *Schriftauslegung*, 191; P. SCHUBERT, in *Ntl. Studien f. Bultmann*, 178 (the climax of the argument from prophecy which has been pursued throughout the gospel).

[188] E. LOHSE, *Auferstehung*, 29: "Vom Ende her will die Bibel betrachtet und gelesen werden, damit aus allen Büchern das eine Wort Gottes über Christus vernommen wird .... Christus also ist Ziel und Mitte der ganzen Schrift." Also J. DUPONT, *Études*, 280: "Pour que les Écritures deviennent intelligibles, il fallait la présence de celui vers lequel, tout entières, elles convergaient."

of facts observed and the *total* publicity of the mighty prophet's career (pp. 110f.). No less than there is the motif meant to work in contrast to the total *incomprehension* of the scriptures *ex parte hominis*. The cutting edge of the Scriptures' christological totality is the helplessness of the man who searches them apart from the presence of the One they *all* proclaim! Such, according to Lk's Paul, was the plight of the Jews who consigned their Saviour to death; they did so ἀγνοήσαντες καὶ τὰς φωνὰς τῶν προφητῶν τὰ κατὰ πᾶν σάββατον ἀναγινωσκομένας (Acts 13,27). The guilty people is reminded by Peter that its action unwittingly served God's purpose to fulfill what he had foretold διὰ στόματος πάντων τῶν προφητῶν, namely, παθεῖν τὸν χριστὸν αὐτοῦ (Acts 3,18). Indeed, the temple speech of Peter illumines the *argumentum* of the Stranger even more effectively than it did the words of Cleopas:

> Peter's call to repentance is joined by the chorus of scriptural voices which the audience had not understood (Acts 3,17), for these days of the apostolic mission were announced by πάντες ... οἱ προφῆται ἀπὸ Σαμουὴλ καὶ τῶν καθεξῆς ... (v. 24). Moses was among that throng of prophets, as v. 22 shows,[189] and the way the preacher appeals to Moses' promise of a prophet like himself sheds light on Lk's scriptural argument. *Dt 18,15.18f.* is used to motivate the call to repentance, for the messiah's persecutors are being reminded of the Mosaic injunction to heed the voice of the prophet who would be "raised up"[190] in Moses' image (v. 23). *That voice is Jesus' own*, now heard through his kerygmatic spokesmen. It is the voice of the *risen Lord*, the key to the meaning of all the Scripture.[191]

Now we know the reason why Lk understands Jesus' ministry in prophetic categories, and what *word* it is that became the unique source of faith and understanding. The *word* of scripture exposition on the

---

[189] The introduction to v. 22 — Μωϋσῆς μὲν κτλ., with corresponding δέ in v. 24 — shows clearly that Moses is to be reckoned with the "holy prophets" ἀπ' αἰῶνος, already spoken of in vv. 18 and 21 (so M. RESE, *Alttestamentliche Motive ...*, 68).

[190] I tend, therefore, to agree with J. DUPONT (*Études*, 249) and F. SCHNIDER (*Prophet*, 93) that it is difficult to ignore the suggestion of the resurrection in the word ἀναστήσας, especially considering Lk's unique use of the transitive form to express God's action at Easter. This is despite the objection that the combination of ἀναστήσας with ἀπέστειλεν in 3,26 appears to favor the application of the verse to the earthly mission of Jesus (so U. WILCKENS, *Missionsreden*, 43, 137, 163; J. ERNST, in *Schriftauslegung*, 182f.; M. RESE, *Altt. Motive*, 70 n. 19).

[191] Rightly E. HAENCHEN, *Apg.*, 169; F. SCHNIDER, *Prophet*, 91f. — The function of the Dt-citation, hence of the Mosaic typology, is thus ultimately to motivate the apostolic summons to the Jewish audience to repent and be converted (cf. F. SCHNIDER, *op. cit.*, 94). Therefore the πρῶτον of 3,26 is developed and elucidated at Acts 13,46.

road to Emmaus became the word spoken by the missionary Church in the full, personally guaranteed authority of the risen Christ. It is the *word of eschatological prophecy foreseen by Moses,* qualifying as such because all the prophecies of Scripture come to their term in it. It is understandable that, prior to Easter — say, when the crowds acclaimed the wonder-worker (Lk 7,16) or a divided public opinion about him was being registered (Lk 9,7f.19), the *Mosaic* dimension of Jesus' prophecy could precisely *not* be accentuated (cf. n. 154 above). The " prophet like Moses " is he who finally " opens " the scriptures with " living words " (cf. Acts 7,38). This is no one other than the *risen* Christ, to whom the ἀναστήσει of Dt 18,15 belongs in a full and proper sense! Only at Easter could the properly *Mosaic prophecy* of Jesus be brought to light.

The Emmaus dialogue and the temple sermon converge also in their characterizations of the OT scriptures. They are considered in both places globally as *prophecy,* and their authors are all *prophets* (cf. Lk 24,27 : πάντων τῶν προφητῶν / πάσαις ταῖς γραφαῖς · cp. v. 32). The same categorical perspective is found frequently in Lk's writing. It probably accounts for the fact that, in the gospel's programmatic episode at the beginning of the public ministry, Jesus' instruction at the synagogue in Nazareth is based on a prophet's text rather than a pericope from the Torah (Lk 4,17ff. / Is 61,1f.).[192] When we look closely at the tailoring of that prophecy for Jesus' use,[193] we find an interesting anticipation of the kerygma's object as the temple sermon defines it. Twice in Jesus' Isaian reading the word ἄφεσις is featured, once in a statement transferred to this context from Is 58,6 : ἀποστεῖλαι τεθραυσμένους ἐν ἀφέσει. The conflation of the Isaian statements results in a doubled ἄφεσις-proclamation; and whatever " liberation " the post-exilic prophet might have been prophesying, there is only *one sense* this noun ever has in NT usage (10x out of 17x in Lk-Acts !) : it always means *God's* " liberation " of men *from sin's bondage,* — his

---

[192] Cf. esp. Acts 13,27, where the interest is solely on the reading of the *prophets* every sabbath ; — and this despite the fact that our author is clearly familiar with the regular practice of *Torah*-reading (cp. Acts 13,15 ; 15,21). Cf. on this H. SCHÜRMANN, *Lk.* I, 229 : " Eine bewusst geübte Kunst des Weglassens will hier das herausstellen, was an den atl. Schriften im Hinblick auf den Christus allein wichtig scheint : der Verheissungscharakter der Schrift."

[193] It is surely not enough to talk of a " free rendition " of the LXX (so H.-W. BARTSCH, *Wachet,* 62), for the Isaian text, as it stands in Lk 4,18f., was clearly not " found " by any reader in the prophet's scroll ; the text is a deliberate Christian fusion of separate passages as a testimony of the messianic fulfillment in Jesus (rightly SCHÜRMANN, *loc. cit.* in n. 192 ; E. HAENCHEN, " Historie und Verkündigung bei Markus und Lukas," in *Die Bibel und wir,* [156-181] 164).

forgiveness.[194] Understood in this way, ἄφεσις ἁμαρτιῶν in Lk-Acts can be simply equivalent to " salvation " (Lk 1,77) or " being justified " (Acts 13,38f.) *simpliciter.*[195] Moreover, the fact that ἄφεσις ἁμαρτιῶν was the precise content of *all the prophets' testimony about Christ* is the final word of Peter's speech in the house of Cornelius, Acts 10,43. This assertion explains with all possible clarity why the prophetic μαρτυρία chosen for programmatic exposition at Nazareth should have a novel linkage of the two ἄφεσις announcements. The one voice from among them *all* has created in Jesus' first recorded instruction a prolepsis of the message which, on Easter, he would commission to be carried forth in his name (Lk 24,47).[196] When Acts then illustrates the fulfillment of that commission in the mission sermons, it can show the summons to repentance and *forgiveness* as consistently the preachers' focus and as pointedly rooted by them in the testimony of *all* the prophets. Such is the motivation of the summons advanced by Peter in the temple sermon, as he argues from Acts 3,19-21 to 3,22-26. The days of the *eschatological prophet* are declared at hand. Indeed, *the same Jesus who spoke out over the closed book to his kinsfolk and countrymen is also the speaker who announces the scriptures' fulfillment in the kerygma of the apostles.* The voice is the *eschatological prophet's* voice,[197] Moses' counterpart, end and fruition of the prophets' line, bestower of the gift of *forgiveness* just as they *all* had foretold.

So far from a vulgarism of the Palestinian masses, therefore, the view of Jesus as eschatological prophet is the idea which confers a conceptual unity upon the two parts of the Emmaus dialogue. It is not a mere foil for the scripture interpretation of the risen One, but a pregnant christological idea with which Lk attempts to elucidate the nature and course of Jesus' messianic ministry. It is no surprise that

---

[194] Cf. R. BULTMANN, *TWNT* I, 507f., who agrees that the implication is necessary also in Lk 4,18.

[195] Cf. Acts 2,38ff.; 26,18; also 5,31; 10,43; Lk 3,3; 24,47.

[196] Given the omission of the ἰάσασθαι-clause from Is 61,1 in favor of the ἄφεσις-clause from Is 58,6, one can agree with M. RESE that, for the evangelist's " program " of the ministry of Jesus, " dem Heilen Jesu nicht so grosse Bedeutung zukommt wie seinem Wirken in Verkündigung und Vergebung " (*Altt. Motive*, 152). On this " forgiveness " announcement of the Nazareth *lectio divina*, cf. also R. TANNEHILL, in *Jesus in Nazareth*, 70f.; R. GLÖCKNER, *Verkündigung*, 136; E. NELLESSEN, *Zeugnis*, 113.

[197] Cf. p. 135 above (and n. 191), and G. VOSS, *Christologie*, 163f.; F. SCHÜTZ, *Christus*, 83. — The sense of the citation is that the call to repentance, which the speaker urges his audience to heed, is spoken by the very eschatological prophet like himself whom Moses promised and whom he enjoined his people to obey (cf. the mixture of Dt 18,19 and Lev 23,29 in Acts 3,23). We shall discuss this further, but we wish to state our emphatic disagreement with CONZELMANN's assessment of the Moses-figure in Lk-Acts as basically neutral and inconsequential to the author (*MdZ*, 155f. n. 2).

Moses is the ἀρχή of the dominical Scripture hermeneutic (*v.* 27 : ἀρξάμενος ἀπὸ Μωϋσέως). This is so because of the whole plan of the dialogue section, and not just to signify that the sacred books were expounded in order or to employ a conventional citation-formula.[198] The way the reproach of v. 25 is taken up in v. 27, and the curious repetition of ἀπό in v. 27,[199] find explanation in terms of Acts 3,22.24 (Μωϋσῆς μὲν εἶπεν ... καὶ πάντες δὲ οἱ προφῆται ... ἐλάλησαν): all the scripture of the Jews is prophecy, and Moses, its first and principal author, is likewise its first and principal *prophet*. Such a classification in Scripture usage is peculiar to Lk among NT authors,[200] and it is occasioned in both our passage and the Acts speech by the Mosaic typology which each develops. Scripture is illumined by the risen Lord in terms of its " alpha " and " omega," Moses and the Messiah : both " mighty " prophets (Lk 24,19 / Acts 7,22), both " saviours " and " leaders " of a wayfaring people (Lk 24,21 / Acts 7,35 ; 5,31 ; 3,15), and both, according to the central mystery of the divine plan, subjected to the people's rejection and " denial " (Acts 7,35 ; 3,13f. ; Lk 24,20). Bounded so harmoniously by the prophetic leaders who begin and end it, all of Scripture can be understood in its christological unity. So too can the Emmaus dialogue be understood as a unity determined by the *Mosaic prophecy* invoked at its beginning (v. 19) and end (v. 27).

Lk 24,26, once again a variation on the familiar passion prophecy formula, is likewise best understood in light of the Mosaic ἀρχή. Several features of this verse have already come under our discussion : the past tense of δεῖ, the restoration of the χριστός-title after the period of the *Leidensgeheimnis*, and the expression of the messiah's vindication as the

[198] *Contra* J. Dupont, in *Misc. Ubach*, 358 ; W. Grundmann, *Lk.*, 446 (a 3-fold division : Law, Prophets, and Writings). Such may be the case in Acts 26,22, however. It is true that Lk's varied formulas for invoking *tota scriptura* — " the prophets " (Lk 24,25 ; Acts 3,18.21.24 ; 10,43 ; 13,27 ; 26,27), " the prophets and Moses " (Acts 26,22), " the Law and the Prophets " (Acts 13,15 ; 24,14 ; 28,23 ; cp. Lk 24,44), " the scriptures " (Lk 24,32.45 ; Acts 17,2.11 ; 18, 28) — are dedicated to expressing the unity and harmony of all sacred writ, never to singling out only one of its components (cf. J. Ernst, in *Schriftauslegung*, 178-179 ; cp. H. Conzelmann, *MdZ*, 148). This is no less the case in the text at hand. All Scripture is considered as prophecy. Corresponding to this perspective is Lk 24,44, where the prophetic function of the law of Moses will be clearly expressed. Also in the same line of thinking is the presentation of David as prophet (Acts 2,25ff. ; Lk 20,42 *diff.* Mk 12,36).

[199] *Contra* A. Plummer, *Lk*, 555, this repetition is not to stress the distinction of the Pentateuch from the Prophets. The phraseology is indeed a " zeugma " (J. M. Creed, *Lk*, 297), for ἀρξ. ἀπό refers only to Moses ; yet the distinction of him from " all the prophets " is precisely being removed by the second ἀπό, not reinforced.

[200] J. Wanke, *Emmauserzählung*, 87. Cp. H. Conzelmann, *MdZ*, 155 (who errs, in our opinion, when he considers this picture of Moses to be accepted by Lk from his tradition and given no particular emphasis by him).

conclusion of a destined course, εἰσελθεῖν εἰς τὴν δόξαν αὐτοῦ (pp. 30, 39ff. above). Now we inquire what more we might learn about the statement when we measure it by the dialogue context in which it is found. Let us consider the three features in their turn.

(a) As we observed before, the recasting of the mysterious δεῖ in the past tense is gaited to presenting παθεῖν and εἰσελθεῖν as stations on *an appointed course*. The messiah's passion was the divinely ordained *transitus* to his heavenly glory, and as such it lies in the past on Easter.[201] Not so its meaning for his followers, however. As we have learned from consistent trends of Lucan editing, the passion's "necessity" derived from a perennial *law of prophetic endeavour* binding on every spokesman of God's word, "beginning from Moses." That law is understood as a destined course which must be followed also by the witnesses who proclaim the messiah, including the Baptist before him (cf. Acts 13,25 with Lk 3,15-20) and Paul after him (cf. Acts 20,23-24). The best expression of this prophetic heritage amongst Jesus' witnesses is found in a statement remarkably close to the one we are studying, found as a summary[202] of the exhortation given by Barnabas and Paul following the latter's *near-death* in Jewish hands at Lystra:

> διὰ πολλῶν θλίψεων δεῖ ἡμᾶς εἰσελθεῖν εἰς τὴν βασιλείαν τοῦ θεοῦ (Acts 14,22).

When one notices not only the clever kerygmatic nuance put into the account of the Jews' attack — τεθνηκέναι/ἀναστάς (14,19f.) — but also the preceding acclaim of the wonder-men (14,11ff.) and the evocative motif of execution ἔξω τῆς πόλεως (14,19),[203] it becomes clear that the sequence was composed according to familiar Lucan blueprint! The law of the prophet's course is inherited by the missionary witness, who must also pass from divine certification by wondrous deeds to violent rejection by the public. But the *telos* of this path, revealed by the

---

[201] Cf. note 86 above (chap. I). Further A. HASTINGS, *Prophet and Witness*, 123; G. KEGEL, *Auferstehung*, 85, 86; S. SCHULZ, *Stunde*, 289; G. SCHNEIDER, *Verleugnung*, 177: "Hier wird die Passion als Durchgang zur Doxa verstanden, als notwendige Station des Gottes Planes. Sie muss zuvor durchschritten werden, soll die folgende erreicht werden." Cf. also E. KÄSEMANN, "Die Heilsbedeutung des Todes Jesu nach Paulus," in H. Conzelmann, *et al.*, *Zur Bedeutung des Todes Jesu*, (11-34) 31; W. RADL, *Jesus und Paulus*, 235. — Cf. n. 134 of chap. IV.

[202] Not only the major "summaries" (Acts 2,42-47; 4,32-35; 5,12-16) but the small, generalizing connective remarks (e.g. Acts 1,14; 6,7; 9,31f., etc.) are valuable signs of Lk's redactional activity in the second volume. They are best understood by analogy to his adaptation and variation of the Marcan "summaries" in the gospel. Cf. H. J. CADBURY, *The Making*, 58; M. DIBELIUS, *Aufsätze zur Apg.*, 15f.; H. CONZELMANN, *Apg.*[2], 9.

[203] Re. Jesus at Nazareth: Lk 4,29; Stephen: Acts 7,58. Cf. Lev 24,14; Dt 17,5; tract. *Sanh.* VI, 1ff.

risen One at Lk 24,26, is the witness's consolation and can be spoken as παράκλησις by the rejected Paul in words directly appropriated from the Lord's own.[204] — We can conclude with reasonable certainty that both Lk 24,26 and Acts 14,22 are from the mind and hand of Lk himself, just as the contexts in which they occur reflect his consistent formula for the combining and amplifying of source-material. We can suggest, too, that the same redactional association of passion-mystery and "journey" motifs as governed Lk 9-18 also directed the fashioning of an Emmaus appearance into "the Emmaus *journey*." (Cf. again pp. 133-134 above.)

(b) On the first appearance of Lk's formula, παθεῖν τὸν χριστόν,[205] we observe only that the title's appearance is based on the plan of Lk's composition not only with respect to v. 7, where "Son of Man" made its last appearance (cf. pp. 39f.), but also with respect to the "prophet" designation of v. 19. This latter transition was rehearsed in the specially tailored sequence of Lk 9,7-20, as we saw (pp. 120f.), and the wayfarers' dialogue is now leading across that great divide which only Jesus himself could cross at the time of Peter's confession. The essence of the mystery which has covered the story since that point is that *God's messiah* (9,20) had to *suffer* (9,22). Between those two terms of the mystery was interposed the *krypsis*: μηδενὶ λέγειν τοῦτο (9,21), indicating that Jesus could not be known as *messiah* until his path *through suffering to glory* was complete.[206] Here the *skandalon* of the gospel story was encountered: the disciples were to remain absorbed in the glitter of the Master's miraculous activity (Lk 9,43f.; 19,37, both *diff.* Mk) while Jesus sought to instill the necessity of his passion (cf pp. 35-36 above). — Yet we have learned, too, that Lk does not view the miraculous and martyrological phases of Jesus' mission in a strictly dialectical relationship, as might be the case moreso in Mk.[207] Rather, as might be expected of him, Lk has tried to put the two phases toge-

---

[204] F. Schütz, *Christus*, 112: "Das Leiden der Gemeinde ... wird als diejenige Form der Existenz in dieser Welt angesehen, die der Gemeinde als Gemeinde des leidenden Christus entspricht." Cf. also W. Radl, *Jesus und Paulus*, 111.

[205] J. Wanke, *Emmauserzählung*, 86, 92: neither the absolute use of παθεῖν (Heb 2,18; 9,26; 13,12; I Pet 2,21) nor, of course, the use of the *Christos*-title with passion statements is peculiar to Lk. But the frequency and contextual variation of this formula in his two books (cf., besides the Mk-parallels, Lk 17, 25; 24,46; Acts 3,18; 17,3; 26,23; also Acts 1,3) indicate that it belongs to the "technical" vocabulary of the Lucan historiography.

[206] Recall chap. I, n. 67, on the one-sentence editorial linkage between 9,21 and 9,22 (*diff.* Mk 8,30f.).

[207] Cf. K. Kertelge, *Die Wunder Jesu im Mk.-Ev.* (cited in n. 138 above) 38; U. Luz, "Das Geheimnismotiv und die markinische Christologie," *ZNW* 56 (1965, 9-30) 26; L.E. Keck, "Mk 3,7-12 ...," *JBL* 84 (1965) 341-358. But cf., on the other side, T. A. Burkill, "Mark 3,7-12 ...," *JBL* 87 (1968) 409-417.

ther in an harmonious, salvation-historical perspective.[208] These were the necessary phases of every *prophet's* career, hence they are the inevitable stations along the *messiah's* way, for he is the goal and promise of all the prophets' missions. The law of the prophet's destiny was articulated in both phases of Lk's account of the public life, both in the violent Nazareth episode which presaged the story's end (Lk 4,24ff.) and in the midst of Jesus' purposeful journey to Jerusalem (Lk 13,33). The motif proper to each stage is yet found in the other: Nazareth anticipates both the power and the rejection aspects, and the miracles do not cease during the " journey " but only right before the entry to the city of all the prophets' demise (19,37; cf. p. 36 above, with n. 104). The two stages are not opposed or mutually exclusive, therefore. They simply express the contrast which the kerygma will make into a searing call for repentance: " the one whom God has certified..., you have put to death " (pp. 125-26 above). — In other words, our dialogue's sequence, *prophet-messiah*, has been the plan of Lk's gradual exposition of the *articulus stantis vel cadentis* of messianic faith: " that the Christ must suffer."

(c) Given the fact that v. 26 has the same structure as kerygmatic pronouncements found elsewhere in Lk-Acts (cf. Lk 24,46; Acts 17,3; 26,23; cp. Lk 9,22 / Mk 8,31), we are finding the phrase καὶ εἰσελθεῖν εἰς τὴν δόξαν αὐτοῦ where we should expect to find καὶ ἀναστῆναι ἐκ νεκρῶν. The well-established schema followed in the texts cited is the schema of the passion predictions, whose basic model we find already at Mk 8,31;[209] hence this response to Cleopas is yet another of our evangelist's variations on the one basic schema. The major innovation here is that he has given εἰσελθεῖν κτλ. the function of the usual ἀναστῆναι affirmation. If, in addition to the sturdy format it follows, we observe how v. 26 functions in the present context, we can only confirm that εἰσελθεῖν depicts the resurrection and not some heavenly exaltation distinct from it.[210] The imperfect ἔδει governs both

[208] This does not mean, *pace* H. KÖSTER, that " as the story of the archetypical martyr, the passion narrative is *no more than* the last chapter of the aretalogy of Jesus " (in ROBINSON-KÖSTER, *Trajectories*, 191 — ital. mine). The difficult question of the redemptive value of the passion in Lk's thought will not be solved by KÖSTER's penchant for the facile tradition-historical contrast.

[209] Cf. G. LOHFINK, *Himmelfahrt*, 237f.: the common elements of the texts cited include the title ὁ χριστός, a passion statement with παθεῖν (cp. Acts 3,18), a resurrection statement with ἀναστῆναι, and an affirmation of agreement with what was written in sacred Scripture (cf. the common ἔδει of Lk 24,26 and Acts 17,3).

[210] G. LOHFINK, *Himmelfahrt*, 238, 239. Likewise J. M. CREED, *Lk*, 297; H. CONZELMANN, *MdZ*, 189 n. 2; H. SCHLIER, in *Besinnung auf das N. T.*, 237; J. WANKE, *Emmauserzählung*, 87; G. FRIEDRICH, in *Orientierung an Jesus*, 58.

verbs that follow it [211] and refers them clearly to the disciple's recital just concluded. Cleopas had listed the recent phenomena of which he could find no explanation: the mighty prophet's death (= παθεῖν) and, in protracted detail, the puzzle of the empty tomb (= εἰσελθεῖν...). If we were successful, therefore, in showing that vv. 19-21 never existed apart from vv. 21b-24 but where composed with the latter in a unified sequence by the evangelist, we can scarcely avoid the conclusion that he meant v. 26 to be the risen Lord's explanation of the sense of those *already verified* happenings which the traveler could not fit together. It is the unexpected resurrection, therefore, to which the disputed phrase refers.[212]

But why Lk's choice of this unusual phrase ?[213] An answer is suggested by comparing v. 26 with another statement adhering to the same schema. It occurs in Paul's *apologia* for his mission before King Agrippa and, like our passage, it stands in the framework of the christological summation of what "the prophets and Moses" had spoken (Acts 26,22 / Lk 24,25.27). Let us observe the two parallel formulations:

Lk 24,26: παθεῖν τὸν χριστὸν καὶ εἰσελθεῖν εἰς τὴν δόξαν αὐτοῦ·
Acts 26,23: εἰ παθητὸς ὁ χριστός, εἰ πρῶτος ἐξ ἀναστάσεως νεκρῶν ...

---

[211] Rightly J. Schmid, *Lk.*, 357f., *contra* A. Plummer, *Lk*, 555 (who has ἔδει governing both verbs grammatically but referring mainly to παθεῖν). Even if we maintain the infinitives are simply coordinated but subordination is to be inferred from the context (parataxis *loco* hypotaxis, as e.g. J. Wellhausen, *Lc.*, 139, and E. Klostermann, *Lk.*, 237, who give εἰσελθεῖν a final sense), the dependence of both upon the past tense of the main verb has still to be reckoned with.

[212] Many exegetes have maintained that it refers to the heavenly exaltation of Jesus as distinct from his resurrection. Perhaps the best known argument along these lines was that of G. Bertram, "Die Himmelfahrt Jesu vom Kreuz aus und der Glaube an seine Auferstehung," in *Festgabe für Adolf Deissmann zum 60. Geburtstag* (Tübingen: J. C. B. Mohr, 1927, 187-217) 202f., following J. Weiss. But cf. also P. Benoit, in *Exégèse et théologie* I, 377f.; W. Schenk, in *Theol. Versuche* II, 79 (v. 26 is therefore cited as "Ausgangspunkt für die Erschliessung einer Urform der Emmausperikope"!); Ph. Seidensticker, *Auferstehung*, 17.

[213] G. Lohfink's reasons (*Himmelfahrt*, 238f.) are not fully satisfying: need for variety, intensification in v. 46 *vs.* v. 26, and allegation that Jesus could not speak explicitly of his resurrection while his disciples' eyes were still held. With respect to the first two reasons, one passes; but regarding the third, it does not seem consistent at all with the way the passion-concealment has been constructed, since concealment was never compromised by explicit language (24, 7!). — In our own assessment of Lk's reasons, we should subscribe to the reservation R. Glöckner expresses re. Lohfink's exegesis: "Dem ist aber nur zuzustimmen, wenn hier "Auferstehungsaussage' das Gesamt der Erhöhung Jesu aus der Erniedrigung des Leidens und seine Einsetzung zum Χριστός meint" (*Verkündigung*, 203). The reasons for this should be clearer in what follows.

The comparison suggests that εἰσελθεῖν κτλ. should be understood as a resurrection statement, *but more*: an assertion of Jesus' *leadership* on the journey to everlasting life, which is also brought out by the title, ἀρχηγὸς τῆς ζωῆς, that is accorded the risen One in Acts 3,15. Both expressions are open-ended towards the heavenly exaltation, which is the goal of Jesus' way as it was of the vindicated prophets, Moses, Elia, *et. al.*, before him. We recall that the ἀρχηγός-title is one of several features of Peter's temple speech which support a dominant *Moses*-typology there, especially in view of the similarly structured statements in Acts 3,14f. and Acts 7,35 (cf. n. 156 above). Jesus, leading his missionary followers διὰ πολλῶν θλίψεων to heavenly life (Acts 14,22), recapitulates the "Saviour" role of Moses (cp. Acts 7, 35/5,31), and this, too, accounts for "all the prophets'" testimony to him under Moses' lead.

The model of Moses can also account for εἰσελθεῖν κτλ. as paschal phraseology in our text, considering the reminiscence here of the transfiguration and its colloquium. Not only does εἰσελθεῖν respond to the dominical ἔξοδος discussed by the heavenly figures (Lk 9,31), but the vision on the mount was declared by Lk (9,32) to be a vision of *his glory* (*diff.* Mk 9,4ff.). Not only does the phrase "his glory" occur only in these two instances, but there is clearly a close connection between the vision of it and the appearance of the two heavenly figures with Jesus. The connection is that the figures already belong to the realm of δόξα,[214] as v. 31 says of them: οἳ ὀφθέντες ἐν δόξῃ. Moses and Elia already resided in the realm which Jesus *entered* after his death. They too, in their time and fashion, had experienced the divine vindication of which the persecuted prophet can be certain. That is why their discussion of Jesus' death and their appearance with him in *doxa* fit together so closely as to be mentioned in the same breath (Lk 9,31). Since the new information Lk gave concerning the two prophetic figures at the transfiguration was almost certainly his innovation (cf. pp. 22ff. above), it is no less probable that this reprise of those special details and complement to them comes from his hand as well. Discerning what the two passages express together about Jesus' death and his glory, we have added conviction that the "two men" at the tomb were deliberately evocative of the two great prophets, as if the latter were right on the scene to witness the vindication of the *summus propheta*.

---

[214] On the expanded use of δόξα in this sense (W. GRUNDMANN, *Lk.*, 446, compares Lk 23,42), in which Lk distinguishes himself from the other Synoptics (who restrict it to parousia-references), cf. J. WANKE, *Emmauserzählung*, 87.

Concluding Remarks on the Dialogue: Looking back, we are surprised to see how much the travelers' dialogue has been governed and unified by the *Mosaic-prophet christology* which also prevails in the speeches of Acts 3 and Acts 7. Both the image of the prophet-thaumaturge and the doctrine of his inevitable rejection derive from that typology, as do the hope of Israel's " redemption " and the exodus-entry motif shared with Lk 9,31. — But resonances between the gospel and the Acts are not sufficient of themselves to prove that our author has composed freely in both places. To demonstrate integral Lucan authorship effectively, one should show that ideas have been *combined* in a passage according to a pattern Lk has provably followed elsewhere in *combining and commenting upon his sources*. This is what we hope to have done in analyzing the travelers' dialogue.

We have found that, in the dialogue, Lk sums up major editorial decisions made in composing his first (and extensively, too, his second) volume. First, Cleopas summarizes the course of Lk's narrative: Jesus' pneumatic prophecy, then his rejection and death. Prophet-thaumaturge and prophet-rejected form the partnership which frequently links and embellishes traditions adopted in both books. It expresses the human resistance over which God makes his rule prevail, and it also locates the *skandalon* that blocks human perceptions of Christ and makes them dependent upon his summoning *word* spoken in unconditioned freedom. This breach between the fact and the faith of Easter is the editorial *Leitmotiv* we are verifying in each of the three episodes of the chapter. — Finally, the use and characterization of Scripture here proved itself equally characteristic of this author. Like the facts which his editing keeps distinct from the truth to be revealed about them, the prophecies of Scripture are not transparent to the human observer either. They too require the illumining word of him who is their goal, the risen Saviour. Under his exposition they can become the harmonious christological chorus our author well knows them to be; and they can become an efficacious call to repentance for those who, though they had them in their possession, never recognized their central figure! This argument will prove a basic structural principle of the apostolic kerygma to the Jews as Lk conceives and transcribes it in Acts.

The conclusion with everything to support it and little to countermand it is that the Emmaus dialogue is wholly a construct of St. Luke, from beginning to end. Even our story's " journey " framework, setting off as it does the discussion and revelation concerning the mystery of the messiah's destiny, must be assessed as the contribution of the evangelist.[215] — What now remains, in our planned progression back-

---

[215] Lk's tendency to instill the " journey " motif can be observed in the introduction he has given to the pericope of the widow's son at Nain: ἐπορεύ-

wards from composition to tradition, seems a very small remnant indeed. Nor can we be satisfied with convenient lines of demarcation, such as narrative *vs.* dialogue. Our author's total control of his source-material resists any but the most painstaking and non-preconceived analysis; and even after that, results in this case will probably be tentative and needful of much further corroboration.

(4) *The Narrative of Recognition at the Meal* (24,15f.28-31)

No mechanistic unravelling can be attempted, we know well. Already in *v.* 15, a search for non-Lucan words, style, or motifs would be completely frustrated.[216] Besides, v. 15 effectively expresses the evangelist's plan for the story's composition as a whole: the association between *the mystery of the passion* (ὁμιλεῖν ... καὶ συζητεῖν [περὶ πάντων κτλ., v. 14]) and the *journey* shared with Jesus (συνεπορεύετο αὐτοῖς). This picture — passion instruction framed in a "journey" — is the structure of the central gospel chapters all over again! The unknown Emmaus disciples are being caused to recapitulate the path already charted by the evangelist, evidently because they are put forth as representatives of the vast body of believers gathered about the nucleus of the historic Twelve.[217] If, therefore, the Emmaus *tradition* recorded some kind of delayed recognition of the risen Christ as a traveler or by travelers,[218] this scarcely provided the basis of the specific expression and management of the "journey" motif in the present pericope. Nor would the older form of this motif still be recognizable in v. 15. We have to look further.

ϑη ... καὶ συνεπορεύοντο αὐτῷ οἱ μαθηταὶ αὐτοῦ (Lk 7,11). This and other interesting compositional parallels between the two passages are noted by J. Wanke, *Emmauserzählung*, 32. But of course, we should not agree with Wanke (146 n. 308) that one of the parallels is a "tacit correction of a prophet-christology," — not, that is, if the meaning is "correction" rather than messianic enhancement or explicitation.

[216] Cf. pp. 20f. above re. the ἐγένετο construction. The word ὁμιλεῖν is exclusively Lucan (2*x* in Acts, besides here), and συζητεῖν, which is both Marcan and Lucan, combines with συμπορεύεσϑαι (cp. Lk 7,11 etc.) to illustrate Lk's predilection for *composita* with συν- (J. Wanke, *Emmauserzählung*, 30). — What v. 15 mainly illustrates, of course, is the essential connection of "journey" and passion mystery, and that connection has been explicitated in the gospel tradition by this evangelist.

[217] A valid insight of C. R. Bowen over 65 years ago (cf. *Biblical World* 35 [1910] 34ff., 43ff.). It is difficult to sustain any more specific identification of the two, e.g. with the Jerusalem community (Rengstorf) or the family of Jesus (*pace* Hegesippus/Eusebius; Grundmann) (cf. J. Ernst, *Lk.*, 657, 658). Such closer identification is certainly not a priority of the evangelist.

[218] The wayfaring situation seems, at any rate, to be a frequent feature of our story's religion-historical parallels (cf. p. 73 and n. 14 above).

A moment of non-recognition would have been essential to any story of the category of *Rekognitionserzählung*, to which many agree on assigning our pericope (cf. p. 75 above). It is possible, therefore, that at *v*. 16, with its remarkable motif of the " *holding* " of the travelers' eyes τοῦ μὴ ἐπιγνῶναι αὐτόν, we are finally in touch with the story as it was told before Lk's writing. Yet there is uncertainty about this,[219] and a closer look at the verse from the vantage point of what we have already learned will convince us that this may not be the solution.

We have already pointed out the force of the passive voice in ἐκρατοῦντο · it is the typical oblique expression of divine agency without mention of the divine name (cf. pp. 104f., 133, nn. 102, 184). Once in Acts, where a listener's heart is " opened " to receive the word of the kerygma, our author makes the agency of this explicit : ὁ κύριος διήνοιξεν ... (Acts 16,14). Obversely here, the point is made that " a supernatural power seems to be obstructing the disciples' normal use of their senses." [220] There is no question of disguise or " altered appearance," such as the Marcan Postscriptor will have it in his version of this episode.[221] Lk's travelers did not recognize the Master not because of his appearance ἐν ἑτέρᾳ μορφῇ (Mk 16,12) but because of the *divinely determined economy of concealment and revelation* whereby the truth of Christ's person and destiny was finally to be disclosed. We have shown that this first *narrated* encounter with the risen Lord in Lk was designed as a reenactment of the gospel's program of christological disclosure : a " journey " framed by instruction on the mystery of the passion, such that those gaited to rejoice in sharing the wonder-working powers of Jesus might be introduced to the necessity of sharing his passion. Looking back to where we first found these ideas explicitly contrasted (Lk 9,43-45), we discover a noticeably parallel statement of the passion-mystery which illuminates the statement of v. 16, even to the point of the final clause (not merely consecutive) accompanying both :

9,45 : τὸ ῥῆμα τοῦτο ... ἦν παρακεκαλυμμένον ἀπ' αὐτῶν ἵνα μὴ αἴσθωνται αὐτό ...
24,16 : οἱ δὲ ὀφθαλμοὶ αὐτῶν ἐκρατοῦντο τοῦ μὴ ἐπιγνῶναι αὐτόν.

---

[219] Recall the difference of opinion between Wilckens and Wanke, n. 33 above.

[220] J. Dupont, in *Misc. Ubach*, 365. The relationship between v. 16 and the statements accompanying the passion prophecies (Lk 9,45 ; 18,34) was observed already by C.R. Bowen, *Biblical World* 35 (1910) 241 ; A. Plummer, *Lk*, 256. Cf. also I. H. Marshall, *TyndB* 24 (1973) 83.

[221] Rightly J. Dupont, *loc. cit.* in n. 220 ; X. Léon-Dufour, *Résurrection*, 211 ; J. E. Alsup, *Appearance Stories*, 196. On the other hand, falling victim to the temptation of " eisegesis " from Mk 16,12, is B. Rigaux, *Dieu l'a ressuscité*, 230.

In each instance the passive form and accompanying successive clause clause express the divinely imposed regimen of the passion-mystery, initituted *for a season* during the earthly course of the messiah and prolonged during the Emmaus walk so that the *moment* and the *source* of the great revelation of Easter might be the more sharply defined. By means of this narrative economy, Lk teaches that the *content* of the Easter revelation is nothing more than *the meaning and effects of Jesus' mission on earth,* which could be grasped only when the Easter Christ *personally* illumined them in retrospect ! [222] The risen Christ reveals the meaning of his earthly " journey " and thus makes it adaptable by his followers as the content and pattern of their own mission (— as we shall explain more fully *ad* 24,47f. and in chap. IV/ii 1-2). — All of which makes the delayed recognition of the Emmaus episode part of Lk's plan of composition rather than purely a break-through of the older Emmaus tradition. V. 16 will scarcely have preexisted his composition, therefore, at least not in a form that would leave it recognizable to us now.

Mention of a version of the Emmaus episode in the *Marcan Postscript* reminds us that the issue of independent traditions contained in that passage (Mk 16,9-20) is not settled. The older criticism tended to brand the whole piece a mere literary compilation drawn from the canonical gospels, intended to bring the seemingly stunted Easter story of Mk into congruence with the others.[223] Some more recent interpreters have shown themselves more receptive of an independent traditional basis for some of Deutero-Mk's material. But even these more favorable *vota* carefully exclude Mk 16,9-13, where nearly everyone judges the *Postscriptor* to be functioning as *compilator*, and concentrate on 16,(14)15-20.[224] — Following the consensus which now

[222] H.-W. BARTSCH, *Wachet*, 25: " God prevents them from recognizing the risen One so that it might be brought out more clearly that he grants that recognition as his gift." Cf. n. 185 above.

[223] So e.g. E. HIRSCH, *Auferstehungsgeschichten*, 9; E. LOHMEYER, *Galiläa*, 6; W. MICHAELIS, *Erscheinungen*, 45f.; J. G. DAVIES, *He Ascended*, 42f., 49; H. GRASS, *Ostergeschehen*, 15. This older consensus has been endorsed more recently by Eugen HELZLE, " Der Schluss des Markusevangeliums (Mk 16,9-20)," *TLZ* 85 (1960) 470-472; H. KASTING, *Anfänge*, 39-40; G. LOHFINK, *Himmelfahrt*, 119f.; and now the fuller analyses of J. E. ALSUP, *Appearance Stories*, 117-124.

[224] The distinction between vv. 9-13 and vv. 15ff. of Mk 16 is most important to E. LINNEMANN, who has recently sponsored the implausible view that vv. 15ff. belongs to the original Marcan composition (cf. " Der (wiedergefundene) Markusschluss," *ZTK* 66 [1969, 255-287] 258f., 264-269). The same held true with W. SCHMITHALS, who followed LINNEMANN with a still more fantastic reconstruction of the " missing " Markusschluss ("Der Markusschluss, die Verklärungsgeschichte und die Aussendung der Zwölf," *ZTK* 69 [1972, 379-411] 404ff.). — More modest and plausible assertions of independent tradition in Mk 16,15ff., which avoid suggesting the same for vv. 9-13, are: C. H. DODD, in *More N.T.*

includes even the recent supporters of "Mk," and making C. H. DODD's explanation of this text's *argumentum* our own,[225] we can hardly urge Mk 16,12-13 as a solid foundation of any hypothesis meant to explain the tradition-history of Lk 24,13-35. Preparing his counterpoint for the great apostolic encounter he reports in 16,14ff., "Mk" discarded all details of the first two appearances except such as built up the threshold of unbelief for that conclusive, mission-founding experience. One detail that is innovated is the appearance to the travelers ἐν ἑτέρᾳ μορφῇ, which cannot be urged as an original Easter-narrative motif with any corroborative evidence from the other canonical accounts. It has to be judged more probably a later generation's *conclusion* concerning the otherwise inexplicable lack of recognition by the Lord's followers *as reported by the canonical account being excerpted.*[226] This conclusion is the more likely considering that the Postscriptor represents a growing, later-generation interest in the anthropological factors of the Easter appearances: the witnesses' reactions and responses, and the motives thereof.[227] Since, because of this redactor's

---

Studies, 110-11, 130f.; F. HAHN, *Mission*, 53f.; O. MICHEL, "Der Abschluss des Matthäusevangeliums," *EvT* 10 (1950-51, 16-26), 20f.; P. STUHLMACHER, *Evangelium*, 256-258; R. H. FULLER, *Formation*, 156-157.

[225] "The most emphatic points of these little stories [i.e. in vv. 9-13 — R. D.] are those which describe not the appearance of the Lord itself, nor the recognition of him by his followers, but the reporting of the incident to others and its unfavorable reception (xvi. 10-11.13). There is therefore no such specific formative motive at work as we can recognize elsewhere .... The whole stress is laid upon the appearance to the Eleven, which serves to introduce the Lord's command to his Church ..., his ascension, and the summary of the early Christian mission which concludes the passage. The two incidents briefly touched upon in xvi. 9-13 serve only to introduce the main incident, and to exhibit the unbelief with which the reports of Mary Magdalen and the two companions are received, as a foil to the faith of the Church. The contrast of belief and unbelief is in fact a prominent theme of xvi. 14-20 ... it does appear that verses 9-13 may be derivative .... we shall be disposed to think that the appearance to the two companions came out of Lk xxiv. rather than directly out of oral tradition" (C. H. DODD, *More N. T. Studies*, 130).

[226] Cf. F. HAHN, *Hoheitstitel*, 124 n. 4: "Wie stark der ganze Markusanhang von jüngeren Anschauungen über den Auferstandenen geprägt ist, zeigt auch das ἐφανερώθη ἐν ἑτέρᾳ μορφῇ in V. 12."

[227] J. E. ALSUP, *Appearance Stories*, 124, who cites (n. 360) the similar interest of the Codex Beza text of Lk's Emmaus story. ALSUP goes on to survey apocryphal versions of the resurrection appearances, in connection with Mk 16,9ff., and shows how the latter shares with them concerns of the later, developing churches (*ibid.*, 139). — Specifically asserting the character of compilation of Mk 16,9-13(14), and compilation based on *Lk* at that, are Fräulein LINNEMANN, *art. cit.* (in n. 224) 258, 267, 269; K. ALAND, "Der wiedergefundene Markusschluss?" *ZTK* 67 (1970, 3-13) 13; C.H. DODD (n. 225 above); J. E. ALSUP, *Appearance Stories*, 194f. — The only scholar I know of who supports the incorporation of independent tradition at Mk 16,12f. is R. ANNAND, (*art. cit.* in n. 12 above) *ScotJT* 11 (1958) 180ff., but no persuasive analysis accompanies the suggestion to offset the weight of every other opinion I have read on the matter.

haste to reach his main point of interest, the risen One's " altered appearance " gets no development in his narrative, we are left neither knowing nor imagining any integral tradition of Christ's appearance to *viatores* which would have developed this motif, or how it would have done so! — The Deutero-Marcan reference can therefore not function positively in our tradition-historical analysis of Lk 24,13-35.

Our conclusion concerning Lk 24,16 is firm, therefore: it accomplishes the deferral of Easter recognition which sustains the evangelist's passion-mystery to the point where, after " journey " and *didachè* have been rehearsed anew, the appointed moment of the great mystery's disclosure can be recorded. The pathos established between ἐκρατοῦντο and διηνοίχθησαν is Lucan dramaturgy in the service of Lucan theology! Consequently, our search for the older matrix of the Emmaus story still shows minimal results at 24,16, where the dialogue sets in.

The Meal-Scene (24,28-31)

Prospects that clues to the tradition might be more substantial in this section look dim at first sight, for there is ample evidence that the meal sequence has been modelled after the third gospel's version of the feeding of the multitude, Lk 9,11-17, and, to a lesser extent, the institution narrative.[228] The expression for the " declining " day (κλίνειν with ἡμέρα)) occurs only here and in Lk 9,12 *diff.* Mk; so too the verb κατακλίνειν (Lk 9,14.15 *diff.* Mk; elsewhere only Lk 7,36 S). The verb εὐλογεῖν, understood as a gesture of blessing rather than the Jewish table-prayer, occurs in this scene (object = the bread, v. 30) and in the feeding account (object = the loaves and fishes, 9,16 *diff.* Mk 6,41 / Mt 14,19).[229] The phrase κλάσας ἐπεδίδου αὐτοῖς in v. 30 echoes Lk 9,16 (cp. Mk 6,41), with the imperfect (= Mk) suggesting the systematic repetition of such distribution (*vis-à-vis* the ἔδωκεν of

[228] J. Wanke, *Eucharistieverständnis*, 38ff., and *Emmauserzählung*, 97-98. — The evidence for this is enhanced by the considerations advanced by H. Patsch: Lk, like Mt, strikes the distribution of fish from 9,16 (cp. Mk 6,41), allowing all the emphasis to fall on the bread. He also strikes the fish from the gathering of the remnants. " Diese Betonung des Brot-Elementes ist ohne Einfluss der Eucharistiefeier nur schwer erklärlich," says Patsch (*ZNW* 62 [1971] 215), who rightly sees the diminished role of the fish as a tendency wherever the eucharistic character of the feeding miracle is being especially emphasized (*ibid.*, 221). This accords perfectly, of course, with Lk's contouring of the Emmaus meal after the model of the feeding, but of the bread-feeding only.

[229] " Wie fremd dem Nichtpalästiner dieser absolute Gebrauch von εὐλογεῖν erscheinen musste, zeigt Lk 9,16, ... hier ist durch Umstellen des (in der Vorlage Mk 6,41 zu κατέκλασεν gehörenden) Objekts aus dem Tischgebet eine Weihung geworden " (J. Jeremias, *Abendmahlsworte*³, 167; cf. also H. Patsch, *ZNW* 62 [1971] 217ff.). — " Lk wird darum nicht bewusst gewesen sein, dass sein stilistischer Eingriff zugleich ein sachlicher war " (Patsch, *art. cit.*, 219 n. 35).

the institution narrative, Lk 22,19 / Mk 14,23). On the other hand, the vocabulary of the institution — λαβὼν, εὐλόγησεν (Mk 14,22 *diff.* Lk), κλάσας, and (ἐπι)διδόναι (v. 30) — had already infiltrated the traditions of the miraculous feeding which Mk adopted,[230] so one should not preclude a similar cross-fertilization between *eucharistic and Easter traditions* as a possible foundation for the meal scene that Lk relates. In fact, if we could find some hard evidence for such a development independent of Lk's writing, we should have to reckon seriously with the likelihood that our evangelist, in giving the Emmaus meal its pointed echoes of his own account of the mass feeding, was only continuing what had already occurred in the Easter-narrative tradition before him.

Now there is just such evidence, and it is to be found in the Easter story of Jn 21, whose relation to our pericope in the history of the tradition has been proposed occasionally in the literature.[231] Already in our analysis of v. 12 above, we voiced our agreement with R. Pesch, *et al.* (chap. I, n. 183), in the view that the miracle of the great catch and the christophany at the meal are separate entities woven together by the Johannine redactor, and not an integral account which had to be either predated by Lk (5,1-11) or postdated for its position in the fourth gospel. — So far as an exact delineation of those prior entities is concerned, of course, *tot sententiae quot auctores*, and we are in no position to treat the matter adequately in the present study. We do think it possible, however, to consider Jn 21,9.12.13 as the irreducible core of the christophany tradition (perhaps with elements of vv. 4 and 8 added) and to maintain that it featured a recognition[232]

[230] H. Patsch, *ZNW* 62 (1971) 219ff., esp. 227.

[231] Cf. n. 25 above.

[232] In this connection, it seems to us that one of the weakest steps in the analysis of R. Pesch was his diagnosis of the (johannine) tradition of the meal christophany, to which he would ascribe elements that can hardly come from other than the author of the postscript chapter (cf. *Fischfang*, 104ff.). Principal among these is the role of the "*beloved disciple*," whose presence opposite Peter at v. 7 was rightly judged by R. Bultmann a redactional preparation for the contrast of the two disciples' mandates in Jn 21,20ff. (cf. *Johannes*, 543). There is good reason to think that "the beloved disciple" is a redactional clasp-factor for the whole postscript construction, uniting the appearance story with the separate tradition of Jn 21,20ff. and uniting the whole piece with the earlier Johannine composition preceding it; hence there is no good basis for including that figure in the appearance tradition (*contra* R. Pesch, *Fischfang*, 97) and every reason for crediting him to the Postscriptor himself (cf. R. Schnackenburg, *Johannesevangelium* III, 412). Then it becomes probable that Peter's leap into the water was related originally by itself, apart from any recognition by a more perceptive companion, and that it was told originally as part of the *miraculous-catch story* rather than the appearance. It is the miraculous-catch story, after all, and not the meal episode which specially features the person of Peter. Indeed, Jn 21,12f. involves all the disciples, and no dominical meal after which this passage might be modelled (including Jn 6,5ff.) gives any part-

of the risen One in the framework of a *meal of bread and fish*, evocative of precisely the mass-feeding miracle.[233]

Our main point in comparing Lk 24 with Jn 21 does not depend on an exact delineation of Jn's *Grundlage*. Whatever his christophany

---

icular role to Peter. On the other hand, the exultant apostle's leap towards the Master through the water could be Jn's counterpart to his act of veneration in the Lucan version of the great catch (Lk 5,8 ; so K. BORNHAUSER, *Sondergut*, 41-42 ; and on the absence of Petrine emphasis in the appearance episode : Th. LORENZEN, *ZNW* 64 [1973] 218 n. 37 ; J. WANKE, *Emmauserzählung*, 104). If the leap became part of the miracle story together with some element of delayed recognition before the postscript was written, this was probably due to cross-currents within the Petrine narrative tradition (e.g. Mt 14,28ff.). Originally, however, the " great catch " would not have included the recognition motif since the renewed fishing undertaken after a fruitless night's work (Lk 5,5 / Jn 21,3) would have been difficult for any narrator to motivate except by a command of the Master fully recognized (R. BULTMANN, 543f.).

If our argument is correct, the recognition motif belongs indigenously to the appearance tradition (rightly R. PESCH, *Fischfang*, 94, 97, 106) and attaches properly to the event of the *christophany at the meal* rather than to any prior recognition by a leading apostle. Since the Postscriptor has nevertheless produced this intervention at v. 7 (to prepare for the guarantor's role for the gospel tradition that he will assign the anonymous figure in v. 24), he has had to suppress the association of the recognition with the meal, leaving only a vestige of this in the curiously self-contradictory v. 12. Here the redactor has added εἰδότες ὅτι ὁ κύριός ἐστιν, just as he added ὁ κύριός ἐστιν twice at v. 7, sustaining his prepositioning of the appearance story's proper climax (rightly on this Th. LORENZEN, *ZNW* 64 (1973) 218f., *contra* PESCH ; J. E. ALSUP, *Appearance Stories*, 202). — It is our judgment, therefore, that the meal-christophany of Jn 21 became separated from the moment of recognition through the activity of the author of the chapter, hence the present sequence of that notoriously uneven and disputed section should not be proposed as a decisive argument for the view that recognition and Easter meal came together first by Lucan innovation in the Emmaus story (so J. WANKE, *Emmauserzählung*, 104f., and *BZ* 18 (1974) 183, 184). Our analysis is close to that of J. E. ALSUP (*Appearance Stories*, 204f.), except that he insists the Johannine tradition has located recognition of the risen One before the meal — perhaps in the invitation ! — even though the anticipation of recognition at v. 7 is, for him too, clearly redactional. — Exact reconstruction of the tradition is not possible ; but what we do have in Jn 21, we think, is sufficient evidence to justify taking the meal scene of the Emmaus story as the *point de départ* of any quest for the Emmaus *tradition*. Cf. R. SCHNACKENBURG, *Johannesev.* III,412.

[233] R. BULTMANN, *Johannes*, 549f. ; C. K. BARRETT, *St. John* (cited in chap. I, n. 183) 484 ; H. PATSCH, *ZNW* 62 (1971) 230. — The parallelism between Jn 21 and Lk 5 consists of elements concentrated in Lk 5,4b-9, with a few items in Lk's vv. 3 and 10. This parallelism allows the discernment of a common story of the miraculous catch, whereas the tensions within Jn 21,2-13 urge the judgment of vv. 5 and 10 as redactional clamps fastening the miracle story together with the appearance story, and v. 7 as a redactional preparation for the originally separate materials in 21,15ff. There is no need for us to rehearse this whole discussion here, however. Cf. R. SCHNACKENBURG, *Johannesev.* III, 411ff., a good summary.

tradition included, it makes unmistakable allusion to the miracle of the multiplication, of which, as E. HAENCHEN has observed, " it works as something of an imitation." [234] When one observes, too, that the noun has changed between the miraculous catch (Jn 21,6.8c.11) and the meal scene (Jn 21,9.13), from ἰχθύς to ὀψάριον, it seems likely that the latter is intended as an echo of the feeding story, where the same noun was used (Jn 6,9.11). The combination of bread and " little fish " also evokes the memory of the meal of the multitude, in which all were filled from the hand of Jesus and acclaimed him the mighty prophet of the last times, ὁ προφήτης ὁ ἐρχόμενος εἰς τὸν κόσμον (Jn 6,14).[235]

Our point is, of course, that in recording a meal in which the risen Lord repeats the messianic gesture of feeding the many, and in portraying it in language deliberately evocative of the miracle story, Lk was following a pattern that is also verified elsewhere in the gospel tradition. Even if the Johannine scene comes from a later stage of the Easter-narrative tradition and the two passages hardly lie in the same path of development,[236] our argument still has validity: Lk was probably not the first to relate an Easter christophany in the setting of a meal modelled after the miracle of the mass feeding.[237] A sign of the tradition-historical pedigree of his account, *vis-à-vis* Jn's, could be the authentic names of place and person attached to the appearance, — although, of course, he has assigned new functions of his own design to both of them. In any case, the hypothesis is quite plausible that Lk's Emmaus *tradition* was the account of the risen Christ encountered as a *wayfaring stranger entertained as a houseguest* (in the house of Cleopas ?) and, while reclining at table with his host, *reenacting the*

[234] *Art. cit.* (in n. 193 above), in *Die Bibel und wir*, 179. Note the similarities: *Jn 21,13* ; ... Ἰησοῦς ... λαμβάνει τὸν ἄρτον καὶ δίδωσιν αὐτοῖς, καὶ ὀψάριον ὁμοίως· *Jn 6,11* : ἔλαβεν οὖν τοὺς ἄρτους ὁ Ἰησοῦς καὶ ... διέδωκεν τοῖς ἀνακειμένοις, ὁμοίως καὶ ἐκ τῶν ὀψαρίων ....

[235] The tendency to amplify miraculous detail in the Johannine wonder stories is exemplified by the choice of the word ὀψάριον, " little fish, " which makes the contrast of the food on hand with the multitude fed overwhelming. On this amplifying tendency in the Johannine source, cf. Jürgen BECKER, " Wunder und Christologie. Zum literarkritischen und christologischen Problem der Wunder im Johannesevangelium," *NTS* 16 (1969-70, 130-148) 137f.

[236] R. PESCH, *Fischfang*, 133 ; J. WANKE, *Emmauserzählung*, 104. — According to WANKE, the disparity of the two passages makes it impossible to draw from their comparison any more than the possibility of a pre-Lucan origin of the Emmaus meal scene (*ibid.*, 105). We are hopeful that our analysis adds support to that possibility.

[237] Stressing the risen Lord's invitation, J. WANKE (*op. cit.*, 104f.) prefers to consider the eucharistic institution accounts the main influence on the Johannine meal scene (cf. also H. KASTING, *Anfänge*, 51). The difference, of course, is that whereas there is explicit echo of the feeding miracle in the " bread " and " little fish," there is no such verbal repetition in δεῦτε ἀριστήσατε, no matter how much it might put one in mind of λάβετε φάγετε, etc.

miraculous feeding of bread and fish, whereupon his astonished hosts-turned-guests recognized his identity.[238] The Stranger's immediate disappearance has counterparts in the ascension of 24,51 and the " translation " of Philip after the similar sequence of Acts 8(cf. v. 39), but it was likely a component of the older tradition because it is a topical item of charismatic prophecy.[239]

We have two directions in which to develop this tradition-historical hypothesis, the first in pursuit of the *milieu* which might have nurtured such a species of Easter story, the second seeking Lk's purpose and motive in adopting the story. (a) First, concerning the *milieu*: we are especially interested in what appear to be signals of *primitive mission practice* in the hypothetical tradition we have proposed. The Stranger hosted at a meal, who turns out to be the Lord in the breaking of the bread, contains a hint of the *self-image of itinerant Christian missionaries of the early years,* as has been occasionally suggested concerning our pericope (cf. n. 29 above). There is the additional feature of the tradition that it records an Easter encounter which commemorates the *thaumaturgy* of the Master in ministering to the masses, and this may point to *charisma and thaumaturgy* as features of the activity of these itinerants who recounted the Easter meal in this fashion. — What is most significant, however, is that the situation of the earthly Jesus as *houseguest* is a strong and recurrent feature of the *traditions proper to the gospel of Lk,*[240] just as Lk's version of the *Q* sayings forming the *instruction to the missionaries* gives prominent play to the directive governing the travelers' acceptance of *hospitality and table-fellowship* in the households along their route (Lk 10,5-7 *diff.* Mt). — At present, we can only raise the question of a possible bonding of these traditions to the old Emmaus story in both common motifs and common pre-evangelical background. We also wonder whether the suggestion of the tradition's stewardship by charismatic missionaries — in Jn's case, at least, such as recorded the mass-feeding miracle itself with popular acclaim of Jesus as the eschatological prophet — might point us in the

[238] I therefore do not think the whole moment of recognition was Lk's contribution, or that the connection of recognition and meal should be regarded as the *specificum* of Lk's scene (*pace* J. WANKE, *Emmauserzählung,* 107). If one wants to determine the Lucan *specificum,* as we have emphasized, he must look to the connection of the meal with the passion instruction.

[239] The expression ἄφαντος ἐγένετο is *hapax legomenon* in the NT but belongs to the most frequently used vocabulary in hellenistic sources depicting heavenly " translations " (so G. FRIEDRICH, in *Orientierung an Jesus,* 58). The similarity of this element in Lk 24,31 to the corresponding moment of the Philip story (Acts 8,39f.) suggests that both are influenced by a *topos* of charismatic mission lore.

[240] Lk 7,36ff.; 10,38ff.; 14,1; 19,1ff.; (cp. 5,29 *diff.* Mk). We shall discuss this feature of the Lucan *Sondergut* in chap. III (2a-iii).

direction of interesting discoveries on long-debated matters: the stewardship of the oldest Jesus-tradition, the archaic complexion of the Lucan *Sondergut*, and the latter's substantial contacts with some of the Johannine traditions. Our intention now is to let these suggestions linger with us as we proceed further in the study of Lk 24. Chances are, if the hypothesis we have put forward has any substance, we will find some further support for it in the analysis of the third pericope. We shall then organize and expand our tradition-historical findings in the first portion of chapter IV.

(b) More properly the business of the moment, in view of the path our inquiry has taken, is Lk's purpose in adopting the tradition of the meal-christophany that we have suggested. We find the answer to this in some retrospect upon our analysis of the Emmaus pericope. In treating *v.* 35, we observed the remarkably consistent pattern of association between the Master's "breaking of the bread" and his instruction in the mystery of the passion (pp. 105ff.). The sequence of these followed in the case of the mass feeding (Lk 9) and the last supper (Lk 22) was reversed in the Emmaus story, as the travelers were caused to retrace their steps, over the path of the gospel's "journey," rehearsing the truth hidden in the scriptures and receiving bread from the Lord's hand. For Lk, it seems, the "breaking of the bread" is the sacramental signature of Jesus' bequest of his own life's mission and destiny to his followers. As such, the rite is the normal and necessary accompaniment of the passion instruction, so that the two are really a *single act*, not two separate moments of the recognition process in our story. — This is the understanding which explains Lk's appropriation of an Easter tradition in which the feeding miracle was recreated. If he was going to record the passion instruction again, it was normal and necessary that the feeding should accompany it. And the fact that the feeding of *the masses* is the first line of reminiscence in the meal-scene, rather than the eucharistic institution (cf. n. 237 above), reminds us of the crowds that were apparently still on hand after the feeding to hear of the messianic destiny of suffering in Lk 9,23ff. (p. 106 above). The law of the messiah's destiny is ultimately binding on all who heed his voice. That is why the miracle and not the institution is the *Vorbild* of the christophany, just as the travelers who experienced it were not of the founding Twelve but anonymous representatives of the expanding (missionary) Church at large.

So it is that, although 24,31.32 feature two applications of the verb διανοίγειν, we know that these cannot be considered separate "openings", nor can they be taken as symptoms of imperfectly fused tradition and composition. The "breaking of the bread" is the sacramental action which renders the teaching Lord present to his congregation, disclosing to her the mystery of his person and laying upon her the burden of his own mission and destiny. As risen Lord, present in word and sacrament, he shows himself the *goal and meaning of all the scriptures,* and he imparts to his followers that ministry of the word which continues to unlock the secret otherwise hidden away in the sacred pages. *His voice* is what continues to be heard in that ministry of the word (thus Dt 18,15.18 can be invoked by his witnesses, Acts 3,22-23), for it is only *in personal encounter with him,* and from that perspective, that the whole mystery of God's plan of salvation is opened to the eye of faith. — That is, in the final analysis, the teaching of the Emmaus story. *It precisely forbids any ironclad separation of the time of Jesus from the time of the Church,* as if the latter saw only an institutionalizing of what could no longer be a real presence or a living word !

(5) *Results for our Further Investigation*

In this detailed study of the first of our two Easter appearance stories, we found a solid fabric of the *evangelist's own writing,* demonstrated mainly by the observation of patterns that are followed consistently through the two Lucan volumes in the *combining and modifying of sources.* Only in the meal scene did we, at length, find a substantial lead towards a hypothetical *Emmaus tradition* that our author might have utilized. This lead will stand or fall with the success of our further investigation of Lk's source-material in the third pericope of Lk 24, the appearance to the apostolic circle. If evidence can be found there of a traditional substratum at all analogous to the one we suggest for the Emmaus christophany, we shall have won a substantial hypothesis for the tradition-historical explanation of this Easter story.

In pursuit of the mind of Lk, the Emmaus pericope brought us further with some substantial strides. It showed how dialectical patterns developed in the editing of the tomb sequence were at last utilized to bring the period of messianic concealment to a close and exhibit the Easter faith's beginning as the pure gift of the risen Lord, personally present to his followers and instructing them. This dialectical pattern will not now be relinquished, as if the light of day had dawned and the darkness were forever past. Just as every act of faith is a leap forward out of the darkness, so, too, every Easter encounter is presented by Lk as a summons out of confusion and blindness, personally bestowed by the risen Lord *sola gratia.* That is why, contrary to our expectation, the third episode will begin as if nothing had occurred and nothing were changed ! — By now, however, we know the pattern ; we shall follow more easily !

Chapter III

THE APPEARANCE TO THE APOSTOLIC CIRCLE (Lk 24,36-53)

(1) Research Survey and State of the Question

The *Forschungslage* for Luke's third Easter pericope is even less gratifying than for the Emmaus account since even the few specific treatises that were available to us in the previous chapter are wanting in this one. Only a handful of essays are dedicated to the third pericope of Lk 24,[1] and their authors' objective is mostly to gain developmental perspective on the apostolic-appearance tradition in general. Otherwise we are relegated once more to treatments within treatments, — that is, studies of this text in the interests of broader arguments, whether Easter in the New Testament,[2] or mission in the New Testa-

[1] To the whole pericope, as we conceive it, one can name only A. George, "Les récits d'apparitions aux Onze à partir de Luc 24,36-53," in P. de Surgy, et al., *La résurrection*, 75-104. — Recently, on the subject of the narrative phase of the episode, vv. 36-43, were added: M.-É. Boismard, "Le réalisme des récits évangéliques," *LumVie* #109 (1971) 31-41; C. M. Martini, "L'apparizione agli Apostoli in Lc 24,36-43 nel complesso dell'opera lucana," in É. Dhanis, éd., *Resurrexit*, 230-245.

[2] If the famous monograph of H. Grass can be taken as exemplary in this respect, it indicates that scholars are inclined to hasten through the appearance narrative (*Ostergeschehen*, 40-43) so as to devote greater space to the uniquely Lucan ascension (*ibid.*, 43-51), with its attendant problems affecting the sequence and nature of the Easter events. Since most scientific studies of the Easter narratives are preoccupied with developmental patterns, as Grass was, the tendency is to emphasize the trend-markers of our passage — its condensation of time and locale, its "surrealistic" picture of the risen One, his *manducatio*, etc. — without giving all its details a patient hearing. As a result, though some more recent treatments have been lengthier than Grass's (e.g. J. Kremer, *Osterbotschaft*, 72-86; R. H. Fuller, *Formation*, 114-123), they prove only slightly more satisfactory as interpretations of Lk's Easter narrative. A most recent example of *Traditionsgeschichte* through trend-sketching is J. E. Alsup, *Appearance Stories*, who devotes very close analysis to our passage but clearly has his eye on the goal of his quest: a basic literary form and tradition-matrix for the group-appearance stories (cf. pp. 147-190). As a result, redactional concerns proper to Lk are assumed, rather than demonstrated, and are mentioned only in passing, as if they were a shelf for storing elements deemed refractory of the trends. Vocabulary statistics are used to diagnose tradition-elements in a manner which, in view of Lk's mastery of his source-material, cannot be sustained. More about this in our analyses to follow.

ment,[3] or matters of *Lukasanalyse*,[4] where the larger issue determines in every instance the selection of data to be considered. We shall not be able to rely on any of these contributions very extensively, nor shall we find any of the commentaries adequately comprehensive and up-to-date.[5] Our culling of suggestions from the literature will thus be even more eclectic here, at least regarding 24,36-49, than elsewhere.

---

[3] In concentrating almost entirely on this important aspect of our pericope, the recent study of J. DUPONT ("La portée christologique de l'évangélisation des nations d'après Luc 24,47," in *N. T. und Kirche, für R. Schnackenburg*, 125-143) is a welcome amplification of numerous broader treatments, such as F. HAHN, *Mission*, 113ff., and (not mentioned by DUPONT) H. KASTING, *Anfänge*, 41ff. But we hope to show that, in prescinding from the appearance narrative, which is preamble to the Lord's instruction and promise, these authors miss an important ingredient of the interpretation of their passage. Superior in this respect, but much too brief, is J. ROLOFF, *Apostolat*, 189ff.

[4] Although the major treatises in this category do not set any direction for our detailed work on this pericope — though many stress the ascension as Lucan *proprium*, just as the monographs on the Easter traditions do — we do find improved examples of up-to-date, unpredisposed exegesis among them. Of the works of general scope, the best, in our opinion, is R. GLÖCKNER, *Verkündigung*, whose treatment of the Easter portion of Lk's story (IV/1) is an antidote to the usual neglect. Of other general treatments which accord this pericope any treatment, C. H. TALBERT, *Luke*, 30ff., is dedicated to what we think is a mistaken rendering of Lk's mind, and H.-W. BARTSCH, *Wachet*, 26ff., saved but little for the last of his three Easter-story treatments. — More productive, for our purposes, have been the recent treatments of special aspects of Lucan thought, notably G. LOHFINK on the ascension and Chr. BURCHARD and E. NELLESSEN on the "witness" motif. LOHFINK managed to include in his outstanding investigation of the ascension in Lk-Acts a full probe of the relation of the gospel's finale to the contents of the third pericope (cf. *Himmelfahrt*, 147-151, 163-176). And on the much-discussed "witness" motif, BURCHARD devoted some penetrating criticism to our passage (all its aspects) in an excursus (*Zeuge*, 130-135), and NELLESSEN gave fuller treatment to Lk 24,44-49 but took less than adequate notice, given his restricted thesis, to the context of which that passage is an integral part (*Zeugnis*, 107-118). As in all categories, a patient hearing of this pericope's testimony on its own terms, fully and methodically, is wanting amongst the redaction-historical works, even after credit is given to the few which proved more satisfactory and insightful than the many have been.

[5] Once again, the new Regensburg commentary of J. ERNST forces revision of this statement only as the thesis is in the final typing stage. ERNST's treatment of the third pericope is much less impressive than he gave to the Emmaus story, however (cf. pp. 666-674), since he stands pat on older criticism of Lk's "apologetic" purposes and finds little nuance in the narrative beyond such straightforward (anti-docetic) argumentation. Nor do we learn much that is new from the remaining portions of the commentary. Citation of older works predominates and, surprisingly, LOHFINK is unmentioned in the ascension treatment. — Among the rest of the commentaries, assessments run much as for the Emmaus pericope (cf. chap. II, n. 6), except LOISY's is much weakened by his eccentric hypothesis re. the post-Lucan edition of the *Opus ad Theophilum*. — The Acts 1 resumé of our passage means we can benefit from some of the superior Acts commentary (HAENCHEN, CONZELMANN) and R. PESCH, *EKK Vorarb.* 3, 7-35.

A survey of all categories mentioned, however, does bring important trends to light, and our investigation will benefit from an attempt to situate it in reference to them. The trends involve the tradition-historical affiliation of vv. 36ff., the nature of the appearance-tradition utilized in these verses, the Lucan character of the risen One's instruction, and the origin and inspiration of the ascension scene. In addition, the matter of the Western omissions in the textual tradition, already familiar to us from the empty-tomb pericope, becomes crucially controversial again at vv. 36, 40, 51, and 52 in the passage before us. — A sketch of the trends of study affecting each of these matters will suffice for placing the present endeavour in context.

(a) *Tradition-historical Affiliation*: It has long been recognized that all the gospels record the risen Christ's appearance to the *coetus discipulorum* in accounts which share a common schema and common motifs.[6] Mt 28,16ff., Lk 24,36ff., and Jn 20,19ff., and the Marcan and Johannine postscripts as well, show a standard sequence of "vision" and "audition" (L. Brun) in which the resurrected One encounters his earthly associates, overcomes their initial uncertainty of his identity, and commissions them to carry out a mission endowed by himself. Although the narratives differ among themselves to the degree that no single ancestor can account for them all, they show enough structural similarity to prove they are ramifications of a mainstream tradition with common roots.[7] Indeed, the endurance of especially two features, the identity-motif and the mission mandate, persuades us to accept variations among them as clues to either the tradition's developmental reflexes or the evangelists' individual literary adjustments. It is easy to see, for example, how the narrators became increasingly concerned to set the witnesses' doubt aside, given that their accounts run the gamut between no demonstration (Mt) and massive demonstration (Lk/Jn) of the apparition's physical reality.[8] But then, when we find

[6] Cf. M. Albertz, *ZNW* 21 (1922) 259, 268; L. Brun, *Auferstehung*, 54-64; E. Fascher, *ZNW* 26 (1927) 5ff.; C. H. Dodd, in *More N. T. Studies*, 104ff., 111, 113; A. Descamps, *Bib* 40 (1959) 739ff.; B. Lindars, "The Composition of John XX," *NTS* 7 (1960-61, 142-147) 143; W. Marxsen, *Auferstehung*, 83f., 87; Ph. Seidensticker, *Auferstehung*, 65ff., 98f.; A. George, in *La résurrection*, 76, 86-93; H. Kasting, *Anfänge*, 46; J. E. Alsup, *Appearance Stories*, esp. 173ff., 189f. Cf. also I. H. Marshall, *TyndB* 24 (1973) 93.

[7] W. Marxsen writes (*Auferstehung*, 87): "Es kann ... kaum ein Zweifel darüber bestehen, dass wir mit einer Tradition zu tun haben, die aus *einer* Wurzel kommt. Diese ist bei Matthäus, Lukas und Johannes aufgenommen und in *Darstellungen* hineingeführt worden, die unterschiedlich erzählen" (italics his). Cf. also A. George, in *La résurrection*, 103; Ph. Seidensticker, *Auferstehung*, 68, 75.

[8] The further development of this in ever more explicit terms is attested by the post-canonical literature, e.g. *Epist. Apostolorum* 12 (E. Hennecke, *N. T. Apocrypha* I, 197); Ignatius, *Smyrn.* 3,2 (*Loeb Classical Library*, Apost. Fathers

bodily demonstration occurring in John's version (20,20) without being motivated by the doubt factor, we can charge this anomaly to an evangelist whose protest against a *fides quaerens evidentiam* caused a postponement of the doubt-motif to the separate Thomas-episode, where it could be tempered with his own perspective (Jn 20,29).[9] Correspondingly, when Luke's appearance is preamble to provisions for a *future* mission rather than the actual mandate and endowment inaugurating one, we suspect again the refractory touch of the evangelist, who has reduced the commission to a mere designation of witnesses and has withheld the actual (Spirit-) endowment in prospect of the separate Lucan Pentecost (Lk 24,48-49).[10] This kind of departure from the tradition's matrix is readily diagnosed according to the established literary patterns and theories of the evangelist responsible for it.

An unusually impressive consensus governs the question of the special tradition-historical bond between Lk's and Jn's apostolic appearances. Nearly all analysts are convinced that Lk 24,36ff. and Jn 20, 19ff. are variant versions of a single account, and while some have posited the two authors' literary interdependence[11] or reliance on a

I, 254). — Cf. Ph. SEIDENSTICKER, *Auferstehung*, 72 ; U. WILCKENS, *Auferstehung*, 74 ; A. GEORGE, in *La résurrection*, 98-99 ; J. E. ALSUP, *Appearance Stories*, 174 n. 504.

[9] E. LOHMEYER, *Galiläa*, 20,24 ; J. KREMER, *Osterbotschaft*, 108ff. ; W. MARXSEN, *Auferstehung*, 65f. ; U. WILCKENS, *Auferstehung*, 72f. ; C. F. EVANS, *Resurrection*, 117f., 125f. ; R. H. FULLER, *Formation*, 141f. ; J. E. ALSUP, *Appearance Stories*, 173f. — That the evangelist intends a critique of the belief that demands supporting evidence, or at least commits his reader to a deeper and more perfect faith in Christ than Thomas came to (R. SCHNACKENBURG, *Johannesevangelium* III, 399), is widely accepted among the Johannine interpreters (cf. R. BULTMANN, *Johannes*, 539f. ; E. HAENCHEN, *Gott und Mensch*, 69, 88 ; J. M. ROBINSON, in *Trajectories*, 254-255 ; and most recently, with both comprehensive literary criticism and theological analysis to support this view, R. SCHNACKENBURG, *Johannesevangelium* III, 381, 390-391, 395, 398-399).

[10] W. MARXSEN, *Auferstehung*, 173ff. ; R. H. FULLER, *Formation*, 118f., 140 ; H. KASTING, *Anfänge*, 42 ; Chr. BURCHARD, *Zeuge*, 131 ; J. KREMER, *Pfingstbericht*, 226f. ; J. E. ALSUP, *Appearance Stories*, 186f.

[11] Some have urged the dependence of Jn upon Lk, e.g. E. HIRSCH, *Auferstehungsgeschichten*, 10f. (in the interests of the unsuccessful argument that Lk was the creator of the official " Jerusalem Easter legend " of the Church — *ibid.*, 12) ; J. FINEGAN, *Überlieferung*, 94f. ; E. MEYER, *Ursprung und Anfänge* I, 29-31 ; also, by inclination, L. BRUN, *Auferstehung*, 57, and with entirely inconclusive arguments by J. A. BAILEY, *Traditions*, 92-94. — On the other hand, suggestions of the Lucan text's derivation from Jn have been, aside from idiosyncratic positions like LOISY's (*Luc*, 585 : second redactor of Lk knew Jn), mostly limited to allegations of interpolations in the ms. tradition (e.g. F. C. GRANT, " Was the Author of John Dependent upon the Gospel of Luke ? " *JBL* 56 [1937, 285-307] 301), especially, of course, involving vv. 36b and 40. Apart from the textual question, however, such a hypothesis is not to be taken seriously in the investigation of Lk's *Vorlage*. — Isolated, and without so much as

common written source,[12] most prefer to appeal to a single appearance tradition, diversified by both oral transmission and the two evangelists' independent adaptations.[13] Especially if v. 40 (and v. 36b) should be authentic in Lk does the common derivation become inescapable; but even if we prescind from these disputed pieces and their punctual Johannine parallels,[14] we still have a sequence of converging features

---

an echo in subsequent research, has been the suggestion of M.-É. BOISMARD that the Johannine Easter narrative (specifically 20,24-31) was subjected to redaction by *Luke* (" Saint Luc et la rédaction du quatrième évangile," *RB* 69 [1962, 185-211] 200-203)!

[12] On the basis of the homogeneity of materials in Lk 24,12/36ff. and Jn 20,3-10/19-22, R. LEANEY suggested each evangelist drew on a common written source and interrupted its sequence with his own inserted narrative, Emmaus (Lk) and Magdalen encounter (Jn) (*NTS* 2 [1955-56] 111). This suggestion was seconded, apparently, by B. LINDARS (*art. cit.* [in n. 6 above], 145-146) but proved hard to secure because of the fragmentary tradition Lk has of the apostolic presence at the tomb (cf. chap. IV below, n. 104). The differences of content and intention between the two evangelists' Easter sequences make a single literary ancestor hard to arrive at. Diversification of common *oral* tradition before Lk and Jn seems the best explanation (cf. G. HARTMANN, *ZNW* 55 [1964] 218 & n. 52). — Also adhering to the common-source hypothesis, but without any attempt to describe or delineate the source: A. GEORGE, in *La résurrection*, 93,97.

[13] This is the most common position by far. Among its sponsors we may list: V. TAYLOR, *Behind the Third Gospel*, 225f.; J. SCHNIEWIND, *Parallelperikopen*, 91-95; K. H. RENGSTORF, *Lk.*, 285; R. BULTMANN, *Johannes*, 534f.; R. E. BROWN, *John XIII-XXI* (cited in n. 9) 1028f.; Paul GARDNER-SMITH, *St. John and the Synoptic Gospels* (Cambridge: Cambridge Univ. Press, 1938) 81-84; J. SCHMITT, *RvScRel* 25 (1951) 230f.; P. SCHUBERT, in *Ntl. Studien f. Bultmann*, 172; H. GRASS, *Ostergeschehen*, 68; Pierson PARKER, " Luke and the Fourth Evangelist," *NTS* 9 (1962-63, 317-336) 323; H.-W. BARTSCH, *Wachet*, 26f.; G. HARTMANN, *ZNW* 55 (1964) 218; J. KREMER, *Osterbotschaft*, 111; U. WILCKENS, *Auferstehung*, 71; R. H. FULLER, *Formation*, 139; X. LÉON-DUFOUR, *Résurrection*, 123ff., 131ff.; H. KASTING, *Anfänge*, 44f., 46; Chr. BURCHARD, *Zeuge*, 130; B. RIGAUX, *Dieu l'a ressuscité*, 262f., 269f.; I. H. MARSHALL, *TyndB* 24 (1973) 91. — J. E. ALSUP (*Appearance Stories*, 173) seems to favor a " common source," but the rest of his detailed comparison of the texts seems rather to support a common tradition rather than a common written document.

[14] C. F. EVANS (*Resurrection*, 108) takes the quite unusual position that once vv. 36b and 40 have been classified as inauthentic additions to Lk's text, there is scant reason to posit a common traditional substratum of the Lucan and Johannine stories. The same conclusion has clearly not been reached by many others who also doubt the authenticity of the variant readings. Most of those cited in n. 13 do not, in fact, defend their authenticity, and no one bases his case for the common tradition upon them. Those who maintain a common *written* source are more likely to hold them authentic (thus R. LEANEY, B. LINDARS, A. GEORGE, cited in n. 12), but it is equally possible — as we shall see — to retain them as supportive of the common-tradition hypothesis, which would both account for their verbal coincidences and allow for their different functions in Lk *vs.* Jn (cf. K. ALAND, *NTS* 12 [1965-66] 206-208; = *Studien zur Überlieferung*, 168-170, and our considerations under § 1-e below).

in the two accounts which makes even their discrepancies into supportive evidence of the common narrative material.

(i) The phrase expressing the preternatural presence, ἔστη ἐν μέσῳ αὐτῶν, is very close to Jn 20,19 (ἔστη εἰς τὸ μέσον) at all events. (ii) Even the *fear* of the disciples, motivated by the apparition in Lk *37*, might have survived in Jn's introduction, where it is attached rather to the hostility of the Jews and can yield to the " peace " and " joy " produced by the Lord's visitation.[15] (iii) The display of the Visitor's *hands and feet* in Lk *39* clearly means to identify him by his wounds as the Crucified (ἐγώ εἰμι αὐτός), where-upon Jn's combination of *hands and side* can be seen to be a secondary accomodation of this scene to his lance episode, which only he relates among the events at Calvary. Moreover, we have already suggested why Jn might have shifted the actual wound-verification (Lk's ψηλαφᾶν) to the separate Thomas-episode, and now we note that he produced it there side by side with phrases repeated from the basic appearance-tradition (Jn *27/26b-c*).[16] (iv) The words of Lk *41*, ἀπὸ τῆς χαρᾶς, echo ἐχάρησαν οὖν κτλ. of Jn *20*, although here Lk does the adjusting, and it is in accordance with his Easter dialectic of experience *vis-à-vis* revelation (as we shall see). (v) Finally, the consequent commissioning word accompanies the demonstration of identity in both accounts, and both times the endowment and the mandated ministry are the same : the Holy Spirit and the forgiveness of sins

---

[15] This suggestion of X. Léon-Dufour (*Résurrection*, 132) is not at all implausible when one considers the Johannine recasting of other gospel traditions involving the disciples. One thinks, for example, of the sequence of Petrine confession and devil-logion in Jn 6,66-70, as compared with Mk 8,27-33 ; it appears that the earlier version had been " corrected " by Jn's involvement of Judas, whether this was on his own initiative (R. Bultmann, *Johannes*, 346 n. 1) or the product of intervening tradition (E. Dinkler, " Petrusbekenntnis und Satanswort ...," in E. Dinkler, hrsg., *Zeit und Geschichte. Dankesgabe an R. Bultmann* ... [Tübingen : J. C. B. Mohr, 1964, 127-153] 145ff.).

[16] This favors the view that the Thomas-story is Jn's own construction, deliberately tailored to correspond structurally to the preceding episode (20,19-23) and composed of elements from the latter (vv. 25b-c/27, omitted by Jn *in situ*, and v. 26b). Earlier, less analytical assertions of this (by J. Finegan (*Überlieferung*, 95 ; E. Hirsch, *Auferstehungsgeschichten*, 10) have now gained more substantial support from G. Hartmann, *ZNW* 55 (1964) 217f. ; X. Léon-Dufour, *Résurrection*, 242 ; B. Rigaux, *Dieu l'a ressuscité*, 237f. ; and most recently and impressively, Anton Dauer, " Die Herkunft der Tomas-Perikope Joh 20,24-29," in H. Merklein und J. Lange, hrsg., *Biblische Randbemerkungen. Schülerfestschrift für R. Schnackenburg* (Würzburg : Echter Verlag, 1974) 56-76. It is not surprising, of course, that Dauer's analysis is now confirmed in his teacher's commentary : R. Schnackenburg, *Johannesevangelium* III, 390f. In view of this situation among the students of this pericope, it can hardly be maintained that its basis in an independent tradition (so R. Bultmann, *Johannes*, 537 ; H. Grass, *Ostergeschehen*, 69) is a matter " generally agreed " on in recent criticism (*pace* R. H. Fuller, *Formation*, 142).

(Lk *49.47*; Jn *22.23*). We mention only in passing the judgment of John's version by his leading interpreters: the language is so uncharacteristic of him that it suggests he is following the tradition closely at this point.[17]

For our part, we are now in a position to complement that analysis with a recognition of the solidly Lucan fabric in which the commission is embedded in our pericope.[18] Indeed, the disparity between the two versions of it must be due mostly to Lk's heavy editing of the risen Lord's instruction according to the Easter *argumentum* he has been developing all along.

If in subsequent discussion, therefore, we give assent to the Lucan authenticity of the Western omissions (vv. 40.36b), our common-tradition hypothesis will furnish serviceable explanation of their strong verbal coincidences with Jn, without requiring any direct literary dependency or interpolation.

(b) *The Nature of the Appearance as Related in vv. 36ff.*: Besides the common narrative substratum of the Lucan and Johannine cenacle appearances there is also, of course, a conception of the risen Lord that is jointly sponsored by the two accounts. And so distinctive is this conception, with its accent on the bodily presence and resumption of earthly operations on the part of the risen One, that it has furnished prime material for all who dedicate their researches to an evolutionary understanding of the Easter tradition. The expression "massive realism" is used quite frequently to characterize our tradition's picture of Christ,[19] and a rather glib distinction is drawn between its apparent "reanimation" of the Crucified and the usual biblical epiphany "from heaven."[20] Particularly attractive to many is the notion that the

---

[17] H. GRASS, *Ostergeschehen*, 68; R. BULTMANN, *Johannes*, 535; R. SCHNACKENBURG, *Johannesevangelium* III, 385, 387f. Cf. also G. HARTMANN, *ZNW* 55 (1964) 215.

[18] Vv. 44-46 function within our chapter's compositional framework as the final and conclusive exposition of the passion-mystery, resuming vv. 6f. and 25-27. Vv. 47-49 create the connection between this exposition and the apostles' instruction in Acts. The whole pericope is thus tailored to the unique project of its author, for whom it is not the crowning conclusion of the ministry of Jesus and the gospel (as its counterparts in Mt and Jn are) but rather the "Brücke zwischen Jesu Wirken und dem der Kirche und darum auch zwischen Lukasevangelium und Apostelgeschichte" (Chr. BURCHARD, *Zeuge*, 131). Cf. nn. 30-36 below.

[19] H. GRASS, *Ostergeschehen*, 40, 49; W. MARXSEN, *Auferstehung*, 57; J. RIEDL, *BibLit* 40 (1967) 104. Cp. R. H. FULLER, *Formation*, 130; P. SCHUBERT, in *Ntl. Studien f. Bultmann*, 172.

[20] Cf. A. LOISY, *Luc*, 585; E. HIRSCH, *Auferstehungsgeschichten*, 8, 32, 59, 67, 68, 90; H. GRASS, *Ostergeschehen*, 45, 48f. ("quasi-earthly, in-between state"); H. CONZELMANN, *MdZ*, 189f.; G. KOCH, *Auferstehung*, 50 ("Rückkehr aus dem Totenreich in die Weltwirklichkeit"); U. WILCKENS, *Auferstehung*, 96; R. H.

reanimation-view gradually replaced the heavenly apparition in Easter narratives within a quickening tempo of polemics with outsiders, whose derision of the Christian faith could well have taken the form reflected in the Lord's reassurance, πνεῦμα σάρκα καὶ ὀστέα οὐκ ἔχει (Lk *36,39*).[21] The same pressure for historical verification might have tended to bring times and places of the apparitions together, so that the empty tomb and the appearances, previously unrelated in the telling, were drawn irreversibly into close proximity and a brief time-span.[22] This condensing of scattered events and experiences is readily placed under the auspices of a distinct " Jerusalem tradition " [23] of which Luke and John are heirs. And in the most extreme evolutionary theory,[24] such a " Jerusalem tradition " is made simply an apologetic mutation of the original, authentic " Galilean tradition."

FULLER, *Formation*, 115 (" resuscitation of the earthly body ") ; X. LÉON-DUFOUR, *Résurrection*, 146, 147 (" comme le surgissement, le réveil de la mort .... une survie "). — One should acknowledge the difference between our tradition's conception and the usual modality of heavenly apparition, rather than citing the preternatural circumstances — sudden comings, disappearances, veiled identity, etc. — for the purpose of harmonizing them completely (as in W. MICHAELIS, *Erscheinungen*, 95-96). The picture drawn in the Lucan accounts is admittedly a *modus loquendi* dependent on contemporary thought-patterns (J. KREMER, *Osterbotschaft*, 81f.), but Acts 9 shows the " heavenly " modality was also familiar enough to Lk and his contemporaries. One must pose the question whether the difference of modality between Lk 24 and Acts 9 is intentional and part of the author's schema of historical periods and personages ; it cannot be simply assumed that there is no difference.

[21] The famous Ignatian echo of Lk's passage (*Smyrn.* 3,2 : ... ἴδετε, ὅτι οὐκ εἰμὶ δαιμόνιον ἀσώματον) occurs in the context of a refutation of docetic heresy : καὶ ἀληθῶς ἔπαθεν, ὡς καὶ ἀληθῶς ἀνέστησεν ἑαυτόν, οὐχ ὥσπερ ἄπιστοί τινες λέγουσιν, τὸ δοκεῖν αὐτὸν πεπονθέναι ... (*Smyrn.* 2 ; cf. *Loeb Classical Libr.*, Apost. Fath. I, 252f., and C. F. EVANS, *Resurrection*, 108f. ; B. RIGAUX, *Dieu l'a ressuscité*, 261f., 276 n. 37). — Cf. also H. GRASS, *Ostergeschehen*, 40 ; P. SCHUBERT, in *Ntl. Studien f. Bultmann*, 172 ; E. LOHSE, *Auferstehung*, 35 ; J. KREMER, *Osterbotschaft*, 81 ; Ph. SEIDENSTICKER, *Auferstehung*, 98 n. 68.

[22] Cf. chap. I, n. 15, and the repeated observations of H. GRASS, *Ostergeschehen*, 86f. ; 91f. ; 120f. Also G. KOCH, *Auferstehung*, 45 ; H. von CAMPENHAUSEN, *Ablauf*, 42f.

[23] E. HIRSCH, *Auferstehungsgeschichten*, 17 ; H. GRASS, *Ostergeschehen*, 120-121 ; G. KOCH, *Auferstehung*, 44f. ; X. LÉON-DUFOUR, *Résurrection*, 145 ; H. KASTING, *Anfänge*, 84 ; Th. LORENZEN, *ZNW* 64 (1973) 221.

[24] E. HIRSCH, *Auferstehungsgeschichten*, 15, 27, etc. Cf. also Ph. SEIDENSTICKER, *Auferstehung*, 64-73 ; Th. LORENZEN, *ZNW* 64 (1973) 219-221. — Most scholars seem to allow for a valid foundation of both Galilean and Jerusalem traditions, following E. LOHMEYER in this respect (*Galiläa*, 97), even if it is not so clear that the two locales correspond to distinct christological viewpoints (*pace* LOHMEYER, *op. cit.*, 9, 23, 97, 99) or separate early Christian centers of influence (*ibid.*, 80-84, 97, etc.). The standard solution of the locality problem is the Galilee-Jerusalem combination of H. GRASS (*Ostergeschehen*, 119), who maintained that the " Easter-happening " began in Galilee amongst the dispersed

We shall return to discuss some of this alleged development of the Easter story, but for the moment it is the redaction-historical impact of the picture drawn by the cenacle story that interests us. No less than the tradition-historians of Easter are the redaction-historians of Luke inclined to capitalize on the story's traits, and this threatens to confuse the portraiture of the evangelist that we hope to derive from chapter 24. Some scholars eagerly make the tradition's "realism" Luke's, and the tradition's apologetic his concern as well. Indeed, we hear with surprising frequency of *Luke's* apologetic intent,[25] *Luke's* anti-docetism,[26] *Luke's* palpable realism.[27] This is an exemplary instance of the crucial relationship, often difficult to discern, between *tradition* and *redaction*: one cannot proceed to expound the latter until he has painstakingly delimited the former and determined how it has been utilized. If there is reason to think the palpation element belonged

disciples who fled back there, whereas the "Easter-proclamation" took up in Jerusalem, with the benefit of further appearances, once the refugees were motivated to the mission by the risen Lord (*ibid.*, 125). — B. STEINSEIFER, surveying the discussion of this matter, took note of the vogue won by GRASS's view (*ZNW* 62 [1971] 239), only then to institute a refutation of it in favor of the exclusive Jerusalem localization favored by H. CONZELMANN, W. MICHAELIS, and very few others. Since CONZELMANN's case is as yet without analytical argumentation, and MICHAELIS (*contra* HIRSCH) and STEINSEIFER (*contra* historicity of "Galilean" passages) have proceeded mostly *via negativa*, it cannot be said that the "Jerusalem" view is gaining substantially in current discussion. Cf. the refutation of STEINSEIFER in Th. LORENZEN, *ZNW* 64 (1973) 209-221.

[25] V. TAYLOR, *Passion Narrative*, 114 ; K. H. RENGSTORF, *Lk.*, 285 ; G. KEGEL, *Auferstehung*, 89 ; R. PESCH, in *EKK Vorarb.* III, 23 ; D. P. FULLER, *Easter Faith*, 230ff. ; F. MUSSNER, *Auferstehung*, 103, 104 ; J. E. ALSUP, *Appearance Stories*, 171. — Especially exuberant and, we think, careless of the precise direction of Lk's argument, is I. H. MARSHALL, *TyndB* 24 (1973) 91 : "Luke piles on the evidence for the resurrection" (!). Is this really his unmixed intention ?

[26] W. GRUNDMANN, *Lk.*, 449 ; H. GRASS, *Ostergeschehen*, 41 n. 4 ; J. ROLOFF, *Kerygma*, 255 ; C. F. EVANS, *Resurrection*, 109 ; J. E. ALSUP, *Appearance Stories*, 169f., 172. Especially has Chas. H. TALBERT sought to make the anti-docetic argument central to Lk's writing, ignoring, as scholars so often do, the dialectical movements in our evangelist's presentation (cf. *NTS* 14 [1967-68, 259-271] 262f., and *Luke and the Gnostics*, 31f.).

[27] R. MORGENTHALER, *Geschichtsschreibung* II, 26f. ; J. KREMER, *Osterbotschaft*, 84 ; U. WILCKENS, *Auferstehung*, 96 ; X. LÉON-DUFOUR, *Résurrection*, 216. — LÉON DUFOUR wavers on the question, refusing to consider "materialisation" Lk's concern, yet making him the apologist nonetheless : "En retenant une expression qui n'est pas lucanienne ..." (i.e. πνεῦμα σάρκα καὶ ὀστέα οὐκ ἔχει) "Lc indique sa véritable intention : l'apparition n'est pas une illusion ..." (similarly C. M. MARTINI, in *Resurrexit*, 233f., 241f.). Responding to LÉON-DUFOUR, one asks if it is really probable that an author who so thoroughly rewrites his sources would need words not his own — indeed, as it turns out, ideas not his own ! — to bring out his basic intent for a passage ! At least this suggestion should arouse some critical resistance. The question we shall want answered is : does Lk pursue an apologetic argument of *any* kind in his use of this tradition ? Is he really

to the account as both Luke and John found it, then it cannot be that either has simply added it as a direct expression of his own idea. Moreover, it is clear that when John transplanted the motif in the Thomas-story (20,[26],27), he did so in order to use it *dialectically*, as a foil for his own statement that the Easter faith of later generations would triumph unassisted by such palpable verification. Can we then simply assume that the same inherited motif is more directly expressive of Luke's point of view ? Or might it function dialectically for him as well ? In fact, our analyses of the other Easter pericopes will put us on the lookout for some dialectical moment in this one as well. Painstaking itemization of empirical facts in both the tomb sequence and the Emmaus dialogue was a foil for faith's beginning rather than a straightforward path to it; and this may no less be the case in the present episode. The invitation to physical verification in v. 39 — especially if the actual display in v. 40 is genuine — amounts to only a frustrated momentum in the narrative, put in check by the witnesses' reaction: ἔτι δὲ ἀπιστούντων αὐτῶν κτλ. (v. 41) Nor is it correct to say that v. 41 makes the doubt persist only as a heightened threshhold for the risen One's *manducatio*, intended to be the conclusive *Identitätsbeweis*.[28] If

---

still in the business of proving what perhaps the original account had sought to instill (so BOISMARD, *LumVie* # 109, 37) ?

[28] So A. LOISY, *Luc*, 586. The widespread assumption that the eating is intended as apologetic proof *ne plus ultra* (J. SCHMITT, *RvScRel* 25 [1951] 231; P. SCHUBERT, in *Ntl. Studien f. Bultmann*, 172; M. BRÄNDLE, *Orientierung* 24 [1960] 87f.; K. H. RENGSTORF, *Lk.*, 285; M. KEHL, *GeistLeb* 43 [1970] 109; E. KRÄNKL, *Jesus*, 144; J. E. ALSUP, *Appearance Stories*, 165, 167f.; J. ERNST, *Lk.*, 668) causes many to overlook the absence of an explicit affirmation that the disbelieving disciples were finally convinced by it. As C. M. MARTINI observes: " In Lc 24,43 la tensione drammatica dell'episodio non si è ancora sciolta. Le prove che Gesu ha dato di sé non sono conclusive per la fede. E' soltanto nei vv. 44-48 che si parla finalmente di ' apertura della mente ', e quindi di capacita' degli apostoli a comprendere ..." (in *Resurrexit*, 231). — Inevitably we are told that the moment of faith can be assumed after 24,43, though Lk leaves it unspoken; thus H. GRASS, *Ostergeschehen*, 41; J. KREMER, *Osterbotschaft*, 74; J. E. ALSUP, *Appearance Stories*, 176. But our exegesis of 24,8 was enough to put us on guard against alleged unspoken sentiments of our evangelist ! R. H. FULLER is correct in taking note of the missing " conclusion " of the " demonstration " here as a datum of importance to literary criticism, perhaps a sign of Lucan modification of the tradition's account (*Formation*, 115f.). This seems to us a sounder judgment than any projection of a traditional account featuring a meal of eucharistic character, shared by Master and disciples (as in Acts 10, 41, or Lk 24,43 *Vulg.*), only to have that eucharistic meal deleted by *Luke* in favor of the present, supposedly apologetic *manducatio* of the Lord only (so F. MUSSNER, *Auferstehung*, 103; J. LANGE, *Das Erscheinen des Auferstandenen*, 466; cp. also M. KEHL, *GeistLeb* 43 [1970] 109; I. H. MARSHALL, *TyndB* 24 [1973] 92). How does such an assessment respect the thrust of vv. 36-43, which all acknowledge to be the raw material Lk worked on ? Was the eucharistic repast part of *that* tradition ? One should think if there was ever an apologetic revision

this were the case, we should certainly expect some explicit notice that the doubt was dispelled, or recognition set in, consequent upon the eating. Yet there is nothing of the kind. Rather, an instruction in the mystery of the passion follows immediately (εἶπεν δὲ πρὸς αὐτούς· v. 44), noticeably parallel to the one which addressed the travelers' *incomprehension* in vv. 25ff. The very first positive response from the disciples is recorded at v. 52, in the participial προσκυνήσαντες αὐτόν, which seems to climax the whole sequence of apparition and instruction in much the same manner as ἐπέγνωσαν αὐτόν did (in the context of the Lord's departure and the return to Jerusalem) at the climax of the Emmaus account. — We shall have to test these observations further in the detailed analyses to follow, but for the moment we are at least put on guard against any hasty assumption that the heightened physical realism of the cenacle *tradition* has been taken over in Lk 24,36ff. as the straightforward apologetic argument of the Lucan *redaction*.[29]

(c) *Instruction of the Risen Lord* (*Lk 24,44-49*): The thoroughly *Lucan* character of this passage, rather abruptly adjoining the apparition's " demonstration " phase, is hardly in need of vigorous argumentation or itemized proof. Nearly every interpreter takes note of it. It was acknowledged long before *Redaktionsgeschichte* was methodically practiced,[30] and it is a commonplace in studies of recent date.[31] After vv. 25ff., of course, the risen One's exposition of the passion-mystery in light of *tota scriptura* can be recognized as the Lucan *Leitmotiv*. But a more frequent observation of interpreters is the full-fledged rehearsal

---

of the meal, it would have occurred in that tradition first, before it ever got to Lk!

[29] Those who affirm the apologetic intent of Lk's *tradition*, contained mostly in vv. 36-43, are, in our opinion, on firmer ground. Thus R. BULTMANN, *GsT*, 314; C. H. DODD, *More N. T. Studies*, 112f.; H.-W. BARTSCH, *Wachet*, 27; A. GEORGE, in *La résurrection*, 97-98; X. LÉON-DUFOUR, *Résurrection*, 217; R. H. FULLER, *Formation*, 115, 130; J. ERNST, *Lk.*, 666-668. — After the good assessments J. ROLOFF made in *Apostolat*, esp. 189, his advocacy of a Lucan apologetic in *Kerygma* (cf. n. 26 above) surprises us.

[30] R. BULTMANN, *GsT*, 310; L. BRUN, *Auferstehung*, 77; J. FINEGAN, *Überlieferung*, 91; J. SCHNIEWIND, *Parallelperikopen*, 92; J. SCHMITT, *RvScRel* 25 (1951) 231-232. Cf. also H. GRASS, *Ostergeschehen*, 292, reviewing the work of WILCKENS, subsequent to his own, with approval.

[31] H. CONZELMANN, *MdZ*, 147; U. WILCKENS, *Missionsreden*, 98 n. 1, and *Auferstehung*, 75; J. KREMER, *Osterbotschaft*, 83; H. KASTING, *Anfänge*, 43f.; G. LOHFINK, *Himmelfahrt*, 149 (" ganz lukanisch "); Ph. SEIDENSTICKER, *Auferstehung*, 99-100; R. H. FULLER, *Formation*, 116ff.; Chr. BURCHARD, *Zeuge*, 130f.; B. RIGAUX, *Dieu l'a ressuscité*, 260; I. H. MARSHALL, *TyndB* 24 (1973) 91; C. H. TALBERT, *Literary Patterns*, 60; E. NELLESSEN, *Zeugnis*, 111-117, esp. 117. — It is only with mechanical vocabulary-analysis and supposition that J. E. ALSUP overrides this consensus and posits extensive " non-lukan " material in the words of instruction and commission (*Appearance Stories*, 184ff.). This author disregards motif-analysis and seems ill-informed concerning recent study of Lk.

of the Acts kerygma which is contained in the substantive clauses of vv. 46ff., complementing οὕτως γέγραπται.[32] Over the course of our chapter's repetitions of the passion-prophecies (vv. 7. 26. 46f.) there has been a " conscious climactic effect "[33] instilled by the evangelist: (i) the messianic enigma has yielded to messianic revelation as the mysterious " Son of Man " gave way to the χριστός, the subject and goal of all scriptural testimony; (ii) Luke's definition of the messianic δεῖ in terms of scriptural disclosures of the divine will has been brought out progressively and is now fully clear in the alternation of δεῖ πληρωθῆναι and οὕτως γέγραπται (vv. 44.46); (iii) to the two phases of the messianic salvation previously expounded, the Saviour's παθεῖν and ἀναστῆναι, a third is now joined, itself also governed by οὕτως γέγραπται· the *universal proclamation of the word of forgiveness* by the disciples of Jesus in their Master's name.[34]

We note how Luke's literary " climax " has brought the awaited process of salvation to full disclosure. Of its several aspects, the death and resurrection of the Christ had been taught frequently but not comprehended; the world-wide mission had been foreshadowed and implied but not explicitly taught; and the mission's content, a κήρυγμα of repentance and forgiveness, is now disclosed for the first time.[35] More-

---

[32] Cf. the detailed comparisons of J. Dupont, in F. Neirynck, éd., *L'év. de Luc. Mém. Cerfaux*, 332-345, 353; now resumed in *N. T. und Kirche*, 130f. Also U. Wilckens, *Missionsreden*, 98; A. George, in *La résurrection*, 80f., and in *De Jésus aux évangiles*, 119, 125, 126; J. Kremer, *Osterbotschaft*, 76; C. M. Martini, in *Resurrexit*, 239ff.

[33] P. Schubert, in *Ntl. Studien f. Bultmann*, 177. C. F. Evans notes how the kerygmatic statement at hand is a combining of the statements contained in the empty tomb story (v. 7) and the Emmaus dialogue (vv. 26-27), and it is presented as spoken by Jesus while he was still with the disciples (v. 44a = v. 6), showing the fulfillment of all the scriptures concerning him and " opening " their minds to understand the sacred writ (v. 44b = v. 27; v. 45 = v. 32). What is to be found in the scriptures is that the Christ must suffer (v. 46a = v. 26a) and *rise* from the dead (v. 46b = v. 7b) (cf. Evans, *Resurrection*, 109). — On the climax-pattern in the chapter, cf. also J. Roloff, *Apostolat*, 188; G. Lohfink, *Himmelfahrt*, 113-114.

[34] The universal preaching also belongs to the divine plan of salvation disclosed in the scriptures; cf. J. Dupont, " Le salut des gentils et la signification théologique du livre des Actes," *Études*, 393-419, esp. 404, and in *N. T. und Kirche*, 134, 142; S. G. Wilson, *Gentiles*, 48, 53, 243f.; F. Hahn, *Mission*, 113f. Hahn's argument that Lk 24,47 is Lk's rendering of Mk 13,10, omitted *in situ* as part of the Lucan revision of the apocalyptic sermon, confirms our evangelist's systematic interpretation of the messianic δεῖ in terms of the fulfillment of Scripture.

[35] Lk 24,47 is the first explicit provision for the Gentile mission, in contrast to prophetic hints in earlier passages (e.g. Lk 2,30-32; 4,25-27; 10,1f.; 14,16-24, etc.). As historian, Lk properly locates the world-mission in the time of the Church rather than the life of Jesus, deferring the development of his view of the mission until the book of Acts (cf. F. Hahn, *Mission*, 112; S. G. Wilson,

over, this final instruction brings all Jesus' instruction of his disciples to final fruition in their appointment as his *witnesses*, a weighty feature of Luke's compositional perspective for his two volumes.[36] In ὑμεῖς μάρτυρες τούτων (v. 48) the risen Christ's self-disclosure *through interpretation of the scriptures* becomes a mandated " ministry of the word " for his disciples, and his Easter instruction of them therefore seems to become the crucial fundament of their μαρτυρία.[37] It precedes their endowment with the Spirit's δύναμις (v. 49) in Luke's sequence and, as we hope to show, by Luke's logic.

This last point touches an issue of basic interpretative consequence: the discursive relationship between the Lord's physical demonstration and his instruction, his gesture and his word, in this Easter preparation of the witnesses. While it may be an overstatement that " nothing

---

Gentiles, 31-58, esp. 52f.). — An anticipation of the content of the universal proclamation can be seen in the mixed Isaian text read by Jesus at Nazareth (cf. pp. 136f. above). The evangelist understands the forgiveness of sins as prominent among the pneumatic works for which the Spirit endowed Jesus and, in turn, his witnesses (cf. M. Rese, *Altt. Motive*, 145ff.). We shall discuss this major motif of our author in chap. IV/ii § 3.

[36] R. P. Casey, in *Beginnings* V, 30-37 ; U. Wilckens, *Missionsreden*, 144-149 ; N. Brox, *Zeuge*, 43-69 ; J. Roloff, *Apostolat*, 190ff. ; W. C. Robinson, *Weg*, 37-39 ; G. Lohfink, *Himmelfahrt*, 267-270 ; Chr. Burchard, *Zeuge*, 130-135, 173-185 ; C.-P. März, *Wort Gottes*, 44-52 ; E. Kränkl, *Jesus*, 167-175 ; V. Stolle, *Der Zeuge als Angeklagter*, 147-154 ; I. H. Marshall, *Luke*, 41-44 ; E. Nellessen, *Zeugnis*, 30-41 (survey) & *passim*.

[37] J. Roloff (*Apostolat*, 191) rightly stresses the prior importance of the Lord's instruction in the equipping of the witnesses, whereas others tend to reduce their witness to a vouching for the factual reality of the resurrection; thus the *Leitmotiv* of C. H. Talbert's *Luke and the Gnostics*, 17-32 ; but also R. Morgenthaler, *Geschichtsschreibung* II, 27ff. ; G. Kegel, *Auferstehung*, 89 ; U. Wilckens, *Auferstehung*, 95-98 ; I. H. Marshall, *Luke*, 42-43, and the treatments of Brox, Lohfink, and Kränkl, listed in n. 36. Although their treatments might have brought them to a more nuanced position, H. Flender (*Heil*, 142f.) and C.-P. März (*Wort Gottes*, 45) also seem to subscribe to the definition of the disciples' witness as a " testimony of the *factuality/reality* of the resurrection." Chr. Burchard, after repeating that notion (" Garanten der Tatsächlichkeit ..."), adds a crucial qualification : " Dabei ist zu beachten, dass es nicht um nackte Tatsachen geht, sondern um die Tatsachen in ihrer vom Auferstandenen *authentisch erläuterten Bedeutung* als Teil des im Alten Testament geschriebenen Plans Gottes " (*Zeuge*, 133 — ital. mine ; cf. likewise V. Stolle, *Zeuge*, 149, 151). — Here is exactly the nuance that is needed ! The Lucan " witnesses " are not mere " historische Gewährsmänner " (rightly U. Luck, in Braumann-*LkEv*, 107), and the timebound images used to describe their Easter experience cannot be taken as legitimating criteria of their testimony (rightly G. Voss, *Christologie*, 145 ; similarly H.-W. Bartsch, *Wachet*, 27). Also placing physical demonstration in proper perspective, according to the instruction of the risen One the priority which the analysis of tradition and composition in vv. 36-49 suggests for it, are Ph. Seidensticker, *Auferstehung*, 100 ; C. M. Martini, in *Resurrexit*, 235f., 241-242 ; apparently also C. F. Evans, *Resurrection*, 112.

would be lost if v. 44 were to follow v. 36 directly" (J. ROLOFF), it is wholly inappropriate to pretend that "the entire witness motif is constructed to guarantee especially the materiality of these events as the valid content of the church's proclamation" (C. H. TALBERT).[38] In addressing ourselves to this key issue in pursuit of the total sense of Lk 24, we have the unusual advantage of comparative material presented at the beginning of Acts in the form of a specific, retrospective summary (Acts 1,2-4).[39] Whatever conclusions we reach concerning the third pericope's components and their interaction, we shall expect to have formulated and confirmed them by recourse to the Acts summation as well as the proper data of the pericope itself. Since the Acts passage includes the ascension in its retrospect upon the end of the πρῶτος λόγος (Acts 1,2), we are reminded that the Lord's mysterious "departure" (24,50-53) is definitely included amongst the elements whose proportionate weight and relation to the third pericope we are obliged to measure.

(d) *The Ascension* (*Lk 14,50-53*): The very fact that we entitle this section as we do indicates that we consider some long-standing questions about the text and meaning of these verses to be more or less settled. In fact, we have no intention of repeating researches which have pushed this old *crux interpretum* decisively towards a consensus. Even though the leading *Redaktionsgeschichtler* was himself still captive of the older interpolation theory,[40] it has been unmistakably the fruit

[38] J. ROLOFF, *Apostolat*, 189f. n. 68, *vs.* C. H. TALBERT, *Luke*, 31. — The reason ROLOFF gives for his assertion is, in itself, quite correct: "der Satz ἔτι δὲ ἀπιστούντων αὐτῶν ἀπὸ τῆς χαρᾶς καὶ θαυμαζόντων (V. 41) sagt noch nichts über den Osterglauben aus." The desirable middle-ground here is held by C. M. MARTINI: vv. 36-43 are understood only in light of, and in unity with, vv. 44ff., which contain the testimony that sheds light upon the meaning of the unique experiences related in the narrative (*Resurrexit*, 231f., 234ff., 242).

[39] Cf. the essay of R. PESCH, cited in n. 5 above (*in fine*).

[40] H. CONZELMANN, *MdZ*, 86, 189 n. 4; unretracted in *Apg.*², 25, 27 (astounding!). — Aside from curious views of the third gospel's genesis like A. LOISY's (n. 5 above), few positions comparable to Conzelmann's on the gospel's finale were found by us (he cites A. N. WILDER, *JBL* 62 [1943] 311, and we would add K. LAKE, *Beg.* V, 3f., and now S. SCHULZ, *Stunde*, 290). The short-lived hypothesis of an originally continuous *Opus ad Theophilum*, joined at Lk 24,49 and Acts 1,6, with passages in between added for the sake of the two-book division at the time of the formation of the NT canon, won some adherents (briefly Ph.-H. MENOUD, in *Ntl. Studien f. Bultmann*, 148-156; subsequently revoked in *Neotestamentica et patristica. Freundesgabe O. Cullmann* [SupplNT 6; Leiden: Brill, 1962] 148-156; also É. TROCMÉ, '*Livre des Actes*', 31ff., following the lead of H. SAHLIN, *Der Messias und das Gottesvolk*, 11-18). — More customary has been the acceptance of the Western readings in Lk 24,51 and Acts 1,2, thus avoiding the precise ascension references in each (ἀνεφέρετο εἰς τὸν οὐρανόν and ἀνελήμφθη), or the ready assertion of interpolated material in the Acts prologue, which became an "Experimentierfeld für Interpolationshypothesen

of advancing redactional study of Lk-Acts that Lk 24,50ff. could be understood as a piece of genuine Lucan writing, complemented rather than contradicted by the apparently clashing details of the Acts preamble.[41] While some scholars still pose the question whether our evangelist could really have meant to portray the self-same event at the end of the gospel and the beginning of Acts,[42] most would now admit both the authenticity of the ascension-language pertaining to the gospel's finale [43] and the representation of *Jesus' final departure from earthly*

und literarkritische Operationen," according to G. LOHFINK (*Himmelfahrt*, 25). — Cf. the brief but excellent survey of the matter in J. DUPONT, *Sources*, 24f. n. 3, and the earlier chronicles of V. LARRANAGA, *L'ascension*, esp. 43-50, 60-64, 75-83.

[41] The simplest expression of this understanding is also the most persuasive: the ascension is an "event which bears different appearances, when looked at from different angles. On the one hand, the ascension is the end of the story of Jesus, who works cures, perishes in Jerusalem, and on the third day is perfected (cf. Luke 13,32) .... On the other hand, the ascension is the beginning of the story of the Church. It is from this viewpoint that we see it in Acts .... There, the ascension closes an epoch; here, it opens another, which will last until it ends with the return of Christ from heaven, where in the meantime he sits at God's right hand ... as the Lord who through His Spirit directs the work of His Church on earth. Out of Luke's double understanding of the ascension arises a second double proposition of even greater importance ... that, in Luke's thought, the end of the story of Jesus is the Church; and, the story of Jesus is the beginning of the Church" (C. K. BARRETT, *Luke*, 56-57).

[42] W. MICHAELIS, *Erscheinungen*, 89-91; P. SCHUBERT, in *Ntl. Studien f. Bultmann*, 168f. and n. 13; E. E. ELLIS, *Lk*, 279; A. R. C. LEANEY, *Lk*, 296; E. LOHSE, *Auferstehung*, 39. These authors favor the handy solution that the gospel's concluding scene is a mere "departure" ending the christophany, hence is comparable to the disappearance in v. 31. They must ignore, of course, the context of the scene: the "last testament" character of the instruction of vv. 44-49, and the fact that a retirement into waiting for Pentecost follows the "departure" (24,52-53) according to the Lord's final instruction (24,49). It is quite true to say, therefore, that the context makes 24,50-53 a *final departure* of the Lord from the disciples *whether or not* ἀνεφέρετο κτλ. be judged authentic (rightly J. M. CREED, *Lk*, 302; E. KLOSTERMANN, *Lk.*, 239, 243; H. SCHLIER, *Besinnung*, 228, 230; W. MARXSEN, *Auferstehung*, 57, 71; J. KREMER, *Osterbotschaft*, 78f.; U. WILCKENS, *Auferstehung*, 93). — A variation of the separate-events hypothesis is the view of A. WIKENHAUSER, for whom Lk's Easter-day ascension (Lk 24) is the real ascension, while Acts 1,9-11 depicts only the termination of the last resurrection appearance (*Apg.*, 32). Here it is the parallelism of Lk 24,50-53 and Acts 1,9-11, with their contexts, that must be ignored (cf. J. G. DAVIES, *He Ascended*, 42). Both passages follow the same basic instruction of the Lord, viz. his "testament" for the mission of the Church; they can hardly be depicting different events, but only the one final departure of the risen Lord to heaven.

[43] Principally, of course, the non-Western καὶ ἀνεφέρετο εἰς τὸν οὐρανόν in Lk 24,51, whose omission occurs in the Sinaiticus exemplar as well as the usual Western witnesses. Corresponding to this is the omission, by fewer authoritative manuscripts, of ἀνελήμφθη from the first-volume resumé in Acts 1,2. It has long been recognized that both readings are *difficiliores*, hence that their second-

existence in both passages.[44] The different portrayals respond to the different perspectives and stages of the composition at these two junctures.[45] On the one hand, the gospel scene brings the story of Jesus to the triumphal, "third-day" conclusion prophesied by himself (Lk 13,32S), putting something of a concluding "doxology" to the gospel narrative.[46] On the other hand, the Acts passage presents the end of Jesus' life on earth as the beginning of the "time of the Church," whose extension was indefinite and whose part in the divine plan could only be obscured by a lingering *Naherwartung*. "Once ... Luke had conceived the notion that the triumphant conclusion of the story of Jesus contained the germ of a historical process which was to unfold in the course of what he knew was already a fairly considerable period, his vocation as a historian was determined. Indeed, it was determined not only that he should write history, but also how he should write it." [47] — In other words, the differing ascension accounts have much to do with the conjunction of the two Lucan books. Both accounts implement the coordination of the two, for they express the author's pers-

---

ary excision in the interests of harmonizing Lk 24 and Acts 1 is more readily defended than their secondary addition (rightly E. MEYER, *Ursprung und Anfänge* I, 32f.; G. BERTRAM, in *Festgabe für A. Deissmann*, 205; A. PLUMMER, *Lk*, 565; L. BRUN, *Auferstehung*, 91; V. LARRANAGA, *L'ascension*, 171-172, 212; P. BENOIT, in *Exégèse et théol.* I, 395). Amongst more recent authors, we should say that this view has become *opinio communis*; cf. e.g. J. JEREMIAS, *Abendmahlsworte*[3], 144; P. A. VAN STEMPVOORT, *NTS* 5 (1958-59) 36; J. G. DAVIES, *He Ascended*, 41f.; W. GRUNDMANN, *Lk.*, 454 n. 24; H. GRASS, *Ostergeschehen*, 43; A. GEORGE, in *La résurrection*, 78; H.-W. BARTSCH, *Wachet*, 19; U. WILCKENS, *Auferstehung*, 92f.; G. LOHFINK, *Himmelfahrt*, 24f.; G. FRIEDRICH, in *Orientierung an Jesus*, 59; R. H. FULLER, *Formation*, 122.

[44] L. BRUN, *Auferstehung*, 55; P. BENOIT, *Exégèse et théol.* I, 399; J. SCHMID, *Lk.*, 363; C. K. BARRETT, *Luke*, 57; H. SCHLIER, in *Besinnung*, 230ff., 240; G. FRIEDRICH, in *Orientierung an Jesus*, 63; S.G. WILSON, *Gentiles*, 97, 100; J. ERNST, *Lk.*, 672.

[45] J. SCHMITT, *RvScRel* 25 (1951) 38; W. GRUNDMANN, *Lk.*, 450; E. HAENCHEN, *Apg.*, 114; D.P. FULLER, *Easter Faith*, 197-198; A. GEORGE, in *La résurrection*, 82f., and in *De Jésus aux évangiles*, 119; U. WILCKENS, *Auferstehung*, 92ff.; S. G. WILSON, *ZNW* 59 (1968) 275ff., and *Gentiles*, 98-105; W. ELTESTER, in *Jesus in Nazareth*, 96; I. H. MARSHALL, *TyndB* 24 (1973) 94. — Cf. also H. FLENDER, *Heil*, 16-18 (a somewhat less satisfactory explanation of the distinct perspectives), and the trend-setting essays of Anton FRIDRICHSEN, *Theol. Blätter* 6 (1927) 337-341, and P. A. VAN STEMPVOORT, *NTS* 5 (1958-59) esp. 36ff., 41-42. Recall, too, the remarks of C.K. BARRETT, quoted in n. 41 above.

[46] P.A. VAN STEMPVOORT, *NTS* 5 (1958-59) 37, 39: "... Luke gives at the end of his Gospel a 'doxological' interpretation of the Ascension. It is a glorious but a limited interpretation, for history goes on and the Church cannot remain in the attitude of the *proskynèsis* and the *eulogia* .... Acts must follow the Gospel, ... portraying the course of Church history" (37). — Cf. also X. LÉON-DUFOUR, *Résurrection*, 219; S. G. WILSON, *Gentiles*, 105.

[47] C.K. BARRETT, *Luke*, 58.

pectives on the sacred times which intersect at the point of the Lord's departure.

Thus far the ground is fairly well tilled and needs little added effort of ours. So far as we can see, however, both the tradition question and, to an extent, the relation of vv. 50-53 to the ensemble of chapter 24 remain matters needful of development and consensus. First, the issue of pre-Lucan tradition in the epilogue has by no means come to rest, despite the impressive and detailed arguments of Gerhard LOHFINK. A search of NT parallels to Lk 24,36-53 revealed to LOHFINK, as to us, that both the recognition scene (vv. 36-43) and the witnesses' commission (vv. 44-49) are accounted for by the traditional schema of the appearance to the Eleven; but the heavenly translation at the conclusion of such an appearance has no counterpart elsewhere in the tradition of the Easter narratives.[48]

> The sequence of recognition and commissioning word is found not only in Mt 28,16-20 and Jn 20,19-23, the main parallels to our pericope, but also in Jn 21,1-23; Jn 20,14-18 (recognition in *14-16*, commission in *17f.*); Mt 28,9-10, and even in the Petrine kerygma in Acts 10,40f.42. The bipartite schema is clearly well established in the tradition, quite independently of Luke. On the other hand, in none of the accounts mentioned is the disappearance or departure of the Lord recorded. Fully five of them end rather with the words pronounced by the risen One: Mt 28,9f.; 28,16-20; Jn 20,14-18; 20,19-23; 21,1-23, without any departure being recorded. — The situation is similar where angels or other heavenly personages appear. Elsewhere in the tradition of the gospels, no notice is taken of an apparition's departure (cf. Mt 1,20f.; 2,13.19f.; 28,2-7; Mk 16,5-7; Jn 20,12f.), whereas the departure is consistently recorded by Luke (Lk 1,38; 2,15; 9,33; Acts 10,7; 12,10), just as in the christophanies (Lk 24,31 and the two ascensions). This state of affairs seems to allow LOHFINK's conclusion: "Therefore within the NT literature this manner of concluding an appearance is typically Lucan. We can consequently assert with much greater assurance that the departure scene, Lk 24, 50-53, did not originally belong to the appearance of Jesus before all the disciples but was first joined to it by Luke. Just as in narrating angelic appearances Luke felt the need to take specific note of the return of the angels to heaven, he obviously also found it necessary to recount the departure of the risen One and not close simply with the latter's last words" (*Himmelfahrt*, 150).

---

[48] G. LOHFINK, *Himmelfahrt*, 147-151. — Cf. also W. MICHAELIS, *Erscheinungen*, 85: "Das Aufhören einer Erscheinung wird ... selten anders als eben durch die Beendigung der Perikope bezeichnet .... (And so) verlangen um so mehr Beachtung die wenigen Fälle (Luk. 24,31.51; Apg. 1,9ff.), in denen das Verschwinden des Erscheinenden vermerkt wird." Also U. WILCKENS, *Auferstehung*, 91.

Attaching " departures " to apparitions is thus a Lucan habit. LOHFINK admits (*op. cit.*, 151) that his arguments, which are effective as far as they go, do not settle the issue of tradition *vs.* redaction in the final scene itself, vv. 50-53. At most they show that any quest for a pre-Lucan foundation of the scene should concentrate on the passage itself, since one cannot assume it originated as an extension of a pre-Lucan christophany account comprised of recognition and mission.

The survey of (deutero- and) extra-canonical literature with which LOHFINK paves the way to his tradition-historical analysis yields results that are somewhat less conclusive. Of witnesses which separate a distinct ascension from the resurrection with intervening appearances, *Epist. Apost.* 51 (62) and *Acta Pilati* 16,6 are surely dependent on Luke, Mk 16,19 very probably is, but *Barn.* 15,9 may or may not be.[49] In this area, LOHFINK's is something less than an open and shut case. One does have to admit that if there was a tradition of resurrection/appearances/ascension comprising the paschal sequence independent of Luke's conception, such a tradition left remarkably few traces outside the Lucan sphere of influence.[50] Not that this argument is inconsiderable, but so long as the few possible traces have not been excluded analytically, one has to add a measure of reserve to the conclusion that " wherever in the early church one hears of a visible ascension of Jesus that is separated from the resurrection by intervening appearances, there is already dependency on the Lucan conception " (G. LOHFINK, *op. cit.*, 134). Consequently, while many have been won over to the view that, as event distinct from the resurrection and terminus of the christophanies, the ascension originated in the thought of St. Luke,[51]

[49] The Barnabas text comes from an author who was not demonstrably acquainted with " any part of our present New Testament *in written form* " (Robert A. KRAFT, *The Apostolic Fathers. A Translation and Commentary* III [ed. Robert M. GRANT ; New York/London : Thos. Nelson & Sons, 1965] 19f.), hence G. LOHFINK must make the admission : " Die Möglichkeit, dass die auffälligen Übereinstimmungen zwischen Lk 24 und Barn 15 vielleicht doch durch eine gemeinsame ältere Tradition mit Ostertermin bedingt sind, kann nicht ganz ausgeschlossen werden " (*Himmelfahrt*, 125).

[50] It is true that Barn. 15,9 *could be* a " schematizing " of Lk 24 and cannot bear *by itself* the burden of proof of a pre-Lucan stage of the ascension tradition (G. LOHFINK, *Himmelfahrt*, 134), but it is also true that the case for purely Lucan origination of the idea cannot be considered settled so long as the derivation of such a text remains in dispute. Cf. the different analysis of H. KÖSTER, *Synoptische Überlieferung bei den Apostolischen Vätern* (TU 65 ; Berlin : Akademie-Verlag, 1957) 146-148.

[51] A. FRIDRICHSEN already proposed the exclusive Lucan accountability for the visible ascension, observing that as Lk's narrative now stands, " kommt man nicht aus mit dem Hinweis auf irgend eine unbekannte volkstümliche Ueberlieferung " (*Theol. Blätter* 6 [1927] 340). It is true, of course, that Lk is alone amongst the NT authors in portraying the heavenly exaltation of Jesus as a visible event, seen by witnesses and separated from the resurrection by an inter-

we should rather keep an open mind towards the possibility, urged by others,[52] that Luke was not the first to recount this terminal episode, hence that either his gospel's ending, or the Acts account, or both, rest upon tradition he received.

As for clues to a conceptual background of the ascension, hence to the milieu of an eventual tradition whence our accounts derive, we find that the model of the *bodily assumption into heaven*,[53] a commonplace in Antiquity, accounts for both the literary genus and the technical language of these passages. The non-Western, longer text of Lk 24,51 employs ἀνεφέρετο εἰς τὸν οὐρανόν, an expression frequent in the tales of bodily assumption emanating from Greek and Roman

val of appearances (cf. P. Benoit, in *Exég. et théol.* I, 370-376 ; J. G. Davies, *He Ascended*, 56-60, 64 ; H. Schlier, *Besinnung*, 227 ; G. Lohfink, *Himmelfahrt*, 81-98 ; E. Kränkl, *Jesus*, 163-166 ; C. H. Talbert, *Literary Patterns*, 113). But this is not yet to say that the dominical exaltation interpreted after the model of the bodily assumption (*Entrückung*) *originated* in Lucan theology (so R. Schnackenburg, " Zur Aussageweise ' Jesus ist (von den Toten) auferstanden '," *BZ* 13 [1969, 1-17] 8 ; G. Lohfink, *Himmelfahrt*, 242 ; G. Frierich, in *Orientierung an Jesus*, 63 ; but cf. 73f.). And it does not lead directly to the conclusion that " the two ascension narratives are the literary composition of Luke " (Lohfink, *op. cit.*, 209). Authors may propose the mainly compositional origin of either the gospel account (so E. Meyer, *Ursprung und Anfänge* I, 32 ; J. Finegan, *Überlieferung*, 92 ; P.A. Van Stempvoort, *NTS* 5 [1958-59] 36f. ; A. George, in *La résurrection*, 96f. ; R. H. Fuller, *Formation*, 122f. ; and cp. R. Pesch, *EKK Vorarb.* III, 18 n. 33, in contrast to *ibid.*, 15) or the Acts account (P. A. Van Stempvoort, *art. cit.*, 39 ; E. Haenchen, *Apg.*, 118 [qualified]) ; R. Pesch, *EKK Vorarb.* III, 15, 19 ; S. G. Wilson, *ZNW* 59 [1968] 269, 274, and *Gentiles*, 101f., 104), but the matter cannot be decided *apriori*, without painstaking analysis, in either case.

[52] It seems to be the disposition of most authors to leave this possibility open. Thus, even among the authors cited in the previous note, R. H. Fuller, R. Pesch, and E. Haenchen are quite tentative in their assertions of the accounts' genesis *manu auctoris*. Among those defending the traditional basis of both accounts, we may cite : H. Schlier, *Besinnung*, 234 ; F. Hahn, *Hoheitstitel*, 106f., and " Die Himmelfahrt Jesu. Ein Gespräch mit Gerhard Lohfink," *Bib* 55 (1974) 418-426 ; U. Wilckens, *Auferstehung*, 95, 97 ; R. Bultmann, *GsT*, 310 (Lk 24) ; H. Conzelmann, *Apg.*², 27 (Acts 1) ; G. Schille, *ZNW* 57 (1966) 184ff. (Acts 1) ; R. H. Fuller, *Formation*, 128-129 (Acts 1) ; G. Bouwman, *BZ* 14 (1970) 260f. (Acts 1 ?). — Individual diagnoses vary greatly, but one may say, at least, that as soon as it is agreed that " Luke would surely not have been the first to tell the story of the ascension " (E. Haenchen, *Apg.*, 118), all possibilities open up in the tradition-historical question, and conclusions about either account must be built upon close and detailed analysis.

[53] Cf. G. Lohfink, *Himmelfahrt*, 74-79 and, especially regarding Lk 24,50-53, 252 : " Der Abschlusscharakter, den diese Erzählung vermittelt, hängt natürlich in erster Linie damit zusammen, dass hier der Abschied Jesu als *Entrückung* dargestellt wird." Also G. Friedrich, in *Orientierung an Jesus*, 59-66 ; W. Grundmann, *Lk.*, 449f. ; Ph. Seidensticker, *Auferstehung*, 18ff. ; U. Wilckens, *Auferstehung*, 97-98 ; R. H. Fuller, *Formation*, 123 ; R. Glöckner, *Verkündigung*, 219 ; J. Ernst, *Lk.*, 671f.

Antiquity.[54] On the other hand, Luke's favored term for the ascension is the verb ἀναλαμβάνομαι, used in Acts 1,2.11.22; and while it plays no noticeable role in the pagan texts, it was also the LXX translators' choice to express the bodily assumptions of Henoch (Sir 49,14; cp. Gen 5,24/Sir 44,16) and preeminently, of course, Elia (2 Kgs 2,9-11; Sir 48,9; cf. also 1 Macc 2,58).[55] — Bearing out this coincidence of terminology is the basic schema and complexus of motifs found among the assumption stories. In contrast to the "heavenly journey" of the apocalyptic seer, the ascension narrator's perspective is *earthbound*: witnesses are on hand and are left behind (Lk 24,51: διέστη ἀπ' αὐτῶν· cp. ἀπὸ τῶν ὀφθαλμῶν αὐτῶν in Acts 1,9), and the description does not follow the departing one beyond the vision of the earthly eye (Acts 1,9f.). In this way the scene is identified as the *ending of an earthly life*, just as Acts 1,1-2 and the parting statements of Acts 1,6-8 and Lk 24,49 bring out with respect to the ascending Jesus.[56] Individual traits of the Lucan passages are also standard features of this genus: the mountain (Acts 1,12), the cloud (Acts 1,9), the *proskynēsis* (Lk 24, 52 *l.v.*), the *angeli interpretes* (Acts 1,11), and the witnesses' praise (Lk 24,53).[57] — No one pre-Lucan story displays all these traits, but the classic *form* of heavenly-assumption story could incorporate them all, hence it furnishes the adequate conceptual framework for interpreting Luke's texts.[58] Indeed, if G. FRIEDRICH is correct, it may also explain

[54] G. LOHFINK, *Himmelfahrt,* 42 (citations in n. 72), 171; G. FRIEDRICH, in *Orientierung an Jesus,* 60 (citations 54 n. 57).

[55] G. LOHFINK, *Himmelfahrt,* 73 (citations in n. 251); J. DUPONT, *Études,* 478f.; G. FRIEDRICH, in *Orientierung an Jesus,* 63; Armin SCHMITT, *Entrückung-Aufnahme-Himmelfahrt. Untersuchungen zu einem Vorstellungsbereich im Alten Testament* (ForBib 10; Stuttgart: Kathoisches Bibelwerk, 1973) 143. Since profane Greek usage gave expression to the bodily assumptions through various other compound verbs with prefix ἀνα- — ἀνάγειν, ἀναφέρειν, ἀναπέμπειν, ἀναρπάζειν — the verb ἀναλαμβάνειν may well be a translator's choice combining this pattern with the usual *verbum simplex* used to render the Hebrew assumption-verb, לָקַח. The Greek verb is uniquely suited to express both the action of Yahweh (passive), the inactivity of the subject, and the upward direction of the assumption (SCHMITT).

[56] G. LOHFINK, *Himmelfahrt,* 75f., 251ff. Also J. KREMER, *Osterbotschaft,* 78f.; H. SCHLIER, *Besinnung,* 228ff., 235ff.

[57] G. LOHFINK, *Himmelfahrt,* 42ff. (hellenistic texts), 73 (Jewish texts), 75 (Lk). Cf. also G. FRIEDRICH, in *Orientierung an Jesus,* 59ff., 65-66.

[58] G. LOHFINK, *Himmelfahrt,* 79: "... wenn die lukanische Himmelfahrtsgeschichte auch nicht von einer uns bekannten *individuellen* Entrückungserzählung abhängig ist, so doch von der *Form* der Entrückung *im ganzen*" (italics his). As the three nonbiblical texts in which most similarities to the Lucan account are found, LOHFINK suggests: Dionysius Halicarnassensis, *Antiquitates Romanae* I 77,2; II Henoch 67 (CHARLES II, 469); Josephus, *Antiquitates Judaicae* IV 8,48 (326). — It will be objected that the assumption-form is inappropriate as a vehicle for portraying the Easter Christ since, while the latter showed himself

other features of this Easter story;[59] and carrying FRIEDRICH's case a step farther than he was willing to go, one could suggest the assumption concept as a comprehensive vehicle for the Lucan soteriology of the Saviour's " journey ".[60] — But we shall return to this suggestion later on (chap. IV/ii).

The prominence of *E l i a* amongst the *assumpti* of the Jewish tradition has produced its own special effects in Lk-Acts. Language borrowed from the Elia texts is most obvious in Acts 1,9-11,[61] but an Elia-tradition has also been discerned at Acts 3,20-21,[62] and Lk 24,49ff.

---

to be the Crucified, raised up *from the dead*, the *assumpti* of Antiquity are mostly spirited off into the heavens *without dying* (cf. H. SCHLIER, *Besinnung*, 228). It is not really crucial to the discussion whether types of " ascensions " which were preceded by death — admittedly exceptions to the rule — ought to be included in our category (so G. LOHFINK, *op. cit.*, 43) or not (so A. SCHMITT, *op. cit.* [in n. 55], 36, 44). The point is that the Lucan narratives have incorporated the terms, motifs, and format of the old assumption stories for illustrative purposes, but not necessarily to fit the mystery of Easter into the assumption category. The adaptation of older ideas seems rather formal and extrinsic, as G. FRIEDRICH rightly insists: " Er (i.e. Lk) erzählt nicht die Entrückung Jesu, aber er zieht Termini der Entrückung heran, weil er sie für geeignet hält, den Griechen die Besonderheit der Auferweckung Jesu nahezubringen " (*Orientierung an Jesus*, 56; cf. also 73f.).

[59] *Orientierung an Jesus*, 55-59.

[60] Contrary to Friedrich's depreciative assessment of the assumption as a theological category of Lk's (*Orientierung an Jesus*, 73), one is attracted by others' observation of how the key Lucan verb πορεύεσθαι connects Acts 1,11 to Lk 9,51 as terminals of the complete itinerary of the Saviour (cf. also Lk 19,36 *diff.* Mk; Lk 19,12 *diff.* Mt; cf. J. H. DAVIES, "The Purpose of the Central Section of St. Luke's Gospel," *StEv* II/1 [1964, 164-169] 166, and others cited in chap. IV, note 134). Given the thematic " journey " connection, it cannot be excluded that the ἀνάλημψις of Lk 9,51 and Acts 1,11 is basically the same, hence that the Saviour's πορεύεσθαι εἰς Ἰερουσαλήμ (9,51) is ultimately his πορεύεσθαι εἰς τὸν οὐρανόν (Acts 1,10.11; cf. P. von der OSTEN-SACKEN, *EvT* 33 [1973] 79f. n. 21).

[61] J. G. DAVIES, *He Ascended*, 52ff.; R. PESCH, *EKK Vorarb.* III, 15ff.; J.-D. DUBOIS, *RHPhilRel* 53 (1973) 170; U. WILCKENS, *Auferstehung*, 98. — Most striking are the following contacts: 4 Kgs 2,9: ἀναλημφθῆναι ἀπό (Acts 1,11; 1,2); 4 Kgs 2,11: ἀνελήμφθη ... εἰς τὸν οὐρανόν (Acts 1,11); 4 Kgs 2,12: καὶ οὐκ εἶδεν αὐτόν (Acts 1,9); 4 Kgs 2,13: ἐπέστρεψεν (Acts 1,12/Lk 24,52); Sir 48,9: ὁ ἀναλημφθείς (Acts 1,11); Sir 48,12: καὶ Ἐλισαῖε ἐνεπλήσθη πνεύματος αὐτοῦ (Acts 1,8/Lk 24,49). This does not suffice to prove that Lk deliberately constructed the parallelism between Acts 1 and the Elia texts (rightly G. LOHFINK, *Himmelfahrt*, 58, *contra* R. PESCH, *EKK Vorarb.* III, 16f., 18 n. 33). In fact, the assimilation seems to have resulted from the free associations characteristic of oral tradition, not the studied citation one expects to find in a purely literary operation.

[62] This need not have involved the Jewish *Grundschrift* postulated by O. BAUERNFEIND (*Apg.*, 66-68, and " Tradition und Komposition in dem Apokatastasisspruch, Apg. 3,20f.," in O. Betz, hrsg., *Abraham unser Vater. Festschr. für Otto Michel* ... [Leiden: E. J. Brill, 1963, 13-23] 16ff.) and endorsed by W.G.

seems not to be without traces of Elianic influence.[63] Now the more clearly the Elia-traditions emerge as inspiration of Luke's portrayals of the ascending Lord, the more acute does our tradition-historical question become, for a definite interest in Elia as " the epitome of the Spirit-filled prophet ... the prophet *par excellence* of the Old Testament " [64] can be detected in both Luke's redactional policies and the *Sondergut* he made use of.[65] Especially the miracle stories in which

---

KÜMMEL, *TRu* 14 [1942] 165f. ; accepted with reservations by F. HAHN, *Hoheitstitel*, 185, and U. WILCKENS, *Missionsreden*, 155; cf. also H. FLENDER, *Heil*, 89). As G. LOHFINK has shown, Lk has more likely constructed this passage out of separate ideas and expressions, perhaps even a partial statement (Acts 3,20a), put together in the manner of a mosaic rather than taken over bodily from an antecedent source (" Christologie und Geschichtsbild in Apg. 3,19-21," *BZ* 13 [1969, 223-241] 239-240). U. WILCKENS now admits that the thesis " dass Lukas ein Traditionsstück en bloc im Wortlaut übernommen habe, lässt sich daraufhin nicht mehr halten " (*Missionsreden*³, 234), and we should agree. We should not wish, however, to reject the Elia-*tradition* along with the alleged Elia-*text*, as G. LOHFINK does (*art. cit.*, 233). The combination of singular concepts in the Acts passage, to wit : the Parousia-reference of ἀποστέλλειν, and the χρόνοι ἀποκαταστάσεως πάντων, is still best accounted for by the Elia-tradition in Mal 3,23f. (rightly BAUERNFEIND ; WILCKENS, *op. cit.*, 153f. ; admitted by LOHFINK, *art. cit.*, 233f.). Moreover, other texts containing Elia-traditions add to the interpretative framework of this passage, especially the Elianic *ascension* texts, Sir 48,9 and IV Ezra 14,9 (G. FRIEDRICH, in *Orientierung an Jesus*, 69).

[63] Particularly the promise of the disciples' investiture with the Spirit's " power," which is the *ductus* of the ascension scene in the gospel (Lk 24,49b), recalls Elia's bequest of his " spirit " to Elisha (4 Kgs 2,9f.15 ; Sir 48,12). Indeed, the form of the promise in Lk, involving the verb ἐνδύεσθαι, may be an allusion to the mantle of Elia (4 Kgs 2,13), the visible symbol of his bequest to his follower (so R. PESCH, *EKK Vorarb.* III, 17). Somewhat less persuasive, on the other hand, is the alleged echo of Elia's command (4 Kgs 2,2.4.6 : κάθου) in καθίσατε ἐν τῇ πόλει (Lk 24,49/Acts 1,4 ; rightly G. LOHFINK, *Himmelfahrt*, 58 n. 177, *contra* R. PESCH and G. W. H. LAMPE, in *Studies in the Gospels*, 177 ; J.-D. DUBOIS, *RHPhilRel* 53 [1973] 170). Tenuous also is the ἐπέστρεψεν of 4 Kgs 2,13 ; Lk 24,52/Acts 1,12. What we should emphasize is the conceptual connection of Spirit-bequest and heavenly ascension, especially since the Elianic spirit was clearly the wonder-working *dynamis*, just as in Lk's understanding (cf. Sir 48,4ff.12-14). Verbal contacts between the gospel finale and the Elianic texts are otherwise scarcely substantial.

[64] W. WINK, *John the Baptist*, 42.

[65] The distinction between tradition and redaction is frequently not made in this as in other respects. Thus the Elianic christology is discussed in reference solely to the evangelist in P. DABECK, " Siehe, es erschienen Moses und Elias,' " *Bib* 23 (1942, 175-189) 180-189 ; C. F. EVANS, in *Studies in the Gospels*, 51-53 ; G. W. H. LAMPE, in *Studies in the Gospels*, 173ff. ; J.-D. DUBOIS, *RHPhilRel* 53 (1973) 167ff. ; W. WINK, *John the Baptist*, 42-45 ; W. RADL, *Paulus und Jesus*, 285ff. — On the other hand, the development of this typology in pre-Lucan traditions, emanating from early circles well worth investigating, is acknowledged but not pursued at any length by F. SCHNIDER, *Prophet*, 109-111. The evangelist's own activity seems to have been primarily a diminishing of the well-established Elianic interpretation of the ministry of John the Baptist (cf. H. CONZEL-

Jesus (Lk 7,11-17) and his witnesses (Acts 9,36-43; 20,7-12) reenact the resurrection miracles of Elia and Elisha (1 Kgs 17,17-24; 2 Kgs 4,8-37) point back beyond our evangelist to special traditions that were at his disposal; and these, in turn, were only intensifying trends already present in the lore of Jesus' thaumaturgy (e.g. Mk 5,21-43; Jn 11). By any chance, could the tradition of Jesus caught up to heaven in the manner of Elia have been nurtured in the same pre-Lucan circles?

Looking to Lk 24,50-53 in particular, we note the association, frequently pointed out in the literature,[66] between this ascension scene and the liturgy of Simon, the highpriest, with which Jesus ben Sira concludes his colorful encomium of the heroes of Israel's past (Sir 50, 20-22; cf. Sir 44ff.). The appeal of this passage to our author, and perhaps his tradition, can be appreciated when we recall that it exults in the bodily ascensions of Henoch (Sir [44,16] 49,14) and Elia (Sir 48,9)[67] and lays special emphasis on the *endowment of powerful prophecy* transmitted through the generations of Israel's wonder-working *viri illustres*: Moses, Aaron, Josua, Samuel, David, Elia, Isaiah, Ezekiel, and Henoch.[68] A conjunction of elements unites the two passages and seems to require more than a merely formal parallelism between them,[69] to wit: the "raising" of hands in levitical gesture (only in Lev 9,22; Sir 50,20; Lk 24,50), the blessing (εὐλογία/εὐλογεῖν), the *proskynēsis* of those assembled and, following the "liturgy", their praise of God

---

MANN, *MdZ*, 18ff.), but this does not account for the Elia-traits in certain accounts of Jesus' ministry (e.g. Lk 7,11-17; perhaps also Lk 9,51ff.; Lk 4,25f. [3 Kgs 17,1f.]; Lk 22,43 [3 Kgs 19,5ff.]; cf. H. FLENDER, *Heil*, 48f. n. 60).

[66] P. VAN STEMPVOORT, *NTS* 5 (1958-59) 34f.: "The conclusion of Luke's gospel is one of his most beautiful 'Septuagintalisms.'" Also W. GRUNDMANN, *Lk.*, 453-454; H. SCHLIER, *Besinnung*, 229, 231; R. PESCH, *EKK Vorarb.* III, 16; G. LOHFINK, *Himmelfahrt*, 168-169; J. ERNST, *Lk.*, 672.

[67] The special emphasis placed on heavenly ascension in the Ben Sira eulogy is brought out in the mention of Henoch at the beginning of the cavalcade (44,16) and at the end (49,14). The authenticity of the former passage is now attested by the Hebrew text from the Cairo Geniza as well as by the LXX (cf. A. SCHMITT, *Entrückung* [cited in n. 55] 177f.), and the special prominence of Henoch probably derives from a tradition which held him to be the wise man par excellence (Jub 4; I Hen; cf. A. SCHMITT, *op. cit.*, 179).

[68] Miracles are attributed to each of these figures in the eulogy: 45,2 (Moses), 45,19 (Aaron), 46,4 (Joshua), 46,15ff. (Samuel), 47,3 (David), 48,3ff. (Elia), 48, 12ff. (Elisha), 48,20.23 (Isaia), 49,8f. (Ezekiel). Of Henoch it is simply said that "no one equal to (him) has been created on the earth" (49,14). Miracles seem to be the measure of the *viri illustres* in Ben Sira's panegyric (cf. Edmond JACOB, "L'histoire d'Israel vue par Ben Sira," in *Mélanges bibliques rédigés en l'honneur de André Robert* [Paris: Bloud et Gay, (1955), 288-294] 290f.). But JACOB's complaint that Ben Sira "ne voit dans les prophètes que les faiseurs de miracles..." (291) may express precisely what appealed to Lk, or the tradition close to him, in hearking back to this passage.

[69] *Contra* G. FRIEDRICH, in *Orientierung an Jesus*, 59ff.

(note the same succession of the two meanings of εὐλογ- in both cases). Then, too, the scenes have the same function of a solemn, impressive *conclusion* in each instance; and not just a literary conclusion at that, since each brings *sacred history's course to a climax* affecting the author and his readers in the present.[70] It is this comprehensive *terminating function,* widely agreed upon now in respect to Lk 24,50ff.,[71] that also defines the relation of the ascension to the rest of the Easter story, particularly its third episode. G. LOHFINK has explained convincingly how the ascension constitutes "the goal and highpoint of Luke's very carefully composed Easter narrative," since "only when Jesus departs into heaven with a blessing is the full faith of the apostles reached: they fall down in prayerful adoration before the departing One and are henceforth filled with a great joy (24,52). Only now have the disciples grasped the height and depth of what has occurred. Only now do they find the real answer to the fact of the resurrection."[72]

Here is the key to the widely acknowledged phenomenon of "compression" in Luke's Easter story. Time and place factors have been compacted here to a point beyond verisimilitude, and the endlessly discussed conflict between the "one day" of Lk 24 and the "forty days" of Acts 1,3 is surely no critics' invention.[73] It is contrary to the lessons taught us by the history of modern gospel criticism to opt first for the harmonist's procedure and posit some intended gap in the narrative — say, after v. 43[74] or v. 49[75] — so that additional, unreported paschal encounters might be inserted to solve the historical problem. Such intervals not only are not mentioned by our narrator,

[70] Cf. G. LOHFINK, *Himmelfahrt*, 169; and on the contemporary circumstances which might have made Simon II Ben Sira's ideal descendant of the *viri illustres*, cf. M. HENGEL, *Judentum und Hellenismus*, 244-245; Th. MIDDENDORP, *Die Stellung Jesu Ben Siras zwischen Judentum und Hellenismus* (Leiden: E. J. Brill, 1973) 167-169.

[71] Cf. nn. 42 and 44 above.

[72] G. LOHFINK, *Himmelfahrt*, 114.

[73] Most of the critics' inventions have been dedicated to solving the problem and reconciling the two passages. Among these: the curtailments of Lk 24,51 and Acts 1,2, which began with the early copyists; the imposition of different meanings on ἀνελήμφθη, and even on ἄχρι ἧς ἡμέρας in Acts 1,2 (e.g. W. MICHAELIS, *Erscheinungen*, 81ff.); the creation of intervals at vv. 43f. and 49f. of Lk 24, illegitimately mingling historical criticism with literary criticism (cf. nn. 74, 75 below).

[74] E. KLOSTERMANN, *Lk.*, 239; J. SCHMID, *Lk.*, 361; H. GRASS, *Ostergeschehen*, 44; D. P. FULLER, *Easter Faith*, 231f.; Ph. SEIDENSTICKER, *Auferstehung*, 99 n. 69. A. PLUMMER (*Lk*, 564) plays it completely safe by imagining intervals both here and at vv. 49f. — *E contra*, rightly stressing the strict connection of vv. 44ff. with the preceding, W. MICHAELIS, *Erscheinungen*, 90; E. NELLESSEN, *Zeugnis*, 108ff.

[75] A. LOISY, *Luc*, 591; J. M. CREED, *Lk*, 300; I. H. MARSHALL, *TyndB* 24 (1973) 93.

they are plainly contrary to the plan of his narrative. All of vv. 36ff., in fact, leads to the departure scene directly and is completed by it. This we learn from, among other things, the parallelism of the second and third pericopes of Lk 24, with their symmetrical sequences of misapprehended appearance, revelation through word and meal, and departure of the apparition. Indeed, as we have seen, the confrontation between uncomprehended phenomena and clarifying word belongs to the structural pattern of this chapter, hence no gap in the narrative can be urged at v. 44. And no less stringent is the connection between the dominical words at vv. 48-49 and the departure following, since the words are unmistakably *final* instructions, having the nature of a "testament" such as typically accompanied heavenly "assumptions."[76] To concentrate on creating room for other events at either of these points, therefore, would only obstruct the integral assertion our evangelist is intent on making.

Furthermore, a narrative that courses to its end so determinedly, with a tension towards the climax[77] created at points like v. 33 (αὐτῇ τῇ ὥρᾳ, p. 92 above), v. 36 (ταῦτα δὲ αὐτῶν λαλούντων), and v. 44 (εἶπεν δὲ πρὸς αὐτούς), is clearly not tailored to suggest space left for other events and a longer time-period! In fact, Luke is not primarily interested — in our chapter, at least — in the external time-framework of the paschal happenings, but in their inner unity and totality. It is the complete Easter occurrence, the sum of its several components, scripturally ordained and editorially condensed "on the third day," that he expounds in the schema of a single day's course.[78] Time here

---

[76] Cf. pp. 176f. above, and G. FRIEDRICH, in *Orientierung an Jesus*, 63f. H. GRASS states the case succinctly: "Dieser (i.e. längerer Zeitraum) kann allerdings schwerlich zwischen V. 49 und V. 50 eingeschoben werden, denn wenn auch erst in V. 50ff. vom Abschied ausdrücklich die Rede ist, so liegt doch schon über den vorhergehenden Versen, besonders über V. 49 so etwas wie Abschiedsbestimmung .... man weiss eigentlich nicht, was (der Auferstandene seinen Jüngern) noch mehr hätte sagen sollen" (*Ostergeschehen*, 44). Taken together with the final instruction, the *blessing* by the departing One in Lk 24,50f. is an especially expressive sign of final departure (G. LOHFINK, *Himmelfahrt*, 160f.; also H. GRASS, *Ostergeschehen*, 50) since blessings are hallmarks of final-departure scenes in Jewish literature (cf. Gen 27,4; 48,15ff.; Dt 33; I Kgs 8,54ff.; Tob 12,16ff.; Jub 22,10ff.; 45,14; II Hen 57,2; cf. U. WILCKENS, *Auferstehung*, 93; G. FRIEDRICH, in *Orientierung an Jesus*, 59f.).

[77] W. MARXSEN, *Auferstehung*, 58: "zielstrebig"; G. LOHFINK, *Himmelfahrt*, 114: "Spannungsbogen ... innere Zeitbewegung." Cf. also J. G. DAVIES, *He Ascended*, 47ff.

[78] E. MEYER, *Ursprung und Anfänge* I, 31ff.; L. BRUN, *Auferstehung*, 87; J. KREMER, *Osterbotschaft*, 80; W. MARXSEN, *Auferstehung*, 71; D. P. FULLER, *Easter Faith*, 197f.; C. F. EVANS, *Resurrection*, 95f.; B. RIGAUX, *Dieu l'a ressuscité*, 261; A. GEORGE, in *La résurrection*, 82f., and in I. de la Potterie, ed., *De Jésus aux évangiles*, 118: "... il veut présenter en une seule scène la totalité

becomes the instrument for expressing the integrity of the paschal mystery as both the gospel- *narrative's terminus ad quem* and the gospel-*proclamation's terminus a quo.* " It is, in reality, the truth and not the chronology (of Easter) that is (Lk's) guiding interest. For him the ascension belongs at the end of the gospel together with the resurrection, joined very closely to the latter in point of essential truth, not chronological fact." [79] — Based on these observations, which we consider to express the evangelist's intention accurately, we shall make the ascension scene's integral connection to the preceding appearance story and its role of solemn conclusion to the chapter and the gospel basic presuppositions of our exegesis, hopefully to be borne out as we proceed.

So much for initial assessments on the issues of main interest raised by Lk 24,50-53. Although we have not yet resolved the tradition-historical question, we have attempted to set down its terms. The influence of Elia-traditions on the Lucan portrayals of a visible ascension points back to the circles in which similar christological appropriations now traceable in this author's *Sondergut* were made. On the other hand, the borrowing of narrative detail for these verses from Sir 50 looks to us like an editorial decision, based on sustained thematic developments of the Easter chapter : the christological exegesis of the Old Testament, and the picture of salvation history summed up and translated into future prospect by the Easter Christ. These are the compositional motifs which suggest to us how the ascension account fits the plan of our chapter as its appropriate concluding statement and the required ending of the appearance to the Eleven.

(e) *The Variant Readings in Lk 24,36-53* : Again in the concluding pericope, our textual decisions are against the " Western non-interpolations," with K. ALAND *et al.*,[80] and in the face of a still vigorous current of opinion favoring certain of the omissions. If the tide has turned against the omission of the technical ascension phrase in v. 51, there are still many scholars, perhaps most, who consider that vv. 36b and 40 of the " neutral text " were interpolated so as to conform Luke's text more closely to Jn 20 (cf. note 14 above). However, since neither the weight of ancient authorities nor the trend of current opinion subsequent to P-75 creates any advantage for the Western readings, the question in all cases seems to require final adjudication at the

---

de la révélation pascale .... Cette journée est le jour de Pâques, le sommet de l'évangile, le terme du temps de Jésus."

[79] G. LOHFINK, *Himmelfahrt*, 115. Cf. also J. SCHMITT, *RvScRel* 25 (1951) 238 : " programme doctrinal ... dans un cadre plutôt fictif que réel." Similarly A. DESCAMPS, *Bib* 40 (1959) 738.

[80] Also NESTLE-ALAND[26], MERK. Cf. K. ALAND, *NTS* 12 (1965-66) 206-209 (= *Studien zur Überlieferung*, 168-171, and note 14 above).

level of *exegesis*. — Let us take the four problem-texts of the present pericope, in turn. Each of them has been resolved by K. ALAND in the new U. B. S. critical edition (1968) in favor of the non-Western variant (long text), but with assignment of the rubric of lowest probability (D).

Lk 24,36b: An argument proper to textual criticism confirms our appeal to the common appearance tradition (Lk/Jn) against the interpolation hypothesis (K. ALAND, *NTS* 12 [1965-66] 207f.). In this case there is no simple alternative of short, Western reading *versus* long, " neutral text " but the complication of two additional variants, each expanding the long text: (Type C) ἐγώ εἰμι, μὴ φοβεῖσθε follows εἰρήνη ὑμῖν (P al aur c f vg verss.); (Type D) ἐγώ εἰμι, μὴ φοβεῖσθε precedes εἰρήνη ὑμῖν (W). It is difficult to make the short text the source of all three longer variants since the latter are closely interconnected, having the very same introduction (καὶ λέγει αὐτοῖς) and word-composition. Type C adds Jn 6,20 (Mk 6,50) directly to the long text, whereas Type D apparently revises Type C in the interests of proper logical sequence. The genetic order of the three is quite clear, as is the fact that only the " neutral text " can explain both C and D. The addition of the dominical ἐγὼ εἰμι was obviously thought necessary by the interpolators for the better motivation of the reproving τί τεταραγμένοι ἐστέ ...; of v. 38, previously coming *before* the self-disclosure.

Now it would seem that similar troubles with the logic of vv. 36ff. motivated the Western omission of καὶ λέγει αὐτοῖς· εἰρήνη ὑμῖν. J. SCHMITT[81] urged this consideration *against* these words' authenticity: " This kind of salutation of the disciples is scarcely compatible with the succeeding narrative, where the author emphasizes that the apostles were seized with ' terror ' and ' dread ' at the sight of the resurrected One (vv. 37-39)." But the same argument can be wielded more effectively in the opposite direction! The apparent inefficacy of the Saviour's *pax* betokens the *lectio difficilior* which, in all likelihood, motivated the greeting's omission. Especially in view of the " Western " redactor's noted reconciling and sanitizing inclinations[82] does this analysis become the more plausible and the interpolation hypothesis lose its allure.

Lk 24,40: As K. ALAND points out, there is enough disparity between this statement and Jn 20,20 (" hands " and " *side* ", reflecting Jn 19,34) to argue persuasively that the two are *tradition*-variants rather than textual variants. If the Lucan verse is secondary in any sense,

[81] *RvScRel* 25 (1951) 230; cp. R. MAHONEY, *Two Disciples*, 61. — SCHMITT's acceptance of v. 40 (*art. cit.*, 230 n. 1) and rejection of v. 36b is an unusual mixture of positions on the " Western " version of Lk 24. Authors are usually consistent in accepting or rejecting the " non-interpolations."

[82] Cf. E. HAENCHEN, *Gott und Mensch*, 205; W. G. KÜMMEL, *Introd. N. T.*[17], 188, 548.

it could more readily have been derived from Lk 24,39 than from Jn 20,20, for v. 39 already contains it in substance. Indeed, since this is so, one sooner imagines a harmonizing copyist striking v. 40 because of its clash with Jn 20,20 (" feet " *vs.* " side ") and leaving v. 39 in a complementary relation to the Johannine text.[83] More typical of the " Western " operation, however, and of a piece with the revision we maintained in v. 36, would be the impulse to avoid making ἔδειξεν αὐτοῖς ineffectual by reason of the immediate sequel, ἔτι δὲ ἀπιστούντων αὐτῶν (v. 41). Once again, the redactor protected the effective power of the Lord's gestures by suppressing one that did not achieve its purpose with edifying speed.

Of *Lk 24,51* we have already observed that the long text's authenticity is lately growing to be *opinio communis* (cf. note 43 above). Here and in the excision of ἀνελήμφθη from Acts 1,2, the " Western " reconciling passion is more obvious than ever, just as the inconsistencies of the two ascension settings in the original text strike even the casual reader. Corresponding to the omission in 24,51, in fact necessitated by it, is the " Western " exclusion of προσκυνήσαντες αὐτόν from v. 52. If, like the latter-day harmonizers mentioned above (note 42), the scribes reduced v. 51 to a temporary taking leave of the disciples (διέστη ἀπ' αὐτῶν · cp. 24,31), then a *proskynēsis* after the departure would, of course, make little sense. It is only towards the ascended, now heavenly Christ that the band of followers could be portrayed in this worshipping posture. Such logical connection of the two " Western " excisions is supported by the alignment of the witnesses, which, with a very few stray exceptions, is the same for both verses (K. Aland, *NTS* 12 [1965-66] 197).

Thus far the arguments are mainly according to the canons of textual criticism. They make a plausible case for the consistent retention of the " neutral " text, but they are not wholly conclusive. We hope in each instance to support the non-Western option with positive exegetical arguments, whereupon our case for the longer readings may be considered decisive.

(2) Tradition and Composition in the Final Pericope

(a) *The Narrative of the Appearance* (*Lk 24,36-43*)

(i) *Narrative Schema*: Since vv. 33-35 have already situated the third pericope in the Easter story's redactional framework, the first words of v. 36 merely accelerate further the story's rush towards its climax (as was brought out already under 1-d). The Emmaus story was still being told by its supporting actors when the main personage,

[83] Rightly J. Jeremias, *Abendmahlsworte*[3], 144.

evoked with the emphatic αὐτός (cp. vv. 15, 39), stood suddenly in the midst of all (ἔστη ἐν μέσῳ αὐτῶν · cp. Jn 20,19). In the use of the intransitive ἱστάναι to state the fact of the appearance we have something of a biblical convention, for the LXX employ this idiom in reference to the advent of heavenly messengers — " angels " — bearing the divine word in the form of an announcement or an interpretation of events (cf. Gen 18,2 ; Dan 8,15 ; 12,5 ; also Num 22, [22-]24 ; 1 Chron 21,16 ; Tob 5,4 S ; Zech 2,3 ; Ez 43,6). The same usage is carried forward in the NT mostly by Luke, undoubtedly as part of his systematic LXX mimicry (Lk 1,11 ; Acts 10,30 ; 16,9 ; but cf. also Apoc. 19, 17). More frequently Luke varies the idiom with the compound verbs ἐφιστάναι (Lk 2,9 ; 24,4 ; Acts 12,7 ; cp. 23,11) and παριστάναι (Acts 1, 10 ; 27,23), but the evocative, biblical style of the scenes is consistent in all instances. What is characteristic of such classical *angelophanies* is their focus upon the *divine message* communicated by the spokesman, rather than any accenting of the apparitions' visual circumstance or sensation.[84] But for a usual mention of the visitors' white apparel or a radiant glow accompanying them, so as to bring out their heavenly origin, the emphasis is wholly upon the *revelation in word* that God grants through the angelic visitation. The appearing angel is only the medium of the revealing word, and the visionary experience of his presence seldom has a special moment of its own. On the other hand, fear and disquiet on the part of the human recipient are frequent features of such narratives, as are words of greeting and reassurance from the messenger.[85] Indeed, we can speak of a certain *form* or idiom of the biblical narrative that recounts the transmission of the divine word to earth by apparition of a heavenly emissary.[86]

Now some accomodation of this " angelophany " idiom to the Easter *christophany* has occurred in the tradition shared by Luke and

---

[84] W. MICHAELIS, *Erscheinungen*, 111-113.

[85] Cf. Lk 1,12-13.28-30 ; 2,9-10 ; 24,5 ; Acts 10,4 ; 27,24. It is interesting to note, in support of the point MICHAELIS makes (prev. note), that Mary's dismay in the scene of the annunciation is said to be ἐπὶ τῷ λόγῳ (Lk 1,29), not the consequence of a dazzling vision.

[86] Cf. M.-E. BOISMARD, *LumVie* # 109 (avr. 1972) 38ff. Such a " form " has been discussed frequently enough in the literature. Given its broadest possible designation, we might call it the schema of the *heavenly embassy*, embracing the announcements of wondrous births (Isaac, Sampson, and the parallelism between the Baptist and Jesus in Lk 1) and the conferral of divine commissions (e. g. Gideon's, Jgs 6,11-24). According to Josef GEWIESS, the recurring elements are : the divine apparition, the fear and alarm, the message itself, the resistance of the recipient, the accrediting sign, — all unfolding with a certain regularity in the accounts (cf. GEWIESS, " Die Marienfrage, Lk 1,34," *BZ* 5 [1961, 221-254] 241f. — citing, for fuller treatment, S. MUNOZ-IGLESIAS, *EstBib* 16 [1957] 329-383).

John,[87] and this is of more than passing interest to us. For one thing, the verb ἔστη expresses the risen One's appearance in Lk 24,36/Jn 20, 19.26 as well as in Jn 21,4 (cp. Jn 20,14). Furthermore, the succession of greeting, disquiet, and reassurance in Lk 24,36-38 seems to be accord ing to convention, just as in Lk 1,28-30,[88] whereupon 24,39-40 can be considered part of the reassurance element accomodated to the Easter situation. When the sequence in Jn 20,19f. is found to be reduced to the greeting and an otherwise unmotivated display of the Visitor's wounds, there is good reason to judge this a secondary constriction of the narrative on John's part.[89] We readily imagine him bothered by the same non-sequitur of dominical *pax* and disciples' disturbance as bothered J. SCHMITT (n. 81 above) and the " Western " scribe who, in our opinion, suppressed the greeting in Lk. The non-sequitur becomes conceivable, on the other hand, if a narrative schema was being followed in the original story, for such formal structures tend to weaken the force and logic of their separate components. Finally, and most significantly, the center of gravity of the appearance story in both versions is the *risen Lord's message*, which contains the *word of divine commission* wherein the objective and focus of the narrative are to be found. Given that such a centrality of the Visitor's message conforms to the classic schema, we might also be inclined to classify the threshold of narrative detail — the display of wounds (Lk/Jn) and the risen One's meal (Lk) — as an equally typical accreditation of the message before its hesitant recipients (cf. Acts 1,3f.). One cannot forget, however, that the Visitor's identity is essential to the content and force of *this* message, and in this respect the appearance story breaks out of the conventional limits of the angelophany.

Even so, what might the original narrator's purpose have been in adorning the "cenacle appearance " [90] with elements of a classic schema

---

[87] So W. MICHAELIS, *Erscheinungen*, 120. Also A. GEORGE, in *La résurrection*, 85 ; M.-É. BOISMARD, *LumVie* # 109, 41. The use of the verb ἔστη highlights the preternatural suddenness and other-wordly initiative of the apparition (BOISMARD ; X. LÉON-DUFOUR, *Résurrection*, 131).

[88] J. GEWIESS (*BZ* 5 [1961] 244) notes the parallelism between the annunciation scene and Acts 10,9-16 in this conventional sequence of summons, resistance, and reassurance.

[89] Cf. n. 15 above. — John clearly understands the Easter greeting to bestow the legacy of the departing Revealer (Jn 14,27 ; 16,33), and he hastens to record, as consequence of the greeting, the inalienable " joy " promised for the day of reunion between Master and disciples (Jn 16,22).

[90] It is only for convenience sake that I take such liberties with the text as to call this the " cenacle appearance." There is no more basis there to assume it took place in the " cenacle " — traditionally, the room of the Last Supper - - than in the " Upper Room," which A.R.C. LEANEY refers to (Lk, 30f.). The trouble is, if one doesn't find a name like that, he finds this appearance awfully difficult to refer to succinctly. One cannot say, " the appearance

that ultimately could not contain it? A pursuit of plausible motives for this can begin with the content of the Lord's greeting, εἰρήνη ὑμῖν. Is this just a neutral alternative to χαίρετε (Lk 1,28; Mt 28,9), or does it have some more specific function in our narrator's plan? Building on our convictions that Lk is closer to the original appearance-*narrative* and that the greeting is genuine in the Lucan version, we inquire after possible relationships between the *pax* and other details of the story. Opinions may differ as to how important the messianic "peace" motif is to Luke himself,[91] but there is at least one important tradition utilized by him in which that motif figures prominently, and that is the *instruction of the missionaries* in its Q rendition. Luke is our prime witness to the dual form of that tradition since he incorporated Mk 6,7-11 at Lk 9,1-6, then redacted the variant "Q" version under the schema of the "mission of the Seventy(-two)" in Lk 10, 2-12.[92] One of the oldest units in this latter compilation, perhaps even its seminal nucleus,[93] is the "protocol for the household" in Lk 10,5-7 (cp. Mt 10,12-13; Mk 6,10), which bids Jesus' emissary bestow the greeting of *peace* on the household he enters and make his dwelling therein, partaking of the *food* of the household. This combination of gestures, the greeting εἰρήνη τῷ οἴκῳ τούτῳ and the boardsharing ἐσθίοντες καὶ πίνοντες τὰ παρ' αὐτῶν, presents a remarkable analogy to the terminal points of our appearance story, where the risen Christ seems to reenact precisely the procedure he had prescribed for his itinerant representatives! — Now we perceive a tighter conceptual bond between the narrative detail and the dominical pronouncement: both give testimony to the world-mission being inaugurated in the cenacle. First,

to the Eleven and the others," or even "the appearance to the assembled disciples" all the time! And of the tradition that the appearance took place in the very room where the Last Supper was held, being also the place where the frightened disciples regrouped after the passion, we can only say: *se non è vero, è ben trovato*! The appearance is to be marked by a wondrous *coena* of sorts anyway, is it not? So wherever the astonished disciples were able to produce food for the risen Master to eat, why not refer to that place — unmentioned by Lk — as a "cenacle" just as memorable as the original!

[91] Seemingly with equal assurance, special Lucan interest is denied by J SCHMITT, *RvScRel* 25 (1951) 230; J. KREMER, *Osterbotschaft*, 73f.; X. LÉON-DUFOUR, *Résurrection*, 131 n. 7, and asserted by A. GEORGE, in *La résurrection*, 77.

[92] Mt's mission discourse is typically a synthesis of these two versions (Mt 9,37-10,16), hence a comparison of Lk 10,2ff. with Mk and Mt permits the tracing of the "Q" mission instruction as an independent entity. Cf. D. LÜHRMANN, *Redaktion*, 59; P. HOFFMANN, *Logienquelle*, 237-287; S. SCHULZ, *Q*, 404-407.

[93] P. HOFFMANN, *Logienquelle*, 288, 296, and *EKK Vorarb.* III, 52. — On Lk 10,5-7 as the oldest form of the household protocol, cf. F. HAHN, *Mission*, 35; S. SCHULZ, *Q*, 405f., 416f. (HAHN's separation of v. 7 as an early addition to vv. 5f. is gratuitous.)

the risen Christ appears in the role of missionary to the chosen household; then he formally commissions his disciples to become his "witnesses." Moreover, in his role of "proto-missionary," the risen One justifies the echoes of the Old Testament visitations by divine messengers which have been produced in this narrative. Indeed, it may not be accidental that, at the beginning of the gospel's "journey" section, the theme of Jesus' dispatch of "messengers" to precede him comes into its own straightway in the idiom of Old Testament angelic embassies: καὶ ἀπέστειλεν ἀγγέλους πρὸ προσώπου αὐτοῦ (Lk 9,52; cp. Lk 7,27/Mal 3,1).

This analysis furnishes some further clues to the understanding of the Lucan narrative. First, the greeting in the ancient mission program was the distinguishing sound of the kingdom's heralds, "almost magically" ferreting out its adherents.[94] Like the commission to perform healings amongst receptive householders (Lk 10,9), the greeting prescription is explained by the content of the mandated proclamation: ἤγγικεν ἐφ' ὑμᾶς ἡ βασιλεία τοῦ θεοῦ (Lk 10,9).[95] Peace-greeting and kingdom-heralding stand in an essential relationship that was provided for already in the Deutero-Isaiah (52,7) and other late prophecy (Nah 2,1); hence those who conducted the early mission according to the household protocol were inspired by the inherited image of the eschatological prophet, bearing the tidings of the end-time in word and gesture.[96] Perhaps this explains why the sequence of greeting and fear in the cenacle appearance was not perceived as self-contradictory by the original narrators. The prophetic *pax* was conceived first as one of the powerful phenomena inaugurating the eschaton, and not an immediate psychological palliative! "Joy" came in its wake, according to the tradition (Lk 24,41/Jn 20,20), but this could only happen in Luke's sequence when the disciples were reassured of the Visitor's identity, hence not completely till gesture and elucidating word were both completed (Lk 24,52: μετὰ χαρᾶς μεγάλης).

[94] P. HOFFMANN, *Logienquelle*, 296, 298. HOFFMANN rightly argues that Mt 10,13, with its interposition of the worthiness issue, is a secondary interpretation of the messenger's *pax*, originally conceived as itself effecting the salvation of its recipient (cf. also HAHN, *Mission*, 34).

[95] It may be that Lk 10,9 was originally part of the household rule and Lk 10,8 is a redactional enlargement of Lk's (so P. HOFFMANN, *Logienquelle* 276-283, and *EKK Vorarb.* III, 42-49), or it may be that the parallelism of Lk 10,8a.9 and 10,10-11 demonstrates a "city protocol" comparable to the one for houses and formulated as a unit alongside the latter (cf. S. SCHULZ, *Q*, 407) "City" and "house" are already combined as the messengers' fora in the secondarily condensed version of Mt (10,11f.14), hence the second possibility appears to be the more probable.

[96] P. HOFFMANN, *Logienquelle*, 301, and *EKK Vorarb.* III, 51. — On the Jewish tradition which interpreted the מְבַשֵּׂר of Is 52 in terms of the eschatological prophet-figure, cf. P. STUHLMACHER, *Evangelium* I, 146ff.

Another anomaly of Luke's narrative becomes intelligible in the framework of the mission procedure, namely, the food taken by the risen One *from* the assembled disciples. It has been pointed out frequently that this feature prevents the cenacle episode from being considered amongst the eucharistic repasts shared with the risen Christ, for in those he is the subject of the διδόναι action (Lk 24,30; Jn 21,13), while here the disciples give and he receives (Lk 24,42f.).[97] Only when he is viewed in the role of proto-missionary following the steps of his own prescription for the households, hence taking as his food τὰ παρ' αὐτῶν, does this unwonted recipient's position at the meal fit the risen Lord. Moreover, it would seem that Luke meant to recall the mission precept even more punctually when he had Peter cite the cenacle happening on the occasion of the conversion of the first Gentile *household*: ... ἡμῖν, οἵτινες συνεφάγομεν καὶ συνεπίομεν αὐτῷ ... (Acts 10,41; cp. Lk 10,7: ἐσθίοντες καὶ πίνοντες). Here the evangelist's cross-reference practice, already observed by us (p. 65), has again produced a "flashback" which contains items of an underlying tradition that were not reproduced in its first rendition (cp. Lk 24,24 *vs.* 24,12). How appropriate, too, that the apostles' appointment as the Lord's "witnesses" should be recalled with remembrance of the Easter *meal* precisely where Peter is acting as missionary to the *household* of Cornelius (Acts 10,22; 11,12.14), and this even to the point of "abiding" there for "some days" (ἐπιμεῖναι, Acts 10,48) and "eating with" his uncircumcized converts (συνέφαγες, Acts 11,3), in strict adherence to the protocol.[98]

---

[97] The differences between the cenacle eating and the tradition shared by Lk 24,29ff. and Jn 21,12f. are easy to recognize (cf. H. Grass, *Ostergeschehen*, 89; J. Kremer, *Osterbotschaft*, 74f.; U. Wilckens, *Auferstehung*, 72; J. Wanke, *Emmauserzählung*, 104), and the secondary additions to vv. 42 and 43 in the textual tradition (esp. to 43: καὶ τὰ ἐπίλοιπα ἔδωκεν αὐτοῖς) show the early copyists' inclination to supply the missing eucharistic overtones (cf. W. Grundmann, *Lk.*, 451f.; E. Lohse, *Auferstehung*, 36; M. Kehl, *GeistLeb* 43 [1970] 109). It is usually maintained that the eating is a demonstrative act, meant to demonstrate the physical reality of the risen One in the manner of the conclusion to the story of Jairus' daughter (Mk 5,43/Lk 8,55; cf. C. M. Martini, in *Resurrexit*, 236f.). If this is indeed how Lk intends the gesture to be understood, it must still be borne in mind that no recognition is recorded with the *manducatio*, hence the latter must function dialectically, as do the vision and palpation motifs here (cf. pp. 166f. and n. 28). — Along with the differences between the *manducatio* of vv. 41-43 and Lk 24,29ff./Jn 21,12f., one ought also to keep in mind the surprising resemblances of these traditions, especially the Lord's question of v. 41, which recurs in Jn 21,5 (cf. p. 193 below, and n. 107). The Johannine tradition also knows the request of the risen Lord for food from his astounded disciples!

[98] Although neither Acts 10,48 nor Acts 11,3 is usually explained in terms of the mission protocols enjoined by Jesus (cf. Haenchen and Conzelmann, *ad loc.*), they by no means stand alone as reminiscences of Jesus' mission directives in the Acts mission accounts (cf. note 100 below). Moreover, it is reasonable

Nor can it be accidental, in such a context, that the first Gentile missionary recalls the word sent by God to Israel, εὐαγγελιζόμενος εἰρήνην διὰ Ἰησοῦ Χριστοῦ (Acts 10,26; cf. Is 52,7; Nah 2,1 LXX).[99] Indeed, the Cornelius sequence is full of resonances of the dominical program for the mission to the households, hence it is a natural occasion for recalling the cenacle christophany, where the risen Lord set the example for that mission.

It would seem that these reiterations of the household procedure, to which one might add the Zacchaeus episode (cf. Lk 19,5ff.) and certain Acts passages,[100] come from the pen and the special interest of

---

to conclude from both Acts 11,3 and the apparent logic of an underlying Cornelius-*tradition* (i.e. the connection between the content and the result of Peter's vision) that Lk omitted mention of a *meal* shared by Peter and the converts which the source had recounted (so Karl Löning, " Die Korneliustradition," *BZ* 18 [1974, 11-19] 10-11). When one takes notice of the " mission-historical " conclusion which Lk himself records at the end of the Cornelius sequence (Acts 11,18), it becomes clear that the issue of (table-) *koinonia* between Jewish and Gentile Christians, which was likely the *tradition's* thorny issue of concern, is no longer the main interest of the author of Acts (rightly K. Löning, *art. cit.*, 15). This may explain his omitting mention of what Acts 10,48 and 11,3 clearly presume. But even if, according to the less satisfying analysis of M. Dibelius (*Aufsätze*, 98f.), Lk embellished the original Cornelius-story with the previously unconnected vision of the foods (Acts 10,9-16) and fused the two items rather by contrivance at Acts 10,28, there is still no doubt that Lk understands Peter's ἐπιμεῖναι (10,48) in terms of " ein wirkliches Verhältnis der Tischgemeinschaft " (M. Dibelius, *op. cit.*, 100).

[99] K. Löning again makes a plausible case for ascribing Acts 10,34-36 to a Cornelius-*tradition* constituted, like the Saul-sequence of Acts 9, by a double-vision structure (cf. *BZ* 18 [1974] 12ff.). The correspondence of the two visions is disclosed in the dialogue of the two visionaries (Acts 10,23b-36), which originally formed the interpretative complement of the vision episodes. Under Lk's editing, the conclusion of this second section (vv. 34-36) became the introduction to the familiar Petrine sermon (vv. 36-43; cf. K. Löning, *art. cit.*, 19), and the well-known grammatical tensions at vv. 36f. were the result of the artificial attachment. However one should understand the grammar of v. 36, it scarcely points to " die ursprüngliche Zusammengehörigkeit des ganzen Passus 10,36ff." (U. Wilckens, *Missionsreden*, 48). — If Löning's ascription of vv. 34-36 can be analytically sustained along with the rest of his delineation of a Cornelius-tradition, we should then have interesting support for our suggestion that the companion gestures of the household protocol, the proclamation of peace and sharing of food, had left their mark on traditions of the early missions that antedated Lk's writing.

[100] Cf. esp. Acts 16,31-34; also Acts 16,15. That Lk himself is conscious of the household as primary mission field is indicated by the summary in Acts 5,42 (cp. 2,46) and Paul's " testament " at Acts 20,20. — Nor is the household procedure the only dominical prescription for the missions to be echoed in the narratives of Acts. The prophetic gesture of " shaking the dust " against unreceptive communities is repeated at Acts 13,51, where it is probably redactional (cf. Lk 9,5[= Mk]; 10,11/Mt 10,14[Q]; cf. E. Haenchen, *Apg.*, 357; W. Radl,

Luke. But we should not draw this conclusion too hastily in view of the noticeably greater interest he appears to have in the *polis* as the mission's real theatre. It is this greater interest which may account for the somewhat awkward translation of the household protocol into a *city*-protocol in Lk 10,8,[101] and it surely accounts for the systematic emphasis in Acts on " whole " cities as the missionaries' forum and audience.[102] So far as the household procedure itself is concerned, one cannot say that it is reiterated systematically in all the instances we have cited. The *pax* and table-fellowship motifs are not superimposed on traditional material in a consistent fashion, as we should expect in redactional arrangements, but are gleaned from here and there, some-

---

Paulus und Jesus, 88), and Acts 18,6. The *Trostwort* concerning the " hairs of your head " (Lk 12,7/Mt 10,30) is repeated in Paul's exhortation at Acts 27,34. And the step is short, as W. RADL points out (*op. cit.*, 365), from the principle, " he who receives you receives me " (Lk 10,16/Mt 10,40), to the appearing Lord's question to Saul (Acts 9,4f.; 22,7f.; 26,14f.), especially in view of the principle's negative extension in Lk (*diff.* Mt): " he who rejects ...." — Although Lk's composition was undeniably dedicated to a systematic parallelism of ministries and destinies between the Master and his mission representatives, this concern by no means originated with our author. Indeed, the mission logia we have cited as echoed in Acts were transmitted to Lk in source-passages (Mk, Q) that were composed to bring out the same comparison (W. RADL, *op. cit.*, 363ff.). Consequently, one cannot decide apriori that the echoes, any more than the original sayings, were inevitably created by Lk's hand. The tradition-historical pedigree of each passage must be decided on its own merits. Lk was surely concerned with the parallelism and is occasionally responsible for bringing it out it detail; but he need not have originated it in all passages of his two volumes where it is verified.

[101] At least this seems likely with respect to the ill-fitting injunction to share the food furnished by the receptive *city* (!) in Lk 10,8b (S. SCHULZ, *Q*, 407 n. 25), even if one prefers not to follow HOFFMANN (cf. note 95 above) in charging v. 8 wholly to Lk's redaction. HOFFMANN does not deny Lk's creation of v. 8b because of its awkwardness (so SCHULZ, *loc. cit.*) but precisely explains the logical sequence Lk meant to create by adding ἐσθίετε τὰ παρατιθέμενα ὑμῖν to echo v. 7a (cf. *Logienquelle*, 282f.).

[102] Besides the well-known publicity of the apostles' ministrations before " all Jerusalem," brought out repeatedly in the early chapters of Acts, we observe that " cities " are the principal objectives of Christian missionaries in our historian's perspective (cf. Acts 8,40; 14,6.21; 15,36; 16,4). Philip's publicity in Samaria (Acts 8,5ff.), Peter's effect on the Judaean cities (9,35; " all Joppa," 9,42), Paul's audience made up of " all the city " at Pisidian Antioch (13,44), and the impact of the Pauline mission on numerous cities along the path to Rome (cf. esp. Acts 14,4; 16,20; 17,5.13; 17,17ff.; 18,10; 19,17, etc.), all attest this predominant interest. Lk means to show that the Christian mission operates with all publicity and with the " whole world " as its objective; hence wherever missionaries come, the " whole world " is moved by their message. In this presentation, " das Stadt-Motiv ist im Rahmen der hellenistischen Stadtkultur ein wirkungsvolles Mittel, diese Intention zu veranschaulichen " (P. HOFFMANN *Logienquelle*, 280). Cf. H. J. CADBURY, *Making of Lk-Acts*, 245-249.

times only by implicit association with companion themes.[103] It hardly seems that Luke was specially concerned to bring out the combination of the two gestures in all fundamental or exemplary mission activity. It looks rather as if the traces of the old rule had been instilled, more or less naturally, in certain traditions he made use of.

More pertinent to our literary analysis at hand is the question whether Luke himself added the risen Lord's meal to the cenacle story, out of concern for the old mission rule or not. After all, this is the one feature of his version which is altogether without analogy in Jn 20, and some scholars believe it is an addition that comes from Luke's hand and Luke's interests.[104] On the other hand, the meal might as readily have been eliminated by John in pursuing the goals of his rendition of the Easter sequence.[105] John has drawn out the cenacle story into a two-stage drama, the first devoted to the mission without the element of doubt and demonstration, the second seizing upon these elements and turning them to the service of the johannine *Leitmotiv* of the faith that conquers the world (cf. notes 9,15-16 above). If the meal had functioned in the older tradition as it *appears* to function in Lk, as a conclusive step in the Visitor's proof-of-identity (cf. note 28), then it is understandable that John suppressed it since, having reduced the doubters to one faltering disciple, he no longer required a *probatio coram omnibus*. But as we have seen, it is by no means clear that the eating is a probative measure even in Lk, or that it was such before Luke wrote. If we may assume that Luke's difficult ἀπιστούντων αὐτῶν ἀπὸ τῆς χαρᾶς in v. 41 (cp. Lk 22,45) is his altered version of a statement like Jn 20,20b, revised in the interests of his Easter dialectic (cf. p. 162 above), then it probably marks the point at which the original story recorded the *recognition* of the Master by his joyous followers, as in Jn. In that case, of course, the *subsequent* meal would not have been a probative measure but part of an exchange illuminated by faith and recognition. Understood in this way, it must have func-

[103] As with " joy " (Acts 16,34) or " salvation " (Lk 19,9) in relation to the *pax*, and " abiding " (μένειν, Lk 19,5 ; Acts 10,48 ; 16,15) in relation to the sharing of board (on the latter cf. J. WANKE, *Eucharistieverständnis*, 43, 56).

[104] Aside from A. LOISY, *Luc*, 586f. ; J. SCHMITT, *RvScRel* 25 (1951) 231 ; apparently C. H. TALBERT, *Luke*, 74 ; and by suggestion, J. SCHNIEWIND, *Parallelperikopen*, 93, I have not found this position very widespread. Cf. also V. TAYLOR, *Passion Narrative*, 114.

[105] So H. GRASS, *Ostergeschehen*, 68 ; R. LEANEY, *NTS* 2 (1955-56) 113f. ; by implication also E. HIRSCH, *Auferstehungsgeschichten*, 10f. ; J. A. BAILEY, *Traditions*, 92ff., and others who maintain Jn was acquainted with Lk's text. The same view is presumably held by those who believe Lk records the cenacle tradition in 24,36-43 " without commentary " (Ph. SEIDENSTICKER, *Auferstehung*, 99), " essentially unchanged " (P. SCHUBERT, *Ntl. Studien f. Bultmann*, 175), although most authors are prudently reticent about reconstruction of the prior tradition in detail.

tioned as we suggested, namely, as the evocative setting for the dominical mission mandate, imposed by the Master while he himself was observing his own prescription for household visitation. Moreover, if the suggested echo of Old Testament angelic missions was truly intended by the first narrators, there may also be an allusion here to those heavenly " missionaries " who ate food furnished by their earthly hosts.[106] In both evocations, house-rule and angelic houseguests, it was essential to have the Visitor *receive* the food from his hosts, — an anomalous situation for the risen Christ, as we have already observed. We should think, therefore, that the meal episode was recounted in the cenacle tradition much as it is in Lk 24,41b-43, and much as it is echoed — " distantly," indeed[107] — in Jn 21,5a. Small wonder that John found no room for such an obscure episode between the points of recognition and commission in the appearance story. It is quite likely that he no longer understood the allusions the tradition had intended. In our opinion, therefore, Luke is faithful to the tradition in recording the Lord's repast in the cenacle; he has not added this element *ex propriis*. — Whether it is for the sake of the same allusions as previously intended that the meal survived at Luke's hand is another question. The setting changed substantially with the introduction of persistent ἀπιστία at v. 41, hence we shall have to reckon with an altered perspective in the Lucan composition. And in search of this, we shall have to follow the argument of vv. 36ff., step by step.

(ii) *Narrative Argument*: If we look for a central assertion in this passage to which the individual steps of the argument all add up, it proves rather easy to locate. It is the assertion that is intended not only in the display of wounds and invited palpation of them, but also in the greeting, the eating, and the retrospective instruction. It is: ἐγώ εἰμι αὐτός.[108] The identity of the risen Christ with the earthly Jesus, hence the unbroken path of the Saviour inaugurated at Lk 9,51 (his ἀνάλημψις), is being proclaimed in each phase of our pericope: narrative, instruction, finale. That is why words are spoken at vv. 44f. which were spoken ἔτι ὢν σὺν ὑμῖν, and why a familiar station on the way into Jerusalem (Lk 19,29) is mentioned again on the way to the

[106] Cf. E. KLOSTERMANN, *Lk.*, 241: Gen 18,8; 19,3; Tob 7,8; 8,1 (but cf. 12,19).

[107] R. SCHNACKENBURG, *Johannesevangelium* III, 422; but cf. J. LANGE, *Das Erscheinen des Auferstandenen*, 465f., 485, for a less reserved assessment. And cf. n. 97 above. — With its expected negative answer (μή τι προσφάγιον ...; Jn 21,5), the Johannine version of the Lord's query (Lk 24,41b) may very well be more than a redactional connective between the previously separate miracle and apparition stories (*pace* R. PESCH, *Fischfang*, 87, 95).

[108] R. GLÖCKNER, *Verkündigung*, 206, 208. Cf. also W. MARXSEN, *Auferstehung*, 172: " Auch *Lukas* geht es ... um Kontinuität mit dem irdischen Jesus." Also F. SCHÜTZ, *Christus*, 95f.

scene of the departure into heaven (Lk 24,50). In this manifest redactional concern, however, Luke is at one with his tradition, for it was the real presence of the *same Jesus* to his own after his death, rather than a polemical tour de force against docetic beliefs,[109] that the pre-evangelical appearance story brought out with its demonstrative elements. It is clear that Luke better preserves the old story's sequence since he logically reports the display of wounds as the Master's response to his disciples' terror and confusion, whereas in Jn the display is unmotivated and the doubt and reassurance are postponed to the derivative Thomas episode.[110] Of Luke's sequence it has been frequently asserted that a three-fold demonstration is featured: the Lord invites the assembled followers first to look upon him, then to feel him, then to give him to eat, and so, by ascending grades of evidence, to have their lingering doubt of his reality dispelled.[111] The trouble with this, of course, is that these evidential steps are not accompanied by any corresponding climax of reaction from the doubters, as we should expect if the narrator was intent on progressive reasoning. In neither evangelist's account do we learn that the physical probing was actually carried out, and in Lk we hear nothing of understanding or recognition until *after* the demonstrations, when the risen One has begun to *speak* (v. 45: τότε διήνοιξεν αὐτῶν τὸν νοῦν τοῦ συνιέναι τὰς γραφάς). Prior to that "opening", the only reaction noted was the mysterious ἔτι δὲ ἀπιστούντων αὐτῶν ἀπὸ τῆς χαρᾶς καὶ θαυμαζόντων (v. 41), which, as we have opined previously, has to be Luke's adjustment of the original burst of recognition (Jn *20*),[112] suppressed at pre-

[109] Rightly U. Wilckens, *Auferstehung*, 77f.; R. Schnackenburg, *Johannesevangelium* III, 383. — Also supporting the identity of the Nazarene with the Easter Christ as the appearance-*tradition's* basic assertion: G. Koch, *Auferstehung*, 45, 48f.; H.-W. Bartsch, *Wachet*, 26f.; W. Grundmann, *Lk.*, 451; W. Marxsen, *Auferstehung*, 70.

[110] Cf. note 9 above. — Also supporting, on this basis, Lk's greater fidelity to the traditional narrative: J. Schniewind, *Parallelperikopen*, 93; A. R. C. Leaney, *Lk*, 30f.; G. Hartmann, *ZNW* 55 (1964) 210ff.; J. Kremer, *Osterbotschaft*, 112; Robert T. Fortna, *The Gospel of Signs* (cited in chap. I, n. 183) 142f.; X. Léon-Dufour, *Résurrection*, 235-238; R. H. Fuller, *Formation*, 141f.; R. Schnackenburg, *Johannesevangelium* III, 382. — Cf. also H. Grass, *Ostergeschehen*, 65ff.

[111] J. Schmitt, *RvScRel* 25 (1951) 231; J. Kremer, *Osterbotschaft*, 74; G. Kegel, *Auferstehung*, 89; M. Kehl, *GeistLeb* 43 (1970) 109; R. H. Fuller, *Formation*, 115. — On the other hand, H. Grass doubted the climax-intention because of the absence of a corresponding movement of the disciples' reaction (*Ostergeschehen*, 41).

[112] Cf. pp. 162, 192 above. — The feeling that ἀπιστούντων ... ἀπὸ τῆς χαρᾶς is a Lucan touch, artificially combining the "joy" which came at this point in the old story with Lk's own dialectic of sense perception and belief, finds confirmation in the similar remark of Lk 22,45 *diff.* Mk 14,37; also Acts 12,14. Cf. J. Wellhausen, *Lc.*, 141; E. Klostermann, *Lk.*, 241 (only there is no "vix"

cisely the point of its original occurrence so that our chapter's dialectic between Easter phenomena and Easter revelation might be sustained. That means, of course, that only the display of wounds, not the *manducatio*, had preceded the recognition, and that other purposes — evoking a classic pattern of heavenly visitations, recalling his own prescription for household evangelization — were served by the Lord's repast. The same sense is found in both the display of wounds and the repast: the mysterious Visitor is the Master and none other. The communion of teacher and disciples was renewed, albeit on a higher and richer level, through evocative gestures which assured his followers that the person and the endeavour of Jesus of Nazareth were truly, uninterruptedly alive!

Consequently, rather than ascending steps of proof towards acceptance of the risen Christ *in corpore*, we should rather see two parallel statements made in response to the fear and misapprehension in the disciples' assembly: *it is really I* (αὐτός, the same), and *it is not a spectre*. These are positive and negative reassurances whose content is cumulative. They are contained in the parallel invitations of v. 39: ἴδετε and ψηλαφήσατε, to which correspond ἔδειξεν in Jn 20,20 and φέρε κτλ. in Jn 20,27. Both versions of the story show the *equivalence* rather than the progression of these invitations, Luke with ψηλαφήσατε ... καὶ ἴδετε in v. 39, John with φέρε τὸν δάκτυλον ... καὶ ἴδε in v. 27. Moreover, after the two invitations in v. 39, Luke recounts only the ἔδειξεν of the crucified limbs in v. 40, noting no additional tactile demonstration. It was here that recognition came in the original story, as it does presently in Jn 20,28. *Recognition*, that is, and not acquaintance with what a risen body is! No anti-docetic or anti-gnostic polemic need be posited here, such as we find when the ψηλαφᾶν is reported to have been carried out in 1 Jn 1,1.[113] More pertinent is a comparison of our episode to the disciples' encounter with Jesus walking the stormy waters (Mk 6,45ff.), a sight which caused them to think they

in Lk's statement, as there is in the comparable Livy text which K. cites); J. KREMER, *Osterbotschaft*, 74; Ph. SEIDENSTICKER, *Auferstehung*, 135. It may be that the ἀπιστία of Lk 24 (vv. 11. 41; cp. Acts 28,24) comes from the evangelist's concern for a special problem of his own generation, as J. LANGE opines, but we shall not follow him immediately to the conclusion: "Es geht Lk nicht zuletzt um eine Sicherung der 'Fakten'" (*Das Erscheinen des Auferstandenen*, 484).

[113] R. SCHNACKENBURG, *Johannesevangelium* III, 383. One can understand, however, that apologetic exploitation of a tradition like this one readily set in under the pressure of rising polemics (cf. the Ignatian text cited above, n. 21). Prior to such intent, one might have associated "proofs" of identity with such a story of delayed recognition, given the convention of producing such proofs in accompaniment of the ἀναγνώρισις motif in the Greek theatre (observed by C. H. DODD, in *More N. T. Studies*, 113 n. 1, 123 n. 2).

were seeing a φάντασμα, a more conventional *vocabulum* for such a context.[114] The Master's reassurance of the terrified band took nearly the same form on that occasion: θαρσεῖτε, ἐγώ εἰμι · μὴ φοβεῖσθε (Mk 6,50). In both cases it is misapprehension of the apparition's *identity* which causes the followers' terror and furnishes the content of the words of reassurance. Both times the fear and perplexity are of the kind that is germane to heavenly-apparition stories, not failure to recognize true corporeal reality. Once again our initial observation of the classic apparition framework in the episode at hand helps us to gain some clarity in discerning its basic intention.

Furthermore, the coincidence of features between the Marcan miracle story and the Easter story is an effective reminder of a familiar motif that has consistently figured in the *redactional plan* of Lk 24. The disciples' fear and misunderstanding in both the Marcan and Lucan passages are products of the messianic *mysterium*: the riddle of the messianic miracles in Mk (6,51f),[115] the mystery of the messianic passion in Lk. That is why we hear of the observers' θαυμάζειν again at v. 41, as we heard of it at the empty tomb (cf. *ad* 24,12 above): in both instances the familiar enthusiasm is evoked by the preternatural phenomenon, but this is no greater advance towards messianic *faith* in either case than it was when it clashed with the dominical passion

prophecy at Lk 9,43ff.[116] In their cenacle cluster, the disciples' " mind "

[114] Understandable, therefore, but only of historical interest, is the substitution of φάντασμα for πνεῦμα in Lk 24,37 by D and Marcion. The use of πνεῦμα in this sense is unconventional for the NT (cf. I Pet 3,19) and altogether unusual in the Lucan writings (comparable is Lk 8,55 *diff.* Mk). — Detailed observations on the comparison between the Lucan appearance and the Marcan miracle story are offered by J. E. ALSUP, *Appearance Stories*, 169ff.; cf. also C. M. MARTINI, in *Resurrexit*, 232f.

[115] G. MINETTE de TILLESSE, *Secret messianique*, 70. Mk 6,52, a redactional statement which fits the overall Marcan treatment of the disciples (*ibid.*, 304), is closely related to the *Verstockungstheorie* with which Mk explains Jesus' speech in parables (Mk 4,11f.; *ibid.*, 269). — J. E. ALSUP is undoubtedly right in saying that the Marcan and Lucan " apparitions " are not to be explained by a redactional operation on the latter's part, but by assimilation of the narrative-traits in the process of transmission (*Appearance Stories*, 170f.). Lk's omission of the Marcan story *in situ* can be explained by his christological contouring in chap. 9, already discussed by us (pp. 37, 106, 120f.) and needs no hypothesis asserting some obscure common origin of the two " apparition " accounts which, because he was aware of it, caused Lk to pass over the earlier occurrence.

[116] J. ROLOFF is correct in saying that v. 41a " sagt noch nichts über den Osterglauben aus " (*Apostolat*, 189f. n. 68). H. FLENDER (*Heil*, 139) modernizes here: " ... eine noch unentschiedene Haltung ... die noch vor der eigentlichen Glaubensentscheidung steht." One need not find a trendy rationalization, however, for the fact that the evangelists constantly judge human θαυμάζειν before Jesus the wonder-worker to fall short of the faith of Christians, and often to be compatible with non-acceptance of Jesus (cf. esp. Lk 4,22/Mk 6,2; pp. 66f.

cannot be " opened " solely by what their eyes observe[117] but only when that is illumined by the same *instruction on the passion by the risen One* which finally illumined the Emmaus travelers (cp. vv. 45f. with vv. 25f.). Here is Easter-story editing in a pattern already well established by our study, and we can see that, in both the Marcan epiphany on the lake and the Lucan appearance to the closeted disciples, a fear and confusion that are apposite to the literary pattern of apparitions have been redactionally augmented with the accents of the *Messiasgeheimnis* proper to each evangelist.

(iii) *Narrative Threshold*: This brings us to the junction of gesture and word in our appearance story, Lk 24,43f. According to the diagnosis of a common tradition that we have made by comparing Lk and Jn, the original story presented a sequence of greeting, troubled reaction, reassuring display of wounds, recognition, evocative repast, and mission mandate. Luke, in a procedure we easily recognize after our study of the previous Easter episodes,[118] postponed the evidence of recognition to the conclusion of the pericope's action-instruction sequence (24,52), creating a typical threshhold of human bewilderment for the decisive utterance of the *revealing word*. — Now if this turn of the argument was truly the evangelist's intention in composing the final Easter episode, we shall be able to find confirmation of it in the two retrospective citations of this narrative that are made in the pages of Acts. The first and nearest of these, of course, is that introductory reprise of the paschal encounter between the Lord and his " chosen "

above). Cf. Ph. SEIDENSTICKER, *Auferstehung*, 135: " Im lukanischen Bericht erreichen die Jünger die Stufe des Glaubens nicht. Ihr (blosses) Staunen, aber ' noch nicht glauben ' ... veranlasst Jesus dazu, vor ihrer Augen zu essen. Aber der Bericht weiss über einen Erfolg des Bemühens Jesu nichts zu vermelden: die Jünger bleiben stumm ...." — Also C. M. MARTINI, in *Resurrexit*, 231: " Le prove che Gesù ha dato di sé non sono conclusive per la fede. E' soltanto nei vv. 44-48 che si parla finalmente di ' apertura della mente ', e quindi di capacità degli apostoli a comprendere (cfr. At 16,14), e che viene esplicitato il senso del ritrovarsi di Gesù in mezzo ai suoi."

[117] Ph. SEIDENSTICKER, *Auferstehung*, 137: " Es ist dem Menschen nicht möglich, angesichts des auferstandenen Herrn ein Experiment zu verlangen und durchzuführen, um so des Auferstandenen gewiss zu werden." Written concerning the Johannine Thomas episode, these words readily apply to the Lucan narrative. SEIDENSTICKER has correctly observed the dialectical moment in both evangelists' versions.

[118] Cf. pp. 18 and 32 above concerning the shift forward of the node of the dialectic between tomb experience and Easter faith; and cf. pp. 110f. on the paradoxical documentation of total empirical observation in the Emmaus story. Cf. J. ROLOFF, *Apostolat*, 190: " ... (es) bleibt als Ergebnis, dass in der heute vorliegenden Form erst die beiden Worte des Auferstandenen, das Demonstrationswort (38-43) und der Schriftbeweis (44) miteinander den Osterglauben wecken: zum leiblichen Sehen muss das Verstehen kommen, das durch den Auferstandenen erschlossen wird (... V. 45)."

disciples that forms part of the second volume's preamble. It happens to be formulated in a manner which makes for easy exploitation by those convinced that factual proof of the Easter gospel was Luke's objective: οἷς καὶ παρέστησεν ἑαυτὸν ζῶντα μετὰ τὸ παθεῖν αὐτὸν ἐν πολλοῖς τεκμηρίοις ... (Acts 1,3). The word τεκμήρια, "persuasive proofs," seems tailored to an apologetic argument that the apostles' Easter faith was "based on a certainty stemming from the empirical realm," indeed that their "knowledge of Jesus as risen was wholly the result of overwhelming empirical evidence."[119] But aside from the risk of exaggeration when one forces on this *hapax legomenon* the technical sense assigned it in Aristotelian rhetoric (cf. *e contra* Wis 19,13; 5,11),[120] it is essential to read the whole sentence in which it occurs in order to learn precisely how our pericope is being resumed. In the main clause of the sentence, we hear an echo of the angels' designation of him who was not to be sought in the realm of the dead (Lk 24,5): οἷς καὶ παρέστησεν ἑαυτὸν ζῶντα μετὰ τὸ παθεῖν αὐτόν ... There is the proper antonym of πνεῦμα in Lk 24,37.39: not physical one, material one, palpable one, but *living one*! The Crucified showed himself to be *alive*, contrary to every expectation and possibility *ex parte humana*. The audience and occasion of his display are fixed by the relative pronoun (referring to Acts 1,2) and the phrase, μετὰ τὸ παθεῖν αὐτόν· it is the third Easter pericope that is being resumed.[121] The τεκμήρια of the risen One's demonstration that he was *alive* are specified in two subordinate clauses that follow: δι' ἡμερῶν τεσσαράκοντα ὀπτανόμενος αὐτοῖς, and λέγων τὰ περὶ τῆς βασιλείας τοῦ θεοῦ. The "forty days" suddenly ruptures the framework of Lk 24, but the structure of the "demonstration" is exactly as it was in our appearance story. The

[119] So D. P. FULLER, *Easter Faith*, 230, 232. FULLER wishes to preserve both the *sola gratia* bestowal (*ibid.*, 222) and the foundation in empirical evidence for Lk's version of the Easter faith, but it is difficult not to see self-contradiction in "such paradoxical thinking" (*ibid.*, 233). — G. KEGEL's presentation of Lk's main concern, "the facticity of the resurrection" (*Auferstehung*, 81-100), is an unrelieved detailing of physical evidence and factual witness whose inadequacy becomes apparent when K. attempts to deal with the ἔδωκεν αὐτὸν ἐμφανῆ γενέσθαι of Acts 10,40 (*ibid.*, 93).

[120] E. g. C. F. EVANS, *Resurrection*, 111. — Cf. Aristotle's *Rhetoric* I,2 (16-18); *Prior Anal.* II, 27; but then cf. *De Arte Poet.* 16 (1454b), 21 (and C. H. DODD, in *More N. T. Studies*, 123 n. 2).

[121] R. PESCH, *EKK Vorarb.* III, 23f. — That the "forty days" intends some typological sense (Moses? Elia? — cf. J. ROLOFF, *Apostolat*, 195; J. G. DAVIES, *He Ascended*, 53ff.; S. G. WILSON, *ZNW* 59 [1968] 270), or at least a symbolic "round number" established in OT preparation periods (so H. SCHLIER, *Besinnung*, 233f.; G. LOHFINK, *Himmelfahrt*, 181ff.; R. PESCH, *EKK Vorarb.* III, 14; Ph.-H. MENOUD, in *Neotestamentica et patristica* [cited in n. 40 above], 148-156), is confirmed by the fact that it is the only narrative detail in Acts 1,2-8 which is not a retelling of the last gospel episode.

risen Lord persuaded his followers he was " alive " by his *appearance* and by his *instruction*. The two steps were necessary *together* to show that this was truly he (αὐτός, Lk 24,39), and it was not until the second step — the instruction that had been given ἔτι ὢν σὺν ὑμῖν (Lk 24,44), the " totality of Jesus' testimony about himself in light of Scripture " [122] — that there could be any report of an " opening " of " their mind." Unquestionably the instruction is to be included amongst the " persuasive signs " of the risen One's identity; and bearing in mind the structural conformity of Acts 1,3 to the *argumentum* of our third Easter pericope, we should have to understand the instruction as the decisive τεκμήριον. This word therefore does not refer exclusively to the physical display of the Lord in the cenacle, any more than Lk 24,36-43 constitutes an integral Lucan statement by itself.[123]

A second Acts " flash-back " to our appearance story occurs in the speech of Peter to Cornelius' household, Acts 10,40-43, a passage whose parallelism with this one includes, as we have found, its traditional narrative setting. Adjoining Peter's resurrection kerygma is the significant formula: καὶ ἔδωκεν (ὁ θεὸς) αὐτὸν ἐμφανῆ γενέσθαι (10,40), which stresses the strictly *divine agency* of the Easter cognition. The word ἐμφανής bids the sense of " revealed," not simply " visible," hence the accent is upon God's giving rather than empirical availability.[124] This is the reason " not all the people " saw the *Christus revelatus*, but only " the witnesses foreordained by God " (10,41). It is also a good reason for understanding the subsequent mention of these witnesses' repast with him as something more than proof of the facticity of their witness.[125] The grammatical coordination of ἔδωκεν ... καὶ παρήγγειλεν in 10,40.42 is basically the same as between ὀπτανόμενος ... καὶ λέγων in

---

[122] J. ROLOFF, *Apostolat*, 190. Cf. also Ph. SEIDENSTICKER, *Auferstehung*, 100: " Man erkennt deutlich, dass Lukas an einer Fundierung des ... Kerygmas gelegen ist und nicht an der so realistischen Begegnung des Auferstandenen mit seinen Jüngern."

[123] That 24,36-43 makes no case by itself, but must be interpreted with vv. 44ff. and as prelude thereto, is the point effectively made in the study of C. M. MARTINI, in *Resurrexit*, 231ff.

[124] Cf. W. MICHAELIS, *Erscheinungen*, 118-119; G. VOSS, *Christologie*, 144f.; R. GLÖCKNER, *Verkündigung*, 205ff.

[125] *Pace* H. CONZELMANN, *Apg.*², 73; H. GRASS, *Ostergeschehen*, 89; P. SCHUBERT, in *Ntl. Studien f. Bultmann*, 172f.; R. PESCH, *EKK Vorarb.* III, 23, 24; C. H. TALBERT, *Luke*, 31. Cf. also M. KEHL, *GeistLeb* 43 (1970) 107. — Others take note of the problem created by the clash of ideas: the demonstrative presence of the risen One, yet the fact that only chosen witnesses were " given " to see him (cf. W. MICHAELIS, *loc. cit.* in n. 124; W. DIETRICH, *Petrusbild*, 285: " ... die Auferstehung bildet kein für die Allgemeinheit erfahrbares Phänomen..."). Cf. H. FLENDER, *Heil*, 142f., whose argument for a dual aspect of the resurrection in Lk might have led him to a more perceptive reading of Acts 10,41, but he, too, seems content to see only the " Tatsächlichkeit des Bezeugten " there.

Acts 1,3, with the same indispensable conjunction of revealing *vision* and revealing *word* brought out in each statement. Clearly, too, the content of the word spoken to the witnesses (10,42-43) presents a nuanced replay of Lk 24,47-48 and Acts 1,4ff. In all three texts, the origin of the Easter witness is located in the *recognition and audition* of the risen Christ, specially vouchsafed by God to the chosen disciples. Indeed, given the close relationship of these texts, we discover that ἔδωκεν in Acts 10,40 expresses pungently and succinctly what Lk's editing has aimed to establish through the three confrontations of phenomena and kerygma in Lk 24. Between the αὐτὸν δὲ οὐκ εἶδον of 24,24 and τότε διήνοιξεν τὸν νοῦν in 24,45 the determining factor is *not* what human senses could perceive, but the gracious gift of God that is imparted with the *complete self-disclosure* of the risen One: *living presence, illumining word*!

If the dialectic of human perception and divine disclosure is still operative at 24,43f., what are we to conclude about *Luke's* adaptation of the risen One's meal? We have set forth, as a result of previous analysis, the traditional provenance of this item, antedating both evangelists' writing and located at a point in the story after the disciples' recognition and evocatively prior to their commissioning. By postponing that moment of recognition, however, has Luke not made the eating into a physical τεκμήριον that it was not in the older story?[126] Is not ἐνώπιον αὐτῶν ἔφαγεν to be rendered: "he ate it *before their eyes*,"[127] in accordance with the preposition's literal sense? — An affirmative answer would probably put us in the mainstream of exegetical poinion on this passage, but we think that opinion should be reconsidered. First of all, the preposition is a septuagintal idiom for "in the presence of," or "with," especially in situations of meals taken by guests "*before*" their host.[128] This is the usage we observe in Lk 13, 26 S; and Acts 27,35 also involves table fellowship (— if ἐνώπιον is demonstrative there, it is surely not because Paul is an apparition proving his substance!). Moreover, if we take the preposition in Lk 24,43 to express the table fellowship of guest *with* his hosts, we find that this is the sense that is echoed in the retrospective references of Acts: συνεφάγομεν καὶ συνεπίομεν (10,41; cp. Lk 13,26!) and συναλιζόμενος (1,4). The evidential force of the meal, on the other hand, is not alluded to in those reprises. Nor is that force of the preposition frequent in Lk-Acts, whereas the septuagintal expression for "with"

---

[126] So F. MUSSNER, J. LANGE, perhaps also M. KEHL, in n. 28 above.

[127] So KLOSTERMANN, GRUNDMANN, SCHMID, ERNST, NAB, NEB. Cf. also J. REILING & J. L. SCHWELLENGREBEL, *A Translator's Handbook on the Gospel of Luke* (Helps for Translators X; Leiden: E. J. Brill, 1971) 762.

[128] E.g. LXX 2 Kgs 11,13; 3 Kgs 1,25; cp. Gen 18,8. Cf. X. LÉON-DUFOUR, *Résurrection*, 218.

or " in the presence of " is favored Lucan usage.[129] — We propose, therefore, that the parallel texts and the range of the preposition's idiomatic usage in Lk both urge the sense: " he ate it *at their table,*" or " ... *in their company,*" " ... *as their guest,*" in Lk 24,43.[130] The repast is not thereby deprived of all demonstrative thrust. It is part of Lk's dialectic of human perception and divine disclosure, after all, and it does build the same kind of threshold for the risen Lord's instruction as we observed at 24,24. What it demonstrates, however, is the *renewal of table fellowship* between the Master and his disciples, just as he had had it with them ἔτι ὢν σὺν ὑμῖν. The point is *continuity, reunion.*[131] The physical substance of the risen body is not the evangelist's concern.

Now the progress of thought is clearer which creates the threshold of the paschal " word " in 24,44ff. Cumulative evidence is given to allay the observers' fears. The Master is truly alive; his limbs are those of the Crucified, showing that his path has not been broken by death. What is more, this real, living person now revives a relationship with the cluster of his followers which should immediately evoke the familiar setting of their communion before his death: the *household meal,* which both reenacts great scenes of his instruction during his earthly ministry and anticipates his reception by future adherents in the person of his itinerant missionary. We are speaking now not of the " eucharistic " repasts in which bread was broken with the followers and instruction concerning their common destiny was given; we mean those repeated *meal scenes* of the gospel in which Jesus was received as a *guest* and made his appeal to prospective followers in that capacity.

---

[129] Cf. A. Plummer, *Lk*, lx. — The use of ἐνώπιον with τοῦ κυρίου or τοῦ θεοῦ is frequent (9 times in Lk-Acts), showing how conscious our author was of the biblical ring of the preposition. — Evidential use, strictly speaking, occurs only at Lk 5,25 and Acts 4,10, both instances of a cure demonstrated " before " the public (cp. Lk 8,47). We notice that, in the one instance of what is apparently an evidential " eating " and is urged as parallel to our case — Lk 8,55 (= Mk 5,43), any such statement as καὶ ἐνώπιον αὐτῶν ἔφαγεν (ἡ παῖς) is not to be found. The eating of the child restored to life remains a command of Jesus whose carrying out is not recorded, hence its demonstrative value to the narrator is muted; and in any case, it is not brought out with the help of ἐνώπιον. Too, the absence of this detail from the comparable resurrection story, at Lk 7,15 S, shows that it is not a self-understood demonstration of resurrection from the dead which Lk brought from the miracle-story tradition to the appearance story (cf. C. M. Martini, in *Resurrexit*, 236f.).

[130] If the position of ἐνώπιον αὐτῶν before the verb here is urged in favor of the strictly demonstrative sense, one does better to look at Acts 27,35 first: εἴπας δὲ ταῦτα καὶ
λαβὼν ἄρτον εὐχαρίστησεν τῷ θεῷ ἐνώπιον πάντων καὶ κλάσας ἤρξ. ἐσθίειν.
24,43: λαβὼν ἐνώπιον αὐτῶν ἔφαγεν.

[131] R. Glöckner, *Verkündigung*, 208.

This happens to be an editorial schema of importance to Luke and of significant bearing upon the sequence we are studying.

J. Wanke writes: " No evangelist beside Luke managed to record so often about Jesus that he accepted the invitation to be a *guest at table* " (cf. Lk 5,29 *diff.* Mk; 7,36 S; 10,38ff. S; 14,1 S; [19,1ff. S]).[132] The hosts of these meals include Levi, the publican, ill-disposed Jewish leaders, Martha and Mary, and the ἀρχιτελώνης, Zacchaeus, who hosted his longer sojourn. The dinner guest offers his teaching and grants salvation to the ἁμαρτωλοί who are usually his table companions (Lk 5,30; 7,37.39; 19,7). Indeed, all of the five scenes are occasions to exhibit the Master's embrace of the lowly.[133] Three of the five become settings for his *forgiveness of sins* (Lk 5,32 *diff.* Mk: καλέσαι ... ἁμαρτωλοὺς εἰς μετάνοιαν [cp. 24,47]; 7,39.48 S; 19,10 S). The " great banquet " parable, which climaxes the dominical instruction in the meal scene of Lk 14, becomes in its Lucan version an allegory of the two-stage Christian *mission*: to the despised and disinherited of Judaism, then to the Gentile outsiders.[134] — This survey of the gospel meals makes the connection much clearer between the *Easter meal with Christ as guest* (24,43) and the announcement of the disciples' *mission to proclaim* " *repentance* (*for*) *the forgiveness of sins* " in his name to all the world (24,47f.). Jesus had already exercized this mission at the meals in which others hosted him and heard his teaching. The same ministry is to continue, uninterrupted, in his " name " and in the familiar setting of the household meal. An integrity of thought thus appears in this third Easter pericope once we declare our emancipation from that scholarly fixation upon the *manducatio* as physical demonstration and apologetic *tour de force*. What is being demonstrated is the continuation of Jesus' earthly ministry in the mission of his witnesses. It is this demonstration that is served by the " recognition " motif and the τεκμήρια of the appearance story.

Some important *conclusions* can now be drawn from our study of

[132] J. Wanke, *Eucharistieverständnis*, 54 (italics mine). As Wanke asserts, " just the frequency of this kind of scene leads us to recognize the special interest with which (Lk) took up such episodes of the Jesus-tradition."

[133] Including Mary, who presumably embodies the renunciation of the accepted piety of deeds (Lk 10,41f.), and the sick man healed on the sabbath (Lk 14,2), as well as the recipients of the new invitations in the banquet parable (Lk 14, 21ff.). It is instructive concerning the evangelist's understanding of the meal scenes that in the middle of the sequence in Lk 14, the Lord, who is *table guest* at 14,1, suddenly becomes *host* of the " great banquet," according to Lk 14,22. The basis of this exchange of roles is the beatitude of Lk 14,15: μακάριος ὅστις φάγεται ἄρτον ἐν τῇ βασιλείᾳ τοῦ θεοῦ (J. Wanke, *Eucharistieverständnis*, 58).

[134] Cf. Éta Linnemann, " Überlegungen zur Parabel vom grossen Abendmahl (Lk 14,15-24; Mt 22,1-14)," *ZNW* 51 (1960) 246-255; W. C. Robinson, *Weg*, 62; H.-J. Degenhardt, *Lukas*, 101-105; J. Wanke, *Eucharistieverständnis*, 57ff.

the narrative threshold here in the third Easter pericope. First, the *nexus* between Jesus hosted at a meal and the universal mission in his name was both argued in the source-narrative and well understood by our evangelist. The gospel data we have reviewed shows that Luke knew and systematically brought out the connection of these themes. — But we found good probability, too, that the Lord's repast belonged to the appearance story as both Lk and Jn received it. With peace-greeting and meal framing the recognition of the risen Lord in the cenacle, the old story clearly meant to reenact the household protocol of the earliest missionaries as a prelude to their Easter commission. Our studies in chap. IV/i will urge that missionaries whose ministrations were governed by that primitive protocol are likely to have recounted the Easter foundation of their endeavour in terms of it. The same pattern of recollection was being followed by the same group, we should think, when the Lord's appearance in the *dwelling* of the Emmaus disciples was recounted, with the invitation: μεῖνον μεθ' ἡμῖν, and the ensuing: καὶ εἰσῆλθεν τοῦ μεῖναι σὺν αὐτοῖς (Lk 24,29). Here is some of the support we augured for our tentative suggestions concerning the Emmaus tradition (pp. 153f., 155 above). A fuller investigation of Lk's *Sondergut* in chap. IV/i should consolidate and amplify these findings.

(b) *The Words of Easter Instruction* (*Lk 24,44-49*)

Once again, by prolonging the pathos of the appearance-story's stage of *non*-recognition, Lk has given conclusive weight to the words uttered by the mysterious cenacle guest. It is fully in accordance with this perspective that most judge vv. 44ff. to be mainly of Lk's own composition, whereas the preceding account of the visual experience came mostly from the appearance tradition.[135] Nevertheless, we shall

[135] Cf. notes 30-31 above. A. GEORGE has sought to confirm this delineation with vocabulary and style analysis (in *La résurrection*, 79, 96f.; likewise B. RIGAUX, *Dieu l'a ressuscité*, 275), but his survey is faulty and does not include "Lucanisms" like πτοηθέντες καὶ ἔμφοβοι γενόμενοι (v. 37), ἀναβαίνειν ἐν τῇ / ἐπὶ τὴν καρδία(ν), ἐνθάδε, etc., which, though their statistics are not impressive, are consonant with Lk's style (e.g. LXX imitation) and mainly or exclusively found in his books in the NT. Neither does GEORGE mention words like θαυμάζειν, a favorite of Lk's (cf. p. 67 above) but not exclusively his (17*x* of 42*x* in NT); or ψηλαφᾶν, rare (4*x* NT) but also used in Acts 17,27 in a rather different *argumentum*. On the vocabulary question cf. also C. M. MARTINI, in *Resurrexit*, 236-238, who prefers not to segregate vv. 36-43 for its non-Lucan language (cf. his n. 9). We have found before, and reiterate here, that a mechanical argument from vocabulary is very fragile procedure in Lk-Acts. A similar method leads J. E. ALSUP to find substantial *non*-Lucan material in vv. 44-49, flying in the face of a massive consensus of which he takes little or no notice (cf. *Resurrection Stories*, 182ff., *vs*. nn. 30-31 above)! This is an author of such versatility and mastery of his sources that holding him accountable to a narrow repertory of frequently used *vocabula* is simply doing no justice to his universally acknow-

bear in mind that at least some version of the commission to announce and/or impart the forgiveness of sins was part of the tradition also (cf. Jn 20,22f.), hence that an Easter event of vision and mission was already recounted before Lk's writing. What makes the mission program in this passage inalienably Lk's own is its relation to the fact and plan of his two volumes. The " commission " is really only an appointment, and the Spirit is promised rather than bestowed; thus the actual inauguration of the mission, which is the very *raison d'être* of the Church, is saved for the second book. The ascension brings the time of Jesus to a close, and the book of the gospel with it. The actual Spirit-outpouring will inaugurate the time of the Church, and with it the matter of the book of Acts. Inspiring the " economy " of the Lord's mission program in Lk 24, therefore, are " deliberate and controlling elements " of the Lucan literary enterprise.[136]

As we have shown, the risen Christ's words take up directly from the threshold of narrative detail (v. 43),[137] as they did at v. 25. Moreover, the words are no less a " demonstrative sign " of his identity, still unrecognized, than the physical traits were. Does not οὗτοι οἱ λόγοι continue in the same line with ἴδετε τὰς χεῖράς μου κτλ., especially in view of the fact that these are words οὓς ἐλάλησα πρὸς ὑμᾶς ἔτι ὢν σὺν ὑμῖν? They are no less implements of the recognition of the risen One as *the very same* as the crucified Master, for their content is the very same *passion instruction* they had heard (and not understood) during their συναναβαίνειν with him from Galilee to Jerusalem. Lk's initiative in shifting the moment of recognition beyond the narrative threshold, thus making it finally the fruit of the story's combination of gesture *and word,* is now illustrated by the demonstrative nature (οὗτοι οἱ λόγοι) of the words. They continue the still unsuccessful demonstration and are part of the dramatic process of bringing the followers' lagging recognition to pass.

The third transcription of the passion formula in the Easter story is typical of Lucan " repetition and variation " (chap. I, n. 110). Details of the earlier prophecies have been augmented in Lk 24 in a cumulative pattern, as we noted before (n. 33 above), so that this final reprise of them can be expected to contain a summation of what Lk

---

ledged breadth of self-expression. In fact, few *vocabula* in 24,36-43 are such as to alert us to the presence of a source because Lk could not, or normally would not, use them. Perhaps πνεῦμα = " ghost " qualifies; or σάρκα καὶ ὀστέα. What else? — At most, the linguistic argument can function as a tentative adjunct to theme-analysis and internal comparisons, — in this case, endorsing in some respects the diagnosis which finds a pre-Lucan appearance story underlying at least the basic narrative-line of the third pericope.

[136] Chr. BURCHARD, *Zeuge*, 131. Cf. p. 160 and n. 10 above.

[137] M. BRÄNDLE, *Orientg* 24 (1960) 88; G. LOHFINK, *Himmelfahrt*, 148.

has intended them to express. — Taking note only of what has been added or altered this time, we observe first that the parallelism of vv. 44b and 46 now defines the δεῖ of the previous formulas explicitly in terms of Scripture fulfillment (just as implicitly in vv. 25f.). Now the perspective is added which the Emmaus instruction brought out (v. 27), that *all* the scriptures (πάντα τὰ γεγραμμένα) obtain their fulfillment in the Christ of Easter. He alone is the definitive revelation of the *whole* bible's meaning,[138] and this is, as we have seen, the sense of Lk's reservation to him of the status of *eschatological prophet* (p. 136 above). Despite the citation of Scripture according to its standard divisions in the present passage — " the law of Moses, the prophets, and the psalms " (v. 44) — the Lucan view of all Scripture as *prophecy* remains essentially unaltered. Moses was *prophet* even as *author*, as we saw in treating v. 27. And the psalms, specified here because they are crucial to our author's christological hermeneutic of the Old Testament, fall into the prophetic category as well. After all, David, their author (Lk 20,42 *diff*. Mk; Acts 1,16; 2,25.34; 4,24), is understood to have been a " prophet " before all else (Acts 2,30), hence his book of sacred songs is considered a " repository of prophecy." [139] If one agrees that the present passage is programmatic of the apostolic preaching in Acts,[140] there can be no surprise that the psalms get special mention among the γεγραμμένα, seeing that they furnish the major Old Testament passages invoked by the Acts preachers as prophecy of the resurrection/exaltation: Ps 16,8-11 (Acts 2,25ff.), Ps 110,1 (Acts 2,34f.), Ps 118,22 (Acts 4,11), Ps 2,7 (Acts 13,33; cp. Ps 2,1-2 in Acts 4,25f.). With their characteristic celebration of God's victories (and the righteous man's — cf. pp. 100-103 above) over human rebellion and wickedness, the psalms offered prime attestation of the divine plan which brought about both the suffering and the resurrection of Christ κατὰ τὸ ὡρισμένον..[141]

On the other hand, ours is not the first passage in the third gospel in which the mysterious δεῖ of the messianic passion is expounded in terms of scripture fulfillment. The last of the Supper instructions, drawn from Lk's *Sondergut* and attached to the dominical meal in the pattern already set in chap. 9 (cf. pp. 106f. above), ends with citation of

---

[138] H. CONZELMANN, *MdZ*, 151. Cf. J. ERNST, P. SCHUBERT, J. DUPONT, H.-W. BARTSCH, E. LOHSE, cited in chap. II, nn. 187, 188.

[139] J. DUPONT, *Études*, 265. Cf. also H. CONZELMANN, *MdZ*, 147 n. 1.

[140] J. DUPONT, *Études*, 246; H. CONZELMANN, *MdZ*, 151 n. 1. Cf. again note 32 above.

[141] On the psalm usage in the Acts sermons, cf. J. DUPONT, *Études*, 283-307. Also M. RESE, *Alt. Motive*, 105f. — On the reason for the specification of the psalms in the present text, rightly E. MEYER, *Ursprung und Anfänge* I, 28 n. 1; J. M. CREED, *Lk*, 300f.; E. KLOSTERMANN, *Lk.*, 241; J. ERNST, *Lk.*, 669.

a specific prophecy, Is 53,12, introduced with phraseology similar to 24,44 (22,37 : τοῦτο τὸ γεγραμμένον δεῖ τελεσθῆναι ἐν ἐμοί, τὸ Καὶ μετὰ ἀνόμων ἐλογίσθη). The *telos* of that specific prophecy in the events of the passion is now just part of the *global realization of all prophecy* that is to be demonstrated in the Easter Christ. Too, what forges a special relationship between that argument from prophecy at the Supper and the present, global argument, is that the Supper instruction concerned a *mission directive* of Jesus which, in view of the new, embattled situation of himself and his followers, he seemed to be revoking (Lk 22,35 ; cp. Lk 10,4 *diff.* 9,3/=Mk 6,8).[142] Luke, by making this tradition[143] the

[142] The famous logion of v. 36b, which would appear to terminate the period of the disciples' mission "like lambs in the midst of wolves," unarmed, unfurnished with this world's goods, etc. (Lk 10,3-4 Q), is probably to be taken as a figurative saying that proclaimed the period of the messianic tribulation. Lk's intention seems to have been to contrast this with the disciples' impression that the Master was calling for armed resistance to his captors (22,38.50), whereupon the response of v. 38b can be taken in light of v. 51 as a stricture on the discussion and a reproof of those who would seek to advance God's cause by violent means (cf. J. Ernst, *Lk.*, 603f. ; also H. Conzelmann, *MdZ*, 74ff. ; G. Voss, *Christologie*, 108f., 111 ; F. Schütz, *Christus*, 22f. ; G. Schneider, *Verleugnung*, 185, 189f.). On the sense of ἱκανόν ἐστιν, "enough of that !" most commentators are agreed ; cf. also Klostermann, Grundmann, *ad loc.*

[143] That Lk 22,35-38 is entirely from Lk's hand (*pace* J. Finegan, *Überlieferung*, 16) is scarcely tenable, as R. Bultmann rightly observes (*GsT* Ergänzungsheft^4, 102). A minimal assessment would make the sword-logion of v. 36b the traditional nucleus around which Lk wove the rest as framework, thus putting the situation of incipient messianic combat in sharp contrast to the receptive atmosphere, hence provisionless mission, of the Master's lifetime (so H.-W. Bartsch, "Jesu Schwertwort, Lukas XXII.35-38. Überlieferungsgeschichtliche Studie," *NTS* 20 [1973-74, 190-203] 199-200). Why such exertion to preserve an isolated and anomalous logion ? Was it just to prepare for the sword scene of 22,49ff., as M. Dibelius proposed (*Formgeschichte*, 201) ? — H. Schürmann maintains the original narrative unit included vv. 35-36 (and 37b) (*Jesu Abschiedsrede*, 131) and was not connected to the passion story. As an independent piece, it would have been directed to challenges developing in the Church of the future, viewing them in the perspective of the eschatological combat (apocalyptic). When the tradition became attached to the passion story, which Schürmann thinks happened at the level of the pre-Lucan passion source (similarly G. Schneider ; cf. chap. II, n. 108), the new context accounted for the addition of the fulfillment-citation, Is 53,12, since the imminent arrest of Jesus was to be carried out ὡς ἐπὶ λῃστὴν ... μετὰ μαχαιρῶν καὶ ξύλων (Lk 22,52/ = Mk 14,58 ; cf. G. Schneider, *Verleugnung*, 176). It is doubtful, however, whether this logic applies only to the scripture-quotation ; would it not also cast doubt on the originality of the whole sword motif ? And since we are personally convinced the hypothesis of a special Lucan passion narrative is not viable, we should rather think that such tailoring of the tradition as took place to make it a prologue to the passion story to follow (G. Voss, *Christologie*, 110f.) was done by Lk himself, and no one before him. This would certainly include v. 38 ; and perhaps v. 37b also. Must it also include the Isaian citation (*pace* Voss ; also M. Rese, *Altt. Motive*, 160, 164) ? Surely not by Schürmann's logic. — Cf. chap. IV, n. 25.

ductus of the arrest scene and keeping it in the framework of a still unbroken enigma of the passion, might have been looking to restrain a charismatic militancy fostered by some of his *Sondergut* (and *Sondertradenten* too, of course). In its present setting, the call to the sword is a misinterpreted announcement of the tribulations to come, its literal interpretation belied and repudiated by the actual course of the *suffering* messiah to death, and beyond.[144]

V. 46, the Easter story's third rehearsal of the passion prophecy, has no new vocabulary, save ἐκ νεκρῶν, the standard modifier of the verbs ἐγείρειν and ἀνιστάναι (Acts 3,15; 4,10; 10,41; 13,30; 17,3.31) which, nevertheless, makes its first appearance here in the gradual crystallization of the Lucan kerygma. Rather than new vocabulary, the reader finds new perspectives in this third recital, and they result from the ensemble of the Easter story which by now lies nearly all behind him. He now knows, for example, that παθεῖν τὸν χριστόν expresses the core of the messianic enigma and the barrier to unaided human perception during the *triduum sacrum* (cf. 24,21). And by now he better understands why the intransitive ἀναστῆναι persists (cf. pp. 48f. above), even though it will be largely supplanted by transitive forms in the Acts sermons. Placed alongside εἰσελθεῖν εἰς τὴν δόξαν αὐτοῦ in v. 26, the intransitive form in v. 46 sustains the movement of the messianic *journey*, which is about to reach its term in the Lord's heavenly ascension (cf. n. 60 above). The Easter story completes the dominical itinerary which began at Lk 9,51 and will terminate in heaven; and it is wholly appropriate that since the journey is really the framework of the formation of disciples, the same passion instruction which inaugurated the itinerary now also brings it to its conclusion. — And while discussing new perspectives, it is hardly necessary to add that the "third-day" resurrection chronology, which is here explicitly traced to scriptural testimony (presumably Os 6,2 and its tradition),[145] is now fully intelligible to the reader as the events of Lk's Easter "day" run rapidly towards their conclusion.

V. 47 presents the great novelty of this third kerygmatic centerpiece of Lk's narrative: it is the new substantive clause added to οὕτως γέγραπται· καὶ κηρυχθῆναι ἐπὶ τῷ ὀνόματι αὐτοῦ μετάνοιαν (εἰς) ἄφεσιν ἁμαρτιῶν εἰς πάντα τὰ ἔθνη. The verse poses problems on the assumption either that the universal mission is not meant to be included

---

[144] Cf. H. CONZELMANN, *MdZ*, 75; G. SCHNEIDER, *Verleugnung*, 189f. — The hypothesis of H.-W. BARTSCH to explain the background of Lk's own interest in this tradition is, we think, rather fragile; cf. *art. cit.* (prev. note) 200ff.

[145] The problem remains, of course, that Os 6,2 is never formally cited amongst the passages of the OT where Christians found forecasts of their Easter message. Cf. the proposed solutions again, chap. I, n. 138.

amongst the provisions of biblical prophecy[146] or that the disciples' witness (v. 48) is essentially the attestation of real *facta salutis* (hence τούτων could refer only to v. 46).[147] Neither assumption is correct, however, according to our understanding of the passage. By taking up each in turn and attempting to correct it, we may hope to gain an adequate understanding of the mission mandate, which must surely qualify as the literary and dramatic peak of both the pericope and the chapter.

First, there is no syntactical or hermeneutical reason to doubt that the universal preaching of repentance and (unto) forgiveness is being presented as part of the Easter fulfillment of Scripture.[148] The strikingly parallel arguments in Acts 26,22f. and Acts 10,43 say it with the fullest clarity: passion, resurrection, *and universal mission of preaching* (*forgiveness*) are the sequential stages in the realization of all the prophecies by the risen Christ.[149] All three infinitives, therefore, — παθεῖν, ἀναστῆναι, and κηρυχθῆναι — are intended and interconnected subjects of οὕτως γέγραπται. In fact, the same alternation of scriptural fulfillment and messianic " necessity " applies to all three: to the passion and glory of the Son of Man (Lk 24,25-26), and to the universal preaching insofar as v. 47 is rightly judged to be Lk's adaptation of Mk 13,10, omitted by our evangelist from its place in the Marcan apocalypse (Lk 21,13).[150] If Mk's δεῖ πρῶτον was the oldest evangelist's modification of an apocalyptic timetable so as to include the evangelization of the

[146] J. Wellhausen (*Lc.*, 141) implausibly suggests that the κηρυχθῆναι clause is independent, *modo hebraico posteriore* (with לְ), obtaining a jussive sense. *E contra*, quite rightly, E. Meyer, *Ursprung und Anfänge* I, 28f. n. 2; A. Loisy, *Luc*, 589; E. Klostermann, *Lk.*, 242.

[147] See notes 37 above, 171 below.

[148] Rightly J. M. Creed (301), E. Klostermann (242), and nearly all of the commentaries (it is no issue any more, apparently, for J. Ernst, 670). Cf. also F. Hahn, *Mission*, 113ff.; H. Kasting, *Anfänge*, 43; J. Jervell, *Luke*, 56; S. G. Wilson, *Gentiles*, 48; J. Dupont, *Études*, 404, and in *N. T. und Kirche*, 128ff. — See again n. 34 above.

[149] J. Dupont has shown the relationship of Lk 24,47 to its counterpart in the Acts prologue (1,8) and the latter's relation, in turn, to the explicit citation of Is 49,6 LXX in Acts 13,47 (... εἰς σωτηρίαν ἕως ἐσχάτου τῆς γῆς). Cf. *Études*, 402-404, and in *N. T. und Kirche*, 135-138. Also J. Kremer, *Pfingstbericht*, 189.

[150] H. Conzelmann, *MdZ*, 199f. n. 4 (also 119); F. Hahn, *Mission*, 111f., 113f.; H.-W. Bartsch, *Wachet*, 120f.; S. G. Wilson, *Gentiles*, 47-48; J. Dupont, in *N. T. und Kirche*, 131ff. It is surprising to find the relation of 24,47 to Mk 13,10 left out of consideration frequently, even in up-to-date works like R. Geiger, *Endzeitreden*, 183. The fact that " repentance for the forgiveness of sins " stands in the Lucan text in place of Mk's τὸ εὐαγγέλιον is not an argument against Lk's dependency, for the substantive εὐαγγέλιον is consistently avoided by our evangelist, being eliminated either in favor of the corresponding verb or altogether in the places where Mk had used it (cf. W. Marxsen, *Markus*, 95; H. Conzelmann, *MdZ*, 206f., 119 n. 1).

world under the urgent momentum of the end-time, Lk's οὕτως γέγραπται is a further modification of the eschatological framework which gives the mission the stability of a sacred epoch, related to the biblical past in the reliable rhythm of promise and fulfillment.[151] A similar modification of eschatological perspective will introduce the parallel mission announcement of Acts 1,8, for Mk's disavowal of the apocalyptist's timetable (Mk 13,32), having again dropped out of the Marcan *situs* in Lk (21,33f.), has been recast as the risen Lord's rejoinder to his disciples' query in Acts 1,6f.[152] — It is interesting, on the other hand, that whereas the world-mission was removed from the tension of the temporal δεῖ πρῶτον by Lk's relocation of Mk 13,10, the *passion of the Son of Man* was precisely inserted into such a framework by the addition of Lk 17,25 to the eschatological sayings of Q (cf. pp. 42ff. above). The tension produced there, however, was not of a temporal sort; it was between the spheres or stages of the messianic itinerary, "the dialectic of glory and suffering,"[153] brought out in prospect of the parousia in Lk 17,24f. as it is in view of the Easter consummation in Lk 24,26. In its context, the eschatological projection of the passion mystery in Lk 17,25 is meant to place the travails of a missionary church, longing for the sight of her hidden Lord (v. 22; cp. Acts 3,21) and afflicted by conditions reflected in Lk's parenetic insertions (e.g. 17,32-33; cp. 21, 12-19), under the challenge and consolation of the Lord's own destiny.[154] It is this same consolation that Paul and Barnabas, stoned and nearly killed at Lystra, are able to offer the faithful on the way back to Antioch, the mission center: ὅτι διὰ πολλῶν θλίψεων δεῖ ἡμᾶς εἰσελθεῖν εἰς τὴν βασιλείαν τοῦ θεοῦ (Acts 14,22; cp. Lk 24,26).

---

[151] Cf. H. CONZELMANN, *MdZ*, 199f. (with n. 4). I should not agree with CONZELMANN that the eschaton has become the end of the mission epoch but not its quality. Lk's concern might as readily be to maintain the eschatological *quality* of the mission once its eschatological *timing* had had to be revised (so J. ZMIJEWSKI, *Eschatologiereden*, 285). I do not think, for example, that the alteration of the Joel-text in Acts 2,17 (ἐν ταῖς ἐσχάταις ἡμέραις) is accidental, merely scribal (*pace* E. HAENCHEN), or refractory of Lk's designs. — On the Marcan text cf. J. ZMIJEWSKI, *Eschatologiereden*, 144ff.

[152] H. CONZELMANN, *MdZ*, 122 (with n. 2); E. HAENCHEN, *Apg.*, 111f.; J. ZMIJEWSKI, *Eschatologiereden*, 284f., 383; R. GEIGER, *Endzeitreden*, 238f.

[153] H. FLENDER, *Heil*, 87f. Cf. also J. ZMIJEWSKI, *Eschatologiereden*, 409; R. GEIGER, *Endzeitreden*, 84.

[154] R. GEIGER, *Endzeitreden*, 83: "The path of Jesus and the path of the congregation coincide in this passage ...." Similarly J. ZMIJEWSKI, *Eschatologiereden*, 420, 429, 525f. — Whereas R. GEIGER (55ff.) interprets the difficult verse (17,)22 in terms of Lk 10,24 Q (but here with future reference), the better explanation seems to be H. FLENDER's (*Heil*, 88f.), followed by J. ZMIJEWSKI (401ff.): relating "days" to "the day" in the case of the Son of Man as in Noah's (17,26f.) and Lot's (17,28f.), one gets the sense of a period determined by the great event of judgment which ends it. The epoch determined by the

The contrasting stages to be traversed by the mission under stress of the messianic δεῖ are also suggested by the formula attached to the preaching program in 24,47, ἐπὶ τῷ ὀνόματι αὐτοῦ. "*The Name of Jesus*" is a well-known Lucan instrument for depicting the reality and vitality of the ascended Christ operative during the age of the Church.[155] The prepositional formulas in which it occurs present mainly two aspects of Christ's representation by his missionaries: the wondrous ministrations that display his powerful, saving presence, and the suffering which fosters the spread of his message, waxing stronger in the face of mightier opposition. When the preposition is ἐπί or, equivalently, ἐν, the formulas are found to apply to all the major activities of the Lord's surrogates: exorcizing and subjecting the demons (Lk 9,49; 10, 17),[156] miraculous healing (Acts 4,10; cp. 3,6f.16), preaching forgiveness (Lk 24,47), baptizing (Acts 2,38; 10,48), and the "speaking" and "teaching" that the mission's adversaries strove in vain to silence (Acts 4,17f.; 5,28.40). The *power and authority* of the disciples to perform these ministrations "comes from Jesus, and in its exercize Jesus is himself present in his *power*. This makes the action a *witness* to him as Kyrios operating in his followers."[157] — The other major segment of *Name*-formulas involves the other essential aspect of the emissaries' witness: their participation in the Lord's destiny of rejection and suffering. This aspect is brought out mainly where ὄνομα (or the proper name or pronouns) occurs with the prepositions διά, ἕνεκεν, and Lk's preferred variation on these, ὑπέρ. These prepositions express a benefit to "the Name" that comes from the tribulations of its exponents, — a benefit to its missionary propagation, in other words.[158]

---

parousia ("the day of the Son of Man") is characterized by the hidden, heavenly existence of the judge and vindicator (Acts 3,20f.), — his "days." To crave to see one of his "days" is the craving to see *him* during this period of the hidden process of the Kingdom's realization (17,20f.). Such is the craving of the *ecclesia pressa* during this period. — Cf. chap. I, nn. 120-123 on Lk's editing of the Q sayings in Lk 17,23ff.

155 Cf. H. CONZELMANN, *MdZ*, 165f.; U. WILCKENS, *Missionsreden*, 179; G. VOSS, *Christologie*, 148-153; J. ZMIJEWSKI, *Eschatologiereden*, 157-161.

156 Cf. also Acts 16,18. — The practically equivalent sense of ἐπί and ἐν in these formulas is illustrated by the wavering of the textual tradition between the two in Lk 9,49.

157 J. ZMIJEWSKI, *Eschatologiereden*, 157. — A similar sense is obtained with the διά formula, both with ὄνομα and with the proper name alone (cf. Acts 4, 30; 10,43 [with ὄνομα]; 2,22; 3,16; 10,36; 13,38; 15,11; 20,28 [with "Jesus Christ," or pronoun substitute, but without ὄνομα]). In all these instances the *mediating* role of the Lord — and therefore of his surrogates — in dispensing the divine gifts is the particular nuance of the preposition.

158 Cf. J. ZMIJEWSKI, *Eschatologiereden*, 160f.; W. RADL, *Paulus und Jesus*, 377ff.; R. GEIGER, *Endzeitreden*, 182. Prepositions: διά · Lk 21,17 (= Mk 13,13); ἕνεκεν · Lk 21,12 *diff.* Mk 13,9; cp. Lk 9,24; 18,29 with Mk 8,35; 10,29; and

The gospel sayings put such suffering for (the propagation of) Jesus' "Name" in the same revised eschatological framework as was produced by Lk's relocation of Mk 13,10. Lk 21,12 is his rendition of Mk 13,9 and, as in Mk, it introduces the paragraph which grimly forecasts the missionaries' fortunes; but it is introduced by the dissociating rubric, πρὸ δὲ τούτων πάντων (instead of δεῖ πρῶτον), which sets these travails apart from both τὸ τέλος and the political upheavals traditionally associated with it (Lk 21,9; cp. Mk 13,7). Such an adjustment seems tailored, of course, to the altered but still afflicting circumstances of the evangelist's christendom.[159] Moreover, at precisely the juncture of Mk 13,9f., Lk makes a separate and generalizing principle out of Mk's εἰς μαρτύριον αὐτοῖς· ἀποβήσεται ὑμῖν εἰς μαρτύριον (Lk 21,13). Rejection and suffering are thus considered the quintessentially necessary mode of witness to Jesus,[160] not just a contingency that should direct

---

Lk's favored variation on these: ὑπέρ · Acts 5,41; 9,16; 15,26; 21,13. — Illustration of this nexus as the basis of a sustained compositional pattern in Acts is offered by F. SCHÜTZ, *Christus*, 109ff.: the first persecution (Acts 8,1ff.) produced the crucial Antiochean community (Acts 11,19ff.); the Jewish rejection of Paul at Pisidian Antioch caused him and Barnabas to turn to the Gentile mission (Acts 13,42-49); Iconium, Lystra, and Derbe were all places visited by the Pauline party fleeing persecution; so also Thessalonica after Philippi, and Beroea after Thessalonica, and Athens and Corinth thereafter (cf. the schema in 19,8-10 also). Finally, of course, it was the ferocious onslaught of the Jerusalem Jews which led to Paul's transfer to Rome, and in Rome he managed to proclaim the word "unhindered," though a *prisoner*!

[159] Lk's revised order is thus: persecutions, political turmoil, cosmic turmoil, the end (H. CONZELMANN, *MdZ*, 120). It is usually maintained that this adjustment reflects Lk's own experience of the *ecclesia pressa* (so above all G. BRAUMANN, *ZNW* 54 [1963] 140ff.; also R. GEIGER, *Endzeitreden*, 178f.; F. SCHÜTZ, *Christus*, 14), but some doubt that he worked from actual experience, preferring to think he was looking *back* upon the travails of the formative period (Acts) and reminding his church that it could expect at any moment a return of those travails (so J. ZMIJEWSKI, *Eschatologiereden*, 151f.). In any case, I think BRAUMANN is right (*art. cit.*, 142) in insisting that πρὸ δὲ τούτων πάντων is not intended to remove the persecutions from the perspective of the eschaton (*pace* CONZELMANN) but precisely to maintain their continuity with it despite the expanded time of the Church. A similarly expanded eschatological process is envisioned in the altered wording of Joel 3,1 LXX in Acts 2,17, as was maintained in note 151. — On Lk 21,13 cf. chap. IV, n. 142.

[160] H. CONZELMANN, *MdZ*, 219: "Das christliche Leben ist ein 'Weg' und führt notwendig (!) durch viele Drangsale, act 14,22. Die geforderte Haltung ist die ὑπομονή ..." (Lk 8,15; 21,19). Cf. also U. WILCKENS, *Missionsreden*², 196, 199; G. BRAUMANN, *ZNW* 54 (1963) 120ff., 133, etc.; R. GEIGER, *Endzeitreden*, 181. Especially well-chosen are the words of F. SCHÜTZ, 105: "... die 'Kreuzessituation' der Gemeinde (entsteht) dadurch ..., dass sie ihrem Herrn nachfolgt. Hier deutet sich die Auffassung an, dass die Gemeinde nicht leidet, *obwohl*, sondern *weil*, sie die Gemeinde des Christus ist. Das Leiden gehört zu ihr als 'Christus'-Gemeinde deshalb, weil der Auferstandene identisch ist mit dem Verworfenen und dem Gekreuzigten."

one's thoughts to the imminent end of things. Because of him whose mission it is, this witness involves " being dishonored *for the sake of* (ὑπέρ) *the Name* " (Acts 5,41), hence the appointment to " *bear my Name* " is equivalently the burden of standing under the same *necessity* as determined Jesus' path: δεῖ αὐτὸν ὑπὲρ τοῦ ὀνόματός μου παθεῖν (Acts 9,15-16).[161]

The concepts of Jesus' " Name " and " witness " stand, therefore, in the closest relationship at the level of Lucan editing,[162] and this shows the source and rationale of the sequence in vv. 47-48 of the cenacle instruction. The two main groups of ὄνομα-formulas provide for a missionary endeavour which faithfully reproduces the contrasting phases of Jesus' ministry as recounted by this evangelist: his *deeds of power* and his *destined passion* (cf. Lk 9,43f.; 13,32f.; pp. 37, 119-126 above). These phases are placed in relation to the goal of the Lord's " journey " in the summation given to the " mission of the Seventy (-two)," also carried out in Jesus' " name " (Lk 10,17ff. S): exorcisms and miraculous powers are celebrated (vv. 17-18), reassurance is given in prospect of adversity (οὐδὲν ὑμᾶς οὐ μὴ ἀδικήσῃ), and heavenly vindication is promised (v. 20: χαίρετε κτλ. ... ἐν τοῖς οὐρανοῖς). — " Witness " to the Lord on the mission thus involves a *comprehensive reenactment of his " journey,"* not a mere vouching for its factual reality (— the second notion we set out to correct on p. 208). The unity of christological kerygma (24,46), mission in the Lord's name (v. 47), and " witness " mandate (v. 48), is a unity of *Lucan conception*, abundantly illustrated in his composition throughout the two volumes. The " journey " to be shared by the " witnesses " with the Lord passes through contrasting stages, including heavenly consummation, which conform to the christological model of the eschatological (Mosaic) *prophet*, as we have argued (pp. 121ff., 131f., 140f., etc.). Understandably, then, when they embark on that same journey and traverse its successive stages, the missionaries also share the Master's *prophetic status* (cf. Acts 2,17,ff, and pp. 123-124, 126 above).[163] This is why, as the church's founding " witnesses " and exponents of a continued " eschatological prophecy," they had to be nourished by the Easter Christ's instruction on the fulfillment of all the prophecies. How we impoverish Luke's " witness "

---

[161] W. Rädl, *Paulus und Jesus*, 80. — On Acts 9,15f. as recognizably Luke's composition, cf. *ibid.*, 71f.; and on the 'passion' content of both verses, *ibid.*, 75ff.

[162] Rightly J. Zmijewski, *Eschatologiereden*, 161.

[163] Pointed out properly, and with good observation of the consequent *equipment* of the prophetic witnesses (i.e. learning the *instruction* of Christ), by B. Rigaux, *Dieu l'a ressuscité*, 263. — For precisely the suffering-*prophet* identity inherited by the disciple of Jesus, cf. Lk 6,23.26 (cp. Mt 5,11-12) and F. Schütz, *Der leidende Christus*, 108f.

concept when we make them mere vouchers for the risen One's return from the tomb! — But more of this *ad* v. 48.

The risen Lord's specification of the preaching's content — μετάνοιαν εἰς (P-75 / *vs.* καὶ· A C D etc.) ἄφεσιν ἁμαρτιῶν — is no less effective in qualifying this appointed ministry as a continuation of his own. First of all, it is significant that the *word* is made the prime medium of salvation, a fact which complements both the decisive role assigned the revealing *word* in the Easter story (24,25ff.44ff.) and the presentation of Jesus' first messianic ministration in Lk 4,14ff. as a "coming in the word" (cf. chap. II, n. 172). Furthermore, although a comparison with Jn's appearance story indicates that the commission to forgive sins was part of the tradition used by both evangelists (cf. pp. 162f. above), the particular combination of "repentance" with forgiveness, as the latter's antecedent condition, belongs to a schema repeatedly invoked by Lk to illustrate the continuity of his story. From John the Baptist to Jesus, and from the Easter mandate to the mission sermons to both Jews and Gentiles, the messianic salvation is invariably announced as the opportunity of repentance (*turning from* sinful ways) and conversion (*turning to* a merciful God).[164] It is upon these human responses to the missionary preaching that the divine gift of forgiveness is bestowed (Acts 10,43; 13,38; 26,18). The one same appeal, "*do penance*," "*be converted*," came from both Jesus (Lk 5,32 [*diff.* Mk]; 10,13; 11,32; 15,7[Q]; 13,3.5[S]) and the missionaries preaching in his name (Acts 3,19; 20,21; 26,20, etc.). Indeed, through the numerous scenes of mission endeavour that Lk has constructed in Acts, one finds a recurrent *ordo salutis* proclaimed with characteristic variations and cumulative exposition.[165] Its steps lead from the Jesus-kerygma to the appeal to repent, then baptism "in the name of Jesus" (Acts 2,38; 8,16), forgiveness bestowed by the power of the "Name" (Acts 10,43; 13,38), and reception of the Holy Spirit (Acts 2,38; 8,17; 11,15). All this constitutes what this author understands as "*being saved*" (Acts 2,40.47; 4,12; 13,26; cp. ζωή· 11,18). And it is all

---

[164] H. Conzelmann, *MdZ*, 213ff.; U. Wilckens, *Missionsreden*, 178ff.

[165] U. Wilckens, *Missionsreden*, 179. — The Acts sermons to mission audiences are uniformly structured so as to have the (call to/announcement of) *repentance* as their logical climax, produced by force of contrasts drawn in the kerygmatic recital: either between the divine vindication and human rejection of the messiah (Jewish audiences) or between worship of idols and the claim of the living Creator (Gentile audiences). Cf. U. Wilckens, *Missionsreden*, 54, 87ff., 98-100, 119-121; and earlier, M. Dibelius, *Formgeschichte*, 15f., and *Aufsätze*, 97f., 142; H. Conzelmann, *MdZ*, 213 n. 1; U. Wilckens, *ZNW* 49 (1958) 225f. Also J. Dupont, *Études*, 433-440, 460-465. — Cf. also pp. 100ff., 125 above.

brought to realization in the one saving act of God, called the " giving" (δοῦναι) of repentance (Acts 5,31; 11,18).[166]

The continuity of the Easter mission-provision with Jesus' inaugural scripture exposition at Nazareth has been brought out by us already (p. 137 above). A conflation of Deutero-Isaian passages permitted a summary depiction of the messianic ministry in twice-emphasized terms of *forgiveness* (= the prophet's ἄφεσις· chap. II, nn. 194-196). That forgiveness of sins was the heart of all the prophets' promises was brought out as early as the canticle of Zachary, where the nature of the Baptist's mission as προφήτης ὑψίστου was forecast (Lk 1,76f. S). Indeed, in Lk's earliest pages we had already learned why the *eschatological prophecy* of Easter would be dedicated to the announcement of God's *forgiveness in Jesus' name,* hence why this gift of the crucified and risen messiah would prove to be the fruition and ultimate exercize of biblical *prophecy.* With respect to this divine gift, the message of Jesus and his successors is related to the prophets' words as fulfillment to promise.

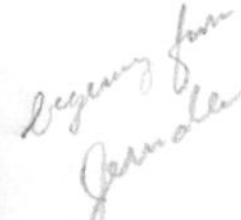

Despite the grammatical difficulty it causes and the manuscript variants it generated, ἀρξάμενοι ἀπὸ Ἰερουσαλήμ should be read as a subordinate clause of vv. 46f., not of v. 48. No less than the death and resurrection of Christ and the universal preaching in his name, the mission's starting point at Jerusalem is understood by Lk to be part of the provisions of OT prophecy.[167] With ἀρξάμενοι, taken almost adverbially, we have the beginning of an abrupt shift to direct address (v. 48), a phenomenon that is repeated in Acts 1,4 with the equally unexpected ἥν ἠκούσατέ μου. In fact, it is the planned complementary parallelism between our vv. 47-49 and Acts 1,8 which brings out that the mission *to the Gentiles* must be inaugurated by a *Jerusalem* " beginning." For the "beginning" in question is substantive, not merely

[166] Cf. H. CONZELMANN, *MdZ*, 90-92, on *metanoia* in the gospel and Acts. The close and necessary connection between repentance, as requisite condition, and divine forgiveness " through Jesus' name " is already reflected in what looks to be Luke's refinement of the injunction to forgive one's brother without limit: ἐὰν ἁμάρτῃ ὁ ἀδελφός σου ἐπιτίμησον αὐτῷ, καὶ ἐὰν μετανοήσῃ ἄφες αὐτῷ· ... καὶ ἑπτάκις ἐπιστρέφῃ πρὸς σὲ λέγων, Μετανοῶ, ἀφήσεις αὐτῷ (Lk 17,3f. / cp. Mt 18, 15-21). Note, too, the prominence of the great paradigms of (repentance and) forgiveness drawn by Luke from his *Sondergut*: the repentant woman (Lk 7,36-50), the parables of the pharisee and publican (Lk 18,9-14) and the repentant son (Lk 15,11-32). In connection with our contention that the summons to repentance and forgiveness is understood by Luke as a *prophet's* message, indeed the realization of the prophets' doctrine of salvation, it is not insignificant that, in the course of the story of the repentant woman, an obviously ironic challenge is heard to Jesus' identity as prophet (Lk 7,39).

[167] G. LOHFINK, *Himmelfahrt*, 264, citing Is 2,3 as typical. For similar uses of ἄρχομαι cf. Lk 23,5; 24,27; Acts 1,22; esp. Acts 10,37 (J. DUPONT, in *N. T. und Kirche*, 126f., with n. 7).

chronological or geographical.[168] It has to do above all with Jerusalem's *privilegium odiosum* of being the place of the prophets' doom (Lk 13, 34[Q]; 13,33[S]; 18,31 [*diff.* Mk]). As we saw in surveying the ἕνεκεν/ὑπέρ formulas involving the "Name" (pp. 210f.), Lk believed the propagation of the word to be fostered by the tribulations of its spokesmen, and this idea inspired schematic patterns of narrating the mission's early history in the book of Acts (cf. n. 158 above). In clear conformity with this idea, it will be Jerusalem's lethal ouslaught against Stephen and his group that compels the community to move outward from the city (Acts 8,1ff.), undertaking mission activity in Samaria and Judaea, and finally establishing the key center of the Gentile mission, Antioch in Syria (Acts 11,19ff.). The geographical conspectus of Acts 1,8 suggests that self same course of missionary development, hence confirms the decisive push *outward* that was furnished by the first martyr's death, — Jerusalem's typical prophet-murder! The "way" that drew Jesus from Galilee to Jerusalem now becomes the "way" outward, with the city's inevitable hostility to God's envoys being, in both cases, the compelling impulse of the journey.[169] In this sense, Jerusalem would furnish an active, nay forceful ἀρχή for the age of the mission, and it would do so in complete accordance with the forecasts of biblical prophecy (Lk 18,31). Only in this sense can the Jerusalem ἀρχή truly participate in the messianic δεῖ, which is thus seen to provide for the course of the universal mission — hence the full sequence of 24,46-47 — following the schema so succinctly captured in Acts 13,45-46.[170]

V. 48 brings us, at length, to the theme which we shall not be able to circumscribe with merely the data that our chapter provides, the Lucan *witness* theme (cf. n. 36 above). Let us point out, first of all, that we have by now an accumulation of reasons for resisting the view that Lk's "witness" is primarily a "guarantor of facts."[171]

---

[168] E. LOHSE, *Auferstehung*, 37. — The masculine plural ἀρξάμενοι accentuates the ἀρχή for the *missionaries and their destiny*, rather than just for the mission itself (*pace* F. HAHN, *Mission*, 114). In other words, Luke's interest in Jerusalem as the prophet's city of doom may account for the unattached and ungrammatical masculine plural participle.

[169] J. ZMIJEWSKI, *Eschatologiereden*, 156f.

[170] Cf. Lk 21,24 *diff.* Mk, which may be connected with this 'Jerusalem' theory; — on v. 47 as a sketch of the mission's course, U. WILCKENS, *Missionsreden*, 98; and on the ἀρχή concept, H. CONZELMANN, *MdZ*, 197 n. 1.

[171] That the Lucan resurrection "witness," insofar as it is a delimiting function of "the Twelve," is essentially "*Tatsachenzeugnis*" (G. SCHNEIDER, *Verleugnung, Verspottung und Verhör*, 204ff.), seems to be generally held amongst the exegetes who follow the analyses of H. CONZELMANN (see e.g. U. WILCKENS, *Missionsreden*, 146f., G. KLEIN, in *Zeit und Geschichte*, 205 [in G. BRAUMANN-*LkEv*, 187], G. KEGEL, *Auferstehung Jesu*, 89, 93, 99). Cf. also, and especially, C. H. TALBERT, *Luke and the Gnostics*, 17-32. — Other exegetes appropriately

(a) First, total exposure to empirical fact in the present pericope, no less than the two preceding ones, led only to perplexity and ἀπιστία, not yet to Easter faith. The latter comes only with the elucidation of the " facts " by the risen Lord expounding the scriptures, hence its witnesses had to be, above all, reliable exponents of his prophetic argument. It is that argument which Lk has made the center of the Easter revelation. (b) Our exegesis of the mission statement of v. 47, in discerning the close connection between activities *in/for* " the Name " of Christ and the concept of witness, brought out a fuller scope of representative embodiment of the Lord than usually comes to light in treatments of this passage. Mission in the name of Jesus meant to Lk nothing short of *total reenactment of the christological " journey,"* embracing both the powerful ministrations of pneumatic " prophecy " and the inevitable prophet's rejection. The relationship and logic of these two phases could come to light only in the risen Lord's demonstration of *all the prophecies' fulfillment* in himself (— the argument spoken of in -a-). This is further reason for emphasizing the *word of instruction*, filling out and illumining the total Easter experience of continuity and identity, as the indispensable equipment of the " witness." [172]

(c) Let us add the argument based on the immediate context of our passage, which is admitted even by the sponsors of a mainly factual witness.[173] In the statement of v. 48, ὑμεῖς μάρτυρες τούτων, the demonstrative pronoun clearly refers to all the aspects of scripture fulfillment in vv. 46-47, and that includes a *future* component, the world-mission, which is certainly not yet factual reality! This makes it quite clear that it is of the paschal " opening " of the scriptures first that the third-day observer is made " witness." Nor is the situation different in the several declarations of the apostles' " witness " stature made in the Acts sermons:[174]

---

waver on the issue. Chr. BURCHARD, for example, speaks of the witnesses as " Garanten der Tatsächlichkeit " (*Der dreizehnte Zeuge*, 132f.), but then specifies the content of their witness as " not bare facts," but the facts given their authentic interpretation and meaning by the risen Christ (*ibid.*, 133, 135). Similarly, despite his heavy emphasis on factual guarantee as Luke's objective, D. P. FULLER, *Easter Faith and History*, 224f. See again note 37 above.

[172] Cf. H. SCHLIER, *Über die Auferstehung Jesu Christi* (Kriterien 10; Einsiedeln, ³1970) 44, and the excellent remarks of K. KIENZLER, *Logik der Auferstehung* (cited in n. 177 below), 254. Cf. also V. STOLLE, *Zeuge als Angeklagter*, 149.

[173] E.g. D. P. FULLER, *Easter Faith and History*, 224f.; G. SCHNEIDER, *Verleugnung, Verspottung und Verhör*, 206; R. PESCH, *EKK* III, 31. — A balanced perspective on the witness's equipment was given by H. STRATHMANN: " ... sowohl die Tatsachen wie ihre *gläubig erfasste Bedeutung* " is what he must attest (μάρτυς κτλ., *TWNT* IV [477-520] 496; cf. also J. KREMER, *Pfingstbericht*, 188; — italics mine). Cf. also E. NELLESSEN, *Zeugnis*, 114f.

[174] J. ROLOFF's argument against WILCKENS on this point (*Apostolat*, 192)

Acts 2,32 includes the witness-statement *after* the scripture argument, not before (at 2,24). — The " witness " of *Acts 3,15* is declared both after scriptural argument (v. 13) and in the context of fuller christological representation by healing " through faith in his name " (v. 16). — *Acts 5,32* declares : καὶ ἡμεῖς ἐσμεν μάρτυρες τῶν ῥημάτων τούτων, and even acknowledging a broader meaning of ῥῆμα than purely linguistic, the content of Acts 5,31, to which this statement directly refers, is not mainly factual data, such that observers could vouch for ! — The same can be said of Acts 10,37-38 as referred to in *Acts 10,39*, and we have already discussed the situation of *Acts 10,40f.* (cf. pp. 199f., and note the substantive clause that completes διαμαρτύρεσθαι in v. 42, as well as the assignment of the witness function to OT prophets in v. 43 !). — Finally, *Acts 13,31* significantly declares the *companions of the Jerusalem journey* to be the risen Christ's μάρτυρες πρὸς τὸν λαόν, and this by reason of the witnesses' complete christological representation, not to prove comprehensive factual exposure ! Reference is made here to the " many days " of Easter appearances, clearly evoking the " forty days " of Acts 1,3 and the Lord's λέγειν τὰ περὶ τῆς βασιλείας τοῦ θεοῦ associated therewith.

Even where the motif of the witnesses' *seeing* is most emphatically developed, namely, in the Acts ascension account (5 separate accentuations in 1,9-11),[175] the purpose cannot be to exhibit their unique factual knowledge when the cloud is said to take the Lord ἀπὸ τῶν ὀφθαλμῶν αὐτῶν and the familiar ἄνδρες δύο, with a reprimand reminiscent of 24,5, must explain the true significance of what has occurred. The ascension story, too, has the familiar dialectic of observable fact and divine revelation, and it is as recipients of the latter, *mediante verbo*, rather than as boasting unique and univocal visual experiences, that the Easter observers obtained the status of " witnesses." Rescued from the dullness of their human senses by the divine word, and experiencing thus the *gift* of Easter faith, the " eye-witnesses " *became* " ministers of the word " (Lk 1,2). Luke's Easter story is, in fact, the story of that " becoming " (cf. chap. IV/ii) !

is therefore not as forceful as he might have made it, for the references of Acts 2,32 and Acts 3,15 are no more to exclusively factual data than is the case in Lk 24,48 or Acts 5,32 ! On the apostolic " witness " declarations of Acts, rightly R. GLÖCKNER, *Verkündigung*, 53 : " Nur ist die Mitteilung irgendwelcher ' bruta facta ' nirgends das eigentliche Ziel der Aussagen. Die Mitteilung bestimmter Ereignisse bedeutet nicht die Reduktion der geschichtlichen Erfahrung auf das Bewiesene oder doch prinzipiell Beweisbare. Das Zeugnis der Zeugen will nicht argumentierend beweisen, es will überzeugen. Damit drängt es aber immer über die reine Mitteilung von Ereignissen hinaus und entfaltet seine innere Kraft von der ansprechenden Bedeutsamkeit des Bezeugten her." Similarly V. STOLLE, *Zeuge als Angeklagter*, 148-150.

[175] G. LOHFINK, *Himmelfahrt*, 186f. ; R. PESCH, *EKK* III, 33.

From our present perspective, we cannot decide the question of what precise *circle of people* are given the " witness " mandate at 24,48 (cf. chap. IV/ii 4), other than to heark back to the broad *coetus* that was present when the pericope began (v. 33: the Eleven and those " gathered " with them, plus the Emmaus duo).[176] The resumé at the beginning of Acts will suddenly presume a concentration of the Easter witness in " the apostles whom he had chosen " (1,2), referring back to Lk 6,13 (*diff.* Mk) and the circle of " the Twelve." But that is by no means yet clear after the story of Lk 24 has been told; and Luke seems readily to interchange references to " the Twelve " and the broader circle of disciples, as if he presumes the whole circle, nucleus and broader membership, were always together, and to speak of one is to speak of the other (cf. Lk 24,9-10, and chap. II, n. 40). It will be from the broader circle, after all, that " the Twelve " are restored to plenary number at Acts 1,21ff., and whatever distinction the latter group obtains in that passage, it cannot be of the order of paschal *experience*, else the choice by lot could never have replenished the group. — But more of this when we consider the Easter story within the total context of Lk-Acts (chap. IV/ii 4). For the moment, we cannot verify any special accentuation of the inner circle of disciples in the " witness " recruitment of Lk 24.[177]

V. 49 concludes the witnesses' instruction with a cryptic promise and a command. Both fit into this setting readily on the basis of our previous study. The parallel passage in Acts 1,8 identifies the " promise " and " power " to be expected by the followers as the Holy Spirit; and we know well by now that this is a component of the original appearance tradition (Jn 20,22; cf. pp. 160, 204 above) that is tailored here to Luke's historiographical schema. But the fact and choice of the circumlocutions for the Spirit in our text hold some interest. It is clear that a certain pathos of expectation is meant to be aroused here at the end of the first volume. The disciples are to await the divine " promise " meant for them, a " power " to equip them for their missionary endeavour. It is this momentum of anticipation, artfully built into the junction of his two books, that must account for Luke's choice of words to begin the momentous Pentecost story, Acts 2,1: ἐν τῷ συμπληροῦσθαι τὴν ἡμέραν τῆς πεντηκοστῆς ...[178] On hearing those

[176] E. Nellessen, *Zeugnis*, 107ff.

[177] N. Brox, (*Zeuge*, 55) admits the distinction between the function of witness and the title apostle, even though he clearly tends to limit the former to the office of the latter. On the other hand, cf. J. Roloff, *Apostolat*, 202ff., and the fine discussion and survey in Klaus Kienzler, *Logik der Auferstehung. Eine Untersuchung zu R. Bultmann, G. Ebeling, und W. Pannenberg* (Freiburger theol. Studien 100; Freiburg/Basel: Herder, 1976) 208ff.

[178] J. Kremer, *Pfingstbericht*, 182.

words, one will know that the period of waiting is over, and he will be ready to hear the astonishing account of the birth of a new people. — But, in a typically Lucan mixture of perspectives, those words will also direct the reader's attention *back* to Lk 9,51, ἐν τῷ συμπληροῦσθαι τὰς ἡμέρας τῆς ἀναλήμψεως αὐτοῦ, whereupon he will know what it is that is being inaugurated on the Pentecost: the ascended Lord's "witnesses" will be *embarking on the "journey" that is to repeat his own*! Such is at least the suggestion that results from the solemn introductions, nowhere repeated in between, that create a certain symmetry between the total "journey" of Jesus[179] and the mission epoch inaugurated at Acts 2,1. Like the baptism of Jesus (Lk 4,18; Acts 10,38), the Pentecost will be an outpouring of the Holy Spirit as *power for mission and ministry*;[180] and in both cases the Spirit instills the power of *prophecy* (Lk 4,24; Acts 2,17ff.), — prophecy in its two essential phases so well known to us by now: mighty works and violent rejection! Indeed, the mission is to be the Lord's "journey" all over again!

So far as the content of the circumlocutions for the Spirit is concerned, it can be dealt with quickly. "The promise of the Father" is nevertheless "sent" by Jesus, a combination which is explained in Acts 2,33 in the recurrent Lucan perspective of the Father's action through Jesus' mediation.[181] The understanding of the Spirit in terms of *power* is already familiar to us as a mark of our author's writing (cf. pp. 114f. above), and it is given special prominence in the Jesus-kerygma at Cornelius' house (Acts 10,38), a passage fraught with programmatic significance for the Gentile mission. More specifically, we have seen that a mission carried out "in Jesus' name" involves ministrations of "power" in which the Lord of the Church makes his presence felt (pp. 210, 212), hence we have a perfect conceptual bond between v. 47 and v. 49b.

By now, once we hear of "power," we expect to hear of sufferings. And so we do, in a veiled way. The command to remain in the city contains the prospect of a mission advanced by the sufferings of the missionaries, such as Jerusalem perennially visited upon the envoys of God. Consequently, the prospect of a *charismatic* and *persecuted prophecy*, actually the continuation of Jesus' *eschatological prophecy* in a worldwide missionary endeavour, is what comes to veiled expression

[179] Cf. n. 60 above, in defense of extending the 'journey' framework to embrace all of Lk 9,51 – Acts 1,11.

[180] J. KREMER, *Pfingstbericht*, 182. In this respect it differs from John's baptism, as Acts 1,5 states, for John's βαπτίζειν was a preparation for the *judgment* of the *Endzeit*, whereas the disciples' βαπτισθῆναι would be an equipping for the *task* of the *Endzeit*, the mission.

[181] Cf. H. CONZELMANN, *MdZ*, 161ff.; U. WILCKENS, *Missionsreden*, 163.

(befitting the pathos of expectancy) in v. 49. It is thus a quite appropriate conclusion of the mandate, which began at v. 46.

Speaking now of the whole mandate: aside from the mission of forgiving sins in the Spirit's power, all of the provisions of vv. 47-49 come from the mind and pen of the evangelist, who has remoulded the christophany tradition most thoroughly at this point for the intersection of his two volumes. The strength of his hand here is such that it must outweigh arguments for prior tradition based on selective vocabulary statistics, or questionable Elianic echoes in καθίσατε and ἐνδύσησθε. V. 49 scarcely offers secure footing for pre-Lucan traditions linking the apostolic christophany and the ascension.[182]

(c) Finale: The Ascension (Lk 24,50-53)

The reader will discover that much of what we have to say about our chapter's concluding verses has been said already, in the section devoted to appraisal of the work done by others (1-d). This is a deliberate allotment, for we have few novel perspectives to add to an already ample discussion. Our interest is mainly in relating the departure scene to our interpretation of the rest of the Easter story; and this we hope to do in two ways: (1) by a closer look at the influence of the literary finale of Ben Sira, noted (pp. 179f.) as a commonplace of commentary on this Lucan passage; (2) by highlighting the importance of προσκυνήσαντες αὐτόν in v. 52, so effectively argued by G. Lohfink (n. 72 above), as the Easter faith's triumph, at long last, over the uncertainty and hesitation of the *triduum* observers. These two points should bring the main currents of our interpretation to a conclusion that is faithful to our evangelist's intentions. Let us preface them, therefore, by raising the important issue of a possible tradition underlying this concluding scene.

Contrary to R. Pesch,[183] we feel the case for pre-Lucan tradition here is too meagre to argue successfully. In our opinion, the situation is the reverse of Pesch's contention: if Luke had any predecessor in narrating the Lord's visible ascension — a possibility we definitely mean to leave open (cf. p. 175) — we should rather explore Acts 1,9-11 for traces of such an antecedent account, rather than posit them here in the gospel's finale. This passage has impressed us as a *literary conclusion* with a *literary origin* (as G. Lohfink contends). The literary origin is, of course, Ben Sira's conspectus of Israel's heroic past, which becomes Luke's model for summarizing the *Easter fulfillment of the*

---

[182] *Contra* R. Pesch, *EKK* III (cited in note 63 above); rightly J. Kremer *Pfingstbericht*, 186f. n. 46 (the ἐνδύεσθαι figure is simply too common a metaphor in the bible to convince one of attachment to a particular tradition).

[183] *EKK* III, 15.

sacred past, which has been the theme of his three episodes of the "third day." The substance of descriptive narration in these terminal verses comes from the sage's book, and we found no other substantial tradition to account for what is here. — Our contention needs further elaboration, however. Precisely how does this biblical ancestor inspire the literary climax to both the Easter story and the gospel that our skillful author required?

The Palestinian sage's account of the heroic past is related to the genre of "lives" of *viri illustres* that was popular at the height of the hellenistic age,[184] and his intent with it was to certify his teaching as a wisdom whose wonder-working exponents showed it far superior to any rival in the flourishing world-culture (Sir 44,3-9).[185] What seems most significant, *vis-a-vis* Lk's argument, is Ben Sira's pains to demonstrate the *succession* of the great tradition's spokesmen,[186] and to show that the great miracles they performed were the fruits of a *heritage of powerful prophecy* which he carefully traces to Moses as its source. E. Jacob's critique that the sage saw the prophets only as workers of miracles (n. 68 above) is precisely the point! The miracles, and the prophecy they expressed, had a precise διαδοχή which the author traces. Joshua is called Moses' διάδοχος ... ἐν προφητείαις (Sir 46,1), and here he locates the fountain-head of the tradition of thaumaturgy (on which cf. n. 68). Moses' tradition was a stream that divided into the separate institutions of prophecy, priesthood, monarchy, and sacred scholarship (Sir 44,3-6); but the primacy of prophecy in it is indicated by the fact that Moses, the first and greatest prophet, "ordained" and "anointed" Aaron to the priestly office (ἐπλήρωσεν Μ. τὰς χεῖρας καὶ ἔχρισεν ... 45, 15), and Samuel, "the Lord's prophet, established the monarchy and anointed rulers over his people" (46,13). In the close relation of prophecy and monarchy, Nathan is shown to have succeeded Samuel just as Solomon succeeded David (Sir 47,1.12: μετὰ τοῦτον ἀνέστη κτλ.). Then, as the monarchy declined, the incomparable Elia arose (Sir 48,4) and anointed prophets to succeed him (48,8), of whom, of course, it was Elisha who inherited his spirit and matched his θαυμάσια (cp. 48, 4.12-14). Afterward came Isaiah, powerful counselor of Hezekiah (Sir 48,20ff.), and finally the prophets, including "the twelve," whose missions accompanied the end of the faithless kings' line and revived a fallen Israel's hopes (49,7-10). — The sense of the διαδοχή is thus to

[184] M. Hengel, *Judentum und Hellenismus*, 248f.; Th. Middendorf, *Die Stellung Jesu Ben Siras zwischen Judentum und Hellenismus* (Leiden: E. J. Brill, 1973) 27.

[185] Robert T. Siebeneck, "May Their Bones Return to Life! — Sirach's Praise of the Fathers," *CBQ* 21 (1959, 411-428) 413.

[186] M. Hengel, *Judentum und Hellenismus*, 249 (as in Eupolemus, and Josephus, *C. Apionem* 1,41: τὴν τῶν προφητῶν ἀκριβῆ διαδοχήν).

show that the prophets' tradition survives in the scholarly wisdom of the present, whose authentic connection with Moses and undiminished vitality for the present are thus effectively exhibited (44,10-15).

If this fuller context of the sage's argument is compared with Luke's interest in chap. 24, the evangelist's choice of a model for his finale becomes more intelligible. In Ben Sira, after all, Luke had a ready-made digest of the *argument from prophecy* that he has urged in each of the three Easter pericopes, most specifically in terms of " Mosaic," thaumaturgical prophecy in 24,19-27. If the risen Christ was to proclaim himself the end and summation of all the contents of the sacred books, *interpreted as prophecy*, reviving the mighty deeds of the illustrious men of Israel and suffering public resistance to the prophetic word, his argument — the one of 24,27 and 24,44f. — could hardly have found a more effective, digested model to follow than the sage's panorama. Just as in Ben Sira the " prophecies " of Moses were the vibrant source of Israel's institutions of prophecy, priesthood, and monarchy, so the Lucan Christ can now merge these functions anew in himself, exercizing them all in fulfillment of *all* the scriptures. Moreover, with the greatest of Ben Sira's *illustres*, Henoch and Elia, the Easter Christ is spirited into the heavens at the end of his ministry and is to return, *modo Eliae*, for the " times of restoration " (Sir 48,9-10/Acts 3,21). One can see that the schematic presentation of sacred history in Ben Sira furnishes a perspective from which to carry out a christological reading of all Scripture, whose traditions of wondrous prophecy find their harmonious completion in the risen *and ascended* Christ.

To those who would like to find in Lk a measure of the sage's special interest in the *priesthood*, considering the identity of the model in Sir 50,20ff., and the apparently corresponding " priestly " scenes at the beginning and end of the gospel,[187] I must confess that I cannot verify this. With J. ERNST,[188] I find the alleged symbolism in a response of the final priestly εὐλογεῖν to the incomplete priestly service of Zachary (Lk 1,8) anything but compelling. Where is the in-between substance of this theologoumenon in the other twenty-two chapters ? Where is any follow-up in Acts ? That Luke's interest in the Jewish priesthood is anything more than casual (Acts 6,7), or that it is more than one among several Old Testament institutions he knew to be terminated and perfected in the Easter Christ, I just do not see ! In the christological portrait this evangelist has been drawing for us in chap. 24, prophecy is central and comprehensive ; priesthood is briefly implicit, otherwise undeveloped.

---

[187] G. VAN STEMPVOORT, *NTS* 5 (1958-59) 35 ; G. LOHFINK, *Himmelfahrt*, 253 ; G. ODASSO, *BibOr* 13 (1971) 112f., 116. Cf. also W. OTT, *Gebet und Heil*, 124f., 128.

[188] *Lk.* 672f.

On the other hand, the argument we have advanced — supposing that Luke was appealing to a broader context of an Old Testament passage than he actually utilized in his composition (as in the case of Ps 31, pp. 100ff. above) — urges that Ben Sira's précis of a heroic history, studded with wonder-working prophets, was just the vision of biblical history that our evangelist had, and just the picture he knew to reach its completion in the risen Lord and the bequest of " power " to carry on his ministrations. As the *terminus ad quem* of a " star-studded " biblical history, Ben Sira's choice of Simon the Highpriest had been definitively superseded with the events of Easter day. Indeed, if our exegesis of Lk 24 has been basically correct, *how could the author of this chapter ever have read Sir 44-50 without craving to change the sage's ending and make it his own ?* — To our knowledge, this deeper probe of Luke's motives in the appeal to Sir 50 has not been undertaken by other scholars. Our conviction that it is proceeding in the right direction is nevertheless undiminished !

(2) The parallel εὐλογίαι in 24,50b and 53 involve a combination of two senses of εὐλογεῖν that is perhaps the surest sign of our author's literary dependency upon Ben Sira. The dominical blessing and worshippers' praise constitute a concluding exchange wholly appropriate to a heavenly ascension with sacred bequest attached (cf. p. 176 above). In the middle of this exchange comes the gesture of worship itself, the *proskynēsis*, which is the first signal we receive that the disciples' fear and disbelief have been replaced by *Easter faith.* In the προσκυνήσαντες αὐτόν of Lk 24,52, still subordinated to ὑπέστρεψαν εἰς Ἰερουσαλήμ which provides for the continuity of Lk's larger story, an interesting editorial phenomenon occurs which G. LOHFINK very persuasively brought out.[189] This is the first time the verb προσκυνεῖν is appearing in this gospel. In the Marcan passages where adoration or homage of the earthly Jesus was recorded, Lk avoided these expressions — γονυπετεῖν (Mk 1,40 *diff.* Lk 5,12 ; Mk 10,17 *diff.* Lk 18,18) and προσκυνεῖν (Mk 5,6 *diff.* Lk 8,28) — in favor of a non-committal verb, (προσ-)πίπτειν, which avoided the sense of *worship.* Bows before Jesus in Lk's story were for the purpose of petition (Lk 8,41), thanksgiving (Lk 17,16), or fear (Lk 5,8 ; 8,47), but not for the solemn purpose of prayer. Proper adoration was saved, so to speak, to be tendered here at the ascension, with the proper term in use, depicting what could only be the relation of the believing disciple to the Christ of Easter. Just as this is the first occasion in the gospel when the Lord " lifts his hands " in solemn priestly blessing of his followers, it is likewise the first occasion when

[189] G. LOHFINK, *Himmelfahrt*, 171ff. ; also " Gab es im Gottesdienst der neutestamentlichen Gemeinden eine Anbetung Christi ? " *BZ* 18 (1974, 161-179) 163ff.

they can enter the relationship to him which will become the permanent attitude of the Christian church towards its ascended Lord: solemn adoration!

Confirming the fact that the *proskynēsis* of v. 52 is actually the point to which the expected moment of recognition was deferred by our evangelist is a noticeable literary relationship between v. 41, where we maintained he intervened to postpone a statement like Jn 20,20b, and the description of the returning disciples in v. 52: μετὰ χαρᾶς μεγάλης. When we hear of their *great joy* at this point, we can hardly fail to recall the *disbelief from joy* which still afflicted them as they observed the risen One take food at their table. The veil of mystery which prevented their recognition of the Visitor has been drawn aside — progressively, indeed — through the totality of his gestures, his revealing word, his bequest, and his final blessing. Recognition thus came about in much the same delayed and tantalizing fashion as held the reader's rapt attention during the Emmaus story.

Finally, the ascension scene's familiar *framework* of movement *from and back to Jerusalem* (v. 50: ἐξήγαγεν · v. 52: ὑπέστρεψαν [cp. 24,9.33]) deserves our comment. The locale of this ascension-scene is reconciled without difficulty with that of Acts 1,12, once it is recalled that Bethany and the Mount of Olives were associated by the evangelist in his tracing of the Master's *itinerary into Jerusalem* (Lk 19,29).[190] That original notice came nearly word for word from Mk 11,1, and the cumbersome ἕως πρὸς βηθανίαν, rather than ἕως βηθ., seems to be Lk's attempt to recreate the locale of entry according to the imprecise data of Mk. "Up to a point *towards* Bethany" would be just where the Mount of Olives stood, according to the Marcan itinerary; hence Lk, in typical fashion, uses complementary rather than repetitive data from a source to locate two versions of the same event. — What is more significant than this locale, however, is that in reporting it first along Jesus' path of entry to the city, Lk had prefaced it with his distinctive "journey" scenario: ἐπορεύετο ἔμπροσθεν ἀναβαίνων εἰς Ἱεροσόλυμα (Lk 19,28). That was his last such notice, indicating that Jesus would take his *departure from earth and his followers at the very point where his path to Jerusalem had reached its end.* Jerusalem, the place of his death, is thus reduced to a *station on the "journey" whose destination is heaven.* Thus the understanding of ἀνάλημψις in Lk 9,51 in terms of the ultimate "ascension," the gospel's ending, gains probability to the point of conviction (cf. n. 60 again).

At *v. 53* and the end of the gospel, the followers of Jesus have come back into full possession (διὰ πάντος) of the temple, the center

[190] V. Larranaga, *L'ascension de N. S.*, 404-416; P. Benoit, *Exégèse et théol.* I, 400; Lohfink, *Himmelfahrt*, 165; G. Odasso, *BibOr* 13 (1971) 111f.

of Jewish religion (cp. Acts 2,46). Easter has documented the full realization of the promises contained in the Jewish scriptures, hence the disciples are rightful possessors of the central worship place. Literary design and theological argument are thus rounded off in the gospel's last sentence, and the way is clear for the emergence of the *true Israel* with full and demonstrable continuity. That is the story Acts will tell.

Conclusion and Prospect:

Our study of the third and final Easter pericope, which organically includes the ascension, has obtained substantial results for both the *tradition*- and *composition*-analysis of Lk 24. — First, with respect to the *tradition*: we found in the appearance-*narrative* substantial remnants of a tradition we had tentatively identified in studying the Emmaus story, viz. the itinerant, charismatic mission to households, where the rigorous precepts of Jesus' mission sayings were closely observed and his appearance to his disciples narrated according to the procedure and ideals of the movement. It is possible such a group furnished Lk's copy of Q, perhaps other of his *Sondergut* too, so we shall now place our findings in the framework of a broader study of the special traditions which have contributed so much of the third gospel.

Secondly, with respect to Lk's *composition*: this pericope brought us at length to the goal of Lk's Easter dialectic of experience and revelation: it was the appointment of *witnesses*, whom the risen Lord had led across the otherwise impassable threshold of faith by the *gift* of his renewed presence and instruction. Climactic patterns of Lk's story have thus led the reader, with the disciples, from the sight of Jesus buried to the worship of him ascended; from obscure passion-*mystery* to effulgent Easter *kerygma*; and from the perplexity of triduum *observers* to the faith of resurrection *witnesses*. These developments our chapter has sketched in a unified, dialectically seasoned, slowly chrystalizing argument which has remoulded three separate traditions as one story.

These two major results yield two parts of our last chapter.

Chapter IV

LK 24 IN THE LARGER CONTEXT OF LUKE-ACTS

Taking as our basic principle of organization the two results we formulated from the analysis of our chapter's final pericope, we move now to organize the fruits of the first three chapters' work into a comprehensive understanding of Lk 24 as part of the greater Lucan opus. The *first step* in this will be to relate the special traditions we found to the larger body of traditions Luke has employed in the gospel (and eventually, too, in the Acts). After drawing as clear a picture as we can of these evangelical "raw materials," striving to understand the ideas and issues, the historical and social framework, perhaps even the movements and audience they represent, we shall then better understand the items among them that were chosen for adaptation to Luke's Easter narrative. Then too, in a *second step*, we shall be able to pursue a sharper definition of Luke's own editorial purposes in coordinating these traditions as he has, distilling their ideas and tendencies in his masterful way so they could contribute to an integral vision of Christian origins. We believe that vision embraces a two-epoch sacred history, and that the Easter story is intended to illustrate the harmonious passage of the one epoch into the other. We thus see our story as a central reservoir of Lucan thought as well as the structural intersection of the greater Lucan project. In the second part of this chapter, we shall attempt a summary exposition of how Lk 24 acquits itself of such crucial functions.

I. Tradition-Analysis

Lk 24 among the special traditions of Luke

Since the space left to us is limited and this topic is massive, what follows in the first part of the chapter will be more general and, in part, more tentative than the literary analysis of the first three chapters. We shall be aiming to draw lines of continuity between our study and its predecessors and potential successors. Consequently, we shall as often be making suggestions and prognosis as drawing firm conclusions from data fully mastered.

1) The Procedures and Ideology of the Itinerant Mission

Much emphasis was given in chap. III to the ideals of the early missionaries that seemed to be reflected in the narrative-sequence of the mission-founding appearance. Suggestion of that relationship came from the tradition of Jesus' instruction on the mission, recorded in differing versions by all three Synoptics. Specifically, the protocol for household evangelizing (Lk 10,5-7), which we heard echoed explicitly in the apostolic appearance, less punctually in the Emmaus meal, was part of a series of directives for journeying missionaries whose extraordinary dearth of provisions for their journeys (Lk 10,4 & par.) clearly had some demonstrative intent related to the radical content of their message: "*the Kingdom of God has drawn near*," faithfully preserved in Lk 10,9.11. Very likely, as we held, such instructions were kept in the early Church by Christians whose lives were governed and styled by them. — This suggestion, of course, is of prime tradition-historical moment, and we are not the first to make it.

The clues to its custody offered by the synoptic tradition of Jesus' sayings have been the object of important studies of the recent past, particularly those which posed the question in terms such as these: what groups in primitive Christendom would likely have expressed themselves in the *forms*,[1] and lived by the *radical*,[2] *demonstrative*[3] eth-

[1] E. Käsemann, "Die Anfänge christlicher Theologie," in *Exeg. Versuche* II, 82-104, and "Sätze heiligen Rechtes im Neuen Testament," *ibid.*, 69-82. Also M. Eugene Boring, "How May We Identify Oracles of Christian Prophets in the Synoptic Tradition? Mark 3 : 28-29 as a Test Case," *JBL* 91 (1972) 501-521. — The presence among the synoptic *Herrenworte* of oracular utterances emanating from early Christian prophets has been quite frequently asserted, following the lead of H. Gunkel, H. J. Holtzmann, and A. Loisy (all quoted by David Hill, "On the Evidence for the Creative Role of Christian Prophets," *NTS* 20 [1973-1974, 262-274] 263) and, more influentially, by R. Bultmann, *GsT*, 134f. (*Ergänzungsheft*[4], 51-52). Form-analysis to support this assertion has been infrequent and, in the judgment of other scholars, inconclusive (cf. D. Hill, *art. cit.*, and G. Dautzenberg, *Urchristliche Prophetie*, 24-28). Of tentative contributions to such analysis, besides Käsemann and Boring, one can list: V. Hasler, *Amen. Redaktionsgeschichtliche Untersuchung zur Einführungsformel der Herrenworte 'Wahrlich ich sage euch'* (Zürich: Gotthelf Verlag, 1969) esp. 71-72, 84; Richard A. Edwards, "The Eschatological Correlative as a *Gattung* in the New Testament," *ZNW* 60 (1969) 9-20; S. Schulz, *Q*, 57-93.

[2] G. Kretschmar, "Ein Beitrag zur Frage nach dem Ursprung frühchristlicher Askese," *ZTK* 61 (1964) 27-67; Gerd Theissen, "Wanderradikalismus ...," *ZTK* 70 (1973) 245-271, and "Legitimation und Lebensunterhalt ...," *NTS* 21 (1974-75, 192-221) 193-200; S. Schulz, "'Die Gottesherrschaft ist nahe herbeigekommen' (Mt 10,7/Lk 10,9). Der kerygmatische Entwurf der Q-Gemeinde Syriens," in H. Balz & S. Schulz, hrsg., *Das Wort und die Wörter. Festschrift Gerhard Friedrich* (Stuttgart: Verlag W. Kohlhammer, 1973) 57-67; S. Schulz, *Q*, 33f., 481ff.

[3] P. Hoffmann, *Logienquelle*, 320ff.

os, that distinctively characterize large portions of the sayings tradition? Despite predictable differences of opinion *in individuis*, there is an exciting convergence of the answers in substance: the ethical radicalism of the sayings represents the life-style and ministry of *itinerant Christian missionaries* — apostles, prophets, teachers (as the various sources designate them) — who founded and ministered to small, rural communities of believers in the bilingual Syro-Palestinian Christendom of the first centuries. These vagabond propagandists, with their scattered, mainly peasant constituencies, represented the first extensions of the earthly mission of Jesus himself in time, place, and concept.[4] On the other hand, the nearly institutional durability of this mission-style, due in part to the remoteness of its natural territory, is exhibited by the relatively unaltered circumstances of its practice recorded in over a hundred years of the region's literature: *Didachē* 10-13, the apocryphal *Acta* (*Thomae*, e.g.), the Ps.-Clem. *Ad Virgines* (3rd cent.).[5] Occasionally the literature shows that these pneumatic preachers could give up the itinerant life in favor of *stabilitas loci*,[6] but for the most part — and certainly insofar as they remained missionaries — their ministry was a prophetic embodiment of the *homelessness*, *penury*, *renunciation of family and property*, and consequent *consignment to society's fringes*,[7] which was all precisely imposed in the sayings they repeated as most earnest *tradentes*.

"Repeated," we say, because there is no call for the notorious skepticism commonly blamed on the form-critic. The radicalism of the roving "charismatics" hardly begat the radicalism of the sayings; we should think the situation is rather the reverse: the radical ethos of Jesus' very words was systematically practicable only under a life-style that G. THEISSEN has called "*Wanderradikalismus*."[8]

---

[4] G. KRETSCHMAR, *ZTK* 61 (1964) 49; M. HENGEL, *Nachfolge*, 92f.; G. THEISSEN, *ZTK* 70 (1973) 257: "Jesus war der erste Wandercharismatiker. Die Tradenten seiner Worte übernahmen seine Lebensweise, die τρόπους κυρίου (Did XI, 8). Was durch ihren Lebenstil geprägt ist, ist deswegen noch lange nicht 'unecht'. Ihr Wanderradikalismus geht auf Jesus selbst zurück. Er ist authentisch." — G. THEISSEN makes much of the mainly peasant audience and rural milieu of the itinerant enthusiasm (*ZTK* 70 [1973] 264ff., and *NTS* 21 [1974-75] 196f.). The mainly Syro-Palestinian locale of the small communities begotten by this movement was a point made by E. KÄSEMANN (*Exegetische Versuche* ... II, 91), reiterated by G. KRETSCHMAR (*ZTK* 61 [1964] 30ff., 36, 47f., etc.).

[5] G. KRETSCHMAR, *ZTK* 61 (1964) 36f.

[6] *Did.* 13,1f. (G. KRETSCHMAR, *art. cit.*, 37). The Pauline constellation of charisms includes prophecy as a stable endowment of the local community, just like teaching. One readily imagines that smaller communities, less developed or more rurally located, continued to await the "charismatics" from without, whereas more self-sufficient congregations, in larger settlements, acquired their own "resident" preachers.

[7] G. THEISSEN, *ZTK* 70 (1973) 249ff.

[8] G. THEISSEN, *ZTK* 70 (1973) 252, 256f.; *NTS* 21 (1974-75) 200. It is

The critical procedure which yielded this explanation of the sayings tradition [9] consisted of the two classical methods of form-criticism enhanced by a third, analogical step. Thus, *analysis* of the sayings' form and content, combined with *construction* of the tradition's course from direct testimonies of usage (e.g. the sub-apostolic witnesses), is supported by the analogy of contemporary propagandists, the vagabond Cynic preachers of the 2nd/3rd centuries, who also operated on hellenistic society's fringes and cultivated a radical, personal freedom by sundering earthly ties.[10] Form-criticism of the dominical precepts of discipleship and mission thus exerts a *sociological scrutiny* of such hard demands as provisionless journeys (Lk 10,4 Q),[11] *hatred* of family and earthly life (Lk 14,26 S). That such ideals were pursued in the religious climate of late hellenism, and that specifically Christian groups pursued them as part of a stewardship of the Saviour's own words, are secure conclusions from the extra-evangelical literature we have cited. If the gospel demands created the marginal social form of itinerant Christian radicalism and made it a limited but surprisingly durable movement in early Church history, we can confidently expect that the movement generated an equally limited but durable tradition of the teachings on which it was founded. And arguing conversely, we can expect that the charismatic life-style thus cultivated and preserved will have extensively determined the selection and casting of dominical words transmitted under its auspices. G. THEISSEN's suggestions in this matter are provocative and occasionally speculative, but it seems possible to work in the direction he has taken and see if it offers access to a better portraiture of the special traditions Luke took up in the gospel, and the Easter chapter in particular.

clearly sounder method to posit subsequent modifications and alterations of the tradition where the radical ethos of the dominical saying appears diluted or extenuated, as Hans G. KLEMM demonstrated in the case of the word about the burial of the dead by the dead (" Das Wort von der Selbstbestattung der Toten. Beobachtungen zur Auslegungsgeschichte von Mt. VIII.22 Par.," *NTS* 16 [1969-1970] 60-75, esp. 74).

[9] G. THEISSEN, *ZTK* 70 (1973) 248.

[10] G. KRETSCHMAR, *ZTK* 61 (1964) 35; M. HENGEL, *Nachfolge*, 31ff.; P. HOFFMANN, *Logienquelle*, 318f.; G. THEISSEN, *ZTK* 70 (1973) 255-256, and *NTS* 21 (1974-75) 210f. Cf. the observations of Epictetus on the Cynic wanderers, in *Diss.* 22,46-48, quoted by G. THEISSEN.

[11] The anomaly of the provisionless journey is documented in contemporary sources by P. HOFFMANN, *Logienquelle*, 315ff. Anyone embarking on a journey so meagerly provided for as the dominical instructions require would inevitably have aroused the curiosity and wonderment of his contemporaries. The messenger of Jesus, like the Baptist and even the Cynic wanderers, sought to implement his preaching by such demonstrative comportment. Renunciation of a traveler's normal provisions, just like the radical separation from family and possessions, functioned as a *prophetic sign* bespeaking a special vocation and a message that dramatically broke through the patterns of everyday. " Ihr ungewöhnliches Verhalten hat die Function eines Zeichens, es dient der Demonstration ihres Programms " (P. HOFFMANN, *op. cit.*, 320; cf. also S. SCHULZ, *Q*, 414-415; M. HENGEL, *Nachfolge*, 84 n. 146).

In point of fact, ideals of primitive radicalism and missionary charisma are found in all of the third gospel's substrata: Mk, Q, and the *Sondergut*. This shows, of course, that the personalization of Jesus' own standards of public ministry *ad rigorem*, in " charismatic " deed and radical ethic, was a uniquely influential factor in the development of a Jesus-tradition such as the gospels preserve.[12] An important step to be taken immediately, therefore, is the discernment of any specific patterns of roving missionaries' influence that might distinguish the special traditions of Luke, from which the appearance stories of Lk 24 were adopted. — Let us begin at the point where we discovered the strong analogy to the sequence of greeting and repast in 24,36ff., namely the journey instructions of the " discourse to the Seventy(-two)," [13] Lk 10,3ff.

---

[12] M. HENGEL, *Nachfolge*, 89-93. — By placing the word " charismatic " within quotation marks, we acknowledge that its use with special reference to the roving, enthusiastic messengers of Jesus is theologically inexact. One gives the word a narrower sense in this connection than it has, say, in I Cor 12. But since our application is widespread in the literature (cf. S. SCHULZ, *Q*, 53, 94-141; M. HENGEL, *Nachfolge*, 71, 97f., and sect. III *passim*; P. HOFFMANN, *Logienquelle*, 312-331, esp. 330), we choose to follow the narrower, but still broad-enough sense given the word by M. HENGEL: " ' Following ' and ' discipleship ', ' vocation ' and radical emancipation from all bonds arise precisely where old forms break up; they are ... dependent upon the activities of the *charismatic* personality that breaks through the restraints of the everyday. And that means, in the religious sphere, the personality of the *prophetic teacher* and *bearer of salvation* " (*Nachfolge*, 37). — A more specific description can be added from the depiction of the ' Q ' harbingers and their " prophetic charism " by P. HOFFMANN: " This charisma was brought to life by them also (i.e. as by the Baptist and Jesus — R. D.) in a world of ideas stamped by Apocalyptic, and it was borne along by proximate Parousia-expectation, revelation, and miracle-working powers " (*Logienquelle*, 330).

[13] For convenience sake, we adopt for the following discussion the originality of the reading " Seventy-two," following P-75 and " a combination of early witnesses that normally carries a high degree of conviction of originality," but acknowledging the ultimate inconclusiveness of both readings (Bruce M. METZGER, *The Text of the New Testament. Its Transmission, Corruption, and Restoration* [Oxford: Clarendon Press, 1964] 243-245). — Beside the studies of the " instruction to the emissaries " listed in chap. III, n. 92, we list the following as having been consulted for the present treatment: F. HAHN, *Mission*, 33-36; H. SCHÜRMANN, " Mt 10,5b-6 und die Vorgeschichte des synoptischen Aussendungsberichtes," in *Traditionsgeschichtliche Untersuchungen*, 137-149; H.-J. DEGENHARDT, *Lukas*, 63-66; M. HENGEL, *Nachfolge*, 82-89; P. HOFFMANN, " Lk 10,5-11 in der Instruktionsrede der Logienquelle," *EKK Vorarb.* III, 37-53; S. SCHULZ, *art. cit.* in n. 2 above.

(A) Rigorism in the " Instruction of the Seventy(-two) " :

We cannot undertake the complicated tradition-analysis of the synoptic *Aussendungsrede* in its several, remarkably divergent forms, but we recall the discussions, previously cited (chap. III, n. 92), which have sought to fix the text of " Q " in this sector. Results have not been conclusive despite the doublet instructions in Lk and the supposition that Lk 10 should furnish a firm basis of comparison with Mt for an ultimate demarcation of the source-text.[14] Whether, and to what extent, Lk 10,2-12(16) represents the Q-text Luke read, we shall not attempt to decide. We shall devote our attention rather to the consistency between the instructions of 10,2ff. and the framework in which they have been placed, the " commission of the Seventy-two " (Lk 10,1.17-20), which is found only in Luke's gospel.

Most seem to judge that the dispatch and return of the " Seventy-two," although it includes fragments of traditions of diverse provenance, is an editorial framework constructed by the evangelist for the Q mission instruction and fitted to the latter by him for the first time.[15] *Transeat*, for the moment, although we think this may not be completely true. We note, first, that the Master's response to the wayfarers on their return makes much more pointed reference than is usually recognized to the *travel without provisions* which was mandated at the outset of the instruction (Lk 10,4/Mt 10,10 ; cp. Lk 9,3/Mk 6,8). Here was the source of the wanderers' radical life-style ! Without a weapon,[16] or footwear (Lk 10,4/Mt 10,10 *versus* Mk 6,9), money or extra clothing (*omnes*), they were truly defenseless " lambs in the midst of wolves " (Lk 10,3/Mt 10,16). Thus drastically did they display their commission as the prophetic harbingers of the *peace* of the imminent kingdom of God (cf. p. 188 above). The only protection they had against the hazards of such unequipped travel was, in fact, their invincible protection : the promise by the Lord of the mission, οὐδὲν ὑμᾶς οὐ

[14] The analyses of P. Hoffmann and S. Schulz, cited in chap. III, n. 92 above, frequently stop short of a final judgment on the original ' Q ' wording in this section, despite the uniquely favorable situation of the texts (i.e. the Lucan doublet instruction) for such a determination. Even if Lk stands systematically closer to the source text than Mt, as both Hoffmann and Schulz opine, the vocabulary differences that defy any decisive source-identification suggest that one may be dealing with *different recensions of the Q instruction* that lay before Mt and Lk respectively.

[15] E. Klostermann, *Lk.*, 113 ; R. Bultmann, *GsT*, 359 ; G. Baumbach, *Das Verständnis des Bösen*, 178-184 ; F. Hahn, *Mission*, 33 ; P. Hoffmann, *Logienquelle*, 249 ; M. Miyoshi, *Anfang des Reiseberichts*, 26, 59-62, 73, 110-119 ; D. Lührmann, *Redaktion*, 60f. ; G. Lohfink, *Sammlung Israels*, 68ff.

[16] The " staff " is prohibited in Mt 10,10 but goes unmentioned in Lk 10,4. On the other hand, the single staff is permitted in Mk 6,8, but prohibited in

μὴ ἀδικήσει (Lk 10,19).[17] As prelude to this promise, and to document it,[18] Jesus points to the successes of the mission just concluded, announcing the authority he has bestowed (*perfect* tense) upon them : ἰδοὺ δέδωκα ὑμῖν τὴν ἐξουσίαν τοῦ πατεῖν ἐπάνω ὄφεων καὶ σκορπίων, καὶ ἐπὶ πᾶσαν τὴν δύναμιν τοῦ ἐχθροῦ. The demonic adversary whose fall was envisioned at v. 18 (echoing Is 14,12)[19] is seen as the *mission's adversary*, and the missionaries' power over him is proclaimed with an unmistakable allusion to Psalm (90)91,13. Unmistakable, indeed, only why are the " scorpions " substituted in the Master's statement for the psalmist's " lions " ? The defenders of a purely symbolic, demonic meaning in v. 19 are embarrassed by this question,[20] whereas a literal

---

Luke's reproduction of the Marcan instruction (Lk 9,3). This would seem to indicate that Luke was correcting Mk in favor of the greater rigorism of the Q instruction, and perhaps he did not record the " staff " prohibition at 10,4 because it had already been spoken at 9,3, just as he avoided Mk's allowance of the travelers' " sandals " at 9,3 in order to record the prohibition at 10,4 (= Mt 10,10). The operation in both Lucan instructions seems to be our evangelist's typical coordination of his sources, so chances are the " staff " prohibition is original in Q (P. HOFFMANN, *Logienquelle*, 266). — On the use of the " staff " as traveler's protective weapon to ward off threatening animals and men, cf. P. HOFFMANN, *op. cit.*, 313f., 324 ; G. THEISSEN, *ZTK* 70 (1973) 258f. n. 36.

[17] G. BAUMBACH, *Verständnis des Bösen*, 182 : " Luk. 10,19 enthält gewissermassen das Motto, das man über die Apostelgeschichte und damit über die gesamte lukanische Darstellung des christlichen Mission stellen könnte." Similarly P. HOFFMANN, *Logienquelle*, 252. — One thinks of Acts 28,3-6, where Paul's snakebite verifies the promise of Lk 10,19 (BAUMBACH, *op. cit.*, 280 ; HOFFMANN, *op. cit.*, 250 n. 58).

[18] As against G. BAUMBACH, *Verständnis des Bösen*, 181, I do not believe the " power to tread upon snakes and scorpions " is simply a figurative expression of " the subjection of the surreptitious and dangerous powers of the evil one," through allusion to Ps 91,13. The comparable texts B. cites are all instances of Satan's role as *tempter* (Lk 4,3ff. ; 22,31 ; Acts 5,3ff. ; 13,10f.), whereas the present case is quite different. Here Satan's defeat is suffered in his role as *source of dangerous hazards to the missionary*, as exemplified in Mk 16,17f. and Acts 28,3-6. That is why I should rather take Lk 10,19a in *literal reference* to the mission's physical hazards, not as mere figurative duplication of καὶ επὶ πᾶσαν δύναμιν τοῦ ἐχθροῦ, κτλ.

[19] J. SCHMID, *Lk.*, 187 ; (and with other Jewish parallels :) A. R. C. LEANEY, *Lk*, 179. J. SCHMID explains that Jesus' vision is not of Satan's fall from divine favor and consignment to the earthly realm (as in Apoc 12,10-12), but of his fall from the position of power over man that he held heretofore (cp. Jn 12,31 ; 16,11). It is thus an anticipation of his final fall from power that will mark the end of the age (*Ascen. Moysis* 10,1 ; *Jub.* 23,29 ; *Test. Sim.* 6 ; *Test. Jud.* 25).

[20] E.g. G. BAUMBACH, *Verständnis des Bösen*, 180f., who is unable to present Jewish texts illustrative of the scorpion as demonic figure, hence can only suggest that it has been substituted for " lions " in our text because scorpions are more secretive and their danger more unforeseen. B. has to admit that the " scorpion " texts adduced in Str.-Bill. II, 168 have a literal rather than a

understanding in terms of special hazards to the *unshodden wayfarer* (→ Lk 10,4) makes the substitution sensible. The Lord's promise is thus the mission's triumph over the "enemy" working against it through harmful forces in nature,[21] as well as any other δύναμις he could muster. His special recourse to natural hazards is a crafty tactic against those vocationally bound, by the very program of the mission given in the preceding verses, to be defenseless and unarmed. A related mission hazard is specified in the Easter commission of the Marcan postscript, a passage closely parallel to the one at hand: "... if they should take any lethal drink, it will not harm them" (Mk 16,18). Again, this promise would appear gratuitous, except it be understood as a protection of those obliged to take their food and drink from others along the road.[22] In other words, the Lord's hard demands on his legates are closely related to the reassurance he gave to them. The two would seem to emanate from *the same tradition*.

A further connection of Lk 10,17ff. to the passage it concludes can be found in the vision of Satan's fall, v. 18, which allusively invokes Is 14,12 after Is 14,13 was explicitly cited in v. 15 (= Mt 11,23 Q) to depict proud Capernaum's punishment. The power of the adversary was exerted through the Galilean cities' resistance to the missionaries,[23]

---

figurative meaning, but insists this proves nothing! Cf. also P. HOFFMANN, *Logienquelle*, 250 and n. 57, who, besides asserting that the boundaries between literal and figurative use of animals in ancient texts are "fluid," was able to add nothing to BAUMBACH's case for a purely figurative sense. Cf. Dt 8,15.

[21] Rightly J. SCHMID, *Lk*, 187f. — That the Q injunction was of *unshodden* travel, not simply a restriction to a single pair of sandals (as in Mk 6,9), is clear from Mt 10,10 and Lk 22,35, so one should not stress the βαστάζειν of Lk 10,4, with its multiple object, as indication that "a change of shoes" is the extent of the Lucan prohibition (*pace* H.-J. DEGENHARDT, *Lukas*, 65; also A. PLUMMER, *Lk*, 273). The Q-text and Lk require the emissaries to journey *barefoot* (rightly J. M. CREED, *Lk*, 145; E. E. ELLIS, *Lk*, 154 [citing the NEB], and most of the commentaries; also P. HOFFMANN, *Logienquelle*, 267, 314f.; S. SCHULZ, *Q*, 414f.; M. HENGEL, *Nachfolge*, 84 n. 146).

[22] An interesting parallel between the Marcan postscript text and Luke's "return of the Seventy-two" is the sense of ἐν τῷ ὀνόματί μου/σου in both instances (Mk 16,17f./Lk 10,17). Just as the "*charismatic*" aspect of acting in Jesus' "Name" is highlighted in Mk 16,17f., in contrast to the liturgical sense of Mt 28,19 (cf. F. HAHN, *Mission*, 54; G. BORNKAMM, "Der Auferstandene und der Irdische," in E. Dinkler, hrsg., *Zeit und Geschichte. Dankesgabe an R. Bultmann* [Tübingen, 1964, 171-191] 179 n. 39), so also is the ὄνομα the source of *miraculous power* in Lk 10,17ff., as in Acts 19,13.17, painting a picture of the missionary as "medium of the power of Jesus" and agent of a "pneumatic demonstration" (cf. D. GEORGI, *Gegner des Paulus*, 213; P. HOFFMANN, *Logienquelle*, 252f.).

[23] E. KÄSEMANN, *Exegetische Versuche* ... II, 98: "Offensichtlich sind auch Chorazin and Bethsaida (in den Evangelien sonst nicht erwähnt) Ziele frühchristlicher Mission in Galiläa gewesen, die man nicht erobern konnte." Cf. also R. BULTMANN, *GsT*, 117f.; D. LÜHRMANN, *Redaktion*, 64; S. SCHULZ, *Q*, 362ff.

hence their doom and his under the sovereign judgment of God can find expression in the same scriptural passage. — This is further evidence that the conclusion of the deputation of the " Seventy-two " looks back upon the words of their instruction and translates them into a promise of their certain success. What has made their mission invincible, despite its material privations, is the only genuine motive of their rejoicing: service of God's rule and membership among his elect (Lk 10,20).[24] One is put in mind here of the Lord's query raised at the end of the Last Supper instruction, likewise drawn from the *Sondergut* and referring explicitly to the instruction of the Seventy-two: ὅτε ἀπέστειλα ὑμᾶς κτλ. ..., μή τινος ὑστερήσατε; to which, of course, the answer: Οὐθένος (Lk 22,35).[25] The certainty of the mission's success is thus a paradox: the messengers are destitute from every human perspective, and yet their imponderable cause, the hidden Kingdom of God (Lk 17,20f.), will not be stopped by the powerful and resourceful enemy!

There is consequently a substantial consistency between these words of consolation to the missionaries, tendered by Luke's special source, and the mission instructions of the common sources. Furthermore, there is this special affinity between the Lucan *Sonderquelle* and the instructions of Q: in both, the demands are of an undiluted *rigor*, whereas Mk begins to display some measures of practical accomodation: *one* staff is permitted in his version, and so are sandals (Mk 6,8f. *versus*

[24] Lk 10,20 does not seem to place an eschatological proviso on the mission's victory over Satan (*pace* H. CONZELMANN, *MdZ*, 98) since the relation of Lk 10,18f. to the mission conquests of Acts suggests itself strongly as our author's perspective (rightly G. BAUMBACH, *Verständnis des Bösen*, 182f.). On the other hand, it does not seem adequate to read v. 20 as simply a warning against complacency after exorcizing successes (*pace* BAUMBACH). It seems more likely to serve the demarcation between the miraculous displays of the heroic past, recounted in the gospel and Acts, and the present phase of the mission that involved the evangelist and his contemporaries. As P. HOFFMANN writes, " Lukas bereitet die Ablösung von der ' heroischen ' Zeit des Anfangs vor, indem er — wiederum schon in der Zeit Jesu — das ' Eigentliche ' nennt, das auch den Späteren — seinen Zeitgenossen nämlich — bleiben wird, (nur noch oder gerade) die Freude über das ihnen geschenkte ewige Heil " (*Logienquelle*, 253).

[25] Cf. pp. 205ff. above. If Lk 22,35-38 does derive substantially from pre-Lucan tradition (but, perhaps, for v. 37a and v. 38), then one can suggest that Καὶ μετὰ ἀνόμων ἐλογίσθη expressed precisely the social stigma that lay upon Jesus' wandering emissaries in view of their departure from mainstream-society's standards. It was conceivably just such a " classification " that was given them when they were *in statu confessionis*, the situation for which, presumably, the reversal of the earlier mission ideals was found necessary (cf. H. SCHÜRMANN, *Abendmahlsbericht*, 61ff.). SCHÜRMANN, too, sensed the " existential " connection of this passage with " Wanderapostel und Evangelisten " (*ibid.*, 67). During times of persecution, provision had to be made for the fact that " doors of hospitality were no longer opened to them " (*ibid.* 63), and this may be the situation reflected in the supper instruction's enigmatic conclusion.

Lk 9,3; → 10,4/Mt 10,10).[26] Similarly stark rigorism over against the Marcan tradition can be seen in the sayings on discipleship, where the Q couplet disqualifying one who does not *hate* family and life with him who fails to shoulder the cross (Lk 14,26f.) has either been softened by Mt (10,37f.; cp. Mk 8,34f.) or hardened in the pre-Lk circle. Whether the rest of the series in Lk 14,26-33 was also transmitted in Q is difficult to decide, but it obviously sustains and thematizes the radical ethic of the two key sayings shared with Mt. One is inclined to think in terms of *different recensions of the Q material*, the one of Luke's employment being produced and amplified by a group of particularly rigoristic ideals! The razor-edge of their mode of discipleship is best felt, in fact, in the apophthegms of Lk 9,57-62, which are actually a Q-series (Mt 8,18-22) giving memorable expression to the complete rupture of earthly ties involved in the following of the Master.[27]

Our tentative suggestion, based on these observations, is that Luke obtained his recension of the Q material from the same auspices as furnished his special tradition of the dominical teachings.[28] At least

[26] The secondary mitigation of the mission instruction's requirements in Mk 6, *vis-à-vis* Q, is noted by F. HAHN, *Mission*, 35; P. HOFFMANN, *Logienquelle*, 239ff., 266; M. HENGEL, *Nachfolge*, 84; S. SCHULZ, *Q*, 415 n. 83.

[27] M. HENGEL, *Nachfolge*, 5: "die harte Bedingungslosigkeit ..."; H. G. KLEMM "Das Wort von der Selbstbestattung der Toten," *NTS* 16 (1969-70, 60-75) 64: "Wer so redet, lässt nicht mit sich reden." Cf. also S. SCHULZ, *Q*, 440ff. — Whether or not the third apophthegm (Lk 9,61f.) belonged already to the Q series that Matthew read (cf. the divided opinions documented by S. SCHULZ, *op. cit.*, 435 n. 239), Luke's passage distinguishes itself also by a special application of the uncompromising dominical summons to the *work of the Kingdom's traveling herald* (v. 60b: σὺ δὲ ἀπελθὼν διάγγελε τὴν βασιλείαν τοῦ θεοῦ. Cp. v. 62: εὔθετός ἐστιν τῇ βασιλείᾳ τοῦ θεοῦ) (H. G. KLEMM, *NTS* 16 [1969-70] 63). The anticipation of the "Kingdom of God," *Leitmotiv* of the mission instruction, in these two instances (cp. Lk 10,9.11) makes it likely that Luke found the vocation apophthegms and the mission instruction already adjoining each other in his version of Q (rightly H. KLOSTERMANN, *Lk.*, 112). It is completely plausible, too, that his version of Q already displayed some of the special touches that differentiate his vocation apophthegms from Matthew's (cf. F. HAHN, *Christologische Hoheitstitel*, 83 n. 4).

[28] It remains an unanswered question of gospel criticism whether the special traditions of Mt and Lk constitute independent entities or further developments of the tradition designated "Q" (S. SCHULZ, *Q*, 41f., D. LÜHRMANN, *Redaktion*, 105ff.), and in the case of Matthew the further development of the same saying tradition in the *Sondergut* has been suggested more than once (cf. O. H. STECK, *Israel und das gewaltsame Geschick* ..., 306f. n. 8, citing G. STRECKER; D. LÜHRMANN, *Redaktion der Logienquelle*, 112f.; but cf. W. G. KÜMMEL, *Introduction*[17], 109). The same suggestion is made re. Lk by D. LÜHRMANN, *Redaktion*, 73f., 82f., 105. The analyses of H. SCHÜRMANN dedicated to tracing segments of "Q" in passages peculiar to both Matthew and Luke (*Traditionsgeschichtliche Untersuchungen*, 116ff., 112ff.) may have proved too hypothetical and mechanical, but a path of investigation was indicated thereby (*ibid.*, 125) that has not been widely followed, perhaps because of the enthusiasms of *Redaktionsgeschichte*.

in some cases, such as the " mission of the Seventy-two " and the severe instruction of Lk 14,26-33, the literary fusion of these strata had already taken place before Luke wrote. Lk 10,1-20(24), allowing for special tailoring by the evangelist in his familiar style (as in v. 1), would thus have been a pre-Lucan literary unit, including a return from the " mission " much like that of the parallel Marcan sequence (Mk 6,30 *ad* 6,7-13).[29] In that case, such distinctive items as the two-step household protocol (10,5-7), not integrally reproduced in Matthew, would derive from the greater rigorism and more punctual transmissions of Luke's *tradentes*.[30] This is the group, we suggest, whose tradition of the cenacle christophany was structured according to the two steps that these austere mendicants undoubtedly followed, as they did all the Lord's directives, *ad rigorem* !

When SCHÜRMANN also argued for the " Q " provenance of Luke's Nazareth episode (*Lk.*, I, 227f., 234, 239, 241) and Lk 10, 17-20 (*Trad. Unt.*, 146 n. 37), his method might still have been faulty but his suggestion of the tradition-historical problem was valuable. — The pursuit of tradition-historical connections between " Q " and *Sondergut* passages is shown to be methodologically sound by the basic fact that material of the sayings source cannot be positively delimited, only inferred when Mt and Lk coincide apart from Mk (W. G. KÜMMEL, *Introduction*[17], 67ff.). Since omissions by either evangelist must always be considered possible, the mere absence of a passage from the Matthean or Lucan parallel text cannot be considered to exclude its derivation from the " Q " substratum a priori. And where one evangelist is found to have material that is thematically or stylistically complementary to that which both share, one can suggest different stages of the common tradition's development, as has been discussed more frequently in relation to S-Mt (cf. also P. HOFFMANN, *Logienquelle*, 2). The different forms of Q in Mt and Lk are " plausible ... (but) quite speculative," according to J. FITZMYER, in *Jesus and Man's Hope* I, (131-170) 154 ; favored by W. G. KÜMMEL, *Introd. N.T.*, 69.

[29] It is equally possible that Lk 10, 17 is a Lucan imitation of Mk 6,30/Lk 9,10 (*pace* P. HOFFMANN, *Logienquelle*, 249), even though neither of those conclusions directly adjoined the words of instruction as this one does ; nor does Luke himself usually express the ἐξουσία exerted in Jesus' name in terms of subjection of the demons alone. Indeed, his practice is to combine exorcisms and healing miracles under the one term, θεραπεύειν (cf. Lk 9,6 [Mk 6,13] with Lk 9,1/Mk 6,7 ; cf. P. HOFFMANN, *Logienquelle*, 246). It is plausible, nevertheless that Lk 10,17 is due mainly to Luke's redaction since it forms a transition from v. 16 to v. 18 and thus creates characteristic literary symmetry between the " missions " of the Twelve and the Seventy-two (H. FLENDER, *Heil und Geschichte*, 26), especially in view of the fact that the perspective of the mission completed (v. 17) seems in less than full accord with the provision for the future mission in v. 19. — Redactional creation of v. 17 on the basis of the " strange Exorcist " episode (Lk 9), *pace* M. MIYOSHI (*Anfang*, 110, 119), is not very obvious to our eye.

[30] The different versions of the " household protocol " in Mt and Lk caused T. W. MANSON to derive Lk 10, 4-7 (as well as 10,1.17-20) from Luke's special source rather than from Q. MANSON considered Lk 10, 1-20 to be compounded of " Q " and " L " source-material, and we believe he had a point in this (cf.

So far, our position is only tentative. It needs further support through motif-analysis, and ultimately it will require the kind of literary analysis and refinement that we cannot give it in the confines of the present study.

(B) Hospitality toward the Indigent Wayfarers:

After renunciation of home and possessions, and travelling without any provisions, the itinerant spokesmen of Jesus could lay claim to food and shelter from those who hearkened to them along the way: ἄξιος γὰρ ὁ ἐργάτης τῆς τροφῆς αὐτοῦ (Mt 10,10). They were not truly beggars, for it was not to their listeners' charity that they appealed; lodging and board was due them in justice, as recompense for the *work* of heralding God's kingdom in word and deed (Lk 10,7.9).[31] The impression of begging and parasitism undoubtedly stigmatized them, as it did their pagan counterparts, in the view of mainstream hellenistic society; hence it is no surprise to find provisions against wayfarers' abuses in the Christian literature that documents their mission activities.[32] Nevertheless, the believer's obligation to take the wandering ἐργάτης in was most sacred and serious, for it was based on the christological principle which inspired this whole " charismatic " endeavour: *the guest thus entertained was really Christ himself*, and one " received " him ὡς Κύριον (*Did.* XI, 2; cp. Mt 10,40/Lk 10,16).[33] The NT vocabulary attached to this hospitality theme, the verb δέχεσθαι (Lk 9,5[Mk]; 10,8.10[Q]; Mt 10,40ff.) with its compounds, and the verb ξενίζειν, happens to enjoy an unusually frequent usage in the

The Sayings of Jesus, 74; and, in agreement, J. Roloff, *Apostolat-Verkündigung-Kirche*, 151 n. 53).

[31] Cf. I Cor 9,4f.14, and G. Theissen, *ZTK* 70 (1973) 260; *NTS* 21 (1974-75) 196, 198f., 205ff., etc. Also Adolf von Harnack, *Mission und Ausbreitung* I, 183f.; H. Conzelmann, *Geschichte des Urchristentums* (NTD Ergänzungsreihe 5; Göttingen: Vandenhoeck und Ruprecht, 1969) 49; P. Hoffmann, *Logienquelle*, 301f.; S. Schulz, *Q Spruchquelle*, 417. — Cf. the application of the principle to " every true prophet who wishes to settle among you " in *Did.* 13,1f.

[32] Cf. *Did.* 11,5-6, placing limits on the hospitality obligation in order to avoid parasitical abuse (cf. J.-P. Audet, *La Didaché: Instructions des Apôtres* [Études bibliques; Paris: J. Gabalda et Cie., 1958] 444f.). It is possible, too, that the synoptic injunction not to pass from house to house (Lk 10,7; Mk 6, 10) was an attempt to avoid the abuses associated with mendicants (G. Theissen, *ZTK* 70 [1973] 259). The contempt in which mainstream society held the mendicants, even in the ancient world, is explained by G. Theissen: " Was sich selbst als religiös begründete Freiheit gegenüber den fundamentalen sozialen Bindungen verstand, konnte von aussen als arbeitsscheues Vagabundentum erscheinen " (*ZTK* 70 [1973] 263).

[33] E. Käsemann, *Exegetische Versuche* II, 89ff.; G. Kretschmar, *ZTK* 61 (1963) 45f.; G. Theissen, *ZTK* 70 (1973) 254 and n. 26.

two Lucan volumes,[34] and in the gospel it occurs prominently where Jesus himself, in the role of protomissionary, is taken in as a wayfaring guest by Martha (Lk 10,38 : ὑπεδέξατο) and Zacchaeus (Lk 19,6 : ὑπεδέξατο). These are both passages of Luke's *Sondergut*, where in fact, as was pointed out before (p. 202), the situation of Jesus entertained as a guest at others' table is a predilection bequeathed to the evangelist. — The special features of the two ὑποδέχεσθαι passages are worth taking note of.

The Martha pericope seems to deal with an equivocation that arose in the hosting of itinerant preachers.[35] Just as, *ex parte hospitis*, there was to be no passing from house to house in quest of finer accomodations (Lk 10,7),[36] so also, *ex parte hospitae*, there was not to be so much care (μεριμνᾶν) lavished on the accomodation of the traveler that his words of instruction, ἡ ἀγαθὴ μερίς, could not be attended to. This admonition, too, came from the rigorous self-renunciation of the wandering " charismatics " : their worldly needs, like the Lord's of whom they were fully authorized surrogates, were minimal and to be met with a sheer sufficiency, nothing more ! " The temptation to riches was to be repulsed by allowing only a sufficiency of earthly life's requirements and maintaining the radical priority of God's kingdom over all else." [37] — Zacchaeus, on the other hand, represents the " charismatic " renunciation from another perspective : the companionship, hence also common board, that Jesus' emissaries were obliged by his example to have with society's outcasts (Lk 19,7). — In both these special Lucan pericopes, the principle of their relevance to the lives of the special tradition's exponents was the " charismatic " conviction of *representing Christ's person* (Mt 10,40) and *being his authentic voice* (Lk 10,16). Therefore, as the story itself was told about the Master, the point was being made for the benefit of his itinerant ambassadors ! [38]

---

[34] H. J. CADBURY, *The Making*, 251-253 ; Erling LALAND, " Die Martha-Maria-Perikope Lukas 10,38-42. Ihre kerygmatische Aktualität für das Leben der Urkirche," *ST* 13 (1959, 70-85) 72f.

[35] E. LALAND, *ST* 13 (1959) 77ff. Some of LALAND's description of the *Sitz-im-Leben* of this pericope is quite speculative, but the basic point is, I think, sound.

[36] At least, such is the interpretation of the saying advocated by THEISSEN (cf. note 32 above) and supported by P. HOFFMANN, *Logienquelle*, 302 (although the latter is not sure it is original to Q since Luke might have adopted it from Mk 6,10 [but cf. Lk 9,4] ; cf. HOFFMANN, *op. cit.*, 274). Cf. the similar explanations advanced by A. PLUMMER, *Lk*, 274f., and H. SCHÜRMANN, *Lk.* I, 502.

[37] E. LALAND, *ST* 13 (1959) 82.

[38] The equivalence of the missionary's roles of spokesman (Lk 10,16) and personal representative (Mt 10,40) is borne out by the fact that the verb δέχεσθαι can take alternately the speaker (Mt 10,40) and his words (Lk 8,13 ; Acts 8,14 ; 11,1 ; 17,11) as object. In materials derived from the "charismatic" mission, as

The episode of Zacchaeus introduces us to the strong motif of *solidarity with the downtrodden* which is an understandable reflection of the vagrant missionaries' consignment to society's fringes. Their rejection of home, family, and possessions, together with their appearance of vagrant beggars, must have made them "prophets," like their Master, no longer δεκτοί in their fatherland (cf. Lk 4,24 *diff.* Mk). It is interesting that, in the Lucan version of this "rejected-prophet" maxim, the adjective has been changed from Mark's ἄτιμοι to one related to the verb of hospitality used in the passages we have been surveying.

(C) Guest and Host of the Unworthy:

The lifestyle of the itinerant enthusiasts would be, of course, a serious breach of polite society's code in any age. Indeed, the harsher and more radical renunciations usually bring the more vehement social ostracism. It is no surprise, therefore, that the special Lucan tradition we are studying, where the radical ethos gets perhaps the severest expression of all the gospel voices, should also record memorable scenes of Jesus, as traveler and guest, ministered to by the lowly and despised (cf. p. 202 above). We might speculate, too, about the existential background of the tradition in Lk 22,35ff., especially in view of its feature of solidarity between Master and disciples, in prospect of tribulations, noting that he (and they ?) "was counted among outlaws" (22,37).

A particularly impressive passage of the *Sondergut*, which ironically combines the prophet-character and unworthy company of Jesus as houseguest, is the account of the sinful woman who attended to the Master and won forgiveness from him, Lk 7,36-50. The unevenness and tradition-historical complexity of this narrative are notorious and cannot occupy us at any length.[39] In a brief treatment of its problems in chapter 1 (cf. note 31), however, we subscribed to a gradual assimilation of traditions that made an original paradigm of repentance and forgiveness into an episode of the *hospitality* denied the Lord by the "righteous" and lavished on him by the disenfranchised. At the level of Luke's redaction, we recall, detail was added from the Bethany

---

M. Hengel has suggested, "'Jesusüberlieferung' und 'Gemeindebildung' in nahezu untrennbarer Weise ineinandergeflossen sind" (*Nachfolge*, 92).

[39] Aside from our brief reference to Lk 7,36-50 above (chap I, pp. 11f. and nn. 29-31), we refer the reader to U. Wilckens' list of principal difficulties raised by the pericope (in *Orientierung an Jesus*, 397f.); (1) relationship of parable (vv. 41-42) to the rest of the narrative; (2) interpretation of the parable (vv. 44-47), applying the latter to the situation narrated in a way that cannot be verified in the narrative's exposition (vv. 37f.); (3) the relationship of the anointing to the action of cleansing and drying Jesus' feet (v. 38); (4) the relationship of the two, clearly reciprocal clauses of v. 47; (5) the forgiveness, on

anointing of Mk 14,3-9, whereupon a note of burial preparation was sounded which was otherwise quite foreign to the story. In her present place in Luke's story, therefore, the repentant woman serves to illustrate the connection between the healed and exorcized women who served Jesus in Galilee and the corps of Easter witnesses (Lk 8,2-3; 24,10). But such was not the pericope's original intention.

As U. WILCKENS has pointed out,[40] the story's élan is diffused over two different exchanges, one between Jesus and the pharisee that terminates at v. 47, the other between Jesus and the woman with terminus at v. 50. The main issue of the first exchange is the love that responds to forgiveness, whereas the issue of the second exchange turns out to be the woman's faith. Although it is difficult to diagnose the points of secondary accretion with detailed accuracy, it is reasonably clear that the dual movement is not perfectly meshed and comes at least partially from secondary additions. The most striking symptom of this occurs at vv. 44-46: Jesus contrasts the woman's penitential gestures with Simon's deficient *hospitality*, although no suggestion of such deficiency was made in the initial exposition (vv. 37-38) and v. 38 hardly depicts gestures a guest would rightfully expect of his host.[41] These verses (44-46) therefore present the strongest evidence of secondary attachment, and so also, therefore, does the theme of hospitality.[42]

---

the one hand already given, according to the parable, and motive of the woman's loving ministrations, on the other hand first pronounced to the woman in v. 48; (6) relationship of v. 50, now pronouncing the woman's faith as motive of her actions, to v. 48 and what precedes it; (7) relationship of this pericope to the Marcan anointing at Bethany, Mk 14,3ff. — These matters raise questions of literary criticism and suggest points of secondary development which cannot be simply passed over, as they mostly are in a study like Hans DREXLER's, *ZNW* 59 (1968) 159-173.

[40] In *Orientierung an Jesus*, 416. — The clear inconsistency of vv. 48-50 with what precedes it is dealt with by most exegetes with a declaration that these verses are a secondary addition, probably the result of Luke's own adaptation of elements from the Marcan healing/forgiveness of the paralytic (Mk 2,5ff./Lk 5,20ff.; cf. R. BULTMANN, *GsT*, 19; E. KLOSTERMANN, *Lk.*, 92; W. GRUNDMANN, *Lk.*, 170; J. SCHMID, *Lk.*, 149f.; H. SCHÜRMANN, *Lk.* I, 440f. [S-Lk, not Luke]; J. DELOBEL, *ETL* 42 [1966] 465; R. GLÖCKNER, *Verkündigung*, 150f.). The analysis of WILCKENS is more nuanced, for he recognized that the considerations urging a secondary assimilation of vv. 48-49 are not necessarily telling against v. 50 (*Orientierung an Jesus*, 411f.). Moreover, H. DREXLER is quite right that v. 47 could not have concluded the "sinful woman" pericope; a direct word to the woman has been awaited and is formally required (*ZNW* 59 [1968] 171).

[41] H. SCHÜRMANN, *Lk.*, I 435-436; U. WILCKENS, in *Orientierung an Jesus*, 399-400.

[42] Advocating the secondary character of vv. 44ff., besides SCHÜRMANN and WILCKENS, are R. BULTMANN, *GsT* Ergänzungsheft[4], 21; E. HAENCHEN, *Weg Jesu*, 471; J. ROLOFF, *Kerygma*, 162f. and n. 204; J. DELOBEL, *ETL* 42 (1966) 467f.; G. BOUWMAN, *ETL* 45 (1969) 174f.

A contrast between the pharisee's and the woman's *accueil* seems not to have been the focus of the oldest version of the story, whereas it was very much the focus of potential interest among the roving missionaries we have been discussing. If they came to narrate this episode at a certain point of its transmission, we can readily imagine their adding to it a reflection of their own experience of a wayfarer's contrasting receptions! Their own accomodations had probably to be found most often amongst people like the repentant woman, whereas citizens of stature offered them scant welcome.[43] It was thus under their influence as his *tradentes,* rather than at Luke's own hand,[44] that the woman's story acquired vv. 44-46 and its hospitality counterpoint.

Correspondingly, one might suggest that, in the itinerant enthusiasts' telling, the story's basic challenge to Jesus shifted from the fact of his forgiving sin to the manner of people whose attentions he accepted. Whether or not they added it, the missionaries would have cherished the irony of the challenge in v. 39, which consists not only in the expectation of a prophetic denunciation of the sinner but also in the basic kind of prophetic word Jesus is expected to speak. The prophet's *scrutinium cordis* is expected to yield a word of condemnation, whereas Jesus' "prophecy" is his word of *acceptance and forgiveness* of the sinner! Here the story's irony yields an understanding of dominical *prophecy* that is displayed prominently in Luke's special tradition. We have already observed the close connection of eschatological prophecy

[43] This *Sitz-im-Leben* for the secondary hospitality-motif of the "sinful woman" pericope has been suggested by G. Bouwman (*ETL* 45 [1969] 177ff.) and, following him, G. Theissen, *ZTK* 70 (1973) 263f. n. 51. Cf. also G. Theissen, *NTS* 21 (1974-75) 198f.

[44] Most of the sentiment documented in n. 42 above seems to favor the contribution of vv. 44-46 by Luke himself, and G. Bouwman specifically made the conflict between "Christian pharisees" and the wandering apostles over accepting hospitality from the unworthy "le *Sitz-im-Leben* générateur de la rédaction de Lc VII,36-50" (*ETL* 45 [1969] 178). But it was precisely by insisting on the hospitality of the unworthy as a special *Lucan* interest, carried over from the gospel to the Acts, that Bouwman became vulnerable to the rejoinder of J. Delobel ("Encore la pécheresse. Quelques réflexions critiques," *ETL* 45 [1969] 180-183) that his was an "affirmation séduisante mais gratuite" (182). Delobel is correct that the motif of unworthy hostesses is not emphasized in Acts, hence it is difficult to prove a redactional consistency between the two volumes in this respect. In our view, on the other hand, the hosting of outcasts by outcasts was a theme of the tradition utilized by Luke, but not necessarily one of his own predilection throughout his writing. We think it possible, therefore, to preserve Bouwman's suggested *Sitz-im-Leben* for the secondary development of the "sinful woman" pericope without making Luke himself responsible for that development. In this, as in the suggestion of pre-redactional associations between this pericope and its present neighboring materials in the gospel (Lk 7,31-35-Q ; Lk 8,2-3 S), we find ourselves in agreement with H. Schürmann, *Lk.* I, 440f., 448, at least so far as Lk 8,2-3 is concerned. (According to S., the pre-redactional sequence was Lk 7,11-17. 36-50 ; 8,2-3.)

and the forgiveness of sins in the construction of the Isaian *lectio divina* at Nazareth (Lk 4,18 ; cf. pp. 137, 214 above). Not only the two-fold ἄδεκτος but the four-fold designation of the messiah's downtrodden audience — πτωχοί, αἰχμάλωτοι, τυφλοί, τεθραυσμένοι — demonstrates the perspective from which the citation was fashioned.[45] Both passages, the " sinful woman " and the Nazareth instruction, come from Luke's *Sondergut*. Both feature references to Jesus as " prophet " (Lk 4,24 ; 7,39), and both locate his " prophecy " in the pronouncement of the forgiveness of sins, which gives the messiah a solidarity with the " poor," the " captive," and the " oppressed," while it makes him a προφήτης ἄδεκτος amongst the righteous householders of traditional Judaism. In the understanding of Luke's rigoristic *Sondertradenten*, the Lord continued to speak the prophetic word of forgiveness, and to find *accueil* only amongst the disinherited, as he extended his mission through his " charismatic " surrogates !

Questions of the special tradition's links with Q can also be raised at this point in our inquiry. The " sinful woman " episode is closely related to the Q passage that precedes it, as both an illustration of Jesus' friendship with τελῶναι καὶ ἁμαρτωλοί (Lk 7,34 Q) and a concrete instance of the sharply contrasting responses given God's prophetic spokesmen by Jewish officialdom and the Jewish subculture (Lk 7,29f./ = Mt 21,32). It is true that Lk 7,29f. shows unmistakable signs of the hand of Luke himself,[46] especially in its separation of πᾶς ὁ λαός (cp. ἀπὸ πάντων κτλ., v. 35) from the pharisaic leadership and its apparent concern to subject only the latter to the verdict pronounced *via* the *mashal* of the discontented children (vv. 31ff.).[47] On the other hand, the two verses also have a recognizable parallel in the logion of Mt 21,32, whose direct-address form and combination of οἱ τελῶναι καὶ αἱ πόρναι might be original but whose wording and placement seem no less redactionally functional than Luke's version is.[48] Considering that

---

[45] R. GLÖCKNER, *Verkündigung*, 148f. On the expressive irony of the use of " prophet " in Lk 7,39, cf. M. RESE, *Altt. Motive*, 151.

[46] Franz MUSSNER, " Der nicht erkannte Kairos (Mt 11,16-19 = Lk 7,31-35)," *Bib* 40 (1959, 599-612) 610 ; also G. BOUWMAN, *ETL* 45 (1969) 175 ; P. HOFFMAN, *Logienquelle*, 194ff. — On the other hand, this passage has its parallel, in direct address by Jesus, at Mt 21,32, hence its basic assertion, opposing " publicans and prostitutes " (Mt) to the Jewish (people ? leadership ?) in the response to John the Baptist, can be considered to have come from Q (rightly D. LÜHRMANN, *Redaktion*, 28 ; W. WINK, *John the Baptist*, 18ff. ; H. SCHÜRMANN, *Lk*. I, 422).

[47] F. MUSSNER, *Bib* 40 (1959) 609ff. ; A. GEORGE, *RB* 75 (1968) 493f. ; H. CONZELMANN, *MdZ*, 136, 153 n. 1 ; G. LOHFINK, *Sammlung Israels*, 43-44 and n. 91.

[48] G. BORNKAMM, *Überlieferung und Auslegung im Mt.-Ev.*, 25. — Matthew's placement of the saying is obviously a transfer from its original Q location, for

Matthew's " publicans and prostitutes " probably yielded to the awkward " all the people and the publicans " to serve Luke's interests in Lk 7,29, we have no trouble imagining a sequence in which the original combination stood in that verse, whereupon the " sinful woman " story would make the more appropriate continuation and exemplification of the preceding passage. Indeed, let us precisely suggest that Luke's recension of Q, developed by his special tradition, already linked the testimony to the Baptist with the *mashal* of the children by means of the statements in Lk 7,29f., perhaps in the direct-address form as well as the older wording of Mt 21,32.[49] In that case, the special tradition would likely have furnished the *sequence* that includes the " sinful woman " episode and the summary account of the journeying Master's redeemed *ministrae* (Lk 8,2-3) [50] as illustrations of the scandalous allian-

---

the sequence in Mt 21-22 is Marcan and has been expanded by Matthew with a view to systematizing the polemical argument of the controversy episodes. It was this project which occasioned the insertion of the " two sons " parable (Mt 21,28-31) between the challenge to Jesus' authority and the parable of the wicked vinegrowers. Since the precedent of John the Baptist was cited by Jesus to confound the challengers of his authority (Mt 21,25-26/Mk 11,30-32), the logion concerning the contrasting responses to the Baptist furnished a convenient interpretation of the " two sons " because it connected the latter to the Marcan sequence.

[49] Reading Mt 21,31b-32 after Lk 7,28/Mt 11,11, one finds a good " Stichwortanscluss " (*ad* βασιλεία τοῦ θεοῦ) to explain the sequence in Q, and this no longer forces the conclusion that Mt 11,12f. was the continuation of the Q " testimony " (*pace* D. LÜHRMANN, *Redaktion*, 28). Most seem to judge that neither evangelist's connective between the " testimony " and the *mashal* of the children is original (so P. HOFFMANN, *Logienquelle*, 194). Mt 11,12f. no longer have the Baptist as their subject but the Kingdom of God, of which John was harbinger (G. BARTH, in *Überlieferung und Auslegung*, 59 ; P. HOFFMANN, *Logienquelle*, 58) ; hence the clearly redactional Mt 11,14 is required to unite these sayings to the series eulogizing the Baptist. Thus, whether or not both evangelists' setting for the difficult " Stürmerspruch " are departures from Q (so W. WINK, *John the Baptist*, 20), Matthew's assuredly is. — In suggesting that Lk 7,29f. faithfully preserves the *situs* if not the wording of the logion reproduced in Mt 21,31bf., we follow H. SCHÜRMANN, *Lk*. I, 442f. No specification of a different audience would have been necessary in the original sequence if the Master's audience was the ὄχλοι of Lk 7,24/Mt 11,7 and Lk 3,7 *diff*. Mt 3,7. The originally intended contrast would have been between the Jewish people and the " publicans and harlots " they scorned, not between these and the Jewish leadership. The " crowds " were the original target of the *mashal* in Q in any case, as G. LOHFINK has shown (*loc. cit.* in n. 47 above), so the adversary perspectives of our sayings do not pose a special problem of their own on that score for a reconstruction of the Q sequence.

[50] As we discussed in chapter I (pp. 10f.), however, Luke placed this report of the Galilean ladies in relationship with the Marcan tomb sequence, probably by producing the introductory statement, Lk 8,1, and by composing Lk 8,3 with pointed echoes of Mk 15,41. This, together with his list of names in 24,10 and introduction of Bethany-anointing elements in Lk 7,37f., gave the sequence 7,36-8,3 an aspect of Easter anticipation for the purposes of Luke's larger narrative

ces already at issue in the matrix Q-material. Again, what emerges as the *specificum* of Luke's special source is this focusing of the unworthy-associations issue on *ministrations by the "unworthy" to the Lord as traveler and guest.* This was the situation which apparently made the "protomissionary" vividly real and present to his followers of the pre-Lucan circle.

If we pursue this suggestive combination of *forgiveness* and *house-guest relationship with the lowly* that has moulded the pericope of the sinful woman, we shall be led to further literary fusions of Q and special material that might be ascribed to our evangelist's *Sondertradenten.* It is natural to think first of the "banquet" sequence of Lk 14, which begins with a situation similar to 7,36ff., has its Q matrix in the parable of the invited guests (Lk 14,15-24), and includes the command to make unfortunate strangers one's *invited guests* rather than the friends and relatives from whom reciprocation is expected (Lk 14, 12-14).[51] Here the downtrodden have the role of guests, but the prescribed *familiaritas* with them is the same.[52] — Further on in Lk, there

---

plan. The women who attended Jesus in Galilee, and whom he delivered from the clutches of Satan, became part of the circle of Easter witnesses referred to first at Lk 23,49. — The mention of "Joanna, wife of Chuza, Herod's steward" in Lk 8,3 (cf. chap. I, n. 27) is by no means a departure from the pattern of Jesus' despised companions. Being the wife of a functionary of Herod's court, "sie gehörte gewiss nicht zu den im Volk beliebtesten Kreisen" (G. THEISSEN, *NTS* 21 [1974-75] 199). The practice of allowing the accompaniment and services of women on the journeys of the wandering missionaries seems to have been continued amongst the "charismatics" of the early Church, at least according to the Pseudo-Clementine *Ad virgines* (cf. G. KRETSCHMAR, *ZTK* 61 [1964] 33f.) and perhaps already *Did.* XI,11 (*ibid.*, and G. THEISSEN, *ZTK* 70 [1973] 253; also R. A. KRAFT, ed., "The Didache," in R. M. Grant, *The Apostolic Fathers* III, 171). The itinerant συνείσακτοι had no reason to think they were not being faithful to a τρόπος κυρίου, even if the Pseudo-Clementine document reveals the inevitable abuse of such "spiritual marriages" that might be expected. — That Lk 8,2-3 belonged to S-Lk as continuation of the "sinful woman" story is also held by H. SCHÜRMANN, Lk. I, 448.

[51] Cf. chap. III, p. 202 above. Cf. J. WANKE, *Eucharistieverständnis*, 59: "In der Mahlgemeinschaft, die Jesus gewährt, wird die Heilszusage aktualisiert. Die Mahlgemeinschaft ist schon Ausdruck der Rettung (vgl. Lk 19,9) ...." This accords perfectly with the old household protocol of the missionaries, which combined the greeting of "peace," with its wondrous discernment of its destined recipients, with a familial meal shared by wanderer and householder (Lk 10,5-7).

[52] H.-J. DEGENHARDT, *Lukas*, 100. — Because the meal shared with the missionary was an "expression of salvation" already come to the household, just as the initial *pax* also was (see previous note), it is easy to understand why the missionary could be conceived alternately as the *guest* and the *host* of such meals. Especially if the meal had eucharistic character, as we should imagine and as the Emmaus meal indicates, the wayfarer would have exchanged his guest's role for the host's, as the risen Lord did at table with the two disciples (Lk 24,29-30). This explains why the wayfarers' tradition, in propounding and exemplifying the dominical ideal of communion with the disinherited,

is the neighboring sequence of chapter 15, devoted to the theme of the *salvation of the undeserving*. The literary association of its three pericopes (the first from Q, the others from S-Lk) has been proposed before as antedating Luke's composition.[53] Here we observe the mixture of forgiveness and banquet motifs in the famous parable of the " lost son " and suggest this is surely not unrelated to the vital concerns and experiences of the stigmatized, wayfaring " charismatics." Moreover, we note in Lk 15,1-2 (and 6) a typical recasting of the Q parable of the lost sheep which relates it to the special tradition's *Leitmotiv*: οὗτος ἁμαρτωλοὺς προσδέχεται καὶ συνεσθίει αὐτοῖς. Jesus again appears as model practitioner of his own directive, Lk 14,13 ! — Indeed, the literary pre-history of Lk 14-15 would be well worth a close analysis.

The messianic forgiveness of the unworthy and solidarity with them found programmatic expression in the inaugural Nazareth instruction (Lk 4,16-30 S), as we have brought out more than once. In that passage the Lucan special source shows its relation to the Q tradition in a different way: not by recasting and amplifying a Q instruction, but by adapting the nucleus of one such instruction to a different occasion and scenario. A partially coinciding selection of self-descriptive prophecies by the Deutero- and Trito-Isaiah is recited to characterize the mission of Jesus in both the Nazareth synagogue instruction (S-Lk) and the answer to John the Baptist's messengers (Lk 7,22f./Mt 11,5 Q). The recited scripture serves in both instances to interpret Jesus' ministry as the *eschatological prophecy*,[54] and the resemblance of the two

---

can assign the responsibility of host to both traveler and householder. Jesus himself plays the host's part with the publicans and sinners, according to Lk 15,2 (cf. J. JEREMIAS, " Tradition und Redaktion in Lukas 15," *ZNW* 62 [1971, 172-189] 187f.), just as he does in the eucharistic repasts and as he will in the banquet of " the kingdom of God " (Lk 14,15 ; 22,16).

[53] H. B. KOSSEN, " Quelques remarques sur l'ordre des paraboles dans Luc XV ...," *NT* 1 (1958) 75-80, esp. 79 (cf. W. GRUNDMANN, *Lk.*, 304f.) ; also, apparently, Emilio RASCO, " Les paraboles de Luc XV," in I. de la Potterie, éd., *De Jésus aux évangiles*, (165-183) 169ff. ; perhaps J. JEREMIAS, *ZNW* 52 (1971) 188. — The position is hardly widespread or emphatically defended. Perhaps the argument of Ingo BROER for the pre-Lucan association between the principle of Lk 15,7 and the parable of 15,11-32 (" Das Gleichnis vom verlorenen Sohn und die Theologie des Lukas," *NTS* 20 [1973-74, 453-462] 459-460) would support the pre-Lucan composition of the three parables under a unified conception. At least BROER has argued effectively against the frequent suggestion that Luke is the *author* of the " prodigal son " (*pace* Louise SCHOTTROFF, " Das Gleichnis vom verlorenen Sohn," *ZTK* 68 [1971] 27-52, esp. 51f.), as has J. JEREMIAS as well (*ZNW* 62 [1971] 181).

[54] This point is persuasively made with respect to the two passages by P. STUHLMACHER, *Das paulinische Evangelium* I, 218-230, who also posits a direct tradition-historical *continuum* between them. We wish to endorse this argument fully. — On the Q passage cf. F. HAHN, *Christologische Hoheitstitel*, 393f. (and 394ff. on Lk 4,16ff.) ; R. PESCH, *Jesu ureigene Taten ? Ein Beitrag*

passages is such that H. SCHÜRMANN suggested Luke had read both in Q (n. 28 above). We think it proves at least the likelihood that Q and S-Lk came to the evangelist from the same circles and the same rigorous stewardship of Jesus' words. If the Nazareth pericope, with its "stylistically and conceptually suitable commentary on the history of the prophets" in Lk 4,23f.25-27, can be considered substantially a pre-Lucan composition, then one can subscribe to the tradition-historical appraisal made by P. STUHLMACHER:[55]

> "... a clear tradition-historical line of connection appears between this Lucan text and the Q-tradition of Mt 11,2-6: out of the old, prophetic and polemical tradition a novelistically expanded, ideal scene has been fashioned, and this served the mission-active, Judaeo-hellenistic community as a foundation of their missionary mandate .... The primitive Christian prophet maxim was transformed in Lk 4 into a historic scene; and Jesus' claim, admittedly only veiled in the Q tradition, to be accorded the status of eschatological prophet, now is thematically expounded (in a form understandable to Gentile hearers) ... We

---

zur Wunderfrage (Quaest. Disp. 52; Freiburg/Basel: Herder, 1970) 40-44; A. VÖGTLE, *Das Evangelium und die Evangelien*, 238ff.; P. HOFFMANN, *Logienquelle*, 205ff. (doubting that the passage should be explained on the basis of authenticating miracles of the prophet prescribed by the Jewish tradition); S. SCHULZ, *Q Spruchquelle*, 195-203. The consensus here is rather impressive. — On the Nazareth passage cf. our note 148 above in chap. II.

[55] *Das paulinische Evangelium* I, 227, 228. — The debate over the origins of the Nazareth pericope, whether it be a Lucan embroidery of Mk 6,1-6 (R. BULTMANN *GsT*, 31; M. DIBELIUS, *Formgeschichte*, 107-108, and *Aufsätze zur Apg.*, 158; H. FLENDER, *Heil und Geschichte*, 132-133; W. ELTESTER, in *Jesus in Nazareth*, 135; Robert C. TANNEHILL, "The Mission of Jesus according to Luke iv 16-30," in *Jesus in Nazareth*, [51-75] 52; E. HAENCHEN, in *Die Bibel und wir*, 167-169; M. RESE, *Alttestamentliche Motive*, 153f. [with recourse to Q]; J. DELOBEL, in F. Neirynck, éd., *L'évangile de Luc*, 217f.) or drawn from a non-Marcan *Sondergut* (so, besides STUHLMACHER, K. L. SCHMIDT, *Rahmen*, 39; W. GRUNDMANN, *Lk.*, 119; F. HAHN, *Christologische Hoheitstitel*, 394; August STROBEL, "Die Ausrufung des Jobeljahrs in der Nazarethpredigt Jesu," in *Jesus of Nazareth*, [38-50] 40; T. SCHRAMM, *Der Markus-Stoff bei Lukas*, 37 [with n. 2]; G. LOHFINK, *Die Sammlung Israels*, 45), is far from settled and still in need of careful literary studies. The difficulties of the matter are such as to persuade even confirmed *Redaktionsgeschichtler* to leave the question open (as H. CONZELMANN ultimately does, *Mitte d. Zeit*, 29-30 n. 2; also E. HAENCHEN, *Der Weg Jesu*, 216; cf. also E. KLOSTERMANN, *Lk.*, 61f.; I. H. MARSHALL, *Luke: Historian and Theologian*, 118f.). — We have already mentioned the hypothesis of H. SCHÜRMANN that this pericope came to Luke integrally from Q (cf. note 28 above; also SCHÜRMANN, *Traditionsgeschichtliche Untersuchungen*, 76, and "Zur Traditionsgeschichte der Nazareth-Perikope Lk 4,16-30," in *Mélanges Bibliques en hommage au R. P. Béda Rigaux* [éd. A. Descamps & A. des Halleux; Gembloux: J. Duculot, 1970] 187-205, esp. 201), and we add that this view has been adopted by Schürmann's students, J. WANKE (*Emmauserzählung*, 61) and C.-P. MÄRZ, (*Wort Gottes*, 43).

are thus considering Lk 4,16-30 as a novelistic development of the old Q tradition of Mt 11,2-6, and as native sphere of this development we think of the hellenistic Jewish-Christian missionary community."

The missionary movement STUHLMACHER speaks of is, we think, the enthusiastic, peripatetic endeavour that we have been attempting to characterize through the contents of S-Lk. If it is correct that the Nazareth story is this group's expansive adaptation of Q's response to the Baptist, then a comparison of these passages should disclose some of its special interests. The lines from Isaiah quoted in each instance, for example, suggest that whereas Q gave the priority to the great prophet's miraculous deeds, Luke's tradition stressed his ministry of the word, specifically the word of *forgiveness and vindication of the lowly* pronounced by him. This is in full accord with both our analysis of the Nazareth reading given above (pp. 137, 214) and our survey of the *Sondergut* in this chapter. The late Isaian prophecies served both traditions as testimonies of the " beginning of the end " that set in with Jesus' ministry. Heralding that end in word and gesture, the Master had discharged the function of *prophet of the eschaton*, harbinger of the Kingdom of God.[56] Moreover, it is clear that the instructions of both Q and S-Lk were transmitted by people who believed that this eschatological prophet's function had been entrusted to the church, at least to the church of the itinerant mission, with its drastic renunciations, its distinguishing word of " peace," and its gestures of healing and exorcism (Lk 10,3-12.17-20, etc.; cf. chap. 3, p. 188 and nn. 94-96). Whether carrying out physical healing or pronouncing the word of forgiveness in the households of the elect, the enthusiastic envoys of the Lord were carrying forward their master's " prophecy of the endtime." The main aspects of this " prophecy," and the various depic-

[56] This is the sense in which we are using the expression " eschatological prophet " in reference to the Q and S-Lk traditions. In Q, according to P. HOFFMANN, this concept is " nicht auf eine Schicht begrenzt, sondern bestimmt die gesamte Überlieferung " (*Logienquelle*, 183). HOFFMANN makes this statement over citation of Mt 11,5; Lk 6,20f.; Lk 10,5-7a.9, — all passages which have undergone expansion under the auspices through which Luke received the Q tradition: the response to the Baptist (as we have seen, expansively developed in Lk 4,16ff.), the beatitudes (expanded with the Lucan woes; cf. D. LÜHRMANN, *Redaktion*, 105, following R. BULTMANN, *GsT*, 117), and the mission directives of Lk 10, whose development in S-Lk we have already discussed. Agreeing with HOFFMANN on the prophetic consciousness of the missionaries who nurtured the Q tradition are the authors cited in note 12 above, and also U. LUZ, "Das Jesusbild der vormarkinischen Tradition" in G. Strecker, hrsg., *Jesus Christus in Historie und Theologie. Ntl. Festschr. f. H. Conzelmann* (Tübingen: J. C. B. Mohr, 1975, 347-374) 349.

tions of Jesus as "prophet" that flowed from it, furnish the next focus of our inquiry into the background of Luke's special tradition.

(2) "ESCHATOLOGICAL PROPHECY"

(A) "CHARISMA" AND THAUMATURGY:

Whether or not Jewish tradition required that the prophet of the *Endzeit* validate his mission through the working of miracles,[57] there is no question that several aspects of this tradition, especially among the voices of hellenistic times, made Jesus' miracles a condign feature of his announcement of the imminent Kingdom of God. For one thing, the late prophets anticipated a revival of the wonders of the exodus to signal the arrival of the final salvation (e.g. Is 35,5f.), and they thus subscribed to the pattern of assimilating *Urzeit* and *Endzeit* which would so permeate the eschatology of intertestamental Judaism. To be sure, the late-Jewish and rabbinical testimonies do not seem to attribute the revival of the classical prodigies to the personal agency of the messiah or "the prophet,"[58] but the tradition which interpreted Dt 18,15ff. as an eschatological promise did increasingly exploit the history and legend of Moses as paragon of the expected "prophet."[59] Foremost in the developing legend as well as the propagated

[57] See chap. II, p. 132. P. HOFFMANN (*Logienquelle*, 205ff.) questions this, demurring against the supposition (of STUHLMACHER, *et al.* — cf. n. 54 above) that the combination of Is 35,5f. (*Heilszeit* miracles) and Is 61,1f. (*Heilszeit* prophet) in Q's answer to the Baptist's query can be adequately explained from the Jewish tradition of the eschatological prophet. HOFFMANN feels the texts usually cited to support this view (e.g. Josephus, *Bell.* 2, 259.261f.; 7,438-440; *Ant.* 20, 97ff.; and *rabbinica* of widely varying pedigree in Str.-Bill. I, 593ff.) lay no special emphasis upon the "prophet" as their agent, hence the combination of Is 35,5f and 61,1f in the response to the Baptist comes from the *de facto* combination of preaching and healing in the ministry of Jesus (*Logienquelle*, 208). — In our opinion, while it may be correct that currents of stricter Jewish tradition do not emphasize the person of the messiah or prophet when speaking of the prodigies of the last times, HOFFMANN may not have considered the new accents of a Judaism responding to the hellenistic world-culture (as in Sir 44-50), where special accentuation of the pneumatic powers of the prophet is concerned. Cf. n. 62 below.

[58] The lack of association between the miracles and the messiah's person in Jewish tradition is, of course, a commonplace of biblical studies (cf. e.g. R. BULTMANN, *GsT* 275, and *Theol. of the N.T.* I, 27; Albert SCHWEITZER, *The Quest of the Historical Jesus* [trans. W. Montgomery; London: Adam & Chas. Black, [3]1954] 345-346; Str.-Bill. I, 593f.; F. HAHN, *Hoheitstitel*, 219; P. STUHLMACHER, *Evangelium* I, 218). — On the eschatological prophet as miracle-worker, see the previous note, and chap. II, p. 126, and n. 169.

[59] The closing verses of Deuteronomy (34,10-12) laid down the qualifications of a prophet like Moses, which no one had fulfilled in Israel: that he know God "face to face," that he perform "signs and wonders," have "wondrous

history, of course, was Moses' role of *hero and thaumaturge*,[60] and these traits could hardly have been omitted for long from anyone's speculation about a "prophet like Moses." A Mosaic eschatology like the Samaritans', for example, was able to translate the central theorem of their Moses-centered doctrine, Dt 34,10f., into a prescription for the awaited figure who would fulfill the Deuteronomic "prophet" *vaticinium, Moses-redivivus*.[61] When one recalls, moreover, the emphasis laid upon miracles as the prophet's authentication by hellenistic-Jewish apologetics,[62] it becomes less difficult to explain the association of

---

powers" and a "mighty hand." Even though the Deuteronomic historian refused to let miraculous performances be the sole criterion for identifying the promised successor (Dt 13,1-5; 18,9-22), it is clear they were to play their part in authenticating that special presence of God that was unknown in Israel after Moses' lifetime (D. L. TIEDE, *The Charismatic Figure as Miracle Worker*, 102f.). — On the Moses tradition in which Deuteronomy and the Deutero-Isaiah independently stand, cf. Gerhard VON RAD, *Theologie des Alten Testaments* II (München: Kaiser-Verlag, ³1962) 273f.; and the uncommonly rich documentation assembled by Juan-Peter MIRANDA, *Der Vater, der mich gesandt hat. Religionsgeschichtliche Untersuchungen zu den johanneischen Sendungsformeln* (Europäische Hochschulschriften XXIII/7; Bern/Frankfurt-am-Main: Herbert/Peter Lang, 1972) 308-388, esp. 334ff., 372ff.

60 D. L. TIEDE, *Charismatic Figure*, 180f., citing Ben Sira (44,23-45,5) and the *Antiquitates Biblicae* of the Pseudo-Philo as effective examples of "the general prevalence of this feature in diverse portraits of Moses ..."; cf. also D. GEORGI, *Gegner*, 148ff.; L. BIELER, ΘΕΙΟΣ ΑΝΗΡ II, 5ff., 30ff.; Géza VERMÈS, "La figure de Moise au tournant des deux Testaments," in H. CAZELLES, et al., *Moise, l'homme de l'alliance* (Paris/Tournai; Desclée et Cie., 1955) 63-92; J. JEREMIAS, Μωυσῆς, *ThWNT* IV, 854ff.

61 The centrality of Dt 34,10 in the Samaritan Moses-doctrine was pointed out by John MACDONALD, *The Theology of the Samaritans*, 197f.: "... Samaritan interest in Moses reaches its zenith with the words of Deut. 34,10. There will never be any like Moses, not in all the world. It was probably because of this belief that they conceived the idea, no doubt derived from their 'proof-texts' Deut. 18,15.18, that if one is to come to prepare the way for God's judgement and restore everything for God, then that person must be *Moses redivivus* ..." It is admittedly in sources datable only to the fourth century A. D. that Dt 18,15.18 is applied to the figure of the Samaritans' "restorer," the תָּאֵב (= ὁ ἐρχόμενος), but both belong to the earliest traditions. The eschatological understanding of the Deuteronomy passage is documented by its noted insertion in the "tenth commandment" of the Samaritan decalogue (i.e. Ex 20,17 in the Samaritan Pentateuch); and two sources of the late first century, Jn 4,25 and Josephus, *Ant.* 18,85 (cf. *Bell.* 3, 207), confirm the antiquity of the *ta'eb*, as documented in the principal Samaritan source outside the Pentateuch, the *Memar Marqah* III § 4; IV § 10-12 (cf. also Justin, *Apol.* I 53-6). The repeated question, "where is there the like of Moses?" (reflecting Dt 34,10), gets its answer in terms of the *ta'eb* in *Memar Marqah* IV § 12. — Cf. J.-P. MIRANDA, *Der Vater* ... (cited in n. 59) 346ff.; J. MACDONALD, *Theology of the Samaritans*, 362-371; Wayne A. MEEKS, *The Prophet King: Moses Traditions and the Johannine Christology* (Suppl. to *NT* 14; Leiden: E. J. Brill, 1967) 250-254.

62 Gerhard DELLING, "Josephus und das Wunderbare," in *Studien zum*

miracle and "prophet"-acclamation in such Christian texts as Lk 7,16; 9,8.19; 24,19; Jn 6,14, etc. Admittedly, Samaritan eschatology and hellenistic-Jewish apologetics are very limited currents of Jewish thought contemporary with our author, but we have ample reason to think that he and the tradition close to him had substantial contacts with both.

Some recent discussion has unexpectedly focused on the *Samaritan contacts* of special traditions in both Lk and Acts.[63] To our knowledge, no attempt has yet been made to link such separate materials in a common *Sitz-im-Leben* that would account for their local color.[64] Yet this might just be the path that can lead us to a comprehensive tradition-history of the *Sondergut* we have been discussing. Let us

---

Neuen Testament und zum hellenistischen Judentum (Göttingen: Vandenhoeck und Ruprecht, 1970, 130-145) 134-136; George MACRAE, "Miracle in *The Antiquities* of Josephus," in C. F. D. MOULE, ed., *Miracles: Cambridge Studies* ... (129-147) 134, 135; G. VERMÈS, *art. cit.* (in n. 60) 66-74; D. GEORGI, *Gegner*, 154ff.; D. L. TIEDE, *Charismatic Figure*, c. 2 *passim*, esp. 180-240. G. VERMÈS and D. L. TIEDE make important distinctions between the cruder, more popularesque portrayals of Moses by Artapanus, which are obviously directed at the competition on a level of lower sophistication and greater syncretism (hence highlight Moses' magical powers), and the more philosophical treatments of Philo, Eupolemos, Aristobulus, and Josephus, who emphasize the wisdom of Moses more than his thaumaturgy and understand the miracles as God's action through him, not powers at his own disposal. — But cf. chap. 2, note 395 against artificially separating Moses' wisdom from his preternatural powers, and cf. on this M. HENGEL, *Judentum und Hellenismus*, 248f., 299.

[63] Cf. John BOWMAN, *Samaritanische Probleme. Studien zum Verhältnis von Samaritanertum, Judentum und Urchristentum* (Franz-Delitzsch-Vorlesungen 1959; Stuttgart/Mainz: Kohlhammer, 1967) Abschnitt 3; Johannes Munck, *Acts of the Apostles* (Anchor Bible 31) appendices V and VII (by Abram SPIRO and W. F. ALBRIGHT); R. PESCH, *Jesu ureigene Taten*? 127ff.; Charles H. H. SCOBIE, "The Origins and Development of Samaritan Christianity," *NTS* 19 (1972-73, 390-414) 390-400. G. SCHILLE (*Anfänge der Kirche*, 71, 73ff.) suggests that these contacts reflect missionary "Gebietsprogramme" and "Gründungsschema(ta)," but his hypotheses are wanting any sound analytical foundation, so far as we can see.

[64] We would include in this assessment the essay of Hans KLEIN, who would make Luke himself a native of coastal Palestine and mediator of local traditions ("Zur Abfassungsort ...," *EvT* 32 [1972] 467-477, esp. 474). Such a diagnosis cannot account for the complexion of the Pauline chapters in Acts nor the faulty geography of the Palestinian phases of Luke's story (cf. chap II, note 52). In our opinion, KLEIN has not managed to revise CONZELMANN's generally accepted appraisal of the Lucan geography of Palestine: "Das ganze Land scheint von Übersee her gesehen zu sein" (*MdZ*, 62). On the other hand, for reasons we hope to be establishing in this section, we should not agree with CONZELMANN's view that the Samaritan episodes of the gospel reflect no local traditions (*ibid.*, 64). The coincidence of Samaritan views and traditions between Lk and Acts furnishes something of the "Beweis" for a local tradition that C. maintained was lacking.

observe, first, that three pericopes of S-Lk have a *Samaritan color*, and all three are located in the " journey section " of the gospel : the Samaritan rejection story (Lk 9,52-56), the " good Samaritan " parable (Lk 10,29-37), and the miracle of the ten lepers (Lk 17,11-19). Except for Mt's mission directive to avoid Samaritan cities (Mt 10,5), which Luke does not reproduce, these are the only references to Samaria and the Samaritans in the Synoptics (in Jn, cf. the special tradition in Jn 4, and elsewhere only Jn 8,48). Moreover, references to the place or its people in the S-Lk passages go beyond a merely neutral information of the kind which can introduce gospel pericopes. In all three instances, special importance is attached to the Samaritan identity of persons involved in the story : the inhospitable townsfolk (οὐκ ἐδέξαντο αὐτόν) whom the Master would not allow his ἄγγελοι to afflict with Elia's " samaritan " curse (Lk 9,54 = 2 Kgs 1,10.12), the parable's model of ministering to the unfortunate, and the one leper won over by his cure. All of these suggest that Luke's tradition accords the outcast Samaritans a special status ;[65] and that status is clearly not without pertinence to the *Christian mission to Samaria*, whose great success through the superior *thaumaturgy of Philip* (Acts 8,5-25) supports its pivotal position in the Acts history as *threshold of the mission to the Gentiles*.[66]

---

[65] F. SCHÜTZ (*Christus*, 119) rightly accounts this to the Lucan Christology of the " Saviour of the outcasts " ; but he does not pursue the origins of such a picture beyond the evangelist. — Cf. also G. SELLIN, " Lukas als Gleichniserzähler," *ZNW* 66 (1975) 43ff. ; I. H. MARSHALL, *Luke*, 140.

[66] Acts 1,8 ; 8,1 ; 9,31 ; 15,3. Note especially how, in the last passage cited, Samaria is associated with " the conversion of the Gentiles " related by Paul and Barnabas. It is as if, in making their pilgrimage to the *sedes apostolica*, the two Gentile missionaries are retracing the steps of the mission's progress. Indeed, in Luke's schema, Samaria is the first mission station outside Jerusalem, and the good news reached there as soon as the Hellenists' *persecution* (Luke's standard impulse to the mission's expansion, as we brought out in chap. III, pp. 214f. and note 158), broke out and scattered that contingent of the mother church. The fact of Samaria's primacy among the mission stations is not accidental, for its people are viewed in our evangelist's tradition as "*foreigners* " (Lk 17,18 : ἀλλογενής ! — cf. G. SELLIN, *ZNW* 66 [1975] 44f. : " Hier geht es also eindeutig um die soteriologische Sprengung der Grenzen Israels "). The " good Samaritan " parable illustrates Samaria's role of connecting link between Israel and the Gentiles, for the parable's hero is shown to understand and keep the law (recall the parable's connection with the preceding apophthegm of the law's prescription for " eternal life " : Lk 10,25ff. S) whereas cultically delimited, orthodox Judaism, embodied in the priest and levite, failed to fulfill the law in this instance (G. SELLIN, *art. cit.*, 45). Biblical authority for the consideration of the Samaritans as non-Israelites could be urged in 2 Kgs 17,24f., although Jewish attitudes towards the sect vacillated in NT times and afterward (cf. on this John BOWMAN, " Samaritan Studies," *BJRylL* 40 [1957-58, 298-327] 298ff.). See note 128 below.

Superficially, it appears that only the fact of Samaria's response to the miracles done in Jesus' name unites the Philip-tradition to the gospel stories, as perhaps vindication of Jesus' forebearance (Lk 9,54f.) and a mission harvest beyond the boundaries of Jewish orthodoxy which the "tenth leper" foreshadowed.[67] But there are profounder influences of *Samaritan tradition* on the composition of Acts which may elucidate and solidify this *continuum* of "charismatic mission." For one thing, we know that appropriation of the Mosaic-prophet status by two legendary "divine men" of Samaria, Simon Magus (Philip's competitor) and Dositheus, was known and combatted by Christian authors of the second and third centuries.[68] More importantly, however, the discourse of Stephen, protomissionary and protomartyr, has been thought to contain an integral fabric of Samaritan traditions, including a discursive use of Old Testament passages which relies on several peculiarities of the Samaritan Pentateuch.[69] Once again, it is the prominently featured

---

[67] For the literary criticism of the "ten lepers" episode, which generally acknowledges the difficult introductory verse (Lk 17,11) to result from the evangelist's geographical schematizing, whereas the thankful leper's Samaritan identity is ascribed to the pre-Lucan story (— an expanded version of Mk 1,40-45 ?), cf. Hans-Dieter BETZ, "The Cleansing of the Ten Lepers (Luke 17 : 11-19)," *JBL* 90 (1971) 314-328 ; R. PESCH, *Taten*, 114-134. If it is true, as both BETZ and PESCH contend, that the Lucan story is a secondary version of the Marcan made into an apophthegm to feature the faith of the "foreigner," then it is not unreasonable to conclude, with H.-D. BETZ (*art. cit.*, 321), that this version of the lepers' story "presupposes the definite breach between Judaism and Christianity" and "the success of the Christian mission to the Samaritans." — On the other hand, whether an initial version of the "ten lepers" without the Samaritan motif ever existed, in view of the story's inherent reminder of the *Samaritan* episode of Naaman and Elisha (2 Kgs 5,1-14/Lk 4,27 ; cf. the terminological echoes throughout listed by R. PESCH, *op. cit.*, 127), we have grave doubts and think BETZ has produced one step too many in the tradition process.

[68] Cf. Karlmann BEYSCHLAG, *Simon Magus und die christliche Gnosis* (WissUntNT 16 ; Tübingen : J. C. B. Mohr, 1974) 48-67 ; Howard M. TEEPLE, *The Mosaic Eschatological Prophet* (*JBL* Monograph series 10 ; Philadelphia : Society of Biblical Literature, 1957) 64f.; J.-P. MIRANDA, *Der Vater, der mich gesandt hat* (cited in n. 59 above) 348. — On Dositheus : Origen, *Contra Celsum* I, 57 (PG 11, 765B) ; on Simon : Ps.-Clem. *Recognitiones* VII 33,1f. (hrsg. B. Rehm & F. Paschke, in GCS 51 [Berlin : Akademie-Verlag, 1965] 213). — K. BEYSCHLAG acknowledges the antiquity of the tradition on which the Simon-Magus presentation of the Pseudo-Clementines is based (*op. cit.*, 58), and this is enough to make our point. We cannot pursue the other issues surrounding Simon, a notoriously enigmatic figure in the research of Christian origins. That the issue of the Mosaic prophet's identity is a key issue of the debates between Peter and Simon the Samaritan, the Pseudo-Clementine author makes abundantly clear (cf. *Recognitiones* I, 40,4 ; 54,4f. ; II 45,3-46,2 ; hrsg. Rehm & Pashke, *GCS* 51, 32, 39, 78-79).

[69] Cf. M. SIMON, *St. Stephen*, 35ff. ; A. SPIRO, in Joh. Munck, *Acts*, 285-288 ; Martin A. SCHARLEMANN, *Stephen*, 31-51, esp. 45ff. ; Robin SCROGGS, "The Ear-

vaticinium of the "prophet like Moses," Dt 18,15 (Acts 7,37), which presents one of the suggested indications of the Samaritan influence.

As mentioned already (note 61), one of the idiosyncrasies of the Samaritan biblical text is its interpolation of Dt 18,15 as part of the tenth commandment in Ex 20,17. Stephen's speech, in turn, is a sweeping review of the Pentateuchal history, featuring a sequential excerpt of the narrative of Genesis and Exodus that can be verified by following the Scripture references footnoted by NESTLE/ALAND. Once this plan is recognized, we can be prepared for the appearance of Dt 18,15(18) at Acts 7,37 only by following Stephen along in the *Samaritan Pentateuch*, where this Mosaic prophecy occurs with the

---

liest Hellenistic Christianity," in *Religions in Antiquity. Essays in Memory of E. R. Goodenough* (ed. J. Neusner; Studies in the History of Religions 14; Leiden: E. J. Brill, 1968) 176-206; C. H. H. SCOBIE, *NTS* 19 (1972-73) 393f. — The main reliance on SP readings would occur at Acts 7,4 (Gen 11,32 SP), Acts 7,32 (plural "fathers," Ex 3,6 SP, *contra* sing. MT, LXX), Acts 7,37 (Ex 20, 17f. SP, interpolating Dt 18,15), Acts 7,5 κληρονομία (Dt 2,5 SP: ירשה, *contra* MT, LXX, Targ). Moreover, instances where Samaritan tradition or viewpoint seems to have shaped the survey of sacred history: (a) the burial of Jacob and "his fathers" at Shechem (i.e., Mount Gerizim) in Acts 7,15f., *contra* "Hebron" in Gen 49,29ff.; 50,13 MT (cf. *opera citata* above: SPIRO 286; SCHARLEMANN 40; SCROGGS 190); (b) the blending of Ex 3,12 and Gen 12,6f. in Acts 7,7, so as to shift words spoken to Moses about Horeb to words directing Abraham that Shechem was to be the worship place (SPIRO 286; SCROGGS 190); (c) Acts 7,47-50 makes the building of the Jerusalem temple (χειροποίητος) the climax of Israel's apostasy and breaks off the survey of sacred history precisely at this point, reflecting a Samaritan vision (SPIRO 288; J. BOWMAN, *Samaritanische Probleme*, 72-73; SCROGGS 178-188; C. H. H. SCOBIE 396); (d) the speech is devoted to the example of Samaritan heroes, overwhelmingly to Moses (more then half!), but also to Abraham, Joseph (ancestor of the northern tribes of Ephraim and Manasseh), and Joshua; (e) the speech is constructed around the *vaticinium* of the Mosaic prophet, Dt 18,15.18 (Acts 7,37). "This figure plays relatively little part in Jewish messianic expectation, but is the key figure in Samaritan eschatology" (SCOBIE 395; SCHARLEMANN 73; cf. SPIRO 290; M. SIMON 37f., 61ff.; SCHARLEMANN 47-49). — Finally, there are non-Pentateuchal citations and allusions which support Samaritan viewpoints, according to these authors: Jer 7,18; 19,13 in Acts 7,42; Amos 5,27 in Acts 7,42-43; Ps 132,5 in Acts 7,45-46; Is 46,1-2 in Acts 7,49-50. The fact that these texts were not sacred scripture for the Samaritans suggests that acceptance of the broader OT canon had been likely a "price of admission" for Samaritan Christians (SCOBIE 400). — In spite of all this data, to regard direct Samaritan influence on Stephen's speech as "indubitable" (M. HENGEL, *ZTK* 72 [1975] 159f. n. 36) may just be premature, in view of U. WILCKENS, *Missionsreden*³, 219; E. RICHARD, *CBQ* 32 (1977) 190-208. — At all events, one should consider any attribution of the speech to the historical Stephen or his movement rather doubtful (cf. M. HENGEL, *art. cit.*, 186f.; also S. C. WILSON, *Gentiles*, 149). Rather than the thoughts of Stephen and the "Hellenists," Acts 7 probably presents the protomartyr's mission through other eyes, perhaps those of its converts who themselves became roving spokesmen of the Lord.

uniquely Samaritan "tenth commandment," bidding the worship of Yahweh on Mount Gerizim (cf. J. BOWMAN, *BJRylLib* 40 [1957-58] 310f.). The flow of Exodus parallels in Acts 7,31ff. is manifest: Ex 3,4-10 (31-34), Ex 2,14 (35), Ex 3,2 (35), Ex 7,3 (36), Ex 14,21 (36), then Dt 18,15 (37), then Ex 19,1-6; 20,1-17 (38).[70] (The sequence ends with Ex 32,9; 33,3.5 in Acts 7,51.) With its "tenth commandment," Samaritan religion established its center and substance: the true worship-place, and the expectation of a renewed Mosaic prophecy. Similarly, Acts 7,37 is the center of Stephen's historic panorama and the only basis of its christological frame of reference (cf. C. H. H. SCOBIE, *NTS* 19 [1972-73] 395; M. SIMON, *St. Stephen*, 61-62; U. WILCKENS, *Missionsreden*³, 211f.; S. G. WILSON, *Gentiles*, 134). — N. B. Earl RICHARD's case against the Samaritan text's influence in Acts 7 appeared during the typing of this thesis: *CBQ* 32 (1977) 190-208. If his arguments are correct, this would remove Lk's source from the direct influence of the Samaritan text (which I think probable anyway) but not from its *tradition*.

Combined with the excerpts from Exodus at the center of the protomartyr's recital of sacred history, the prophecy of the prophet in Moses' image creates a christological typology[71] remarkably similar to the portrait drawn by Cleopas in the Emmaus dialogue (Lk 24,19ff.). Moses, worker of "wonders and signs" (7,36/Ex 7,3), was yet resisted by his people (*7,35*/Ex 2,14; *7,39-40*/Ex 32,1.23). On the one hand, the "wonders and signs" are understood in their function of legitimating the true prophet, which made them part of Samaritan expectation of the Moses to come.[72] On the other hand, rejection by the people follows, antithetically, as the true prophet's destiny (7,39f.52f.). Both essential aspects of the prophetic ministry occur in adaptations of Exodus passages and stand on either side of Stephen's quotation of the Mosaic-prophet text. These were the hallmarks of prophecy which

[70] A confirming argument for the Samaritan text's inspiration of our passage could be the parallel beginnings of Acts 7,37 and 7,38: οὗτός ἐστιν κτλ. The common expression closely connects the prophet-announcement of Moses to his receiving λόγια ζῶντα δοῦναι ἡμῖν, referring, of course, to the commandments of the law (v. 53). In other words, the commandments and the future Moses stand in precisely the relationship here that they have, uniquely, in the Samaritan decalogue.

[71] H. CONZELMANN, *Apg.*², 54; M. RESE, *Altt. Motive*, 78-80. Even those who do not interpret the whole treatment of Moses as typological, as U. WILCKENS (*Missionsreden*³, 217) and R. GLÖCKNER (*Verkündigung* 165) are inclined to do, maintain that v. 37 introduces the typological exegesis (so J. C. O'NEILL, *Theol. of Acts*, 75; S. C. WILSON, *Gentiles*, 134).

[72] Cf. note 61 above; also Moses GASTER, *The Samaritans: Their History, Doctrines and Literature* (Schweich Lectures of 1923; Oxford Univ. Press, 1925). 91. On Moses' incomparable miracles in Samaritan perspective, cf. J. MACDONALD, *Theology of the Samaritans*, 196, 208ff., 424f.

furnished an editorial schema for our author's arrangement of both the Jesus-tradition and the story of the early mission (cf. chap. 2, pp. 121ff.). Does this mean that the crucial turn of Stephen's argument came from his pen, or is this the tradition which inspired the schema ?

We are inclined to rule in favor of the pre-Lucan tradition at this point. It is certainly reasonable to maintain that Stephen's sequential Exodus citations – (including Ex 20,17f. SP ?) – represent a single conception and a single author,[73] and what we have seen inclines us to agree that is *not* St. Luke.[74] If this is correct, we now have a finger on a most important tradition-historical landmark in the pre-history of his work. Stephen's speech, separable completely from the surrounding Acts narrative of his ill-fated ministry,[75] contains a vision of sacred history and Old Testament exegesis that acquaint us with a distinctive Jewish-Christianity : hellenized but not Pauline,[76] north-Palestinian, amply nourished by Samaritan tradition and expectation, therefore witness of the native culture and temperament of its recruited constituents. Moreover, as an utterance of Stephen, this tract meant to illustrate the prophetic credentials and destiny of the protomissionary, whom the *martyrium* narrative presents as " exemplary Spirit-bearer "

[73] Rightly R. GLÖCKNER, *Verkündigung*, 168.

[74] We should therefore be inclined to agree with WILCKENS, STECK, and HAHN (cf. chap. II, note 182) that the substance of the speech has been received by Luke from his source. Because of the sustained sequence of Exodus excerpts, we do not agree with those who follow M. DIBELIUS in maintaining that Luke broke in as redactor in 7,35ff. (so CONZELMANN, HAENCHEN, RESE, HOLTZ, ERNST, cited in chap. II, note 182). Not that we wish to hold the speech as a document of the real thoughts of Stephen and the hellenists (so A. SPIRO, in J. Munck, *Acts*, 293f., 297f. ; M. SCHARLEMANN, *Stephen*, 50, M. SIMON, *St. Stephen*, 37f., 59ff.) ; rather, it seems best to characterize it as a pre-Lucan document of the mission to Samaria that comes to be narrated, with the same aura of pneumatic enthusiasm, in Acts 8 (so R. SCROGGS, *art. cit.* [in n. 69] 197ff. ; C. H. H. SCOBIE, *NTS* 19 [1972-73] 396ff.). Cf. n. 69 *in fine* above).

[75] In this M. DIBELIUS was quite right (*Aufsätze zur Apg.*, 143ff.) and has general agreement among the interpreters, e.g. H. CONZELMANN, *Apg.*², 57; R. SCROGGS, *art. cit.* [in n. 69] 182ff. ; U. WILCKENS, *Missionsreden*³, 208f. ; J. BIHLER, *Stephanusgeschichte*, 37f. ; S. G. WILSON, *Gentiles*, 132 ; R. GLÖCKNER, *Verkündigung*, 169 ; M. HENGEL, *ZTK* 72 (1975) 195. It should be remembered, of course, that the original independence of the speech from its present context does not free the interpreter from facing the problem that the Lucan context presents. Even if the speech does not inherently bear upon the situation of Stephen before his persecutors or the charge made against him, it is clear that Luke understood the speech to answer the charge (J. C. O'NEILL, *Theol. of Acts*, 73), and so one must pursue the sense in which that could be so.

[76] H. CONZELMANN, *Apg.*², 57 ; " wir lernen hier die Bibel- und Geschichtsbetrachtung eines hellenistischen Judenchristentums vom ausserpaulinischen Typ kennen, von dem sich auch sonst noch Spuren finden." Cf. also U. WILCKENS, *Missionsreden*³, 217ff.

(Acts 6,8.10), " paradigm of the earliest Christian, Spirit-guided enthusiasm." [77] Hence we may well be learning from Stephen a substantial measure of the ideology and self-understanding of the itinerant, " charismatic " missionaries who, from their Palestinian fatherland, penetrated the world of St. Luke.

The gospel pericopes with Samaritan locale complement this picture, as we have suggested. The Samaritan leper won over by the miracle of Jesus (Lk 17,15ff. S), foreshadowing the success of Philip's thaumaturgy in the mission to Samaria (Acts 8), proves to be the counterpart of the " foreigner," Naaman, whom Elisha, " charismatic " heir of Elia, miraculously healed at Samaria (2 Kgs 5,1-14/Lk 4,27 S). By evoking the ancient prophet's deed in both the Nazareth scene and the miracle on the Jewish frontier, Luke's *Sondergut* inculcated the same classic phases of the great prophets' careers as Stephen taught about Moses: on the one hand, the authenticating wonder of their deeds, on the other hand, the resistance to their ministry in Israel. Moreover, the tradition is also aware of the correlation between Israel's refusal and the prophetic call to the " outsiders," for this seems to be implicit in the parable of the good Samaritan. The parable's hero enters into a solidarity with the wretched victim which also exists between the two classes of newly invited to the " great supper " (S-Lk *vs.* Mt): first the lowly and the wretched, and then the " outsiders " (Lk 14,21-24; cf. chap. 3, n. 134). Here we discover an added reason why the bearers of Luke's special tradition would have reveled in the memory of the Master's table fellowship with the unworthy! Not only their radical renunciations but their association with the mission to Samaria — whether as Samaritans themselves or at least counting Samaritans now as co-religionists and co-workers — made them ἄδεκτοι among the Jews, perhaps even among many strict Jewish Christians. The " prophet's rejection " was doubtless a reality of which Luke's *tradentes* had vivid experience, despite their " charismatic " words and deeds.

(B) Rejection in Israel:

Using the speech of Stephen as a tradition-historical *terminus a quo* for the Lucan books, as U. Wilckens has done also in the third edition of *Missionsreden* (p. 221), we feel we have discovered the raw materials for our evangelist's schematic conception of Jesus and his

---

[77] M. Hengel, *ZTK* 72 (1975) 193, 194. Cf. also J. Bihler, *Stephanusgeschichte*, 17f., 25f., who points out the significance of the speech's insertion between Acts 6,15 and 7,55, therefore between the protomartyr's angelic transfiguration and his heavenly vision of the Son of Man. Clearly, Stephen is speaking " als geisterfüllter Visionär." hence as an embodiment of the Lord's " charismatic " spokesman *in statu confessionis* (Lk 12,11-12/Mt 10,19).

witnesses as *wonder-working prophets repudiated in Israel.* The student of the Jewish scriptures who assembled Stephen's mosaic of Pentateuchal passages managed to bring out the historical continuity between the ministries of Moses and Jesus, on the one hand, and between both of them and the protomartyr: all were mightly in deed and speech (Acts 7,22; Lk 24,19; Acts 6,8.10), and all experienced rejection in Israel (Acts 7,39ff.51ff.)[78] because of this people's perennial "opposition to the Holy Spirit" (Acts 7,51), the agent and power of all prophecy. — With this traditional motif of rejection *and murder of the prophets,* we find ourselves in a current of ideas which O. H. STECK has delineated in the final verses of the speech, Acts 7,51-53 (his analysis now used by U. WILCKENS with approval).[79] It is the tradition of "the violent destiny of the prophets," which, framed by a Deuteronomic summation of Israel's history of infidelity to Yahweh, became a fixed schema for preaching repentance and conversion in postexilic (especially hellenistic) Judaism. In stereotyped succession, the elements of the schema in Jewish usage were: (a) Israel's stubbornly persistent disobedience (so Acts 7,51);[80] (b) Yahweh's repeated dispatching of prophets to instruct, rebuke, and encourage his rebellious people (so Acts 7,52b);[81] (c) Israel's response rejecting, persecuting, and murdering the prophets (so Acts 7,52a);[82] (d) as a consequence of this, Yahweh's terrible judgment and

[78] A. HASTINGS, *Prophet and Witness,* 134.

[79] O. H. STECK, *Israel,* 265-269; also 99ff. Cf. also U. WILCKENS, *Missionsreden*[3], 215f.

[80] This is consistently found wherever the Deuteronomic historical framework is relied upon: e.g. Ezr 9,6ff.; Neh 9,5ff.; Pss 78; 106; Zech 1,4; 7,11-14; 2 Chron 29,6; 30,7; Dan 9,11-13; Bar 1,15-22; I Hen 93,8; Jub 1,8-14; 4 Ezr 14,27-35, etc.

[81] In Deuteronomic perspective, the prophets were sent to urge obedience to the *law* and warn of the consequences of its transgression. Observing Neh 9,26, for example, we note that element (b) of the prophet-schema typically embraces all the nation and all its pre-exilic history in the land, presupposing its habitual disobedience to the law (cp. Ezr 9,10f.) and making its conversion the prophets' objective (O. H. STECK, *Israel,* 62f.). Typically, too, the addressee of the prophetic missions is also the object of the statement being made *via* the schema, viz. *all Israel.* Conforming to this pattern, Stephen's concluding words identify the audience with their ancestors' misdeeds and summarize the latter under disobedience to the *law* (Acts 7,53; STECK, *op. cit.,* 266, n. 2).

[82] Neh 9,26 is the first expression of Israel's resistance to the prophets in generalized terms of her *killing* them! Comparison with texts of similar construction reveals that, while Israel is blamed for rejecting the prophets *habitually* in 2 Kgs 17,13ff. (applied to the Northern Kingdom); Jer 44,4-6; 2 Chr 36,14-16; Ezr 9,10ff., only in the Neh text is that inevitable reaction to the prophets depicted as *murder of the prophets* (cp. Neh 9,26 with 9,30; O. H. STECK, *Israel,* 71). This *novum* of the Neh text is also the *specificum* of the developed schema to which Acts 7,51ff. belongs. The rejection statement shows a gradual development to the point where, in order to express the pre-exilic people's total and

punishment of Israel, prototypified in the tragedy of the Babylonian exile[83] and auguring the dreaded catastrophe of the last judgment.[84] In Christian adaptation, of course, the schema's third member often specifies the violent death of Jesus (as Acts 7,52c), the ultimate rebellion that brings on the ultimate catastrophe (70 A.D.).[85] Just as earlier preachers saw Israel's misfortunes as the divine judgment upon her repudiation of the prophets, the Christian preachers anticipated the new tragedy that came in the wake of her violent rejection of the Master *and themselves.*

Indeed, the occurrence of this schema in Christian adaptation has explicit reference on at least two occasions to *Christian preachers' violent fate* rather than the Lord's. It is no surprise that these are two of the three *Q sayings* that feature the schema (Lk 11,47-51/Mt 23,29-36;[86] Lk 6,22f./Mt 5,11f.[87]), for as we have seen, the sayings tradition was stewarded by the kind of prophetic enthusiast who confidently identified his own word and acceptance with the Lord's (Lk 10,16; Mt 10,40, etc.). Considering that both prophet-sayings from Q are strikingly close to Acts 7,52 in identifying the present generation of prophet-persecutors with their "fathers," we are inclined to judge that the missionary circle behind the Stephen tradition was also a transmitter of the Q tradition, and only the latter furnished the schema for preaching Israel's perennial

---

constant resistance to Yahweh, she was made the agent of a *violent killing* visited upon Yahweh's spokesmen (STECK, *op. cit.*, 79f.). A reflex of that development can be observed between the two texts in which Josephus employs our schema and the OT texts on which he depends: *Ant.* IX 13,2 (2 Chr 30,6-10) and *Ant.* IX 14,1 (2 Kgs 17,7-20). In the first text the schema emerges in Josephus *vis-à-vis* his source and prophet-rejection becomes prophet-*murder* (cp. *Ant.* X 3,1); in the second text, the historian respects his source and there is no violent-fate statement.

83 The schema could also be applied to the twin catastrophe of the Northern Kingdom in 722 B.C. (2 Kgs 17,18; Josephus *Ant.* IX, 14,1), understood by analogy to the catastrophe of Judah in 587 B.C. (Neh 9,27; Ezr 9,13.15; Jer 44,6; 2 Chr 26,16b).

84 Ezr 9,14b; (2 Chr 36,16b). — The eschatological dimension of the catastrophe is apparent in the Christian adaptations of the schema that are listed in n. 85.

85 Cf. Mk 12,1-9; Mt 22,1-7.8ff.; 1 Thess 2,15f. (apocalyptic perspective without specific reference, of course, to 70A.D.); Lk 13,34f./Mt 23,37-39; Lk 11, 47-51/Mt 23,29-36. The judgment statement is lacking in Acts 7,51-53 but may be anticipated in 7,43 if the latter be taken in analogy to 70 A.D. (F. HAHN, *Hoheitstitel*, 383; U. WILCKENS, *Missionsreden*³, 216 [but cf. 212 n. 1]; *e contra* H. CONZELMANN, *Apg.*², 55).

86 O. H. STECK, *Israel*, 26-33, 51-53, 222-227. Cf. F. SCHNIDER, *Prophet*, 136-142.

87 O. H. STECK, *Israel*, 20-26, 257-260: an artificial mixture of two strands of ideas, not a complete realization of the schema under discussion. Cf. F. SCHNIDER, *Prophet*, 133-136.

attack on God's spokesmen. The Acts rehearsal of the protomissionary's dying testimony would then be an expansive historical validation of 7,51-53 focused on the figure of Moses.

Our suggestion of the Q sayings' inspiration of Stephen's invective can be confirmed by several observations. First, if it is correct to identify the *tradentes* of the gospel *Sondergut* and the Stephen-Philip cycle, it is also true that S-Lk did not independently develop the Deuteronomic prophet-rejection schema beyond the *loci* of Q.[88] Luke may have developed and varied the pattern in the mission discourses of Acts,[89] but his treasury of the Lord's sayings was not specifically enriched along these lines by his special source. Furthermore, the other traits and background features of Acts 7 that we explored are not found to have any traditional association with the prophet-schema. That is, O. H. STECK was unable to find the schema in the major Samaritan documents,[90] nor does it have any pre-Christian association with the Mosaic-prophet theologoumenon or the ideal of the prophet-thaumaturge.[91] We thus conclude that Stephen's accusation against his captors is based on a conception and form obtained from the Q tradition. This is a further confirmation of the close association of Luke's *Sondertradenten* with the sayings tradition, and it is a further instance of their concern to identify the " charismatic " missionary with his Lord, ultimately even in the destiny of (violent) rejection ! [92]

(C) HEAVENLY ASSUMPTION : THE PROPHET'S VINDICATION

We have only a few suggestions under this heading, based mainly on our special tradition's obvious interest in the example of the proto-

---

[88] For reasons set forth in chapter II, note 149, Lk 13,31-33 is taken to be an artificial unit, in which v. 33 does not fit harmoniously with v. 32 and is probably a construct of the evangelist, whether or not the prophet maxim is his conclusion from Lk 13,34f.-Q or a preexistent, independent saying like Lk 4,24.

[89] Such is the revised opinion of U. WILCKENS, who has incorporated STECK's researches into his third edition of *Missionsreden* (cf. esp. pp. 219-224).

[90] *Israel*, 211 n. 15. STECK reports having searched the *Memar Markah* and the *Asatir*, two sources to which prime importance is attached by J. MACDONALD, *Theology of the Samaritans*, 42ff.

[91] O. H. STECK, *Israel*, 240ff. According to STECK, " in der Tradition der (deuteronomistischen Prophetenaussage) fehlen die Momente des Wunders und der Erlösungsfunktion völlig " (240 n. 1). Where the motif of the prophet's violent fate appears together with that of Elia, prophet of the end-time, that combination is judged to be a Christian innovation without demonstrable Jewish antecedents (as e.g. in Mk 9,[11-]13).

[92] Cf. A. HASTINGS, *Prophet and Witness*, 134. Cf. also F. SCHÜTZ, *Christus*, 83f. — Remarking the analogy between Lk's Q-material and the Acts 7 *Vorlage* : O. H. STECK, *Israel*, 268f.

types of pneumatic prophecy, Moses, Elia, and Elisha. For one thing, our tradition has supplied rare ecstatic and visionary elements in the words of Jesus (e.g. Lk 10,18) as well as the Stephen-Philip cycle.[93] Beyond that, however, its two classic prototypes are figures with whom late-Jewish tradition had increasingly associated the *bodily assumption* motif: Elia naturally, since the tradition was unanimous on him, but probably Moses also, given the developments in late sources and the Samaritan doctrine of later generations.[94] If the " Elianic " episode of Acts 1,9-11 could be counted, in its substance, among the contributions of the special source, then the " two men " who interpret the event for the " Galileans," in cryptic form and apocalyptic accents, might well have been intended to represent the two great prophets who had preceded the Master into the heavens,[95] and this already at the level of the pre-Lucan account. The evangelist would then have altered the scene at the tomb in imitation of the inherited ascension story (cf. chap. 1, pp. 21ff.), with the result that the two " ascended " prophets of Israel's golden age are, so to speak, " guides " and witnesses of Jesus'

---

[93] Cf. M. Hengel, *ZTK* 72 (1975) 193-195, 194 n. 142.

[94] The tradition which Josephus witnesses in *Ant.* IV, 8,48, with strong critical reserve, has undoubtedly begun to interpret Moses' death in terms of a bodily assumption, under the inspiration of Dt 34,5f. (cf. G. Lohfink, *Himmelfahrt*, 62). Even though the historian himself does not favor the idea, the text itself obviously relies on a tradition with elements strikingly similar to the Acts ascension account: the mountain, the final discussion with a trusted circle of followers, the cloud, and the departing figure's ἀφανίζεσθαι (cp. *Ant.* IX 2,2 [28] re. Elia and Henoch), all of which are *topoi* of the bodily assumption legends. In general, however, the vast Moses tradition does not include accounts of a bodily assumption of Moses, no doubt because of most narrators' respect for the scriptural account of the great man's death and burial. However, the appearance of Moses with Elia in the oldest transfiguration story, Mk 9,4, might indicate that there were *speculations* along these lines in some circles in the first century of the Christian era (cp. Apoc 11,3-12[?]; G. Lohfink, *Himmelfahrt*, 68-69). Isolated texts of later date attest such speculation (*Siphre Dt.* ad 34,5; *Acta Pilati* 16,7; Hier. *In Amos* 9,6 [*CSEL* 32,343f.]; Aug. *In Jn-Evang.* 124,2), and a vigorous tradition based thereon developed in later Samaritan literature (with the mountain and cloud, but more of the nature of an ascent of the soul, as J. Macdonald shows in *Theology of the Samaritans*, 219, 442f.). There was undoubtedly influence of the Christian sacred literature upon the Samaritan *Memar Markah*, where the exuberant legends of Moses' departure are found. But considering the Josephus text, it is not unreasonable to postulate some degree of traditional speculation that might already have been abroad in the Samaritan-Christian milieu of Luke's *Sondertradenten*.

[95] The pre-Lucan origin of the Acts ascension, and redactional anticipation of that scene in the empty tomb story of Lk 24,4f., seems a much more likely process to us than the opposite (Acts 1,10f. composed in imitation of Lk 24,4ff., *pace* G. Lohfink, *Himmelfahrt*, 196-198, and M. Miyoshi, *Anfang*, 20). The formal elements in each case are indeed true to the *angeli-interpretes topos*, and the latter are not infrequently on the scene of bodily assumptions. But these observations do not create conclusive cases for or against Lucan authorship.

complete " journey," from its outset (Lk 9,30 – Mk) *via* death and the grave (Lk 24,4 *diff.* Mk) to heavenly glory (Acts 1,10 – S).

We should emphasize the limits of the judgment we are making here. It is a *motif-historical*, not a literary judgment. Our position is, if the enthusiastic missionaries we have sought to portray in this chapter did recount the episode of Acts 1,9ff., with its Elianic allusions and central instructional content spoken by the ἄνδρες δύο, this would have been wholly consistent with the tenor, background, and *Sitz-im-Leben* of their tradition as we have analyzed it. Whether in fact they did transmit that episode to Luke, so that it, not the gospel finale, represents the ascension *tradition* Luke used,— this we could decide only after close literary analysis of the Acts passage. We have already registered our analytical judgment that the gospel ascension scene is a literary conclusion we owe to the evangelist. We feel our present suggestion is a plausible step towards identifying the nature and source of an ascension account that antedated his writing. But that is all we are putting forth in the matter.

(3) Jerusalem and the Prophet Tradition

In discussing the traditional prophet-rejection schema as adopted by Luke's tradition in Acts 7, we did not consider the one logion from Q which, for the first and only time in O. H. Steck's history of the schema, names *Jerusalem as the prophets' murderess.*[96] The saying is Lk 13,34f./Mt 23,37-39, and like its counterpart in Lk 11,47ff., it was likely once an independent Jewish utterance using the city as representative of the nation. It is related to its counterpart also in its contacts with the wisdom tradition, which has probably furnished the image of the mother-bird and her nest (Sir 1,15) along with the concept of the divine wisdom taking up residence in Jerusalem (Sir 24,8-12 ; cp. Prv 1,20ff.).[97] In pre-Christian usage, such sayings might have come from Jewish wisdom teachers who adapted the prophet-rejection schema to their own usage (as e.g. Prv 1,24ff.). In Lk, as we know, the Jerusalem logion from Q is prefaced by the puzzling apophthegm Lk 13,31-33, which frames the Lucan norm of prophets' death in Jerusalem yet is not representative of Steck's Deuteronomic schema.[98] Moreover,

[96] *Israel*, 227f. ; also 45-58 ; Also F. Schnider, *Jesus der Prophet*, 142-147.

[97] O. H. Steck, *Israel*, 230-234 ; but cf. F. Schnider, *op. cit.*, 144ff.

[98] O. H. Steck, *Israel*, 46 n. 4. As Steck points out, the tradition of the violent destiny of the prophets in Israel could account for the location of a prophets' death at Jerusalem, or could even make Jerusalem herself the murderess (Lk 13,34f.) insofar as the city assumed a representative role for the whole nation. But such ideas do not yet represent the assertion of Lk 13,33b, which is that a prophet *cannot die elsewhere than* Jerusalem ! This rule is not

since the apophthegm does not really fit together and seems a synthetic fusion of vv. 31f. and 33, we repeat our agreement with STECK that Luke composed v. 33 as a *ductus* to the Q saying that follows.[99] Whether the οὐκ ἐνδέχεται principle contained in v. 33 is Luke's own conclusion from the Q saying or an independent prophet logion (like Lk 4,24), it hardly represents a broad interest or substantial innovation of S-Lk. Nowhere else in the *Sondergut* is the prophet-schema or Jerusalem's violent treatment of the prophets brought out. In our opinion, the sacred necessity of *Jerusalem's* onslaught against the divine messengers is *an editorial motif of Luke's,* based on Mark's journey sequence (cf. Lk 18,31 *diff*. Mk 10,33) illuminated by the Jerusalem saying from Q.

Confirmation of this judgment can be found in the nature of Lk 13,33: it is a literary guidepost, a thematic explanation of the urgent " journey " pattern built into the composition of Lk 9-18. Reduplicating v. 32, which might well have expressed our missionaries' " charismatic " program and determination in the face of repression,[100] v. 33

found in the tradition of the Deuteronomic prophet-statements, or anywhere else in the late Judaism or primitive Christian tradition, for that matter.

[99] Cf. chap. II, note 149. Is not STECK's view that even 13,33b is Luke's own composition (*Israel*, 46f) confirmed by the very singularity of its language and conception (as indicated in the previous note)? The singularity can be explained if the evangelist was creating a connection faithful both to the sequence of the source-material and to his own rationale for the " journey " (cf. also K. LEHMANN, *Auferweckt*, 234, and already K. L. SCHMIDT, *Rahmen*, 265-267).

[100] The widespread conviction among exegetes that Lk 13,32 is so enigmatic because it is an authentic logion of Jesus is probably quite accurate (cf. K. L. SCHMIDT, *Rahmen*, 266f. [32a]; R. BULTMANN, *GsT*, 35; W. GRUNDMANN, *Lk.*, 287f.; G. BORNKAMM, *Jesus*, 142; J. BLINZLER, in *Synoptische Studien*, 42-46; K. LEHMANN, *Auferweckt*, 236f., *inter alios*), and it may again be the itinerant mission's direct continuity with the ministry of Jesus which accounts for what R. BULTMANN acknowledges to be the biographical element " im eigentlichen Sinne " in 13,31-32. The meaning of the words in Jesus' mouth depends, of course, on what meaning is ascribed to τελειοῦμαι (" I bring [my activities] to a completion "; cf. the possibilities in J. BLINZLER, *art. cit.*, 43 n. 61, and cf. chap. II, n. 43 above): is the saying a " somewhat veiled passion prophecy " (J. SCHMID, *Lk.*, 240), or does it intend mainly to set an urgent time-limit on Jesus' *works* (O. H. STECK, *Israel*, 44f.)? Luke's two other uses of τελειοῦσθαι (Lk 2,42; Acts 20,24) do not support the pregnant sense given the verb in Heb 2,10; 5,9; 7,28, (*contra* E. KLOSTERMANN, *Lk.*, 147f.; A. DENAUX, in *L'év. de Luc. Mém. Cerfaux*, 272f.), but then neither does the parallel statement of Paul exclude a reference to impending *martyrium* (Acts 20,24; rightly W. RADL, *Paulus und Jesus*, 157). We are inclined to agree with K. LEHMANN (*Auferweckt*, 235f.; cf. also M. MIYOSHI, *Anfang*, 22-23) that Lk 13,32 announces the " coming to term " of Jesus' saving works, the exorcisms and healings, and that this, rather than the end of his life, is the proper (albeit not exclusive) scope of the statement. The works are to be *carried out within a brief, divinely guaranteed period*, whereupon they will be " *completed*," not simply ended. The nuance of divine determination and eschatological finality is expressed, by biblical convention, in the sequence " today," " tomorrow " (Jos 22,18; Sir 20,15; Jas

employs the evangelist's key-word of the section in course, πορεύεσθαι, and makes it complement the familiar δεῖ in a sense that will be expounded in the third passion prophecy, at the " journey's " end (Lk 18,31). Jerusalem inexorably draws the traveling Master by the same salvation-historical necessity as she will impell his traveling witnesses outward to the wide world beyond (explained in chap. 3, p. 215): she is perennially ἀποκτείνουσα τοὺς προφήτας, archetype of the persecutor who, as Luke will illustrate repeatedly in Acts, paradoxically fosters the mission's progress (chap. 3, n. 158). As " the very heart of Luke's theology of Jerusalem," motivating the " journey " that brings the two divinely appointed participants in the passion together, Jesus and Jerusalem,[101] Lk 13,33 really explains the whole dynamism of the Christian mission. And that is the real subject matter of Luke-Acts!

What has just been said also explains Luke's programmatic elimination of Galilee as a site of resurrection appearances (Lk 24,49; Acts 1,4). We quite agree with G. LOHFINK[102] that there is no tradition-historical foundation for this exclusion in principle, whatever should then be said of the so-called Galilean *vs.* Jerusalem Easter traditions and their comparative claims. In any case, Jerusalem as the *divinely appointed and exclusive* site of his witnesses' communion with the risen Christ is Lucan theology of the mission, not information contributed by Luke's sources.

(4) CONCLUSIONS:

Let us be clear about what we have argued here and what we have *not* argued. We have sought to obtain a profile of the group that gave to St. Luke much of the material that is peculiarly his; and we proceeded by analysis of recurrent *motifs* of S-Lk and Acts 6-8. We did

4,13-14), and " the third (day) " (Ex 19,10-11.16; Os 6,2, etc.; K. LEHMANN, *Auferweckt*, 176-181; A. DENAUX, in *L'év. de Luc. Mém. Cerfaux*, 279ff.). The challenge of the human adversary cannot prevail against the ministry of Jesus, to which a short but nevertheless determined period of time has been assigned by God himself. Consequently, the works will come to term, they will not be interrupted by hostile forces (similarly A. DENAUX, *art. cit.*, 271f., who is probably right in taking τελειοῦμαι as *passive* expression of divine agency). For the sense of our statement's time-framework, cf. also E. KLOSTERMANN, *Lk.*, 148; W. GRUNDMANN, *Lk.*, 288f. — Gleaning thus what we might consider a core of commonly accepted meaning from the exegetes' discussion of this enigmatic verse, we might suggest that the Lord's statement was repeated by his " charismatic " emissaries as an assurance of the fulfillment of their own labors in the short time remaining before the parousia. The context of an embattled mission could be the same as we suggested for Lk 22,35ff. (chap. IV, p. 240).

[101] A. HASTINGS, *Prophet and Witness*, 109, 120.

[102] *Himmelfahrt Jesu*, 123f.; cf. also B. STEINSEIFER, *ZNW* 62 (1971) 238; Th. LORENZEN, *ZNW* 64 (1973) 220.

not attempt to characterize the *type of documentation* that group furnished to the evangelist, hence this study takes no position in the age-old Proto-Lk debate. As a tentative opinion in this matter, one could say that, since S-Lk has shown itself to us several times as a probable development of the Q sayings tradition, it was likely that kind of documentation (including his version of Q) that Luke received from this circle. This assessment is confirmed, we judge, by the predominant *word-character* of the material we have studied: most of it has been centered on words of instruction by the Master, and even the miracle stories of the *Sondergut* — instance Lk 17,11-19 — tend to be apophthegms developed out of older, simpler stories,[103] or feature the prophet-status (Lk 7,11-17) or mission summons (Lk 5,2-10) of Jesus. Just as miracle stories tended to acquire words of instruction as their focus when told by these *tradentes,* so did the *martyrium* of Stephen and the account of Philip's wonders at Samaria acquire major instructional sections, and probably did so before Luke incorporated them into Acts. Considering this uniformity of word-orientation, we are not inclined to think of S-Lk in literary dimensions beyond those of Q in the classic two-source hypothesis. We have no reason to think of a full-fledged *gospel* employed as Luke's *Sonderquelle* and, in fact, do not mean to suggest that all the special material came to the evangelist in written form. All such judgments take the kind of lengthy literary analysis that we could not undertake in this chapter.

What we do hope our motif-study has accomplished is a tentative picture of the kind of movement and circumstances which nurtured the special Easter traditions of Lk 24. We have projected a circle of (a) itinerant, " charismatic " missionaries who (b) strove to personalize the Master's radical renunciation, hence (c) relied on the hospitality of receptive households in their incessant travels and, (d) given their severing of earthly ties, experienced ostracism and frequent reliance on service and accomodations from others on the periphery of mainstream society, that is, the very sinners and pariahs who had experienced the Lord's companionship and forgiveness. Enhancing the last observation, we learned from the Stephen-Philip cycle of Acts that the *Sondertradenten* were probably associated with (e) the early Christian mission to

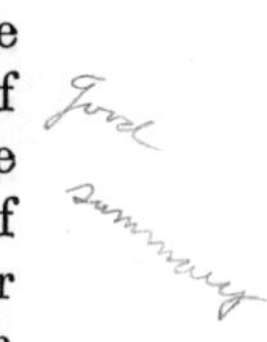

[103] Demonstrated in the case of Lk 17,11-19 by the two studies listed in note 67 above. Is the same true of the story of the miraculous catch, shared by Lk 5,2-11 with Jn 21,2ff., but acquiring the " catcher of men " logion (cp. Mk 1,17) only in the S-Lk version ? The story of the repentant woman acquired at least the sayings on the hospitality of the unworthy (Lk 7,44-46), if not the parable of vv. 41-42 as well, under the auspices of S-Lk. Notice also the substantial infusion of instructional content into the story of the woman with the spirit of infirmity (Lk 13,11-17 S), which may well be an apophthegmatically developed variant of Mk 5,25ff. And observe also Lk 14,1-6, comparing with Mk 3,1-6. — On the pattern of such development in S-Lk, cf. R. PESCH, *Taten,* 129.

Samaria, as perhaps both its agents and its recruits. Not only would such a milieu better explain (f) the missionaries' experience of alienation from Israel and incentive to evangelize the Gentile "outsiders," it would also account for (g) the eschatological-prophet Christology and strains of Elia/Elisha narrative that so often underlie the *Sondergut* pieces.

Applying these results to the narrative of Lk 24, we find: (1) points a to c account for the christophany situation that is common to the Emmaus and "cenacle" pericopes, viz. the traveling (Emmaus) Master entertained as a guest, either turning host for the eucharist (Emmaus) or taking food from the receptive household (cenacle); (2) in point d comes the rationale for the household mission-situation used as prologue for the appointment to proclaim the *forgiveness of sins* to *all the nations,* a feature we have judged all along to have belonged to the pre-Lucan pericope; (3) points e and f reinforce the last finding, especially the Gentile-mission aspect; (4) point e indicates the source of the prophetic christology in Lk 24, particularly the "charismatic" portrait of Lk 24,19 which Luke insisted must be integrated with that of the rejected and murdered prophet (the pattern of such integration already furnished in the Scripture mosaic of Stephen). (5) Finally, point e may also suggest the traditional *point de départ* for the Lucan ascension, perhaps already recounted by S-Lk as it now stands in Acts 1,9-11 (cf. point g).

If this tradition-historical picture adequately supports the literary analysis of previous chapters in delimiting the pre-Lucan source-material of chapter 24, we may proceed to a final summation of the personal statement of our evangelist in his Easter story.

II. REDACTION-HISTORICAL SUMMATION:

THE WORLD-MISSION'S PRELUDE AND PREPARATION

(*Lk 24 at the Intersection of the Two Volumes*)

It is principally *vis-a-vis* his source-materials that the voice of the gospel's redactor must be individuated. If one has managed to discern the contours, provenance, and separate affirmations of such *Vorlagen* in a given segment of the canonical book, he may then proceed to measure the assertions intended by the one who combined and embellished the sources for the final product. In Lk 24 we dealt with two main source-auspices, Mk in the tomb story and S-Lk in the two christophanies. It may be that some literary combination of these episodes came already from S-Lk — say, the tomb-story and the apostolic appearance, as R. Leaney thought[104] — but we were unable to verify that analytically to our satisfaction. Nor is it necessarily the case that all the *Sondergut* came to the evangelist in written form, much less as an integral " gospel " of Marcan dimensions. In point of fact, the connective tissue presently joining the three Easter pericopes has proved so clearly and consistently the *redactor's work* that any pre-existence of the three *in sequence* appears doubtful. They were more likely bequeathed to Luke in spoken form, or in rudimentary written compilation, as we suggested regarding the Stephen- and Philip-traditions. In sum, the literary analysis of our first three chapters fully confirmed the judgment of J. M. Creed, among others, that the Easter episodes' order and interconnection " has been imposed by the historian upon his materials, and the links are the least original part of the story " (*Lk*, 289).

On the other hand, we were able to demonstrate a strong affinity of *Sitz-im-Leben* between the two Lucan appearance stories. Both feature the risen Lord as an itinerant stranger hosted at a meal, which was the very circumstance that often attended the ministry of the wayfaring missionaries who, we assert, had been the bearers of S-Lk. Because mission prototypes and ideals thus dominate Lk 24, as they dominate much of the *Sondergut*, we do well to choose the *mission enterprise* as our focal point for distilling and refining the message of St. Luke that chapter 24 conveys. We have already looked to that *Sitz-im-Leben* to diagnose the special tradition, its often archaic, Judeo-Christian complexion,[105] and the problematic linkage of such material with the Gentile author of Lk-Acts. Now we pose the question whether, because the Easter chapter clearly functions as both the gospel's conclusion and its point of connection with the story to be told in Acts (so the retrospect in Acts 1,2ff. demonstrates), the chapter's mission focus was intended by *the evangelist* to serve precisely as the *connection and transition motif* between the two great divisions of his history. If the second volume will tell the story of Jesus' missionaries reenacting his ministry and propagating his message, then the transition chapter

---

[104] Cf. chap. III, note 12. — It may be that S-Lk presented in sequence a version of the tomb story similar to Jn 20,3-10 (severely condensed in Lk 24,12) and the christophany before the assembled disciples, in which Lk 24,36ff. and Jn 20,19ff. are found in close parallel. In that case, of course, Luke would have preferred his Marcan source for the substance of the empty tomb episode, for reasons we have explored at length. This editorial decision, however, together with the lone appearance of Mary Magdalen in Jn 20, makes the argument of R. Leaney very difficult to put on solid analytical footing. For a view similar to Leaney's, cf. most recently Hans Klein, " Die lukanisch-johanneische Passionstradition," *ZNW* 67 (1976, 155-186) 186 n. 92.

[105] O. H. Steck, *Israel*, 269 : " puzzling ... fact that Luke obtained the sayings documentation in very archaic form."

must be a programmatic statement of this divinely ordained *continuum.* Let us see if and how this is verified.

(1) The Mission's Content

A major vehicle of the evangelists' self-expression was their way of combining and interrelating source materials. In so subtle a gesture as combining the Galilean suppliants of his special source with the Marcan women at the tomb (Lk 24,10/8,2 ; cp. Mk 16,1), Luke also meant to combine the pardoned sinners featured as the Teacher's constituency in S-Lk with the paschal witnesses of the common synoptic tradition. The combination forms a true Easter assembly, the *ecclesia in partu.* How appropriate it is that *this* assembly should be appointed to carry out the universal proclamation of μετάνοια εἰς ἄφεσιν ἁμαρτιῶν in Jesus' name (Lk 24,47f.). The women healed and forgiven (recall 8,2f. adjoining 7,36-50 !) embodied Jesus' own earthly ministry being translated into the universal mission's content.[106]

A similar blending process can be observed with respect to the sources' divergent christological portraits. Mark's was a portrait of the Son of God progressively revealed by his *deeds,* but recognizable for who he was only when the deeds were retroactively illumined by the Cross.[107] The Q/S-Lk combination, on the other hand, presented the Master as prophet of the imminent Kingdom of God and executor of the judgment, whose *words* and *regula vitae* were to be disseminated by his followers as the standard of membership among God's elect.[108] The risen Christ of Lk 24 is both of these, in carefully measured combina-

[106] On the implied inclusion of the forgiven sinner among the female attendants (Lk 7,36-50/8,2-3), cf. chap. I above, p. 12. The women's presence among the recruited witnesses betokens the comprehensive paschal fulfillment of the earthly "way of Jesus," a Lucan editorial interest effectively brought out by R. Glöckner, *Verkündigung,* 202ff.

[107] Cf. Mk 15,39. This seems to be an emerging consensus concerning the "book of secret epiphanies." According to M. Dibelius, who coined that popular characterization of the Marcan gospel (*Formgeschichte,* 232), Mark included specimens of Jesus' teaching only by way of occasional illustration and confirmation of the identity of Jesus, the kerygma's object ; it was not his concern to document the Master's words for systematic repetition by the Church (*Formgeschichte,* 237ff., 259ff.). — On the cross as the awaited moment of the messianic confession and the goal of Mark's narrative pathos, see chap. II above, note 138.

[108] This much seems to be matter of common agreement in the recent treatises on Q. Cf. H.-E. Tödt, *Menschensohn,* 224-249 ; D. Lührmann, *Redaktion,* 96-100 ; P. Hoffmann, *Logienquelle,* 153-158 ; S. Schulz, *Q,* 481-489. — We pass over the refinements of each position, of course. The influence of the Easter kerygma and Son of Man Christology (Tödt, Hoffmann) is not agreed upon, nor should one overlook the differentiated stages of the Q tradition in, say, the gradual diminishing of imminent expectation (rightly S. Schulz, *op. cit.,* 29f.).

tion. He is the messiah whose death and resurrection gives meaning and fulfillment to the earthly ministry just concluded; but he is also the Teacher whose words once spoken, ἔτι ὢν σὺν ὑμῖν, become the key to understanding and participating in the eschatological events at hand. Moreover, the pattern of this combination is intriguing since the dominical *words* brought forward to illumine the events are the kerygmatic prediction-formulas of *Mark,* inserted as the centerpiece of all three Easter episodes. In the appearance stories, indeed, the usual contributions of the sources have been reversed: the narratives come from S-Lk, usually dedicated to Jesus' teachings, as we have seen,[109] while the inserted *dicta Jesu* are the statements of the mystery of the passion adapted from Mark. These formally exceptional ingredients accurately represent their sources, however. The *narratives* from S-Lk betray the norms of the wayfaring mission which was to disseminate the sayings tradition, and the *sayings* from Mark reflect the kerygmatic orientation and finality of the narrative gospel. Luke is clearly intent on making both traditions the content of the church's mission. His approach is to *reconcile and harmonize* them, not to validate one at the expense of the other.[110]

This observation contains a valuable clue to Luke's literary intentions which we can better understand by referring back to his statement of objectives in the much-discussed gospel prologue. In introducing the present study, we announced as one of its targets the widespread view that, as "the first Christian historian," Luke made historical narrative (διήγησις, Lk 1,1) a separate category alongside gospel catechesis (Lk 1,4),[111] superadded to the latter as its authenticating argument, establish-

[109] Cf. the remarks on p. 265, and n. 103 above. It is clear that formal differences in their material cannot adequately differentiate the Marcan and Q/S-Lk traditions. The first is dedicated to proclaiming the Son of God through telling of his saving deeds, while the other stewards his teaching as key to the salvation imminently breaking in upon human affairs. One proclaims the gospel through the medium of historical narrative, the other through the medium of charismatic prophecy. Sayings in Mk and narrative in Q/S-Lk serve the selfsame purpose as the more usual content of each source; they are not exceptions to the rule which alter the prevailing literary objective.

[110] As against the inclination of some exegetes to read ἐπεχείρησαν in Lk 1,1 pejoratively, as an editorial resolve to correct faulty predecessors (so G. KLEIN, in *Zeit und Geschichte*, 195f.; S. SCHULZ, *Stunde*, 244), R. GLÖCKNER correctly argues: "Lukas sieht sich mit seinem Versuch also nicht in Rivalität oder gar in Bruch zu den vorgegebenen Traditionen und bestreitet weder ihr Recht noch ihren Wert. Sein γράψαι beansprucht eher den Charakter eines vervollständigenden und in etwa auch überbietenden Neuversuches" (*Verkündigung*, 12). The verb in question obtains its nuance from the context in each case and does not carry an automatic adverse judgment, even in Lk-Acts. Rightly also, against KLEIN: I. H. MARSHALL, *Luke*, 40f.; H. SCHÜRMANN, *Traditionsgeschichtliche Untersuchungen*, 259).

[111] Cf. p. IX above. — DIBELIUS's judgment of Luke's "gospel," "nicht

ing its factual content and legitimate spokesmen while no longer conveying its direct kerygmatic summons. The exegetical analysis of Lk 24 has substantially undermined that categorical theorem of mainline *Lukasanalyse*. For one thing, in none of the Easter pericopes did " a succession of historical facts " amount to the adequate *Glaubensgegenstand* or *Glaubensgewissheit*,[112] for painstakingly articulated " facts " in each of them created only a heightened threshold of human uncertainty for the repetition of words from the earthly Jesus' prophecy about himself. It was clear the facts did not speak for themselves, any more than Jesus' miracles automatically generated faith in him among the onlookers.[113] Only when wondrous fact and interpreting word coincided in the conclusive self-disclosure of the Easter Christ did the messianic enigma dissipate and the messianic salvation become accessible. Such is the indispensable partnership of fact and word (Lk 24,19), of seeing and hearing (Lk 7,22 ; 10,23f.), hence of *narrative* and *sayings* traditions, which must constitute both the credentials of the Easter witness and the content of the Easter message. Moreover, since the crucial words illumining each episode of the " third day " were presented as rehearsals of the earthly Jesus' explanation of all scriptural prophecy in reference to himself, they are clearly to be taken as summations of all his λόγοι (Lk 24,44f.), not just a *caput princeps* thereof.

We believe this analysis is supported by the language of the prologue, even though the drastic brevity of that passage invites manipulation in support of predetermined arguments. It seems correct, at

---

Inhalt der Predigt ... sondern Bürgschaft für diesen Inhalt " (*Formgeschichte*, 14) seemed to enunciate mutually exclusive categories which lend themselves to CONZELMANN's " Zweites zum Kerygma ... (das) nicht selbst Kerygma (ist), sondern gibt dessen geschichtliche Voraussetzungen " (*MdZ*, 3). In our opinion, U. LUCK successfully demonstrated how the Lucan historiography was aimed at arguing the divinely instilled unity of all sacred history in the Spirit, hence at showing the direct connection between the sacred past and the salvation of the gospel's audience in the present (*ZTK* 57 [1960] 56ff./Braumann-*LkEv.*, 101ff.). " Lukas hat in seinem Evangelium die Aufgabe zu lösen versucht, vergangene Geschichte vom gegenwärtigen Wirken des Geistes her als Gottesgeschichte zu verstehen. Darin wurzelt das Problem seines Evangeliums " (*ibid.*, 65/ = 113). Viewed in this perspective, of course, the Lucan historiography and kerygma are " nicht auseinanderzureissen," we quite agree.

[112] G. KLEIN, in *Zeit und Geschichte*, 216.

[113] Cf. Lk 6,11, where rejection and hostility are the aftermath of the healing miracle ; Lk 13,10ff., where the same miracle affects different groups in different ways (v. 17) ; Lk 17,11ff., where the miracle begets faith and confession in only one of ten beneficiaries. R. GLÖCKNER is correct to cite these passages as refutation of any inherent saving power of facts and deeds in Luke's understanding (*Verkündigung*, 17). Just as the deed of Jesus required believing acceptance in its object before it could be a *saving* deed, so also do the πράγματα of Luke's historical narrative require the dimension of believing, faith-awakening *word* before they can be considered πεπληροφορημένα ἐν ἡμῖν (see note 115 below).

all events, to interpret Lk 1,1f. in terms of the unified testimony of dominical deeds and words, carried forward as tidings of the Christian mission through the *combined* offices of the " *eye-witnesses* become *ministers of the word.*" [114] The evangelical διήγησις is a product of both ingredients, the αὐτοψία and the διακονία τοῦ λόγου (Acts 6,4), which distinguished the original Easter witnesses and their *paradosis*. In turn, the two ingredients correspond to the two phases of salvation enunciated in Lk 1,1 : the basic *facta salutis* (πράγματα) and their " coming to fruition " (πληροφορεῖσθαι) in circles removed from the " eyewitnesses " in time and/or place (cf. ἐν ἡμῖν 1,1 ; παρέδοσαν ἡμῖν 1,2).[115]

---

[114] G. Klein confines the participle γενόμενοι to the second part of this phrase (Lk 1,2), rather than rendering it " were " and referring it to both αὐτόπται and ὑπηρέται (cf. *Zeit und Geschichte*, 204f. ; likewise W. Grundmann, *Lk.*, 44 ; H. Schürmann, *Lk.* I, 9 n. 55 ; and on both possibilities, E. Nellessen, *Zeugnis*, 232). Against the objection that, had he wished to restrict the participle with the sense of "become," Lk would have repeated the definite article after καί, one can insist that this would have implied that the αὐτόπται and ὑπηρέται were at least partially different groups, whereas Lk clearly intends to characterize *one and the same group* in two successive stages. Moreover, the parallel positions of ἀπ' ἀρχῆς and γενόμενοι seem to indicate confinement of each to the phrase it is in (— as is certainly the case with ἀπ' ἀρχῆς). Cp. Jerome's Vulg. with the standard renderings of RSV, NEB, NAB.

[115] The interpretation of the prologue's πληροφορεῖσθαι in terms of the historical events' salvific *effect* among believers of a different time and locale (so H. Schürmann, *Traditionsgeschichtliche Untersuchungen*, 268, and *Lk.* I, 8f. ; E. Lohse, " Lukas als Theologe der Heilsgeschichte," in Braumann - *LkEv*, 70ff. ; G. Klein, in *Zeit und Geschichte*, 198ff.) seems to us to be the only way to coordinate the ἐν ἡμῖν in v. 1 with παρέδοσαν ἡμῖν in v. 2. R. Glöckner does not seem to have satisfied both expressions, for if one is determined to translate πεπληροφορημένων with merely " happened," even meaning a " vollendetes Geschehensein," it is difficult then to declare the " us " of v. 1, Luke's circle, to be " contemporaries " of the events who must nevertheless have the events " handed down " to them by eye-witnesses (v. 2 ; cf. *Verkündigung*, 19-20). The concept of *traditio* does not usually imply " Gleichzeitigkeit ... mit den Heilsereignissen selbst und mit deren Augenzeugen ...," and in any case the inception of Christian faith in Luke's circle is not found in the happening of the events but in the παρέδοσαν ἡμῖν, the same *traditio* as κατηχήθης refers to in v. 4. — Consequently, one is inclined to look for the nuance of " *come to full conviction* " in πληροφορεῖσθαι (cf. usage with personal subjects in Rom 4,21 ; 14,5 ; Col 4,12). It is not really possible to obtain this meaning directly from the passive form, as suggested by A. Schlatter (*Lk.*, 20), K. H. Rengstorf (*Lk.*, 14), and W. Grundmann (*Lk.*, 43f.), since it is the active voice which can mean " create full conviction " (W. Bauer, *Wb.*[5], 1329f.), hence only πράγματα πεπληροφορηκότα could express " things that have created full conviction among us " (rightly G. Klein, in *Zeit und Geschichte*, 197 n. 33 ; cf. also J. M. Creed, *Lk.*, 3 ; H. J. Cadbury, in *Beginnings* II, 495f.). Nevertheless, the form Luke wrote qualifies at least as the typical passive expression of divine agency (rightly E. Lohse, in Braumann - *LkEv*, 71 ; U. Luck, *ZTK* 57 [1960] 60/ = Braumann *Lk.-Ev.*, 106f.), and if " the use of this verb suggests that Luke is thinking of events which were promised and performed by God, ... (hence) conveys the idea of

The " fruition " of the πράγματα is thus the continuing business of the mission, and it is accomplished only where the events of the *historia Jesu* are rendered signs of messianic recognition by the clarifying, summoning *Anrede* of the preaching. Since, in Luke's perspective, this *praedicatio Christi* was already furnished in the λόγοι of the earthly Jesus interpreting his own person and mission, it follows that the Christian preacher's interpretative word will be simply a faithful stewardship of the tradition of Jesus' words. It is the Easter chapter which establishes this Lucan equation, and it is an ultimate coherence of narrative and sayings traditions which is achieved thereby ! Having imposed such a consensus on the sources, of course, Luke could not but understand his historical διήγησις as itself a *preaching of the kerygma,* and not an historicizing rationalization thereof.

The implications of this argument for other bones of contention in Lucan studies are clear, notably the kerygmatic vitality of " *today* " in Lk 4,21 [116] and the two-epoch schema of Lk 16,16.[117] These, too,

---

fulfillment " (I. H. MARSHALL, *Luke*, 41), the perfect tense accentuates the *perduring effect* of this divine " carrying to completion." The " events " are thus not to be conceived apart from their *impact upon the believer in the present,* which means their " completion " involves their fruition in a believing adherence to their tradition. The perfect tense may achieve what the exact sense of the verb in the passive voice could not communicate !

[116] H. CONZELMANN's consignment of Luke's " *today* " to the sacred past, contrasting it to Paul's " *now* " in II Cor 6,2 (cf. *MdZ*, 30, 156, 158, 182), has not won the day, thanks to H. FLENDER, *Heil*, 135ff. ; E. E. ELLIS, *NTS* 12 (1965-66) 36f. ; O. BETZ, *Interpr* 22 (1968) 134-138 ; H. SCHÜRMANN, *Lk.* I, 233 ; W. ELTESTER, in *Jesus in Nazareth*, 140f. ; M. RESE, *Altt. Motive*, 147f. ; S. G. WILSON, *NTS* 16 (1969-70) 347, and *Gentiles*, 66f., 86f. ; E. SCHWEIZER, *Jesus*, 140f. ; I. H. MARSHALL, *Luke*, 120f. ; C.-P. MÄRZ, *Wort Gottes*, 41ff. ; R. GLÖCKNER, *Verkündigung*, 132-133 ; E. FRANKLIN, *Christ the Lord*, 71.

[117] As is well known, H. CONZELMANN found in Lk 16,16 the key-statement of Luke's alleged (by C.) *three-epoch* schema of salvation-history, of which the ministry of Jesus constitutes the *Mitte*, without any pre-history in the age of " the Law and the Prophets " which John terminated, and differentiated from the age of the Church in that it was an ideal *Heilszeit*, free of Satan and his onslaughts (cf. *MdZ*, 9f., 17, 20, 92ff., 103f., 104f., 149f., 172f. ; cf. also " Zur Lukasanalyse " in Braumann - *LkEv.*, 62f.). Whatever might be said in favor of the schema C. advocates, it is widely agreed that he chose a particularly dubious text to support it in Lk 16,16f. By now, the remark of Paul MINEAR on this issue has become a favorite quotation against C. : " It must be said that rarely has a scholar placed so much weight on so dubious an interpretation of so difficult a logion " (in *StLA*, 122). A particularly detailed and devastating critique of C's exegesis of 16,16 was made by W. G. KÜMMEL, " ' Das Gesetz und die Propheten ...," in Braumann - *LkEv.*, 398-415, where the difficulty of the Q source-text, the ambiguity of Luke's ἀπὸ τότε, the uncertain extent and emphasis of the Lucan editing, and — perhaps most telling — the *de facto* mention of only two epochs, the " law and the Prophets " and the Kingdom's proclamation, in the disputed logion, are all argued with lethal effect on the three-epoch hypothesis. — As a result, despite the punctual agreement C. won

are articles of the *consensus fontium* imposed by the evangelist. Already the gift of " forgiveness " is announced at Nazareth as the substance of the eschatological prophecy, and the same message is the continuation of the Easter kerygma in Lk 24,46-47.[118] Similarly, the *terminus ad quem* of the prophetic scriptures is defined at Lk 16,16 in terms of the subject-matter of the sayings tradition: ἡ βασιλεία τοῦ θεοῦ εὐαγγελίζεται. And the same subject-matter is attached to the instructions of the risen Christ in Acts 1,3. It seems to us that Luke's historical schema embraces *two epochs*, not three, and that the present stands over against the past as the *age of the eschatological prophecy*, the bequest of the Lord to his missionary church.[119] Here, of course, the voice of the Lucan *Sondergut* is heard clearly over the other sources, furnishing a hermeneutical principle by which to combine the deeds and sayings of the Master, and the traditions devoted to each, into a unified content of the Christian missionaries' propaganda.[120] Then, as his own special accent added to the concept of eschatological prophecy, we recall Luke's

---

from some scholars on 16,16 (e.g. E. HAENCHEN, *Apg.*, 86; S. SCHULZ, *Stunde*, 284; E. GRÄSSER, *Parusieverzögerung*, 182f., 187ff., 215; G. SCHNEIDER, *Verleugnung*, 208-209), one agrees with the broader consensus of C's critics that Lk 16,16 is not a programmatic statement of Lucan *Heilsgeschichte* (cf. even U. WILCKENS, *Missionsreden*, 105 n. 2; also U. LUCK, *ZTK* 57 [1960] 53 n. 5 [= Braumann-*LkEv.*, 97 n. 12]) and the schema presupposed in that verse is rather a two-epoch arrangement (up to John the Baptist, and since John the Baptist), the first related to the second as " promise " to " fulfillment " (rightly H. FLENDER, *Heil*, 112f.; W. C. ROBINSON, *Weg*, 29, 60ff.; O. BETZ, *Interpr* 22 [1968] 132f. & n. 5; H. ZIMMERMANN, *Methodenlehre*, 217; H.-J. DEGENHARDT, *Lukas*, 15 n. 1, 132f.; S. BROWN, *Apostasy and Perseverance*, 97f. n. 404; W.-G. KÜMMEL, " Luc en accusation ...," in *L'Év. de Luc. Mém. Cerfaux*, 102 f. [= Braumann, *LkEv.*, 428]; S. G. WILSON, *NTS* 16 [1969-70] 333ff., and *Gentiles*, 63ff.; I. H. MARSHALL, *Luke*, 145-146; J. ZMIJEWSKI, *Eschatologiereden*, 283f., 422; C.-P. MÄRZ, *Wort Gottes*, 43f.; O. MERK, in *Jesus und Paulus*, 207; R. GLÖCKNER, *Verkündigung*, 88f.; E. FRANKLIN, *Christ the Lord*, 85f.). Other authors take issue with CONZELMANN on the latter's exclusion of John from the era of salvation, either without addressing themselves to the three-epoch schema (thus G. BRAUMANN, *ZNW* 54 [1963] 122ff.; E. KRÄNKL, *Jesus*, 93-97), or retaining the schema and simply adjusting the second epoch to include John (thus W. WINK, *John the Baptist*, 55f.).

[118] We took note of the relation of these two passages in chap. II (p. 137) and chap. III (p. 214).

[119] Here one learns the significance of the Joel-prophecy quoted by Peter on the Pentecost, with its editorial repetition of καὶ προφητεύσουσιν, of which we took special note in chap. 2 (p. 126 and n. 168). Cf. F. SCHNIDER, *Prophet*, 57.

[120] We recall that, in the Emmaus disciple's recollection of Jesus as προφήτης δυνατός κτλ. (Lk 24,19), the combination of " work and word " cited corresponded to the combination of " seeing and hearing " with respect to Jesus' activity (Lk 7,22; 10,24) and his witnesses' testimony (Acts 4,20; 22,15) (cf. F. SCHNIDER, *Prophet*, 125).

portrayal of the Easter Christ as the term of all biblical prophecy,[121] coordinating, as we saw, the two parts of the Emmaus dialogue.

(2) The Mission's Pattern

More clearly still is the third gospel's "journey" plan the fruit of a blending of Luke's sources. Mark had already given his *theologia crucis* the literary form of a "journey" connecting Galilean and Jerusalem narrative sequences,[122] and Luke strained the very same framework with a vast insertion of non-Marcan materials, bounded by the second and third passion predictions and artificially subsumed into the Marcan *anabasis* (Mk 10,32).[123] On the other hand, most of the material of Lk 9,51 – 18,14 is from S-Lk (with characteristic Q admixture), hence the section's "journey" framework was in complete harmony with the ideals of the wayfaring mission which we have shown to form much of the content of the combined sayings tradition. The influence of the special source is also apparent in the keynote *mission instructions* which inaugurate the "journey" section: the Samaritan embassy (Lk 9,52ff.), the recruitment of fellow wayfarers (Lk 9,57ff.) and, of course, the mission program itself (Lk 10,1ff.), all of which represent either *Sondergut* or Q-material mediated, as we suggested, by the *Sondertradenten*. We wish to suggest that this coordination of Marcan and non-Marcan source material in Lk 9-10 furnishes an important clue to the rationale of our Easter story's composition.

Luke's redaction of Mark's passion preview and connected disciple instructions is joined to the mission passages at Lk 9,51f., a sentence (including καὶ ἀπέστειλεν κτλ.) whose origin at the evangelist's hand has been successfully argued by the *Redaktionsgeschichtler*.[124] The direct

[121] Cf. chap. II, pp. 134f. Also chap. III, pp. 205, 222.

[122] Note the editorial pattern established with the word ὁδός in Mk 8,27; 9,33.34; 10,17,32,46,52; 11,8. The thematic statement of the "way" motif is Mk 10,32 and its climax is Mk 11,8. Cf. W. Wrede, *Messiasgeheimnis*, 96-101; K. L. Schmidt, *Rahmen*, 245ff.; R. Bultmann, *GsT*, 361; H. Conzelmann, "Zur Lukasanalyse," in Braumann-*LkEv.*, 54, and *MdZ*, 54 n. 2, 55 n. 3, 66; also in *Zur Bedeutung des Todes Jesu*, 41ff.; Johannes Schreiber, *Theologie des Vertrauens. Eine redaktionsgeschichtliche Untersuchung des Markusevangeliums* (Hamburg: Furche-Verlag, 1967) 190ff.; D. Gill, *HarvTR* 63 (1970) 218ff.; R. Pesch, *Markusevangelium* I, 37.

[123] Cf. W. G. Kümmel, *Introd. N.T.*[17], 133, 134, 141; J. Blinzler, in *Synoptische Studien* (*f.* A. Wikenhauser), 34f.; J. Schneider, *ibid.*, 211; H. Conzelmann, in Braumann-*LkEv.*, 54, and *MdZ*, 65; W. C. Robinson, *JBL* 79 (1960) 20ff., and *Weg*, 53; W. Grundmann, *Lk.*, 197-200; W. Eltester, in *Jesus in Nazareth*, 83-85.

[124] H. Conzelmann, *MdZ*, 58; H. Flender, *Heil*, 35; E. Lohse, "Lukas als Theologe," in Braumann-*LkEv.*, 72f.; W. C. Robinson, *Weg*, 34, 53 n. 310; G. Voss, *Christologie*, 140ff.; F. Schütz, *Christus*, 68f.; G. Lohfink, *Himmel-*

sequence of the *doctrina passionis*, the dispatch of ἄγγελοι πρὸ προσώπου αὐτοῦ (Lk 9,52a), and the lesson of the Samaritans' rejection (Lk 9,53: καὶ οὐκ ἐδέξαντο αὐτόν),[125] is coordinated by the announcement that forms the title-sentence of the gospel's "travelogue": αὐτὸς τὸ πρόσωπον ἐστήρισεν τοῦ πορεύεσθαι εἰς Ἰερουσαλήμ. It could not be clearer that the Master's own ἀνάλημψις is the course charted for his missionaries.[126] This is the *nexus* Luke furnished between the two source-segments and their main ideas. He discerned the fundamental coherence between the

---

fahrt, 215-217; C. H. TALBERT, in *Jesus and Man's Hope* I, 176f.; A. GEORGE, in *De Jésus aux évangiles*, 109-110; G. FRIEDRICH, in *Orientierung an Jesus*, 70ff.; M. MIYOSHI, *Anfang*, 15; P. von der OSTEN-SACKEN, *EvT* 33 (1973) 479ff.; D. GILL, *HarvTR* 63 (1970) 200ff.; R. GLÖCKNER, *Verkündigung*, 73. — Even before redaction analysis, the Lucan character of this verse was recognized, e.g. by M. DIBELIUS, *Formgeschichte*, 44 n. 3; K. L. SCHMIDT, *Rahmen*, 259-260; cf. also R. BULTMANN, *GsT*[4] *Ergänzungsheft*, 23. The few voices raised against this broad consensus, e.g. J. BLINZLER, in *Synoptische Studien* (*für A. Wikenhauser*), 39ff.; G. OGG, "The Central Section of the Gospel according to St. Luke," *NTS* 18 (1971-72, 39-53) 40, remain isolated and do scant justice to the compositional design of the third gospel. One can scarcely agree, for example, with BLINZLER's contention: "Lukas legt dem Rahmen der Jerusalemreise keine tragende Bedeutung bei..." (*art. cit.*, 41), and yet one inevitably undermines the crucial journey-conception of the evangelist by insisting that a statement like 9,51 has to come from some pre-Lucan *Quelle*. More appropriate is J. SCHNEIDER's judgment, at least with respect to 9,51, where he follows K. L. SCHMIDT (cf. *Synoptische Studien*, 212).

[125] M. MIYOSHI (*Anfang*, 12) rightly judges that, while the account of the Samaritan rejection is drawn from Luke's *Sondertradition*, its placement at the beginning of the travel-narrative represents the redactor's decision. Cf. also K. L. SCHMIDT, *Rahmen*, 267-269. — The intentionally inaugural position occupied by the Samaritan episode is confirmed by the obvious literary relationship between Lk 9,52a and Lk 10,1 (noted by M. MIYOSHI, *op. cit.*, 25f.). Luke clearly intends that the universal mission of the Church after Easter should be foreshadowed, and provided for, in the journey of the Master to Jerusalem. See note 128 below.

[126] The importance of the section preceding the *Reisebericht* for the latter's interpretation was noticed by J. SCHNEIDER (*Synoptische Studien*, 210f.) and established by H. CONZELMANN (*MdZ*, 56). Cf. also W. GRUNDMANN, *Lk.*, 199; H. FLENDER, *Heil*, 70; G. SCHNEIDER, *Verleugnung*, 199; D. GILL, *HarvTR* 63 (1970) 220f.; P. von der OSTEN-SACKEN, *EvT* 33 (1973) 479, 484. — It is clear to these interpreters that the journey-narrative's placement, introduction, and individual components are meant to inculcate, in concert, the necessary participation of Jesus' missionary envoys in the harsh destiny of their Master. Cf. esp. D. GILL, *HarvTR* 63 (1970) 213-214, 218-221; P. von der OSTEN-SACKEN, *EvT* 33 (1973) 495 (rightly insisting there is no "either/or" of christological and ecclesiological purposes in the journey-narrative, 494); M. MIYOSHI, *Anfang*, 26; H. FLENDER, *Heil*, 76; W. ELTESTER, in *Jesus in Nazareth*, 85; G. SCHNEIDER, *Verleugnung*, 199: "Der Zug Jesu nach Jerusalem ist nicht einfach Ausdruck des Leidensbewusstseins Jesu, sondern er ist im Sinne des Luk als dem Lebensweg des Christen vorgängiger und vorgeordneter Weg des Christus durch Passion und Tod zum himmlischen Heil zu interpretieren."

Marcan discipleship of the suffering Son of Man and the contradicted "eschatological prophecy"[127] transmitted in the sayings tradition. Moreover, by making *Samaria* the dominical mission's first station and first *échec*, Luke signifies that it is the way of the mission *beyond Israel*, the mission to the Gentiles, that was being inaugurated and charted in the commencement of the Master's journey to Jerusalem.[128] — Now one can see that the gospel's Easter story, with its threefold reprise of the passion instruction and its concluding charter of the world-wide mission in Jesus' name, was composed with deliberate echoes of the sequence in Lk 9-10, showing the essential continuity between the earthly Jesus' "journey" and the course of the missionary Church. The destined association between the passion of Jesus and the fortunes of his missionaries, editorially stated already at Lk 9,51f., became the *Leitmotiv* of the "witnesses'" recruitment on Easter day, which is the story Lk 24 tells.

Recognizing this important and expressive editorial symmetry between the beginning and end of the gospel's "journey,"[129] we are better prepared to spot certain intentional cross-references between the passages in question. Early on in our study we had occasion to notice the deliberate, anticipatory references that this evangelist had introduced into the transfiguration story (cf. chap. 1, pp. 22ff., 40f.): the ἄνδρες

---

[127] The wolf/sheep figure of Lk 10,3, for example, seems to place that saying in line with the Q theorem of the prophets' dire fate in Israel (cf. Lk 11,49-51/ Mt 23,34; Lk 13,34/Mt 23,37; Lk 6,22-23/Mt 5,11-12; Lk 7,33-35/ Mt 11,18-19; cf. P. HOFFMANN, *Logienquelle*, 295; S. SCHULZ, *Q*, 413). "Sheep" symbolize the good people oppressed by the evil, and the poor oppressed by the rich, in Sir 13,17. On the other hand, it is not the familiar motif of the Gentile nations' hostility to Israel that should be taken as the saying's proximate inspiration, *pace* T. W. MANSON, *Sayings*, 75.

[128] J. SCHNEIDER, in *Synoptische Studien*, 225f.; A. GEORGE, in *De Jésus aux évangiles*, 111f.; D. GILL, *HarvTR* 63 (1970) 202f., 215; M. MIYOSHI, *Anfang*, 17. — Cf. note 66 above.

[129] That the symmetry represents a deliberate redactional proceeding, meant to bring Luke's soteriological thought to expression, we find confirmed by the connection between Lk 9,51 and Acts 1,11 as termini of the complete itinerary of the Lord (argued above in chap. III, note 60). As many have correctly insisted, the plural "days" of Lk 9,51 refers to "the paschal mystery in its entirety: passion, death, resurrection, and ascension" (J. DUPONT, in *Études sur les Actes*, 479), hence the ἀνάλημφις begun at 9,51 is the integral "journey" of the Lord whose terminus is in heaven (see below, note 134). What the vocabulary-echoes between Lk 9,51 and Acts 1,11 (ἀνάλημψις / ὁ ἀναλημφθείς and πορεύεσθαι/πορευόμενον) bring out, the parallel associations and *argumenta* of Lk 9 and Lk 24 also express, viz. the soteriology of the dominical "journey" as the foundation of the missionary church. The theological expressiveness of such symmetries in Luke's arrangement of larger literary blocks was sensed by R. MORGENTHALER (*Die lk. Geschichtsschreibung* I, 159-194), developed to some extent by H. FLENDER (*Heil*, sect. I).

from heaven, their cryptic conversation with Jesus, and the silence of the disciples about the vision " in those days " (Lk 9,36/*diff*. Mk 9,9). The redactional *nexus* between the celestial conversation (Lk 9,31) and the " journey " undertaken by Jesus *and his envoys* (Lk 9,51f.) effectively displays the connection Luke saw between the mystery of the passion and the élan of the mission. By then modifying Mark's statement placing the heavenly vision under the veil of the messianic secret (Lk 9,36), Luke gave his story a momentum of expectancy towards the *day* when both the messianic destiny of the passion and its crucial pertinence to the Christian mission would be revealed by the risen Lord. Unlike Mark, Luke chose to narrate the course of that revelation fully, which is what he has done in the twenty-fourth chapter. This is the reason why the chapter's two appearance stories contained those " flash-backs " to both the passion instruction and the mission program which our analytical study brought out. The " journey " setting in which the Emmaus disciples were instructed in the mystery of the passion was deliberately evocative of the sequence of passion prophecy and mission " journey " in Jesus' own ministry, with intersection of the two at Lk 9,51. Consequently, it may not be inappropriate to consider the travelers to Emmaus representatives of the " Seventy-two," thus participants in the proleptic world-mission of Lk 10,[130] who returned to join the Eleven at Jerusalem and experience the world-mission's enactment and enlistment there by the risen Lord. Indeed, the designation of those travelers as merely δύο ἐξ αὐτῶν in Lk 24,13 might reflect the dispatch of the Seventy-two ἀνὰ δύο, whether or not this means Luke has contributed both the travel-setting and the twofold travelers' number to the underlying tradition.[131] The resonances of Lk 9-10 are, in any case, part of an editorially superimposed union of the two appearance narratives, the one depicting pioneer missionaries' adherence to the Easter faith understood as their ἀνάλημψις with Christ διὰ πολλῶν θλίψεων (Lk 24,26/Acts 14,22), the second depicting the mission as continuation of the Lord's earthly ministry, according

[130] This suggestion of J. SCHMITT (*RvScRel* 25 [1951] 236) was thus undeserving of the rejection out of hand which it got from J. DUPONT (*Misc. Ubach*, 350f.).

[131] In view of the fact that the missionaries' dispatch " two by two " belongs to the instruction of the Seventy-two in Lk 10,1 and seems to have been transferred there from the Marcan instruction of the Twelve (Mk 6,7, without parallel in Lk 9,1ff. or Mt), we ought to reckon with Luke's redaction at Lk 24,13 to recapture the two-fold embassy prescribed by the Lord of the mission. This is the more plausible when we consider that Cleopas is the only name we learn in the course of the narrative, as if before the story acquired its present dimensions (largely at Luke's hand, as we argued), this had been the name attached to the household in which the journeying Lord was welcomed, his the guise of the itinerant missionary of post-Easter days. Cf. chap. II, pp. 83f.

to the norms and model established by his own "journey." It is quite appropriate, in fact, that the second appearance, being a kind of rehearsal of the universal mission, included among its recipients both "the others" instructed at 10,1ff. (cp. Lk 24,9.33) and "the Eleven," who learned the ways of the mission at 9,1-6. The Eleven are the guarantors of full continuity with Jesus' historic ministry and teaching, while "the others" embody the wide world beyond Israel's borders that is destined to receive the word about him. Both groups' mission recruitments frame the gospel's pivotal mid-section (9,1ff./10.1ff.), where christology and missiology are blended into a Lucan program for the age of the universal church.[132] What the Easter story does is simply reaffirm that program, formerly reserved under the messianic *krypsis*, as the content of the revelation made by the risen Lord.

We wish to suggest that this Lucan blending of christology and ecclesiology, drawing out the *missiological consequence* of the Master's path to glory through passion and death, contains the key to Luke's much debated theological appraisal of the death.[133] It is clear to us, and seemingly to most students of this evangelist, that "the days of his ἀνάλημψις" inaugurated at Lk 9,51 include the death as but one of the stations on an itinerary whose completion is the ascension to heaven.[134] This may indeed reduce the death to a *Durchgangsstadium*,

[132] As P. von der OSTEN-SACKEN correctly observes, the conjunction of passion instruction and journey commencement in Lk 9f. gives to the journey section an "indissoluble unity of christological and ecclesiological aspects" (*EvT* 33 [1973] 495). He adds (n. 80): "This unity can be perceived if we consider the similarity between the fate of Jesus and that of the disciples in the age of the Church," citing Acts 14,22.

[133] See again chap. I, note 84. Revaluations of the Lucan *theoria crucis* (not to beg the question by saying "theologia"!) have been among the principal signs of vitality in *Lukasanalyse* after CONZELMANN. H. FLENDER was an important stimulator of this trend, although his own rather unsatisfactory "existentializing" of the evangelist's thought will not carry us far towards a resolution of the issue (cf. *Heil*, 140-142). A good survey of views refractory of the CONZELMANN doctrine is now available in R. GLÖCKNER, *Verkündigung*, 103-113, with mention rightly given to G. VOSS and F. SCHÜTZ as proponents of a necessary reassessment of the death's Lucan significance. GLÖCKNER himself advances several perspectives of Luke's which are often neglected (*ibid.*, 155-201), and these are perhaps the best alternate views to be probed in our own pursuit of a meaning of the death that might be consistent with the explanations of the Easter chapter that we have advanced heretofore. We shall be especially interested in the remarks on the death's salvation-historical rationale and *martyrium* character, which are significant features of GLÖCKNER's treatment even though they do not seem to have led him to a well-coordinated conclusion on the question.

[134] (Cf. chap. III, note 60). Also E. KLOSTERMANN, *Lk.*, 111; E. LOHSE, "Lukas als Theologe," in Braumann-*LkEv.*, 72f.; J. G. DAVIES, *He Ascended*, 40; H. SCHLIER, in *Besinnung*, 227; H. FLENDER, *Heil*, 35, 88; J. DUPONT,

as some are disposed to call it,[135] but by no means is it thus deprived of soteriological value. After all, the whole itinerary comes under the salvation-historical συμπληροῦσθαι in 9,51, and the fact that Luke concentrates the messianic *mysterium* in the phrase παθεῖν τὸν χριστόν plainly implies that he found primary *salvational* significance there.[136] In order to assess that significance correctly, Luke's interpreter must refocus his inquiry in two ways. First, he must broaden his requirements for a *theologia crucis* beyond the familiar atonement category of the Deutero-Isaiah and the Corinthian *paradosis*.[137] Next, he must carefully probe the relationship our evangelist perceived between the dominical " journey " and the whole course of sacred history that was summed up in it. — Let us address these points in turn.

(3) The Mission's " Witness " Mandate

First, an alternate soteriological category under which to pursue Luke's understanding of Jesus' death is that of *martyrium*, suggested once by M. Dibelius.[138] This is a concept which offers to connect the death with functions of *prophecy* and *mission*, which have proved so

Études, 479 ; J. Schneider, in *Synoptische Studien*, 212 ; G. Voss, *Christologie*, 141f. ; C. G. Talbert, in *Jesus and Man's Hope* I, 173, 176f., and *Literary Patterns*, 112 ; M. Miyoshi, *Anfang*, 19 ; D. Gill, *HarvTR* 63 (1970) 202 ; P. von der Osten-Sacken, *EvT* 33 (1973) 479f. ; E. Kränkl, *Jesus*, 166 ; W. Radl, *Paulus und Jesus*, 122f. — The view which restricts the ἀνάλημψις of Lk 9,51 to Jesus' death (J. Schmid, *Lk.*, 176 ; W. Michaelis, *Erscheinungen*, 82 ; G. Lohfink, *Himmelfahrt*, 220 ; G. Friedrich, in *Orientierung an Jesus*, 73) now seems to be exceptional. And it is even rarer and, we think, quite as inappropriate to restrict the word in that passage to the heavenly ascent alone, thus applying it in its strict technical sense (so P. Schubert, in *Ntl. Studien*, 184f.).

[135] Cf. Käsemann, et al., as cited in chap. II, note 201.

[136] Rightly H. Flender, *Heil*, 141 ; R. Glöckner, *Verkündigung*, 156f. The same thing might be said, of course, concerning the fact that Luke puts Jesus' death with his resurrection as points " in the series of promises coming to fulfillment " (E. Lohse, in Braumann-*LkEv.*, 76). The very fact that the evangelist makes the death part of the fulfillment of the scriptures, attaching his fulfillment terminology to it (e.g. Lk 18,31f. ; 22,37, etc.), means that he views it as a *saving event*, coming to pass as assured by divine promises.

[137] Rightly R. Glöckner, *Verkündigung*, 110ff., emphasizing, with E. Lohse, that the interpretation of Jesus' death as atoning or guilt-purging sacrifice is only one of several views of the event in the NT, which does not uniformly attest the atonement theology. Nor does one have to resort to that conception in order to salvage any salvific value for the death.

[138] *Formgeschichte*, 202 (cf. chap. II, note 92), although Dibelius wrongly dissociated martyrological from soteriological aspect. — Cf. also H. Flender, *Heil*, 53 ; G. Voss, *Christologie*, 110f., 118ff. ; S. Schulz, *Stunde*, 289f. ; A. George, *RB* 80 (1973) 207ff. ; R. Glöckner, *Verkündigung*, 183ff. Also G. Schneider, *Verleugnung*, 21, 181, 187, who, however, uses the martyrological traits as pointers to an uncertain pre-Lucan passion account emanating from S-Lk.

important in the course of our study of Lk 24. It is by no means accidental that Luke, alone among the evangelists, concluded his account of the crucifixion with the report that the bystanders, as if responding to the centurion's acknowledgement of "the righteous one," beat their breasts and retreated from the scene (Lk 23,48). Thus did the sufferer's testimony reduce his tormentors to repentance. Accordingly, too, the Acts sermons will urge God's vindication of his "righteous one" after death as motive of the repentance and conversion to which they summon their Jewish audiences (cf. esp. Acts 3,14-19, and chap. 2 above, n. 92, p. 125). According to martyrological *topoi* used in both Jewish and hellenistic specimens,[139] the innocent sufferer is shown to be the victim of God's/truth's own enemies, and so he meets death with a prayer of serene trust and satisfaction on his lips, obtaining thus both a victory over his tormentors and a radiant example for his followers. Luke's recourse to this pattern in his own passion account[140] does indeed appear to be part of his concern to demonstrate continuity between the missions of Jesus and his post-Easter followers, particularly *in statu confessionis*. We observed once before the repetition of martyr-motifs from the passion story in the account of Stephen's death (chap. 2, n. 91), and some aspects of Paul's sufferings, too, seem to be portrayed in Acts, *mutatis mutandis*, with the martyr's model in mind.[141] But something of an explicit statement of the martyrological quality of the confessing Church's torments occurs in Luke's editing of the Lord's apocalyptic prophecies. A Marcan qualification of those trials ἕνεκεν ἐμοῦ εἰς μαρτύριον αὐτοῖς (Mk 13,9) gets the greater moment of an independent statement in Lk 21,13:

ἀποβήσεται ὑμῖν εἰς μαρτύριον.

Luke's addition of ἀποβήσεται and substitution of ὑμῖν for the Marcan *dativus commodi* αὐτοῖς, together with the elimination of Mk 13,10,

[139] Surveyed by H.-W. SURKAU, *Martyrien in jüdischer und frühchristlicher Zeit* (FRLANT 54: Göttingen: Vandenhoeck und Ruprecht, 1938), and more recently by Detlev DORMEYER, *Die Passion Jesu als Verhaltensmodell. Literarische und theologische Analyse der Traditions- und Redaktionsgeschichte der Markuspassion* (NTAbh, n. F. 11; Münster: Verlag Aschendorff, 1974) 43ff.

[140] Cf. particulars in H.-W. SURKAU, *Martyrien* (prev. note) 90-100; M. DIBELIUS, *Formgeschichte*, 202-204. In the martyr tales, seen in their late-Jewish model in such books as 2 and 4 Maccabees, the sufferer is shown to be the victim of the forces of evil, himself proved innocent by the patience, endurance, trust in God, and pious words he manages during the heat of his ordeal and the moment of his death, all of which make him a model for pious followers. The Lucan *propria* in the passion story which display these traits are too familiar to require a full listing, but one thinks immediately of Lk 22,53; 23,4.14.22.27f. 34*l.v.* (cp. Acts 7,60); 23,41-43,46-48.

[141] Acts 20,22-24 (cp. 20,36-38). Cf. R. GLÖCKNER, *Verkündigung*, 182; W. RADL, *Paulus und Jesus*, 147f., 167, 261f., 363, 383-385.

amounts to a clearer involvement of the confessors' *sufferings* in the content of their *testimony*.[142] In fact, Lk 21,13 in its context makes much the same affirmation as we found in Lk 24,48, ὑμεῖς μάρτυρες τούτων, with the demonstrative pronoun referring to the whole christological testimony of the scriptures (24,46-47): *witness to Jesus meant the total reenactment of his " journey "* (Acts 10,39!), not just a vouching for the tradition about him (cf. chap. 3, pp. 215-217). Lk 21,12-19 is, in effect, a commentary on the risen Lord's commission from the standpoint of the *ecclesia pressa*; indeed, the redactional insertion of 21,18 brings out the confessor's passage *through death to salvation* in the footsteps of the Master (cp. Acts 14,22; 27,34 in context). Salvation " through Jesus' name " is, in essence and by necessity, *passage through death,* and so it is that passion and death belong to the structure of Christian " witness." We are convinced, therefore, that Luke took the step towards the later Christian understanding of *martyrium* which many still insist was never taken by NT authors.[143]

---

[142] As against J. ZMIJEWSKI, *Eschatologiereden*, 161-169, I do not believe that Luke's ἀποβ ὑμῖν. εἰς μαρτύριον is an abandonment of any idea of witness for Christ in favor of the completely singular notion (for Lk-Acts) of a " testimony " of the exalted Lord *in favor of* the suffering disciples, as if the statement should be read in strict parallel with Phil 1,19 (εἰς σωτηρίαν) and in anticipation of v. 19 (so also H. von CAMPENHAUSEN, *Die Idee des Martyriums in der alten Kirche* [Göttingen: Vandenhoeck und Ruprecht, 1936] 26 n. 1). The dative ὑμῖν goes with ἀποβήσεται, after all, not with μαρτύριον, and v. 13 is intended to carry forward the thought of v. 12 (just as the parallel Marcan expression functions), not to break with it, *pace* the less creditable textual witnesses which insert δέ, which Merk accepted but Nestle and Aland reject (cf. E. NELLESSEN, *Zeugnis*, 102f.). It is for the gospel, not for the confessors, that witness is given in the *status confessionis* (rightly E. KLOSTERMANN, *Lk.*, 201; W. GRUNDMANN, *Lk.*, 381, and most commentators). Nor do we think that it suffices to make ἀποβ. designate the opportunity which the disciples are given of making their " witness " (H. STRATHMANN, μάρτυς κτλ., *TWNT* IV [477-520] 510; likewise N. BROX, *Zeuge und Märtyrer*, 29). One should rather agree with E. NELLESSEN, (*Zeugnis*, 105, 106) that our redactor meant to bring out the quality of " testimony " in the complete event of a Christian confessor's prosecution by an adversary tribunal (*ita* GRUNDMANN). The word-character of his " witness ", which Mk 13,10 accentuated, gets secondary or, rather, complementary status in Lk (v. 15), whereas the violent treatment, prison, and even death (v. 16) for Jesus' " name " (cf. chap. II, p. 211) brings Christian *martyrium* to its fulness because it is the disciple's total appropriation of his Master's destiny (W. RADL, *Paulus und Jesus*, 361-363). In the master's own apocalyptic prophecies, Lk 21,18 is our evangelist's insertion to complete the " passage " *through death* to salvation that is forecast for the church's confessors (cf. Acts 14,22 and chap. III, pp. 211ff.).

[143] Concerning Stephen's case (Acts 22,20), I agree with H. STRATHMANN (*TWNT* IV, 498) that, while we do not have yet the later ecclesiastical " martyr " concept, we have a step taken towards it in ἐξεχύννετο τὸ αἷμα Στεφάνου τοῦ μάρτυρός σου (*e contra*, N. BROX, *Zeuge*, 63, 66, 119). STRATHMANN correctly observes that the genitive σού keeps us within the sphere of " confessional "

That our evangelist should have made suffering a component of confessional " witness " (cf. Acts 22,20 ; 23,11 ; cp. 9,16 with 22,14 ; 26,16)[144] seems to be a corollary of his systematic view of salvation history, expressed in his δεῖ statements *inter alia*. Passion and death at the hands of " sinful men " (Lk 24,7) was a matter of both the prophets' words about the Christ (Lk 24,25f.44-46 ; 18,31-32 ; 22/37) and *their experience* which prepared for him (Lk 13,33 ; cp. Acts 10,43/39). Such a comprehensive version of the prophets' christological testimony was gathered by Luke from his sources : the Marcan passion formulas, of course, but also the Q sayings mentioned above (p. 259) and the " survey of *unredemption*-history " attributed to the proto*martyr* in Acts 7[145] (pp. 258ff. above). The tradition of late-Jewish parenesis mirrored in the Q sayings and the martyr's speech was, as we have learned, the Deuteronomic schema of *the violent destiny of all Israel's prophets*, and we think that tradition may furnish the inherited point of connection between " prophet " and " witness " roles in the Lucan argument.[146]

---

witness : " Stephen is not called a witness because he dies ; he dies because he is a witness of Christ and because of his evangelistic activity." But the step taken here towards incorporation of the Lord's sufferings and death into his " witnesses " experience is also present, we think (*contra* STRATHMANN, *art. cit.*, 509f.), in Lk 21,13 in its context. — The view that NT authors never associated the μάρτυς vocabulary with the tribulations of the *status confessionis* is saying more than that they did not develop the later, ecclesiastical " martyr " concept ; and so far as Luke is concerned, we think it is denying too much. Typical of this view, however, is N. BROX, *Zeuge und Märtyrer*, 129ff., 232ff.

[144] The distinction advanced by STRATHMANN between " witness " of facts and " witness " of truths or viewpoints (*TWNT* IV, 480ff.) is not appropriate to the usage of the word-group in Lk-Acts (rightly O. MICHEL, in *Neues Testament und Geschichte*, 19, 27 ; E. NELLESSEN, *Zeugnis*, 277). We think our exegesis of Lk 24,48 above (pp. 215ff.) fully justifies the avoidance of such a distinction in interpreting the Lucan " witness " passages. The very fact that the designation of μάρτυρες is never given to the apostles during their earthly companionship of Jesus, but only when their instruction by the risen Lord has been completed (24,48), shows that it was not the mere observation of events which made them *Jesus*' witnesses, but a complete appropriation of his prophetic destiny ! It will be the " adversary proceedings " of Acts which will bear out the totality of that appropriation, for they will create a " present reality of the passion of Jesus for the time of the Church and the destiny of the followers " which would become the *Leitmotiv* of later Christian " martyr " tales (e.g. the " Martyrdom of Polycarp," or that of James reported by Hegesippus ; cf. H.-W. SURKAU, *Martyrien* [cited in n. 139] 122ff., 130) (quotation from G. SCHNEIDER, *Verleugnung*, 176 ; but cf. esp. R. GLÖCKNER, *Verkündigung*, 61f.).

[145] Characterization used by R. GLÖCKNER, *Verkündigung*, 166 ; emphasis mine.

[146] Following the suggestion of O. H. STECK, *Israel*, 162ff., and O. MICHEL, in *Neues Testament und Geschichte*, 19ff. — On the " prophet "-" witness " connection, cf. also A. HASTINGS, *Prophet and Witness*, 97.

A syntactically precise association of these words in OT and late-Jewish texts is admittedly wanting, but a potential association which finally emerged in the process of their *translation* can be traced in uses of the verb הֵעִיד (עוד *hiph.*). The root עוד (= " repetition," " continuance ") yields the causative nuance " instill," " teach," " warn," " admonish," which are the first meanings of the *hiph'il* conjugation. A second group of meanings, to which the noun עֵד (" witness ") is related, includes " to call to witness," or " to bear witness," depending on sentence structure and combination with prepositions. The noun עֵד is applied to " the servant of Yahweh " (= Israel) in Is 43, 8-13, a portrayal of Yahweh's contest against heathen nations and their gods, but is not elsewhere applied to the prophets or prophetic figures. Used in such a forensic setting, the verb would depict a *confirming* of facts which the " witness " has experienced, hence which he is able to " repeat " for others reliably. But where the verb is applied to the activity of the *prophets* — as it precisely is in texts belonging to the Deuteronomic prophet-rejection schema : 2 Kgs 17,13 ; 2 Chron 24,19 ; Neh 9,26.29f. — such a forensic contest-setting is absent, and both context and syntax call for the meaning " *warn* " or " *admonish,*" which more recent versions display (BJ, NAB, NEB) in contrast to older ones (RSV) (cf. O. H. Steck, *Israel*, 69f. n. 2). In all these texts, the prophets' function is portrayed as that of bearing the *admonition* of Yahweh, his *call to conversion* ; this was the call that stiff-necked Israel repeatedly ignored, violently suppressing its spokesmen. The schema's purpose in post-exilic Judaism was clearly to urge *conversion* upon the audience of the present, lest this congregation continue the cycle of " unredemption " to which their forefathers were prey (cf. O. H. Steck, *op. cit.*, 321). Nevertheless, though the prophets' role in the Deuteronomic parenesis was intended to be that of " warning " or " admonishing " for Yahweh, the tradition of the representative texts' *translation* does show a movement towards characterization of their role as " *testifying.*" The LXX διαμαρτύρεσθαι (cf. Acts 10,43) retains the Hebrew verb's duality of meaning, hence the original texts are quite faithfully rendered in 4 Kgs 17,13 ; 2 Paralip. 24,19 ; 2 Esdr 19[= Neh 9], 26. On the other hand, Yahweh's action towards his people *through* (בְּיַד) his prophets (2 Esdr 19,29f.) was rendered with the verb ἐπιμαρτύρεσθαι (" call to witness," " appeal to evidence," " conjure "), which contained a nuance of *legal contest* which was not lost on Jerome (*contestare*). This evidence, as yet hardly conclusive, prepares us for the fact that when the same prophet-rejection schema is taken up in the second-century (B. C.) *Book of Jubilees*, the Ethiopic translation in which the book is most reliably transmitted to us has God forecast to Moses the rejection of his " *witnesses* " :

> " *And I will send witnesses unto them, that I may witness against them, but they will not hear, and will slay the witnesses also ...*"
> (Jub 1,12 ; Charles II,12).

The familiar schema is recognizable (O. H. STECK, *Israel*, 159-162), and the Hebrew original had probably substituted a new designation, likely "*admonishers*" (מְעִידִים, considering the subsequent purpose clause), for the now obsolete נְבִאִים (*ibid.*, 163f.). The envoys' function was still the one which this tradition assigned to the prophets, viz. preachers of repentance. It was the translator who saw them as "witnesses" for Yahweh in an adversary proceeding.

We know already that Luke is heir of the tradition to which the texts just examined belong. We are inclined to think, with U. WILCKENS,[147] that having known it through Q and his special material (Acts 7,52), our author adapted it to his own purposes in the apostolic mission sermons to Jewish audiences (Acts 2-5.13), which are also, like the speech of Stephen, admonitions addressed to a sinful people with a history of unredemption and unrepentance. Of course, only Acts 13, 16ff. duplicates the kind of historical survey which Stephen gave, and the sermons have generally the character of salvation-preaching rather than the invective (*Scheltrede*) of the protomartyr's speech. Nevertheless, the latter acquaints us with a christianized version of the Deuteronomic prophet-murder parenesis, certainly pre-Lucan (cf. p. 256 and n. 74 above), where the basic, lamented fact of Israel's repudiation of the call to repentance/salvation is demonstrated at the beginning (Acts 7,26-28) and the end (Acts 7,52f.) of her dealings with the prophets, of whom Moses and Jesus are the terminal figures. This argument appears in Lucan adaptation at a closely related point of the Petrine kerygma, where Jesus' relation to Moses as *eschatological preacher of repentance* gets a crisp, one-sentence statement: Acts 5,31. Here the exalted Christ is endowed with the "Mosaic" titles of ἀρχηγός and σωτήρ, whose effect is simply δοῦναι μετάνοιαν τῷ Ἰσραὴλ καὶ ἄφεσιν ἁμαρτιῶν. What makes the exalted Lord's offer *eschatological*, it seems, is the component of *forgiveness*,[148] announced as the gift of the last days by all the prophets (Acts 3,19-26), more effective and extensive, Paul would claim, than could ever have been obtained under Moses (Acts 13,38). After the declaration of Acts 5,31 appears the typical Lucan "witness" statement: καὶ ἡμεῖς ἐσμεν μάρτυρες τῶν ῥημάτων τούτων, uniting the apostles' "witness" with that of "all the prophets" in Acts 10,43: ἄφεσιν ἁμαρτιῶν λαβεῖν διὰ τοῦ ὀνόματος αὐτοῦ πάντα τὸν

[147] *Missionsreden*³, 221, 223f., following O. H. STECK, *Israel*, 268. Cf. again note 89 above.

[148] Forgiveness as gift of the exalted Christ: also Acts 10,43; Lk 24,47 (E. KRÄNKL, *Jesus*, 181). As KRÄNKL points out, "die Erhöhung als Tat Gottes zielte weniger auf die Person Jesu als auf seine Funktion gegenüber seiner Gemeinde" (*ibid.*, 162).

πιστεύοντα εἰς αὐτόν. In both instances the " witness " embraces the whole of the kerygma which precedes it,[149] and the striking parallelism of the two statements has the effect of inserting the apostolic missionaries into the historic pattern of Israel's relations with her preachers of repentance. It is that pattern, we think, which makes them properly " witnesses " *in Lucan perspective*, that is, spokesmen for the God of Israel in his perpetual *adversary-proceeding* against his people ! In fact, it is often in the framework of such a proceeding between the exalted Lord's missionaries and their reluctant (Jewish) audiences that the term μάρτυς, and also the verb μαρτυρεῖν, are employed in our author's account of the early mission.[150]

---

[149] On Acts 5,32, where a particularly close parallelism with Lk 24,46-48 can be observed (μετάνοια καὶ ἄφεσις ἁμαρτιῶν included in the testimony, and Holy Spirit mentioned as source of it), cf. E. NELLESSEN, *Zeugnis*, 88. — In Acts 10,43, the comprehensive christological (= kerygmatic) content of the prophets' μαρτυρεῖν is brought out by the demonstrative τούτῳ, which precedes the verb (E. NELLESSEN, *op. cit.*, 258). — It should be clear from the kerygmatic reference of the " witness " in both texts that no artificial distinction should be introduced between the " witness " and preaching roles of the missionaries, as, for instance, between vouching for the truth and propagating it (*pace* Chr. BURCHARD, *Zeuge*, 132f.). This distinction, like the one between factual and confessional witness, is foreign to Luke's argument. The μάρτυς concept is in the service of Luke's demonstration of continuity between Jesus and his missionary preachers *in ministry, message, and destiny*. The appointment to witness is the appointment to proclaim Christ and to appropriate the full context of his ministry in doing so ; hence the alternative of guarantor vs. preacher of the kerygma is false (rightly E. NELLESSEN, *Zeugnis*, 114f., 115 n. 268).

[150] This insight has been sponsored in recent discussion by K. LÖNING, *Saulustradition*, 148ff., and (with respect exclusively to Paul and Stephen) V. STOLLE, *Der Zeuge als Angeklagter*, 144-147, 153f., 224f. LÖNING's statement may be too broadly generalized : " A Christian preacher is also called a μάρτυς to the extent that his message — whether from its content or its intended audience — provokes contradiction amongst the Jews " (*op. cit.*, 149). Whether or not it can be maintained that μαρτυρεῖν has frequent reference to disputed subjects, it is remarkable that the two instances in which the term μάρτυς is applied to Paul both belong to accounts of Paul on trial (Acts 22,15 ; 26,16) ; and the verbs μαρτυρεῖν and μαρτύρεσθαι are applied to him in the same context (26,22) or reference (23,11). Cp. 28,23 ! The case of Stephen was similar, of course (Acts 22,20), and the earlier application of the noun to the apostles in their mission to Jewish audiences (Acts 2,32 ; 3,15 ; 5,32 ; 10,39.41 ; 13,31) cannot be without reference to their accusation (ὑμεῖς ἐσταυρώσατε, etc.) and call to repentance, always the main target of the mission discourses. Even where a present audience is not being summoned to repentance, the crime of messiah-murder and its perpetrators get mention in the same breath with the " witness " statement (as in 10,39). It seems the data can be summed up at least as follows : " Opposition, persecution, and fear for life and limb are regularly the consequences of coming forward as a witness. Admittedly, these contretemps are never directly associated with the function of witness and the vocation thereto. At most, one might speak of an indirect component of the Lucan witness conception, a conclusion drawn from the circumstances of its use." (E. NELLESSEN, *Zeugnis*,

The Christian *martyrium* before an accused and unreceptive audience proved to be a continuation of the classic trend of salvation-history. Or should we call it " unredemption " history after all ? And should it not lead to a misanthropic dispair, — not to mention those forms of anti-semitism which were thought to be founded on the testimony of the apostles ? No, this would be viewing the Lucan *martyrium* from the wrong side. As brought to its climax in the apostolic kerygma, the tradition of prophets rejected finally displays *not* the irredeemable perversity of mankind but *the invincible persistence of divine forgiveness* ! It is of this, ultimately and essentially, that the embattled missionaries are " witnesses " : *witnesses of his resurrection* ! [151] They carry forward the announcement of repentance and forgiveness (Lk 24,47f.) which generations of men, *including the present generation* of messianic times, have violently rejected. The word of forgiveness will yet prevail, with its spokesmen, because it is God's word, God's rule ! Of this inevitable triumph the risen and exalted Christ is the unimpeachable " witness " ! [152]

This fuller perspective on Luke's " witness " motif, and his adaptation of the prophet-rejection schema, finds support in a closer look at the message of Peter within the context of the sanhedrin hearing, Acts 5,27-42.

278). — To our way of thinking, this is a minimalizing of the motif, but we believe its roots in the prophet-murder tradition might better explain the " circumstances " which NELLESSEN causes to appear almost accidental.

[151] Cf. V. STOLLE, *Der Zeuge als Angeklagter*, 150 : " Die Auferweckung als Tat Gottes fasst dann den Heilsplan Gottes in diesem einen Punkt zusammen (2,32 ; 3,15 ; 10,40 ; 13,30f.) .... Im Leidenden, Auferstandenen und Erhöhten hat Gott in der Welt auf die Welt hin in einer endgültigen und entscheidenden Weise gehandelt, die die βασιλεία gebracht hat. Die Zeugen Jesu sind deshalb Zeugen der sich für alle Menschen durch seine Jesustat erweisenden Herrschaft Gottes."

[152] This seems in basic accord with the evaluation of Jesus' death which R. GLÖCKNER reaches after his survey of the Lucan data (cf. *Verkündigung*, 185-187, 194f.). In his concluding remarks, G. opines : " Sein (i.e. Jesu) Weg in die Niedrigkeit des Lebens und in die Erniedrigung des Todes ist die Vollzugsform, wie Gott durch ihn seinen Heilswillen in die Unheilsgeschichte verwirklicht " (201). Cf. also Paul ZINGG, *Wachsen*, 299. — The " kingdom of God " is the object of " witness " in Acts 28,23, where we have arrived in the world-capital, yet we are brought back to a scene of the Jewish audience challenged and divided by the message. It is a scene of Paul διαμαρτυρόμενος τὴν βασιλείαν τοῦ θεοῦ, and the witness meets partial *success*, partial rejection (28,24). M. VÖLKEL correctly observes that this passage shows Luke's ultimate objective in Acts to be the *success* of the mission to Israel, hence the ultimate realization of the divine promise (cf. *ZNW* 65 [1974] 69f.). The story told in Acts is not of the rejection of Israel and the access of the Gentiles to salvation. Rather, it is of the gradual emergence of a universal people of God, comprised of believers of every stock, won over to the message of forgiveness through the instrumentality of the prophetic preachers and their sufferings.

Luke's composition in this passage seems deliberately evocative of the μαρτύριον for " the Name " forecast in Lk 21,12-19.[153] The scene has all the ingredients of the *status confessionis* [154] previewed in Jesus' prophecies : the trial situation (5,27), " the Name " at issue (5,28.40f. ; cp. esp. v. 41 with 21,17), the resolve to murder the confessors (5,33 ; cp. Lk 21,16), and their ultimate " salvation " because their message was the invincible word of God (5,39/cp. Lk 21,15 ; 5,32/cp. Lk 12, 11f.[S] ; 5,41f./cp. Lk 21,18f.). — On the other hand, hints that this *martyrium* is the inevitable continuance of God's spokesmen's perennial experience at the hands of His people are furnished by the accusation against the prosecutors which they themselves enunciate (5,28), and by their plan to murder the apostolic confessors (5,33), which yet again verifies the accusation. Like other scenes of the missionary preaching *in statu confessionis*, however, this situation only appears to be leading towards the destruction of the witnesses and the suppression of the word. It can have no such outcome, of course, in the story Acts tells. The persecutors' plan does not prevail, and moreover, the basic principle validating the Christian mission is enunciated by Gamaliel, *en dépit de soi* (5,39, verifying Lk 21,15). We can now confirm how much Lk 21,15.18f. was edited, against its Marcan exemplar, with the Acts scenes of the missionaries' deliverance and the gospel's conquests in our author's mind (cf. J. ZMIJEWSKI, *Eschatologiereden*, 136, 138f., 175).

The confessors of the mission whose story is told in Acts are " witnesses of Jesus' *resurrection* " insofar as they are bearers of the invincible word of God's forgiveness (Lk 24,46-48), which only waxes stronger under the human onslaughts against it. It is that word of grace, making its way inexorably from Jerusalem to Rome, which is the harbinger and effective medium of what is called " the kingdom of God." This inherited eschatological term can thus be applied to the present salvation in, say, Acts 1,6-8 (cf. 8,12 ; 28,23.31), for it depicts the saving reality of the risen Christ, rendered present to ever-widening circles of recipients through the missionary preaching of his followers.[155]

---

[153] The composition of Lk 21,12-19 with the narratives of Acts in view is repeatedly brought out in literary analysis of the section by J. ZMIJEWSKI, *Eschatologiereden*, 130-139 ; cf. also 177 : " Man kann sagen : Der Abschnitt Lk 21,12ff. verhält sich zur Apostelgeschichte wie Verheissung und Erfüllung, wie Voraussage und geschichtliche Entfaltung."

[154] U. WILCKENS, *Missionsreden*, 62.

[155] The risen Christ, that is, who represents the fulfillment of God's promises and the triumphant realization of his saving plan. We note the synonymous parallelism of κηρύσσων τὴν β. τοῦ θεοῦ and διδάσκων τὰ περὶ τοῦ κυρίου Ἰησοῦ Χριστοῦ in Acts 28,31, and also the nuance (and promise !) of triumph in μετὰ πάσης παρρησίας ἀκωλύτως. — On the relationship of the Lucan βασιλεία concept with the progress and success of the missionary preaching, cf. M. VÖLKEL, *ZNW* 65 (1974) 67ff., and O. MERK, in *Jesus und Paulus*, 204ff., 211, 214f., 218ff.

God, invincibly drawing to repentance and forgiveness the very mankind that strives to still His voice: such is the story of the advance of His " kingdom," the story recounted in the Lucan *opera*. The perennial contrast between divine grace and human rebellion has thus a Lucan version, corresponding to the Pauline redemption *sola gratia*. Indeed, this is an aspect of our evangelist's theology mostly ignored by the redaction-historians who are committed to the portrait of Luke as standard-bearer of *Frühkatholizismus*.[156] Already in his exegetically neglected infancy narrative, he placed the event of the virgin-birth in the service of a vision of God still able to accomplish πᾶν ῥῆμα when all man's resources are spent and his calculations confounded (cf. Lk 1,35-37).[157] In the same vein, as we have observed in full detail, the Easter narratives which conclude the gospel have divine revelation *sola gratia* as their basic pathos, three times documenting the complete *échec* of human perceptions before the third-day phenomena, building thus *ratione contraria* a heightened threshold for the risen Christ's self-disclosing word. Now we can better understand what it was that *only he* could reveal. It was the climax, in his own death and rising, of the age-old conflict between God's people and the prophetic harbingers of his forgiveness. He showed the divine purpose triumphant at the point where the people's rejection was most drastic and most sinful.

The path of argument is the same in all these cases: *where human failure is total, there does God rule most powerfully*! Our historian accentuates and solemnizes the first moment of this dialectic so as to argue the second the more effectively. Yet he argues precisely a dialectic,[158]

[156] It is therefore only his good grace, undoubtedly a certain *noblesse oblige*, too, which prevented W. KLAIBER from taking note of the irony of his contribution to the KÄSEMANN Festschrift: " Eine lukanische Fassung des Sola Gratia. Beobachtungen zu Lk 1,5-56," in *Rechtfertigung*, 211-228. The jubilarian's analysis of Rom 4 is invoked to illustrate the Lucan theology of grace in the birth story (219 n. 37), the virgin birth is declared an instance of *creatio ex nihilo* (217), a favorite phrase of the KÄSEMANN *Rechtfertigungslehre*; but no mention is made of the characterization of Lucan theology as that " welche sich von der urchristlichen wesentlich unterscheidet und in ihrem Zentrum wie in vielen ihrer Einzeläusserungen als frühkatholisch bezeichnet werden muss," — and this because, among other things, " an die Stelle der Eschatologie tritt eine merkwürdig kontrollierbare, kontinuierliche und trotz allem Wunderglanz immanente Heilsgeschichte " (KÄSEMANN, *Exegetische Versuche*, II, 30).

[157] Brought out in the essay of W. KLAIBER in the KÄSEMANN Festschrift, cited in the previous note. KLAIBER makes his own, and specifically pertinent to the Lucan presentation, the remark of Josef RATZINGER: " Die Jungfrauengeburt bedeutet weder ein Kapitel Askese noch gehört sie unmittelbar der Lehre von der Gottessohnschaft Jesu zu; sie ist zuerst und zuletzt Gnadentheologie, Botschaft davon, wie *uns* das Heil zukommt; in der Einfalt des Empfangens, als unerzwingbares Geschenk der Liebe, die die Welt erlöst " (*Einführung in das Christentum*, 228, quoted by KLAIBER, *art. cit.*, 217f.).

[158] The recognition of this important but underestimated feature of Lucan

not separate and conflicting historical processes. Human failure and divine forgiveness are aspects of *one and the same process of God's ruling amidst the débris of man's illusions.*[159] Christ *natus ex Maria virgine* is surely God's doing, even though it fits the historic pattern of the births God bestowed beyond human possibilities, hence was a *testimonium paupertatis hominis,* as they were.[160] Moreover, the physical phenomena and impressions of Easter had a *positive* function in the Easter revelation, not merely a negative one; the risen Lord addressed himself to them (Lk 24,19ff.39ff.), he did not negate or trivialize them. — So too, therefore, is the Lord's *death* a *positive component of his eschatological prophecy,* not a mere " malfunction of world history " which " God repaired at Easter ..., as he repairs all things in due course."[161] The death of Jesus was in accordance with the divine will, not a momentary dominion of human error (cf. Acts 3,17f.; 13,27). It followed the recurrent historical pattern of his prophets' fortunes,

---

theology is credited to H. FLENDER, *Heil,* 14-37, who found it permitted Luke to approach the *facta historiae Jesu* as both real events in time and place, yet also matters of divine initiative which resist, rather than endorse, the inherent thrust of human affairs. Thus the event of Jesus is displayed as historical reality without sacralizing history itself, which is under man's regime (*op. cit.,* 24). Thus, too, the glory of the Son of God is concealed in suffering and death, which can be grasped, even appropriated, as *saving* destiny only through the faith which overcomes the world (*ibid.,* 37). The importance of this insight to the new ferment in Lucan studies is acknowledged by R. GLÖCKNER, *Verkündigung des Heils,* 103ff.

[159] This must be so, as KÄSEMANN has pointed out so often and so well, if God is to be truly the Father of Jesus Christ, the God of the ungodly, the creator of the world. The dialectic between history and divine design must never be relinquished if this understanding is to be safeguarded (rightly KÄSEMANN, *Paulinische Perspektiven* [Tübingen: J. C. B. Mohr, [2]1969] 121ff.; *Exegetische Versuche* II, 195ff.), and it is a superficial reading of Luke's history which contends he has relinquished the paradox. The death of Jesus, after the pattern of the prophets' fate in Israel, is precisely the salvation which, " measured by human criteria, fundamentally masks itself... as non-salvation," thus shattering all human claims to privilege and prior right (as also occurred at Nazareth, according to the programmatic Lucan pericope 4,16-30; rightly H. CONZELMANN, *MdZ,* 31: " ' Verwandter ' Jesu ist man sola gratia "). Surveying the history of men's dealings with the messengers of God, one learns the Pauline lesson: " God has confined all in disobedience that he might have mercy on all " (Rom 11,32). Why insist that the point of the missionary sermons is substantially different ?

[160] W. KLAIBER, in *Rechtfertigung,* 216f., 220f. Cf. also R. GLÖCKNER, *Verkündigung,* 116f. — KLAIBER makes the suggestive association of the " swaddling clothes " and the " manger " of Lk 2,7.12 and the cross, which is quite logically forecast in Simeon's σημεῖον ἀντιλεγόμενον (Lk 2,34). " Die Funktion, die bei Paulus die Verkündigung des Kreuzes zu Gericht und Gnade einnimmt, wird bei Lukas schon in der Vorgeschichte dem Bericht vom Wirken Jesu und vom Widerstand gegen sein Wort und Werk zugedacht " (*art. cit.,* 226).

[161] E. KÄSEMANN, *Der Ruf der Freiheit*[3] (Tübingen: J. C. B. Mohr, 1968) 167.

willed by God (Lk 24,25f. : ἔδει), and thus concluded the *positive prophetic testimony* of God's undaunted purpose to forgive, which becomes most effective where man's resistance is mightiest ! Here is where the death of the Crucified finds its soteriologically positive Lucan evaluation, in our judgment. It was the most powerful of the historical Jesus' " prophecies," fully continuous with the ministry of ἄφεσις-*proclamation* which he inaugurated at Nazareth.

Calvary's connection with Nazareth, already expressed at the end of the hometown episode (Lk 4,28f.), suggests the role played by Jesus' death in the gradual liberation of the gospel from the restraints of its institutional ancestry. The series of rejections of his message, from the kinsfolk at Nazareth (Lk 4,24) to the religious establishment at Jerusalem (Lk 24,20), and then to the Diaspora communities of Pisidian Antioch (Acts 13,46) and Rome (Acts 28,24-28), show the painful but ineluctable *disentanglement* of the word from all prior claims and ligatures, whether blood relation, birthright, tradition, or institution. Concurrently, and just as painfully, a new people is assembled in response to the word : the disadvantaged and disinherited from Jewish ranks, and Gentile outsiders who had never entered the holy city's gates (Lk 14,21-23). This divinely ordained " disenfranchisement " of the saving message,[162] brought about with the death of Christ and continued repudiations of his missionaries, could give birth to a truly universal ἐκκλησία τοῦ θεοῦ, of which only God's giving and men's believing would be the criteria (Acts 13,48f. ; 28,24.28). Thus " disentangled," the word could be proclaimed ἀκωλύτως (Acts 28,28-31), and its worldwide audience could be truly said to have been " acquired " by the blood of God's own Son (Acts 20,28: ἣν περιεποιήσατο διὰ τοῦ αἵματος τοῦ ἰδίου) [163].

[162] Cf. Lk 8,21 (*diff.* Mk) ; 11,27-28 (S), and H. CONZELMANN, *MdZ*, 31 ("' Verwandter ' Jesu ist man sola gratia "); H. FLENDER, *Heil*, 28 ; C.-P. MÄRZ, *Wort Gottes*, 68.

[163] R. GLÖCKNER, *Verkündigung*, 183 : " Der Hinweis darauf, dass die Kirche durch das Blut Christi erworben worden ist, kann nicht als Ausdruck einer rechtfertigenden Sühnevorstellung gelten, sondern er charakterisiert den Kreuzestod als Zeichen einer bis zum äussersten gehenden Liebe und Hingabe für die Kirche." We quite agree that the statement from Paul's " testament " at Miletus is an expression of Luke's own thought concerning the death of Christ (rightly A. GEORGE, *RB* 80 [1973] 211f.), not simply an occasional recourse to a traditional formula (*pace* H. CONZELMANN, *MdZ*, 187f., 215 n. 2, and *Apg*^{2}, 128f. ; U. WILCKENS, *Missionsreden*, 185 n. 2, ^{3}197 n. 2 ; E. KRÄNKL, *Jesus*, 123). Rightly G. LOHFINK, *Sammlung Israels*, 90-92, who can speak of both traditional language and determined purpose of the author in the composition of the verse. " ... Lukas zeigt, dass bereits im Kreuzestod Jesu der kirchengründende Wille Gottes am Werbe war " (92).

(4) The Witnesses' Identity

On the question of precisely *who* is prepared for the universal mission in Lk 24, we have only to coordinate what we have already said in chap. 3 (pp. 215-218) with the additional perspectives on the " witness " motif which we obtained in the preceding section. Let us first reiterate : Lk 24 supports no restriction of the " official " witnesses' circle to the Eleven ; quite the contrary, we saw that a purposeful redacting of the two Easter appearance stories into a direct sequence (Lk 24,33-36) brought together " the Eleven " and " those who were with them " as recipients of the great mission deputation. Moreover, the various reprises of Lk 9-10 in Lk 24 favor a mingling in the risen Lord's audience of the separate mission groups he had recruited at Lk 9,1-6 and 10,1-20, " the Twelve " and " Seventy(-two) others," their original sequence being then reversed in the sequence of Easter apparitions (cf. pp. 277f. above). Luke undoubtedly means to take account of a witness-mandate to disciples other than the " apostles," " just as he took account of a mission of the Seventy-two disciples (Lk 10,1-20) alongside that of the Twelve (Lk 9,1-6)." [164] Whether he then proceeds to define something of an " official witness " of the apostles in Acts 1, when reporting that group's restoration to its plenary number (Acts 1,21ff. ; cp. Acts 10,41 ; 13,31),[165] we shall not attempt to decide in this study. Let us be content with the fruits of our analysis of Lk 24,48 and its context.

What we shall attempt here is a suggestion of guidelines for the debate over the Acts " witnesses " which we believe our study has contributed.

(1) Foremost among our convictions nurtured by this study is the disqualification of an exclusively factual " witness " in the mission

[164] A. George, in *La résurrection du Christ*, 54. The comparable status of the Twelve and the Seventy(-two) as witnesses of Jesus' earthly life is correctly observed by G. Lohfink : " Lukas kann durch 10,1-24 zeigen, dass Jesus von einem relativ grossen Jüngerkreis begleitet wird, der mit dem Zwölferkreis zwar nicht identisch ist, der aber wie dieser mit Verkündigungsaufgaben betraut werden kann und der wie dieser zum Zeugen des gesamten Wirkens Jesu wird (vgl. 10,23f.) " (*Sammlung Israels*, 70).

[165] Rather than the gradual accumulation of unique " witness " credentials by the Twelve, as postulated by G. Klein (in *Zeit und Geschichte*, 204-205), I should prefer the explanation of G. Lohfink, who acknowledges the special focus on the Twelve which Acts 1 begins, but understands this in terms of the numerical nucleus which maintains the direct continuity between Israel and the universal Church (*Sammlung Israels*, 77, 78). In any case, E. Nellessen has quite convinced me that the Acts treatment of the Twelve does not endow them with special experiences of the earthly Jesus or the risen Christ which would not be attributed also to the wider circle that is present in both Lk 24 and Acts 1 (cf. *Zeugnis*, 118ff., 127f., 177, 197, 209f.).

recruitments of Lk 24. The view of Lucan historiography as guarantor rather than proclaimer of the gospel has, in turn, favored the evangelist's portrayal of " the Twelve " as vouchers for the *historia Jesu* and the unassailable reality of the *facta paschalia*.[166] Since we found, however, that the potential witnesses' observations constituted a frustrated momentum in the Easter narratives, reducing them to a confusion and disappointment whence only the decisive word of the risen Lord could rescue them, we cannot subscribe to any notion of the Lucan apostles as uniquely qualified vouchers for the historical *facta salutis*. So far as we can see, their rescue from confused and frustrated sense-perceptions by the risen Lord's instruction was substantially the same as the Emmaus disciples required. A close compositional symmetry between the two appearance stories brought out the similar structure of both experiences, as we have observed.[167] Indeed, the two phases of the Easter faith's awakening in both instances are reflected in the prologue's characterization of the founding witnesses: οἱ ἀπ' ἀρχῆς αὐτόπται on the one hand, καὶ ὑπηρέται γενόμενοι τοῦ λόγου on the other hand. Only the Lord's revealing *word* of instruction made " eye-witnesses " of uncomprehended facts into potential " ministers of the word " (γενόμενοι!),[168] for without his word they remained only the " foolish and slow of heart to believe ..." of Lk 24,25, the " startled and frightened ... (who) supposed they saw a ghost " of Lk 24,37. This transformation of puzzled observers into believing witnesses is the same at Lk 24,25ff. and Lk 24,44ff., and those who were thus transformed are all the *ecclesia in partu* specified by the evangelist in his fusion of the two episodes: " the Eleven and those who were with them," rejoined by the Emmaus travelers (Lk 24,33-35). Considering the nature of their experiences, these Easter disciples qualify as " witnesses " of the *pure gift* of God's revelation, not as specially competent vouchers for its empirical foundation or historical verity.[169] Moreover, in their capacity

[166] Chr. Burchard betrays the influence of the apologetic assessment of Luke's historiography at the end of his monograph (*Zeuge*, 185) after his earlier *prise de position* in full favor of the witnesses as " guarantors " (*ibid.*, 132ff.). In our opinion, if the witnesses can be said to " guarantee " anything, it is the continuity of mission between the Master and the Church, not the facticity of the events of the *Jesuszeit*.

[167] Cf. our treatment of Lk 24,44ff. above, and cf. E. Nellessen, *Zeugnis*, 117 with n. 286.

[168] Cf. note 114 above on the separate function of γενόμενοι with ὑπηρέται κτλ. Klein makes the " becoming " a matter of progressive delimitation by unique experience, whereas we maintain it reflects the two stages of the Easter revelation to the " witnesses," empirical observation and revelatory instruction, hence would apply to all the paschal *coetus* of Lk 24, not the Eleven alone. Rightly R. Glöckner, *Verkündigung*, 21f.

[169] The remarks of R. Glöckner on the ἀσφάλεια which Luke makes his work's objective (Lk 1,4) prove especially pertinent to this conclusion we have

of " witnesses," they are propagators of a faith which will presumably happen to others as it happened to them: *sola gratia Dei*, not with a kind of evidential guarantee that meets skeptical human listeners on their own terms.

(2) If our study dissuaded us from classifying the Easter witnesses as " guarantors of the facts " of the *historia Jesu*, it fully confirmed the view that they are meant to embody the continuity between the

---

drawn (cf. *Verkündigung*, 26-41). First of all, the " security " Luke aims for affects the λόγοι of the believer's instruction: it is an ἀσφάλεια λόγων, not primarily an ἀσφάλεια πραγμάτων. Moreover, the λόγοι involve Luke's typical depiction of the whole of Christian preaching, based upon the αὐτοψία of the witnesses *and* their ὑπηρεσία τοῦ λόγου. " Λόγος and λόγοι bezeichnen umfassend die christliche Verkündigung, die prinzipiell auf eine Annahme im Glauben ausgerichtet ist." What that preaching solicits from the hearer, in the Lucan portrayals, is not simply listening and perceiving, but " ein Annehmen im spezifischen Sinn des Glaubens (vgl. Lk 1,20, 8,11ff.; Apg 2,41; 4,4; 8,14; 11,1), der sich im Tun ausweist (Lk 6,47; 8,21; negativ: Apg 8,21). Der λόγος ist ein Wort, das die in den ' Missionsreden ' geforderte Glaubensumkehr hervorruft (Apg 13,26-49) und in die Doxologie einmünden kann (13,48)." As this survey shows, the program of Luke's writing is not worked out in such fashion that " Lukas konsequent die folgende Verkündigung unter dem Gesichtspunkt historischer Zuverlässigkeit verengt und mit seinem Evangelium nur rationale Einsicht in historisch gesicherte Sachverhalte vermitteln will." With ἀσφάλεια τῶν λόγων is clearly intended an ordering of different aspects of the tradition to one another, so as better to convince the adherent of the significance of it all for his own life and times, " ... ohne dass einer den anderen einengt oder sogar ausschliesst " (GLÖCKNER, *op. cit.*, 34). — At this point, GLÖCKNER adheres to H. FLENDER's exposition of the *dialectical* modes of Lucan presentation, insisting, as FLENDER had, that our author precisely avoided reducing his material to a rational argument based on the immanent logic of historical events, and did so by juxtaposing different views or aspects of the events, sometimes complementary, sometimes climactic, often antithetical (cf. FLENDER, *Heil*, 36f.). As we have seen, a principal Lucan dialectic is observable between the aspects of wonder-working and passion-destiny in the portrait of Jesus, and correspondingly between divine certification and human rejection of his prophetic ministry. When this dialectical picture is drawn in the Pentecost sermon of Peter, its conclusion is a call for believing recognition in Israel: ἀσφαλῶς οὖν γινωσκέτω κτλ. (Acts 2,36). This " secure knowledge " is a preacher's objective, and it clearly is not historical conviction of facts separable from what the preacher then calls for: μετανοήσατε, καὶ βαπτισθήτω ἕκαστος κτλ. (Acts 2,38). There is no reason to maintain that the ἀσφάλεια pursued by the Pentecost preacher is any different from the ἀσφάλεια pursued by the Lucan opus as a whole, nor that the one is any more or less *authentically kerygmatic* than the other. — Therefore, in researching anew the historical dimension of faith's claim upon the hearer, Luke is not inventing the category of *Heilsgeschichte* (rightly W. G. KÜMMEL, in *L'év. de Luc. Mém. Cerfaux*, 101; = Braumann-*LkEv.*, 426f.), he is simply carrying further what " many " have done before him in presenting the kerygmatized διήγησις of the narrative " gospel." Nor is Luke, any more than his predecessors, preempting " die Aufgabe der eigenen, den Glauben fordernden Neudeutung und Annahme des Erzählten " on his reader's part (R. GLÖCKNER, *op. cit.*, 38).

ministry of Jesus and the mission of the Church.[170] This function will be stipulated at Acts 1,21f., where the larger reservoir whence Matthias is chosen will show that full " exposure to the facts " was no property of the Twelve. Acts 13,31 will specify the shared *anabasis* of the Master from Galilee to Jerusalem as the witnesses' credentials, and we suspect the only reason Paul cannot speak yet of his own μαρτυρία on that occasion is that his own *anabasis* to Jerusalem, with its strong ingredient of Lucan *theologia crucis*, is still in the offing (Acts 19,21ff.).[171] The Easter narratives had the continuity argument as perhaps their major focus, from the μνήσθητε of the angels (24,6) through the agitated travelers' recital of τὰ γενόμενα (24,18) to the risen One's illumination of unheeded signs of his return (24,39-43) with the words he had spoken ἔτι ὤν σὺν ὑμῖν (24,44). Even the subtle touches which brought the healed women of Galilee to the Easter scene (24,10) told us that " the third day " marked an integral transition of the ministry of Jesus of Nazareth into the worldwide mission in his name (24,47f.). In our evangelist's plan, the integrity of the transition depends on the paschal witness of πάντες οἱ γνωστοὶ αὐτῷ (23,49), and this is why Luke is at pains during the paschal sequence to stress the *togetherness* of the Eleven and the wider circle, not the smaller group's separateness and distinctness (cf. chap. II, n. 40, and p. 218 above).

[170] Cf. the argument concerning the central point of the third Easter pericope, chap. III, p. 193; also pp. 204, 212, 216 of chap. III. G. KLEIN is right, of course, that such continuity is guaranteed by the ἀπ' ἀρχῆς αὐτόπται καὶ ὑπηρέται τοῦ λόγου (Lk 1,2; cf. *Zeit und Geschichte*, 199ff.; also J. ROLOFF, *Apostolat*, 199; H. CONZELMANN, *MdZ*, 197-198, 201f. with n. 2; N. BROX, *Zeuge*, 54; G. LOHFINK, *Himmelfahrt*, 267-270; G. SCHNEIDER, *Verleugnung*, 206f.; H. SCHÜRMANN, *Lk.* I, 8f.; C.-P. MÄRZ, *Wort Gottes*, 50-51; E. KRÄNKL, *Jesus*, 174f.; P. ZINGG, *Wachsen*, 72; W. C. ROBINSON, *Weg*, 37-39.) The tendency of these scholars to narrow the embodiment of historical continuity between Jesus and his Church to the twelve apostles, occasionally to the extent of positing an exclusive ecclesiastical " office " of the Twelve in this respect (G. KLEIN, *Apostel*, 209; S. SCHULZ, *Stunde*, 260ff.), is resisted and rightly modified by R. GLÖCKNER, *Verkündigung*, 45ff., and E. NELLESSEN, *Zeugnis*, 115ff., 231ff. The Twelve are indeed at the center of the corps of witnesses which covers the entire dominical ἀνάλημψις (in the comprehensive sense of Lk 9,51), but they are not the entire number thereof. And their nuclear position amidst that group, already defined in the *mise-en-scène* of Jesus' first " sermon " (Lk 6,13ff.), has another continuity to express, viz. the continuity between the Israel of God's original choice and the church of Christ (cf. note 172 below).

[171] Therefore, I should not agree that the experience of Jesus' *anabasis* to Jerusalem ought to be deemphasized as basic requirement of " witness " (*pace* E. NELLESSEN, *Zeugnis*, 207, at least by implication [n. 849]). I rather agree with W. C. ROBINSON (*Weg*, 39) that the " journey " represents an essential " qualification of Christian witness," highlighting the passion as the journey's climax and observing that Paul's self-designation as " witness " could be made only as accused missionary on trial (Acts 22,15; 26,16), after his own " journey to Jerusalem " had been completed (Acts 19,21ff.). Cf. H. FLENDER, *Heil*, 118f.

Luke's schematic picture of concentric circles of humanity around Jesus — the Twelve, the disciples, the crowd (e.g. 6,13-20) — was intended, as we learned, to illustrate the true Israel's emergence from the ranks of the old (cf. p. 55, and n. 160 there). That great array of listeners is in the process of being restored by Easter and Pentecost; and in the work of ministering to the outer circle, humanity at large, the Twelve and the disciples are at one, without distinction in the content or quality of their witness.

The mention of the " true Israel " reminds us of the unique status the Twelve did have. They exhibited the continuity of *Israel* as the people of divine election and recipient of Jesus' message.[172] At the last supper, in conversation with the " apostles " (Lk 22,14/cp. Mk 14,17), the Master promised them the role of judges over the twelve tribes (Lk 22,30b Q). That promise stands in the unique framework of their solidarity with the Master ἐν τοῖς πειρασμοῖς μου (Lk 22,28 S). Is it not Luke's understanding that the Twelve stood with the Lord in his preaching to Israel (cf. Lk 6,13-17),[173] victims with him of her age-old persecution of the prophets (Lk 6,22f.; 22,35-37; Acts 5,27ff.), and participants, finally, in her judgment (Acts 10,42f.)? At least this is the direction our study favors for future investigations of the apostolate in Lk-Acts.[174]

---

[172] Brought out with special emphasis by H. FLENDER, *Heil*, 107-122, and most recently and impressively by G. LOHFINK, *Sammlung Israels*, 63-84.

[173] G. LOHFINK, *Sammlung Israels*, 64-65, notes the concentric circles of listeners arranged for the " sermon on the plain ": the Twelve, a " great crowd of his disciples," and " a great crowd of the people (λαός) from all Judea and Jerusalem ..." " In erster Linie sind die Jünger angesprochen, aber zugleich geht die Feldrede an ganz Israel. Die ekklesiologische Relevanz dieses eigentümlichen Phänomens wird uns noch beschäftigen." We might add that the salvation-historical relevance of this audience comes to be illustrated in the beatitudes, particularly Lk 6,22f.26, where the sufferings of Master and disciples are situated in the history of this people's dealings with the prophets.

[174] G. LOHFINK's more recent study (n. 172) represents a substantial step forward with respect to his repetition of the conventional, "Twelve" -centered criticism in *Himmelfahrt* (n. 170 above). Perhaps this development of LOHFINK's thinking might augur corresponding improvement of the discussion by other exegetes. — How it is that, despite the texts we have mentioned in this paragraph, H. SCHÜRMANN can still suppose that Luke was unconscious of the " older " rationale for the election of Twelve, viz. their relation to the twelve tribes (*Lk.* I,315) quite escapes us. SCHÜRMANN himself simply pays no attention to the larger contexts in which our author develops the role of the Twelve through his two volumes: the classic pattern of Israel's dealings with the prophets, on the one hand, and the mission to Israel, centered at Jerusalem, on the other. It is not accidental that once the theatre of missionary endeavour has shifted from Jerusalem in the Acts narrative, the Twelve simply disappear from the scene!

(3) Luke thus places the traditional reason for the calling of the Twelve into the framework of passion solidarity (Lk 22,28ff.). This is in harmony with his " witness " concept : *total reenactment of the Lord's journey* (Acts 10,39 ; 13,31), meaning the complete embrace of the prophet's destiny (Lk 13,33). This is the reason why instruction in the mystery of the passion, from the perspective of its Easter termination, was found to be the thematic bond uniting the three Easter pericopes into an integral literary statement. This was the revelation which prepared observers of the *triduum paschale* for their mission as "witnesses," inaugurating "from Jerusalem" a church history in which the gospel's propagation and the witnesses' suffering were to be essentially, necessarily interrelated.[175]

There is the point in which the Lucan Easter story has its compositional unity and focus, for its feature of *mission recruitment and rehearsal* is what works its pivotal function in the design of Lk-Acts. With the traditions of an early, itinerant Christian mission furnishing the matrix of the two appearance stories, Luke, in conscious dialogue with these and with Mk, showed us how the Easter events contained the seminal beginnings of the disciples' mission to the world, — hence also formed the crucial intersection between the story of Jesus and the story of his Church.

EPILOGUE

I bid the reader judge how the issues raised on pp. ix to x of my introduction have been dealt with. The positions taken on them have been mostly advanced in chap. IV, as a result of the analysis pursued in the preceding chapters (except where other references were made in the introduction itself). I have answered most of those questions differently than many of the contemporary representatives of Lucan scholarship would answer them ; but I do find the support of an increasing number of more recent *Redaktionsgeschichtler* in presenting a viable alternate approach to the one sponsored in *Die Mitte der Zeit*. Wherever the right answers lie (assuredly not in any systematic view of Lk's theology), our investigation has assured us that Lucan studies are very, very much alive, — and far from settled !

[175] H. CONZELMANN was correct to cite this as an essential feature of Lucan ecclesiology (*MdZ*, 195f. n. 2).

BIBLIOGRAPHY

(A) Abbreviations:

(1) In general, abbreviations are used from the list furnished in the *Elenchus bibliographicus biblicus* 55 (1974) v-xxx, with reliance on older numbers of the same in a few instances where entries were not included in vol. 55.

(2) It is assumed that the reader is familiar with standard biblical reference works, hence special listing is not made of them here. Reference is made in our pages to the Aland *Synopsis Quattuor Evangeliorum* (1964), the W. Bauer *Wörterbuch*[5] (1963), the Blass-Debrunner (Bl-Deb) *Grammatik*[10], Charles' *Apocrypha and Pseudepigrapha of the Old Testament*, Hennecke-Schneemelcher, *New Testament Apocrypha* (tr. R. McL. Wilson; London: Lutterworth Press, 1965, 2 vols.), *Loeb Classical Library*: The Apostolic Fathers, trans. Kirsopp Lake (2 vols.), and H. Strack – P. Billerbeck, *Kommentar zum Neuen Testament aus Talmud und Midrasch* (5 vols. with index) (Str-Bill).

(3) Besides these common works, we also abbreviate certain frequently cited resources with special bearing on the subject-matter at hand. They are the following:

R. Bultmann, *GsT* (= *Die Geschichte der synoptischen Tradition*, listed p. 300 below);

Beginnings (= F. J. F. Jackson/K. Lake, eds., *Beginnings of Christianity*, listed p. 298 below);

Braumann-*LkEv* (= G. Braumann, hrsg., *Das Lukas-Evangelium*, listed p. 300 below);

Conzelmann, H., *MdZ* (= *Mitte der Zeit*, listed p. 301);

StLA (= *Studies in Luke-Acts*, ed. L. E. Keck & J. L. Martyn, listed below, p. 305).

(4) Presumed: R(evised) S(tandard) V(ersion), N(ew) A(merican) B(ible), N(ew) E(nglish) B(ible).

(B) Commentaries on Luke and Acts:

Bauernfeind, Otto. *Die Apostelgeschichte*. Theologischer Handkommentar zum Neuen Testament 5; Berlin: Evangelische Verlagsanstalt, 1939.

Creed, John Martin. *The Gospel according to Saint Luke*. London: Macmillan, 1957 (repr. of 1930 original ed.).

Conzelmann, Hans. *Die Apostelgeschichte*. Handbuch zum Neuen Testament 7; Tübingen: J. C. B. Mohr, 1963; 2. Aufl., 1972.

Ellis, E. Earl. *The Gospel of Luke*. The Century Bible, new edition. London/New York: Thos. Nelson Sons, 1966.

Ernst, Josef. *Das Evangelium nach Lukas*. Regensburger Neues Testament, neue Auflage. Regensburg: F. Pustet, 1977.

Grundmann, Walter. *Das Evangelium nach Lukas*. Theologischer Handkommentar zum Neuen Testament 3; Berlin: Evangelische Verlagsanstalt, ²1961.

Haenchen, Ernst. *Die Apostelgeschichte*. Meyerkommentar, 3. Reihe, 14. Auflage. Göttingen: Vandenhoeck und Ruprecht, 1965.

JACKSON, F. J. F., and Kirsopp LAKE, eds., *The Beginnings of Christianity.* Part I. The Acts of the Apostles. 5 volumes. London: Macmillan, 1920-1933.

KLOSTERMANN, Erich. *Das Lukasevangelium.* Handbuch zum Neuen Testament, 2. Auflage. Tübingen: J. C. B. Mohr, 1929.

LAMPE, G. W. H., in *Peake's Commentary on the Bible* (ed. M. Black & H. H. Rowley; London/New York: Thos. Nelson Sons, 1962): Lk 820-843; Acts 882-926.

LEANEY, A. R. C. *The Gospel according to St. Luke.* Harpers New Testament Commentaries; New York: Harper and Row, 1958.

LOHMEYER, Ernst. *Das Evangelium nach Lukas.* Meyerkommentar, hrsg. mit Ergänzungsheft von G. Sass. Göttingen: Vandenhoeck und Ruprecht, 1953.

LOISY, Alfred. *L'évangile de Luc.* Paris: Émile Nourry, 1924.

MUNCK, Johannes. *The Acts of the Apostles.* Anchor Bible 31; New York: Doubleday, 1967.

PLUMMER, Alfred. *St. Luke.* International Critical Commentary. Edinburgh: T. & T. Clark, [5]1928.

RENGSTORF, Karl Heinrich. *Das Evangelium nach Lukas.* Das Neue Testament Deutsch 3; Göttingen: Vandenhoeck und Ruprecht, [13]1968.

SCHLATTER, Adolf. *Das Evangelium des Lukas aus seinen Quellen erklärt.* Stuttgart: Calwer Verlag, [2]1960.

SCHMID, Josef. *Das Evangelium nach Lukas.* Regensburger Neues Testament. Regensburg: F. Pustet, [3]1955.

SCHNIEWIND, Julius. *Das Evangelium nach Lukas.* Das Neue Testament Deutsch 3; Göttingen: Vandenhoeck und Ruprecht, [6]1952.

SCHÜRMANN, Heinz. *Das Lukasevangelium.* I. Teil: Kommentar zu 1,1 – 9,50. Herders theologischer Kommentar zum Neuen Testament III/1; Freiburg/Basel/Wien: Herder, 1969.

STÄHLIN, Gustav. *Die Apostelgeschichte.* Das Neue Testament Deutsch 5; Göttingen: Vandenhoeck und Ruprecht, [10]1962.

WELLHAUSEN, Julius. *Das Evangelium Lucae.* Berlin: Georg Reimer, 1904.

WIKENHAUSER, Alfred. *Die Apostelgeschichte.* Regensburger Neues Testament 5; Regensburg: F. Pustet, [4]1961.

(C) OTHER LITERATURE:

ACHTEMEIER, Paul J., " Gospel Miracle Tradition and the Divine Man," *Interpr* 26 (1972) 174-197.

——, " The Lukan Perspective on the Miracles of Jesus," *JBL* 94 (1975) 547-562.

ALAND, Kurt, " Neue testamentliche Papyri II," *NTS* 12 (1965-66) 193-210. Now excerpted in " Die Bedeutung des P-75 für den Text des Neuen Testaments. Ein Beitrag zur Frage der ' Western non-interpolations '," in K. ALAND, *Studien zur Überlieferung des Neuen Testaments und seines Textes* (Berlin: W. de Gruyter, 1967) 155-172.

ALBERTZ, Martin, " Zur Formengeschichte der Auferstehungsberichte," *ZNW* 21 (1922) 259-269.

ALSUP, John E. *The Post-Resurrection Appearance Stories of the Gospel Tradition. A History-of-Tradition Analysis.* Calwer theologische Monographien 5; Stuttgart: Calwer-Verlag, 1975.

AMMASSARI, Antonio. *La Risurrezione nell'insegnamento, nella profezia, nelle apparizioni di Gesu.* Roma: Città Nuova Editrice, 1975.

BAILEY, John Amedee. *The Traditions Common to the Gospels of Luke and John.* SupplNT 7; Leiden: E. J. Brill, 1963.

Barrett, C. K. *Luke the Historian in Recent Study.* London: Epworth Press, 1961. Now in Facet Books, bibl. ser. 24; Philadelphia: Fortress Press, 1970.

Bartsch, Hans-Werner. *Wachet aber zu jeder Zeit. Entwurf einer Auslegung des Lukas-evangeliums.* Hamburg-Bergstedt: Evangelischer Verlag Herbert Reich, 1963.

——. *Das Auferstehungszeugnis. Sein historisches und sein theologisches Problem.* Theologische Forschung 41; Hamburg-Bergstedt: Evangelischer Verlag Herbert Reich, 1965.

Baumbach, Günther. *Das Verständnis des Bösen in der synoptischen Evangelien.* Theologische Arbeiten XIX; Berlin: Evangelischer Verlagsanstalt, 1963.

Benoit, Pierre, "L'ascension," *RB* 56 (1949) 161-203. Now in P. Benoit, *Exégèse et théologie* I (Paris: Editions du Cerf, 1961) 363-411.

——, "Marie-Madeleine et les disciples au tombeau selon Joh 20,1-18," in Walther Eltester, hrsg., *Judentum-Urchristentum-Kirche. Festschrift für Joachim Jeremias* (BZNW 26, 2 Aufl.; Berlin: A Töpelmann [W. de Gruyter], 1964) 141-152.

——, and M.-E. Boismard. *Synopse des quatre évangiles.* 2 vols. Paris: Editions du Cerf, 1972.

Bertram, Georg. *Die Leidensgeschichte Jesu und der Christuskult. Eine formgeschichtliche Untersuchung.* FRLANT 32; Göttingen: Vandenhoeck und Ruprecht, 1922.

——, "Die Himmelfahrt Jesu vom Kreuz aus und der Glaube an seine Auferstehung," in *Festgabe für Adolf Deissmann zum 60. Geburtstag* (Tübingen: J. C. B. Mohr, 1927) 187-217.

Betz, Hans-Dieter, "Jesus, the Divine Man," in F. Thomas Trotter, ed., *Jesus and the Historian. Written in Honor of Ernest Cadman Colwell* (Philadelphia: Westminster Press, 1968) 114-133.

——," Ursprung und Wesen des christlichen Glaubens nach der Emmauslegende (Lk 24, 13-32)," *ZTK* 66 (1969) 7-21.

Betz, Otto, "The Kerygma of Luke," *Interpr* 22 (1968) 131-146.

Bieler, Ludwig. ΘΕΙΟΣ ΑΝΗΡ. *Das Bild des "göttlichen Menschen" in Spätantike und Frühchristentum.* (Vienna, 1935-36) Repr. Darmstadt: Wissenschaftliche Buchgesellschaft, 1967. 2 Bde.

Bihler, Johannes. *Die Stephanusgeschichte im Zusammenhang der Apostelgeschichte.* Münchener theologischer Studien I/30; München: Max Hueber Verlag, 1963.

Blinzler, Joseph. "Die literarische Eigenart des sogenannten Reiseberichts im Lukasevangelium," in J. Schmid and A. Vögtle, hrsg., *Synoptische Studien, A. Wikenhauser zum 70. Geburtstag ... dargebracht* (München: Karl Zink Verlag, 1953) 20-52.

——, "Die Grablegung Jesu in historischer Sicht," in E. Dhanis, éd., *Resurrexit. Actes du symposium int. sur la résurrection de Jésus.* (Rome: Libreria Editrice Vaticana, 1974) 56-107.

Bode, Edward L. *The First Easter Morning. The Gospel Accounts of the Women's Visit to the Tomb of Jesus.* AnBib 45; Rome: Biblical Institute Press, 1970.

Boismard, M.-&. "Le réalisme des récits évangéliques," *LumVie* 109 (1971) 31-41.

Bornhauser, Karl. *Studien zum Sondergut des Lukas.* Gütersloh: Verlag C. Bertelmann, 1934.

Bornhamm, Günther. *Jesus von Nazareth.* Urban-Bücher 19; Stuttgart: W. Kohlhammer, [4]1960.

——, Gerhard BARTH and H. J. HELD. *Überlieferung und Auslegung im Mattäusevangelium.* WissMon ANT 1; Neukirchen: Neukirchener Verlag, [5]1965.

BOUWMAN, Gilbert, "Die Erhöhung Jesu in der lukanischen Theologie," *BZ* 14 (1970) 257-263.

BOWEN, Clayton Raymond, "The Emmaus Disciples and the Purpose of Luke," *The Biblical World* n.s. 35 (1910) 234-245.

BOWMAN, John. *Samaritanische Probleme. Studien zum Verhältnis von Samaritanertum, Judentum und Urchristentum.* Franz Delitzsch-Vorlesungen 1959; Stuttgart/Mainz: Kohlhammer, 1967.

BRÄNDLE, Max, "Auferstehung Jesu nach Lukas," *Orientg* 24 (1960) 85-89.

BRAUMANN, Georg, "Das Mittel der Zeit. Erwägungen zur Theologie des Lukasevangeliums," *ZNW* 54 (1963) 117-145.

——, hrsg. *Das Lukas-Evangelium. Die redaktions- und kompositionsgeschichtliche Forschung.* Wege der Forschung 280; Darmstadt: Wissenschaftliche Buchgesellschaft, 1974.

BROER, Ingo. *Die Urgemeinde und das Grab Jesu. Eine Analyse der Grablegungsgeschichte im Neuen Testament.* StANT 31; München: Kösel-Verlag, 1972.

BROWN, Schuyler. *Apostasy and Perseverance in the Theology of St. Luke.* AnBib 36; Rome: Pontifical Biblical Institute, 1969.

BROX, Norbert. *Zeuge und Märtyrer. Untersuchungen zur frühchristlichen Zeugnis-Terminologie.* StANT 5; München: Kösel-Verlag, 1961.

BRUN, Lyder. *Die Auferstehung Christi in der urchristlichen Überlieferung.* Giessen: Verlag A. Töpelmann, 1925.

BULTMANN, Rudolf. *Theology of the New Testament.* 2 vols. Trans. Kendrick Grobel. New York: Chas. Scribner's Sons, 1952, 1955.

——. *Die Geschichte der synoptischen Tradition.* FRLANT 29; Göttingen: Vandenhoeck und Ruprecht, [3]1957; Ergänzungsheft, hrsg. Gerd Theissen and Philipp Vielhauer, [4]1970.

——. *Das Evangelium des Johannes.* 17. Auflage. Meyerkommentar; Göttingen: Vandenhoeck und Ruprecht, 1962.

BURCHARD, Christoph. *Der dreizehnte Zeuge. Traditions- und kompositionsgeschichtliche Untersuchungen zu Lukas Darstellung der Frühzeit des Paulus.* FRLANT 103; Göttingen: Vandenhoeck and Ruprecht, 1970.

BUSSE, Ulrich. *Die Wunder des Propheten Jesus. Die Rezeption, Komposition, und Interpretation der Wundertradition im Evangelium des Lukas.* FzB 24; Stuttgart: Katholisches Bibelwerk, 1977.

CADBURY, Henry J., "Acts and Eschatology," in W. D. Davies and D. Daube, eds., *The Background of the New Testament and Its Eschatology. Essays in Honor of C.H. Dodd* (Cambridge: Cambridge University Press, 1956) 300-321.

——. *The Book of Acts in History.* London: Adam and Chas. Black, 1955.

——. *The Making of Luke-Acts.* London: S. P. C. K., [2]1958.

CAMPENHAUSEN, Hans Freiherr von. *Der Ablauf der Osterereignisse und das leere Grab.* Sitzungsberichte der Heidelberger Akademie der Wissenschaften, philosophisch-historische Klasse; Jahrgang 1952, 4. Abhandlung. Heidelberg: Carl Winter Universitätsverlag, [3]1966.

CERFAUX, Lucien. "La composition de la première partie du livre des Actes," *ETL* 13 (1936) 667-691. Now in L. Cerfaux, *Recueil Lucien Cerfaux II* (Gembloux: Editions J. Duculot, 1954) 63-91.

——. "La première communauté à Jérusalem," *ETL* 16 (1939) 5-31. Now in L. Cerfaux, *Recueil Lucien Cerfaux II* (Gembloux: Editions J. Duculot, 1954) 125-156.

——, et J. CAMBIER, "Luc," *DBS* V (Paris, 1953) 545-594.

CONZELMANN, Hans. *Die Mitte der Zeit. Studien zur Theologie des Lukas.* Beiträge zur. hist. Theol. 17 ; Tübingen : J. C. B. Mohr, [1]1954, [5]1964.

——, " Zur Lukasanalyse," *ZTK* 49 (1952) 16-33.

——, " Luke's Place in the Development of Early Christianity," in Leander E. Keck and John L. Martyn, eds., *Studies in Luke-Acts. Essays Presented in Honor of Paul Schubert* (Nashville/New York : Abingdon Press, 1966) 298-316.

——, " Historie und Theologie in den synoptischen Passionsberichten," in Aritz Viering, hrsg., *Zur Bedeutung des Todes Jesu. Exegetische Beiträge* (Gütersloh : Gerd Mohn, 1967) 35-53.

——, " Literaturbericht zu den synoptischen Evangelien," *TRu* 37 (1972) 220-272 (esp. 264-272).

CREHAN, Joseph H., " St. Peter's Journey to Emmaus," *CBQ* 15 (1953) 418-426.

CROSSAN, John Dominic, " Empty Tomb and Absent Lord (Mark 16 : 1-8)," in Werner H. Kelber, ed., *The Passion in Mark* : *Studies on Mark* 14-16 (Philadelphia : Fortress Press, 1976) 135-152.

DAUTZENBERG, Gerhard. *Urchristliche Prophetie. Ihre Erforschung, ihre Voraussetzungen im Judentum und ihre Struktur im ersten Korintherbrief.* BWANT 104 ; Stuttgart/Berlin : Verlag W. Kohlhammer, 1975.

DAVIES, J. G. *He Ascended into Heaven. A Study in the History of Doctrine.* The Bampton Lectures, 1958. New York : Association Press, 1958.

DEGENHARDT, Hans-Joachim. *Lukas — Evangelist der Armen. Besitz und Besitzverzicht in den lukanischen Schriften. Ein traditions- und redaktionsgeschichtliche Untersuchung.* Stuttgart : Katholisches Bibelwerk, 1965.

DELLING, Gerhard, " Die Jesusgeschichte in der Verkündigung nach Acta," *NTS* 19 (1972-73) 373-389.

DELORME, Jean, " Résurrection et tombeau de Jésus. Marc 16, 1-8 dans la tradition évangélique," in P. de Surgy et al., *La résurrection du Christ et l'exégèse moderne* (Lectio divina 50 ; Paris : Editions du Cerf, 1969) 105-151.

DENAUX, A., " L'hypocrisie des Pharisiens et le dessein de Dieu. Analyse de Lc., XIII, 31-33," in F. Neirynck, éd., *L'évangile de Luc* : *Problèmes littéraires et théologiques. Mémorial Lucien Cerfaux* (Bibliotheca *ETL* XXXII ; Gembloux : Editions J. Duculot, 1973) 245-285.

DESCAMPS, A., " La structure des récits évangéliques de la résurrection," *Bib* 40 (1959) 726-741.

DHANIS, Edouard, " L'ensevelissement de Jésus et la visite au tombeau dans l'évangile de saint Marc (Mc., XV,40 – XVI,8)," *Greg* 39 (1958) 367-410.

DIBELIUS, Martin. *Die Formgeschichte des Evangeliums*, hrsg. Gerhard Iber. Tübingen : J. C. B. Mohr, [3]1958.

——. *Aufsätze zur Apostelgeschichte.* FRLANT 60, hrsg. Heinrich Greeven ; Göttingen : Vandenhoeck und Ruprecht, [4]1961.

——. *Botschaft und Geschichte. Gesammelte Aufsätze I* : *Zur Evangelienforschung.* Tübingen : J. C. B. Mohr, 1953.

DIETRICH, Wolfgang. *Das Petrusbild der lukanischen Schriften.* BWANT 94 ; Stuttgart : Kohlhammer, 1972.

DODD, C. H. *The Apostolic Preaching and Its Developments.* New York : Harper and Brothers (orig. 1935) 1961.

——. *According to the Scripture. The Sub-structure of New Testament Theology.* New York : Chas. Scribner's Sons, 1953.

——, " The Appearances of the Risen Christ. An Essay in Form-Criticism of the Gospels," in D. E. Nineham, ed., *Studies in the Gospels* : *Essays in Memory of R. H. Lightfoot* (Oxford : Basil Blackwell, 1955) 9-35. Now in C. H. Dodd, *More New Testament Studies* (Manchester : Manchester University Press, 1963) 102-133.

DUBOIS, Jean-Daniel, " La figure d'Élie dans la perspective lucanienne," *RHPhilRel* 53 (1973) 155-176.

DUPONT, Jacques. *Les problèmes du livre des Actes d'après les travaux récents* (1940-1950). Louvain : Publications universitaires, 1950.

——. *Les sources du livre des Actes : état de la question.* Bruges : Desclée de Brouwer, 1960. ET, *The Sources of Acts.* Trans. Kathleen Pond. London : Darton, Longman & Todd ; New York : Herder, 1964.

——. *Études sur les Actes des Apotres.* Lectio Divina 45 ; Paris : Editions du Cerf, 1967.

——, " Les pèlerins d'Emmaüs (Luc xxiv, 13-35)," *Miscellanea Biblica Bonaventura Ubach.* Scripta et Documenta I ; Montserrat, 1953. Pp. 349-374.

——, " Les discours de Pierre dans les Actes et le chapitre XXIV de l'évangile de Luc," in Frans Nierynck, éd., *L'Evangile de Luc : Problèmes littéraires et théologiques. Mémorial Lucien Cerfaux* (Bibliotheca Ephemeridum theologicarum Lovaniensium 32 ; Gembloux : Editions J. Duculot, 1973) 329-374.

——, " La portée christologique de l'évangélisation des nations d'après Luc 24, 47," in J. Gnilka, hrsg., *Neues Testament und Kirche, für Rudolf Schnackenburg* (Freiburg/Basel : Herder, 1974) 125-143.

EDWARDS, R. E., " The Redaction of Luke," *JRel* 49 (1969) 392-405.

EHRHARDT, A., " The Construction and Purpose of the Acts of the Apostles," *ST* 12 (1958) 45-79.

——, " The Disciples of Emmaus," *NTS* 10 (1963-64) 182-201.

——, " Emmaus. Romulus und Apuleius," in A. Stuiber und A. Hermann, hrsg., *Mullus. Festschrift Theodor Klauser* (*Jahrbuch für Antike und Christendum*, Ergänzungsband 1 ; Münster : Aschendorff, 1964) 93-99.

ELLIS, E. Earle. *Eschatology in Luke.* Facet Books, bibl. ser. 30. Philadelphia : Fortress Press, 1972.

——, " Present and Future Eschatology in Luke," *NTS* 12 (1965-66) 27-41.

——, " Die Funktion der Eschatologie im Lukasevangelium," *ZTK* 66 (1969) 387-402.

——, " The Composition of Luke 9 and the Sources of Its Christology," in G. F. Hawthorne, ed., *Current Issues in Biblical and Patristic Interpretation. Studies in Honor of Merrill C. Tenney* (Grand Rapids : Wm. B. Eerdmans, 1975) 121-127.

ELTESTER, Walther, " Israel im lukanischen Werk und die Nazarethperikope," in Erich Grässer, et al., *Jesus in Nazareth* (BZNW 40 ; Berlin : Walter de Gruyter, 1972) 76-147.

ENSLIN, Morton S., " Once Again, Luke and Paul," *NT* 15 (1973) 59-71.

ERNST, Josef, " Schriftauslegung und Auferstehungsglaube bei Lukas," in Josef Ernst, hrsg., *Schriftauslegung. Beiträge zur Hermeneutik des Neuen Testaments und im Neuen Testament* (Paderborn : Verlag Ferdinand Schöningh, 1972) 177-192.

EVANS, C. F. *Resurrection and the New Testament.* StBibT, 2nd ser., no. 12. London : SCM Press, 1970.

——, " The Central Section of St. Luke's Gospel," in D. E. Nineham, ed., *Studies in the Gospels. Essays in Memory of R. H. Lightfoot* (Oxford : Basil Blackwell, 1955) 37-53.

——, " The Kerygma," *JTS* 7 (1956) 25-41.

FASCHER, Erich, " Die Auferstehung Jesu und ihr Verhältnis zur urchristlichen Verkündigung," *ZNW* 26 (1927) 1-26.

FINEGAN, Jack. *Die Überlieferung der Leidens- und Auferstehungsgeschichte Jesu.* BZNW 15 ; Giessen : Alfred Töpelmann, 1934.

FLENDER, Helmut. *Heil und Geschichte in der Theologie des Lukas.* BEvT 41 ; München : Kaiser Verlag, 1965.

FRANCIS, F. O., " Eschatology and History in Luke-Acts," *JAmAcRel* 37 (1969) 49-63.

FRANKLIN, Eric. *Christ the Lord. A Study in the Purpose and Theology of Luke-Acts.* Philadelphia: Westminster Press, 1975.

FRIDRICHSEN, Anton, " Die Himmelfahrt bei Lukas," *Theologische Blätter* 6 (1927) 337-341.

FRIEDRICH, Gerhard, " Lk 9,51 und die Entrückungschristologie des Lukas," in Paul Hoffman, hrsg., *Orientierung an Jesus. Zur Theologie der Synoptiker, für Josef Schmid* (Freiburg/Basel: Herder, 1973) 48-77.

FULLER, Daniel P. *Easter Faith and History.* GrandRapids: Wm. B. Eerdmans, 1965.

FULLER, Reginald H. *The Formation of the Resurrection Narratives.* New York: Macmillan, 1971.

GEIGER, Ruthild. *Die Lukanischen Endzeitreden. Studien zur Eschatologie des Lukas-Evangeliums.* Europäische Hochschulschriften XXIII/16; Bern/Frankfurt-am-Main: Herbert/Peter Lang, 1973.

GEORGE, Augustin, " Jésus Fils de Dieu dans l'évangile selon saint Luc," *RB* 72 (1965) 185-209.

——, " Tradition et rédaction chez Luc. La construction du troisième évangile," in Ignace de la Potterie, éd., *De Jésus aux évangiles. Tradition et rédaction dans les évangiles synoptiques* (Bibliotheca *ETL*, XXV: Gembloux: Editions Duculot, 1967) 100-129.

——, " Israel dans l'œuvre de Luc," *RB* 75 (1968) 481-525.

——, " Les apparitions aux Onze à partir de Luc, 24,36-53," in P. de Surgy et al., *La résurrection du Christ et l'exégèse moderne* (Lectio divina 50; Paris: Editions du Cerf, 1969) 75-104.

——, " Le sens de la mort de Jésus pour Luc," *RB* 80 (1973) 186-217.

GEORGI, Dieter. *Die Gegner des Paulus im 2. Korintherbrief. Studien zur religiösen Propaganda in der Spätantike.* WissMonANT 11; Neukirchen: Neukirchener Verlag, 1964.

GILL, David, " Observations on the Lukan Travel Narrative and Some Related Passages," *HarvTR* 63 (1970) 199-221.

GILS, Félix. *Jésus prophète dans les évangiles synoptiques.* OrBiLov II; Louvain: Publications universitaires, 1957.

GLÖCKNER, Richard. *Die Verkündigung des Heils beim Evangelisten Lukas.* Walberger Studien, theol. Reihe, Bd. 9; Mainz: Matthias-Grünewald-Verlag, 1975.

GOLLWITZER, Helmut. *Jesu Tod und Auferstehung nach dem Bericht des Lukas.* München: Kaiser-Verlag [1941], [5]1963.

GOUDOEVER, J. van, " The Place of Israel in Luke's Gospel," *NT* 8 (1966) 111-123.

GRÄSSER, Erich. *Das Problem der Parusieverzögerung in den synoptischen Evangelien und in der Apostelgeschichte.* BZNW 22; Berlin: Walter de Gruyter, 1957.

——, " Die Apostelgeschichte in der Forschung der Gegenwart," *TRu* 26 (1960) 93-167.

——, " Acta-Forschung seit 1960," *TRu* 41 (1976) 141-194; 42 (1977) 1-68.

GRANT, Robert M., et al., eds. *The Apostolic Fathers. A New Translation and Commentary.* London/New York: Thomas Nelson, 1964-1968. 6 vols.

GRASS, Hans. *Ostergeschehen und Osterberichte.* Göttingen: Vandenhoeck und Ruprecht, [4]1970.

GRASSI, Joseph A., " Emmaus Revisited: Luke 24,13-35 and Acts 8,26-40," *CBQ* 26 (1964) 463-467.

HAENCHEN, Ernst. *Gott und Mensch. Gesammelte Aufsätze.* Tübingen: J. C. B. Mohr, 1965.

——. *Der Weg Jesu. Eine Erklärung des Markus-Evangeliums und der kanonischen Parallelen.* Berlin: Alfred Töpelmann, 1966.

——. *Die Bibel und wir. Gesammelte Aufsätze II.* Tübingen: J. C. B. Mohr, 1968.

——, "Tradition und Komposition in der Apostelgeschichte," *ZTK* 52 (1955) 205-225. Now in E. Haenchen, *Gott und Mensch*, 206-226.

——, "Judentum und Christentum in der Apostelgeschichte," *ZNW* 54 (1965) 155-187. Now in E. Haenchen, *Die Bibel und wir*, 338-374.

——, "The Book of Acts as Source Material for the History of Early Christianity," in Leander E. Keck and J. Louis Martyn, eds., *Studies in Luke-Acts. Essays Presented in Honor of Paul Schubert* (Nashville/New York: Abingdon Press, 1966) 258-278.

Haes, P. de. *La résurrection de Jésus dans l'apologétique des cinquante dernières années.* Studia Gregoriana; Rome: Pont. Univ. Greg., 1953.

Hahn, Ferdinand. *Christologische Hoheitstitel. Ihre Geschichte im frühen Christentum.* FRLANT 83; Göttingen: Vandenhoeck und Ruprecht, 1963.

——, *Das Verständnis der Mission im Neuen Testament.* WissMonANT 13; Neukirchen: Neukirchener Verlag, 1963.

Harnack, Adolf von. *Beitrag zur Einleitung in das Neue Testament. III: Die Apostelgeschichte.* Leipzig: J. C. Heinrich, 1908.

——. *Lukas der Arzt. Der Verfasser des dritten Evangeliums und der Apostelgeschichte.* Beiträge zur Einleitung in das Neue Testament 1; Leipzig: J. C. Heinrich, 1906.

——. *Die Mission und Ausbreitung des Christentums in den ersten drei Jahrhunderten.* Band I. Leipzig: J. C. Heinrichs, [4]1923.

——, "Die Verklärungsgeschichte, der Bericht des Paulus (I. Kor. 15, 3ff.) und die beiden Christusvisionen des Petrus," Sitzungsbericht der preussischen Akademie der Wissenschaft, philosophisch-historische Klasse, VIII (Berlin, 1922) 62-80.

Hartmann, Gert, "Die Vorlage der Osterberichte in Joh 20," *ZNW* 55 (1964) 197-220.

Hastings, Adrian. *Prophet and Witness in Jerusalem. A Study in the Teaching of St. Luke.* London: Longmans, 1958.

Hawkins, Sir John C. *Horae synopticae. Contributions to the Study of the Synoptic Problem.* Oxford, 1899.

Hengel, Martin. *Nachfolge und Charisma. Eine exegetisch-religionsgeschichtliche Studie zu Mt 8,21f. und Jesu Ruf in die Nachfolge.* BZNW 34; Berlin: Alfred Töpelmann (W. de Gruyter), 1968.

——. *Judentum und Hellenismus. Studien zu ihrer Begegnung unter besonderer Berücksichtigung Palästinas bis zur Mitte des 2. Jh. v. Chr.* WissUnNT 10; Tübingen: J. C. B. Mohr, 1969.

——, "Maria Magdalena und die Frauen als Zeugen," in Otto Betz et al., hrsg., *Abraham unser Vater. Juden und Christen im Gespräch über die Bibel* (Leiden/Koln: E. J. Brill, 1963) 243-256.

——, "Zwischen Jesus und Paulus. Die 'Hellenisten', die 'Sieben' und Stephanus (Apg 6,1-15; 7,54-8,3)," *ZTK* 72 (1975) 151-206.

Higgins, A. J. B., "The Preface to Luke and the Kerygma in Acts," in W. Ward Gasque and Ralph P. Martin, eds., *Apostolic History and the Gospel. Essays presented to F. F. Bruce* (Grand Rapids: Wm. B. Eerdmans, 1970) 78-91.

Hirsch, Emmanuel. *Die Auferstehungsgeschichten und der christliche Glaube.* Tübingen: J. C. B. Mohr, 1940.

Hoffmann, Paul. *Studien zur Theologie der Logienquelle.* NTAbh 8; Münster: Aschendorff, 1972.

HOLTZ, Traugott. *Untersuchungen über die alttestamentlichen Zitate bei Lukas.* TU 104 ; Berlin : Akademie-Verlag, 1968.

HOLTZMANN, Heinrich Julius. *Synoptiker.* Handkommentar zum Neuen Testament, I-1 ; Tübingen/Leipzig, [3]1901.

HOOKE, S. H. *The Resurrection of Christ as History and Experience.* London ; Darton, Longman and Todd, 1967.

HUFFMAN, Norman, "Emmaus among the Resurrection Narratives," *JBL* 64 (1945) 205-226.

JEANNE D'ARC, Sœur, " Un grand jeu d'inclusions dans ' les pèlerins d'Emmaüs,' " *NRT* 99 (1977) 62-76.

JEANNE D'ARC, Sœur. *Les pèlerins d'Emmaüs.* Série " Lire la Bible " 47 ; Paris : Éditions du Cerf, 1977.

JEREMIAS, Joachim. *Die Abendmahlsworte Jesu.* Göttingen : Vandenhoeck und Ruprecht, [3]1960.

JERVELL, Jacob. *Luke and the People of God. A New Look at Luke-Acts.* Minneapolis : Augsburg Publishing House, 1972.

KÄSEMANN, Ernst. *Exegetische Versuche und Besinnungen.* 2 vols. Göttingen : Vandenhoeck und Ruprecht, 1960, 1964.

KAESTLI, Jean-Daniel. *L'eschatologie dans l'œuvre de Luc. Ses caractéristiques et sa place dans le développement du Christianisme primitif* : Genève : Labor et Fides, 1969.

KASTING, Heinrich. *Die Anfänge der christlichen Mission. Eine historische Untersuchung.* Beiträge zur evangelischen Theologie, 55 ; München : Verlag Chr. Kaiser, 1969.

KECK, Leander E., and J. Louis MARTYN, eds. *Studies in Luke-Acts. Essays Presented in Honor of Paul Schubert.* Nashville/New York : Abingdon Press, 1966.

KEGEL, Günter. *Auferstehung Jesu — Auferstehung der Toten. Eine traditionsgeschichtliche Untersuchung des Neuen Testaments.* Gütersloh : Verlagshaus Gerd Mohn, 1970.

KEHL, Medard, " Eucharistie und Auferstehung. Zur Deutung der Ostererscheinungen beim Mahl," *GeistLeb* 43 (1970) 90-125.

KELBER, Werner H., ed. *The Passion in Mark. Studies on Mark* 14-16. Philadelphia : Fortress Press, 1976.

KILGALLEN, John. *The Stephen Speech : A Literary and Redactional Study of Acts* 7,2-53. AnBib 67 ; Rome : Biblical Institute Press, 1976.

KLAIBER, Walter. " Eine lukanische Fassung des sola gratia. Beobachtungen zu Lk 1,5-56," in J. Friedrich et al., hrsg., *Rechtfertigung. Festschrift für Ernst Käsemann* (Tubingen : J. C. B. Mohr, 1976) 211-218.

KLEIN, Günter. *Die zwölf Apostel. Ursprung und Gehalt einer Idee.* FRLANT 77 ; Göttingen : Vandenhoeck und Ruprecht, 1961.

KLEIN, Günter, " Lukas 1,1-4 als theologisches Programm," in W. Eltester, hrsg., *Zeit und Geschichte. Dankesgabe an R. Bultmann zum* 80. *Geburtstag* (Tübingen : J. C. B. Mohr, 1964) 197-216 ; now in G. Braumann, hrsg., *Das Lukas-Evangelium. Die redaktions- und kompositionsgeschichtliche Forschung* (WdF 280 ; Darmstadt : Wissenschaftliches Buchgesellschaft, 1974) 170-203.

KLIESCH, Klaus. *Das heilsgeschichtliche Credo in den Reden der Apostelgeschichte.* BBB 44 ; Köln/Bonn : Peter Hanstein Verlag, 1975.

KOCH, Gerhard. *Die Auferstehung Jesu Christi.* Beiträge zur historischen Theologie, 27 ; Tübingen : J. C.B. Mohr, 1959.

KRÄNKL, Emmeram. *Jesus, der Knecht Gottes. Die heilsgeschichtliche Stellung Jesu in den Reden der Apostelgeschichte.* BibUnt 8 ; Regensburg : Pustet, 1972.

KREMER, Jacob. *Die Osterbotschaft der vier Evangelien. Versuch einer Auslegung der Berichte über das leere Grab und die Erscheinungen des Auferstandenen.* Stuttgart: Verlag Katholisches Bibelwerk, [3]1969.

——, " Zur Diskussion uber ' das leere Grab '," in E. Dhanis, éd., *Resurrexit. Actes du symposium international sur la résurrection de Jésus* (Rome: Libreria Editrice Vaticana, 1974) 137-168.

KRETSCHMAR, Georg, " Ein Beitrag zur Frage nach dem Ursprung frühchristlicher Askese," *ZTK* 61 (1964) 27-67.

KÜMMEL, Werner Georg. *Introduction to the New Testament.* Revised edition, translated from the 17th German edition by Howard Clark Kee. New York/ Nashville: Abingdon Press, 1975.

——, " Das Urchristentum," *TRu* 14 (1942) 81-95, 155-173; 17 (1948) 3-50, 103-142; 18 (1950) 1-50; 22 (1954) 138-170, 191-211.

——, " Luc en accusation dans la théologie contemporaine," *ETL* 46 (1970) 265-281; — German version: " Lukas in der Anklage der heutigen Theologie," *ZNW* 63 (1972) 149-165. — French also in F. Neirinck, ed., *L'év. de Luc. Mémorial L. Cerfaux* (cf. listing below) 93-109.

——, " ' Das Gesetz und die Propheten gehen bis Johannes '. Lukas 16,16 im Zusammenhang der heilsgeschichtlichen Theologie der Lukasschriften," in O. Böcher und K. Haacker, hrsg., *Verborum Veritas. Festschrift für Gustav Stählin* (Wuppertal: Verlag Rolf Brockhaus, 1970) 89-102; now in Braumann-*LkEv.*, 398-415.

KUHN, Hans-Wolfgang, " Der irdische Jesus bei Paulus als traditionsgeschichtliches und theologisches Problem," *ZTK* 67 (1970) 295-320.

LAMPE, G. W. H., " The Holy Spirit in the Writing of St. Luke," in D. E. Nineham, ed., *Studies in the Gospels. Essays in Memory of R. H. Lightfoot* (Oxford: Basil Blackwell, 1955) 159-200.

LANGE, Joachim. *Das Erscheinen des Auferstandenen im Evangelium nach Mattäus. Eine traditions- und redaktionsgeschichtliche Untersuchung zu Mt* 28,16-20. ForBib 11; Würzburg: Echter Verlag, 1973.

LARRANAGA, Victorien. *L'ascension de Notre-Seigneur dans le Nouveau Testament.* Scripta Pontificii Instituti Biblici; Rome: Institut Biblique Pontifical, 1938.

LEANEY, Robert, " The Resurrection Narratives in Luke (XXIV, 12-53)," *NTS* 2 (1955-56) 110-114.

LEHMANN, Karl. *Auferweckt am dritten Tag nach der Schrift. Früheste Christologie, Bekenntnisbildung und Schriftauslegung im Lichte von* 1 *Kor.* 15.3-5. Quaestiones Disputatae 38; Freiburg/Basel: Herder, [2]1968.

LEON-DUFOUR, Xavier. *Résurrection de Jésus et message pascal.* Série " Parole de Dieu "; Paris: Editions du Seuil, 1971.

LINDSEY, F. D., " Lucan Theology in Contemporary Perspective," *BS* 125 (1968) 346-351.

LINNEMANN, Eta. *Studien sur Passionsgeschichte.* FRLANT 102; Göttingen: Vandenhoeck und Ruprecht, 1970.

LIGHTFOOT, R. H. *History and Interpretation in the Gospels.* Oxford: Oxford University Press, 1935.

LÖNING, Karl. *Die Saulustradition in der Apostelgeschichte*, NtAbh, n. F. 9; Münster: Verlag Aschendorff, 1973.

LOHFINK, Gerhard. *Die Himmelfahrt Jesu. Untersuchungen zu den Himmelfahrts- und Erhöhungstexten bei Lukas.* StANT 26; München: Kösel-Verlag, 1971.

——. *Die Sammlung Israels. Eine Untersuchung zur lukanischen Ekklesiologie.* StANT 39; München: Kösel-Verlag, 1975.

LOHMEYER, Ernst. *Galiläa und Jerusalem.* FRLANT 52; Göttingen: Vandenhoeck und Ruprecht, 1936.

LOHSE, Eduard. *Die Auferstehung Jesu Christi im Zeugnis des Lukasevangeliums.* Biblische Studien no. 31 ; Neukirchen : Neukirchener Verlag, 1961.

——. *Die Geschichte des Leidens und Sterbens Jesu Christi.* Gütersloh : Gerd Mohn, 1964.

——, " Lukas als Theologe der Heilsgeschichte," *EvT* 14 (1954) 256-275 ; now in Braumann-*LkEv.*, 64-90.

LOISY, Alfred. *Les évangiles synoptiques.* Ceffonds, 1907-08. 2 vols.

LORENZEN, Thorwald, " Ist der Auferstandene in Galiläa erschienen ? Bemerkungen zu einem Aufsatz von B. Steinseifer," *ZNW* 64 (1973) 209-221.

LOSADA, Diego Adolfo, " El episodio de Emaus, Lc 24,13-35 " *RBibArg* 35 (1973) 3-13.

LUCK, Ulrich, " Kerygma, Tradition und Geschichte Jesu bei Lukas," *ZTK* 57 (1960) 51-66 ; now in Braumann-*LkEv.*, 95-114.

LÜHRMANN, Dieter, *Die Redaktion der Logienquelle*, WMANT 33 ; Neukirchen ; Neukirchener Verlag, 1969.

MACDONALD, John. *The Theology of the Samaritans.* New Testament Library Series ; London : S. C. M. Press, 1964.

MÄRZ, Claus-Peter. *Das Wort Gottes bei Lukas. Die lukanische Worttheologie als Frage an die neuere Lukasforschung.* Erfurter theologische Studien 11 ; Leipzig : St. Benno-Verlag, 1974.

MAHONEY, Robert. *Two disciples at the tomb. The background and message of John* 20,1-10. Theologie und Wirklichkeit 6 : Bern/Frankfurt-am-Main : Herbert/Peter Lang, 1974.

MANSON, T. W. *The Sayings of Jesus.* Cambridge : Cambridge University Press (London : S. C. M. Study Edition), 1949.

——, *The Teaching of Jesus: Studies of its Form and Content.* Cambridge University Press, [1]1931 ; [2]1935.

MARSHALL, I. Howard, " Recent Study of the Gospel according to St. Luke," *ExpTim* 80 (1968-69) 4ff.

——, " The Resurrection in the Acts of the Apostles," in W. Ward Gasque and Ralph P. Martin, eds. *Apostolic History and the Gospel. Essays presented to F. F. Bruce* (Grand Rapids : Wm. B. Eerdmans, 1970) 92-107.

——. *Luke, Historian and Theologian.* Grand Rapids : Zondervan Publishing House, 1971.

——, " The Resurrection of Jesus in Luke," *TyndB* 24 (1973) 55-98.

MARTIN, Ralph P., " Salvation and Discipleship in Luke's Gospel," *Interpr* 30 (1976) 366-380.

MARTINI, Carlo M. *Il Problema Storico della Risurrezione negli Studi Recenti*, Analecta Gregoriana 104 ; Roma : Libreria Editrice dell'Università Gregoriana, 1959.

——, " L'apparizione agli Apostoli in Lc 24,36-43 nel complesso dell'opera lucana," in É. Dhanis, éd., *Resurrexit. Actes du symposium international sur la résurrection de Jésus* (Rome : Libreria Editrice Vaticana, 1974) 230-245.

MARXSEN, Willi. *Die Auferstehung Jesu von Nazareth.* Güttersloh : Verlagshaus Gerd Mohn, 1968.

——, Ulrich Wilckens, Gerhard Delling, H. G. Meyer, *Die Bedeutung der Auferstehungsbotschaft für den Glauben an Jesus Christus.* Gütersloh : Verlagshaus Gerd Mohn, [7]1968.

——. *Der Evangelist Markus. Studien zur Redaktionsgeschichte des Evangeliums.* FRLANT 67 ; Göttingen : Vandenhoeck und Ruprecht, [2]1959.

——. *Einleitung in das Neue Testament. Eine Einführung in ihre Probleme.* Gütersloh : Gerd Mohn, 1964.

MASSON, Charles, " Le tombeau vide (Marc 16 : 1-8)," *RTPhil* 32 (1944) 161-174.

MATTILL, A. J., Jr., " Naherwartung, Fernerwartung, and the Purpose of Luke-Acts : Weymouth Reconsidered," *CBQ* 34 (1972) 276-293.

——, " The Purpose of Acts : Schneckenburger Reconsidered," in W. Ward Gasque and Ralph P. Martin, eds. *Apostolic History and the Gospel. Essays presented to F. F. Bruce* (Grand Rapids : Wm. B. Eerdmans, 1970) 108-122.

MENOUD, Ph-H., " Le plan des Actes des Apôtres," *NTS* 1 (1954-55) 44-54.

MERK, Otto, " Das Reich Gottes in den lukanischen Schriften," in E. Earle Ellis & Erich Grässer, hrsg., *Jesus und Paulus. Festschrift für Werner Georg Kümmel zum* 70. *Geburtstag* (Göttingen : Vandenhoeck und Ruprecht, 1975) 201-220.

METZGER, Bruce M. *A Textual Commentary on the Greek New Testament* : *A Companion Volume to the United Bible Societies' Greek New Testament* (*Third Edition*) : On behalf of and in cooperation with Kurt Aland, Matthew Black, Carlo M. Martini, and Allen Wikgren. London & New York : United Bible Societies, 1971.

MEYER, Eduard. *Ursprung und Anfänge des Christentums I* : *Die Evangelien.* Repr. of 4./5. Auflage. (Stuttgard and Berlin, 1924). Darmstadt : Wissenschaftliche Buchgesellschaft, 1962.

——. *Ursprung und Anfänge des Christentums III* : *Die Apostelgeschichte und die Anfänge des Christentums.* Stuttgart/Berlin, 1923 ; Repr. Darmstadt : Wissenschaftliche Buchgesellschaft, 1962.

MEYER, Rudolf. *Der Prophet aus Galiläa. Studie zum Jesusbild der drei ersten Evangelien.* Leipeig, 1940 ; Repr. Darmstadt : Wissenschaftliche Buchgesellschaft, 1970.

MICHAELIS, Wilhelm. *Die Erscheinungen des Auferstandenen.* Basel : Verlag Heinrich Majer, 1944.

MICHEL, Otto, " Zeuge und Zeugnis. Zur neutestamentlichen Traditionsgeschichte," in H. Baltensweiler & Bo Reicke, hrsg., *Neues Testament und Geschichte. Historisches Geschehen und Deutung im Neuen Testament. Oscar Cullmann zum* 70. *Geburtstag* (*gewidmet*) (Zürich : Theol. Verlag/Tübingen : J. C. B. Mohr, 1972) 15-31.

MINETTE DE TILLESSE, G., *Le secret messianique dans l'évangile de Marc.* Lectio Divina 47 ; Paris : Éditions du Cerf, 1968.

MIYOSHI, Michi. *Der Anfang des Reiseberichts Lk* 9,51-10,24. *Eine redaktionsgeschichtliche Untersuchung.* Analecta biblica 60 ; Rome : Biblical Institute Press, 1974.

MORGENTHALER, Robert. *Die lukanische Geschichtsschreibung als Zeugnis. Gestalt und Gehalt der Kunst des Lukas.* Abhandlungen zur Theologie des Alten und Neuen Testaments 15 ; Zürich : Zwingli-Verlag, 1949. 2 vols.

MORTON, Andrew Queen, and George Hogarth Carnaby MacGregor. *The Structure of Luke and Acts.* New York : Harper and Row, 1965.

MOULE, C. F. D., ed. *Miracles* : *Cambridge Studies in their Philosophy and History.* London : A. R. Mowbray, 1965.

MUDDIMAN, John, " A Note on Reading Luke XXIV.12," *ETL* 48 (1972) 542-548.

MUSSNER, Franz. *Die Auferstehung Jesu.* Biblische Handbibliothek 7 ; München : Kösel-Verlag, 1969.

NAUCK, Wolfgang, " Die Bedeutung das leeren Grabes für den Glauben an den Auferstandenen," *ZNW* 47 (1956) 243-267.

NAVONE, John. *Themes of St. Luke.* Rome : Gregorian University Press, 1970.

NEIRYNCK, Frans, " La matière marcienne dans l'évangile de Luc," in F. Neirynck, éd. *L'évangile de Luc* : *Problèmes littéraires et théologiques. Mémorial Lucien Cerfaux.* (Bibliotheca *ETL* 32 ; Gembloux : Éditions J. Duculot, 1973) 157-201.

——, " The Uncorrected Historical Present in Lk XXIV.12," *ETL* 48 (1972) 549-553.

NELLESSEN, Ernst. *Zeugnis für Jesus und das Wort. Exegetische Untersuchungen zum lukanischen Zeugnisbegriff.* BBB 43 ; Köln/Bonn : Peter Hanstein, 1976.

ODASSO, Giovanni, " L'ascensione nell'evangelo di Luca," *BibOr* 13 (1971) 107-118.

O'NEILL, J. C. *The Theology of Acts in its Historical Setting.* 2nd. revised edition. London : S. P. C. K., 1970.

ORLETT, Raymond, " An influence of the Early Liturgy Upon the Emmaus Account," *CBQ* 21 (1959) 212-219.

OSTEN-SACKEN, Peter von der, " Zur Christologie des lukanischen Reiseberichts," *EvT* 33 (1973) 476-496.

OTT, Wilhelm. *Gebet und Heil. Die Bedeutung der Gebetsparänese in der lukanischen Theologie.* StANT 12 ; München : Kösel-Verlag, 1965.

PAYNE, D. F., " Semitisms in the Book of Acts," in W. Ward Gasque and Ralph P. Martin, eds., *Apostolic History and the Gospel. Essays presented to F. F. Bruce* (Grand Rapids : Wm. B. Eerdmans, 1970) 134-150.

PESCH, Rudolf, " Der Anfang der Apostelgeschichte : Apg. 1,1-11. Kommentarstudie," *EKK Vorarbeiten* 3 (1971) 7-35.

——. *Der reiche Fischfang, Lk 5,1-11/Jo 21,1-14 : Wundergeschichte – Berufungserzählung – Erscheinungsbericht.* Düsseldorf : Patmos-Verlag, 1969.

——. *Jesu ureigene Taten ? Ein Beitrag zur Wunderfrage.* Quaestiones disputatae 52 ; Freiburg/Basel ; Herder, 1970.

——. *Das Markusevangelium.* 1. Teil. Herders theologischer Kommentar zum Neuen Testament II/1 ; Freiburg/Basel : Herder, 1976.

PLÜMACHER, Eckhard. *Lukas als hellenistischer Schriftsteller. Studien zur Apostelgeschichte.* StUmweNT 9 ; Göttingen : Vandenhoeck und Ruprecht, 1972.

RADL, Walter. *Paulus und Jesus im lukanischen Doppelwerk. Untersuchungen zur Parallelmotiven im Lukasevangelium und der Apostelgeschichte.* Europäische Hochschulschriften XXIII/49 ; Bern/Frankfurt-am-Main ; Herbert/Peter Lang, 1975.

REHKOPF, Friedrich. *Die lukanische Sonderquelle. Ihr Umfang und Sprachgebrauch.* WissUntNT 5 ; Tübingen : J. C. B. Mohr, 1959.

REILING, J. L. and J. L. Swellengrebel. *A Translator's Handbook on the Gospel of Luke.* Helps for Translators X ; Leiden : E. J. Brill, 1971.

RENGSTORF, Karl Heinrich. *Die Auferstehung Jesu. Form, Art und Sinn der urchristlichen Osterbotschaft.* Witten/Ruhr : Luther-Verlag, [5]1967.

RESE, Martin. *Alttestamentliche Motive in der Christologie des Lukas. StNT* 1 ; Gütersloh : Gerd Mohn, 1969.

——, " Zur Lukas-Diskussion seit 1950," *WoDie* n.F. 9 (1967) 62-67.

REUMANN, John, " Heilgeschichte in Luke : Some remarks on its background and comparison with Paul," in *Studia evangelia* IV (TU 102, ed. F. L. Cross ; Berlin : Akademie-Verlag, 1968) 86-115.

RIEDL, Johannes, " ' Wirklich der Herr ist auferweckt worden und dem Simon erschienen ' (Lk 24,34). Entstehung und Inhalt des neutestamentlichen Osterglaubens," *BiLit* 40 (1967) 81-110.

RIGAUX, Béda. *Dieu l'a ressuscité. Exégèse et théologie biblique.* Gembloux : Éditions J. Duculot, 1973.

——. *Témoignage de l'évangile de Luc.* Pour une histoire de Jésus IV. Bruges : Desclée de Brouwer, 1970.

ROBINSON, James M., and Helmut KOESTER. *Trajectories through Early Christianity.* Philadelphia : Fortress Press, 1971.

ROBINSON, W. C., "The Theological Context for Interpreting Luke's Travel-Narrative (9,51ff.)," *JBL* 79 (1960) 20-31.

ROBINSON, William C., Jr. *Der Weg des Herrn. Studien zur Geschichte und Eschatologie im Lukas-Evangelium. Ein Gespräch mit Hans Conzelmann.* Theologische Forschung 36 (aus dem Manuskript übersetzt von Gisela und Georg Strecker); Hamburg-Bergstedt: Evangelischer Verlag Herbert Reich, 1964.

ROHDE, Joachim. *Die redaktionsgeschichtliche Methode. Einführung und Sichtung des Forschungsstandes.* Hamburg: Furche-Verlag, 1966.

——. *Rediscovering the Teaching of the Evangelists.* Trans. by Dorothy M. Barton, with revisions and additional material from the author. "New Testament Library" series; Philadelphia: Westminster Press, 1968. Pp. 153-239 (Lk).

ROLOFF, Jürgen. *Apostolat-Verkündigung-Kirche. Ursprung, Inhalt und Funktion des kirchlichen Apostelamtes nach Paulus, Lukas und den Pastoralbriefen.* Gütersloh: Gerd Mohn, 1965.

——. *Der Kerygma und der irdische Jesus. Historische Motive in den Jesus-Erzählungen der Evangelien.* Göttingen: Vandenhoeck und Ruprecht, 1970.

SAHLIN, H. *Der Messias und das Gottesvolk. Studien zur protolukanischen Theologie.* Acta seminarii neotestamentici Upsaliensis; Uppsala, 1945.

SCHARLEMANN, Martin A. *Stephen: A Singular Saint.* Analecta biblica 34; Rome: Biblical Institute Press, 1968.

SCHENK, Wolfgang. "Die Einheit von Wortverkündigung und Herrnmahl in den urchristlichen Gemeindeversammlungen," in Joachim Rogge und Gottfried Schille, hrsg., *Theologische Versuche II* (Berlin: Evangelische Verlagsanstalt, 1970) 65-92, esp. (on Lk:) 76-81.

SCHENKE, Ludger. *Auferstehungsverkündigung und leeres Grab. Eine traditionsgeschichtliche Untersuchung von Mk* 16,1-8. SBS 33; Stuttgart: Verlag Katholisches Bibelwerk, [2]1969.

SCHILLE, Gottfried. *Anfänge der Kirche. Erwägungen zur apostolischen Frühgeschichte.* BEvT 43; München: Kaiser-Verlag, 1966.

SCHLIER, Heinrich, "Jesu Himmelfahrt nach den Schriften des Lukas," *GeistLeb* 34 (1961) 91-99; now in H. SCHLIER. *Besinnung auf das Neue Testament. Exegetische Aufsätze und Vorträge* II (Freiburg/Basel: Herder, 1964) 227-241.

SCHMIDT, Karl Ludwig. *Der Rahmen der Geschichte Jesu. Literarkritische Untersuchungen zur ältesten Jesusüberlieferung.* Berlin, 1919; Repr. Darmstadt: Wissenschaftliche Buchgesellschaft, 1964.

——. *Die Stellung der Evangelien in der allgemeinen Literaturgeschichte.* FRLANT 36/2; Göttingen: Vandenhoeck und Ruprecht, 1923. Pp. 50-134.

SCHMITHALS, Walter, "Der Markusschluss, die Verklärungsgeschichte und die Aussendung der Zwölf," *ZTK* 69 (1972) 379-411.

SCHMITT, Joseph. "Le récit de la résurrection dans l'évangile de Luc. Étude de critique littéraire," *RvScRel* 25 (1951) 119-137; 219-242.

SCHNACKENBURG, Rudolf. *Das Johannesevangelium.* Herders Theologischer Kommentar zum Neuen Testament IV, 1-3; Freiburg/Basel: Herder, 1965 (I), 1971 (II), 1975 (III).

SCHNEIDER, Gerhard, "' Der Menschensohn ' in der lukanischen Christologie," in R. Pesch & R. Schnackenburg, hrsg., *Jesus und der Menschensohn, für Anton Vögtle* (Frieburg/Basel: Herder, 1975) 267-282.

——. *Die Passion Jesu nach den drei älteren Evangelien.* Biblische Handbibliothek xi; München: Kösel-Verlag, 1973.

——, "Das Problem einer vorkanonischen Passionserzählung," *BZ* 16 (1972) 222-244.

——. *Verleugnung, Verspottung, und Verhör Jesu nach Lukas* 22,54-71. *Studien zur lukanischen Darstellung der Passion.* StANT 22; München: Kösel-Verlag, 1969.

SCHNEIDER, Johannes, " Zur Analyse des lukanischen Reiseberichtes," in J. Schmid & A. Vögtle, hrsg., *Synoptische Studien, A. Wikenhauser zum* 70. *Geburtstag... dargebracht* (München : Karl Zink Verlag, 1953) 207-229.

SCHNIEWIND, Julius. *Die Parallelperikopen bei Lukas und Johannes*². Hildesheim : Georg Olms, 1958.

SCHNIDER, FRANZ. *Jesus der Prophet.* Orbis biblicus et Orientalis 2 ; Göttingen : Vandenhoeck und Ruprecht, 1973.

SCHNIDER, Franz – Werner STENGER, " Beobachtungen zur Struktur der Emmausperikope (Lk 24,13-35)," *BZ* 16 (1972) 94-114.

SCHRAMM, Tim. *Der Markus-Stoff bei Lukas. Eine litararkritische und redaktionsgeschichtliche Untersuchung.* SNTS 14 ; Cambridge/New York : Cambridge University Press, 1971.

SCHUBERT, Paul, " The Structure and Significance of Luke 24," in Walther Eltester, ed., *Neutestamentliche Studien für Rudolph Bultmann, zu seinem siebzigsten Geburtstag am* 20. *august* 1954 (dargebracht) (BZNW 21 ; Berlin : Verlag Alfred Töpelmann, 1954) 165-186.

SCHÜRMANN, Heinz. *Jesu Abschiedsrede Lk* 22,21-38. *III. Teil einer quellenkritischen Untersuchung des lukanischen Abendmahlsberichtes Lk* 22,7-38. NTAbh XX/5 ; Münster-Westf. : Aschendorff, 1957.

——. *Der Abendmahlsbericht Lucas* 22,7-38. Paderborn, 1957.

——. *Traditionsgeschichtliche Untersuchungen zu den synoptischen Evangelien.* Düsseldorff : Patmos-Verlag, 1968.

——, " Zur Traditionsgeschichte der Nazareth-Perikope Lk 4,16-30," in A. Descamps & A. de Halleux, éds., *Mélanges bibliques en hommage au R. P. Béda Rigaux* (Gembloux : Éditions J. Duculot, 1970) 187-205.

SCHÜTZ, Frieder. *Der leidende Christus. Die angefochtene Gemeinde und das Christuskerygma der lukanischen Schriften.* BWANT 89 ; Stuttgart : Kohlhammer, 1969.

SCHULZ, Siegfried. *Die Stunde der Botschaft. Einführung in die Theologie der vier Evangelisten.* Hamburg : Furche-Verlag, 1967. Pp. 235-296 (Lk).

——. *Q. Die Spruchquelle der Evangelisten.* Zürich : Theologischer Verlag, 1972.

——, " Gottes Vorsehung bei Lukas," *ZNW* 54 (1963) 104-116.

SCHWEIZER, Eduard. *Jesus.* Trans. David E. Green. Richmond, Va. : John Knox Press, 1971.

SCOBIE, Charles H. H., " The Origins and Development of Samaritan Christianity," *NTS* 19 (1972-73) 390-414.

SEIDENSTICKER, Philipp. *Die Auferstehung Jesu in der Botschaft der Evangelisten. Ein traditionsgeschichtlicher Versuch zum Problem der Sicherung der Osterbotschaft in der apostolischen Zeit.* SBS 26 ; Stuttgart : Katholisches Bibelwerk, 1967.

——. *Zeitgenössische Texte zur Osterbotschaft der Evangelien.* SBS 27 ; Stuttgart : Katholisches Bibelwerk, 1967.

SELLIN, Gerhard, " Lukas als Gleichniserzähler : die Erzählung vom barmherzigen Samariter (Lk 10,25-37)," *ZNW* 65 (1974) 166-189 ; 66 (1975) 19-60.

SIMON, Marcel. *St. Stephen and the Hellenists in the Primitive Church.* The Haskell Lectures, Oberlin College, 1956 ; London/New York : Longmans, Green, & Co., 1958.

SNAPE, H. C., " The Composition of the Lucan Writings. A Re-assessment," *HarvTR* 53 (1960) 27-46.

STECK, Odil Hannes. *Israel und das gewaltsame Geschick der Propheten. Untersuchungen zur Überlieferung des deuteronomistischen Geschichtsbildes im Alten Testament, Spätjudentum und Urchristentum.* WMANT 23 ; Neukirchen : Neukirchener Verlag, 1967.

STEINSEIFER, Bernd, "Der Ort der Erscheinungen des Auferstandenen. Zur Frage alter galiläischer Ostertraditionen," *ZNW* 62 (1971) 232-265.

STOLLE, Volker, *Der Zeuge als Angeklagter. Untersuchungen zum Paulusbild des Lukas.* BWANT 102 ; Stuttgart/Berlin : W. Kohlhammer, 1973.

STRECKER, Georg, "Die Leidens- und Auferstehungsvoraussagen im Markus-evangelium (Mk 8,31 ; 9,31 ; 10,32-34)," *ZTK* 64 (1967) 16-39.

STREETER, B. H. *The Four Gospels. A Study of Origins Treating of the Manuscript Tradition, Sources, Authorship and Dates.* London : Macmillan, 1924 (now New York : St. Martin's Press, 1964).

STUHLMACHER, Peter. *Das paulinische Evangelium. I. Vorgeschichte.* FRLANT 95 ; Göttingen : Vandenhoeck und Ruprecht, 1968.

TALBERT, Charles H. *Luke and the Gnostics. An Examination of the Lucan Purpose.* Nashville/New York : Abingdon Press, 1966.

——. *Literary Patterns, Theological Themes and the Genre of Luke-Acts.* Society of Biblical Literature, Monograph series, vol. 20 ; Missoula, Montana : Scholars Press, 1974.

——, "The Redaction Critical Quest for Luke the Theologian," in David Buttrick, ed., *Jesus and Man's Hope* I. Pittsburgh Festival on the Gospels, 1970 (Perspective Books 1 ; Pittsburgh : Pittsburgh Theological Seminary, 1971) 171-222.

——, "Shifting Sands : The Recent Study of the Gospel of Luke," *Interpr* 30 (1976) 381-395.

TANNEHILL, Robert C., "The Mission of Jesus according to Luke IV 16-30," in Erich Grässer, et al., *Jesus in Nazareth* (BZNW 40 ; Berlin : W. de Gruyter, 1972) 51-75.

TAYLOR, Vincent. *Behind the Third Gospel. A Study of the Proto-Luke Hypothesis.* Oxford : Clarendon Press, 1926.

——. *The Formation of the Gospel Tradition.* London, 1935 (now New York : St. Martin's Press, 1968).

——. *The Passion Narrative of St. Luke : A Critical and Historical Investigation.* SNTS 19, ed. by Owen E. Evans ; Cambridge/New York : Cambridge University Press, 1972.

THEISSEN, Gerd, "Wanderradikalismus. Literatursoziologische Aspekte der Überlieferung von Worten Jesu im Urchristentum," *ZTK* 70 (1973) 245-271.

——, "Legitimation und Lebensunterhalt : Ein Beitrag zur Soziologie urchristlicher Missionare," *NTS* 21 (1974-75) 192-221.

THÜSING, Wilhelm. *Erhöhungsvorstellung und Parusieerwartung in der ältesten nachösterlichen Christologie.* SBS 42 ; Stuttgart : Katholisches Bibelwerk, 1969.

TIEDE, David Lenz. *The Charismatic Figure as Miracle Worker.* S. B. L. Dissertation series 1 ; Missoula, Montana : Society of Biblical Literature, 1972.

TÖDT, Heinz Eduard. *Der Menschensohn in der synoptischen Überlieferung.* Gütersloh : Gerd Mohn, 1963.

TRITES, Allison A. *The New Testament Concept of Witness.* SNTS 31 ; Cambridge/New York : Cambridge University Press, 1977.

TROCME, Étienne. *Le 'Livre des Actes' et l'histoire.* Paris : Presses Universitaires, 1957.

TROMPF, G. W., "La section médiane de l'évangile de Luc : L'organisation des documents," *RHPhilRel* 53 (1973) 141-154.

VAN STEMPVOORT, P. A., "The Interpretation of the Ascension in Luke and Acts," *NTS* 5 (1958-59) 30-42.

VAN UNNIK, W. C., "Luke-Acts, A Storm Center in Contemporary Scholarship," in Leander E. Keck and J. Louis Martyn, eds., *Studies in Luke-Acts. Essays presented in Honor of Paul Schubert* (Nashville/New York: Abingdon Press, 1966) 15-32.

VIELHAUER, Philipp, "Zum 'Paulinismus' der Apostelgeschichte," *EvT* 10 (1950-1951) 1-15; 12 (1952-53) 481-484; now in Ph. Vielhauer. *Aufsätze zum Neuen Testament* (Theologische Bücherei 31; München: Kaiser-Verlag, 1965) 9-27, and in *StLA* (Eng. trans.).

VÖGTLE, Anton. *Das Evangelium und die Evangelien. Beiträge zur Evangelienforschung.* Düsseldorf: Patmos-Verlag, 1971.

VÖÖBUS, Arthur, "Kritische Beobachtungen über die lukanische Darstellung des Herrenmahls," *ZNW* 61 (1970) 102-110.

VÖLKEL, Martin, "Der Anfang Jesu in Galiläa. Bemerkungen zum Gebrauch und zur Funktion Galiläas in den lukanischen Schriften," *ZNW* 64 (1973) 222-232.

——, "Zur Deutung des 'Reiches Gottes' bei Lukas," *ZNW* 65 (1974) 57-70.

VOSS, Gerhard. *Die Christologie der lukanischen Schriften in Grundzügen.* Studia Neotestamentica, Studia II; Paris/Bruges: Desclée de Brouwer, 1965.

WANKE, Joachim. *Beobachtungen zum Eucharistieverständnis des Lukas auf Grund der lukanischen Mahlberichte.* Erfurter theologische Schriften 8; Leipzig: St. Benno-Verlag, 1973.

——. *Die Emmauserzählung. Eine redaktionsgeschichtliche Untersuchung zu Lk* 24, 13-35. Erfurter theologische Studien 31; Leipzig: St. Benno-Verlag, 1973.

——, "'... wie sie ihn beim Brotbrechen erkannten'. Zur Auslegung der Emmauserzählung Lk 24,13-35," *BZ* 18 (1974) 180-192.

WILCKENS, Ulrich. *Die Missionsreden der Apostelgeschichte. Form- und traditionsgeschichtliche Untersuchungen.* WMANT 5, 2. Auflage; Neukirchen: Neukirchener Verlag, 1962. — 3., überarbeitete und erweiterte Auflage, 1974.

——, "Kerygma und Evangelium bei Lukas," *ZNW* 49 (1958) 223-237.

——, "Der Ursprung der Überlieferung der Erscheinungen des Auferstandenen. Zur traditionsgeschichtlichen Analyse von 1. Kor. 15,1-11," in Wilfried Joest and Wolfhart Pannenberg, eds., *Dogma und Denkstrukturen, Edmund Schlink in Verehrung und Dankbarkeit zum* 60. *Geburtstag* (dargebracht) (Göttingen: Vandenhoeck und Ruprecht, 1963) 56-95.

——, "Die Perikope vom leeren Grabe Jesu in der nachmarkinischen Traditionsgeschichte," in *Festschrift für Friedrich Smend zum* 70. *Geburtstag, dargebracht von Freunden und Schülern* (Berlin: Verlag Merseburger, 1963) 30-41.

——, "Interpreting Luke-Acts in a Period of Existentialist Theology," in L. E. Keck and J. L. Martyn, eds., *Studies in Luke-Acts. Essays in honor of Paul Schubert* (Nashville/New York: Abingdon Press, 1966). 60-83.

——, "Die Überlieferungsgeschichte der Auferstehung Jesu," in W. Marxsen – U. Wilckens, et al., *Die Bedeutung der Auferstehungsbotschaft für den Glauben an Jesus Christus* (ed. Fritz Viering; Gütersloh: Verlagshaus Gerd Mohn, 1968) 43-63.

——. *Auferstehung. Das biblische Auferstehungszeugnis historisch untersucht und erklärt.* Themen der Theologie, hrsg. von H.-J. Schultz 4; Stuttgart/Berlin: Kreuz-Verlag, 1970.

WILCOX, Max. *The Semitisms of Acts.* Oxford: Clarendon Press, 1965.

WILSON, S. G., "Lukan Eschatology," *NTS* 16 (1969-70) 330-347.

——. *The Gentiles and the Gentile Mission in Luke-Acts.* SNTS 23; Cambridge/New York: Cambridge University Press, 1973.

——, "The Ascension: A Critique and an Interpretation," *ZNW* 59 (1968) 269-281.

WINK, Walter. *John the Baptist in the Gospel Tradition.* SNTS 7; Cambridge: Cambridge University Press, 1968.

WINTER, Paul, "The Treatment of His Sources by the Third Evangelist in Luke XXI-XXIV," *StTh* 8 (1954) 138-172.

——, "On Luke and Lucan Sources," *ZNW* 47 (1956) 217ff.

WREDE, William. *Das Messiasgeheimnis in den Evangelien. Zugleich ein Beitrag zum Verständnis des Markusevangeliums.* Göttingen: Vandenhoeck und Ruprecht, [2]1913 (repr. 1963).

ZIMMERMAN, Heinrich. *Neutestamentliche Methodenlehre. Darstellung der historische-kritischen Methode.* Stuttgart: Katholisches Bibelwerk, 1967.

ZINGG, Paul. *Das Wachsen der Kirche. Beiträge zur Frage der lukanischen Redaktion und Theologie.* Orbis Biblicus et Orientalis 3; Göttingen: Vandenhoeck und Ruprecht, 1974.

ZMIJEWSKI, Josef. *Die Eschatologiereden des Lukas-Evangeliums. Eine traditions- und redaktionsgeschichtliche Untersuchung zu Lk* 21,5-36 *und Lk* 17,20-37. BBB 40; Bonn: Peter Hanstein Verlag, 1972.

INDEX OF SCRIPTURAL REFERENCES AND CITATIONS OF OTHER ANCIENT SOURCES

Note: Extended treatments of given passages are indicated by page-numbers in bold-print.

OLD TESTAMENT

APOCHRYPHA

PSEUDEPIGRAPHA

TESTAMENTS OF THE XII PATRIARCHS

NEW TESTAMENT

ROMANS